The Muse of Urban Delirium

Also from New Academia Publishing

REAL AND PHANTOM PAINS: An Anthology of New Russian Drama, compiled and edited by John Freedman

Read an excerpt at www.newacademia.com

The Muse of Urban Delirium

How the Performing Arts Paradoxically Transform Conflict-Ridden Cities into Centers of Cultural Innovation

Blair A. Ruble

NEW ACADEMIA PUBLISHING

Washington, DC

New Academia Publishing, 2017

Printed in the United States of America

Library of Congress Control Number: 2016952428
ISBN 978-0-9974962-9-1 paperback (alk. paper)

NEW ACADEMIA
PUBLISHING

4401-A Connecticut Ave., NW, #236, Washington DC 20008
info@newacademia.com

More titles by New Academia Publishing at www.newacademia.com

For Slava and Pep, Pavel and Sasha and Grisha, Edisio and Richard, Elena and Natalia, and Andriy and Svitlana — who taught me to ask:

"What is the point of living in a city
if you can't take its poetic measure?"

—Robert Farris Thompson,
Tango: The Art History of Love, 2005

For what does a city consist of? Everything that has been said there, dreamed, destroyed, undertaken. The effected, the disappeared, the imagined that never came to be. The living and the dead. The wooden houses that were torn down or burned, the palaces that might have existed, the bridge which was drawn but never built, the houses still standing where generations have left their memories. But there is much more than that. A city is all the words that have been uttered there, an unceasing never-ending muttering, whispering, singing, and shouting that has resounded through the centuries and been blown away again. This cannot have vanished without having belonged to the city. Even that which is never to be retrieved is part of the city because once, in this place, it was called out or uttered on a winter night or summer morning. The open-field sermon, the verdict of the tribunal, the cry of the flogged, the bidding at an auction, the ordinance, the placard, the discourse, the pamphlet, the death announcement, the calling of the hours, the words of nuns, whores, kings, regents, painters, aldermen, hangmen, shippers, lansquenets, local keepers, and builders, the persistent conversation along the canals in the living body of the city, which is the city. Whoever wishes can hear it.

—Cess Nootebom, "Amsterdam,"
in *De Filossof Zonder Ogen*, 1997

Contents

List of Illustrations

Preface

The Devil Is a Local Call Away

So urbanists, tune in to the beats.

—Edgar Pieterse, "Youth Cultures and the Mediation of
Racial Exclusion or Inclusion in Rio de Janeiro and
Cape Town," 2010

At the height of the Cold War, Soviet wags loved to tell ironic tales about their political leaders. Communist Party general secretary Leonid Brezhnev inspired a number of particularly endearing stories, which always somehow related to his being slightly at sea in the middle of the world events swirling around him.[1] One such *anikdot* pitted the witless Brezhnev against a wily Richard Nixon.

Brezhnev and Nixon, it seems, were meeting in the White House when the American president decided to call God for advice. He summoned an aide, who brought a large white phone. A few moments after he had completed his consultation with the Divine Being, another assistant came in with a receipt. Nixon approved the bill of some $20 million for the call.

Flying back to Moscow, a furious Brezhnev inquired of the cowering Red Army officers how it was that the Americans could call God but he could not. He demanded that the entire Soviet military research complex dedicate itself to establishing phone service with God.

A few months later, it was time for Nixon to visit Moscow. The two leaders sat in Brezhnev's Kremlin office. At a critical juncture in the negotiations, Brezhnev summoned an aide, who brought a red phone that was even bigger than the white one Nixon had used in the Oval Office. Brezhnev dialed a number and had a brief conversation. A few moments later, an obsequious aide shuffled into the meeting with a receipt for just 2 kopecks (or 0.02 ruble). Brezhnev was pleased, but perplexed. Why, he asked his assistant, once the Americans had departed, had it cost Nixon $20 million to place his call, but he, the Communist general secretary, had to pay only 2 kopecks? The subordinate quickly responded, "Because calling the Devil from Moscow is only a local call."

Yet paradoxically, this very Moscow where Hell was just a local call away also happened to be one of the planet's most creative cities. Internationally acclaimed authors were penning their best works, noble ballerinas were training, world-class actors were perfecting their craft, and perhaps the greatest collection of mathematicians in recent centuries were engaged in thought. Brezhnev's Moscow was the headquarters and command center for an ideological empire that extended to nearly every continent—it oversaw massive military and prison kingdoms on a scale that was previously unknown; and it stood at the center of an enormous hinterland covering a dozen time zones. Clocks from Prague to Pyongyang marked Moscow time. People with vast differences came and went every day; they jostled on streets that, indeed, resembled visions of Dante's *Inferno*. Moscow under Brezhnev underscored the reality that creativity does not necessarily coexist with virtue.

Living in and traveling to Brezhnev's Moscow forced me to ponder the apparent contradiction between the gray and repressed existence of everyday life in the Soviet Union (Stalin's terror had subsided, and had been replaced by an eerie, enervating inertia) and the bright and impressive personalities who seemed to abound. I found myself thinking about how beauty can emerge full blown from the most unbeautiful places. I began to understand that the urge to create beauty is a natural response to ugliness; it is a way for individuals and communities to establish their presence in a certain place at a specific time. Thus beauty and creativity can thrive in bleak environments such as Brezhnev's unhappy and dark capital.

But Moscow wasn't just any place; it was one of the largest cities in the world. How did its "urbanness" matter?

Over the course of my career, I have written about a diverse group of cities: Saint Petersburg (aka Leningrad), Moscow, Yaro-slavl, and Yekaterinburg in Russia; Kyiv and Odessa in Ukraine; Montreal in Canada; Osaka in Japan; and New York, New Orleans, Chicago, and Washington in the United States. On the face of it, this is a rather random collection of cities. Yet there was a logic to their selection. My research and writing have been animated by the deep belief that one of humankind's primary challenges in the twenty-first century is to avoid repeating the slaughters of the twentieth. And because most humans live in cities, I am convinced that we need to figure out how people who can barely stand one another can nonetheless manage to live on top of one another in cities without killing each another. My writing about each of these cities encouraged me—and, hopefully, my readers—to try to think creatively about such larger questions of human existence.

I came to consider cities through an intellectual back door. During the mid-1970s, I conducted dissertation research in Leningrad for a study of Soviet trade unions. Once I had published my revised doctoral thesis as *Soviet Trade Unions*, I began to look for a new project.[2] The editors at the Institute of Governmental Studies at the University of California, Berkeley, happened to be searching for a Western political scientist with research experience in Leningrad who might want to write a volume about the city for their Lane Series in Regional Government. The appropriate connections were made, and I began to think about how to place metropolitan government in Leningrad within a broad, comparative framework.

Examining the development of the Soviet Union's second-largest metropolis during the late Soviet period in my Lane Series monograph titled *Leningrad*—which appeared just as the city was once again being renamed Saint Petersburg—I argued that shaping the face of a great city is a complex task.[3] Order within a metropolitan region is the result of the accumulation of layer upon layer of social, economic, cultural, and political sediment. For the vast majority of residents, much of what takes place in a city seems spontaneous. To the extent that conscious rationality determines a city's fate, it emerges as the sum of the rationalities of its constituent parts.

This process of city building is particularly exposed at moments of great societal transformation, such as the one after the Soviet

Union's implosion and during the emergence of a new, market-oriented economic system in Russia. The Soviet collapse prompted a sweeping reorganization of Russian social, political, and economic life, which dramatically altered entrenched patterns of urban existence. As I demonstrated in *Money Sings*, social differentiation and fragmentation increase as market mechanisms take hold.[4] New cleavages generate previously unknown—or at least submerged—conflicts and competition, which alter the distribution of urban political and economic power. And this contention produces diverse interests, which appear, at times, to undermine the social, economic, and political underpinnings of urban life.

Growing competition among diverse groups requires those with custodianship of cities to confront this diversity, manage it, and convert it into an asset. In *Second Metropolis*, I explored the evolution of three burgeoning industrial metropolises—Chicago, Moscow, and Osaka—that were among the world's largest and fastest-growing cities at the dawn of the twentieth century. These cities' explosive capitalist industrialization spurred their wild expansion.[5] In this context, their political entrepreneurs were spurred to develop shared strategies, whereby groups and people that could hardly tolerate one another learned how to choose their battles carefully so they could enter into alliances that enabled them to move beyond the destructiveness of zero-sum competition. The result was a "pragmatic pluralism," which maximized any group's capacity to achieve its most important goals. However, in the cases of these three cities, practically minded municipal regimes collapsed in the face of a failure to institutionalize the practice of pragmatic pluralism in local political and social life.

I continued my investigation into the pragmatic acceptance of urban diversity by exploring the impact of transnational migrants in three communities that had long been divided by binary definitions of language and race: Montreal, Washington, and Kyiv. In *Creating Diversity Capital*, I argued that the growing presence of individuals who do not fit within long-standing group boundaries fundamentally alters the social, cultural, and political contours of such traditionally bifurcated regions.[6] For me, "diversity capital" provides a menu of responses to diversity that advances accommodation to differences. Like monetary capital, over time "diversity capital" can accumulate interest and grow, be invested, be spent, be lost, and be put to good or bad use. And this entire repertoire can expand or contract. The rationale for developing diversity capital need not be as ambitious as convincing intolerant people of the virtues of tolerance. More simply, the objective can be to establish rules of the game that make it advantageous for intolerant people to act as if they are tolerant.

I came to understand through my research and writing that effective responses to diversity must become embedded in official — usually democratic — institutions. And just as important, they must promote customs and norms, and thus habits of acceptable behavior and thought. In other words, what happens on a bus or in a shop can be as important — perhaps even more important — as what happens at city hall. This insight led me to appreciate the critical role of the arts and sports in promoting cross-group contact.

In my next book, *Washington's U Street*, I argued that perhaps the greatest of all human achievements is the ability to add beauty to the world in the face of injustice, horrors, and stupidity.[7] This observation — which is drawn from the Washington novelist Olga Grushin's haunting debut novel *The Dream Life of Sukhanov* — allowed me to better grasp the connection between artistic and urban achievement.[8] Grushin's insight drew me toward an investigation of how particular urban settings promote creativity.

With the passage of time, I have come to believe that cities, because of their density and diversity, are a natural environment for the sort of cultural creativity that fascinates me: the creation of beauty in the midst of ugliness. Urban decay is not the only stimulus for humans to try to step out of themselves to add a note of splendor to the world; nor are cities a unique venue for creativity. But cities are places where people who often can barely tolerate one another crash together while coming and going to their houses and apartments, places of worship, doctors' offices, funeral parlors, restaurants, cafés, bars, theaters, stores, stadiums, and schools. Cities, together with the arts, Benjamin Barber has argued, "reflect a common creativity, a shared attachment to openness and transparency, and a core commitment to play and playfulness."[9] Cities are where people meet with a purpose and, just as important, without one. Indeed, providing spaces for aimless wandering may be one of the most creative functions of any street or neighborhood or town. Such jagged urban edges are where cities both fail and succeed.

The urban experience in inherently contradictory and conflict-ridden places—such as Brezhnev's Moscow and Washington's segregation-plagued U Street—in almost any era are the urban wetlands of our lives. Like wetlands in the natural environment, such mixing bowls of urban diversity often appear to outsiders to be little more than wastelands. They are the first places to be reconceived, redesigned, rebuilt, and reconstituted when "reformers" grandiosely decide to "improve" our lives. Yet this arrogant reforming is a terrible mistake. Like wetlands, a city's jagged edges are among its most fertile and productive corners. And like wetlands, cities must be revitalized from time to time for them to continue to enrich society.

This book seeks to explore the relationship between urban life and creativity through a series of chapters examining the vibrant invention and reinvention of the various performing arts in specific cities—and even neighborhoods—at particular historical moments. It is more of a slide show than a video, and thus it offers a variety of snapshots rather than a panoptic, synthetic overview. My hope is that I have been able to select a half dozen examples, drawn from different eras and continents, to illustrate my three primary arguments: humankind needs more places where diversity can be converted into an advantage; cities offer the most likely venues for such a conversion; and the performing arts offer potent opportunities for doing so.

The selections of cities, performance styles, and eras that follow are highly personal. Some obvious stories—such as the emergence of jazz in New Orleans at the turn of the twentieth century, and the birth of hip-hop in the Bronx a century later—have been omitted. I make no claim to comprehensive inclusion, though I have tried to incorporate examples that reflect different dimensions of the perpetual conflict between shocking urban realities and the beauty of human creativity.

More specifically, the book's journey begins with two examples—Naples and Osaka—drawn from among the many eighteenth-century cities controlled by early modern autocratic rulers that were being transformed by a rising middling merchant class preoccupied with creating its own sense of self. Next, we turn to two of the great immigrant cities of the early twentieth century—New York and Buenos Aires—where longtime residents were forced to accommodate previously unimagined neighbors as new communities burst forth, seemingly out of thin air. And finally, we find the creative impulse in two contemporary cities—Cape Town and Yekaterinburg—struggling with postauthoritarian transitions and reincorporation into globalized economies and cultural practices.

Like flickering images on a computer screen, these chapters highlight how the dislocations of urban life during periods of intense and rapid social transformation spurred the invention of compelling new forms of the performing arts, which eventually transcended the boundaries of any one community or city. All six cases explored here represent moments when the lived experience of urban delirium has become the muse for extraordinary outbursts of human creativity.

This book, then, is about such moments of urban healing that emerge from the creation of new forms in the performing arts. It rests on the belief that cities are more than places of production and consumption. Cities heal through the joy of creativity. In the face of real and profound sorrow and grief, humans need joy. Successful cities nurture spaces where emotions are transformed into new forms of being. As the South African urban observer Edgar Pieterse argues, if you want to understand why the city is important, "tune in to the beats" of creative urban invention.

Acknowledgments

I dedicate this volume to eleven friends and colleagues who have encouraged my explorations of the urban condition and taught me profound lessons about the meaning of life: Edesio Fernandes, Vyacheslav "Slava" Glazychev (1940–2012), Pavel Ilyn (1936–2015), Grigorii "Grisha" Kaganov, Andriy Puchkov, Svitlana Shlipchenko, Richard Stren, Josep "Pep" Subirós (1947–2016), Elena Triubina, Natalia Vlasova, and Alexander "Sasha" Vysokovsky (1948–2014). I can only hope that the pages to follow provide a modicum of their insights about the city.

I could not possibly have written these chapters—which often go far beyond my comfort zone of knowledge and specialization—without the help of many, many others. In particular, I would like to thank my Woodrow Wilson Center colleague, Janet Spikes, and her husband, Daniel Spikes, for their observations about Naples; my former Wilson Center colleague, Joseph S. Tulchin, and my close family friends, Valeria Varea and Mauricio Varea, for their always-wise insights about Buenos Aires; and the Kyoto University professor Kengo Akizuki, the University of Pittsburgh professor emeritus Thomas J. Rimer, and the University of Hawai'i Kabuki specialist Julie Iezzi for their good-spirited commentary about Osaka and my approach to that city. The George Washington University historian James Miller provided particularly needed encouragement as I considered writing about Cape Town, and my Wilson Center colleague Steve McDonald taught me many necessary lessons about South Africa.

Turning to Yekaterinburg, I am the beneficiary of profound wisdom from many people who know far more about the city than

I could ever hope to learn, including Leon Aron of the American Enterprise Institute; Pilar Bonet, the *El País* Moscow correspondent; Leonid Bykov and Valentine Lukyanin, Yekaterinburg writers and literary leaders extraordinaire; John Freedman, the *Moscow Times* theater critic; Maxim Khomiakov (formerly) and Elena Trubina (presently), of the Urals Federal University; Natalya Vlasova, of the Urals State Economics University; Nikolai Kolyada, dramatist, teacher, and playwright; Andrei Malaev-Babel, of Florida State University's Asolo Conservatory for Acting Training; and Sergei Zhuk, of Ball State University in Indiana.

More generally, Joe Brinley, the director of the Woodrow Wilson Center Press and my longtime friend, offered sage advice along the way. An army of interns—all of whom deserve my deepest gratitude and respect—made this project possible. Before suggesting that you, the reader, move further into the pages of this book, please allow me to thank several among my research assistants, Jared Barol, Oleksandr Chornyy, Elizabeth Hipple, Raughly D. Nuzzi, and Yan Slavinskiy. Intern extraordinaire Irina Kuzemkina, a native of the Siberian prison camp and mining center of Norilsk, is living proof of one of the central themes of this book: that extraordinary people can be found in the most unordinary places.

Master editor Alfred Imhoff has greatly improved various infelicities in my writing and, as he has so often, enhanced the final product. Noreen Banks has identified the illustrations throughout, which similarly enrich the book. Aaron Winslow has added a comprehensive index. I especially want to acknowledge Anna Lawton and the team at New Academia Publishing who consistently have believed in this project. I am grateful for their work.

Materials in some of the chapters that follow appeared previously in these publications:

Blair A. Ruble, *Second Metropolis: Pragmatic Pluralism in Gilded Age Chicago, Silver Age Moscow, and Meiji Osaka* (Washington and New York: Woodrow Wilson Center Press and Cambridge University Press, 2001);
Blair A. Ruble, *Washington's U Street: A Biography* (Washington and Baltimore: Woodrow Wilson Center Press and Johns Hopkins University Press, 2010);
Blair A. Ruble, *Performing Community: Short Essays on Community, Diver-*

sity, Inclusion, and the Performing Arts (Washington: Woodrow Wilson Center, 2015);

Blair A. Ruble, "Ethnicity and Soviet Cities," *Soviet Studies* 41, no. 3 (1989): 401–14;

Blair A. Ruble, "Cultural Ethnicity among the Tatars of Leningrad: An Ethnographic Report," *Canadian Review of Studies in Nationalism* 13, no. 2 (1986): 275–82;

Blair A. Ruble, "A Paradise Inhabited by Devils: Opera in Viceregal and Bourbon Naples," *Perekrestki/Crossroads*, no. 1 (2013): 19–39; nos. 3–4 (2013): 125–46;

Blair A. Ruble, "Seventh Street: Black DC's Music Mecca," *Washington History* 26 (Spring 2014): 1–11;

Blair A. Ruble, *Urals Pathfinder: Theater in Post-Soviet Yekaterinburg*, Kennan Institute Occasional Paper 307 (Washington: Woodrow Wilson Center, 2011);

Blair A. Ruble and Mary Elisabeth Malinkin, "A Political Economy of Tolerance: The Reception of Migrants in Krasnodar, Nizhnyi Novgorod, and Yekaterinburg," in *Nauchnoe izdanie: Modernizatsionno-innovatsionnye protsessy v sotsial'no-ekonomicheskom razvitii regionov i gorodov, Kniga 1*, ed. M. V. Bausova et al. (Yekaterinburg: Izd. Ural'skogo Gosudarstvennogo ekonomicheskogo universiteta, 2013), 312–22; and

Blair A. Ruble, "Adding Human Diversity to Urban Political Economy Analysis: The Case of Russia," in *Segmented Cities? How Urban Contexts Shape Ethnic and Nationalist Politics*, ed. Kristin Good, Phil Triadafilopoulos, and Luc Turgeon (Vancouver: University of British Columbia Press, 2014), 37–59.

Also, some materials previously appeared in these electronic postings by Blair Ruble:

With Barbara Lanciers, "Tracking Political Turmoil through the Prism of Theater Culture," *New International Theatre Experiment World Theatre News*, New York, February 5, 2014;

"Putin's Punitive Theater of the Absurd," *Newsweek*, New York, January 9, 2015; and

"Physical Theatre and Public Policy Hooliganism," *HowlRound: Theater Community Knowledge Commons*, Boston, July 31, 2015.

Overture

David Akers's Smile: Urban Delirium and Cultural Innovation

I like cities that destroy themselves. Triumphant cities smell of disinfectant.

> —Manuel Vázquez Montalbán,
> *The Buenos Aires Quintet*, 1997

In 2010, I published a history of Washington's premier African American neighborhood, U Street, NW.[1] As I researched and wrote the book, I began to hear more and more about the Howard Theatre, which had opened its doors in 1910 as the first major theater in the United States promoting African American performances. A half century later, the Howard fell prey to the ravages of civil unrest, poverty, and crime that swept across the U Street neighborhood during the late 1960s and early 1970s. Throughout the remainder of the twentieth century, its hulking shell crumbled at the intersection of T and Seventh streets, NW, as a reminder of a greatness that seemed gone forever.

As I met with community groups to talk about my book, I came to appreciate just how important the Howard Theatre had been to African American Washington. The Howard's day-long performance schedule offered a home away from home for many young African Americans. The theater inspired people who would transform entire cultural fields—the composer Duke Ellington and the Atlantic Records founder and music promoter Agmet Ertegun; the writers Langston Hughes and Jean Toomer; the singing group the Supremes and the Chitlin' Circuit founder S. H. "Uncle Dud" Dudley. Perhaps more important, scores of wonderful—if less well known—musicians got their start at the Howard before moving on to play with the likes of Elvis Presley and James Brown. Nearly every African American over forty living in Washington at the outset of the twenty-first century had gone to the Howard on their first, second, or third date.

The more I spoke with people about the old theater, the more I understood that the building's abandoned carcass was like an open wound in the psyche of DC. Therefore, I never doubted for a moment that T Street, where the theater actually stood, was the only place where I could be on April 9, 2012, when the theater was scheduled to reopen after a long process of rebuilding, dating back at least a quarter century, that included several false starts, insufficient funding, bureaucratic intrigue, falsely optimistic projections, and incomplete planning. That day turned into my best day ever living in Washington (figure 1).

The organizers of the reopening seemed to have planned for a couple of hundred people. But several hundred, if not a couple of thousand, folks showed up. Somehow, the resulting moments of chaos added to the emotions of the day—one that was all about "Hometown DC" at its very best.

The theater's dedication ceremony was what one would expect, as DC mayor Vince Gray, DC congressional delegate Eleanor Holmes Norton, the local city councilmember Jim Graham, and DC "mayor-for-life" Marion Barry—plus various business folks and neighborhood representatives—held forth for an hour or so (actually for more). But the day wasn't about any of them.

The proceedings began with an African incantation to the ancestors, performed by a group that included the neighborhood drummers who play every Sunday at nearby Malcolm X Park. A cousin of the famous mid-twentieth-century American contralto Marian Anderson sang the Lord's Prayer, while a well-known local pastor—the Reverend Doctor Sandra Butler-Truesdale—was among the masters of ceremony. Duke Ellington's descendants were there to personify a link with the past. All the folks who had made the reopening possible were rightfully proud after literally decades of hard work.

But ceremonies are ceremonies. This beautiful spring day— with temperatures in the 70s moderated by a steady breeze—be-

Figure 1. The renovated Howard Theatre in Washington.
Source: Photograph by Blair Ruble.

longed to the people in the street. Sandra greeted me with a big smile and a hug. A George Washington University vice president, Bernard Demczuk—and Ben's Chili Bowl historian (yes, Ben's has a historian)—recalled his days as a community organizer. The jazz saxophonist Marshall Keys seemed pleased; the guitarist Greg Gaskins, who had played with Elvis, was beaming; and James Brown's drummer, "Mousey" Thompson, could not have been prouder. But the person who best captured the moment for me was David Akers, a local DC musician and novelist whose father had worked at the Howard. David's smile of blissful reconciliation made the entire day worthwhile. Such greetings and exchanges of goodwill were happening everywhere.

I waited for more than an hour in a disorganized line to get inside to see the renovations. But this delay didn't matter in the least. Mousey Thompson's James Brown Experience was holding forth onstage, and was soon followed by other groups. I stood waiting between Sylvia and Ed, old friends who hadn't seen one another in a couple of decades. From what I could tell, they had graduated from Armstrong High in 1952, and had hung out at the Howard back in the day. Sylvia's respirator and walker didn't stop her from boogalooing to the James Brown songbook. They had both been lured back by fond memories of their old haunt, and their story was being played out hundreds of times all around me.

The renovated theater is, in the words of one of its developers, "a twenty-first-century venue" in every way. But its somewhat-updated appearance didn't stop tears of recognition from falling as people entered for the first time. And the place is a beauty, with its quasi-baroque 1910 facade gorgeously restored—crowned by a colorful statue of a trumpet-blowing jazzman—and its new nightclub-chic interiors.

When I walked out, music and dancing were going on all over a freshly cobblestoned T Street. I strolled over to see a new statue of homeboy Duke Ellington, who is represented seated at a keyboard that soars to the heavens in the form of a treble sign. Kids were crawling along its sensuous curves. I spotted the sculptor Zachary Oxman nearby with his family. He told me that he knew he had accomplished his vision when he saw the first child climb onto the treble sign.

On the Metro subway train riding back to work, I found myself seated with a distinguished African American couple whom I had noticed at the ceremony. We started talking. All three of us found the same word to describe what we had just experienced: "healing." This was what we felt—from the initial African incantation to David Akers's smile, from Sylvia and Ed's rediscovery of one another to a five-year-old climbing up on Duke Ellington's lap. Our long-tormented city was healing just a little bit.

What is it about a theater and the music performed there that can heal a city? Entire libraries have been penned about this subject. But what is it about a city that produces the magic of a Howard Theatre? In particular, what is it about a city as divided as Washington by the demons of race and inequality that makes people such as David Akers devote their lives to the pursuit of lasting beauty? These questions have been asked much less frequently.

The chapters that follow cannot hope to answer such grandiose inquiries. Focused as they are on a handful of creative moments in just a half dozen cities on five continents—Naples, Osaka, New York, Buenos Aires, Cape Town, and Yekaterinburg—the chapters can do little more than prompt readers to ask similar questions about their own communities as they move through their own lives. This book will be a success if it inspires those who spend time with it to constantly be on the lookout for David Akers's smile.

Odessa as Inspiration

Traveling throughout my adult life to the part of the world once known as the Soviet Union opened up a multitude of wondrous opportunities. The region is full of natural beauty, exciting cities, and larger-than-life personalities. Yet even in the Carnivalesque wreckage of the region's collapsed political system, nothing quite compares to the city of Odessa. Odessa is not just a place, of course. It is more of a state of mind—or, at the very least, Web sites for a virtual Odessa that exists in the imaginations of the thousands of former residents who have moved to places as varied as Moscow, Tel Aviv, Sydney, Toronto, and Brooklyn.[2]

A "real" Odessa exists as much in the ironic short stories of the *Odessa Tales* by Isaac Babel, who was arrested and shot by Stalin's

NKVD, as it does in the compelling stage productions of Babel's grandson, Andrei Maleev-Babel, who teaches acting in Florida.[3] Odessa, in other words, is not just city with a promenade with a famous staircase overlooking the Black Sea; psychically, it also extends from Siberia to Sarasota. It does so because, throughout its brief yet extravagantly tawdry history, Odessa has inspired people to create.

Odessa was officially established in 1794, and Catherine the Great's frontier settlement and Black Sea port quickly emerged as a randy mix of nationalities and cultures. It has remained so ever since. The anthropologist Tanya Richardson drew on the city's complexities to explore how diversity and place can combine to nurture innovation. Richardson wanted to understand how the city's presumed peculiarities—its mix of nationalities, tolerant attitudes, cuisines, dialects, joie de vivre, sense of humor, Southern temperament, resourcefulness, and entrepreneurial spirit—defined a distinctive Odessan sense of place and history within a newly independent Ukraine (figure 2).[4]

Figure 2. The inner courtyard at 57 Bolshaya Arnautskaya Street in Odessa, on July 2, 2009, showing the city's disorder.
Source: Photograph by Alexey Sergeev; used by permission.

During this quest, Richardson found herself drawn to the work of a literary scholar—Rebecca Stanton—who was examining the Odessa School of writers (including Babel) at the outset of the twentieth century. For Stanton, these authors viewed the city as a Russian cultural space formed by the interaction of multiple lenses, which shifted as if through the prism of a kaleidoscope.[5]

The kaleidoscope—the Scottish physicist David Brewster's contraption combining chips of colored glass and interior mirrors within a tube, much like a telescope—became the rage of Europe as soon as it was invented in 1817. Though today it is only an inexpensive child's toy, the kaleidoscope once came in all sizes, including giant open air versions, for which customers paid willingly to have a look. The "kaleidoscope" soon became a popular metaphor in social criticism, with its mirrors seen as providing an ever-shifting and constantly distorted reflection of more than just physical reality. As early as 1823, the seminal writer Honoré de Balzac suggested that his own depictions of contemporary Parisian society provided a "veritable moral kaleidoscope with its millions of inflections."[6]

Richardson builds on this tradition by arguing that "places are similar to kaleidoscopes in the way they refract history and geography. Ukraine's many localities share fragments of imperial, national, ethnic, and social histories, yet the salience and influence of these histories on the present differ radically."[7] She set out to explore the various ways in which different actors at different times have refracted the complex and multilayered realities of Odessa by shifting perspective—by rotating an analytical/ideological kaleidoscope, as it were. As she tells her story of the Odessan kaleidoscope, she explains how urban communities with incomprehensible differences encourage those living in them to create beauty in order to establish meaning in their own lives.

The Odessan kaleidoscope began spinning from the very beginning.[8] The city took shape in the mind of a Neapolitan soldier of fortune—José Pascual Domingo de Ribas y Boyons (Osip Mikhailovich Deribas)—before it assumed physical presence. De Ribas was the child of a Spanish consul and his aristocratic Irish wife. He had entered into Russian service in the 1770s after a brief stint in the Neapolitan army. While he was serving on the staff of Catherine's lover and imperial strategist, Grigorii Potemkin, de Ribas caught the attention of his superiors by watching over and covering for the multiple offenses of the dissolute American rear admiral John Paul Jones, who also had come to Russia in search of fortune.

Following the ultimate Russian victory over the Ottomans, de Ribas convinced Catherine and Potemkin that a patch of land near the mouths of four major European rivers—the Danube, Dniester, Dnieper, and Bug—would make an excellent location for a city. On May 27, 1794, Catherine ordered that a port be built on the site. Following the Russian practice of identifying settlements in the empire's recently acquired lands in the south—an area that became known as New Russia (following the pattern of New England, New France, and New Spain)—de Ribas's town was to be named after a classical Greek hero. In this case, the name Odysseus was feminized to Odessa in order to honor the empress.

De Ribas set out to create a newer and more orderly version of his hometown, Naples. However, Odessa's sketchy origins—relying on a multitude of fortune hunters and adventurers representing any number of the corners of the late-eighteenth-century world—made coherence difficult to achieve. In some ways he succeeded, as the city grew outward along a logical grid. Nonetheless, there was nothing well ordered about the people who filled it up. The new city's residents came from a variety of backgrounds, having been pulled together by a presumed opportunity to get rich quickly.

Catherine's grandson, Alexander I, replaced de Ribas as Odessa's "city chief" (*gradonachal'nik*) with a French aristocrat, Armand Emmanuel Sophie Septimanie du Plessis, the duc de Richelieu (a great-nephew of the famous Cardinal Richelieu). De Richelieu was on the lam at the time, fleeing revolutionaries in Paris. He is still fondly remembered, and his statue stands atop Odessa's iconic Potemkin Stairs, an urban ladder on which one climbed 200 (now 192) steps from the city's docks to its central districts.

As the governor of New Russia, de Richelieu transformed Odessa into a city of Russia's least-respected "estate" (*soslovia*, social class): the petit bourgeoisie (*meshchane*). Arriving semiskilled workers, tradesmen, shopkeepers, former serfs, Jews, and other outcasts came seeking a new life, and they found it. The *meshchane* were much taken with themselves, even if others were not, and their love of reading and hearing about their lives fostered new forms of Russian literature, theater, song, and media.

Odessa's urban biographer, Charles King, captures the city's "taste for the witty and the absurd; a veneer of Russian culture laid over a Yiddish, Greek, and Italian core; a boom-and-bust economy; a love of the dandy in men and the daring in women; a style of music and writing that involved both libertine abandon and controlled experimentation; and an approach to politics that swung wildly between the radical and reaction."[9] The resulting urban delirium produced, in King's words, a city that "has continually sought to unleash its better demons, the mischievous tricksters that are the vital muses of urban society and the restless creators of literature and art. But it has often loosened its darker ones instead, those that lurk in alleyways and whisper of religious loathing, class envy, and ethnic revenge."[10]

Throughout its history, Odessa as a place—as a city—has prompted a constant rejuxtaposition of different historical, cultural, and political fragments of past and present. It is a community that seems to encourage a turning of the kaleidoscope as residents seek new meaning in endless layers of cultural, religious, ethnic, political, and class differences. The city itself encourages a melding, reconciliation, and mutual borrowing of diverse cultural expressions and traditions to produce ever-new amalgams.[11]

Why is this so? What is it about certain cities that prompts kaleidoscopic refraction of differences? What is it about cities like Odessa that produces a mythologized sense of history and diversity that adds an attractive patina to personal identity? As the Tulane University history professor Samuel Ramer has pondered in relation to New Orleans, what is it about certain cities that drives residents to pause and think: "Yes, this place may have endured tragedy in the past, but it was not a wilderness: Important dramas with major repercussions in our own time took place here. This city, in short, is significant, and by extension, I am also significant."[12]

New Orleans on the Mind

Ramer's own city of New Orleans similarly reflects the power of kaleidoscopic urban serendipity. Like Odessa, New Orleans was, from the beginning, a coincidence of empire. Ramer's Tulane historian colleague, Lawrence Powell, explains what happened: "The accident that had called New Orleans into existence had become the locus of an improvisational way of life. It was as though the entire town had been populated with inhabitants parachuted in from a Hieronymus Bosch painting."[13]

Although every city contains its contradictions, as Louis Eric Elie notes, New Orleans is "in many ways a segregated city, its populations form blurry, complex checkerboards, whose inhabitants also intermarry, mingle in various ways, and don't lend themselves readily to being mapped."[14] Indeed, in addition to everything else that New Orleanians have done since their city was founded, they play music by riffing on what everyone else is playing, no matter what their origins. As the former Tulane president Scott Cowen puts it, "In New Orleans, music is the medium and the message. The whole history of the city, dating back to its origins as a slave-trading center in the seventeenth and eighteenth centuries, is written in its music."[15]

The city's improvisational style has influenced every aspect of its life. For Powell, the distinctive local cuisine contains the essential elements that have made New Orleans its own place:

> The kitchens may have been French, but the cooks were slaves, tossing in the same kettle culinary ingredients plucked from three continents. They received direction from the mistress of the house, but they were the ones who occupied the nexus between town and country. Not only did they cook the food but they purchased the groceries from petty tradesmen and footloose trappers, themselves slaves; and in the process, they skimmed off something extra— "lagniappe," as later generations would describe it—in the form of income and victuals. . . . In other words, African slaves not only stirred the pot; they filled it too.[16]

What was true in the pots and pans that hung over the stoves of this swamp metropolis proved equally true when New Orleanians put down their spoons and knives and picked up musical instruments, which similarly had been created on three continents. The results, of course, became known to the world as "jazz." Jazz, to a considerable degree, is the music that emerged more than a century ago from the rough-and-tumble streets of the city's Storyville neighborhood, a so-called red light district, through the powerful collision of African musical traditions, at times filtered through the Caribbean idiom, and European instrumentation.[17]

As Powell makes clear, this clash has occurred since the city's founding. French and later Spanish colonial administrators allowed—and even encouraged—African-born slaves and their descendants to congregate on Sundays to form drum and dance circles, trade, and practice the traditions of their homelands on a barren patch of land in the "back of town" that became known as Congo Square.[18] These gatherings persisted into the American period, until a fearful antebellum elite led by local slave owners brought them to a halt. Such gatherings nonetheless continued elsewhere in the city, with Congo Square and the nearby Tremé neighborhood remaining focal points for musicians and musical forms that combined African, Caribbean, European, and American traditions. The historian Susan C. Pearce correctly observes that "New Orleans jazz, in fact, was rooted in neighborhoods. The jazz form arose organically within and across neighborhoods, and the performance spaces and musicians were able to place their own local stamps on the compositions that resulted."[19]

The historian Freddi Williams Evans records the story as well:

Alongside European-derived dances, some African descendants continued to dance in the ways of their tradition. Several of the eyewitness accounts of Congo Square gatherings, given during the 1840s, indicate that the dance and the music were African. Dance descriptions given in the 1940s, around one hundred years after the gatherings ceased, show that black New Orleanians continued to employ those rhythms, dances, musical instruments, or cultural practices. The use of handkerchiefs when dancing and the receiving of money for impressive, informal street performances became standards in New Orleans culture. . . . Thus, African-based rhythms that both stimulated and accompanied dance steps undergirded indigenous New Orleans styles. Indeed, the music and the dance continuously influenced each other.[20]

This new music flowed over racial, ethic, class, and gender divisions. "Because of the open-air nature of much music in New Orleans (parades, ballyhoos, lakefront picnics, lawn parties)," Charles B. Hersch adds, it "could not be completely segregated, for it could be heard by all."[21]

The New Orleans story did not end with jazz. The city's musicians played pivotal roles in developing at least three more of the twentieth century's most potent musical forms: Gospel, rock 'n' roll, and hip-hop. Although each of these later genres has multiple claimants for parenthood, there is no doubt that the Crescent City nurtured some of the most seminal figures in each. A cappella quartets such as the Zion Harmonizers moved Gospel from the storefront to established churches during the 1920s and 1930s; and Water Street–born Mahalia Jackson helped to secure Gospel's acceptance nationwide.[22] Every African American performer of note during the 1940s and 1950s cut his or her musical teeth in the city, driving jazz- and blues-laced rhythm & blues into what is now known as rock 'n' roll.[23]

Underneath all this music, from the drums of Congo Square to the electrified rubber bands at the Magnolia Projects a couple of centuries later, lies the most distinctive element of all New Orleans music: a powerful bass line. Bass defines New Orleans music, whether it has been played by African drums or snare drums, acoustic or electrified basses, tubas or foghorns, or chanted by Mardi Gras Indians. Let the music get "dirty and lowdown" and "muddy as the Mississippi," and whatever is happening up above doesn't matter. It's New Orleans.[24]

Almost a half century ago, the bass guitar master George Porter Jr. defined a particular form of bass line on his Fender long-neck guitar that would become known as "funk."[25] Funk has underlain everything since, from rock 'n' roll to rhythm & blues, from hip-hop to "bounce" (the local dance party music that emerged from public housing projects in the 1990s, hence known as "Project Music").[26] New Orleans Bounce is "rip-roaring call-and-response" music with raunchy lyrics and a "propulsive, swinging beat."[27] It is the music of the poor who, though warehoused in increasingly dysfunctional housing projects, still managed to use music to define for themselves who they were.

More recently, New Orleanian rap singers have joined with performers from Houston and Atlanta to fill the gap left in the world's most popular commercial music style.[28] Local hip-hop artists developed something the city had never had before: a powerful recording industry. The rapper Master P (Percy Miller) has sold more recordings than any other New Orleans musician in history, including the legendary Louis Armstrong and Fats Domino.[29] Others—such as Master P and his brothers, Zyshoon (Silkk the Shocker) and Corey (C-Murder), as TRU; Lil' Wayne (Dwayne Michael Carter Jr.); Mystikal (Michael Tyler); Mia X (Mia Young); Fiend (Ricky Jones); and Kane and Abel (David and Daniel Garcia)—have not been far behind.[30]

Just as in Richardson's and Stanton's kaleidoscopic, literary Odessa, the incredibly fertile musical atmosphere in New Orleans for more than two centuries is no accident. It is a result of a vibrant mixing of cultures (Native American, European, African, and Caribbean) within the physical context of shared space (Congo Square, Storyville, Plymouth Rock Baptist Church, the Dew Drop Inn, the Calliope, and Magnolia Housing Projects), as multigenerational musical families (e.g., the Marsalises, the Bastiles, the Nevilles, the Harrisons, and the Millers), and shared institutions (including churches, bars, clubs, so-called social aid and pleasure clubs, radio stations, heritage music festivals, and everything associated with Mardi Gras) come together to confront the demons arising from poverty and disenfranchisement.

In other words, despite differences in style, New Orleanian musicians long have shared a culture. Ned Sublette points out, for example, that "rappers' relatives played in brass bands and [joined in second-line parades] in social and pleasure clubs. Because in New Orleans, people knew that genres weren't locked doors, so they all coexisted. It was all one community."[31] Music, in short, was a way ahead, and a way of claiming one's right to be alive.[32]

The musical history of New Orleans underscores the importance of cities for the creation of art. Cities are where individuals come to terms with who they and their communities are, within the context of constant challenges. "The city," as the notable Kenyan–South African urbanist Caroline Wanjinku Kihato reminds her readers, "is not only an ensemble of policy regimes and the modes of control drawn upon by planners, policy makers, and city officials to manage the city. It is also comprised of urban dwellers' own systems of knowing and understanding their experiences—the codes and symbols *they* use to interpret their experiences, the tactics they employ to navigate it, the vocabularies they use to describe it, and the images they see in their imaginings of it."[33]

The performing arts are not the only vocabularies available for interpreting experiences or for establishing a claim to a particular place at a particular time. They nonetheless are an important component among the many ways in which human beings respond to the delirium of the too-rapidly spinning kaleidoscope of urban life. There are moments when they help urbanites make sense of who they are; and these moments, in turn, are when deep innovation in the arts becomes a necessity as the old ways of telling stories no longer prove sufficient.

Music is thus as ubiquitous in New Orleans as literature is in Odessa.[34] A musical cornucopia finds common roots in the city's deep traditions linking music and community. This connection is perhaps best personified by the now-honored-but-once-persecuted Mardi Gras Indians, as well as the "social and pleasure clubs" of the urban poor.[35]

Such connections have remained just below the surface of "proper" New Orleanian society for most of the city's existence.[36] It is doubtful, for example, that more than a handful of the white shoppers making their way down busy Canal Street in 1915 trying to finish their daily errands even noticed two teenage "colored boys" playing their hearts out for 50 cents a day on a flatbed advertising wagon. None of these shoppers probably ever thought for a moment that they were listening to a free concert by players who would become two of the most important musicians of the century—Sidney Bechet on clarinet, and Louis Armstrong on cornet.[37]

Urban Jagged Edges and Contact Zones

The stories of Odessa and New Orleans suggest how cities of great diversity nurture human creativity. One reason why this is so rests in what the ancient Greeks understood was true of the polis, as captured many centuries ago. As the contemporary French political philosopher Pierre Manent has observed, the city is at a scale where it becomes possible for humans to shape their environment, to "govern themselves and know that they govern themselves."[38]

Such self-government, in turn, creates possibilities for urbanites to define their own meaning in life—to define what they themselves and the community around them mean. Kristof Van Assche and Petruța Teampău go to the heart of the matter when they observe that civic identity is "always local, is always tinged by local histories and identifications and networks as visible and transformed in governance."[39] Community identity is negotiated and renegotiated by members through governance practices and public cultural expressions.

The contemporary British theologian Philip Sheldrake makes the same point somewhat differently. "Cities," he writes, "have always produced vibrancy. They not only have a particular capacity to create diverse community but, historically, they have been the primary sites of human innovation and creativity."[40] However, he cautions, "human community in a fully developed sense is not something that is simply automatic and unconscious. It demands our commitment, a quest for shared values, and a measure of self-sacrifice."[41] This is where the performing arts enter into the equation.

Odessa and New Orleans, of course, are hardly singular instances. To add a more contemporary example, on August 11, 1973, the residents of the high-rise apartment building at 1520 Sedgwick Avenue, in the Morris Heights neighborhood of New York City's impoverished and crime-infested South Bronx, probably were no more aware than those who heard the young Bechet and Armstrong playing on the back of a truck a century earlier that they were witnessing a globally significant moment of cultural invention. New Orleanians walking down Canal Street were hearing the creation of jazz. And the Sedgwick Avenue residents whose walls were vibrating on that August evening with the extraordinarily loud beat emanating from DJ Kool Herc's giant amplifiers at a back-to-school party were experiencing the birth of the late twentieth century's signature musical genre—hip-hop (figure 3).[42]

As with jazz in New Orleans, rap and hip-hop emerged from a long and deep engagement among diverse groups—especially

Figure 3. 1520 Sedgwick Avenue in the Bronx, New York City.
Source: Photograph by Bigtimepeace; used by permission.

the Puerto Ricans and African Americans of poor Bronx neighborhoods—years before any particular evening in 1973. Cultural
engagement between Puerto Rican and other Caribbean migrants
with African Americans in New York dates from at least the 1940s
and 1950s. Protean musicians such as the towering Machito began to perform with Dizzy Gillespie and Charlie Parker; and activist writers such as Jésus Colón, Piri Thomas, and the young
"Nuyorican" poets, including Felipe Luciano and Victor Hernandez Cruz, explored new ways to express racial and national pride.
Often sharing poor neighborhoods, these artists drew from each
other as well as from their often-shared African roots. Like Bechet
and Armstrong, by learning from those who had come before, DJ
Kool Herc simultaneously built on and transformed already-con-
solidated African, Caribbean, Puerto Rican idioms.[43]

If, as a leading historian of Weimar Germany, Eric Weitz, has
proclaimed, "jazz is the sound of the city elevated to art," then the
music pounding through the walls of the Morris Heights high rise
along the Major Deegan Expressway in the Bronx on that hot summer evening more than four decades ago raised the sounds of the
city to a new art form.[44] Clive "DJ Kool Herc" Campbell had moved
to the Bronx from Kingston in 1967. Once in New York, Kool Herc
became witness to an emerging record-based disc jockey street culture. He developed a style known as "break," in which he used
records as a percussion instrument. By doing so, he brought the
distinctive sounds of Jamaican dub music, a subgenre of Reggae,
to partying New Yorkers.[45] They responded with acrobatic forms
of "break" dancing. The amplified sounds of break music quickly
combined with an emerging street-poet scene forming around the
griot traditions of West African storytelling to create rap and hip-
hop.[46]

As these legends attest, kaleidoscopic cities depend on kaleidoscopic neighborhoods, those places of indeterminacy that force
residents to redefine themselves. The spirit of cultural innovation
grows in those urban spaces that confront and confound, constantly challenging people to rethink who they are, and with whom
they share common fates. In this context, the French economist
Jacques Attali presciently argues that music often has presaged
broad social, political, and ideological shifts.[47] Music and the other

performing arts reflect a future being born because they give form and structure to people's deepest fears and hopes about the world around them.

In some cases, urban cultural novas like the birthplaces of jazz and hip-hop can be found on the city's disorderly metropolitan fringe; in others, they exist in the very heart of the city itself. For instance, consider Russian literature in the late nineteenth and early twentieth centuries. Marveling at how, in the span of barely two generations, Russia's age of underdevelopment produced one of the world's great literatures, Marshall Berman increasingly found himself drawn to one particular street—the Nevsky Prospekt in Saint Petersburg, also variously known as Petersburg and Leningrad—for an explanation:[48]

> Finally, the Nevsky was the one place in Petersburg (and perhaps in all Russia) where all the existing classes came together, from the nobility whose palaces and town houses graced the street at its starting point near the Admiralty and the Winter Palace, to the poor artisans, prostitutes, derelicts, and bohemians who huddled in the wretched fleabags and taverns near the railroad station in Znaniemsky Square where the Prospect came to an end. The Nevsky brought them all together, whirled them around in a vortex, and left them to make their experiences and encounters what they could. Petersburgers loved the Nevsky, and mythologized it inexhaustibly, because it opened up for them, in the heart of an underdeveloped country, a prospect of all the dazzling promises of the modern world.[49]

Berman writes of the Nevsky Prospekt at its height under the Romanovs, when the boulevard served as the Russian Empire's *grande allée*. But this street continued to play an elemental role in Russian cultural life long after power and majesty had departed for Moscow because it remained an essential place of contact among the great city's various contradictory components.[50] The Nevsky has always provided meeting places for all sorts of "poor artisans, prostitutes, derelicts, and bohemians," it seems.

Recalling his student days in Leningrad, Kamas Ginkas—the

groundbreaking Jewish-Lithuanian theater director who helped to define Russian-language theater over the past half century—was drawn to his recollections of the Nevsky's Saigon Café. Having been celebrated in cultural histories of the late Soviet era, the Saigon was just the sort of place where those on the edge of society reshape all that is around them. This shabby and unexceptional—but well-located—low-end Soviet eatery was home to precisely the sort of urban—and often vodka-fueled—delirium that undermines urban propriety and cultural authority. As Ginkas evokes this place, the Saigon

> really was not even a café, and its name was not the Saigon. That is just what people called it. It was a dinky street-corner place, maybe 30 square meters, with no seats or tables, where they served lousy coffee. It was basically just a dirty little hole. You stood at these elbow-high counters to drink your coffee, which cost a couple of kopeks, or you brought along something stronger of your own. It was on the corner of Liteiny and Nevsky Prospekt. If you look down Nevsky toward the Admiralty, it would be at your left on the farthest corner from the center. It was around for a long time, into the late 1970s, before it eventually fell apart. This semi-underground place attracted alcoholics, unemployed people, dissidents, crazies, and geniuses. It brought together all of Leningrad's outsiders with an intellectual and bohemian bent. The KGB naturally knew all about it. Its agents were always there listening to what was going on. Everything avant-garde in Leningrad was connected to this spot in one way or another. It was a place where all the rejects of the Soviet era congregated.[51]

Those "rejects" included not just the student Ginkas and his theatrical friends from Georgy Tovstonogov's nearby Bolshoi Drama Theatre around the corner, such as the epochal actor Innokenty Smoktunovsky. They also included the creators of the city's influential underground music culture—Boris Grebenshikov, Viktor Tsoi, and Sergey Kuroykhin—who dropped by, as did such seminal writers as Sergei Dovlatov, Yevgeny Rein, and the future

Nobel laureate Joseph Brodsky. Before its destruction in the 1980s, the distinctly seedy Café Saigon was arguably one of the most creative patches in a country that covered one-sixth of the Earth's land mass. This spot is now, at the beginning of the twenty-first century, the site of a high-end bathroom fixtures store, and thus has been gentrified to the point of destroying even a scintilla of inspiration.

Areas such as the Nevsky Prospekt, to borrow from Robert Alter, are "compelling arenas of incoherence," bringing together those with purpose and those without, thereby defining a city's meaning for its residents.[52] They can be central to a city's life—as is the Nevsky—or much more mundane fringe areas. Russia's first "urbanist"—and most famous satirist—Nikolai Gogol' observed in 1842 that creativity emerges first and foremost in unexceptional neighborhoods and on typical streets that are not of "cardinal importance," because, in such places, a city lives rather than being put on display.[53] Today's social scientists "problematize" these places of group interaction as "zones of contact."[54]

A Study of How Cities and the Arts Interact

Art, as the detective writer Donna Leon observes, is "a mugger that can knock us down whenever it wants. It can lie lurking in a poem and surprise us with joy; it can hide in the lines of a drawing, the curve of the *R* in an illuminated manuscript. Or it can slide out from behind Iago's sneer. For some of us, it comes most powerfully in those perfect moments when the voice, always the voice, goes there and rests just there and, in the doing, sets our spirits free."[55]

No city in the world is more associated with the creative delirium produced by improvised relationships, "co-presence," "zones of contact," and artistic muggings than New York. Rem Koolhaas argued in his path-breaking exhortation of New York during the 1970s, *Delirious New York*, that "the Metropolis strives to reach a mythical point where the world is completely fabricated by man, so that it absolutely coincides with his desires." In the case of New York, he continued, "Manhattan's architects performed their miracles luxuriating in a self-imposed unconsciousness."[56] Urban diversity in and of itself offers an inescapable invitation to impose an inner world onto a cityscape of immense complexity.

Koolhaas's influential manifesto for delirious urbanism has taught urban thinkers to consider the contradictions of urban life as a well-spring for social and physical invention. This approach has in turn encouraged a fulsome appreciation of the sudden, disconcerting juxtaposition of opposites—of high and low culture, good and evil—within a cityscape.

The cases portrayed in the chapters that follow seek to begin responding to the challenges of urban diversity, conflict, and creativity by examining the emergence of musical and theatrical originality in a series of very specific cities at very particular times. Each case uses one of the various performing arts—opera, dance, theater, or music—as a window into the creativity of urban life. And in each case, the members of local proper society—whether aristocratic, merchant, bourgeois, or revolutionary—looked down on the larger communities surrounding them. These were urban societies where the kaleidoscope was turned with such delirious speed as to become the muse for many among their most creative inhabitants. Moreover, none of the cities considered in this volume were prim and proper at the time explored here—or at any other time. "A certain vestige of disorder," the Berlin observer Peter Schneider has written, "and laxer attitudes regarding building rules, business closing times, and nighttime noise limits stand for something that, if anything, is more important than cleanliness: tolerance and open-mindedness."[57]

At their core, the cities examined here have sparked creativity precisely because they have been profoundly tolerant and open-minded places. This volume explores the relationship between creative, open minds and their urban muses rather than the arts that they have produced. In other words, it is a book about urban place, not about the performing arts.

In his elegant social history of opera, *The Gilded Stage*, Daniel Snowman cautions his readers that he is more interested in the broad context within which opera took shape than with opera itself.[58] He continues that he wants to explore how opera has been created, financed, produced, received, perceived, and changed rather than reporting on what takes place onstage. Like Snowman's volume, this book is about the performing arts not as discrete cultural phenomena but rather as reflections of the broader social and political contexts in which they emerged and flourished. It remains, in the end, first and foremost a book about the city rather than a book about the arts.

This volume's chapters build upon a long tradition of works exploring the relationship between cities and creativity that is almost as old as cities themselves. Most well-read Americans of a certain age no doubt will recall perusing Lewis Mumford's *The City in History* at some point during their educations.[59] The argument here differs slightly from that of Mumford, for it hews more closely to that offered by Peter Hall in his astonishingly impressive volume *Cities in Civilization*.[60]

Hall's landmark book opens up the golden ages of more than two dozen cities across nearly three millennia, from Classical Athens to twentieth-century Los Angeles. Searching for the "key to creativity," Hall argues that talent may be more important for urban success than wealth, given that talent comes from all corners of cities' known worlds. "The creative cities were nearly all cosmopolitan," he explains.[61] And he observes that "probably no city has ever been creative without continued renewal of the creative bloodstream."[62]

Hall takes his line of thought a step further, writing that "as a massive generalization, but one that stands up surprisingly well, they are cities that were in a state of uneasy and unstable tension between a set of conservative forces and values—aristocratic, hierarchical, religious, conformist—and a set of radical values which were the exact opposite: bourgeois, open, rational, skeptical. These were societies troubled about themselves, societies that were in the course of losing the old certainties but were deeply concerned about what was happening to them."[63] In other words, as P. D. Smith summarizes Hall's larger point in his own *City: A Guidebook for the Urban Age*, "creative cities are complex, even disorderly, cosmopolitan communities. They are certainly not the easiest and safest places in which to live. . . . Such cities are often overwhelming and intense environments."[64]

If Hall looks to cities experiencing their belle époques, the cases explored in the present volume focus on the periods leading up to—or down from—a city's apotheosis. The chapters that follow delve into the hidden corners of towns, neighborhoods, and quarters that were never belle to begin with. It argues that the edgy conflict of social transformation and social difference, affected by the density of urban life, generates a form of delirium that produces new ways of thinking about life and expressing one's feelings through performance as the kaleidoscope of urban life spins ever more quickly.

The delirious behavior, places, and imaginations incited by an ever-too-quick turning of the kaleidoscope of urban incongruities have produced some of humanity's greatest as well as its most disturbing achievements. Those cities that are most full of contradictions force residents and visitors to choose their own meaning to impose on a constructed reality, thereby fostering intense creativity. Such "foundries in which the old models [are] regularly melted down to be cast into new ones" are those places where urban delirium becomes converted into cultural creativity.[65] They provide the moments that make innovators such as David Akers smile.

Act One: Going for Baroque

A Paradise Inhabited by Devils: Opera in Viceregal and Bourbon Naples

Some cities are born for commerce, some for religion, others for reasons of state. Naples began with a song.

—Barringer Fifield, 1996

Naples under Spanish Habsburgian viceregal administration between 1503 and 1700, and under Bourbon rule, which lasted with interruptions from 1734 until 1861, was a place where the future of European music became its present.[1] Neapolitans successfully interjected middle-brow and low-brow musical forms into high-brow forms. In doing so, they added the verve and energy of their own city to propel European classical music forward. Naples was more than "the capital of the world's music."[2] It was a mixing bowl in which European music became supercharged with the vitality of the nonaristocratic. Neapolitan performers and composers reshaped opera by bringing the contradictions of everyday Neapolitan life to the stage. From there, they moved on to reshape European music as they spread out across the continent. Traces of seventeenth- and eighteenth-century Neapolitan invention can be heard in operas and symphonies throughout the nineteenth and into the twentieth centuries.

The Bourbons' quest for legitimacy lent financial and political support to a blend of music that remained distinctively Neapolitan. Opera in particular provided both the rulers and the ruled in Bourbon Naples with opportunities to come together in conflict and in unity. Opera in eighteenth-century Naples, in other words, became a bountiful venue for creative "conversations" among the city's various paradoxes. Nonetheless, the centrality of music to Habsburg-ian viceregal and Bourbon Neapolitan life hardly distinguishes the era from any other period in the city's millennia-long history. After all, according to legend, the city was founded on a song.

Ulysses, if Homer is to be believed, was the first mariner to escape the temptations of the Bay of Naples. According to *The Odyssey*, Ulysses had heard of the bay's infamous sirens—part women, part bird or nymph-like creatures—who lured sailors to their death by singing so beautifully that no one could sail on without succumbing. Thus, when returning from the Trojan War via the bay, Ulysses plugged the ears of his crew with beeswax and bound himself to the mast until they had sailed safely out of range of the sirens' audible temptation. Then, one of the sirens—Parthenope—angry over their failure to seduce their prey, drowned herself in the sea. The original settlement on the bay was said to have grown on the spot where she washed ashore, claiming her name as its own.[3]

The various communities huddled around the Bay of Naples date, in one incarnation or another, back to the second millennium before the birth of Christ. Ever since, this urban area has remained one of the world's great cultural fulcrums. "The wonder of the place," as the novelist and writer on the arts Benjamin Taylor reminds us, "is that it has not been annihilated by so much history. Ask yourself what New York or Chicago or Los Angeles will be twenty-five centuries from now. Imagination falters."[4] Although Taylor is correct in asserting that our imagination falters, the Neapolitan imagination rarely has.

Between Apollo and Dionysus

Greek colonizers made the town of Parthenope—which was on the site in Naples where the medieval Castel dell'Ovo stands today—a beachhead for further colonization of the western Mediterranean Sea region. Their cities—including the "new town" of Neapolis—sprang up along the bay's shores as colonizers paid their devotion to the god of reason, Apollo. Nearby, the mountain we know as Vesuvius reminded them of Nisa, the sacred mountain of Dionysus back home. They soon traveled up its slopes to organize seductive rites of fertility and renewal. Ancient and Byzantine Greeks dominated the bay's towns for centuries, creating a local culture that manically swings between Apollonian rationality and Dionysian sensuality.[5]

As the Greeks quickly appreciated, the Bay of Naples promises humans one of the most salubrious habitats on the planet. The bay's environment, in fact, is so perfect that local residents have rarely been forced to be enterprising. They have merely needed to live off the land and sea as the mild Mediterranean climate, safe harbor, turquoise sky, and indigo sea have sustained lush vegetation boosted by a deep layer rich volcanic soil and an easy growing season. In 326 BC, the victorious Romans assumed control over the area. The local Neapolitan Greeks did all they could to make sure that the arriviste Romans remained under their spell. As Taylor puts it, though it had been defeated militarily, "Naples proceeded to conquer Rome culturally."[6] Prominent Romans, including the conqueror of the Orient, Lucullus, started building large villas for their retirement as they turned the area into an elite resort.[7]

Two millennia later, Peter Robb, the Australian writer on art and crime (a very Neapolitan combination), explains what happened: "By staying Greek and not being a political player in the region at all, Naples became everything Rome was not. The price of its security involved a psychic diminution for the more ancient city, but the arrangement was also immensely liberating for Naples. Neapolitans were free not to be serious. Free to cultivate their Greek garden, and not unaware how deeply Romans remained in awe of Greek culture. Being Greek was a kind of revenge, a soft power of its own subtle kind."[8]

Yet all was not quite idyllic. The inhabitants of this earthly paradise constantly faced the possibility of near-instantaneous annihilation by Mount Vesuvius. Categorized as a "red" volcano for the lava that periodically spews from its crater, Vesuvius has erupted cataclysmically over the centuries, as when it eradicated the Roman port cities of Pompeii and Herculaneum in AD 79.[9] A Neapolitan of any century only needed to peer at the menacing mountain looming over the city to be reminded of the transitory folly of human existence.

Mount Vesuvius necessarily makes tangible Percy Bysshe Shelley's observation that Naples is a "Metropolis of a ruined Paradise."[10] And Shirley Hazzard, the graceful Australian-Anglo-American interpreter of Naples, contends the Neapolitan sense of life is "profoundly informed by [an] awareness of death that values the smallest pleasure as god-given, fatalistically attributing misfortune to the gods' sterner associate, Il Destino."[11] Time in Naples, Hazzard continues, is long, "but a town with a volcano is no place to forget mortality."[12]

Under such circumstances, Neapolitans have naturally looked for salvation to whatever source is available. A persistent and "living interdependence between Christian and pagan emotions," in the words of Taylor, marks the local culture to this day.[13] For example, tens of thousands of Neapolitans over the centuries have believed that they have been saved at critical junctures in the city's history by the intervention of San Gennaro (Januarius), a decapitated Christian martyr who is the city's patron saint. Gennaro's liquefying blood—which miraculously occurs three times each year—is believed to stave off the worst effects of the earthquakes, lava flows, ash clouds, and poisonous gas emanations that have struck the city with worrisome regularity across the centuries.[14] This extravagant delirium stands at the core of what it means to be "Neapolitan." And of particular importance, as the twenty-first-century urban explorer Moses Gates observes, the city's "chaos isn't chaos at all, not once you figure out a few things."[15]

Hallucinatory Effervescence

Political excitability seems to accompany the natural volatility of living on top of a geological powder keg, as the Romans learned during the great Pompeian slave rebellion led by Spartacus in 73 BC.[16] Over the years, Naples has been ruled and misruled by a succession of leaders and dynasties, many with only a tangential connection to the Neapolitans themselves. The ancient and Byzantine Greeks dominated the area even after the Romans had arrived. Effective independence ended with the appearance of the Normans in the middle of the twelfth century, with a succession of foreigners holding sway for some six centuries.[17]

Even the most straightforward chronological listing of the city's changing ruling regimes communicates something of its political affliction. Naples has been lorded over by the Etruscans, Cumaeans, Greeks, Romans, Byzantines, Ducal princes, Normans, Swabian Hohenstaufens, Angevins from today's France and Aragonese from today's Spain, Spanish and Austrian Habsburgs (including periods known as " parentheses"), Bourbons, Parthenopean Republicans, Bonapartean French (in yet another "parenthesis"), restored Bourbons, Risorgimento revolutionaries, Savoy Italian royalists, Fascists, American occupiers, and Italian Republicans.[18] The city's history is so complex, in fact, that the distinguished British historian John Julius Norwich was reduced to offering sympathy to the readers of his magisterial history of the Mediterranean region, *The Middle Sea*. Writing about dynastic conflicts in fourteenth-century Naples, Norwich threw up his hands and warned that "the reader is not expected to follow the rest of this paragraph and its successor, briefly included only to illustrate the level to which Neapolitan politics had sunk."[19]

Any city that is able to survive gaggles of years classified as historical "parentheses" necessarily has suffered through more than would be expected from even predatory and rapacious regimes. Consequently, Neapolitans learned to distrust their foreign rulers and nurtured a culture in which, as Barringer Fifield records, "the lie is truer than the truth, [as] the lie reveals the liar's true dreams and desires."[20]

Not surprisingly, Naples, the long-impoverished Campania region of which it is the capital city, and all of Southern Italy have emerged from this delirious mélange as poster children for political failure.[21] Pick a century, and during it Naples was overflowing with poor folks piled on top of one another, rampant diseases, periodic plagues and vicious epidemics, human exploitation of every conceivable form, grotesque social deformities, and mundane foolery. It is no wonder that the city has been known widely since the Middle Ages as a "paradise inhabited by devils."[22]

Whoever these Neapolitan devils might have been, they have proven to be profoundly human. Their deeply ingrained humanity has inspired intellectual, cultural, and sensual beauty. The city's combination of natural appeal and peril has nourished a lively culture marked from the time of its original settlers, the Epicureans, by a distinctive blend of sensuous, joyful hedonism and rigorous, stern sanctity—of paganism and piety. Thus, Naples has been home both to the inventors of pizza and chocolate ice cream, on one hand; and to countless religious orders, on the other. For some visitors, the city has been little more than an agglomeration of churches, convents, and monasteries combining a local religion and architecture of straitlaced redemption with hallucinatory effervescence.[23] Yet religious piety carried only so far in a city where attempts by Spanish overseers to impose the Inquisition were twice turned back by popular revolts, in 1510 and again in 1547.[24]

Even the most cursory listing of thinkers and performers who have been born, raised, or spent a significant productive sojourn in Naples inspires awe: Virgil, Pliny the Elder, Pliny the Younger, Thomas Aquinas, Giovanni Boccaccio, Francis Petrarch, Giotto, Caravaggio, Miguel de Cervantes, Giambattista Basile, Atommaso Campanella, Jusepe de Ribera, Farinelli, Alessandro and Domenico Scarlatti, Metastasio, Giambattista Vico, Gioachino Rossini, Gaetano Donizetti, Mary Shelley, Enrico Caruso, Gabriele d'Annunzio, Pablo Neruda, Benedetto Croce, Alberto Moravia, Sophia Loren, Sergio Bruni, Lina Wertmuller, Massimo Ranieri, Peppe Barra, Elena Ferrante, and Maradona—all products to some degree of the joy and pathos that so mark Naples.[25]

Any city that can claim such a list of brilliant daughters and sons must be more than a cesspool of human degradation. The well-deserved censure that so often has been leveled against Naples must be tempered with an equal appreciation of its creativity. Censure and admiration may not be distinct phenomena at all, but merely multifaceted aspects of a single chemical reaction among nature and humans over millennia of habitation. Arguably, this fusion of Heaven and Hell—of so-called high and low cultures—stands at the center of the Neapolitan creative impulse.

Peter Robb captured this distinguishing urge at the end of the twentieth century. For Robb, Naples was

> an intricate society of crowded urban spaces and a promiscuous mixing of classes, a culture that made a great deal out of the immaterial, the precarious, and the ephemeral, whose highest arts were music and theatre, and whose distinctions were rhetorical, erotic, comic, baroque, carnal, metaphysi-

cal, a sensibility that was lazily sensual and austerely abstract by turns, choral and instinctive, solitary and systematic. Naples gave the world ice cream [*sic*], pizza, opera buffa, and transvestitism as an art form. Naples ravished Virgil, Boccaccio, Stendhal, shocked and disgusted Sade, Ruskin, Sartre. Naples filled the paintings of the visitor Caravaggio and the operas of the visitor Mozart. Naples was the motherland of the polymorphous perverse, and parts of it still recognizably the Greek city of Petronius's *Satyricon* in the late twentieth century.[26]

How have these Neapolitan angels and devils inhabiting this paradise together been so creative for so many millennia? Over the centuries, authors—including some of these very same Neapolitan angels and devils—have tried to provide an answer, demonstrating that every approach to Naples somehow falls short of the mark. But my line of attack here is less ambitious. By focusing on only one very small moment in the grand sweep of Neapolitan history—the creation of distinctive forms of opera over the course of the seventeenth and eighteenth centuries—this chapter attempts to uncover some of the ways in which the kaleidoscopic delirium of a city such as Naples transforms culture.

Opera during Spanish Rule

The explosion of Neapolitan opera during the eighteenth century came after a complex period of accomplishment and failure in every aspect of local life. Two centuries of Spanish viceregal rule shambled to an end when the Habsburg Charles II of Spain died without an heir in 1700, setting off the War of Spanish Succession across Europe. It is important to consider the origins of Spain's domination of Naples in order to appreciate the meaning of its collapse.

Spanish rule was a complex era for Naples. The fifteenth and sixteenth centuries were a time of constant maritime warfare between Islam and Catholic Christendom for control of the Mediterranean Sea region.[27] Because France, Spain, Venice, and Rome were increasingly threatened by Muslim incursions and coastal raiding parties, these European states desperately looked for ways to contain the bleeding of wealth and young men at the hands of Islamic raiders, such as relying on the fearsome Barbarossa brothers and scores of other self-designated naval defenders of their faith.[28]

The battle was one that the Spanish simply could not afford to lose. This fundamental reality sparked a protracted power struggle between Spain and its French rivals following the collapse of Aragonese power in the late 1490s. Naples eventually was brought securely under Spanish control in 1503, much to the initial delight of the locals. However, as Robb notes, Spanish rule proved to be "not the solution Naples imagined for itself. Neapolitans had no idea how long those people were going to stay. Two hundred years later, they were still there. Naples realized too late the cost of joining an empire. The earlier kings of Naples, who had been French or Spanish, had been foreigners who became Neapolitan and identified their interests with those of this city where they now lived. Now, however, the kingdom was a vicerealm and Naples was a vassal city governed by a viceroy taking orders from Madrid. Neither the barefoot crowds nor the plumed nobility on their best mounts imagined, at the end of 1503, that their city would be seen from Madrid as a military staging post, a source of revenue and labor power for fighting Spain's foreign wars. Spain had locked Naples into a global empire, which soon showed signs of being seriously overstretched."[29]

Spanish hegemony would last until the early years of the eighteenth century. As that new century began, the city fell to Charles's Austrian Habsburg cousins, with the former Kingdom of the Two Sicilies being divided into separate entities, as it had often been in the past—one with a capital on the island of Sicily at Palermo, and the second with a capital on the Italian Peninsula at Naples.[30] When the dust finally settled in 1734, both Palermo and Naples found themselves under the rule of Charles of Bourbon, and Naples would remain under the Bourbons for a century and a quarter.[31]

Two centuries of Spanish and Austrian Habsburg rule between 1503 and 1734 served Naples well in many ways. The city's rulers encouraged displays of "magnificence" and "splendor," in part by patronizing grand buildings with rich decorative details made from sumptuous materials.[32] They simultaneously relied on public rituals, street displays, and festivals to establish their legitimacy and to reach out to a population that persisted in being deeply suspicious of, feeling betrayed by, and experiencing alienation from its foreign overseers.[33]

Spanish Naples had become one of world's great metropolises, as both the largest city under the Spanish Crown throughout the first half of the sixteenth century, and, throughout much of the century to follow, as a competitor to Paris for runner-up to London among European cities.[34] Naples's growing population, spacious palaces, ornate churches and monasteries, theatrical cityscapes, and booming foreign trade set it apart from nearly anyplace else on the Continent.[35] It was what scholars and tourist promoters today would call a "world city."[36]

The Spanish ensured that Naples could not easily fall to either an outside invasion or an internal insurrection. The indefatigable Spanish viceroy, Don Pedro Alvarez de Toledo—who ruled the city for Spain with an iron hand between 1532 and 1552—transformed the town by rebuilding or constructing a major network of old and new fortifications that control the commanding heights around the city as well as its bustling waterfront.[37] His refurbished "splendid and scared Sant'Elmo fortress loomed over the city, visible from it every part and never out of mind. On the seafront stood the Castel Nuovo, massive, buttressed, turreted, moated, and symmetrical; and a mile away, thrust out over the water, the seriously military brutalism of the Castel dell'Ovo clanked in readiness to repel navies, garrison troops, and incarcerate enemies of the state." Finally, the Castle Capuano, at the city's eastern gate, completed the defensive lines that continue to dominate Naples's cityscape today.[38]

Viceroy Toledo laid out and built the arrow-straight street that still bears his name to facilitate the movement of troops around the occupied city.[39] To house his soldiers, he, subsequent viceroys, and officials turned to developers to set down a dense street grid lined with tall, barrack-like buildings filled with soldiers and the local population, who depended on the soldiers for their living. Long known as the Spanish Quarters (Quartieri Spagnoli), the area has been renowned for its toughs, brigands, and sex service industry workers. "Filled with riotous foreign soldiery and the locals who serviced their needs," Robb notes, "the Quarters were never one of the most desirable residential areas in Naples."[40]

On a continent where most buildings at the time were three, or maybe four, stories tall, Naples's cramped location—wedged between volcano and sea—encouraged buildings to grow to six and seven stories.[41] It was, in the words of Lady Emma Hamilton's twenty-first-century biographer, Kate Williams, "a town of big-time glamour and massive spending, an eighteenth-century Las Vegas." Williams continued: "Neapolitan buildings were painted bright colors—garnet, sapphire, blue, pink, and mint green. . . . [This] extravagant architecture suited Naples. People, noise, and color spilled out of every doorway. Even travelers from London, a city more than twice as populous, gazed openmouthed at the throngs. Unlike London, where the poor congregated in hidden slums, the Neapolitans seemed to live almost entirely outdoors."[42]

This theatrical city benefited in innumerable ways from having been integrated into the world's most powerful global empire.[43] Vibrant foreign communities settled in, bringing new wealth, ideas, and business contacts as Catalan, Dutch, Flemish, Florentine, French, German, Genoese, Greek, Jewish (before their expulsion), Milanese, Portuguese, Venetian, and, eventually, English merchants set up shop in the flourishing city.[44] The constant presence of foreigners enriched the local scene, though diminishing its value in the eyes of subsequent art historians (e.g., Giorgio Vasari and a host of Anglo-American authors), who have valued the "authenticity" of culture rooted in place.[45] The city's dynamic transnational presence made Naples different from other cities on the Italian Peninsula.[46] As Robb argues, the flowering of local painting emerged from this mix, as when Michelangelo Merisi arrived from the town of Caravaggio in the early seventeenth century—and eventually became known as the notorious, prodigally creative Caravaggio.[47]

Instead of interpreting the cultural achievements of Naples as proof of the city's modernity and innovation, historians have denigrated these accomplishments for not having been home grown, as were those of Tuscany.[48] But in contrast to smaller cities to the north, Naples remained a place where artists came for work, quite often leaving town when the task for which they had been hired was complete. It was a city where royalty and its representatives— rather than mercantile princes and grand dukes, as in Tuscany— commissioned rather than purchased art. Local customs and practices tended to convert those who created works of art into mere employees, rather than encouraging them to become independent actors or, perhaps, guild members, as elsewhere in Italy and Europe.[49] Thus Naples' most creative minds, pens, brushes, chisels, and voices, once tied to Church institutions and to the Court, failed to present as compelling a tale of heroic genius, as defines so much of the writing of art history, artistic self-promotion, and Renaissance lore. Instead, prosaic economic ties embedded them in highly complex and culturally varied institutions.[50]

A Center of Difference

Diversity was nothing new for the communities surrounding the Bay of Naples, because the area had become and remained a mixing bowl of languages, cultures, and religions starting well before the Romans arrived. In this regard, the British Classicist Mary Beard observes with reference to Pompeii at the time of its destruction in AD 79 that this Roman city was full of "Greek art, Jewish dietary rules, Indian bric-a-brac, Egyptian religion, and so forth," as "indigenous peoples speaking the native Oscan language rubbed shoulders with Greek settlers" (figure 4).[51]

Syncretistic, cross-cultural blending can be seen throughout the area's history, as when the retired Roman general Lucullus planted cherry trees plundered during his conquests of the Roman East around his luxury villa along the shore of the bay.[52] Later, likewise, the French Angevins brought master masons and gothic architecture to adorn their Neapolitan capital.[53] Carrying on this tradition of cross-cultural propinquity, local gourmets invented chocolate ice cream in 1690 by combining the Roman traditions of enjoying flavored ice with sugar imported from Ottoman Asia and the "newly discovered" cacao that had begun to be imported via Spanish colonial trade with the Americas.[54] Less prosaically, more than three thousand churches, convents, and monasteries promoted the arts and theological inquiry.[55] And the University of Naples—Italy's third-oldest, and Europe's first state-sponsored, university, having been founded in 1224—served as one of the continent's major intellectual centers; important scientific societies—including the Accademia de' Secreti, Accademia degli Oziosi, Accademia degli

Figure 4. A view of Pompeii in Roman times.
Source: Library of Congress.

Incogniti, Accademia degli Ardenti, and Accademia degli Investi-
ganti—began to flourish; and orphanages and major public hospitals opened their doors.[56]

Vesuvius exploded pitilessly in 1631, with certain annihilation
staved off in popular imagination only by an intervention from San
Gennaro, who appeared in the sky before 300,000 terrorized Neapolitans and commanded that the mountain cease its eruption.[57]
Earthquakes, famine, and plagues claimed many lives, as some of
the most crowded neighborhoods in Europe became petri dishes for
all forms of natural and social contagions. The famed Neapolitan
criminal organization known as the Camorra took shape around a
Spanish precursor, the Confraternita della Guarduna, which had
been formed in Seville by soldiers and petty criminals.[58] An insurrection of the poor—led by a fishmonger, Masaniello (Tommaso
Aniello), in 1646 and 1647—temporarily drove the viceroy from
power, whereas the Macchia Conspiracy in 1700 attempted to secure local independence.[59]

Against this backdrop of anxieties over their unruliness and
depravity—complicated by volcanic eruptions and other natural
calamities—the Neapolitans turned across the centuries to music,
frivolity, and prayer for solace and salvation.[60] Local celebrants
were spurred on by their Spanish overlords, who sought to legitimate their power by observing an intricate annual series of public
spectacles tied to the agricultural calendar, individual life cycles,
and pivotal events in the lives of the royals.[61] Twenty-eight new
patron saints—each worthy of a grand public festival—joined the
city's original seven.[62] The local hero Gennaro alone merited three
fêtes a year when his blood liquefied.[63] This is perhaps fitting, given
that tolerant Naples produced few homegrown Christian martyrs
of its own. Even Gennaro had his head cut off in nearby Pozzuoli,
not in Naples proper.[64]

Viceroys and the lesser nobility, for their part, often celebrated their positions with additional public spectacles. The result, as
the historian John Marino notes, is that "in Spanish Naples during
the reigns of the three Philips [Philip II, 1556–98; Philip III, 1598–
1621; and Philip IV, 1621–65], public ceremonies in the streets and
squares, courts and churches of Naples—recurrent performances
of fixed, movable, and extraordinary feasts in religious processions,

devotional rites, civic festivals, and popular demonstrations—not only combined the religious and the secular but also most often found the two inseparable."[65]

In the theater, the centuries-old commedia dell'arte tradition of stylized farce spoken in local dialect—a performance art that itself had descended from Latin *fabulae atellanae* first staged in the Campania town of Atella in the fourth century BC—flourished in Habsburgian Naples, just as it had in Roman Neapolis.[66] The masked jester Pulcinella—who appears as Punch, alongside his sidekick Judy, in the English-speaking world—was well on his way to becoming a symbol of Neapolitan life by the Middle Ages.[67] The buoyant custom of vernacular madrigal singing that had been formalized by the Benedictine monk Paul Warnefrid in the mid-900s continued to flourish long thereafter.[68] Popular music merged with sacred music, as the vernacular and the formal flowed together with wild music—including the *villanelle*, *frottole*, and the musical accompaniment to the *tarantelle* dance—wafting into the classrooms and studios of the city's four major Spanish-era conservatories. By the seventeenth and eighteenth centuries, Naples had become one of the indisputable music capitals of Europe.[69]

Opera in Bourbon Naples

Naples was growing rapidly throughout this period, with the city doubling in population throughout the eighteenth century, from 215,608 in 1707 to 435,903 in 1798.[70] The majority of the city's residents included the abjectly poor, together with the impoverished schemers known as the Lazzaroni (named after the patron saint of lepers, Lazarus), whose bravura set the tone for local urban life. The Bourbons arrived just as the city's growth was accelerating still further.

On May 10, 1734, King Charles of Bourbon—the son of King Philip V of Spain and his second wife, the Italian Elizabeth Farnese—triumphantly arrived, just after his eighteenth birthday, in this burgeoning and reinvigorated capital to claim his throne. Enthusiastic crowds carried the young monarch to the Cathedral to pay homage to San Gennaro (figure 5).[71] The saint responded by performing the miracle of his blood's liquefaction, as the jubilant

Neapolitan crowds luxuriated in their good luck. Naples was a fully independent realm for the first time in nearly eight centuries. The city celebrated its new status as a capital. The twenty-first-century chronicler Jordan Lancaster records, "The period of Bourbon rule . . . was perhaps the city's happiest time, offering a certain degree of political stability and independence, albeit incomplete implementation of the civic ideals of the Enlightenment."[72]

King Charles found a city that had been much abused by Spanish colonial rule and the ill-fated Austrian "parenthesis." As regime builders invariably do, he and his minions confronted the challenge of legitimizing their rule by creating a new state ideology. Just as their Spanish predecessors had done upon claiming the kingdom as

Figure 5. *San Gennaro Intercedes with the Virgin, Christ, and God the Father to End the Plague,* by Luca Giordamo, circa 1650.
Source: Museo Nazionale di Capodimonte, Naples.

their own two centuries earlier, Charles initially sought to impose a new physical order on the capital by reconstructing the cityscape.

The Bourbons, in fact, had few opportunities to rebuild the city in their preferred image. By the time of their arrival, the population had recovered from a devastating epidemic of the plague during the mid–seventeenth century. The Naples entered by Charles and his court was once again among the largest in Europe, with a population fast approaching 300,000, and was far more densely settled than anywhere else on the Continent.[73] The majority of these inhabitants were migrants from the increasingly impoverished countryside, which was being racked by an economically lethal combination of feudal rights and widespread brigandage.

Previous rulers had left behind a collection of architectural monuments that asserted their intention to control the city—such as the thirteenth-century Castel Nuovo in the harbor; the glowering fourteenth-century Sant'Elmo fortress; and dozens of large, seventeenth-century, High Baroque Roman Catholic religious institutions of every conceivable kind.[74] The fortress in particular took on ever darker significance after being renovated by the indefatigable Viceroy Toledo, who converted it into an icon of Spanish domination. As noted above, he similarly built the unswerving Via Toledo through the city's heart to allow the free flow of troops around town (as well as of patrons to the street's prestigious shops).[75] Yet, as Robb records, the grand changes wrought by Toledo and other Spanish overseers "failed to impose their grandeur on the people who lived among them. . . . Naples itself lived in the interstices, and that life was harder to see."[76]

King Charles would have to leave his mark in other ways. His capital's periodic outbreaks of both violence and multitudinous ills provoked some of Europe's most brilliant social thought of the era.[77] The city's notable social ingenuity can be seen, for example, in the writings of Paolo Mattia Doria, Celestino Galiani, Ferdinando Galiani, Antonio Genovesi, Saverio Mattei, Giambattista Vico, their peers, and their antagonists at some of Italy's oldest and newest academies, literary societies, and universities.[78] As one twenty-first-century Risorgimento skeptic—the British journalist David Gilmour—forcefully argues, "After Florence and Austrian-ruled Milan, Naples was the best place for intellectuals to be, living under the sympathetic eyes of its new Bourbon monarchs and their talented ministers. Rome or Turin would not have tolerated the presence of Antonio Genovesi, who inspired many people with his advocacy of radical economic and humanitarian reforms. Yet in the tolerant atmosphere of Bourbon Naples, he could enjoy a successful public career as a professor of metaphysics and ethics, becoming in 1754 the first professor of political economy in Europe."[79]

Another twenty-first-century writer, Benjamin Taylor, has been drawn to the deeply humanistic efforts of Giambattista Vico to overturn the rampant rationalism and natural philosophic thought of Descartes and others by creating "a new science of human things" (*le cose umane*).[80] Vico's attack on reductionism is a precursor to the historicist perspectives of the modern and postmodern eras.[81] His belief in the verification of truth through creation and invention rather than observation reflects the realities of a vast, sprawling, contradictory city where everyone improvises to survive.

Naples sustained top-flight social thought in part because of its rulers' indifference to intellectual inquiry and in part because of the sheer number of human beings living on top of one another.[82] The complexity of the city's social order prompted leading social thinkers to consider the meaning of ancient urban patterns that rendered social, economic, and political reform and renewal maddeningly confusing.[83]

The painter Caravaggio's late-twentieth-century biographer, Helen Langdon, tried to capture what the city must have been like when the artist sought refuge there after fleeing a death sentence in Rome in 1606. What Caravaggio found would have been familiar to Charles as he entered the city a century later. Langdon wrote:

> The beauty of the bay celebrated since antiquity was proverbial and from the shores there rose, as in a vast theater, tiers of buildings, churches, palaces, and monasteries, encircled by the city walls. Everything was subject to the visible power of Spain. . . . A wealth of *palazzi* and ecclesiastical buildings made the city one of the marvels of Europe. It retained its ancient Greek grid plan, and within the ramparts, immensely long, straight avenues, most famous and fashionable among them, the new Via Toledo, thrust dramatically

across the center. . . . Grandiose and massively rusticated portals, crowned by heraldic shields, and imposing facades, with heavily barred windows, proclaimed the mighty status of the ancient families, while the saturation of the city center was intensified by the palaces of the new nobility, the high-ranking functionaries of the Spanish state, and the great Spanish families who had settled there. . . . The palaces and the religious buildings took up so much space that the rest of the population was packed into crowded dwelling quarters, and a vital, noisy and violent life took place on the streets.[84]

More often than not, given such an entrenched and constricted built environment, Bourbon urban renewal involved the mundane tasks of improving commerce (e.g., port and road improvements, as well as demolishing old city walls), establishing order (building new cavalry barracks), and creating strategically placed symbolic sites (modernized the Royal Palace in town, together with building new palaces and parks at Capodimonte overlooking the city, as well as at Portici and at Caserta outside town).[85] The Bourbons initially embraced the local penchant for theatricality with a triumphalist Baroque style, which lent many of their projects an air of majesty far in excess of their urban function.[86] In reality, however, the dark, winding, labyrinthine crowded alleys and backstreets towered over by six- and seven-story tenements exerted their domain over the cityscape.

Beyond building projects, King Charles and his brilliant minister, Bernardo Tanucci, set out to elevate the city's stature more broadly, turning to music and a native neoclassicism in all the arts that received fresh impulse in the period following the midcentury rediscovery of Herculaneum and Pompeii.[87] They encouraged music in general—and opera in particular—as a means for underscoring the city's new capital status and for elevating Naples's reputation throughout Europe.[88] This strategy to cement the Crown's relationship with its own subjects simultaneously raised the young kingdom's prestige as one of the great centers of European music.[89] By 1739, the French travel writer Charles de Brosses declared the city to be "the capital of the world's music."[90]

Singing for Legitimacy

Many visitors from Northern Europe agreed with de Brosses, observing that the quality of Italian music improved the further south one traveled along the peninsula.[91] A quarter century later, at the end of the 1760s, Joseph-Jerome LeFrançais de Lalande addressed the issue in a guidebook for French travelers to Italy. "Music is the Neapolitans' triumph," Lalande started. "Apparently," he continued, "eardrums are more sensitive, more attuned to harmony, more sonorous, in this country than in the rest of Europe; the entire nation sings; gestures, inflections of voice, the way each syllable is emphasized, conversation itself, all show and manifest a sense of harmony and music. Naples is the principal source of Italian music, of great composers, and of excellent operas." He urged visitors to attend performances at one of the city's five opera theaters: the San Carlo, the Fiorentini, the Teatro Nuovo, the San Carlino (for opera buffa), and the Teatro del Fondo.[92] Charles of Bourbon's magnificent San Carlo Opera House was not only the grandest among them; it was also the largest in Europe when it opened on November 4, 1737.[93]

Charles assumed the Spanish crown in 1759, leaving eight-year-old Ferdinand IV on the Neapolitan throne. Ferdinand—who would become known affectionately to his subjects as *il re nasone* for his large beak nose—remained in power for nearly seven decades, among the longest reigns in European history.[94] Historians have attached any number of disparaging sobriquets to the monarch and his tenure in power. Even the sympathetic Gilmour records that "Ferdinand emerged as a boisterous, bonhomous, rough-edged youth who loved hunting as much as his father and hated reading, writing, and even signing his own name."[95] Norwich is characteristically more direct, observing that "Ferdinand—'the scoundrel king,' as he was universally known—*il re lazzarone*'—was a childish boor who loved only hunting and horseplay, possessed not a shred of natural dignity, and boasted of never having read a book."[96]

For many of his subjects, Ferdinand was perhaps better known for selling a day's catch of fish at a small stand in the city's main market than for his prowess in governance or courage in battle.[97] By contrast, his strong-willed wife, Maria Carolina—the daughter of Austrian empress Maria Theresa and the elder sister of Marie Antoinette—proved herself a close-minded reactionary who encouraged her husband's conservative inclinations.[98]

Maria Carolina's brother, Emperor Joseph II of Austria, succinctly recorded his impressions of Ferdinand following a 1768 visit with the Neapolitan royals. Joseph wrote that he detected in his brother-in-law "so definite an aversion from all innovation, so great an indolence of mind and a distaste for all reflection, that I almost dare assure you that the man has never reflected in his life either about himself or his physical or moral existence, his situation, his interests, or his country. He is quite ignorant of the past and present and has never thought about the future; in fact he vegetates from day to day, merely engaged in killing time."[99]

By the time Ferdinand died in 1825, his realm had been racked by unending conflict between the provinces and the capital; massive migration into Naples by thousands of the poorest of the poor from an impoverished countryside; grinding famine in 1763–64; violent earthquakes, such as that of 1783; a failed, bloody revolution; military occupation by the Napoleonic French (the French Emperor temporarily placed his brother Joseph on Ferdinand's throne before entrusting the city and region to his brother-in-law Joachim Murat); an unsuccessful transition from an absolutist to a constitutional monarchy; Masonic plots; maladroit administration of justice; bureaucratic incompetence; massive corruption; widespread brigandage; and periodic bouts of Absolutist repression.[100] As Lancaster wryly notes, "Ferdinand was not the enlightened statesman his father had been, and nothing so clearly sums up the differences between father and son as the two eponymous theatres they established: the San Carlo for opera seria, and the San Ferdinando for opera buffa."[101]

Charles and Ferdinand were hardly hopeless dilettantes in focusing so much attention on opera as a source of legitimacy for their reigns. The music historian Martha Feldman argues that the link between an emerging operatic form of eighteenth-century musical drama—known as opera seria—and sovereignty was quite explicit and direct. "Scholars of the past know the genre well but found it unintelligible," Feldman writes. "Yet," she continues, "opera seria reigned supreme among all musical and theatrical genres across most of eighteenth-century Europe. Getting to write the music or, even more prestigiously, the poetry for an opera seria was like getting to write a feature for Dreamworks.[102]

Feldman extends her argument by observing that "everywhere, whatever forms of rule prevailed, opera seria thrived in the glow of old regime sovereignty. In this sense, it thrived in the glow of a world endlessly marked by the reiteration of social hierarchies whose implications were nothing short of cosmological — implicit assertions of a world order in which ranks cascaded downward in the great chair of being from God to sovereign or ruling class to the various classes and orders below. All the concrete spaces and operations of such theatres were rooted in this fundamental political model, even as some practices put it in doubt."[103]

Feldman warned that the form was politically paradoxical. On one hand, it was kept afloat by wealthy patrons who were looking for confirmation of existing social and political hierarchies; on the other hand, opera houses were commercial operations, reflecting the economic ethos of an emerging protocapitalist bourgeoisie that would eventually rise to challenge royal and aristocratic domination across the continent.[104] In this context, opera in Bourbon Naples represents the fundamental contradictions of the historical moment, as the San Carlo Theater attached to the Royal Palace remained dependent both on the earnings from single-performance ticket sales and also on the long-term rentals of luxurious boxes.

A Night at the Opera

The construction of the San Carlo Theater had been one of Charles's first acts upon assuming power over the newly formed Kingdom of the Two Sicilies, and the speed of its construction was remarkable (figure 6). Feldman records that the "theater throughout the eighteenth century remained unabashedly pledged to Bourbon glory and to the privileged classes, with an exclusive and unusual menu of opera seria used to articulate the annual lineup of Bourbon celebrations centering on dynastic birthdays and name days. Its suggestions of divine kingship were brash and concerted, not least in naming the theater for the temporal king by calling on the immortality of his eponymous saint."[105]

As if unprecedented grandeur was somehow insufficient,

Figure 6. The interior of the San Carlo Theater, showing the royal box.
Source: Photograph by Giorgio Sommer (1834–1914), from Naples: San Carlo Opera House (http://en.wikipedia.org/wiki/Giorgio_Sommer).

Charles allegedly complained to the San Carlo's architect, Angelo Carasale, upon entering his box for the inaugural performance that he would have preferred not to need to walk outside from his palace next door to attend a performance. Legend has it that Carasale scrambled to please his patron, throwing up—by the time the last note of the evening had been sung—a walkway directly to the palace that would serve Charles and both his regal and not-so-regal successors.[106]

Opera was a relatively young art form when Charles opened his theater. The new dramatic genre had emerged from the attempts of late-sixteenth-century Florentines and their neighbors in other commerce-dominated Northern Italian principalities to recreate the music of the ancient Greeks.[107] Although recent historiographical research has altered some of the details in the story, it is clear that new theatrical forms combining drama, dance, song, and instrumental music came together in Northern Italy just before 1600 as something that was qualitatively new. This innovative performance style—which eventually would become known as "opera"—emerged in response to debates over the extent to which the emotional impact attributed to ancient Greek drama was related to the music provided by the chorus.[108] Many of opera's originators, including Galileo's father, Vincenzo Galilei, desired to break out of the limitations of medieval polyphonic choral music and looked to imagined Greek roots for validation of the new style.[109]

Whatever the details of its origins, opera quickly proved to be an ideal form of propaganda for the numerous Absolutist rulers who were busy establishing their sovereignty across Europe.[110] In Russia, four eighteenth-century empresses—Catherine I (1725–27), Anna (1730–40), Elisabeth (1741–62), and Catherine II, the Great (1762–96)—embraced opera as a means for merging European notions of legitimacy with indigenous Russian myth.[111] Anna promoted dance within her court, especially Russian *khorovods* (circle dances), while Elisabeth, a fervent dancer herself, brought ballet to court, sponsored the first Russian theater in Yaroslavl, and enlarged the court chapel chorus.[112] The German-born Catherine the Great went so far as to draw on Russian folk tales to write the libretti for four operas of her own.[113] An active patroness and supporter of opera and other music, she used imperial ceremonials to demonstrate her sovereign power over an expanding empire.[114]

The Neapolitan Bourbons were not alone in their use of opera to secure authoritative domain over their realm. As they and their French, Austrian, and Russian counterparts quickly appreciated, this pioneering dramatic form of vocal dramatic theater was not only strikingly new, like many of the royal regimes of the time. Opera was associated as well with Greek and Roman classicism, the core of legitimacy in European culture. These young rulers hoped that such legitimacy would attach itself to their own sovereignties.

Initially, opera's words were more important that its music. The poet Ottavio Rinuccini began writing the librettos for increasingly sophisticated *intermedi* during court theatrical performances in the latter years of the sixteenth century.[115] The *intermedi* at a performance of *La pellegrina* during the May 1589 wedding of Ferdinand I de' Medici and Christine de Lorraine marked a departure, as small musical skits interspersed throughout the evening constituted a single, integrated story bringing together verse and music for the first time.[116]

After experimenting with a number of alternative performance forms blending music and drama under the patronage of prominent Florentine Jacopo Corsi, Jacopo Peri set Rinuccini's verse to music in a retelling of the ancient legend of Daphne. In so doing, Peri and Rinuccini produced what many historians consider to have been the first opera.[117] Other similar works followed Peri and Rinuccini's *Dafne*, including their own *Euridice*, which was written two years later in honor of the wedding of Maria de' Medici and Henri IV, king of France.[118] The first opera to be performed in Rome—Emilio de' Cavalieri's *La rappresentazione di Anima e di Corpo*—was staged in the Oratorio di Santa Maria in Vallicella as early as February 1600.[119]

Significantly for what would follow, early operatic performances frequently were entertainments produced for the celebration of the pre-Lenten Carnevale. The association of opera with Carnevale would last for decades, expanding the new art form's social role from that of aristocratic party favor to one of dramatic public spectacle.

Claudio Monteverdi is credited with consolidating the new performance art during the first decades of the seventeenth century.[120] He was born in Cremona, and had won fame as a composer and performer of madrigals working in the court of Vincenzo I of Gonzaga.[121] The 1607 performance of his *Orfeo* in Mantua's Ducal Palace is considered by many to mark the initial consolidation of opera as a distinct art form.[122] Monteverdi moved to Venice in 1613 to become the conductor in residence at the Basilica of San Marco, where he wrote operas and liturgical music that are still performed today.[123]

Monteverdi established opera as a genre that could express the complexities of the human condition, and he secured Venice's claim as its most important center.[124] "At his hands," Donal Hay Grout and Hermine Weigel Williams observe, "the genre acquired a wealth of musical resources and a power and depth of expression that make his musical dramas still living works almost four hundred years later."[125] Monteverdi and his colleagues in Venice also transformed opera in other ways, turning what had been the play-thing of dukes and princes into a genuinely public art, for Venetian performance favored grand spectacle. In this regard, Monteverdi produced operas intended for a broader audience than the small circle of aristocrats who could fit into a ducal drawing room.[126]

Following the opening of Venice's first opera house in 1637, Monteverdi and his colleagues began to write for stages that were constructed expressly for the presentation of musical drama.[127] These purpose-built theaters took the form of amphitheaters. Bal-conies were arranged around the theaters' outer edges, as if they were the windows of palazzos overlooking the city's numerous public squares, where festive performances took place during the ever-longer Venetian Carnevale (Carnival) season.[128]

As Daniel Snowman tells the story, the opera house's "original inspiration may have been the amphitheatre of ancient times, but its more modern reincarnation opera house design derives from the piazzas in which street theatre would have taken place. Imagine a small, more-or-less enclosed Venetian piazza with a performing troupe in the middle. Watching it is a crowd of passersby—while above, a second, more-privileged audience looks down, semivis-ible from the privacy of their surrounding balconies. Cover the pi-azza with a domed roof and you have the rudiments of an opera house."[129]

Opera arrived in Naples not long thereafter. The Spanish vice-roy of Naples, Count Ognatte, invited the Febi Armonici opera company to visit from Rome in either 1651 or 1652. The company took up residence at the San Bartolomeo, a commercial theater, just a few years later.[130] Neapolitan opera thus began as an explicitly commercial entertainment, though one simultaneously associated with viceregal patronage.[131]

A Culture of Divertimenti

Opera's remarkable role in Neapolitan life gained sustenance from the city's well-established musical and theatrical cultures. The commedia dell'arte tradition of stylized farce, which dated from Roman times, remained wildly popular. As elsewhere in Europe, vernacular music—such as madrigals and dance tunes—long had established its rightful place alongside sacred scores.[132] Naples participated in these European-wide phenomena, to which Neapolitans made their own meaningful contributions. For example, the above-mentioned tenth-century monk Warnefrid formalized the madrigal, and the local, eighteenth-century luthiers Gennaro and Antonio Vinaccia modernized the mandolin.[133]

The local love of the theatrical, music, and dance greatly impressed visitors from the North. The seventeenth-century English diarist John Evelyn recorded that the city's "women are generally well-featured but excessively libidinous. The country people [are] so jovial and addicted to music that the very husbandmen almost universally play on the guitar, singing and composing songs in praise of their sweethearts, and will commonly go to the field with their fiddle."[134] Communal musical forms were immediately incorporated into the increasingly popular performance art of opera, as librettists drew on such stock comedic characters as nurses, pages, magicians, and allegorical figures in their works.[135]

Ever-more-extravagant pre-Lenten Carnevale celebrations combined with an endless array of saints' festivals to prepare the Neapolitan ground for the arrival of opera. Conservatory students and their professors had begun to participate in such festivities during the late seventeenth century, thereby raising their musical significance.[136] The Neapolitan Carnevale blended Spanish and local traditions.[137] For example, celebrants wore satirical masks, engaged in public food fights among the city's nobility (led under Ferdinand by the king himself), and publicly pillaged carts bearing food prepared by the local guilds, known as the *cuccagna*, which, over time, became formalized as dazzling stage sets.[138] Patients of the Incurabili lunatic asylum were released to join in the *cuccagna* frenzy.[139] The resulting hysteria encouraged city residents of all classes and ages to participate in the celebrations, distinguishing the Neapolitan Carnevale from the more standard merriment of most other pre-Lenten celebrations across Catholic Europe.[140] By the mid–eighteenth century, the city's Bourbon monarchs had extended the festival from its traditional launch in January into the previous year so as to mark Charles's name day, November 4.[141]

As Martha Feldman notes, theater and festivity, the sacred and the profane, became inexorably linked together by music, dance, and light—by opera.[142] The powerful connection between opera and Carnevale in Naples was well established almost from the beginning. By 1701, the union of the two was so strong that local rulers tried unsuccessfully to prohibit operas from being performed during Carnevale. A number of spontaneous *bambocci* (marionette) performances of popular operas sprang up around the city, often with new libretti making fun of those in charge.[143]

The Neapolitan cultural dyad of Dionysian sensuality and paganistic hedonism on one hand and Apollonian rationality and stern piety on the other hand reinforced the local embrace of opera. Naples under Spanish rule had been dominated by an endless number of religious institutions—churches, chapels, monasteries, convents, hospitals, orphanages, schools—connected to various orders within the Catholic Church. Fifield comments that "Neapolitans have usually felt estranged from the working of government. This alienated relation to power differs radically from Naples' relation to religion which has always been visceral. Geographically the spaces of power tended to be at the city's edge—at the sea, or along the walls—partly because power came from without. Religion occupied the inner spaces. The city suffers power; it generates religion. In fact, churches and monasteries and convents do not so much dot the face of Naples as riddle it."[144] These religious oases of both metaphysical calm and magnificence contrasted with the chaos of the streets outside their high, protective walls.[145]

Many of these establishments required choral and instrumental music to celebrate God's glory.[146] As a result, Baroque Naples consumed musicians of talent. The musicologist Dinko Fabris argues that the hiring of musicians rested more on merit than in other European cities because the Spanish viceroys remained for more-or-less fixed terms. Consequently, permanent patterns of patronage associated with a dominant family could not be sustained as the preferences of successive viceroys changed over time.[147] A hierarchy of privilege and power evolved, often becoming linked to the changing status of the religious institutions at which a musician worked. Fabris writes:

> At the top, the most important musical institution was the one in direct contact with the viceroy, that is, the Real Cap-

pella. Similarly, the most prestigious events were those relating to the court in the Palazzo Reale: *festini*, balls, comedies, and operas, plus religious celebrations, birthdays,
marriages, and occasional ceremonies. The other steps of
the pyramid reflect the status of the institutions involved
in the government of Naples: the Duomo with the archbishop as the religious leader of the city; the *Eletti*, holding five
noble "seats" (*seggi*) and one popular; the most important
religious institutions connected to different orders always
in competition with each other (Jesuits, Filippini, Theatines,
Dominicans, Franciscans, et al.). Then [there were the] charitable institutions, from which emerged the conservatories,
confraternities, and other popular devotional or lay associations.[148]

Musicians in Naples, as elsewhere, were artisanal employees
of their patrons. However, the Neapolitan environment—like that
of Venice—was dominated by institutions rather than by wealthy
families.[149] This system created a stable demand for musical talent, with various employers hiring outsiders as well as musicians
from socially unacceptable groups who demonstrated talent. Some
of the most important contributors to Neapolitan opera, such as
the Sicilian-born Alessandro Scarlatti—who moved to the city from
Rome—came from elsewhere because they could compete more or
less fairly to earn appointment in a relatively open system.[150] Others
were products of the city's remarkable conservatories, which were
unmatched elsewhere, with the important exception of Venice.

The Neapolitan Music Machine

According to some estimates, there were 7 conservatories and 617
religious institutions (including 248 churches) in mid-seventeenth-
century Naples offering musical education to 368 boys in 1660, a
number that later increased.[151] The four most prominent conservatories—the I Poveri di Gesù Cristo (founded in 1589), Sant'Onofrio
a Capuana (1578), Pietà dei Turchini (1583), and Santa Maria di
Loreto (1537)—fell under civic and viceregal control. Once again,
Venice was Naples's primary competitor, with several vibrant con-

servatories of its own. However, Venetian musical education was concentrated at orphanages for girls, whereas Neapolitan conservatories catered to boys.[152] This meant that, upon reaching adulthood, the graduates of the Neapolitan conservatories were more likely to pursue professional careers in music.[153]

Orphanages sponsored conservatories in order to provide their boys with a livelihood. As in the famous orphanages for girls in Venice, some parentless children were the illegitimate offspring of the wealthy and notable.[154] Poor families often attempted to send their sons to the conservatories because they provided free room and board.[155] Some conservatories recruited from particular regions around the kingdom—Apulia provided the most students—while others specialized musically.

Boys who had been castrated were of particular value given the popularity of virtuoso castrated vocalists—the castrati—who were thought to supercharge female ranges with male lung capacity.[156] Perhaps the most famous, Carlo Maria Broschi (known by his stage name, Farinelli), followed precisely this path from Apulia to Naples on to trans-European eighteenth-century rock star status.[157]

Some of the best musicians in the city earned their living by teaching at the conservatories. The opera master Francesco Provenzale, for one, taught at two of the four conservatories during a forty-year career.[158] At its height, this system produced a constant stream of innovative musicians who transformed the musical landscape of the era, including, among many, Francesco Feo, Johann Adolph Hasse, Leonardo Leo, Francesco Mancini, Giovanni Battista Pergolesi, Nicola Porpora, Francesco Provenzale, Domenico Sarro, Alessandro and Domenico Scarlatti, Giuseppe Sellitti, and Leonardo Vinci.[159]

Michael Robinson has identified more than forty graduates of Neapolitan conservatories who had significant eighteenth-century professional careers as performers and composers across Europe.[160] They came from a variety of backgrounds, and rose through recruitment and educational networks that reached from the top to the bottom of Neapolitan society. The seventeenth-century Neapolitan music machine incorporated local devils into the paradise of the well off, and in turn invigorated music. The city's musicians formed what became known as the Neapolitan School, whose members were avidly sought by impresarios and aristocrats from Paris to Saint Petersburg, from Madrid to Vienna to London.

Such energy could not last forever, however. Over the course of the eighteenth century, political and economic crises eviscerated the Neapolitan institutions' capacity to employ musicians. Faculty members remained in place too long to allow replenishment of their ranks from below, so dozens of highly sought-after conservatory graduates spread across the face of Europe.[161] Nonetheless, by the early nineteenth century the Neapolitan music community was still renowned for its technical virtuosity. The San Carlo's orchestra, for example, was known as the best in Europe.

Some of the era's more inventive musicians held Naples in contempt because of the city's supposed conservatism in taste. According to Gioachino Rossini's biographer, Gaia Servadio, local composers made even Rossini, an astoundingly popular opera creator, feel unwelcome. His most vociferous local critics attacked Rossini's music as "licentious" when he appeared in 1815 to take up the baton as director of the San Carlo.[162] Before too long, he had moved on to Paris. And after the 1829 premiere of *Guillaume Tell*, he stopped writing operas altogether, even though he would live for another four decades.

Rossini walked away from opera at the height of his fame. "It is no exaggeration," the German historian Anselm Gerhard writes, "to call him the most successful opera composer of his day. . . . He achieved what no composer before him had done, in subsuming the regional differences of Italian schools of opera within his style, and his works were constantly before the public, in opera houses all over Europe and even in the Americas, from Lisbon to Odessa and Saint Petersburg, from London through Vienna to Corfu and Malta, and from New York to Buenos Aires."[163]

Earlier, Rossini's arrival in Milan from his native Bologna had not been by chance. He had been embraced by a master Milanese impresario, the flamboyant Domenico Barbaja, who set out to reinvent the local opera scene in an effort to maximize profits.[164]

A native of a small village near Milan, Barbaja went to work as a waiter at a coffee shop. Seeing opportunity, he secured a subcontract for the 1805 Carnevale season's gambling concession at La Scala.[165] Having thus struck it rich, he took his newfound wealth to Naples in 1806, where he negotiated the gaming contract for the royal theaters with Joseph Bonaparte, and later with Joachim Murat. Ferdinand extended the license when he returned in 1815.[166]

Ferdinand employed Barbaja to divert his subjects' attention from the king's craven exodus before the arriving Bonaparte.[167] Barbaja was more than a talented manager who filled his coffers with gambling profits; he was also a gifted talent scout.[168] During the half dozen years while Rossini was under contract in Naples, he would write and produce twenty operas for Barbaja—including some of his most famous, such as *Il Barbiere di Siviglia, Othello,* and *La Cenerentola*—before moving on to Vienna and Paris.[169] After a falling-out with Rossini, Barbaja promoted such talented young composers as Vincenzo Bellini, Giovanni Pacini, Nicola Vaccai, and Gaetano Donizetti, who wrote some of their best works for the San Carlo.[170] Among the numerous stars within Barbaja's stable were the legendary sopranos Isabella Cobran, Giuditta Pasta, and Maria Malibran, as well as the star tenors Andrea Nozzari, Giovanni Batista Rubini, and Adolph Nourit.[171]

On February 12, 1816—just as Ferdinand, Barbaja, and Rossini were reinventing opera to in turn reinvent the Bourbon Monarchy—the San Carlo caught fire during a ballet rehearsal and was destroyed. Ferdinand scrambled to have it rebuilt in less than a year, on an even larger and more splendid scale.[172] The wily Barbaja brought the project in ahead of schedule and under budget, probably relying on his own funds to finish the job. Barbaja ensured that the new San Carlo was a state-of-the-art theater that favored (though not completely) performance over demonstrations of social status.[173]

Ferdinand began curtailing gambling at his royal theaters as early as 1815. By 1820, Barbaja's strategy of relying on gaming profits to pay for his productions had come to an end.[174] With his revenues dramatically curtailed, he branched out to manage theaters in Vienna and La Scala in Milan.[175] Yet he maintained his connection with the San Carlo until his death in October 1841, and he kept both a primary residence in a grand palazzo on Via Toledo and lavish summer homes at Mergellina and on Ischia.[176]

Ferdinand, his ministers, and his hired musical guns could not turn the clock back, given that both opera as an art form and Naples as a city were being transformed. Gerhard argues that the years around 1800—precisely when the Bourbons were forced off their throne—mark a divide in opera's development, observing that many operas composed thereafter are still in the standard repertory, but many earlier operas "cannot be performed nowadays without some kind of mediation."[177] There are exceptions to this transitional era of roughly 1800 to 1830, such as the operas by Wolfgang Mozart and his librettist Lorenzo Da Ponte, Beethoven's *Fidelio*, and Weber's *Der Freischutz*. Simultaneously, composers were replacing librettists as opera's star creators.

As the opera world's center of gravity moved to Paris, the genre itself, Gerhard contends, became "urbanized." Furthermore, he suggests that "it was only under the extreme pressure exerted by the new modes of perception, and the expectations springing from them, that the operas composed for Paris in the middle decades of the nineteenth century developed new forms and conventions that have nothing to do with the historical predecessors of grand opera. At first sight, a large number of these characteristics still appear nothing out of the ordinary today, for the majority of these models of perception that came into existence after 1800 have scarcely changed."[178] Such alterations, however, undermined efforts to restore Neapolitan opera to the glory years of the previous century.

Naples and the Neapolitan music machine already had been "reformed" in 1806 under the direction of France's Grande Armée. Joachim Murat, appointed to the Neapolitan throne by his brother-in-law, Napoleon Bonaparte, consolidated the conservatories into a single school as part of a general rationalization and reform of local artistic institutions.[179] This school—San Pietro a Mailella—inherited the remarkable music libraries and manuscript collections of its predecessors and continues to train musicians today."[180]

The French were changing more than physical and institutional arrangements. As Gerhard records, "In 1791 France had been the first state to pass a copyright law in the modern sense, giving writers and composers not only material protection in respect to their works, but, also, and more importantly, rights in respect of the content." This new legal regime rendered impossible the free and easy mix-and-match that had long characterized Neapolitan productions.

A much-lamented decline in musicianship followed the Italian Peninsula's run-in with the Bonaparte family.[181] Although the half century following the French emperor's demise witnessed a boom in theater production across Italy—with about six hundred play-houses being constructed—few could sustain the number of musicians required to mount sophisticated performances. As a result, "the most successful composers," Gilmour tells his readers, "were eager to have their premieres only in the finest opera houses—the San Carlo in Naples, La Fenice in Venice, and La Scala—before they earned renown to have them in Paris."[182] And though Neapolitan music became embedded in these larger Italian and European trends, it retained a considerable degree of distinctiveness and reputational excellence. Numerous twentieth- and twenty-first-century musicologists and historians have toiled mightily to deny the actuality of such a Neapolitan "School" in music in any period. But few contemporaries had any doubts about its existence.[183]

Many of the same religious institutions that promoted local musicianship similarly embraced theatrical performances as a means for promotion of the faith. The Jesuits, who had arrived in the city in 1552 to establish a college, were especially active advocates of missionary street theater around the city and the surrounding countryside. The similarity between Jesuit productions and popular theatrical productions became one among many reasons why the Bourbon Court asked the Jesuit Order to leave the kingdom in 1773.[184]

In keeping with Saint Ignatius Loyola's commitment to an urban ministry, Jesuit productions took place in neighborhood churches and on local streets and piazzas. Employing contemporary stagecraft that embraced long-standing traditions, the Jesuits used comedians who drew directly on the local infatuation with commedia dell'arte in order to connect with audiences. Their street performances relied on both scripted dialogue and improvisation, thereby eroding rigid formulas from the past. Their plays similarly relied on local dialects and languages, thereby promoting new theatrical forms, which would find their way onto the stage in opera buffa. Much to the dismay of more staid religious and secular authorities, the Jesuits simultaneously promoted Neapolitan hedonism and piety by making use of public theatricality. This theatricality cemented opera's place in Neapolitan life, enabling the genre to transcend the city's raucous and uncertain political life.

Feldman, trying to explain opera's origins on the peninsula, observes that "Italy's roaring public sphere made it an utterly operatic place—not just a place that had birthed opera and loved it like a child but one where opera and its personnel could reseed themselves almost without end and where public opinion was continually vented."[185] Seventeenth- and eighteenth-century Naples contained, in a most concentrated form, a number of these general Italian traits, which had given rise to opera as a performance art.

Sounds of the City

Naples arguably was typical of other Italian cities in its embrace of public theatricality, though perhaps it was an especially intense example.[186] Most observers at the time—and ever since—have agreed that the city's ingrained musicality made it exceptional.[187] Foreign visitors uniformly commented on the distinctive sounds of Neapolitan everyday life, lyrically finding ever-new ways of documenting how music was in constant earshot whenever they were visiting Naples.[188] Travelers marveled at both the ubiquity and diversity of local musicality. Some, such as the seventeenth-century French visitor Jean-Jacques Bouchard, became so mesmerized by the sounds of the city that he kept an eight-month-long diary of the ever-shifting musical seasons of Naples, from Holy Week through the summertime maritime festivals to the fall harvest celebrations.[189] Twentieth-century biographers of such Neapolitan composers of the era as Domenico and Alessandro Scarlatti and Francesco Provenzale observe that a newborn Neapolitan never experienced silence.[190] Their childhood soundscapes were so encompassing that Roberto Pagano calls the Scarlatti household a "musical factory."[191]

The merely domestic combined with the communal, audible sensations of life in Europe's most densely packed city, where people lived literally on top of one another. Ralph Kirkpatrick writes:

> In the narrower passages an occasional clatter of hooves drowned out the muffled sounds of bare human feet. In the streets that were broad enough could be heard the rattling

of carriage wheels, the lashing of whips, and the soft belch-
ing cry of the Neapolitan carter to his horse, or, more probably, a very Vesuvius of curses, as rich and as colorful as
the piles of melons and peppers on the street corners and as
odoriferous as the fish of the nearby market. Only slightly
subdued at the hour of siesta, this racket gave place at night
to guitars and strident Neapolitan voices raised in quarrel
or in amorous lament.[192]

It was a world where children did not take music lessons; they
learned simply by becoming aware of their surroundings.

Song, perhaps more than any other genre, dominated Neapolitan musicality. Verse was sung on the street in a local dialect, in
church in Latin, and on an aristocratic stage in some vague approxi-
mation of how erudite scholastics thought a Greek chorus might
have performed. The city cultivated poets as well as composers.
One particular Roman child prodigy, Pietro Trapassi (later known
as Metastasio), came to the city to study the Classics. He discovered
the city's musical and theatrical circles and began to write librettos
for operatic melodramas.[193] Working at a time when librettists were
better known than their partner composers, he would stay in the
city between 1719 and 1724.[194] Metastasio became perhaps the most
famous author of operatic verse in his day.[195] His fame and success
eventually enabled him to move to Vienna in 1730, where he became the court poet of the Habsburgs.

Metastasio is credited with standardizing the libretto form and
dramatic structure for opera seria and for shaping what came to
be understood as the most appropriate operatic balance between
drama and music, between recitatives and arias.[196] In this regard,
he followed in the footsteps of the Venetian Apostolo Zeno, who
tried to rationalize operatic plots by removing "supernatural interventions, machines, irrelevant comic episodes, and the bombastic
declamation that had reigned in the seventeenth century."[197] Together, they elevated the role of poetry in opera, bringing it closer
in importance to that of opera's music.

Although Naples had competitors for leadership in the seven-
teenth- and eighteenth-century European musical world—Venice,
Vienna, Paris, and London were among the Continent's alternative

centers of musical leadership—local tastes created an environment where Charles's decision to build the Continent's largest opera house—and his successor Ferdinand's quick reconstruction of this same theater—became appropriate instruments for effective state-craft. Unlike the Bourbon monarchy itself, opera was not merely an import imposed on Naples. Opera became a cultural phenomenon very much rooted in this particular place.

Baffo for Buffa

The experience of attending opera in Naples proved disconcert-ing to many visitors. The venerable Teatro di San Bartolomeo had served as the city's prime opera venue for eight decades preceding the first performance at the San Carlo in 1737. As the venues for some of the best operas by the Scarlattis and the greatest triumphs of Metasasio, the San Bartolomeo and the Teatro dei Fiorentini had become places where Neapolitan society came to be seen, though not necessarily to listen.[198] As the Barbaja saga reveals, there was frequently gambling in the lobby.[199]

The serious classical allegory of opera seria produced far too earnest a backdrop for such social preening. Therefore, by the early eighteenth century, librettists, composers, producers, and perform-ers had begun to look for ways to enliven the evening by interject-ing comic interludes in between the acts of the main performance.[200] These exuberant entr'acte creations drew on local characters from the streets of Naples, as opposed to Greek and Roman heroes. Their performers sang their roles in local dialect rather than more formal Italian, Latin, or Greek. Their stories—which were often incoher-ent and unstructured—were natural and spontaneous. Their music favored straightforward melody. Their comedy favored broad buf-foonery and ridicule that often bordered on the crude.[201] And their undeveloped characters came straight from the stock of traditional commedia dell'arte storylines.

Over time, these short entr'acte performances, which were done in front of the closed curtain, were used to deflect attention from the stage set changes taking place behind. Performers developed standardized forms engaging the audiences, so these short inter-ludes gained a popularity of their own. Eventually, these small diversions evolved into their own art form, the Neapolitan opera buffa.

The members of the local aristocracy, who were rooted in the customs of their former conservative Spanish overlords, were appalled by the chaos unfolding onstage in these opera buffa. By contrast, middle-class Neapolitans, students, and others who could secure a ticket loved these representations drawn from their own daily lives. Unlike the nobility, many prosperous merchants, professionals, traders, and manufacturers earned their livings close to the ground and enjoyed seeing themselves caricatured onstage.[202] Local composers began to write intermezzo buffo with the coherence of a well-told tale. And these stories that began between acts one and two continued in between subsequent acts, so audiences were actually attending two operas at one time—a serious story interspersed with a comedic alter ego.

Opera buffa came of age in 1733, when twenty-three-year-old Giovanni Battista Pergolesi's *La Serva Pardona*, based on Gennaro Antonio Federico's libretto, premiered as the Teatro di San Bartolomeo.[203] The intermezzo buffo performed that evening revolved around two characters backed by a quartet. The play was reconstituted and performed in Paris in 1746, setting the stage six years later for the Querelle des Bouffons, the "war" between Buffonists and Antibuffonists. This battle became a riotous conflict between the pro-Italian partisans of Niccolò Piccinni and the pro-French proponents of the music of Christoph Willibald Gluck, which consumed Parisian cultural and intellectual circles throughout much of 1752, 1753, and 1754.[204]

Opera buffa achieved its greatest heights during the last half of the eighteenth century. This was a time when Neapolitan librettists such as Francesco Cerlone and Giambattista Lorenzi collaborated with composers such as Saverio Zini, Giuseppe Millotti, Valentino Fioravanti, and Giovanni Paisiello. Jointly, they set the stage for the genre's pinnacle achievements: Mozart's three collaborations with his librettist, Lorenzo Da Ponte—*Le Nozze di Figaro*, 1786; *Don Giovanni*, 1787; and *Così fan tutte*, 1789–90—and Gioachino Rossini's *Il Barbiere di Sivigile* in 1816.[205] Mozart and other composers of the era simultaneously drew heavily on the shorter intermezzo buffo form in developing the early symphony (figure 7).[206]

Figure 7. Mozart at his billiard table.
Source: An etching by Oswald Charles Barret (known as Batt).

Opera buffa had emerged as an operatic genre in its own right by the time Charles opened his theater. It was but one form of the intermezzi that filled the blank spaces when an act ended and stage sets had to be changed during the main opera seria of the evening. And though opera buffa spread throughout Europe—Venice competed with Naples as a preeminent center of operatic comedy—it nonetheless remained quintessentially Neapolitan.[207]

Opera Buffa in the Stalls

Performances of opera buffa were staged before Neapolitan audiences whose etiquette frequently offended visitors to the city. The San Carlo was built so that those sitting in the boxes—which were arranged according to social status—could look at the goings on in the audience more easily than at what was happening onstage. Each private box became a small drawing room fitted out according to the tastes and desires of its lessor.[208]

An Englishman, Samuel Sharp, recorded in 1765 that

> it is customary for gentlemen to run about from box to box
> between the acts, even in the midst of the performance; but
> the ladies, after they are seated, never quit their box the
> whole evening. It is the fashion to make appointments for
> such and such nights. A lady receives visitors in her box
> one night, and they remain with her the whole opera; an-
> other night she returns the visit in the same manner. In the
> intervals between the acts, principally between the first and
> second, the proprietor of the box regales her company with
> iced fruits and sweetmeats.[209]

The audience talked constantly, encouraging composers and
librettists to insert longer arias to allow singers to showcase their
virtuosity as a means for holding spectators' attention.[210]

The regal Charles seems to have been one of the worst offend-
ers in ignoring the performance onstage. Michael Robinson begins
his history of Neapolitan opera suggesting that Charles "was not
devoid of cultural interests: he brought the Farnese collection of
paintings to Naples from Parma, founded a porcelain factory at
Capodimonte, and concerned himself with the excavations at Herculaneum. But no one has attempted to credit him with love of music."[211] Charles embraced opera out of political rather than personal
interest. "It was a fact of life," Robinson continues, "that opera had
become the European court entertainment par excellence, a recognized means of propaganda and prestige."[212]

Charles's tastes and demeanor exerted a strong influence over
the shape of Neapolitan opera. Servants could not enter the stalls;
court protocol was to be followed at all times; no applause was permitted for individual singers; and only the king—or, in his absence,
his official deputy, the auditor of the army—could request an en-
core.[213] Most significantly, Charles proclaimed that only ballet could
be performed during intermissions, thereby effectively banishing
the vibrant opera buffa and intermezzo traditions to other theaters
such as the San Fernando, which was to be favored by Charles's
son, Ferdinand.[214] The king and the rest of the audience turned their
full attention to the stage only during such dance interludes.[215]

Elsewhere in Europe, the Italian distinction between opera seria and opera buffa increasingly became viewed as antiquated and artificial. The 1752 contretemps between Parisian Buffoonists and Antibuffoonists revolved in part around Gluck's ultimately successful efforts to reform opera by refocusing the genre on the drama of human existence and by elevating its words and music to equal status.[216]

As noted above, the political reforms of Joseph Bonaparte and Joachim Murat between 1806 and 1815 transformed the institutional and cultural contexts for all music in Naples. The conservatories merged, theaters reorganized, and French rationality imposed order on opera performances.[217] The San Carlo Theater was burned and rebuilt.[218] Barbaja arrived in 1809, enticing the likes of Rossini, Bellini, and Donizetti to work in Naples during his tenure, which lasted until 1824. Barbaja maintained a connection with the San Carlo Theater until his death in 1841, even as he assumed responsibility for La Scala in Milan in 1826 and ran two theaters in Vienna.[219]

Opera buffa—and Neapolitan opera, more generally—enjoyed a reprise of sorts with the coming of age of Gioachino Rossini, Ruggero Leoncavallo, and others.[220] But the world had changed, and opera with it. The startling reaction of the sacred with the profane—of the elevated and the plebeian—that so enlivened Neapolitan musical culture in the seventeenth and eighteenth centuries carried less meaning as the ancien régime faded from view.

Opera and Delirium

The deeply embedded contradictions of Neapolitan life were never more apparent than during the horrid famine years of 1763 and 1764, among the worst to ever hit the Italian Peninsula. The city's authorities scrambled to purchase grain for municipal storehouses. The kingdom's government—led by the Bourbons' crafty senior minister, Bernardo Tanucci—responded vigorously, dispatching agents to the countryside to hunt down speculators and seize hidden grain reserves.[221] Blinded by their Absolutist ideology, officials—no matter how well intentioned—only made matters worse. The Bourbons proved incapable of confronting the myriad structural challenges facing their realm (including the feudal method of organizing rural land tenure, which increasingly became the focus of criticism by some of Europe's sharpest social thinkers at the city's academies and university).[222]

As the full effects of the starvation cause by the famine ground deeper into the countryside, thousands of desperate peasants flooded the capital in search of food. They came in waves throughout the autumn and into the winter.[223] In a moment of profound self-delusion, the king, his ministers, and other city leaders proceeded with the pre-Lenten Carnevale celebrations of 1764, including the ritualistic pillaging of grandiose theatrical floats piled several meters high with mountains of free food — the *cuccagna*.

Feldman describes the *cuccagna* in eighteenth-century Naples:

> The official Carnival season was traditionally elaborated in various outdoor rituals. The official Carnival season extended through four successive Sundays, on each of which the king would appear on his royal balcony to bestow food on the city's beggars, who gathered before him in the great piazza that faced the palace, the Largo del Palazzo. Fronting the palace, a vast architectural structure would be erected many stories high, decked with allegorical and mythological figures bearing food and gazing down upon livestock, fountains of wine, and rivers of milk. Both the architecture and the event were known as *cuccagna*, after the fabled utopian land of leisure and plenty (*le pays de Cockaigne* in French). Although the structure took months to produce, it was almost wholly ephemeral. On the first Sunday of Carnival, and by royal sanction, it was ritually sacked by the makes of the beggar class, who stripped it of comestibles, leaving it much the worse for wear. The structure was patched of any injuries and the same exercise repeated on three subsequent Sundays leading up to the beginning of Lent.[224]

Predictably, the act of setting up these gigantic towers of free food in a city full of desperately starving people did not end well.

The Carnevale opera season began uninterrupted by the tragedy unfolding in the countryside. After attending a gala performance at the San Carlo on January 20, 1764, the French abbé Coyer recorded that famine "does not diminish the fury of spectacles a bit, because the bon vivants are not yet hungry."[225] A few weeks later, on Saturday, February 11—the day before the first *cuccagna* was to take place—workmen under the direction of the royal architect, Luigi Vanvitelli, filled the palace square with displays of free food to be given out the next day. A couple of hours after sundown, restive citizens broke through barricades, looting the food and moving on to stores around the city. A few meters away, upper-class Neapolitans were attending another grand spectacle at the San Carlo. Some among the audience, having been warned by servants, hid as the mob lost control. Others took cover where they could. Generalized disorder continued until the authorities restored calm late on Sunday afternoon.[226]

Tanucci and the nobles in the Council of the Regency demanded that the remaining three *cuccagna* take place so as not to undermine royal authority in the face of mob rule. Now being better prepared, the authorities were able to carry off the remaining bacchanals without losing control of the city. But the contradictions and hypocrisy of Bourbon rule had been fatally exposed.

The Bourbons never quite recovered from this fiasco. Ferdinand won few friends along the way, and he lost even more legitimacy during the short-lived Parthenopean Republic and the rule of the Napoleonic pretenders Joseph Bonaparte and Joachim Murat who followed.[227] Murat, in particular, undertook a number of reforms that began to pull Naples into the world of more modern Europe. The now murderously vindictive Ferdinand did all he could to turn the clock back when he returned to the throne of the newly created Kingdom of the Two Sicilies in 1815 with the support of the Continent's great powers at the Congress of Vienna.[228] But he could not repair his shattered authority.[229] His son and grandson—Francis I and Ferdinand II (aka King Bomba, for having bombed Sicilian insurrectionists in 1848)—fluctuated in their policies between liberalism supporting economic modernization and more authoritarian reactions to rising popular discontent.[230]

Bomba's son—the young and inexperienced Francis II (also known as Franceschiello, Little Francis), together with his bride, Maria Sophia of Bavaria—assumed power in 1859. Never having had the opportunity to perfect the skills of statecraft, Francis failed to prevent the kingdom from succumbing to the popular nationalism of Giuseppe Garibaldi and the disingenuous diplomacy of Piedmont's crafty prime minister, Camillo Benso, the count of Cavour.[231] The monarch and Maria Sophia made a valiant and honorable final defense of their throne during a brutally tragic siege of the Bourbon fortress at Gaeta, on the coast just south of the kingdom's border with the Papal States. After their defeat, the couple embarked for a long life of exile in Rome and Munich. Following Francis's death, Maria Sophia presided over a salon outside Paris that was notable for the presence of anarchists and socialists.[232]

With the Bourbons having been dispatched from their capital, Garibaldi quietly entered Naples by train on September 7, 1860, in advance of his ragtag, populist army, the Red Shirts, known to posterity as "the Thousand." The soldiers arrived in Naples following a victorious march through Sicily in support of a popular uprising on the island. Within months in 1861, the kingdom was incorporated into an increasingly united Italy under Victor Emmanuel of the House of Savoy.[233]

History's victors write the story of the vanquished. In this instance, many of the kingdom's most noteworthy successes—such as its distinguished legal and court system, its tolerant acceptance of urban diversity, its promotion of science, and its musical inventiveness—were quickly passed over amid talk of "non-European" squalor.[234] Few Italians today realize that their country's first railroad opened in Naples in 1839 (and has become part of the region's Circumvesuviana commuter rail system); or that the Kingdom of the Two Sicilies maintained a positive balance of trade with the United States throughout its waning days.[235] Instead, Naples was transformed from being a capital city into becoming a symbol of the new nation's most impoverished region.

Naples still plays by different rules than the rest of Italy. It remains a city where the successful struggle to survive is valued more than, say, politesse. Thus, the contemporary Neapolitan novelist Elena Ferrante's main character, Elena, on returning home upon graduation from her university in Pisa during the mid-1960s, tells herself that "Naples had been very useful in Pisa, but Pisa was no use in Naples, it was an obstacle." She continues: "Good manners, cultured voice, and appearance, . . . [were seen under the Neapolitan glare as] immediate signs of weakness that made me a secure prey, one of those who don't struggle."[236] Ironically, Ferrante's Elena, as an impoverished, neighborhood Neapolitan girl before she went off to see the world, had struggled mightily all along the way. She offers this observation just as she is about to achieve her breakthrough moment.

Like Elena, Naples constantly struggles against how outsiders imagine it to be. The city's multiple travails have been further compounded by a twentieth century that proved to be as unkind to Naples as it was to the great cities of Europe's eastern half.[237] Yet Naples carries on.

"Napule è"

If, as the anthropologist Tanya Richardson argues in relation to twentieth-century Odessa, "places are similar to kaleidoscopes in the way they refract history and geography," with different actors at different times turning analytical and ideological lenses to shift perspective, then Naples is a place where the contradictions of a rich history frequently have spun too quickly.[238] A hint of hallucination has slipped into the Neapolitan psyche as the cylinders have ground on across the centuries. Urban delirium overwhelmed common sense, as during the Carnevale season of 1764, when only those deluded by their own social position could have failed to understand the consequence of piling up mountains of food in the main public square in a city overflowing with starving residents. Yet, across the twenty-eight centuries of its existence, Naples reveals the wisdom of the urbanist Rem Koolhaas, who famously argued in his evocation of New York during the 1970s—*Delirious New York*—that "the Metropolis strives to reach a mythical point where the world is completely fabricated by man, so that it absolutely coincides with his desires."[239]

Since its founding, Naples has been such a city of sudden and disconcerting juxtaposition of opposites—the sort of place that creates and re-creates over and over again the kind of delirious urbanism that constantly bursts forth with invention and creativity. The Naples of paradise and devils—of delirium and creativity—is a place where the devils make the music. And, as is compellingly captured in Giuseppe "Pino" Daniele's 1977 anthem to his home, "Napule é," what great music it is:[240]

Naples is a thousand colors,	Napule è mille culure
Naples is a thousand fears.	Napule è mille paure
Naples is the voice of the children	Napule è a voce de' criature che
That raises slowly, gently and	saglie chianu chianu
You know you are not alone.	e tu sai ca' nun si sulo
Naples is a bitter sun,	Napule è nu sole amaro
Naples is the smell of the sea.	Napule è addore e' mare
Naples is a dirty piece of paper	Napule è na' carta sporca
And no one cares about it	e nisciuno se ne importa e
And everyone awaits their fate	ognuno aspetta a' sciorta
Naples is a stroll	Napule è na' camminata
In the alleys among the people.	int' e viche miezo all'ate
Naples is a dream	Napule è tutto nu suonno
And the whole world knows it	e a' sape tutto o' munno
But they don't know the truth.	ma nun sanno a' verità.

A Passionate and Slippery City: Puppetry and Kabuki Theater in Tokugawa Osaka and Beyond

Osaka people are impatient and love to disobey rules.

—Alex Kerr, *Lost Japan*, 1996

Late in the troubled 1980s, an experimental New York theater director, Lee Breuer, and an audacious composer, Bob Telson, teamed up to tell the story of "the birth of the warrior ant, his descent into hell to find his termite father, his dalliance with a death moth that proves his undoing."[1] They decided to do so on a stage that teemed "with a Trinidadian carnival, augmented by bands on circling, gaudily painted trucks," which were joined by "narrators in eighteenth-century costume, and others who are West African griots or Brazilian singers" telling the story to musical accompaniment combining "Caribbean, Afro-Cuban, Western chamber music, American rock," against the backdrop of battling eighteen-foot mechanical ants, Egyptian belly dancers, Chinese glove puppets, Moroccan Gnawa invocations, and a Bunraku puppet show.[2]

Breuer and Telson originally intended their multicultural phantasmagoria to run for twelve hours. But in October 1988, they settled for just three hours, after being given the opportunity to bring their massive enterprise to the stage of the Brooklyn Academy of Music.[3]

Urban delirium here wasn't only onstage. BAM—as the Brooklyn Academy of Music is known—had established itself as perhaps New York's most cutting-edge large-scale arts institution. The very auditorium in which Breuer and Telson's *The Warrior Ant* was performed was a carefully—and, undoubtedly, expensively—renovated ruin, in which each crack in the plaster, peeling painted wall, and exposed pipe had been carefully planned. The venue had just the right touch of studied decay for such an extravaganza.

More striking, however, was the real decay just outside, on the blocks along downtown Brooklyn's Atlantic Avenue. The city was in the throes of a horrifying crack cocaine epidemic that was tossing a proverbial match into the borough's noxious mix of violence, racial tensions, crime, and poverty. The domesticated decrepitude inside the BAM auditorium was nothing compared with what was happening outside on the neighboring streets. By turning their stage over to Breuer and Telson's wild imaginations, BAM's overseers hoped to produce a manufactured delirium. But there was nothing manufactured about the delirium outside.

New York's critics never quite figured out what to make of this giant, sprawling display of multicultural egotism, though Brooklyn audiences cheered enthusiastically to the jarring juxtapositions of strange and diverse realities that mirrored their daily lives. *New York Times* theater critic Eileen Blumenthal recorded that "the splashing together of diverse cultures has been a hallmark of twentieth-century Western experimental arts. But mere transhemispheric, cross-currents wax timid alongside the new global bug extravaganza. The show's air of car-chase eclecticism is characteristically Breuer—as are its careens between weighty and glib. But nothing in the fifty-one-year-old writer-director's previous work with the Mabou Mines Company attempts the wild sweep of *Ant*. Even the last Breuer–Telson collaboration, *The Gospel at Colonus*, melding the ancient Greek tragedy of Oedipus with a gospel service, seems restrained compared with the new leap across cultures and eras."[4]

What did seem to be clear to everyone was the brilliance of the Bunraku performer Tamamatsu Yoshida. "Mr. Yoshida, an artist of the classical Bunraku doll theater of Japan, is the core performer in this Breuer-Telson-calypso-Disney-Arabian-African-Kurosawa-free-for-all insect war. The hero critter he manipulates is an eighteenth-century-style human puppet," Blumenthal wrote.[5]

Bunraku's addition to the evening's fare was hardly capricious. Breuer, it turned out, had fallen in love with Bunraku theater when he first saw a performance in 1968. "I was completely totaled, instantly," he told the *Times* reviewer. "It was the most brilliant theater I'd ever seen," he continued, "and still is."[6] The New York critics loved the contrast between a "conservative artistic tradition" from a country that, at the time, seemed on a path to "number one" status in the global economy and the multicultural mess playing itself out on a main stage of a city seemingly headed for oblivion.[7]

Yoshida loved the contrast as well. Having grown up as the son of a puppet master, he was looking for ways to bring new energy to Bunraku. "It's very delicate," he told Blumenthal. "You have to do certain things traditionally, but you need to create your own technique, adding and making something new." In Yoshida's case, he admitted to borrowing ideas from television commercials, films, and musicals. "Whatever I see, I always try to steal some elements."[8] Blumenthal noted that "experimenting now to determine how a Bunraku character can best play an Afro-Latin messianic insect, Mr. Yoshida first assumes the ant role himself. He tries out moves he will have the doll perform: 'I become the puppet. I measure the playing area and the space in the music—seeing where I should stop and make *mie'*—feeeze-frame poses—'finding the form.'"[9] Find the form he did. Yoshida's bongo-playing puppet hero brought the house down as 18-foot-tall mechanical insects pranced around stage getting ready for battle.

The critics were correct that, by 1988, the atmosphere at BAM was as far removed from what Bunraku had become as one might imagine. Bunraku had been consolidated into a "national treasure" dominated by performers drawn from generations of the same families.

They were wrong in thinking that Bunraku's origins were like its contemporary form. Bunraku, in fact, emerged in a seventeenth-century Japanese analogue of Brooklyn—a city full of life, vibrating with the energies of people who were looked down on by elites yet were building a distinctive future all their own. Bunraku was a product of the same sort of urban delirium that drove artists like Breuer and Telson to mount a spectacle such as *The Warrior Ant* in the first place. This city was Osaka, and its delirium was generated by an unbridled quest for money.

A Slippery Crowd Atop Swift Waves

Osaka has long been Japan's leading commercial center. The city naturally profited greatly from its Tokugawa era (1603–1868) role as Japan's major staging area and transshipment point for the provisioning of food and household and luxury goods to the Imperial capital upstream along the Yodo River at Kyoto as well as Edo (Tokyo) much further away.[10] Its financiers dominated Tokugawa merchant life, positioning their trading houses at the center of the nation's all-important rice trade.

Inventive and agile, Osaka merchant houses established Japan's first credit system.[11] It was in seventeenth-century Osaka, for example—and not in nineteenth-century Chicago, as many Americans assume—where commodities traders invented futures trading.[12] Osaka's banks dominated Japanese commercial life to such an extent that, as early as the 1670s, they developed credit mechanisms and methods of exchange that quite possibly would have outwitted even the most sophisticated twenty-first-century Wall Street trader. "The Osaka rice brokers," one such Wall Street magician, Al Alletzhauser, would write, "gained a well-deserved reputation for being a particularly passionate, underhanded, slippery crowd."[13] Osaka long has been a city given over to the delirium of personal enrichment.

Osaka is a classic commercial city that just seemed to grow on its own organically almost from the very beginning.[14] According to legend, the Sun goddess Amaterasu Omikami's great-great-grandson, Jimmu, set out from Kyūshū in the seventh century to bring all the Japanese islands under his control.[15] Reaching the mouth of what is today the Yodo River, Jimmu came ashore among "swift waves," *nami-haya*, which later became the settlement Naniwa. The Naniwa moniker has remained closely associated with the region— it still designates one of the city's central wards—even after the name Ō-saka, meaning "large slope," assumed prominence at the turn of the sixteenth century. Jimmu crowned himself Japan's first "emperor" and set up court at Kashiwara.

The archeological record suggests more prosaic origins, revealing that the area's first resident *Homo sapiens* arrived as long as a dozen millennia ago, with substantial settlements appearing sometime around 2,500 years ago. Political power accompanied development. Naniwa became the seat of successive Yamato chieftains, making today's Osaka the site of Japan's first Imperial capital in the seventh century.[16]

Divine authority quickly followed secular power when, in AD 593, Prince Shotoku Taishi established one of Buddhism's earliest Japanese temples near what is today the city's Tennōji district. Local developments took an even more distinctly ambitious turn in 645, when Emperor Kōtoku constructed the Naniwa Nagara-Toyo-saki Palace. Although Kōtoku would move his capital within a decade to what is now Nara Prefecture, the city's function as a vital trade link to other Japanese costal towns and cities as well as to Korea and China had been firmly established. The town once again served briefly as the capital in the eighth century before the Imperial Court decamped to the new capital at Nara.[17]

Imperial Naniwa was, by all accounts, impressive. The city was always far more than a place of political power, as the historian Wakita Haruko notes. "Naniwa's fleeting brilliance as an imperial capital," Haruko observes, "should not be allowed to overshadow completely its significance as a center of commerce and shipping."[18] Warehouses, landing docks, temples, palaces, and the homes of people who worked for a living made Naniwa a complete town.

Naniwa's fate took another formative turn in 1496, when the True Pure Land (Jōdo Shinshū) school of Buddhism established its fortified headquarters at Ishiyama Hongan-ji, on the site of the original Naniwa imperial palace. Now that it was home to one of the country's largest confessions—a religious organization of considerable earthly as well as spiritual power—Naniwa continued to prosper. The Tennōji market was built during these years, selling rice, sake, salt, dyed textiles, straw matting, salted fish, paper, cast-metal goods, bamboo, and various types of wood to be transshipped to villages around the Inland Sea.[19]

The town's fate changed forever with the arrival of Toyotomi Hideyoshi, who, in 1583, decided to construct a castle on the original Ishiyama Hongan-ji site. By 1590, his Osaka Castle was considered Japan's most inviolable fortress—and its most luxuriously magnificent (figure 8).[20] As he increased his power and authority, Hideyoshi eliminated all his opponents, getting rid of the last of

Figure 8. A view of Osaka Castle (reconstructed) from the Nishinomaru Garden in 2005.
Source: Wikipedia (https://en.wikipedia.org/wiki/Osaka_Castle#/media/ File:Osaka_Castle_Nishinomaru_Garden_April_2005.jpg).

them in 1590 at the Siege of Odawara. He threw Christian missionaries out of his domain, and prohibited all but samurai from owning weapons. In 1597, he ordered the crucifixion of twenty-six Christians (including twenty Japanese) in Nagasaki. But still unsatisfied with his growing power, Hideyoshi launched disastrous invasions of the Korean Peninsula with an eye toward conquering China.[21]

Hideyoshi died in September 1598, leaving his young son, Hideyori, in no position to compete for power. Tokugawa Ieyasu took advantage of this vacuum and quickly became the country's most formidable military figure. Emperor Go-Yōzei recognized Ieyasu's supreme power following the Battle of Sekigahara, naming him shogun in 1603. Hideyori, now eight, was married off to Iseyasu's seven-year-old granddaughter and sent back to Osaka Castle, where he grew increasingly vengeful.[22]

Ieyasu "retired" in 1605, passing the shogunal power to his son, Tokugawa Hidetada. The Tokugawas consolidated their regime around Edo Castle in today's Tokyo, which was then a wild frontier town far to the east from the imperial intrigues in Kyoto. Ieyasu returned from retirement to lead the forces of the Tokugawa clan against a growing army rising around the now-twenty-two-year-old Toyotami Hideyori in Osaka. Ieyasu unleashed a fearsome siege of Osaka Castle, leveling it to the ground. Defeated by June 1615, Hideyori and his mother committed ritual suicide (*seppuku*), his son was beheaded, and his daughter was sent to a convent.[23]

The Tokugawas now stood alone atop Japan's power structure. Their military dictatorship continued until 1868, with supreme power being passed from father to son, until the regime succumbed to the growing pressure of restive *daimyo* (i.e., feudal lords under the shogun) in the face of the country's opening up to the West after the visit of US admiral Matthew C. Perry's "Black Ships" in 1853 and 1854.[24]

Beginning in 1620, the Tokugawas began to rebuild Osaka Castle on an even grander scale—this time, as a symbol of outside domination rather than internal ambition. Nearly fifteen years later, during the summer of 1634, Tokugawa Iemitsu, the family's third shogun, arrived in Osaka with forty thousand retainers to inspect the new castle. Osakans awoke the next morning to find a gold banner flying from the castle's main tower, welcoming local merchants and artisans and declaring a tax holiday on land assessments. The city's residents interpreted this gesture of reconciliation as a sign that it was acceptable to enrich themselves as much as possible.[25]

Osaka was hardly alone in having the new Tokogawa regime redefine the city's place in the nation's urban hierarchy. Following their victory at Sekigahara, the Tokugawas launched major urban transformations in all of Japan's major towns. By locating power in Edo, they changed that city's fate. Similarly, their major interventions in Kyoto shifted the Imperial capital's major axis to the east, created new noble districts, and subtly altered major ceremonial spaces, especially after rebuilding Nijo Castle as their Kyoto base of operations.[26]

With aristocratic life concentrated on the increasingly irrelevant emperor and his court in Kyoto—and with political power rest-ing on the samurai attached to the military regime at Edo—Osaka found a niche for itself in the new Tokugawa urban hierarchy dominated by three giant cities—Edo, Kyoto, and Osaka—rather than by a single urban center.[27] Osaka's religious institutions remained, as did its port. Most important for what would transpire, the absence of a military threat meant that the presence of samurai remained minimal, so that, as David Rands points out, "The footprint of the warrior class was much less visible than in other military towns. The commercial nature of the city was undeniable, and the built environment reflected such."[28] This relative military presence meant that the love of money that drove Osaka's merchantry was given free reign to convert the city into a model of ambitious, frenzied townspeople practicing thrift and inventiveness.

The Kitchen of the County

Osaka recovered from the destruction of the country's long internal strife as the military regime closed Japan to the outside world and imposed a new social order. Samurai warriors sat atop the system, including the shogun as well as the regional *daimyo* who controlled enormous territories and maintained their own private armies. Farmers—who were prohibited from moving to town—enjoyed privileged status, despite their dependency on difficult physical labor. Townspeople (*chōnin*), a group that included craftspeople and merchants, found themselves near the bottom of the Tokugawa social order. Only several groups of outcasts—often tied to "unclean" professions associated with death, such as tanners; and also Kabuki actors—were lower in social status than merchants. As a result, status and wealth were not necessarily associated, as poor farmers attained privileged status over wealthy merchants.[29]

Tokugawa overseers welcomed thousands of merchants, artisans, and laborers into the city, and these newcomers rebuilt the local infrastructure to support their entrepreneurial ventures.[30] In particular, they expanded the network of canals, developing a sophisticated web of docks and warehouses where large riverboats could offload onto more than a thousand smaller "tea boats" (*chabune*) to supply workshops and retailers around the city.[31] The city's population grew to more than 400,000 by 1634, before declining by about 140,000 after the construction of the castle was completed, and subsequently climbing back to 350,000 by the Genroku era (1688–1704).[32] Osaka's voracious townspeople specialized in the rapid movement of goods along coastal shipping routes to Edo, thereby bypassing mountainous terrain and inadequate land routes.

Governments from surrounding domains (*han*) constructed large warehouse compounds in the Osaka port area to facilitate the shipment of their produce to a seemingly insatiable consumer market in Edo. A multifaceted system of authorized brokers and wholesalers grew to include some 1,300 by 1688 just in the famous Dōjima rice market, in what is today the centrally located Kita-ku between the Umeda Station complex and Nakanoshima. Merchants and financiers were linked with each other and to the rest of Japan by signal fires, flag communication, and carrier pigeons.[33] Trading began each morning at eight and lasted as long as a slow-burning rope suspended in a wooden box from a central beam in the Dōjima market remained aflame.[34]

Osaka came to dominate the emerging national rice market—and with it, Japan's capital markets—by combining innovation with tradition. Nestled among some of Tokugawa Japan's most advanced agricultural lands, Osaka developed close ties to nearby villages and farmers. The city became a major transshipment point for agricultural products—especially rice. Osaka's financiers controlled the flow of capital in Tokugawa Japan, just as the city's rice merchants established a monopoly over the country's primary food source.[35] They cornered the market on cotton—both raw and ginned—and cottonseed oil, which lit lamps all across Japan. Osaka's financiers and tradesmen busily made their town "the kitchen of the country."[36]

The American historian of Japan William Hauser notes that, as "a townsmen city," Osaka was a city "which served the interests of the common people who made up the vast majority of its population."[37] This focus on common townspeople defined Osaka's personality. The relative absence of privileged merchants in Osaka created a more flexible and less restricted climate for merchants' expansion and development in the seventeenth century. Thus, Osaka had neither as long a history of privileged merchants associated with aristocratic houses as did Kyoto, nor as large a concentration of warriors and their merchant purveyors as in Edo. Instead, Osaka developed a dynamic business culture.[38]

Osaka's merchants and their families—though coarse, crude, vulgar, greedy, and increasingly prosperous by the standards of Kyoto court and Edo political life—were uncharacteristically direct. They cultivated a most unrefined taste for a sort of "gaudy excess" that was atypical for their compatriots elsewhere.[39] This distinctive approach to living was reflected in Osaka's active theater life; in the city's unique tradition of puppetry and Kabuki; in its distinctive local humor; and in its local dialect and an accent that brands an Osaka native even today.[40]

In Tokyo and Kyoto—where status and authority dominated—humor was thought to bring dishonor, insulting one's position in the social hierarchy. In commercial Osaka, a good laugh was thought to bring people together—laughter being an all-important component of merchant relations.[41] Even as the traditional Japanese humorous storytelling tradition, Rakugo, is often associated with Tokyo's "Low City" (the Shitamachi district, which had long been home to townspeople rather than samurai and officials), the genre in fact first emerged in Kyoto and Osaka.[42] Osakan *rakugoka* consistently have been among Rakugo's most accomplished practitioners throughout its history as a performance art.

Seventeenth-century Osakans demonstrated a fearsome social intelligence. As the historian James McClain notes,

> As Osaka grew in size and changed its shape and physical appearance, it affirmed its place as one of the three jewels nestled at the apex of Japan's urban hierarchy. In common with all great world cities, however, Osaka's silhouette did not represent a mere tracing of the broad economic, social, and political trends of the times; rather what happened within the city helped to define and breathe life into the great historical impulses that were reshaping society in general. Throughout the early modern epoch, Osaka's merchant and artisan families moved to the vanguard of a samurai created world, and in doing so unleashed changes felt across the country. Osaka's craftspeople and entrepreneurs

improved processing techniques, discovered new products, and reinvented old ones, and its wholesalers and jobbers crafted distribution systems throughout Japan. . . . The city's playwrights, artists, intellectuals, and clerics enriched the nation by creating new genres of literary and dramatic production and new ways for the people of Japan to conceive of themselves, their relationship with their Gods, their cultural past, and even their place in the world of the future.[43]

Osaka's townspeople—merchants, artisans, retailers, and small-scale producers all jumbled together—wanted to enhance their self-worth in the face of low social status by making money; but once they made it, they wanted to show it off. Neither the haughty refinements of aristocratic form nor the adrenaline-soaked martial arts of the samurai quite matched their taste. They demanded their own culture—coarse, gaudy, and humorous.

Pre-Tokugawa Theater and Dance

Japan had a long and distinguished tradition of the performing arts by the time the Tokugawas extended their domain across the country. Itinerant storytellers and traveling musicians were established well before the time when the inhabitants of the islands forming today's Japan began to record their history on paper. Their performances gradually became structured and formalized, melding along the way with musical and narrative styles arriving from China and, eventually, with more formal rites of religious worship. Well-developed art forms, religious and court rituals evolved by the early years of the Murmomachi period (1533–68) to include raucous rural musical and dance festivals marking rice planting (*dengaku*); circus-like celebrations that had come from China before the eighth century (*sarugaku*); an elegant, twelfth-century male and female dance tradition in which dancers are dressed in court garb with white kimono and gold caps (*shirabyoshi*); and the austere classical court music dating from the seventh century (*gagaku*). Together, they provided Japanese thespians with the building blocks for a revolutionary new dramatic form, one that took shape during the fourteenth century as Nō musical drama.[44]

Nō theater transported Japanese performance culture to a new level. In the words of Ronald Cavaye and Paul Griffith, "the medieval theater of Japan [was] perfected during the Muromachi period. It includes musical accompaniment and dance, but its plays are performed in a solemn, dignified, and measured manner. Richly symbolic and performed in beautiful costumes with some actors wearing finely carved masks, Nō plays are pared down to their barest essentials. Even the stage is magnificent in its simplicity: Nō actors perform on a bare stage in front of a permanent wall on which is painted a solitary great pine tree."[45]

Nō developed in part from *sarugaku* entertainments, in which visiting troupes performed outdoors in small structures thrown up on the grounds of temples and shrines. These performances combined music, dance, and song interspersed with dialogue-based short—usually comedic—plays. The somber dance performances became Nō, while the more humorous spoken interludes—somewhat the functional equivalent of the early Italian intermezzo buffa—eventually evolved into Japanese comedic theater, Kyōgen.[46]

Each troupe developed its own distinctive mark, with four of them—Enamani-za, Sakado-za, Tobi-za, and Yūzaki-za—forming the cores of the great Nō "schools" that still exist today—Kanze, Hōshō, Komparu, Kongō, and Kita. During the mid–fourteenth century, the playwright and actor Kan'ami brought his Yūzaki-za players to the Imperial capital at Kyoto, took the stage name "Kanze," and refined the rhythmic music of *dengaku* with the melodic songs of *sarugaku* to consolidate the Nō tradition.[47]

A Kanze performance in 1374 overwhelmed Shogun Ashikaga Yoshimitsu, so much so that he invited the troupe into court life, where it enjoyed the patronage of the Japanese aristocracy for centuries to come.[48] (This patronage—which was given by the Ashikaga shogunate's military aristocracy, rather than the Imperial court—continued, into the Tokugawa period, as the Tokugawa shogunate continued its patronage of Nō. After the fall of the shogunate, it was partly Imperial patronage that enabled Nō to survive.) Kanze's son, Zeami, continued in his father's footsteps as a theater manager, director, playwright, and actor. He became the new drama's formative author, creating plays as well as central characters that still remain alive on the Nō stage.[49]

Figure 9. A Kyōgen theater performance at the Nō festival at the Castle in Himeji in 2009.
Source: Photograph by Corpse Reviver (https://commons.wikimedia.org/wiki/ File:Himeji-jo_Takigi_Nou_39_37.jpg).

As time passed, Nō became ever more elegant and austere as it conformed to the status-conscious elitism of a court that valued abstraction for its stark beauty. Of particular importance, Nō plays — of which there are now about two hundred and forty, and there once were hundreds, if not thousands, more — typically are performed with ethereal accompanying music in five play sets, with breaks for humorous Kyōgen satirical romps (figure 9). Together, these art forms became firmly ensconced as the definition of Japanese high classical culture.[50]

Nō developed several distinctive characteristics, which would shape subsequent Japanese theater before the arrival of Western drama in the late nineteenth century. Performances featured musicians who moved the action along, surrounding the actors with animating sound. Over the course of centuries, actors came to wear elaborate masks and spectacular costumes of multicolored brocade robes of the richest materials, punctuating the stark abstraction of the stage with a luxurious beauty quite familiar to its aristocratic audiences. The actors played out the story with distinctive gliding movements and stances of stillness, accentuating critical moments in the tales being recited by a chanting chorus. The actors danced alone, often moving in circles, in which the action was smooth and flowing.[51]

The Kyōgen interludes, by contrast, were full of slapstick buffoonery and clever repartee. These interludes were performed with highly stylized and abstract staging similar to Nō, and Kyōgen evolved side by side with Nō to form an integrated theatrical art form known as Nōgaku.[52]

Nōgaku entertainments shared another defining characteristic: They were performed on the distinctive *nogakudo*, or stage pavilion.[53] Actors' troupes built their stages on temple grounds—in some instances, literally adjacent to the temple buildings, which became part of the set—placing carefully trimmed cypress boards over earthenware pots designed to amplify the stomping of actors' feet. The back wall always displayed a painted twisted pine tree. This 20-foot-square/6-meter-square main stage sat under a pavilion roof adjoining a bridge-like walkway (leading to a backstage area called the "mirror room"). This room was separated from the walkway by a special curtain, which was raised for the entrances of all the characters except the musicians and the chorus members, who entered through a half curtain that was pulled aside for them, and who sat to the side.[54] This basic arrangement would come to be repeated in altered form by the subsequent performance arts taking shape during the Tokugawa period.

Nō and Kyōgen were paradigmatic entertainments of pre-Tokugawa Japan. They represented the values and tastes of the court's aristocratic and the samurai warrior classes. More traditional entertainments, such as rice-planting *dengaku* festivals and itinerate circus-like *sarugaku* troupes, captured the imagination of Japanese farmers and country folk. (However, the origins of Nō were in *sarugaku*; the troupe of Zeami, mentioned above, was a *sarugaku* troupe.) Like the regime itself, entertainers generally did not cater to the déclassé craftsmen and artisans of Japan's scattered towns and cities.[55]

Everything changed once the Tokugawas began to consolidate

their power. Edo, long a small frontier settlement, exploded into a wild, rough-and-ready samurai town as it became home to national power. Merchant Osaka enriched itself as quickly as possible. Townsfolk wanted to be entertained, seeking fun and games geared toward their own values and tastes. Japan, it turned out, was full of gifted performers who were more than ready to "bend" art forms to garner new and increasingly prosperous audiences in town.

Okuni's Dance

On a warm summer's evening just as the Tokugawas were settling into power in 1603, the priests at the Grand Shrine of Izumo dispatched the daughter of a blacksmith working on their grounds—a beautiful young dancer, singer, and shrine maiden (*miko*) named Izumo no Okuni—to solicit funds for their shrine. According to legend, Okuni and her husband, a displaced warrior (*rōnin*), Sunzaburō Nagoya, collected various female misfits, including prostitutes, formed their troupe, and headed off for the Imperial city.[56] They set down a small stage (modeled on those where she had seen Nō performances) on the dry Kamo River bed in Kyoto and performed a wildly provocative sultry dance full of sexual taunts.

Okuni and her company drew on existing traditions, melding them in new ways. Much learned scholarship has been produced over the years trying to discern what precisely transpired that evening.[57] What is clear, as the Kabuki historian Andrew Tsubaki has noted, is that Okuni's dance "was no mere accident. From a historical perspective, we can now see diverse forces contributing to the process by which such an art form was molded, forces that were operating in the late Muromachi and Momoyama eras" long before.[58]

Okuni's troupe was successful beyond their dreams, raising prodigious amounts of money, which according to legend was sent back to the shrine. In the process, they launched a new form of theater, in which performers were labeled as *kabuki-mono* (roughly "strange things" or "slanted people"). The "bent" nature of the new performance style went beyond sexual provocation. Okuni and her troupe, which included men, sometimes cross-dressed as a means of ridiculing members of the opposite sex, provoked the authorities by wearing crucifixes, and appeared at times as spirits or ghosts.[59]

This new performance art of "Kabuki" would become Tokugawa's Japan quintessential art form, reconfiguring Japanese theater
and dance. Over time, *"ka-bu-ki"* would be written with characters
meaning "song," "dance," and "skill" rather than "bent" theater.
This altered recording of its name accurately reflects the essence
of Kabuki as performance that integrates other artistic forms into
a single genre.[60] It is a total artistic union that, in the words of the
Kabuki historian Toshio Kawatake, "is identical to what Richard
Wagner advocated in his discussion of 'music drama,' or *'Gesamt-
kunstwerk,'* a deep synthesis of arts."[61] Kabuki, Kawatake argues, is
a truly "Baroque" fusion of the arts.[62]

The notion of a fusion of various arts amplifies Kabuki's core
theatricality. Unlike Nō, Kabuki scripts generally are less appreciated than, in the words of Barbara Thornbury, "the special multiple
interrelationships between actor, role, and character."[63] Perhaps
this emphasis on performance reflects the underlying reality that
there is nothing particularly grand about Kabuki's origins. Wild,
flamboyant, daring, gaudy, provocative, salacious, rude, and crude,
Kabuki immediately won a hearty band of passionate fans. Townspeople loved it. Okuni continued performing with her troupe, as
did many other female and male performers. She traveled around
the Kyoto–Osaka area for seven years, ignoring increasingly desperate entreaties by the Izumo monks to return home. Many followed in her footsteps.

Okuni's success inspired women's Kabuki (*onna kabuki*), which
remained rather basic in its storytelling and ambition. Initially, Kabuki music involved little more than some drums and sticks. To
critical observers, Kabuki dancing consisted of young females—
and males (there were many mixed troupes)—of ill repute showing
themselves off to potential customers. Although this was an overly
simplistic characterization, early Kabuki performances seemed to
many observers to be primarily about selling sex. Tokugawa Ieyasu
himself became increasingly disturbed by the generally obstreperousness, drunkenness, insubordination, and licentiousness that
accompanied Kabuki performances. In 1608, he expelled the Kabuki troupes from the Suruga military base. He became enraged
a short time later, when courtesans and courtiers associated with
his household caroused and publicly engaged in sex acts while

strolling around Edo. The miscreants paid a heavy price—execution and banishment.[64] Such scandals continued until the Imperial authorities lost patience and banned women from performing on the Kabuki stage a quarter century later, in 1629.[65] They would not be allowed back on the stage until the late 1800s.[66]

Young boys took off where the women had been forced to stop.[67] They perfected female roles, creating a new type of actor—males who specialized in female roles (*onnagata*), distinguishing a new "young men's Kabuki" (*wakashū kabuki*) from anything that had come before in Japan.[68] Kabuki audiences continued to grow, especially among the increasingly prosperous townspeople of Osaka and young samurai in Edo. Authorities came to see Kabuki performances as threatening the public order, with homoerotic suggestiveness replacing heterosexual lasciviousness.[69] Officials banned the new art form once again in 1652, after two samurai fought publicly over the favors of one of the boy actors.[70]

The shogunal authorities gave in and lifted the ban the following year. However, they prohibited women from performing on the Kabuki stage and required men to cut their forelocks, thereby signaling maturity.[71] Performing guilds (later to be known as *gekidan*), similar to those that would come to dominate Nō and Kyōgen, established their territories, building theaters licensed by the authorities—such as Edo's Nakamura-za—as early as 1624. Several years later, the authorities had restricted theaters to only a few areas: Sakae-cho, Fukiya-cho, and Kobiki-cho in Edo (by 1657); Shijoga-wara in Kyoto; and Dōtombori in Osaka. Kabuki theaters generally remain in these same neighborhoods centuries later (though new regulations forced Edo's theaters to move to Saruwaka-cho—now known as Asakusa—in 1841).[72]

Such periodic outbursts of regulation—both petty and expansive—reflected a general official discomfort with an art form that represented the evolving social norms and values of a class—townspeople—who were not viewed as completely honorable by the aristocrats or by the military men who ran Tokugawa Japan. The authorities tried to regulate who would perform, and where; to determine appropriate dress and makeup; to prohibit private passages that led directly from the theaters to adjoining teahouses and other places of assignation; and to censor dialogue fraught with indecency, along with even more explicit movements onstage. They would give up regulating in the 1890s.[73] Before then, Kabuki had established itself as a powerful, fully developed art form, just a half century after Okuni had pounded her feet on the Kamo River bed.[74]

Melding Time and Space

As Kabuki reached maturity in the second half of the seventeenth century, it did so on the boards of a distinctive stage that both respected the original Nō model, as Okuni had done during her dance, and bent it in new directions.[75] Unlike their counterparts performing classical Nō, Kabuki actors integrated their performances into the experience of their audiences, moving out and about the theater. Toshio Kawatake speaks of Kabuki as a "free and flexible theater space" that unleashes actors from the constraints of a conventional stage. Starting with an early 12- to 18-foot-square / 3.6- to 5.5-meter-square area, Nō actors developed the *hashigakari* walkway.[76] The *hanamichi* walkway, which went into the audience, was used as a temporary structure as early as 1687 and became a permanent feature in the 1720s. Over time, they added trapdoors and rotating stages as well as flyways overhead, so Kabuki became a "vertical theatre; its theatricality [being] the product of unlimited freedom of its theatrical space where stage and auditorium merge and the actor and audience fuse sympathetically into one" as a "free and flexible space."[77]

The *hanamichi* "flower path" thrust stage remains Kabuki's most distinctive physical structure.[78] Originating some time before 1687, the *hanamichi*—which initially was placed at a right angle to the main stage—had gained widespread use by the 1720s.[79] Various theories associate the evolution of the *hanamichi* with possible Nō and Sumō antecedents.[80] Whatever its origins, the *hanamichi* became a defining element of Kabuki staging as the art matured over the course of the seventeenth century. Presently, it is an aisle-like passageway approximately 1.5 meters wide running from stage right through the audience to the back of the auditorium.[81]

With a hidden passageway running underneath, the *hanamichi* is an integral part of the Kabuki performance, allowing for dramatic entrances and departures. The passageways function as a distinct stage, with action taking place independent from that on the main stage, thereby opening up a production's psychological and physical space beyond the limits placed by a single performance space.[82] Actors fade in and fade out of view, circle the audience returning to stage left, and otherwise add fresh dimensions to a performance on a fixed stage.[83] The *hanamichi's* floorboards are left exposed, or are concealed at times with symbolic coverings (colored white for snow, blue for water, gray for the Earth, or straw tatami matting for a house).[84]

The Kabuki stage evolved further, with a number of trapdoors being added, only to be followed in the mid–eighteenth century by a revolving stage (*mawari butai*)—the first in the world—and many other stage tricks (*keren*), levels, pulleys, and trapdoors that allow performers and sets to rise from the floor, turn in place, and fly over the audience.[85] Set and costume changes became instantaneous, magical illusions became the norm, acrobatic interludes were dazzling surprises, and conventional drama was turned on its side.[86] Theater was being "bent" into new forms, to the delight of audiences. The Kabuki stage became an animate object, one that is in keeping with Baroque operatic and theatrical staging of the same era in Europe.[87] The Kabuki stage liberated performers from being limited by the force of gravity and human limitations.[88] It emancipated its actors from the abstract strictures of classical Nō.

These changes in physical presentation were not accidental. Having originated in flashy, eroticized display, attended by déclassé townspeople and randy samurai, Kabuki appealed to audiences looking for flash, shock, and the fun of the new. Kabuki has always been about an opulent show.

Kabuki promoters and performers constantly pushed the edge of the theatrical experience to keep audiences flocking to their doors. Seating arrangements were borrowed from Nō, Sumō, and other robust entertainments. Tatami-matted box seats were arranged so that tea and tobacco could be served with boxed lunches and intermittent snacks.[89] Free to cheer, heckle, and jeer the actors from close range, spectators turned the theater into a single space in which they became one with actors. The actors, in turn, eschewed the masks of Nō, which some historians have argued had distinguished them from spectators.[90] Social hierarchy melted as the performance began.

Shamisen's Siren Song

Kabuki originated in dance and has retained an intimate relationship with music.[91] "The whole of the Kabuki performance," as the United States' lead theatrical censor in occupied Japan after World War II, Earl Ernst, wrote nearly four decades ago, "is surrounded with music and with what, for lack of a better phrase, can be called musical sound effects; they are literal and usually have a strong rhythmic quality."[92]

The aural quality of Kabuki washes over the audience before the curtain is raised, as white oak wooden clappers announce the beginning of the show with an accelerating beat.[93] Clappers also punctuate the action, announcing critical scenes, entrances, exits and endings, and curtain openings and closings.[94] The action on-stage plays out against the backdrop of elegant music and sound effects produced backstage by musicians who make sophisticated use of a variety of drums (some held in the hand, others on the shoulder or hip; some hit with a stick, others with the hand), gongs, and flutes. For dances and plays in the style of the puppet theater, musical narrators sit onstage throughout the performance.[95]

This reliance on sound underscores Kabuki's sensuous and formalized preoccupation with the external manifestations of inner emotions.[96] As the accomplished actor Bandō Mitsugorō VIII explained to the American Kabuki scholar Samuel Leiter in January 1964, "interiorization" is not "absolutely essential to kabuki acting. The exterior is enough. However," he continued, "the external form developed from an interior need and it is almost impossible to have this surface style unless the emotions are in communication."[97]

The master actor Onoe Baikō VII concurred in another interview with Leiter at that time, noting that "the beauty of kabuki is said to be the beauty of form. Exterior form, however, is not everything. In acting there must be a certain spirit that comes from the heart." Later, he added that "young and inexperienced actors depend too much on outward technique and not enough on feeling."[98] Music, in this context, becomes an integral aspect of Kabuki art, as it expands on the exterior, stylized beauty of its visual impact while augmenting the performance with an additional emotional level of engagement.

Derived from Nō, sacred *gagaku*, and popular song, Kabuki musical performance generally is more diversified than its fore-runners, relying on a larger number and range of instruments than its classical predecessors. Such expansion appealed to less-refined audiences of *chōnin* fans in Osaka, as well as in Kyoto and Edo.[99] Similarly, Kabuki, like Nō, is moved along by integrated musical interludes, song, and storytelling. In keeping with the onstage action, narrators and musicians are visible and active participants, supported by the distinctive sounds of the three-stringed, banjo-like *shamisen*.

The *shamisen* became the quintessential Kabuki instrument, quickly replacing the earlier *biwa* after having arrived in Japan via the Ryukyu Islands (Okinawa) and China in the 1560s.[100] The *shamisen* was first used for narrative storytelling and to accompany puppet performances, before being used in Kabuki. Okuni and many of her sister performers made the *shamisen* their preferred musical accompaniment.[101]

Originally a sheepskin percussive instrument from Egypt, the *shamisen* was modified in China on its way to Japan as silk strings were used over a snakeskin surface covering a resonating chamber.[102] The *shamisen* reached the main Japanese home islands via the port of Sakai in Izumi Province, near Osaka, during the mid–sixteenth century. The instrument would be modified yet again once it reached in Japan. Now made with cat skin, the instrument became immediately popular.[103] The instrument's portability, simple materials, complex tone, and distinguishing sound provided a perfect accent to plebian storytelling.

Within a century of its arrival, the *shamisen* became the primary accompaniment to Jōruri storytelling based on the romantic tales surrounding the fabled heroine Princess Jōruri—often done with puppets—in which the narrative was more important than the music.[104] From Jōruri, the path was a short one to Kabuki. Significantly, the great Osaka narrator and playwright Takemoto Gadyū promoted the use of the *shamisen* at the end of the seventeenth and beginning of the eighteenth centuries, both in the city's increasingly popular puppet and Kabuki theaters.[105] In doing so, Gadyū and others were bringing the merchant city's popular culture onto the stage.

Narrators and playwrights—such as Gadyū and his fellow Osa-

ka contemporary, the incomparable Chikamatsu Monzaemon—
were more than simple storytellers. Some of them (though not
Chikamatsu) were also musicians, who used the rhythmic cadences
of their recitations and poetry as instruments themselves.[106] They
were rap singers centuries before rap.

Arguably, Gadyū and Chikamatsu became Japan's greatest
playwrights and dramatists of their era as they struggled to domesticate their city's brash and gaudy prosperity by showcasing it
before audiences who themselves were its chief beneficiaries and
creators. They initiated an essential conversation about the nature
of their societies by converting their city's raucous social diversity
into an advantage. As Ernst notes, the rise of Kabuki "was linked
with the rise of the townsman, for it was the *chōnin* who principally
attended the Kabuki, and the Kabuki became the expression of the
townsman's artistic tastes and ethical beliefs. Nō theater was familiar to the commoner, but the Kabuki was lustier stuff, more accessible and suited to the tastes of a newly important economic class
than the esoteric Nō."[107]

An Actor's Theater

Movement stands at the center of the Kabuki actor's art.[108] The
actor's skill lies in his ability to order a series of clearly defined
movements and poses (*mie*)—at times in place with stillness—to
form a sequence of nonrepresentational images leading the viewer
through a story.[109] Kabuki performance, as Ernst argues, stands "at
a point about midway between the abstract movement of Western
social dancing and the surface realism of the movement of the rep-
resentational actor."[110] Like the spare haiku poem, it seeks the clarity of the literal in the penetrating precision of the economically
rhythmic.[111]

Over time, Kabuki dance developed three basic categories of
movement: *mai*, or dance, meaning "circling or rotating movements" that are "often slow and deliberate"; *odori*, also meaning
dance, for a "looser kind of movement, in which the body breaks
out of the constrictions of *mai*," with faster, lighter, more rhythmi-
cal movements; and *furi*, or gestures and mime.[112] These motions
represent the acting out of the words recited by the narrator.[113]

Kabuki actors specialize in particular character types, as is most apparent in the men who play female characters, the *onnagata*.[114] Actors are placed onstage in juxtaposition to one another so as to achieve carefully planned visual balance. Much depends, in the words of Ernst, on the isolated expressiveness of the individual actor and the sculptural quality of his figure.[115]

Expressive, symbolic makeup; elaborate wigs; and luxurious, kaleidoscopically colored costumes add dazzle and emotional impact.[116] As mentioned above, Kabuki—unlike Nō—does not use masks, thereby bringing the actors closer to the audience.[117] In the end, however, it is the individual actor who dominates the performance, creating the emotional impact of the action onstage. For these reasons, fans naturally come to idolize the actors who dominate the art.[118] Kabuki has been first and foremost an actor's theater.

Acting careers follow hierarchical patterns inherited from Japanese theater traditions, such as Nō. Kabuki demands high levels of skill and discipline, acrobatic muscularity, and delicate movement, which take a lifetime to cultivate and master. Students move up an extremely hierarchical system, in which the very best assume names of historical significance (e.g., there have been twelve performers since 1675 who have assumed the honored stage name of Ichikawa Danjurō).[119] Hierarchical networks are connected with the members of stage families, who have passed the acting tradition down from one generation to the next, often adopting talented youngsters into the clan over the centuries.[120]

Honored onstage, Kabuki actors have held an uncertain status outside the theater.[121] Supported by officials and feted by merchants, actors have avoided becoming social outcasts. But they nonetheless have never quite fit into the formal Confucian social hierarchy. They were prohibited, for example, from entering the warrior class. Consequently, they relied on the economic power of commoners for artistic and financial sustenance. (It needs to be noted that in the Confucian social order, all people were officially prohibited from changing class—e.g., farmers could not become samurai.)

Kabuki offers few moments when comedy perniciously undermines the social order, and it has no great comedic characters.[122] Rather, as Ernst records, Kabuki has embodied "for good or bad the complex attitudes, beliefs, customs, and aspirations of . . . society." In a static society, such as Tokugawa Japan, "the vocabulary of expression tends to endure." As *chōnin* cult figures, Kabuki actors offered a new representation of society reflecting social change without challenging the underlying order.[123] They were joined, especially in Osaka, by master puppeteers, who similarly renewed the Japanese performing arts so that they became fully entwined with the Kabuki stage and spirit.

The Birth of Osakan Ningyo-Jōruri Puppetry

As Kabuki came under greater official oversight, the master storyteller Takemoto Gadyū joined with enterprising Osaka puppeteers intent on cashing in on the genre's wildly lucrative popularity to use puppets to regain increasingly constricted artistic freedom.[124] In 1684, Gadyū set up a new theater in Osaka bringing together puppets, Jōruri storytelling, and *shamisen* accompaniment, thus building on theatrical practices and performance standards that already were at least several decades old.

Decades before the appearance of Kabuki, Japan's puppet masters had tried to attract an audience away from Nō performances to their theaters. Their strategy failed, for Nō seeks beauty by imposing a new aesthetic on natural human movement, but puppets attract audiences when their appearance and movement approximate living humans.[125] By adapting Jōruri tales to the puppet stage, the genre's masters were able to reorient their performances around a more popular, human-like vision.[126] Their success paved the way for Gadyū, whose company won passionate fans, garnering box office revenues that attracted some of the finest musicians and narrators of the day.[127]

Gadyū had plenty of competition, with a popular narrator-actor and former Gadyū student, Toyotake Wakatayū, joining with a playwright, Ki Kaion, to establish their own puppet theaters — as did other, perhaps less memorable performers.[128] Within a few years, the era's best playwrights were writing for the puppet stage. Their scripts, in turn, began to make their way into the parallel Kabuki repertoire as early as 1708 and proliferated by the 1740s. The result was a new genre of puppetry that quickly attained as high a level of artistic accomplishment as human Kabuki had managed to secure.

Originally called "Ningyō Jōruri," for puppet Jōruri storytelling, Osakan puppet theater is known more widely today as "Bunraku," after Osaka's Bunraku-za Theater, which was founded by Uemura Bunrakuken in 1872.[129] But its origins lay in the far more distant past. Japanese storytellers had been using puppets for centuries, beginning with a lone puppeteer operating a diminutive, hand-held artificial companion.[130] A distinctive style of narrative chant with *shamisen* accompaniment grew out of the tradition of itinerant—often blind—performers, similar to the European ballad singers of the Middle Ages, who traveled around the countryside telling both religious and secular tales. These stories included the twelfth-century *Tale of Heike* (*Heike monogatari*) as well as other works dealing with that century's civil wars.[131] Princess Jōruri, one of the heroines of the non-Heike stories, was the lover of the Genji clan's most illustrious general, Ushiwakamoru (Minamoto no Yoshitsune).[132]

Stories about Princess Jōruri became widely popular as they combined the eternal subjects of military glory, love, sex, betrayal, and conflicting loyalties. By the late sixteenth century—just a few years after the arrival of the *shamisen* from China—celebrated narrators became recognized for chanting her story against the backdrop of this newly Japanized instrument. Such narration to the sounds of the *shamisen* and the earlier *biwa* became known as Jōruri.[133]

Uji Kaganojō was the first great Jōruri narrator, gaining the sort of rock star notoriety for which many successors have striven for centuries. Born in 1635, he drew on Nō styles and tales to expand his repertoire. He began writing plays, increasingly setting out specific instructions for the narrators as part of an effort to elevate Jōruri to the aesthetic level of Nō.[134] His following grew, with more and more performers striving to become his apprentices. One of these students—a certain Gorōbei—was a lad only fifteen years younger than Uji Kaganojō himself.

A Tennōji market neighborhood boy, Gorōbei began performing in and around Osaka, eventually becoming Kaganojō's apprentice. Both Kaganojō and Gorōbei developed a rabid band of followers, sparking a creative competition that invigorated the Osaka theater scene. Gorōbei eventually changed his name to Gidayū, and, in the late 1600s, established the Takemoto-za Theater.[135]

Gidayū's distinctive style of chanting—which involved reciting the lines in a pure form so as to refine their emotional content—placed the highest value on the technique of delivery as well as on the words' meaning. This approach became so well known that his stage name, Gidayū, eventually served as the appellation for all Jōruri puppet narration—and continues to be highly valued by puppet and Kabuki actors and audiences today.[136]

Gidayū's creative narration and compelling writing arrived simultaneously with a new style of puppet. After his death in 1714, inventive puppet makers—such as the Toyotake Theater puppet master Yoshida Bunzaburō—advanced the art further by perfecting team puppetry, whereby figures were manipulated by three men.[137] This new technique promoted fluid and complex movement—especially by an increasingly expressive complex head, *kashira*, of which there are now some seventy types.[138] The additional operators allowed the puppets to grow in size throughout the eighteenth century, to as tall as 4 to 5 feet.[139]

Gidayū and his colleagues, along with his competitors, continued to draw heavily from Nō traditions in building their puppet theaters—both directly and indirectly. As in pre-Tokugawa Japanese theater, the puppet stage is demarcated into separate areas for different functions. Narrators and musicians remain visible, as do the teams of puppet manipulators. Backdrop scenery and curtains as well as side screens are similar to those in Kabuki, often being moved to simulate the passing countryside, city street, or wide open scene from an exposed house interior, as the puppets themselves cannot walk. A cutaway working area lower than the main stage (*funazoko*) hides the puppeteers' lower bodies so as to enhance the illusion that the puppets themselves are moving around the stage.[140]

The opening of Gidayū's puppet theater coincided with the fortuitous arrival of another young performer, Sugimori Nobumori, who was the son of a samurai family who became a master-less *rōnin* following his father's death and set out to make his way in the world. He eventually landed in Kyoto and began writing and performing. Assuming the pen name Chikamatsu Monzaemon, after the Chikamatsu Temple in today's Shiga Prefecture, he grabbed the opportunity to write for the new puppet theater that was gaining in popularity. This decision drew him to Osaka, where he teamed up with Gidayū.[141]

Chikamatsu's personal decision transformed Japanese theatrical and literary art, as he established himself as Japan's premier playwright and one of its leading poets.[142] Writing first for the puppet stage, he later added Kabuki scripts to his repertoire. This movement between both styles built on the several shared characteristics between the two, including stylized narration and the use of some of the same instruments such as the *shamisen*, flute, and drum.[143] Chikamatsu is the confirmed author of more than 130 plays in both genres, and he may have written many more plays by the time of his death in 1725 (less than three months after Gidayū's demise, in October 1724).

Gidayū and Chikamatsu were the leading lights of an explosion of artistic creativity on the Osaka stage, as actors, musicians, writers, and narrators scrambled to keep up with an insatiable audience who were seeking outlets for their ever-increasing prosperity, and who were embedded in a commercial culture that encouraged congenial group gatherings. Their students expanded the puppet and Kabuki repertoires, carrying their traditions into the eighteenth century. Namiki Sōsuke, Takeda Izumo II, Miyoshi Shōraku, Chikamatsu Hanji, and Takada Izumo II penned what are now the classical works of both theatrical traditions.[144]

As Gidayū's and his fellow performers, promoters, and writers established a vibrant theatrical form drawing on and refracting the delirious energy of Osaka itself, they set down a spirit of individualism that remains the mark of Bunraku to this day. As the historian of Japanese art Andrew Gerstle tellingly observes, "Bunraku did not develop family lineages, only lineages based on apprenticeship, discipline, skill, innovation, and achievement. Occasionally sons did join the troupe, but they were (and are) as likely as not to choose a different specialization from that of their fathers, opting perhaps to become a *shamisen* player rather than a chanter. In this regard, the practices that characterized *bunrakun* in Osaka diverged from those associated with Kabuki in Edo." Osaka and the performing arts that it nurtured remain noteworthy for a fierce spirit of independence, despite the general Tokugawa preoccupation with conformity and loyalty to hierarchy.[145]

But times had changed. Another great Osaka playwright, Namiki Gohei I, who wrote for the Kabuki stage from the end of the eighteenth century until his death in 1808, moved to Edo in 1794, bringing innovations to theater there.[146] Just a little later, Tsuruya Nanboku IV penned *kizewamono* plays portraying the horrors of life among Edo's lower strata.[147] Kabuki's center of gravity shifted to Japan's ever-more-powerful shogunal capital in the west.

A Golden Age of Playwriting

The creative outburst of seventeenth-century Japanese dramatic writing performed on puppet and Kabuki stages left an enormous, rich, and varied opus. Both theatrical forms achieved many of the central features that would characterize them throughout the century to follow.[148] This impressive body of work has been analyzed, categorized, and divided according to any number of criteria.[149] The original simple skits taken on the road by Okuni and her sisters produced comical portrayals of the "floating life" (*ukiyo*) found in urban pleasure districts. A little later, the action-packed "*aragoto*" warrior style developed by Ichikawa Danjūro I became most popular in Edo.[150] Ghost plays similarly became a favorite genre of Edo audiences.[151]

Around the beginning of the eighteenth century, "Jidaimono" plays focusing on upper-class nobles, samurai, and priests came into vogue, while still later, extravagant "Shosagoto" plays showcased luxurious costumes and backdrops. For the most part, all these plays could be performed by Kabuki actors as well as by puppets. In either case, they were divided into five acts performed over as long as an entire day.[152]

One of the primary points of differentiation within the Kabuki repertoire became that between the rough-housing of the energetic and muscular "*aragoto*" plays developed by Ichikawa Danjūrō dominating the Edo stage and the more elegant and sedate "*wagoto*" fare perfected by the actor Sakata Tōjūrō I, which was preferred by the Kyoto and Osaka audiences of the Kamigata region.[153] Both styles emerged contemporaneously at the end of the seventeenth and beginning of the eighteenth centuries, and were performed on the stages of all three Kabuki centers—Edo, Kyoto, and Osaka.

They nonetheless increasingly became associated with regional preferences.[154] Chikamatsu's mastery of language and style, for example, mirrored Kamigata (Kyoto and Osaka) taste, as in his 1703 "domestic" (*sewamono*) play *Sonezaki shinjū*.[155]

Chikamatsu's genius lies in his ability to take true incidents drawn from the everyday life of his *chōnin* audiences and present them with ordinary language and settings. Initially written for puppets, many of his greatest scripts were easily adapted by Kabuki theaters almost as soon as they reached the stage. Underneath such surface familiarity, he delved into the underlying psychological and emotional forces that drove everyday life to produce some of Japan's most powerful literary works.[156]

In this sense, Chikamatsu and his successors and imitators in the *wagoto* tradition were the products of the realities experienced by townspeople throughout the Kamigata region. Two stories ripped from the proverbial headlines of the day—those of the "Five Men of Naniwa" and the "Forty-Seven *Rōnin*" (leaderless samurai)—illustrate the manner in which Osaka performers drew on the streets around them for their inspiration, as did their counterparts in Edo.

For all its prosperity, Osaka was a tough town full of dirt and intrigue, success and failure, skilled financial magicians and ordinary street criminals. Karigana Bunshichi led one band of criminals whose exploits captured the local imagination. Known as "samurai hooligans," these "Five Men of Naniwa" were a local version of Robin Hood: bandits who challenged state authority by promoting gambling, extortion, racketeering, and protection rackets while victimizing everyday *chōnin*.[157] Their lives of crime ended badly, with some gang members having their heads cut off in public executions and displayed as a warning for all to see. Others died in prison from torture and cruel treatment. Their brazen exploits inspired endless legends, which in turn led any number of local writers to retell their story. Various versions of the tale appeared on the puppet stage as early as 1702, with Kabuki versions to follow in the decades ahead. Popular fiction writers joined in, and, centuries later, film directors discovered their story still could lure audiences into movie houses.

In reality, the five men of Naniwa—and other thugs like them—brutalized ordinary townspeople, attacking the rich and prosperous only in the imaginations of *chōnin* bystanders. Osaka's puppet and Kabuki theaters domesticated their violence and enabled the city's disaffected to live vicariously precisely because their tales were so prosaic.[158] The Kabuki fascination with blood, torture, combat, and humiliation became part of a process similar to that which transpired in Elizabethan drama, whereby the trauma of violence and economic instability at a time of dramatic social change was rendered less frightening by its appearance onstage.[159]

Similarly, the turn-of-the-eighteenth-century story of the forty-seven *rōnin* was taken from everyday life and assumed legendary stature.[160] In this instance, a group of samurai left leaderless by the ritual suicide of their lord avenged their master's honor by waiting two years to kill his nemesis before rituality killing themselves. Dramatic in its own right, the story was especially prone to compelling embellishment because the honored lives of samurai warriors provided plentiful opportunity for dramatic license. Puppet and Kabuki producers seized on the story for their stages. Plays—some more artfully conceived than others—followed, with plentiful literary works, woodblock prints, and, in the twentieth century, operas and films drawing on the *rōnin* tale for their own artistic purposes.

Myriad other plays drawn from daily life constantly moved back and forth between the Kabuki and Jōruri puppet stages. For example, Yō Yōdai's eleven-act extravaganza about intrigue within the lady's quarters of a high-ranking samurai—*Kagamiyama kokyo no nishiki-e*—premiered as a Jōruri production in 1782, before being taken to the Kabuki stage a year later.[161] *Kagamiyama*, like many of its Jōruri and Kabuki counterparts, evolves into a melodramatic soap opera of unrequited love and justice delayed, in which loyalty emerges as the key virtue holding society together.

Taken from an incident that transpired in Edo in 1724, *Kagamiyama* and plays like it feature chicanery of all sorts, sword fights, ritual suicide (with those killing themselves often mistakenly believing they have been dishonored, when in fact they were the victims of perfidious wrongdoing by their social betters), and revenge performed with verisimilitude and mastery. Audiences then and now drift into an imaginary world onstage, until a concluding samurai Gotterdammerung brings everyone in the theater back to their senses.[162]

To cite one more example of life coming to the stage, the famous

"Amagasaki Scene" in Chikamatsu Yanagi and Chikamatsu Kosui-ken's 1799 puppet play *Ehon taiko ki* continues to be performed by Kabuki and Banruku troupes.[163] The scene tells the story of how the samurai rebel General Akechi Mitsuhide mistakenly killed his mother just days after he had assassinated his lord, the powerful daimyo Oda Nobunaga, in an attempted coup d'état at Kyoto's Honno-ji Temple in 1582. Mitsuhide had been in Nobunaga's service before his perfidious revolt. Three days later—the play's thirteen acts follow each of Mitsuhide's thirteen days in power—Hashiba Hideyoshi avenged Nobunaga, defeating Mitsuhide's army at Yamazaki and assuming the position of supreme military commander.

In this instance, the playwrights renamed the protagonists in order to avoid conflict with censors, who frowned upon portrayals that cast the Tokugawas—who were sworn enemies of the Hideyoshi clan—in a bad light. But their obscuration fooled no one in the audience. Such plays as *Kagamiyama kokyo no nishiki-e* and *Ehon taiko ki* were the sort of pop cultural diversion that twenty-first-century audiences seek out on plasma screens, both miniature and gigantic.

The speed with which such stories could find their way onto local stages underscored the deep connection between Osaka's popular theater—and its two dominant performance genres of Kabuki and Jōruri puppetry—and commoner life. The city's distinctively *chōnin* culture nurtured its own brand of creativity that was neither as refined as that of aristocratic Kyoto nor as brawny as samurai Edo. Osaka's Kabuki and puppet theaters reflected the values and culture of a merchant class that was rising in importance well above its status in the official social hierarchies.

Chōnin Osaka's Contributions to Kabuki and Jōruri Puppetry

Osaka theater's great era began to wane after Gidayū and Chikamatsu died. Edo companies offered more money and recognition. Kabuki's focus was beginning to shift eastward—as was that of Rakugo comic storytelling—and thus they were to eventually, by the end of the century, become more quintessentially Edo art forms.[164] This change, however, did not diminish the remarkable outburst of Osakan creativity in the half century on either side of the turn of the eighteenth century. The city gave rise to some of

Japan's greatest writers, best musicians and actors, most stunning production techniques (including inventions that contributed to Kabuki's use of traps, flyways, and movable and rotating stages), and greatest philosophical insights. Through its Kabuki and puppetry performers, Osaka gave Tokugawa Japan's most popular art form some of its most innovative productions, best writers, and most beloved performers. The city brought Tokugawa culture's most distinctive instrument, the *shamisen*, to center stage.

Kabuki and Jōruri puppetry hardly died in Osaka, even as the center of Japan's creative life shifted to Edo. The city's merchants were as prosperous as ever, and they loved a raucous good time as much as before. By the late Tokugawa period, Osaka had perfected another lasting theatrical legacy, which once more altered Kabuki. Its printers started turning out hundreds of inexpensive playbills featuring local actors for the city's insatiable fans on a scale beyond what was happening elsewhere.

As noted above, Kabuki has long been an "actor's theater," in which fans enjoy a direct and passionate relationship with the stars onstage. "Actors and audience," Timothy Clark and Osamu Ueda argue, "inhabited the same world—the close-knit, downtown world of crowded two-story tile-and-timber buildings—a world which was very much the preserve of the artisans and merchants, the so-called townsman (*chōnin*) class."[165] As time went on and Kabuki left its burlesque origins behind, the theater became increasingly popular among the wives and daughters of the newly enriched merchants, who began to find that their husbands' newfound wealth gave them the luxury of free time and disposable incomes.

Women flocked to theaters, as a distinctive Tokugawa urban culture solidified, in particular in Osaka and Kyoto. Actors became the objects of erotic fantasy for their audiences, and fans became avid readers of the latest backstage gossip. Enthusiasts followed their favorite performers, such as Miyamoto Tomijūrō, Arashi Hinasuke, Arashi Kichisaburō II (Rikan), and Nakamura Utaemon III (Shikan) (figure 10).[166] These "matinee idols"—as they would be called two centuries later and a world away in Hollywood—animated celebrity-dominated Tokugawa popular culture every bit as much as gossip about Charlie Sheen, Lindsey Lohan, and Caitlyn Jenner drives internet blogs and scandal sheets today.

Figure 10. A portrait of the actor Shikan.
Source: Library of Congress.

Urban culture in Tokugawa Japan was one of the world's first popular print cultures, presaging the boulevard press of turn-of-the-twentieth-century Europe and North America. Fans yearned for keepsakes, and, in 1805, Rikan gave them what they wanted. The Osaka superstar and female favorite published the first woodblock prints promoting his own theatrical troupe through pop-culture-like images of the company's stars, beginning with his own visage.[167] In Edo, Katsukawa Shunshō and his protégés similarly launched their own "school" of Kabuki woodblock posters.[168] Though such posters had existed before, they had never appeared on such a scale. They became a characteristic Tokugawa art form as a new genre of graphic art—the actor woodblock print (then known as *yakusha-e*, and today as *buromaido*, for "bromide")—took shape.[169]

Andrew Gerstle has observed that "an obsession with celebrity is not . . . only a modern phenomenon. London in the eighteenth century, for example, promoted the celebrity of its courtesans and actors in print. A print of the famous actor David Garrick shows him at his histrionic best. It is fascinating to witness many of the same elements that characterize our contemporary obsessions in a relatively remote Japanese society of two hundred years ago, long before modern technologies had their impact."[170]

Gerstle's larger point is, perhaps, most telling. Despite all the differences between Tokugawa Japan, Georgian London, and contemporary Los Angeles, the delirium of exploding urban centers creates similar responses. Fast-changing daily life forces humans to render their world comprehensible. But the performing arts are one way for them to leave a distinctive mark that allows them to say that they belong in a particular place at a particular time. Commercialized performing arts, such as those that dominated Elizabethan and Georgian England as well as Tokugawa Japan, in turn require the wealth and attention of an audience—which, until the twenty-first century, depended on the crazed proximity of urban density.[171] These were societies that remained open to the free flow of information and people, as their great commercial cities emerged from earlier eras of feudal control to become major entrepôts promoting exchanges of all kinds.[172]

Kabuki fandom was not merely a group of passive consumers of the theatrical arts. Robust amateur groups sprang up around Osaka, promoting poetry, art, theater, dance, and music, while creating "utopian spaces" (*za*) for social interaction. Amateur groups gathered to recite their favorite plays, imitate their favorite dances, and argue about their favorite performers. Rabid factions formed, pitting the two great actors of the era, Rikan and Shikan, in an intense rivalry that dominated the Kabuki stage throughout the early years of the nineteenth century.[173] A vibrant civil society formed within the larger feudal Japanese world, which valued hierarchical dependence and obeisance.[174] Such a civil society and its social mixing—rooted fundamentally in the city's *chōnin* culture and economy—made Osaka distinctive even among the commanding Tokugawa cities of court-dominated Kyoto and samurai-dominated Edo. Osaka's commercial swagger became subtly subversive.[175]

Kabuki's producers, troupe leaders, and theater owners encouraged fans to invest as much enthusiasm, passion, and money as possible in their theatrical addictions. They encouraged patrons to sponsor banners, decorations, and lanterns above the stage and by the door. Fan clubs dressed in branded costumes and gave gifts of theatrical kitsch to one another.[176] The mutual support of fan and actor and theatrical promoters was fervent and mutually beneficiary.[177]

To encourage fan participation in theatrical frenzy, Kabuki producers picked up a long-standing Nō tradition of publishing texts in playbooks to be read before a performance, much like a libretto in European opera. Jōruri puppeteers copied the idea. By about 1700, reading and owning increasingly elaborate booklets—complete with "official" texts and musical notations, ever-more-lavish illustrations, and concise summaries—became de rigueur for both the Jōruri and Kabuki fans.[178]

Rikan's woodblock actor prints—which appeared before 1800—proved to be a logical next step in this progression.[179] Fans collected the prints, programs, and other souvenirs in scrapbooks. Their insatiable demand supported a local printing and publication industry that was among the largest of any city in the world.[180] Literally hundreds of thousands of such posters and cards appeared during the second half of the Tokugawa period, fostering an ever-more-extravagant local Osakan culture that influenced other Kabuki centers in Kyoto as well as in Edo.[181]

A Time of Urban Frenzy

Kabuki's success should not obscure Osaka's more complex and difficult realities. Increasing tax rates, regional differences, rural-versus-urban tensions, and internal class and clan conflicts bubbled beneath the surface of eighteenth-century Tokugawa Japan. As the historian Uchida Kusuo has written,

The 1720s and 1730s were not easy times for merchant and artisan families in Osaka, or more generally for much of the commoner population throughout Japan. To an unprecedented degree, collective violence and organized dissidence scarred those two decades, providing an index of growing popular antipathy with the shogunate and regional *daimyo* governments. Flames of discontent flared up in every quadrant of the rural countryside, from Kyūshū to Tōhoku, and residents of Japan's major cities were equally restive. In Edo, the poor and angry employed violence as a tactic of protest for the first time in the city's history in 1733, when they attacked the shop of a rice dealer who was closely identified with the shogunate. Just three years later, thousands of merchants in Osaka gathered to express their unambiguous dissatisfaction with the economic conditions and with shogunal policies that threatened to jeopardize their well-being.[182]

Times were difficult, and the dividing lines of urban life were becoming more challenging to hide, as the enervated Tokugawa regime exhausted itself. Popular responses ranged from violence to the embrace of new religious movements, such as more fervent worship of the Shinto fox deity of fertility, rice, and agriculture, Inari okami. Neighborhood shrines honoring Inari sprang up across the country during the second half of the eighteenth century, prompting mass pilgrimages and carnivalesque festivals.[183]

In Osaka, the historian Wakita Osamu records,

the latter half of the eighteenth century was an unhappy period, as the people of the city and its environs lived through a trying sequence of unsettled weather, serious famines, riots protesting high food prices, devastating fires, and the human suffering and spiritual trepidation that followed in the wake of such disasters. As these events piled one upon the other the influx of migrants . . . drove the population of Osaka to levels that the city's commercial production and infrastructure could not sustain and exacerbated inflationary pressures that impinged on everyone. The propensity of the government periodically to impose unscheduled extraordinary tax levies on Osaka merchants and the difficulties experienced by wealthier peasants, who had provided a degree of stability in rural areas by carrying their tenants through hard times in previous generations, complicated matters and further eroded economic conditions and around the city. In the midst of such economic instability, few individuals or their families could count on a certain future.[184]

Kabuki and puppet theater thrived during this period of urban delirium as the Tokugawa regime slowly unraveled, eventually to be overturned by the forces unleashed by the visits of Admiral Perry in the 1850s. As the quintessential Tokugawa popular art form, Kabuki ironically assumed increased meaning as the regime weakened. Kabuki's status and popularity ensured that it would survive the Tokugawa period, often as something of a museum piece honoring a lost time. The restoration of Imperial rule under the Emperor Meiji opened Japan to an avalanche of outside forces, as modernizing Japan tried to find its place in the world.

Kabuki continued to reach out to loyal fans in Kyoto, Osaka, and especially Edo throughout the Meiji period. The traditional Japanese arts—including Nō, Kyōgen, Rakugo, Kabuki, and Jōruri—competed with the performing arts imported from the West. Shakespeare's plays—which were often being adapted in strange ways to hold the attention of Meiji audiences—became especially popular.[185] One legendary production of *Hamlet* allegedly featured the Danish prince riding a bicycle, a not startling turn of events for local spectators to whom both bicycles and Danish royalty were equally and bizarrely foreign.[186]

Early-twentieth-century actors, directors, and playwrights successfully staged the era's Western plays, including a notably popular repertoire of dramas by Anton Chekhov, Henrik Ibsen, and Bernard Shaw.[187] Japanese theaters and translators became ever more serious about performing the Western classics, especially the works of Shakespeare.[188] And the Shinpa Movement—an entirely new genre, sometimes called a hybrid of Kabuki and Western realism—emerged from political protest plays in the late 1880s.[189]

Deep transformations in Japan's society and economy dramatically altered how Kabuiki operated on a daily basis. As in all spheres of Japanese life, old restrictions were lifted and new opportunities for artistic and commercial freedoms opened up. Small, unofficial playhouses and touring companies visiting such venues as temple fairgrounds catered to those who could never afford to enter theaters. Censorship came to an end, as did controls over costume fabrics and colors.[190]

Brian Powell has identified three ways in which the Meiji reforms had a direct impact on Kabuki. First, leading actors and playwrights, such as the actor Ichikawa Danjūrō IX and the playwright Kawatake Mokuami, initiated a movement demanding greater historical accuracy, which led to a new genre of "living history" plays (*katsureki*). Second, the Theatrical Reform Movement (Engeki Kairyō Undō), featuring such luminaries as the actor Ichikawa Danjūrō IX and the impresario Morita Kan'ya XII, attempted to reinvent Kabuki as an art form worthy of Western attention.[191] The promise that once-outcast Kabuki could be transformed into an "official" Japanese theater spurred Kan'ya to invest heavily; but Kabuki never did achieve this official status. Third, the brothers Shirai Matsijrō and Ōtani Takejirō ruthlessly commercialized Kabuki through newly formed joint stock companies, eventually creating the Shōchiku Syndicate, which came to dominate Kabuki—by homogenizing it, by adopting one mode of production, and by eliminating regional differences and character, especially that of Osaka.[192]

The intrepid English adventurer Isabella Bird traveled to Japan during the spring of 1878 "to recruit my health," in the certainty that Japan "possessed in an especial degree those sources of novel and sustained interest, which conduce so essentially to the enjoyment and restoration of a solitary health-seeker."[193] As she attended a performance at Tokyo's Shintomi-za, Bird was bemused by the strange mix of old and new that was coming to the Japanese stage.

"When delay had become nearly insupportable," she reports, "and the noisy music of marine and military bands, which performed alternately, had rasped sensitive nerves to the extreme limit of endurance, a curtain at the side of the stage was drawn aside and Morita [the theater's proprietor], accompanied by forty actors in European evening dress, advanced to the front and right of the stage, those who perform as females grouping themselves on the left, dressed in *kimono* and *hakama*. The actors in European dress arranged themselves in a dismal line, an awkward squad."[194] Morita and the lead actors expressed, in Bird's words, "the desire for *reform from within*," and "sympathy with the great Japanese movement in the direction of Western civilization" (emphasis in the original).

She continued that "after an interval, during which tea and champagne were provided in the galleries, and much feasting went on in the pit, the curtain rose upon the Nō stage and its performers."[195] Although she appreciated the "splendor of the dresses, and the antique dignity of the actors," she nonetheless found the performance "most tedious, and the strumming, squalling, mewing, and stamping by which the traditional posturings are accompanied, are to a stranger absolutely exasperating."[196] Some Japanese members of the audience could well have been just as perplexed by the imitation of European sensibilities at the performance's outset.

Bird, it turned out, had found herself at a pivotal turning point in Kabuki history: June 7, 1878. On that day, with Isabella Bird in attendance, Morita Kan'ya (whose family had managed theaters since the seventeenth century) opened a Kabuki theater sporting the highest Western amenities of the day.[197] Kan'ya's goal was to align Kabuki with the government's ambitious modernization plans, thereby linking the theater to the future rather than to its past. He succeeded, in that his Shintomi-za became the government's semi-official theater, a destination to show off the country's unique blend of tradition and modernity to visiting dignitaries, such as former US president Ulysses S. Grant just a few months later.[198] As the historian William Lee has argued, Kabuki, "long subject to official scorn and regulation, became an object of interest for the educated and governing elite, an interest that itself provided the context for the innovations attempted within the theatre world."[199] In less than a decade, Kan'ya's company would perform before the emperor himself.[200]

The Meiji transformation created tens of thousands of such awkward juxtapositions, as all sorts of Japanese institutions fumbled their way toward a new world. Kan'ya Morita's Shintomi Theater Company was just one of hundreds of drama groups trying to accommodate new ways with the old. These vast changes taking

place swept away the social structure that had produced both Kabuki and Osaka's puppetry tradition at the outset.[201]

Empire and Theater

Change in many ways came slowly, as Kabuki insinuated its way
into a new Japan. A handful of families dominated the Kabuki
stage, often operating within a Tokugawa hierarchy in which the
descendants of some families controlled casting for the best parts
while the heirs of others continued to languish in more obscure
roles.[202] The difference was that space now existed within the
worlds of Jōruri and Kabuki for new groups to emerge. The Tsukjii
Little Theater (Tsukiji Shōgekijō), for example, opened in 1924 to
cater to the tastes of the era's young, European-oriented intellectuals. The Marxist "Theater of the Masses" (Taishū-za) similarly was
founded in 1929 to bring Kabuki and other performances to a wide
public.[203] Actors from several lower-ranked acting families joined
the Taishū-za, which continued to perform well into the years of the
Great Pacific War.[204]

Audiences nonetheless shrank as Kabuki competed with Western performance genres and also, in time, with new electronic
media such as phonograph recordings and film. Many theaters
closed—especially in Osaka and Kyoto—while others revamped
their programming.[205] The Great Kantō Earthquake of 1923 destroyed several traditional Edo theaters, a catastrophe that amplified the sense that classical Kabuki was slowly slipping away.[206]
Kabuki—together with other traditional Japanese performing arts,
such as Nō and Rakugo—was compelled to compete for audiences
and resources in new ways.[207] In the case of Kabuki, stages added
new lighting and configurations, along with other improvements
being made since the 1880s.[208]

Post-Tokugawa Kabuki remained full of contradictions—at
times, seemingly resistant to change; at other moments, rushing off
in new directions. Yet the theater never quite became caught in an
amber amulet that preserved performance styles and language that
would have struck many Japanese as archaic and stale. Early-twentieth-century Kabuki remained a vibrant art form, as new players
and writers expanded its repertoire with plays that reflected new
social realities.

Lady Kate Lawson, a longtime English resident of Japan and member of the Red Cross Society of Japan, described the lasting impact of going to the theater in Japan at the turn of the twentieth century. Describing Kabuki performances of the era, she wrote, "managers of to-day encourage realism, and modern plays depict everyday life with a detail and minuteness thoroughly Japanese. Red paint oozes forth from slaughtered victims; the tragedies are very tragic and the villains very villainous; and when the hero, or all the several heroes, dies the honourable death of *seppuku* or *harakiri*, it is so realistic that we are haunted by the gory scene for weeks afterwards."[209]

The Kabuki historian James Brandon has looked back at the period and has made similar observations:

> Although it might appear to the untrained eye that Kabuki was a monolithic art form, as were Nō and Bunraku, artistically it was schizophrenic. Presented to the public as a compound art of song, dance, and acting skill (*ka-bu-ki*), it also contained within itself numerous elements of earlier theater forms, Nō, Kyōgen, and Bunraku among them. But even more important, Kabuki occupied an indeterminate social status. It is an "old theater" (*kyūgeki*) bound to the Tokugawa feudal past whose classic plays promoted the virtues of bushido, loyalty to one's feudal master, and the duty of honorable self-sacrifice (*gisei*). At the same time, it was a creature of the moment, capable of being molded to suit the unique spirit of the times (*jikyokusei*). These two faces of Kabuki's nature were in constant tension and often in open war with each other.[210]

Post-Tokugawa Kabuki continued to produce new plays while revising and renovating previous productions to remain current with the world swirling around it. This is particularly true, Brandon demonstrates, as fighting continued throughout the Fifteen-Year War in the Pacific between 1933 and 1945. During this period, Kabuki theaters drew on the headlines of the day, cranking out more than one hundred "overnight pickle plays" (*ichiyazuke*) related to battlefront events.

Playwrights and performers similarly adapted contemporary popular culture to enliven new plays, as when Hisamatsu Issei incorporated Western-style tap dancing into his 1933 dance scene in *Takatsuki*. In that scene, a lord on a mountain excursion to view cherry blossoms asks his retainer to purchase a small table (*tatatsuki*). The hapless and increasingly inebriated servant purchases traditional wooden platform sandals (*takaashi*) instead. The young man begins to dance as the mistake becomes clear, ending with a Hollywood-style tap performance.[211]

More than sixty "new history" plays (*shinjidaigeki*) appeared during the 1930s—often in response to rising nationalism and militarism, and often set in the Meiji Era—and continued to enlarge Kabuki's repertoire.[212] But then ordinary Japanese life collapsed under the onslaught of American firebombs and military victories beginning in late 1943.[213]

Brandon is careful not to blame the Americans for Kabuki's postwar near death experience. "Considering that American military forces had annihilated Japanese garrisons in one Pacific battle after another," he writes, "and formations of free flying B-29s were turning Japan's cities and theaters to ashes, it would be easy to attribute Kabuki's near demise in the late summer of 1945 to American actions. But we would be wrong to do so. We have seen that policies determined by Japanese bureaucrats, politicians, and military officers five and ten years earlier reduced Kabuki's status long before war's end."[214]

Following the war, the Kabuki repertoire froze into a well-defined set of historical plays with little contemporary content. The Americans were partially to blame, as the US Occupation Force briefly imposed censorship on Kabuki between 1945 and 1949.[215] The Americans simultaneously promoted the introduction of contemporary plays advancing democratic values. In 1950, for example, the fashionable novelist and screenwriter Yamamoto Shūgorō wrote a highly realistic "ghost play," *Yurei Kashiya*, which presents the life of late Edo Era townspeople in great detail using the everyday patter of postwar Japanese language.[216] *Yurei Kashiya* was closer in form to the productions of Konstantin Stanislavski's Moscow Art Theater than to the traditional Kabuki stage. The story's sense of dramatic movement drew on Shūgorō's cinema experience. Its content and storyline nonetheless derived from the Kabuki "ghost play" genre.

Set in late Edo days, *Yurei Kashiya* is the tale of how the ghost of a middle-aged hostess visits a lazy neighborhood keg maker who has lost his will to work following the death of his mother. Having been left by his wife, the keg maker risks eviction as a landlord frustrated by the absence of rent receipts repeatedly knocks at his door. After seducing the keg maker in a suggestive erotic romp witnessed by snooping neighbors (and the audience), the ghost hostess convinces the keg maker that they can start a rent-a-ghost business in order to pay off his debts. Their venture begins well enough, until some of the ghosts hired to help mere mortals quarrel with one another as well as with their customers. Ultimately, the keg maker is saved by a Buddhist "born again" moment. The newly pious craftsman turns into a beloved neighborhood figure following a pattern established by Dickens in *A Christmas Tale* a century before.

The play fell from favor, despite Shūgorō's fame and popularity (a prestigious literary prize in his name was established in 1987 to mark the twentieth anniversary of his death). Ultimately, popular film, television, and Kabuki actor Bando Mitsugo X set forth on a personal mission late in the twentieth century to bring it back into the Kabuki repertoire.

Against this background, General Douglas MacArthur's aide-de-camp, Faubion Bowers, convinced the United States' lead theatrical censor, Earle Ernst, to be lenient in his interventions in Kabuki companies, thereby earning Ernst the soubriquet "the man who saved Kabuki."[217] It must be added that Kabuki's primary production company, the Shōchiku Corporation, led by its president Takejirō Ōtani, resisted American pressure at every turn, choosing to narrow the Kabuki repertoire to several dozen "classical" plays dating back to before the Meiji Era. After having continued to produce new plays about contemporary subjects throughout the war, Ōtani and the ever-more-powerful producers at Shōchiku "preserved' Kabuki by "classicizing" it. The space for new productions, such as Shūgorō's *Yurei Kashiya*, almost disappeared for the next half century or so—though there was an uptick in new Kabuki plays in the 1960s, after the US Occupation ended.[218]

The puppet theater simultaneously confronted its own twenti-eth-century challenges. Always more of a local Osaka rather than a national performance art, Jōruri puppetry retained its audiences as a sign of local "patriotism." The theater's golden age had ended long before, perhaps even before the closing of the Toyotake-za and Takemoto-za theaters in the mid-1760s. The changes associated with the Meiji Restoration exacerbated artistic and financial strains that had been challenging puppetry performers, writers, and pro-moters for some time, even before the difficult years before and af-ter the war had arrived.[219]

On a positive note, the great performer Masai Kahei reinvigo-rated the art form at the turn of the nineteenth century. He adopted the stage name Uemura Bunrakuken, and his protégés named a new theater in his honor in 1871. The name of this theater, Bunraku-za, eventually became, as noted above, the internationally recognized appellation for the entire performance genre.[220]

Bunraku's performances faced numerous reversals of fate. In 1926, fire destroyed its venues in Osaka, along with puppets, costumes, and sets. A new theater opened in 1929, and, just four years later, Bunraku was declared a "national cultural treasure." This new designation elevated the art form beyond the limitations imposed by its singular identification with one city, making it eli-gible for national government coffers to open up and provide criti-cal support.[221] Two innovative performers—Yoshida Bungorō and Toyotake Yamashiro no Shōjō—simultaneously injected new life into the theater.[222]

Although the wartime destruction of Osaka devastated its the-aters, Bunraku appears to have faced less interference from US Occupation Force censors than had its artistic cousin, Kabuki. The puppet theater confronted a different challenge, however, as bitter disputes among union factions nearly destroyed Bunraku in 1947. Only concerted efforts by the Osaka Prefecture and the national broadcasting company, NHK, eventually were able to force the em-bittered parties to reassociate themselves in 1963.[223]

These upheavals led to other changes that enriched the puppet tradition. The legendary female narrator Komanosuke Takemoto began her more-than-sixty-year career around this time. She was a native of Awaji Island in the eastern Seto Inland Sea (a known center for Bunraku), and she traveled to Osaka as a teenager to study with some of the most exalted masters of the era, including Wakatayu Toyotake X and Koshijidayu Takemoto IV.[224]

Other new legends emerged to sustain the tradition, such as another transformative narrator—Sumitayu Takemoto VII (Kin'ichi Kishimoto)—a native Osakan whose 2014 retirement at the age of eighty-nine years rightly garnered national press.[225] Of particular importance, legends are not only in the past. In early 2015, Tamame Yoshida achieved the performance level required to assume the mantle of his mentor, Tamao Yoshida, who had died nine years before. In April and May of that year, Tamame debuted as Tamao Yoshida II at celebratory performances in Osaka and Tokyo, demonstrating a continued commitment to Bunruku's future as a treasured art form.[226]

Their collective efforts produced a formidable National Bunraku Theatre in Osaka. The new national company consolidated the art on a splendid new stage in Osaka's Sennichimae District in 1984, where it thrives today.[227] Puppetry was once more on a path to artistic, managerial, and financial well-being.

Meiji Osaka and Beyond

Throughout Kabuki's and Bunraku's various vicissitudes, Osaka itself was adjusting to the enormous transformations taking place as Japan reentered the world following the 1853–54 visits of Perry's "Black Fleet" and, most especially, following the final collapse of the Tokugawa military regime in 1876. Osaka had already passed its peak of Tokugawa prosperity by the end of the eighteenth century.[228] The city still harbored some remarkable achievers throughout the entire Tokugawa period, to be sure. Yet Osaka's traders, craftsmen, and manufacturers were fundamentally in trouble long before the new Meiji government set out to "modernize" Japan.[229] Reform measures initially hit Osaka particularly hard, most especially the local *fudasashi* (rice brokers and agents), who had previously dominated Japan's rice trade.[230]

Osaka eventually made a successful transition to become a major industrial center, reinventing itself from a "sea of roof tiles" to a "forest of smokestacks."[231] Japan's "Venice"—much of its trade had moved along an intricate network of canals—would become in just over a quarter century or so a "city of furnaces, factories, and commerce; the centre of the modern spirit of feverish activity in manufacturing and commercial enterprise."[232] As a result, the city exploded from a town of about 350,000 residents to approximately 2.2 million during the half century beginning in 1870.[233]

Osaka managed to remake itself into an industrial dynamo with remarkable alacrity, given the magnitude of its economic and social transformation. Industrial development was delayed in Osaka, as elsewhere in Japan, until the 1880s, when the Japanese government abandoned notions that the state could engage directly in industrial production on its own. The policy shift of the 1880s toward government's encouragement of private-sector industrialization through indirect connections with networks of private banks and firms—a system that eventually evolved into the *zaibatsu* system—prepared the way for the country's great leap into the industrial age.[234] Cartelization reduced the displacement generated by erratic market demand and prices while simultaneously conforming to behavioral expectations rooted in traditional Japanese family management practices.[235] Osaka, with its dense matrix of interrelated financial houses, was well positioned to take advantage of Meiji Japan's indirect industrial policy.

Osaka was hardly alone in enjoying Japan's astonishing economic launch. Nearly every Japanese participated in their nation's improving living standards throughout the half century following the consolidation of Meiji power.[236] Individual wealth exploded as consumption patterns became more diverse and discretionary. Outlays for food, heat, and light as a percentage of household income declined significantly between the late 1870s and early 1920s, while expenditures for clothing, culture, and entertainment all increased in absolute and relative terms.[237]

Development continued, with the local manufacturing base becoming ever more diversified.[238] The Sumitomo clan successfully moved from Tokugawa merchant riches to industrial capitalist wealth; Baron Fujita Denzaburo built a spectacular empire—and an Asian art collection. By 1912, there were 6,415 registered factories, while 27 banks maintained their headquarters in the city.[239] The total value of Osaka's industrial production exploded—increasing by

400 percent between 1901 and 1907.[240] Another spurt, prompted by the "Great War" in Europe, would leave 21,600 factories of various sizes working away by 1923.[241]

Early-twentieth-century Osaka changed both physically and socially in a pattern that would accelerate into the 1920s and 1930s. The city was transforming itself from a traditional large Japanese town into a twentieth-century *"Megaroporisu."*[242] The teens were further notable for the arrival of the forerunners of Osaka's large—and Japan's leading—Korean community following Japanese occupation of the peninsula in 1910.[243]

Osaka was becoming a quite different city than it had ever been before. Its place as a center of economic integration assured its niche in an emerging national structure uniting economic and political power.[244] The Osaka bourgeoisie sought to beautify their surroundings—frequently by pushing the poor and their slums out of sight.[245] Yet the poor hardly disappeared—they never do, as a consequence of such "beautification" projects. Instead, pockets of poverty and clusters of day laborers' cheap inns (*doya*) came to ring the city to the north, east, and south. Strict building codes made the Osakan streetscape decent and orderly, while appalling conditions merely moved inside. The antagonisms of industrial capitalism were omnipresent.

A major port revitalization project helped Osaka sustain its share of trade in a ceaseless competition with nearby Kobe by constantly modernizing its port facilities.[246] The new harbor became integrated into a rail system that encouraged the further development of Japan's largest industrial complex—the Osaka metropolitan region—throughout the period before the Great Pacific War. For a brief moment in the early 1930s, the Osaka region surpassed Tokyo in the size of its population.[247]

Osaka stood at the forefront of urban social policymaking in Japan. The City of Osaka, as Jeffrey Hanes notes, "put together an impressive array of social facilities in the late 1910s and early 1920s. The most important of these facilities were municipally run retail markets, a central wholesale market, employment offices, pawnshops, lunch counters, public baths, technical schools, maternity hospitals, nurseries, day care centers, hospitals, and municipal housing. The concept behind these programs was proactive social reform."[248]

The city could not escape the fate of a Japan hurtling toward the precipice of war. World War II destroyed Osaka, with recovery taking at least two decades. The city physically rebuilt itself following near-total wartime destruction, a quarter-century effort topped off by the Expo '70 World's Fair in 1970. The war left less visible, yet more profound wounds. Osaka's port had been oriented toward Japan's Asian empire—a hinterland lost in 1945.

The increasingly centralized postwar Japanese state posed a more pernicious challenge for Osaka. Political and economic power has come to rest ever more squarely in Tokyo, drawing all but a few symbolic corporate headquarters and much-needed financial capital away from Osaka. Some of Osaka's inner-city neighborhoods became among Japan's most dangerous. The city's heavy industries became less competitive during the postwar period, leaving Osaka's leaders with a number of festering socioeconomic dilemmas similar to those faced by such cities as Chicago, Manchester, and Marseilles.

Osaka remains a place apart—a town of directness and impatience with rules that place the city as much at odds with Tokyo's culture today as they did when the city was home to a vibrant yet disreputable *chōnin* culture while Kabuki and Bunraku were being born. Tellingly, an early-twenty-first-century study of Japanese subway habits noted that Osakans bolt to board their trains 3.2 seconds before the last exiting passenger disembarks, as opposed to more polite Tokyo people, who wait almost two seconds longer.[249]

Puppets and Players Take to the Road

Simultaneously with domestic Japanese trends, Kabuki extended its influence abroad. Kabuki troupes did not travel outside the Japanese Empire with any frequency until the first half of the twentieth century. Even then, Kabuki's international outreach remained largely within the Greater East Asia Co-Prosperity Zone enforced by Japanese occupation armies.[250]

Although few foreigners outside the Japanese Empire had opportunities to experience authentic Kabuki performances, popular and more professional accounts steadily made their way well beyond Japan. Kabuki woodblock posters and other Japanese artistic representations of the Kabuki form became widely known, as did scripts and tales. The emergence of cinema eventually permitted audiences around the world to see films of Kabuki performances. Kabuki, in other words, was known indirectly to anyone who wanted to know about it. There was, however, one single and very noteworthy exception to this new reality.[251]

In 1928, a professional Kabuki troupe under the direction of the leading Japanese stage director of the era, Kaoru Osanai, visited Moscow at the height of its era of theatrical invention.[252] The performers electrified a theater community that was trying to define a new social order onstage. Kabuki sets and costumes appealed to directors, actors, and designers struggling with new angular abstract forms that radiated bright colors. The distinctive Kabuki use of sound proved particularly appealing at a time when leading Soviet cinematographers were trying to invent their craft.

Osanai visited Rome on his way home, being sufficiently impressed by Italian prime minister Benito Mussolini that he wrote a biographical play about the Italian dictator upon his return to Tokyo.[253] Kabuki, however, did not touch quite the same artistic nerve in Rome as it had in Moscow.

Kabuki's Soviet escapade extended its artistic influence in startling ways. Arriving in Moscow, Grand Kabuki encountered a society and artistic community going through just the sort of rapid social and ideological changes that had provoked such an immediate response to Okuni's dance three centuries before. Bolshevik Moscow was a cauldron of contradictions, where intellectuals and artists struggled to define their brave new world. Those various aspects of its pedigree that had once made roguish Kabuki of questionable taste and standing to Japanese aristocratic elites now captivated audiences in delirious, early-Soviet Moscow.

The great stage director Vsevolod Meyerhold drew heavily on Kabuki techniques in developing his revolutionary approach to staging drama. In particular, he was taken by the biomechanics of Kabuki movement as well as the manner in which Kabuki audiences became integrated into performances. Meyerhold similarly integrated graphic qualities from Bunraku as well as *mie* dramatic poses from Kabuki into his work.[254]

For the film master Sergei Eisenstein, seeing Kabuki live was a "moment of epiphany."[255] "The Japanese," he wrote, "have shown us another extremely interesting form of ensemble, the monistic ensemble. Sound-movement-space-voice here do not accompany (nor even parallel) each other, but function as elements of equal significance. . . . Directing himself to the various organs of sensation, [the actor] builds his summation to a grand total provocation of the human brain, without taking any notice which of these several paths he is following."[256]

The Moscow performances of Kabuki also dramatically affected other Soviet stage and film directors and performers. Meyerhold's and Eisenstein's fascination proved to be particularly noteworthy, for both became protean figures in the era's internationalizing artistic avant-garde.[257] These Soviet cultural titans took Kabuki into places where the Japanese theater could never go. Struggling with creating new art forms at a time of tremendous political and economic dislocation and transformation, the Soviets, to some extent, returned Kabuki to its roots. The Soviet avant-garde artists of the era were creating their own "bent" culture that sought to tilt reality off its traditional axes. In this very real sense, they rediscovered aspects of Kabuki that had been lost in Japan itself. Those "strange" and "slanted" elements, in turn, led back to Kabuki's founding as the explosive outburst of fresh theatrical forms confronting a new Tokugawa social order.

Kabuki's creative reach eventually extended worldwide in the increasingly globalized era of the late twentieth century. By the 1950s, books began to appear in English and other languages describing Kabuki. New visual media brought Kabuki performances to movie, television, video, and eventually cyber screens around the globe, while the invention of the Boeing 747 made international tours increasingly affordable for Kabuki companies and their fans.[258] Kabuki courses were offered at schools for the performing arts and university arts departments around the world and, by the end of the 1960s, foreigners were performing Kabuki.[259] Kabuki dramatically expanded its horizons by launching a series of highly successful international tours, beginning with a 1960 expedition to the United States.[260]

Kabuki, with time, has become widely recognized as one of the world's leading forms of theater; and it has remained so for the past half century. Simultaneously, Kabuki ossified as it became recognized as a "national cultural treasure." As Brandon observes, "Kabuki-za audiences today cannot imagine seeing plays about modern Japan on that stage, whereas such plays are commonplace before 1945. Today's Kabuki audiences are exposed to a construct-ed repertory of constantly repeated classics. . . . It is said only partly in jest that if you attend the Kabuki-za regularly for three years, you will see the entire Kabuki repertory."[261]

Significantly, there have been important exceptions to such stultification. For example, actors associated with the Zenshin-za joined forces with the Japan Communist Party in 1949 to create tour-ing companies that would produce traditional Kabuki and modern plays into the 1960s and beyond.[262] As recently as 2013, the *Japan Times* noted that young actors "are stepping up to the challenge. A recent production of the play *Ghost of Chibusa Enoki* . . . [was] per-formed in front of a packed audience at the Akasaka ACT Theater in central Tokyo. Facing a younger crowd at the theater with no *hanamichi*, . . . [the thirty-one-year-old actor] Kankuro dazzled the viewers with a series of moves that saw him nimbly flip between three characters."[263]

Bunraku similarly went abroad to reclaim its original urban vibe—though at different times than Kabuki, and in its own inimi-table ways. Although Tokyo-based performers, producers, and di-rectors increasingly dominated twentieth-century Kabuki, Bunraku has remained quintessentially Osakan in character. Its connections with the world at large are less publicized, often failing to produce the same rhapsodic response abroad as that prompted by Kabuki masters (figure 11).

By century's end, an experimental "little theater" (*shōgekijō*) movement explored inventive brands of contemporary Kabuki, which led to various "new," "neo," "super," and "rock" Kabuki movements (all with Anglicized names), melding Edo with Las Vegas.[264] In the case of "Super Kabuki," innovations extend well beyond the introduction of new stage technologies. Older scripts are rewritten into contemporary language, as today's Japanese au-diences generally have as much difficulty understanding the clas-sical speech of the original Kabuki playwrights as English audi-ences have with Shakespeare's plays performed in his original Eliz-

Figure 11. A performance by a Bunraku puppet troupe.
Source: A drawing by Lily Eversdijk-Smulders; Europeana Collections
(http://www.europeana.eu/portal/record/2021657/232674.html).

abethan verse. Some playwrights are penning new plays as well around contemporary plots and themes.[265]

Such inventiveness recovers something of Kabuki's original "bent" form after a prolonged period as a stultified official art form. Slowly and in small ways, new approaches to the classical art form are being pursued, though Kabuki remains under the long-standing domination of a single major corporation—the Shōchiku media conglomerate, founded by the Meiji entertainment magnates Shirai Matsijrō and Ōtani Takejirō more than a century ago. Impressively, Kabuki is attracting younger performers, who are dedicating their careers to continuing the art form well into the twenty-first century.[266] In doing so, new writers, performers, producers, and audiences are reinvigorating Kabuki as a living art.

Okuni's Delirious Dance Continues

The theatrical cousins Kabuki and Bunraku are products of a distinctive urban culture at the height of a delirium created by social and economic transformations so rapid that they turned life on its head. Kabuki and Bunraku became more than forums for popular entertainment, though they succeeded in providing a multitude of theatergoers with great delight. They became venues in which an emerging class of townspeople defined who they were. They have lasted for centuries ever since, precisely because they gave meaning to a new and chaotic urban reality.

Both Kabuki and Bunraku exerted powerful influences over the shape and character of twentieth-century stagecraft worldwide. They did not do so by basking in the reverence of aficionados of rarified high culture, either in Japan or abroad. Rather, they have exerted their most profound influence at precisely those moments when they have encountered both deep social upheavals and also economic and political transitions similar to those that produced them in the first place.

Okuni danced in a world where traditional Nō performances had become untethered from a new Tokugawa society dominated by wild samurai and shady *chōnin* merchants and artisans. Meyerhold embraced Kabuki aesthetics, just as Soviet society was about to embark on one of the most brutal periods of social transformation in history. Breuer and Telson saw in Bunraku puppetry an expression of the mayhem swirling around them on the streets of 1980s Brooklyn. As in early Tokugawa Osaka, these were moments when the performing arts responded to the delirium of urban life in transition to produce art forms of lasting beauty and meaning.

Stage Notes for Act One

Opera and Kabuki have become deeply encrusted in the sheath of cultural pretension. Both genres face the double burden of having become clichés of classical ambition while confronting the economic reality of being among the most expensive performing arts to stage. Junichi Sakomoto—the president of the Shochiku Company, which purchased its first theater in Kyoto in 1895, and became the primary producers of Kabuki in the 1920s, after it had purchased many theaters in all the major cities—revealed the genre's contemporary pretensions at a 2013 press conference celebrating the reconsecration of Tokyo's contemporary Kabuki "shrine," the Kabuki-za. "Sakomoto revealed," according to the *Japan Times* correspondent, Tomoko Otake, "that his ambition for the new Kabuki-za is to boost the number of annual visitors from the 900,000 before its 2010 closure to 1.1 million. He wants it to outperform the world's 'Big Three' (La Scala in Italy, the State Opera House in Vienna, and the Metropolitan Opera in New York), each of which draws 500,000 to 900,000 visitors per year." In our time, opera and Kabuki have become, for some, symbols of ossified affectation; and, for others, popular spectacles whose success is measured by attendance records.[1]

However, during their formative decades in the seventeenth and eighteenth centuries, opera and Kabuki were intensely innovative and popular theatrical forms that expressed the ambitions, desires, and disappointments of their societies. Naples and Osaka were isolated from one another; as were opera and Kabuki. They existed in parallel universes, because Japanese culture remained cut off under the embrace of enforced autarky. Opera did not influence Kabuki; nor did Kabuki shape opera. The practitioners of each genre probably did not even know that the other one existed. Yet they had very real similarities in their form, content, and development. Why? Part of the answer lies in their profound connection to urbanity.

Naples and Osaka were among the largest and wealthiest cities in the world when opera and Kabuki were coming into being. Their dynamism reflected the energy of new political regimes and the broadening of commerce. The prospect of wealth drew tens of thousands of migrants from the surrounding countryside into town. Although far too many of these arriving travelers were simply refugees from villages where they could not support their families, many—perhaps even most—were opportunists intent on grabbing their cities' exploding wealth. They saw the hoisting of Tokugawa Iemitsu's gold banner proclaiming the desirability of becoming rich—and its more metaphorical equivalents in Naples—as signals to pursue lucre as quickly and as intensively as possible. And once they achieved material prosperity, they had plenty of disposable income to spend for their own entertainment. Opera and Kabuki thus catered to the desires of ambitious, rising nouveaux bourgeoisie to learn about their social betters through theater as they dreamed of ascending ever higher in the social hierarchy.

However, because both Naples and Osaka remained embedded in hierarchical societies where the ultimate heights of acceptability could be obtained only by birth, these merchant social climbers could dream for only so long. When the reality of their contradictory status as wealthy parvenus could no longer be denied, these audiences looked for action onstage that reflected the world around them. Thus, the broad comedies of opera buffa were sung in the language of the street by characters similarly lifted out of everyday life. Kabuki was even closer to the ground, having originated in the Tokugawa sex trade. Seventeenth- and eighteenth-century Neapolitan comic opera and Osakan puppet and Kabuki theater were, in some ways, the Las Vegas floorshows of their day—though they also often went beyond spectacle into the realm of literature.

Yet neither opera nor Kabuki was only about commerce and the crude new rich. Both Naples and Osaka were living through regime change just as these performing arts took shape. Opera was explicitly about the legitimation of the new Neapolitan Bourbon monarchy; Kabuki added legitimacy to the Tokugawa shogunate by subtraction, as those with hegemony over society tried to stamp it out. In both instances, new art forms favored by a variety of social groups interacted with political authority in intricate and at times contradictory ways. Economic realities insinuated mercantile self-interest into the cultural mix. If the San Carlo Opera House was built by and for a king, it survived on the private subscriptions of his merchant subjects.

Opera and Kabuki, then, were products of the deep, unresolved tensions and paradoxes of two societies that were undergoing dramatic, systemic change. They provided opportunities for society to initiate a dialogue with itself about what the future would be. Whether filtered through the metaphorical antics of a commedia dell'arte jester or a silk-embroidered puppet, profound social, economic, and political change animated what transpired onstage.

From the very beginning, both opera and Kabuki were intensely urban in their character. Neither could have gained life anyplace other than in the era's great cities, such as Venice, Naples, Kyoto, Osaka, and Edo. Opera, of course, initially began at court, often in small towns. Venice and Naples—and later London, Paris, and Vienna—were where it secured a lasting place in European culture. Kabuki, from its earliest performances on the dusty Kamo River bed in Kyoto, was always about the town, even if its plots transpired in an imagined countryside or on an aristocratic estate. Both were fundamentally urban—and not just because they were performed in cities, though both required the sort of concentrated disposable income that only a city could provide. Both responded to the kaleidoscopic urban delirium that characterized Naples and Osaka. The writers penning poetry, the social thinkers writing treatises, the librettists and composers creating their operas, and the playwrights producing scripts for puppets drew inspiration from the city life that surrounded them as they moved around their neighborhoods. Urban delirium was their muse. Opera and Kabuki took shape and flourished in the commercial, get-rich-quick ethos and verve of Naples and Osaka. Without this nourishing context of their distinctive hometown cultures, both genres would have developed in very different ways—as becomes evident from the high formalism of the opera that emerged in Paris and the warrior-oriented Kabuki that took shape in Edo.

Opera and Kabuki therefore reflect the creative sparks of these two particular cities, Naples and Osaka, and their societies when they were caught in a time of political and economic regime change. Act Two moves the action across time and space to what were then the two largest cities of the Western Hemisphere, New York and Buenos Aires—both marked by a disorientation resulting from the all-too-quick spinning of the urban kaleidoscope by immigrants with great cultural differences.

A century ago, New York and Buenos Aires were overflowing with ambition fueled by the tens of thousands of immigrants who were arriving from all across Europe. Of the 40 million or so immigrants who crossed the Atlantic between 1870 and 1914, somewhere near a quarter landed at the docks along the Hudson River in Manhattan, while almost 10 percent more came ashore on the Rio de La Plata in Buenos Aires. The world had never seen anything quite like it before; nor has it since.

These newfangled New Yorkers and *porteños* (from the Spanish for "port people," as the residents of Buenos Aires are known) in many cases were abandoning the very same European towns and villages. And along with their suitcases, they brought with them distinctive values, cultures, hopes, and fears. Their energy and presence challenged assumptions that had taken root in European-colonized America, and their cultural creativeness elevated American culture. Indeed, it is possible to argue that because of this immigrant presence, the Americas came to dominate twentieth-century global culture every bit as much as Europe had the nineteenth century.

In coming to the New World, these immigrants were arriving in societies predicated on integration. For about two centuries, culture throughout the Americas had been forming based on locally distinctive blends of native, African, and European elements. Now the same would be true in Buenos Aires and New York. Buenos Aires, a city that had once been more than a quarter African, retained its Africanness through distinctive music and dance that outlived the physical presence of the very African slaves who gave tango its name and distinctive rhythms. And in New York, the descendants of the first- and second-generation immigrant performers and pro-moters who largely created New York's Broadway musical theater have long since assimilated into the broader American culture.

Commerce and greed completely dominated the Americas' two great commercial urban leviathans as they were inventing the modern city. Thus, in the cultural creativity of Buenos Aires and New York, there was hardly any of the political transformation that had been so visible in Naples and Osaka. Politics moved so far back-stage as to be invisible to the audience enjoying the action onstage. Readers interested in the world of politics, however, should be patient. Politics will dominate culture with a vengeance when we move to Act Three.

Act Two: Modernity's Shores

Milonga: The Buenos Aires Conversation of Diversity

There is no one step to *milonga*. Watch it danced, and the style will suggest itself, intimating its identity in rich variations but never reducing to one formula. *Milonga* emerges in cultural encounters that fuse. It is lived cultural theory, optimistic and amiable. To follow its motions, steps, and offbeats is to learn to connect roots with new voices. . . . *Milonga* in this sense refers to reconciling cultures until the pieces all fit. Ritual common denominators emerge and take hold: build a drum, move a body, sing a song, honor ancestors. *Milonga* in this sense sees cultural difference not as predicament but as amiable argument, an argument solved by generosity, shared values, and celebratory spirit.

— Robert Farris Thompson,
Tango: The Art History of Love, 2005

On a lazy late summer Thursday evening in Buenos Aires a few years into the twentieth century, an imaginary immigrant from Italy—let's call him Alberto—might well have made his way wearily up a steeply inclined, cobblestone street from the small shoe repair shop where he worked as an assistant, and walked past the old medical school that had just been turned over to neighborhood children to his right and the Church of Our Lady of Bethlehem (Iglesia Nuestra Señora de Belén) to his left.[1] This was the oldest church in the city, built by the Jesuits in the 1730s, and it had become the Parish of San Pedro Telmo once the Spanish had banished the Jesuit Order from the empire in 1768.[2] Alberto would have continued on, making his way to the newly renovated and reconfigured Plaza

Dorrego, which was the central focus of his neighbors' lives. Reaching Defensa, a main north–south street, he would have turned left for half a block before going through the gate of one of the city's infamous *conventillos* (tenements) on his right.[3] He had been working hard since he left at 4:30 that morning and was happy to be home.[4]

Alberto's life in Buenos Aires was similar in important ways to that of his former neighbors back in Italy who had instead chosen to travel to New York. Robert Anthony Orsi, writing about the life of East Harlem's Italian community about this time, observed that "the men who lived in rooming houses set up small households. They lived with their *paesani*, pooled expenses for food and rent, and shared household responsibilities. They cooked for themselves to save money, washed their own clothes, even made their own wine. Other immigrants lived as boarders with relatives and friends, a practice which Italians valued for the extra money it brought the families and Americans excoriated because of the imagined moral abuses that such close living was said to encourage."[5]

Although New York's brick slum apartments differed physically from the seemingly open, courtyarded Buenos Aires *conventillos*, their residents' daily existence often did not. Alberto, like his former compatriots in New York, fell in with a community of other Italian immigrant neighbors who pooled their resources to make ends meet.

For his part, the imaginary Alberto was fortunate because his particular *conventillo* had once been the reserve of one of the city's wealthiest families before a yellow fever outbreak a generation before had encouraged anyone who was able to move to higher and healthier ground on the city's increasingly upscale North Side.[6] The formerly luxurious building—now broken up into small rooms for several individual immigrants like Alberto, with slightly larger rooms reserved for families—retained a faded elegance that was missing from the tenements in New York that had been purpose built for immigrants (figure 12).[7]

Alberto was lucky to share this small *conventillo* community with fellow immigrants from Genoa who had made their way among thousands of other Italians to this Belle Époque, blue-collar boom town.[8] Frenchified, Genoese-accented Italian filled the air, comforting him as he closed the courtyard gate. His native language

Figure 12. An eviction from a Buenos Aires *conventillo* in the early twentieth century.
Source: *La fotografía en la Historia Argentina, Archivo General de la Nación.*

blurred together with the neighborhood's pungent, Italian-laced Spanish-language criminal slang of the *compadrito* (street thugs), known as Lunfardo, to squeeze out the proper Castilian preferred by his customers at the shop down the hill.[9] If all went well, Alberto hoped to have his own shoe repair shop in a year or so, and then he would bring his wife and daughter across the Atlantic to join him. He very much wanted to move into a larger room closer to the ground—and to the front of the building—rather than staying on his tiny perch way up on the third floor in the back.

Turning around after shutting the gate, Alberto confronted a scene full of life—one quite different from the silence he had left behind when he set out for work before dawn. Children scampered about the first courtyard, while he could see the smoke of the outdoor kitchen rising from the third courtyard. Women cooked, boiled the laundry, and watched over the *conventillo*'s comings and goings from the balconies flying over the scene, in between the first and second and the second and third courtyards. Songs hit his ears at the same moment as the smells of dinner reached his nostrils. This sad, laconic music was both somewhat familiar and completely alien to anything he had heard back in Italy. To Alberto, these sounds represented his new hometown, Buenos Aires. In a few years, he would find himself agreeing with the great tango lyricist Enrique Santos Discepolo that this music, called "tango," is "a sad thought danced."[10]

As Alberto moved into the second courtyard, he saw his friends Giuseppe, Guido, and Antonio seated under a tree with their instruments—a guitar, a violin, and a strange German instrument, a *bandoneón*, that looked like an accordion but sounded like an organ. Alberto was especially indebted to Giuseppe, who had traveled on the same boat from Genoa and Barcelona and knew someone who knew someone who knew someone who knew about this particular *conventillo*.[11] Alberto walked over to relax a couple of moments before climbing to his tiny room up on the third floor. Alfonzo and Carlo grabbed each other, as if about to launch into a waltz, turning their faces toward their outer arms, which stretched out, pointing into some indefinite future. The fact that they had to practice this dance with one another rather than with a female partner was natural, given the large preponderance of males in the city, especially in immigrant communities.[12]

The Germans had invented the *bandoneón* just a few decades earlier for small churches that could not afford organs.[13] It was a kind of upgraded concertina, and during the 1860s it had found new life once arriving in Argentina, where it was exiled to the most bizarrely secular venues imaginable.[14] As Guido pumped away in a rhythm that even Alberto recognized as African, Alfonzo and Carlo started practicing their complicated steps for Saturday night's dance at the brothel in the nearby sailors' quarter of La Boca.[15] Their feet moved in accord with patterns that had traveled to Buenos Aires from Andalusia via the Argentine steppes known as the Pampas, and from Congo via slave ships. They strove to hold their upper bodies rigid, as if they were dancing at some ball back in Vienna. Guido sang of faraway, unrequited love in the district's distinctive Lunfardo slang. Without knowing it, Alberto was watching Giuseppe, Guido, Antonio, Alfonzo, and Carlo add their own personal, improvisational lagniappes to what would become one of the signature dances of the century that had just dawned. Joined by hundreds of others sitting in *conventillo* courtyards, cafés, and houses of ill repute all over the great city's South Side, they were giving form and fresh style to a dance that had probably originated just a handful of decades earlier among Angolan and Congo slaves in the nearby Montserrat district.[16]

Dances of Diversity

By the last decades of the nineteenth century, increasingly wealthy Argentine oligarchs sought to turn their back on more than a half century of postindependence foreign invasions, wars, separatist provinces (including much of what is today's Bolivia, Paraguay, and Uruguay), and civil wars among local warlords by inviting immigrants to inundate local natives, gauchos, *mesozajes*, *pardos*, *morenos*, and Afro-Argentines under a sea of European-ness.[17] Tens of thousands of migrants from Southern Europe—such as Alberto and his friends Giuseppe, Guido, and Antonio—took up the invitation. They streamed into the great port city's downscale neighborhoods—both older quarters abandoned by the rich and newer areas built just for them—bringing along their languages, religions, folk traditions, and music.[18] There, they met with displaced rural farmhands and cowhands—the gauchos—and the descendents of a once-vibrant Afro-Argentine community to create a distinctive new urban culture. The explosive fusion of these groups changed eating habits, courting patterns, religious practices, and the language of everyday life, while producing three vibrant new dances: the *milonga*, the *candombe*, and the tango.

The tango historian Robert Ferris Thompson recounts how the eminent Argentine author Jorge Luis Borges liked to refer to one of those dances—the *milonga*—as "one of the great conversations of Buenos Aires."[19] The *milonga*, Thompson explains, is "African solo dancing [that has been] absorbed in the two person embrace. . . . Dancers become translators, reconciling styles from two different worlds. This situation is fluid and changing. European ballroom impacting on Kongo; Kongo distilling expressions from Russian Jewish dance."[20]

Thompson writes about how, for half a century between the early 1920s and the early 1970s, some of the city's best dancers hung out at the famous Shimmy Club. This club was renowned for the way in which different groups of dancers enjoyed different styles on different floors. The "black saints" danced the *candombe* in the basement after midnight, as patrons of all races performed the tango on the first floor.

The Shimmy Club, which had been named in honor of Harlem's jazz culture a third of a world away, attracted aficionados of gaucho, country-styled, heel-stomping, Andalusian *toconeo*, and the improvised *sentadas* of the city, blending them with the Congo-based legacies of the *bumbakana* and the vibrant *habanera* drum rhythms from Cuba's centuries-old slave quarters. Aggressive dance battles, often accompanied by verbal sparing contests, brought the country poetic jousting of the rural *payada*, crashing together with the ancient, rap-like, ritualized verse call-and-response battles of Congo and Angola. Street dance melted into an improvisational, ballroom terpsichorean delight. "Dancers," in the words of Thompson, "translate[d] strong winds from Africa and Europe into maneuvers that lead to a Creole safe harbor."[21]

The *milonga, candombe,* and tango forcefully embody the complex cosmopolitanism of a supposedly "European" city established as a smugglers' and slavers' outpost at the back door of what had once been the world's largest empire.[22] These three distinct—though related—dances draw in various combinations on the mix of music and dance cultures that formed around the Río de la Plata estuary by the mid–nineteenth century.

The *milonga*—which, in contemporary parlance, can also signify a place where the tango is danced—emerged in Argentina, Uruguay, and Southern Brazil by the 1870s. Having originally been an improvisational mélange of several popular European dance traditions, the *milonga* predated the tango (though it shares many of the better-known tango's steps and movements, in a simplified form danced at a faster rhythm).

The *candombe* arrived in the Río de la Plata delta with African slaves. Having been associated with the complex percussive patterns of drumming troupes, the *candombe* can be a form of dance, a public event at which that dance is performed, or the social organizations that emerged in the early nineteenth century to organize and promote African dance traditions. Some *candombe* dancing and percussion patterns also appear in the religious ceremonies of the Afro-Brazilian Candomblé religion.

The tango, the third component of the delta's distinctive dance trilogy, took shape at the end of the nineteenth century. Drawing in part on elements of both the *milonga* and the *candombe*, the tango was the product of the poor migrant and immigrant settlements on the South Side of the exploding metropolis of Buenos Aires. This dance was originally focused on the historically Afro-Argentine Montserrat neighborhood, but over time the focal point of tango life drifted to the predominantly immigrant neighborhoods of nearby San Telmo, the port district La Boca, and the market quarter Abasto.

Because its formation was heavily influenced by immigrants from Southern Europe who arrived after the *milonga* and the *candombe* had been danced for years, the tango is both a dance and a *tango-cancion*, a song. Although its origins are subject to spirited debate, the tango is a union of various predecessors and influences. As such, it is a perfect symbol for the city that was itself a cosmopolitan immigrant center at the edge of the Atlantic world.

Taken together, as happened quite often in spirited and sometimes shabby *porteño* dance halls such as the Shimmy Club, the Río de la Plata dance trinity reveals what happens when cultures collide and meld into a new element under the pressure of a densely packed urban center receiving thousands of immigrants. And few cities in history have had more immigrants who recently arrived than Buenos Aires at the dawn of the twentieth century.

"The history of tango," as the political theorist and anthropologist Marta Savigliano has observed, "is a history of exiles."[23] More to the point, the history of the tango is the history of those exiles becoming true *porteños*—the history of outsiders becoming insiders. The tango culture is inclusive, mutating to absorb new influences. Once submerged into the tango culture, the outsider and the newcomer become one with the great city itself. The precise origins of the tango were lost long ago.[24] Like American jazz and the Brazilian samba, the tango is what happens when European, African, and American rhythms, music, instruments, and bodies collide.[25] Yet unlike jazz, the tango has no definitive legend of its origins. By the late 1890s, it just *was*.

The task of identifying the origins of the tango is so difficult because this art form emerged from the improvisational mixing of numerous musical, lyrical, and dance traditions and styles. Rather than being about tradition, the tango is about place—the incredibly rich cultural mixing bowl of Buenos Aires's déclassé southern barrios, and the more rural *arrabal* settlements on the city's outskirts. This is an art form that literally came from a little of this and a little of that. Consequently, its origins have been hotly debated by those with deep ideological investments in one or another particular telling of the story. The tango is African; no, it is Mediterranean; not so fast. . . . It is the legacy of genuinely Argentine gauchos coming to town; or perhaps the tango came off the ships from Havana and Rio de Janeiro, together with those ports' distinctive *habanera* and *maxixe* beats. Each claimant to the tango's authentic origins has a certain degree of merit. But to focus on any single story line is to lose sight of the larger truth: The tango became the tango because Buenos Aires was—and remains—one of the globe's great cultural mixing bowls.

The tango historian Simon Collier underscores the essential role that Buenos Aires played in the emergence of the art form a century and a half ago. "As New World cities go," Collins writes, "Buenos Aires has a certain antiquity—founded by a Spanish expedition in 1536, abandoned five years later, and founded again this time for good in 1580. For its first three centuries, however, nobody thought much of it as a place."[26] In other words, Buenos Aires is a city without a firm grounding in history, social standing, political power, or economic dynamism; it is a ballast-less city prone to urban delirium, as its residents search for identity and meaning in a world given to rapid turns of the kaleidoscopes of historical and geographical refraction.[27]

From Back Door to Front Door

As Collier's remarks suggest, Buenos Aires did not get off to the most propitious start. The wide, slow, and muddy delta of the Río de la Plata initially held scant fascination for either the Spanish or the Portuguese, because it was too far from the continent's vast mineral resources in what are today Bolivia and Peru. The nomadic Querandi Indians drove off the first colonists in 1541, five years after Pedro de Mendoza and a handful of settlers putting down roots, more or less on the site of what would become the La Boca neighborhood of Buenos Aires.[28] Other than leaving behind horses and cattle that thrived on the nearby grasslands, the Pampas, the first settlement gave the place a European name, Ciudad de Nuestra Señora Santa María del Buen Ayre (City of Our Lady Saint Mary of the Fair Winds).

In 1580, Juan de Garay, leading an expeditionary force down the Paraná River from Asunción (in today's Paraguay), reestablished the town just north of today's Casa Rosada.[29] Following the then newly proclaimed Law of the Indies, Garay set out a grid of 120-square-yard blocks surrounded by 30-foot-wide streets, thereby establishing the city's underlying morphology.[30] Within a few years, the Río de la Plata region was being called "Argentina"—which means "silvery" in Spanish—reflecting the hope that the riches flowing from what was then the world's most productive silver mines at Potosi (in today's Bolivia) would find an easier exit to the sea—and to Spain—via the Río de la Plata than that offered by the trek to Cartagena (in today's Colombia) and other Caribbean ports. But such a rotation of South American trade routes never happened. Buenos Aires and Colonia de Sacramento—a city across the river (in today's Uruguay) that was founded a century later—languished as poorly patrolled contraband ports leading to the imperial heartlands further north. Buenos Aires and Colonia eventually were joined along the winding coastal area by Montevideo (capital of today's Uruguay), which was established by the Spanish in 1726 to protect the region north of the Río de la Plata from Portuguese incursions.[31]

Local settlers with scant means of income turned to cattle, hides, meat, and the slave trade to survive.[32] By the mid–eighteenth century, Buenos Aires had become the largest slave port in South America, and the city's newfound wealth from contraband and slave commerce were enriching its founding merchant families.[33] A Spanish military garrison grew quickly at the end of the century, as Madrid tried to assert control over the port's bustling—and often illicit—trade. In 1776, the Spanish Crown established the Viceroyalty of the Río de la Plata, with its administrative headquarters in Buenos Aires. Soon thereafter, in 1778, Charles III—the same Charles who had previously been king of Naples and Sicily—launched the Bourbon Reforms, liberalizing trade and reorganizing colonial administration.[34] An increasingly entrenched local bureaucracy followed, at times advancing imperial policies and at times impeding their implementation for personal gain.[35]

The city's population grew beyond 30,000 by the century's end, and about a third of the local residents were Afro-Argentine slaves. Nascent artisanal and merchant classes were lorded over by an expanding corps of viceregal bureaucrats, officials, and soldiers.[36] The increasingly hearty settlement managed to throw out and later repel British invaders in 1806 and 1807, a legendary insurrection against foreign occupation that would in time become a major point of local pride.[37]

The British troops took both Buenos Aires and Montevideo as part of the European wars unleashed by Napoleon Bonaparte. These wars would have much more monumental significance for South America in just a few months. By the end of the decade, Napoleon had invaded Portugal, forcing the Portuguese royal family to decamp for Brazil; had overthrown Charles IV from the Spanish throne; had arrested his heir, Ferdinand VI; and in their place had installed his brother, Joseph Bonaparte. Final royalist opposition crumbled, leading to the fall of the last loyalist holdout in Seville by early 1810. Spanish control of the Americas collapsed in the wake of these events.

Recognizing the absence of imperial rule, the Buenos Aires elite convened a *cabildo abierto* (special open assembly) to establish a junta to assume control over the viceroyalty. On May 25, 1810, the junta took power, swearing allegiance to the deposed Ferdinand VI.[38] José de San Martín, a Spanish-educated military officer who had been born in Argentina's Corrientes Province, returned to his native land after having fought with the Bourbons against Napoleon in Spain. Assuming command of the junta's military forces in 1812, San Martín embarked on a series of brilliant victories that carried him north, then west across the Andes to Chile, and north once more along South America's Pacific coast to Guayaquil in Ecuador. There he met with the Venezuelan Simón Bolívar, who had defeated the Spanish forces in the northern part of the continent. San Martín, fed up with the continued political infighting taking place across Spanish America, returned briefly to Argentina before moving to Europe, where he died in 1850.[39] Meanwhile, delegates from across the viceroyalty gathered in Tucumán after Napoleon's final loss at Waterloo, just before San Martín set off across the Andes. They declared the country's formal independence on July 9, 1816, as the Provincias Unidas del Río de la Plata (United Provinces of the River Plate).[40]

These events largely left Buenos Aires untouched, aside from having provided many of the soldiers who fought in San Martín's various campaigns, including a large number of Afro-Argentine slaves who were promised liberation after independence.[41] The city would not be so lucky in the decades ahead.[42] The collapse of Spanish rule unleashed more than a half century of internecine conflict, which pitted — in numerous guises — the emerging oligarchic rancher, urban commercial, and merchant elites oriented toward the port of Buenos Aires against everyone else.[43] Several of the viceroyalty's territories successfully fought for independence, some joining the newly created Bolivia and Peru and others forming newly independent Paraguay and Uruguay.

During this period of conflict, Unitarians (*unitarios*), who were promoting centralization in Buenos Aires, fought with Federalists (*federales*), who were promoting greater power sharing with the interior. Provincial strong men, caudillos, fought with one another, while various constellations of leaders negotiated and renegotiated a parade of constitutions and other similarly grand covenants.[44] Finally, in 1853, a Constitutional Congress adopted a document that—with some interruptions—has shaped Argentine political life ever since. Even with this Constitution, however, the Province of Buenos Aires did not submit to the Argentine Confederation's new founding accord until late 1859. Nor did peace and tranquillity prevail, for Argentine president Bartolomé Mitre joined with Brazil and allies in Uruguay to attack Paraguay in the brutal War of the Triple Alliance. This devastating war of attrition destroyed not only the regime of Francisco Solano López in Asunción but also led to the loss of Paraguayan territory and reduced Paraguay's population from 525,000 before the war to 221,000 in 1871, including only 28,000 men.[45] For Buenos Aires, this conflict meant the loss of hundreds of soldiers, who were drawn to battle from the lowest social ranks, including large numbers of Afro-Argentines.

Turning the City Red

For Buenos Aires, the continuing struggle between the Unitarians and Federalists took a particularly violent turn in late 1828. Following the British-brokered granting of independence to the Republica Oriental del Uruguay (consisting of the former viceroyal provinces east of the Río de la Plata), General Juan Manuel de Rosas—a Federalist caudillo from Buenos Aires Province—emerged as the most powerful figure in Argentina.

Rosas earned his spurs as a military man fighting against the British as well as in various battles among local warlords that spread across the Pampas following independence. He joined forces with other provincial strongmen to march on Buenos Aires after the provincial rejection of an ill-fated Constitution of 1826 and the accompanying resignation of President Bernardino Rivadavia. Officially, Rosas would serve as governor of Buenos Aires Province between December 1829 and December 1832, returning to power between March 1835 and February 1852. In fact, he was the country's dictator throughout this period.[46]

Rosas was a harsh taskmaster. He was viewed by many as arrogant and disdainful, no less so by foreign diplomats and investors than by his domestic competitors. The United States had more than its share of conflicts with him, while the British and French eventually sent gunboats to the Río del la Plata in response to what they saw as his intransigence on many issues. Although he did not seem to be concerned about what other nations thought of him, his opponents reached out to Argentina's international rivals—especially the British—as they undertook the final insurrection that brought down his regime. As a leading English-language historian of Argentina, David Rock, notes, "Contemporary opponents reviled Rosas as a bloody tyrant and a symbol of barbarism, while a later generation canonized him as a nationalist here, but he is more accurately depicted as the embodiment of the Federalist caudillo, a conservative autocrat dedicated to the aggrandizement of his own province and to its ranchers and *saladeristas* [slaughterhouse workers]. For Rosas, all other concerns were secondary, to be ignored, circumvented, or obliterated."[47]

Rosas's rule is important to the story of the tango, for two reasons. First, his regime embraced the less fortunate members of Buenos Aires's and Argentine society—the *gente del pueblo*, particularly Afro-Argentines—as opposed to the proper *gente decent*. Second, the ferocious backlash that he provoked eventually led to the consolidation of a liberal, Europe-oriented Unitarian opposition that would shape Argentina and its capital later in the century.

The protestations by Rosas on behalf of the dispossessed had a hollow ring. The Mexican novelist Carlos Fuentes observes in his reflections on the Spanish legacy in the Americas that "Rosas' wealthy allies were further enriched by outright confiscation of the property of their political enemies. And the landed interests were supremely gratified by Rosas' expansion of territory for grazing through wars against the Indians. It took a nimble politician to pull off this balancing act, and Rosas was up to the task, . . . posing as a friend of the people while actually furthering the interests of the landowning minority."[48]

Afro-Argentines constituted somewhere between a fifth and a quarter of the city's population when Rosas arrived on the scene.[49] Buenos Aires had become the largest slave port on the continent by the close of the colonial period. Precise data concerning the number of slaves entering the port are unknown, because many slavers transported their human chattel as smuggled contraband to avoid paying taxes. Most of the slaves appear to have come from Angola, Congo, and Mozambique, though perhaps as many as a third arrived from West Africa. Considerable movement of slaves took place between Portuguese-controlled Bahia and Spanish-controlled Montevideo and Buenos Aires.[50] Other free Argentines of African descent arrived from the Cape Verde Islands, Cuba, and Brazil.

The city required few slaves, so most were transported into the interior after only a brief stay in massive slave markets, which where held in what is today the area around the Retiro train and bus stations. Given the absence of a plantation economy and the urban nature of Buenos Aires's environment, most slave holders either used their property for domestic work or promoted their ability to earn income outside the household as artisans. They were joined in these professions by mestizos and Indians, creating a diverse layer of artisans (though Afro-Argentines were usually prohibited from moving beyond journeyman and apprentice levels). This pattern of hiring out slaves to others loosened the masters' control. Many black men became street vendors, while women earned extra money washing clothes for a variety of clients. Slaves worked the docks and slaughterhouses. Many slave and free Afro-Argentines headed into the countryside to work on *estancias* (ranches).[51]

Although few Afro-Argentines were able to break through the discriminatory barriers imposed by slavery and racism, they nonetheless benefited from a more lenient system found in the large plantation economies elsewhere in the Americas. Spanish laws and customs permitted slaves to purchase their freedom and to be granted freedom for special services, such as tutoring children or fighting foreign invaders. This possibility partially explains why so many Afro-Argentine troops fought so valiantly in the never-ending string of wars between the British invasions of 1806 and 1807 and the end of the War of the Triple Alliance in 1871.[52] Their legal status improved as blacks gained the ability to form legal households and as increasing restrictions were placed on the slave trade following independence. Postcolonial governments outlawed the slave trade in 1813 (a ban enforced with increasing vigor under British pressure), granted the children of slaves freedom of birth as *libertos,* and abolished slavery altogether in the Constitution of 1853 (which took effect in Buenos Aires city and province only upon their delayed 1859 accession to the confederation).[53]

The gradual process of emancipation produced a highly variegated racial landscape. If, in the United States, a black cowboy was always a black, in Argentina, black gauchos became gauchos. Analogous processes were also under way in town. As Afro-Argentines became ever freer, they "disappeared." George Reed Andrews reports in his landmark history of the Afro-Argentines that the presence of blacks in the city's population declined precipitously in both percentage and absolute terms from roughly 1830 to 1880. According to Andrews, the absolute number of Afro-Argentines in Buenos Aires in 1887 represented 53.7 percent of the city's 1836 black population, while the community's share of the overall population declined from nearly a third to negligible during the same period.[54] The disappearance of blacks from Argentina has largely been explained by four factors: the abolition of the slave trade; high mortality rates, combined with relatively low fertility rates resulting from very high death rates among males during the wars of the era; the gradual mixing of races, exacerbated by the shortage of males as a consequence of wartime loses; and the arrival of hundreds of thousands of immigrants from Europe.[55]

The "disappearance" has been overstated in a society intent on being viewed as the most European country in the Americas. African Argentine mutual aid societies, newspapers, magazines, and informal associations, ranging from Church-sponsored *cofradas* to self-organized ethnic associations known as "nations," existed into the twentieth century, long after Afro-Argentines themselves were said to have "disappeared."[56] Twentieth-century blacks, unlike immigrants, were citizens and remained visible as orderlies in Congress and in service jobs within government offices.[57]

Try as official Argentina might, the record of Afro-Argentine soldierly glory could not be erased easily. Afro-Argentines fought in separate—as well as in a surprising number of integrated—units in all the wars of postindependence Argentina. They served as foot soldiers, and as senior officers under San Martín, Rosas, and any number of other commanders. Black faces are visible in galleries of portraits of the country's early military leaders.[58] There were rumors that Argentina's first president, Bernardino Rivadavia—often caricatured by opponents as "Dr. Chocolate"—had African ancestors.[59] For a people who no longer existed, Afro-Argentines are to be seen with surprising frequency in portrayals of rural folk and in paintings of city streets. They appear in real life in country towns and on the streets of the Buenos Aires neighborhoods where they were concentrated, such as San Telmo and adjoining Montserrat.

Afro-Argentines are prominent in the history of Argentine letters, arts, and music, most especially that of the tango.[60] Stunningly, for a community that allegedly "disappeared" well over a century ago, 5 percent of Argentines living in 2005 claimed having African ancestors, as did another 20 percent who acknowledged that there might be Africans in their families' pasts.[61]

Dancing in the Streets

The rise and fall of Afro-Argentines in both reality and proclamation is inexorably tied to the Rosas regime. Rosas increased patronage for Afro-Argentines, reined in the slave trade, promoted black military men, and offered financial assistance to African mutual aid societies. His wife, Doña Encarnacion Ezcurra de Rosas, and their daughter, Manuelita, took particular interest in Afro-Argentine causes; and Afro-Argentines returned their support in kind. The blacks of Buenos Aires were among Rosas's staunchest supporters, and remained so to the end.[62] The Women of the Congo Nation mutual aid society, for example, composed a lengthy "Hymn to Doña Manuela Rosas" to honor the president's wife on her birthday in 1848.[63]

Interest in and support for Afro-Argentine music proved to be one of the most visible ways in which the Rosas family reached out to blacks. Rosas removed a ban on the raucous public dances organized by African nations—the *candombe*—that had scandalized the *gente decent*.[64] As Andrews notes,

> the biggest black dances of the year were held on the Day of Kings (January 6) [i.e., the Feast of the Epiphany, the day when the Three Wisemen reached Bethlehem], Saint John's Day, Christmas, Easter, and especially Carnival, the week-long holiday in February before the abstinence period of Lent. The Carnival celebrations of Brazil, particularly in Rio de Janeiro, are justly famed for the Afro-Brazilian dances performed there—they are the throbbing heart of the week's festivities. The same was once true of Buenos Aires. . . . Even as late as 1900 [well after Afro-Argentines had "disappeared"] ten to fifteen Afro-Argentine groups participated in the merriment each year.[65]

In an observation with important implications for the emergence of the tango, Andrews continues, "with the passage of time the original purity of the various national dance steps was lost and the process of melding occurred. Africans from the different nations living in close contact with each other gradually developed a sort of composite dance, the *candombe*, which borrowed elements from a number of African dances. . . . Though such other African and Afro-American dances as the *bamboula*, the *chica*, and the *calenda* were also done in Buenos Aires. . . . The *candombe* may be considered the representative Afro-Argentine dance of the first half of the nineteenth century."[66]

The country's oligarchic rancher-merchant elite was not nearly as forgiving of African-infused street dancing as the Rosas clan. Victims of Rosas's brutality and corruption joined together with the friends and relatives of those who had been imprisoned, disappeared, or murdered—including many of the country's leading intellectuals, who had fled to Chile and Uruguay—to organize an increasingly potent opposition to the dictator's rule.[67] The caudillos, who were tired of having Rosas subvert their power, along with the country's wealthy ranchers and the neighboring governments of Uruguay and Brazil, had had enough of Rosas.

In February 1852, a former ally—the governor of Entre Ríos, General Justo José de Urquiza—raised an army that defeated Rosas at Caseros, sending him into exile in England, where he died in 1877.[68] Uriquiza and a cohort of European-oriented intellectuals, including future president Domingo Sarmiento, took power. One of Sarmiento's first actions upon becoming president in 1868 was to ban the *candombe*.[69]

The *candombe* moved underground. Less politically meaningful in neighboring Uruguay, the *candombe* would be kept alive on the streets of Montevideo by growing numbers of *comparsas*—some black, some white, and some white dancing in blackface under black names—to become that country's national dance form. As the proud legacy of the city's Afro-Uruguayan community, the *candombe* dominates one of the world's largest annual Carnival seasons with thunderous drums, scantily clad parade leaders known as *vedettes* (from the French word for sentry), and twirling, top-like dancers.[70]

Making the Country White

David Rock underscores the momentous transition that took place once Rosas left the scene:

> The fall of Rosas was followed by a wave of change. Politically, the country ceased to be a segmented imbroglio of caudillo chieftainships, and it gradually surmounted its

interregional conflicts to form a national state that gained undisputed authority throughout the republic. Economic expansion occurred on an unprecedented scale. The frontiers advanced rapidly as the Indians were driven away and the free gauchos at last suppressed. A massive network of railroads superseded the old system of transportation by ox carts and mules. In the River Plate steam packets eventually replaced sailing ships, and railways and steamships together revolutionized production and commerce. The concurrent social change was of comparable magnitude. The first national census in 1869 revealed a country in which four-fifths of the population was illiterate and housed in mud and straw shacks. Twenty years later, although conditions varied greatly among the regions, in some areas education, housing, and consumption standards bore comparison with the most-advanced parts of the world. By the late 1880s the nation's population was increasing by threefold every thirty years. Argentina was now becoming a society of white immigrants and large cities. Meanwhile, its landowners and merchants gathered hitherto unknown riches from the fertile Pampas.[71]

New generations of European-oriented oligarchs—the "Generation of 1837" and the "Generation of 1880"—produced a procession of carefully selected presidents who set out to make Argentina more European than Europe itself.[72] President Bartolomé Mitre and the gifted writer Domingo Faustino Sarmiento used their terms to open schools, universities, and libraries; enact legal codes; build railroads; and create a national vision that had little sympathy for the "barbarism" of the Rosas past. Their Argentina was to be transformed into a "civilized" and "European" (i.e., white) nation that would be as "modern" as any in the world. And Buenos Aires was to become the ultimate reflection of their modernity.[73]

The regime of this modernizing, European-oriented liberal elite brought about a profound transformation in Argentina. In the countryside, President Nicolás Avellaneda and President Julio Argentino unleashed their brutal "Campaign of the Desert," which destroyed the free-wheeling life of the gauchos and other less-than-

European Argentines with barbed wire, railroads, refrigeration, and the extermination of Native Americans.[74] Simon Collier succinctly captures the impact of these transformations for the Argentine countryside: "The pressures of civilization and the disciplines of economic growth bore down harshly on the independent gaucho way of life, which had effectively vanished by the end of the nineteenth century."[75]

Many gauchos, dispossessed of their livelihood and culture, moved to the rough-and-tumble outer barrios of Buenos Aires, retaining one foot if possible in the countryside and the other in increasingly marginalized urban fringe neighborhoods known as *arrabal*. "Lawless, landless, and lonely," Fuentes writes, "the former gauchos were left stranded on the pavements of Buenos Aires. They met the immigrants from Europe in the bars and brothels of the city, in solitude. This was a city of lonely men, men without women. They recognized themselves in the tango, the music of immigrants in a transitional, lonely city."[76]

This world of colorful and desperate "toughs"—men who had previously been free to roam as the stars guided them—captured the imagination of two of Argentina's most famous writers: the great nineteenth-century national bard José Hernández, whose epic poems about the frontier hero Martín Fierro defined the very meaning of "Argentineness";[77] and twentieth-century master poet and story teller Jorge Luis Borges, who set many of his most compelling tales among just such ruffians.[78] Argentina's leaders and most international visitors, however, ignored the *arrabal* as best they could. For them, the increasingly elegant and modern capital of Buenos Aires was a world unto itself.

The liberal oligarchs who controlled the country wanted their capital city to be among the most modern in the world, and in many ways they fulfilled their desires. James Scobie's classic history, *Buenos Aires: Plaza to Suburb, 1870–1910*, traces the city's transformation from a "big village"—*la gran aldea*—to the "Paris of South America" in great detail.[79] Not only did the city grow in size as its population exploded sevenfold from 180,000 in 1870 to more than 1.2 million in 1910—but it also improved, according to any measure a modernizing elite might chose to consider: Kilometer after kilometer of streets were paved; water and sewers were brought to tens of thousands of residents; electricity lit entire neighborhoods; streetcar lines sprouted, ferrying ever more proper passengers further and further along elegant boulevards into quiet suburbs; an extensive commuter rail system took them even further along; a new system of docks could accommodate both passengers and goods more efficiently; fancy hotels multiplied; one of the great theaters in the world—the Teatro Colón—opened its doors; industry diversified; white-collar professions grew; and local streets bustled with purposeful commerce among people who had moved to Buenos Aires from every corner of the "civilized" world.[80]

Industry—which in many ways dominated the daily lives of those in the *conventillos*, such as the imaginary Genoese immigrant named Alberto—and the *arrabal*—such as the characters found in Borges's fiction—remained out of view in hundreds of small manufacturing shops scattered about the outer reaches of town. For the Argentine elite, Buenos Aires was, in Scobie's words, a model of a "commercial-bureaucratic" city, in which economic activity remained concentrated in commerce and government. It was every bit as modern as the other great modern cities of the era—Paris, London, New York, Chicago, and Berlin—in which the international exchange of ideas fostered a culture rooted in new forms of institutions oriented toward science and technology.[81] Life in the Barrio Norte was as luxurious as that to be found anywhere. "The legend of Argentina's wealth was mesmerizing," the novelist and nonfiction writer Miranda France reminds her readers. "Here was a country of apparently infinite natural resources. The Pampas could claim to offer the most fertile soil anywhere on Earth. . . . [Argentina] was a country of easy money."[82]

By 1910, Buenos Aires was the "Showcase of Latin America," a city that could hold its own with any other city in the Americas, including such North American dynamos as New York.[83] Its geographic sweep was recognizably characteristic of the New World, as new technologies and open prairies allowed expansive growth in every direction. Albert Londres, a British observer of Buenos Aires's seamier side, noted, "Napoleon sometimes drew up his troops in a square; when the order came, they could open fire on four sides. Buenos Ayres is drawn up like the armies of the late General Bonaparte. The city advances, square by square, to give battle to the pampas."[84]

Simultaneously, the city offered the solidity of Europe, as its banks and offices recalled the solid grandeur of Victorian London.[85] The twenty-first-century Russian urban chronicler Petr Vail' underscored this evolution by noting that

> Buenos Aires actively developed at the beginning of the century, and then successfully reproduced its own style. It is *art nouveau, Jugenstil', moderne*—call it what you like, it has the same essence: fluidity, plasticity, swimming lines, the rejection of straight corners, asymmetry, ornamentalism. But mainly it has the idea of synthesis, an effort to unite the esthetic and the utilitarian. This is the architecture one meets elsewhere: in Paris, Moscow, Vienna, Nancy, Barcelona, where Antonio Gaudi worked, in Prague, which holds probably the world's record in the number of art nouveau facades. Buenos Aires is part of this center, united in a single style.[86]

By the beginning of the twenty-first century, this divide between what has become known as the "informal" and "formal" city had come to be widely understood. But a century ago, this arrangement—of poor, often-self-built neighborhoods on the outskirts of a well-organized and bejeweled central city dominated by the well-to-do and their middle-class accolades—shocked some people. The urban patterns established at the time the tango was born—that of the informal southern barrios and the formal northern ones—remain broadly visible today.

The city simultaneously displayed a social openness and a set of connections between the informal and the formal that was more at home in the Americas than Europe. Of nineteen turn-of-the-twentieth-century cities ranked by measures of ethnic and class segregation, Buenos Aires was less differentiated residentially than any city except Toronto (with South African cities already setting the standard for the world's most residentially segregated cities).[87]

More than anything, however, Buenos Aires was shockingly rich, giving rise at the time to the French expression *"riche comme l'Argentine"* ("wealthy as an Argentine") (figure 13). Its new subway—which opened in 1913, almost contemporaneously with those of New York and Paris—sported beautiful tile and ornate woodwork with munificent mirrors.[88] Most impressively, the city's French Renaissance–style central water pumping station, built between 1877 and 1894 by the Swedish Argentine architect Carlos Nystömer, was covered with more than 300,000 glazed terra cotta tiles imported from the Royal Doulton factory in Britain.[89] And at the Water Palace—Palacio de Aguas Corrientes—caryatids, the mansard roof, busts of great engineers, and the grand, palm-landscaped front entrance inspire even today, though often in a churlish manner, as when one of the novelist Tomás Eloy Martínez's characters feels compelled to quote the poet Rubén Daríio's sly remark that the building "imitated the sick imagination of Ludwig II of Bavaria."[90]

For all this munificence, the liberal dream of a "European" and "modern" Argentina proved to be ephemeral. It would be the "barbarians" whom those in power loathed—rather than "civilized" engineers and architects in the employ of the wealthiest of the wealthy—who were busy inventing Argentina's most enduring symbol, the tango. *Porteños* such as the imaginary Giuseppe, Guido, Antonio, Alfonzo, and Carlo in Alberto's San Telmo *conventillo* moved up to an expanding middle class and constructed a lasting Argentina for themselves.

Mixing the Shadows of Africa, Andalusia, Cuba, and the Pampas

The history of the tango is ideologically charged and replete with contradictions, lacunae, and mysteries. The tango emerged from the poor neighborhoods of Buenos Aires as an amalgam of traditions brought to those quarters by the poorest of the poor—a mixture of many of the same global and local forces that rendered Argentine nation building tragically conflict-ridden. The dance's pedigree is anything but honorable, evolving from brothels and bars reeking of alcohol and besotted with violence.

Marta Savigliano has noted that any retelling of the tale of the tango confronts myriad contentious ideological mandates, which themselves can reproduce the divisiveness of the country's troubled history.[91] Although "authenticity" is impossible, the broad outlines of the story emerge from the haze of historical and ideo-

Figure 13. A high-end scene on the Avenue de Mayo in Buenos Aires in 1910.
Source: Library of Congress.

logical complexity, even if the boldness and dominance of any one line over another varies according to where one stands. Far more important, however, the tango is not about the various cultural streams that melded together to create it as much as it is about the place—the outskirts and port neighborhoods of the great city, Buenos Aires—where these streams came together. In other words, the tango is less about African or Andalusian heritage than it is about the delirium produced by intensified urban propinquity.

As Savigliano tells the basic story,

> Since the 1930s musicologists and dance specialists have tried to put some systematic order into the tango's origins. The story goes like this: In Cuba the African slaves developed new music and dances intermingling their traditional rhythmic sounds with a variant of the French *contre* dances already appropriated by the Spaniards; the resulting *habanera* (from Havana) made its way into Europe and simultaneously into other New World colonies where it intermingled with local styles. The *tango andaluz* (Andalusian tango), Brazilian *maxixe* and the *tango rioplatense* (from the Río de la Plata region in Argentina and Uruguay) were offsprings of this process; the last in particular was nurtured by the *milonga*, a local product itself of a certain Spanish troubadour style. When the *milonga* carried by the gauchos moved to the developing urban harbors (Buenos Aires and Montevideo), it collided with the *tangos de negros* (tangos of the African slaves) and the *tango andaluz* that was performed by the Spanish theater companies touring South America.[92]

The tango thus is a distinctive composite of native Argentine musical forms and dance traditions, African musical forms and dance traditions—both directly, as brought by Afro-Argentine slaves, and indirectly, as mediated by slaves in the Caribbean and Brazil—and European musical forms and dance traditions, as performed on European instruments. But how African? How Argentine? And how European? These have been points of great contention ever since the folklore scholar Vicente Rossi argued in the 1920s that the tango was created primarily by Afro-Argentines—a proposition that was immediately and vociferously challenged by such Argentine cultural leaders as Julio Mafud and Borges.[93]

To begin with the tango's most indigenous roots, the nomadic gaucho life of herding cattle and working the sheep ranches in the country's interior, produced a cornucopia of folk musical forms and songs—estilos, cifras, triunfos, gatos, tonadas, cielitos, zambas, and perhaps the grandest gaucho music tradition, the payada.[94] Something demonstrably identifiable as tango entered this rich repertoire of popular music by the early 1880s, drawing on the native Argentine milonga together with the Spanish Cuban variant on the Spanish contradanza and the French contredans, la habanera.[95] Gauchos, both black and white, inculcated a number of Moorish customs into life on the Pampas, including "clipping the manes of their horses in sharp saw tooth patterns," dancing escondido with star-shaped, silver-tipped spurs, and employing flamenco-related heel stamping and toe tapping. Many of these forms became inculcated into early versions of the tango—such as canyengue—together with Arabized elements found in flamenco singing.[96]

These various traditions from the interior made their way to the downtrodden Buenos Aires exurbs. As Simon Collier explains, "It is more probable that the tango grew up across several such arrabales, in makeshift dance halls (some with earth floors) and brothels. Its social background was poor, marginal, and semi-criminal."[97]

The gaucho payada tradition based on the poetic sparing of competing singer-guitar players served as glue binding many elements together. The genre—which easily lent itself to long evenings around campfires, afternoon breaks under giant ombú and gomero trees, and cocktail hours in makeshift bars across Argentina and Uruguay—aligned with the call-and-response traditions evident in many African musical traditions transplanted to the Americas from the time the first slaves arrived until today's North America in the form of rap and hip-hop. The connection is direct. Perhaps the greatest payadores (performers in payada competitions) of the era—or of any era—Gabino Ezeiza and Higino Cazon—were Afro-Argentine, as were many other leading practitioners of the art.

Ezeiza, who was born in San Telmo in 1858, began singing at the age of sixteen, just as the payada musical form arrived in the city. He traveled around the interior on both sides of the Río de la

Plata, establishing his reputation as a master of the art following legendary singing "duels." One such verbal marathon, in the small town of San Nicolas in 1894 with Pablo J. Vasquez from Pergamino, lasted two days, as Ezeiza and Vasques matched each other rhyme for rhyme and verse for verse.

Robert Ferris Thompson tries to communicate Ezeiza's brilliance by relating his performances to the musical genres of the late twentieth century. "Living in verses," Thompson writes, "Ezeiza would not be matched in this hemisphere until 1940s calypso and 1990s rap. If Ezeiza spoke English and were magically transported to our time, could rappers defeat this brother in rhyme? Ezeiza took the world's measure in five hundred *payadas*. He trained first as a newspaperman, which helps explain his cultural breadth, from gaucho-like jousting to learned allusions to the Tower of Pisa. He once sang as three people, dramatizing their differences by accent, . . . made arguments within arguments. No one could touch him."[98]

The *payada* tradition, in turn, rested on the foundation of an even older gaucho tradition, the *milonga*. *Milongas*, which are vocalized in Spanish and Portuguese, come closer to the North American cowboy song, often sung by improvising gaucho guitar players in Iberian-style verse of eight syllables encompassed by a descending melody, which began on high notes and ended on low ones. *Milonga* singers engaged in lighthearted singing duels, sang at country dances, and mixed tough guy posturing with a melancholy yearning for the disappearing itinerant life. Once in town, the *milongas* incorporated the *habanera* rhythms arriving on ships from Brazilian and Cuban ports to produce an improvisational precursor of the tango, the *candombe*.[99]

By the time Ezeiza died, after being helped off stage a final time in 1916, a new singing duo specializing in Pampas-tinged provincial folk music—Carlos Gardel and José (Pepe) Francesco Razzano—was sweeping the country.[100] Gardel, an illegitimate immigrant child from France, and Razzano, who grew up in Montevideo, had been making a name for themselves singing in small bars around their local barrios. They began to hear of one another, because they were often performing in the same clubs, and they finally ran into one another in 1911.

Razzano was already cutting records for the Victor Company,

embracing the new technology that would spread his fame and that of his partner worldwide. Within months, Razzanno needed a partner for a tour of small provincial theaters scattered around Buenos Aires Province, and he tracked down Gardel. Thus, one of the great entertainment collaborations of the twentieth century was born, an artistic and business partnership that would last until an ugly financial dispute led to their estrangement two decades later.[101] The duo never totally abandoned their original Pampas-infused repertoire, even after Gardel perfected the *tango-canción* genre with his epic recording of Pascual Contursi and Samuel Castriota's "Mi Noche Triste" (My Sad Night).

Although the early tango was the music of dance rather than song, the verbal traditions of the troubadours from the Argentine interior exerted considerable influence over what eventually emerged as tango verse. Savigliano argues that this poetry is a "spectacle of sex, race, and class," in which "a male–female embrace tried to heal the racial and class displacement provoked by urbanization and war. But the seductive, sensual healing was never complete, and the tensions resurfaced and reproduced."[102] Tango verses often became lamentations on melancholy, violence, and sex, combined into a single tale that echoed life on the great Ríoplatenese steppe as much as in the slums of Buenos Aires. The loss and longing of early tango songs—such as Enrique de Maria's verse, accompanying Eduardo Garcia Lailane's music in *Ensalada Criolla*—adds urban decadence to the mix, without traveling very far from the gaucho verses of the Argentine cowhands.[103]

The machismo cult of virility that infuses the tango is evident in country song. The traditional tango characters—such as *el compadrito* and *la milonguita*—have rural equivalents.[104] De Maria and Lailane's 1898 *Ensalada Criolla* and José Hernandez's epic poem *El gaucho Martin Fierro* of a quarter century before are equally recognizable as "Argentine." As Thompson argues, the rural permeates the city via the tango.[105] If Collier is correct that the tango is about the "endless vicissitudes of love, . . . vengeance killings, . . . and the inevitable passage of time," so too are many of the lyrics sung by gauchos roaming the interior; the tango's "strong feeling that the world does not measure up to human expectations" is hardly unknown in Argentine folk music.[106]

The tango exploded in Argentina so powerfully and suddenly because it represented an extension of long-loved musical, poetic, and dance traditions. The tango became more than an expansion of rural folk traditions to fit a new reality. The anthropologist Julie Taylor correctly argues that the tango reflects the insecurities of a nation in the Americas that conceived of itself as somehow "European."[107] The aspiration to be one of the world's great "white" civilizations did not exist on the Pampas. The tango blended these contradictions and traditions with the potent diversity and energy of the city; but not just any city. The collision of rural and urban—of "barbarian" and "civilized"—occurred in one of the fastest-growing and culturally ambitious cities in the world, in a town where the Argentine interior confronted both an Africa and a Europe that had taken shape after Argentine independence. The tango is what happened from the chemical explosion of all these traditions, under the pressure cooker of a Buenos Aires on the make.

The Beating of Congo Drums, the Stomping of Congo Feet

If the tango had indigenous roots from the life of the Pampas, it also had origins in the urban communities of African slaves and their descendents. Indeed, as early as the late 1920s, following the publication of Vicente Rossi's *Cosas de Negros* (*Things Related to Blacks*), some Argentine cultural historians and social commentators began to argue that the tango was more than a country tune that had moved to town.[108] Rossi highlighted the African contributions to both rural and urban manifestations of "Argentineness." His thesis argued that Africans brought in bondage to Argentina lost their language, religion, and tribal affiliation. Therefore, they embraced their local identity as strongly as possible, with many becoming gauchos and launching a distinctly black tradition in Argentine *payada* musical duels. As elsewhere in the Americas, music and dance became among the few means of ancestral cultural expression remaining open to Afro-Argentines, though even then they had to adapt their traditions to European instruments, such as the guitar. The tango emerged from this forced blend of African traditions and European musical implements, as did distinctive forms of black *payador*.[109]

This thesis parallels and does not necessarily contradict the narrative of the tango mediating between town and country. At the time, many Argentine cultural commentators—including the towering Mafud and Borges—rejected the possible African roots of the tango. It has become something of a new conventional wisdom. This position accepts the presence of strong Afro-Argentine influences in the original musical blend that created the initial, identifiable *tango criollo* in the 1890s. Collier summarizes the debate by concluding that "the contribution of the Buenos Aires black community to the invention of the tango was indirect but nevertheless fundamental, in the sense that without it there would have been no tango at all."[110]

How does Africa enter into the tango story? Thompson, a twenty-first-century proponent of Rossi's thesis, goes further by arguing that

the black impact on the tango entails more than one single line of influence, from the civilizations of Central Africa to the *candombes* of Buenos Aires to the tango. The sources are multiple and sometimes indirect, ranging from the coming of the beat of the Afro-Cuban *habanera* to Argentina after 1850, to the integration of key solo moves, from *candombe* in *milonga* couple dancing in the Buenos Aires of the mid–twentieth century and earlier. In addition, cakewalk and ragtime arrived in Buenos Aires in 1903. . . . As if a triple black dosage—*candombe, habaera,* and jazz—were not enough, North African-related qualities factor in too: Andalusian syncopation and percussive heel-stomping (*taconero*), which trace back to the Moorish era in Spain, also enhance the traditions. . . . That most *tangueros* today are white no more hides the original—and continuing—black presence than Elvis Presley conceals the heritage of Albert Johnson or Benny Goodman masks the contribution of Fletcher "Smack" Henderson and Count Basie.[111]

The very name "tango" may be among the most direct African influence on the art form. The word exists in numerous African languages, with meanings that might connect to the *porteño* dance.

"Tango" is a place name in twenty-first-century Angola and Mali; it means "closed place" or "reserved ground" in several African languages, and "drum," "place of dance, "dance motions," and "funeral celebration" in others.[112] Numerous African words have passed directly into Latin American dance terminology, including *nezengolo*, meaning cut; *mumbo*, which was transformed into *mambo* in Cuba; and variations on terms for "sugar" throughout the continent, such as *meringue* in both Haiti and the Dominican Republic.[113] *Candombe*, a term borrowed from Ki Kongo to refer to the dancing societies founded by persons of African descent in nineteenth-century Buenos Aires, would expand to mean "black culture and self-governance" in the late colonial Belgian Congo.[114]

Alternative etymologies point to European roots, though again often with an African accent. For example, some argue that the word "tango" is derived from the Latin verb *tanhere*, to touch, which had been incorporated into the pidgin Portuguese used in the major slave trading post on the island of São Tomé in the Gulf of Guinea. Others suggest an onomatopoeic source somehow representing the beat of a drum.[115] Whatever its origins, the word "tango" most likely was spoken in the New World before anyone else by African slaves; and in any event, it quickly became associated with a variety of black dances throughout South America.[116]

The frequency with which the word "tango" is connected to black dance reflects the considerable presence of African dance forms in the Spanish and Portuguese colonies throughout the Americas. As noted above, for Argentines the African-derived word *candombe* has several meanings, including both a particular dance step (e.g., "he is doing the *candombe*") and the public dances as a social event ("she is at the *candombe*"). This second use of the word is crucial for appreciating the place of African dance in Argentine culture.[117]

George Reed Andrews emphasized the importance of public dance in local black expression. As Andrews records:

> Their public dances were cultural events in the fullest, broadest sense of the term. They brought the community together on a regular basis, strengthening the ties of friendship and community identity. They provided a source of

recreation and rejuvenation and a means of self and group affirmation to a people denied this all-important right. Furthermore, their political significance was unmistakable, as may be seen in the continuing conflict between the community and the government over whether or not the dances were to be allowed to take place.

It is not clear exactly when the Afro-Argentines started holding their public dances, the *candombes*, though surviving documents show that by the 1760s they had caught the unfavorable attention of the authorities. The viceroy banned the blacks' dances twice in 1766, again in 1770, and again in 1790. But these bannings referred only to gatherings held without official supervision—the viceroy specifically allowed the Africans and Afro-Argentines applying the permission to hold special dances for their own nations. In 1795 permission was granted the Congo blacks to dance on Sundays and holidays, and in 1799 a similar permit was granted to the Cambunda blacks. The viceroys were careful to stipulate one absolute prohibition, however; these affairs could only be held as long as no black man was crowned or recognized as king of one of the African nations. . . . On the whole, however, the royal administration was fairly lenient in the matter of the dances, perhaps recognizing their value as a release for the community's frustrations and dissatisfactions.[118]

Andrews's reference to both Congo and Cambunda peoples intimates that the composition of participants in such public festivities was markedly diverse, with as much variation lurking under Argentine black skin as could be found under Argentine white skin. Though largely from Congo and Angola directly across the South Atlantic, numerous captives from West Africa found their way to the Río de la Plata delta, populating slave barracks in what are today Southern Brazil, Uruguay, and Argentina. Though maddeningly incomplete—more slaves were smuggled through Buenos Aires than were ever officially registered—ship manifests, public auction records, and favored Afro-Argentine names reveal the presence of conscripts from the Yourba, Fon, Nupe (Tapa), Hausa

Bornuy Toruba (Mina Nago), Youbaized Mahi, Dahomeans, Quidah (Fida), Yombe, Sundi, and Mboma peoples shipped from the Bight of Benim Oyo and other empires.

Slaves, in other words, came from anywhere accessible to a 300-mile coastline between Cabinda in Congo to the north to Luanda in Angola to the south. They brought their diverse languages with them—and also brought their distinct traditions of worship, music, and dance—only to be forced to merge under the single criterion of skin tone in the New World. The result is a mélange that had very concise and authoritative meaning for Afro-Argentines, while remaining lost on the clueless Euro-Argentines who viewed anyone with a black skin as one and the same.[119]

These traditions were on display in weekly and monthly as well as annual holiday celebrations, at which increasingly well-organized African dance societies reflecting the diverse ethnic and national origins of the city's blacks competed with one another and, at other times, joined together in communal revelry. Funeral dances similarly became a mainstay of Afro-Argentine religious and community life, as is apparent from diaries and artistic representations of the city during the period.[120] Public African dance celebrations reached something of an apex in the 1830s and 1840s, during the Rosas era. The dictator and his family warmly embraced the Afro-Argentine community in return for its steadfast support.[121]

Various Roman Catholic orders, particularly the Jesuits, appreciated how the spiritual release so visible during the *candombe* celebrations could be molded to glorify the Virgin Mary and her Son, Jesus Christ.[122] The challenge, from their perspective, was to celebrate the visible hierarchy of African communities and dance cultures while substituting Spanish royalty and Roman religious authorities for Congolese kings. Some of the most powerful images of *porteño* African street dancing survive in paintings depicting processions organized by the Roman Catholic Church.

Local officials—especially those merchant and colonial elites desperately trying to cover themselves with the veneer of "civilization"—found the presence of dark-skinned Argentines to be a profound embarrassment—a shame only heightened by the constant public display of what, to them, was lascivious barbarity. As early as the 1760s, city councils banned public African dancing whenever they could, citing the offenses against God of vast displays before innocent girls, boys, and adults. Even more profoundly, the dances were sponsored by black national associations—*cofradias*—which collected money to organize the dances and to provide invaluable informal social and economic support to their members. To the self-righteous and self-important *porteño* merchant elite, mere slaves and servants could garner such capital only by stealing it from their owners and betters. Blacks, they complained, were "in a continual state of agitation" because of the dances and were hardly capable of hard work.[123]

Afro-Argentine support for Rosas proved to be more than sufficient justification to ban public forms of African dance following the dictator's downfall. With Rosas out of power, *candombes* either had to take place in deep secrecy or become sublimated within other music forms that were deemed acceptable (e.g., the popular European *danza*, polka, and mazurka).

Audio records from this period do not exist, so precise knowledge of rhythmic content is impossible to discern. In all probability, Ki Kongo beats pounded out on African-style percussion instruments that had been recreated as faithfully as possible using available local materials. Paintings and diaries recount the powerful drumming that filled the air at such events. Thompson describes the presence of such drums in Catholic religious art: "In Trinidad, across the Paraguayan border from Posadas, Argentina, a sculptor for the local Jesuitic mission carved, around 1760, a frieze of angel musicians. One strums a harp, another bows a violin, but one vivid angel beats time with one foot and shakes a huge bass *maraca* as large as his head. Heaven includes dance percussion."[124]

Later, after the 1860s, the muscular syncopation of the Bakongo *habanera* arrived from Cuba via Montevideo. *Habanera* rhythms emanating from primarily West African slaves (most often Yoruba) in Cuba underlay much of what has become known as "American" music, including music in such diverse locations as North Carolina, Louisiana, any number of Caribbean islands, Bahia, Rio de Janeiro, Montevideo, and Buenos Aires. Without it, there would be no blues, jazz, calypso, salsa, samba, or tango. *Habanera* is the urtext of musical life along the entire western edge of the Atlantic (figure 14).

African-derived rhythms found a ready home in *porteño* bars,

Figure 14. Afro-Cuban *habanera* drummers, playing for a rumba, in 2014.
Source: Photograph by Nicole Melancon (www.thirdeyemom.com); used by permission.

dives, and brothels. Such places were so offensive that they escaped the attention of the righteous and well-heeled. They were the perfect spots to conceal Afro-Argentine spiritual gatherings preserving a *candombe* tradition that, in some instances, had arrived in Buenos Aires directly from the shores of Africa and, in other cases, had been modified and reinvented in Cuba and other American homes.

Many of these beats faded long ago into the languid, humid air of the Río de la Plata delta. Yet the dance steps they encouraged have remained. Thompson offers perhaps the most extensive catalogue of Ki Kongo and other African steps and styles that infiltrated Argentine dance forms, including the tango: line (*milona*) and circle (*lukongolo*) formations; dancing in the distance; dancing without embracing, freeing arms, trunk, and legs, for full action; multimetric dancing; embodied percussion; overlapping call-and-response dancing; "hot" dancing, where fire invades the dance, including a sexy "winding" of the hips; the supreme spiritual expression of *mayembo*, ecstatic trembling of the shoulders; African knee flexion; and the concluding *bumbakana*, when men and women dance forward, approaching each other from their positions in opposed lines, or in opposed segments in a circle, and briefly strike their abdomens together. This is the point at which dancing can turn feisty and combative, as partners seem to withdraw into their own worlds.

Moreover, Thompson reports, there are moments in Ki Kongo dance when a single person might cup his chin within his palm as a sign of sadness, of the blues. Feet can "test the water" by freezing the right foot flat while moving the left foot slowly, as if to probe the currents of a river.[125] Better chronicled, perhaps, are the indirect importation of African dance via the beat of *habanera* from Cuba; the hip movements of the *maxaxie* from Brazil; the Africanized forward-leaning cakewalk from North America, together with the more direct local mimicking of African-style counterclockwise cycling; and the swinging of legs in the air and suddenly around the knee of a partner.[126]

African movements joined with other dance steps in the *milonga*, which is a local up-tempo version of the *habanera*; and in the *canyengue*, which is composed of steps that would become the earliest foundation of the tango: *ochos*, *sentadas*, *corridas*, *cortes*, and *quebradas*, plus drags of the feet called *arrastres*.[127] The *milonga* drew energy from the African-style call-and-response patterns enlivening the singing (*payadas*) and the drum duels (*tapadas*) of the *compadres* who had come to town after the 1860s and 1870s. Perhaps more than any other African import, the call-and-response form has become deeply embedded in local performance arts throughout the Americas, marking a distinctive New World improvisational form that has become the core of twenty-first-century global artistic expression. Displaced internal refugees from the Pampas found it to be a means for expressing their anger and aggression in the face of the collapse of their world on the plains.

African influences are evident throughout the tango, as are those from the country's interior. Together, they define a distinctive character that makes the dance something more than a Creole repetition of cultural imports from the metropolis. They were present when the tango was born; and they have remained an ever-evolving and innovative presence. They are the underlying broth of the tango stew.

Polka, Anyone?

Part South American, part African, the tango is also part European. The rural cattle-and-sheep herders and Afro-Argentines who were busy inventing a new art form in the *arrabales* on the city's fringes encountered thousands of European immigrants who brought their own distinctive contributions to the tango. Like the imaginary Alberto, Giuseppe, Guido, Antonio, Alfonzo, and Carlo, real-life immigrants embraced much in their new hometown's culture, including the tango. Life in their *conventillos* ensured that such an embrace would take place in the protected semipublic spaces of courtyards as well as makeshift plazas, bars, cafés, public markets, and open yards. Their neighborhoods—first San Telmo, then La Boca, and, still later, the vibrant, rambling Jewish and Italian market district of Abasto (the city's version of Covent Garden in London and Les Halles in Paris)—spawned the music, verse, and performers that would dominate the tango for years to come.[128] Their adjustment to Argentine life and culture was relentlessly communal, in part because their families more often than not remained in Europe; and in part because both they and their hosts exhibited the habits of Mediterranean sociability.

The newcomers, as is the case everywhere, provoked merriment among the well established, as can be seen in the popular one-act comedies of the 1890s and 1900s about immigrant foibles, the *sainetes.*[129] At other times, their enormous numbers altered the rules of social contact. Generally, immigrants learned to fit into Argentine life with alacrity, changing local culture in the process. Social adaptation and cultural transformation were as visible in the development of the tango as they were in nearly every aspect of *porteño* life. Immigrants introduced popular European dances to the local scene, created a rich and juicy argot that would form the base for tango verse, introduced themes of longing and displacement into popular and folk singing, and brought new instruments with them to the delta's shores.

The *candombes, canyengue, maxixes, habaneras,* and *milongas* that evolved into the tango drew on a well-developed European dance culture that included wildly popular mazurkas and pol- kas and *schottische, contradanzes,* and waltzes, as well as the Jew- ish line dances from Russia and Ukraine—the *karakhod, skotschne,* and *hopke*—and other European folk traditions. At a basic level, these local inventions took shape as non-European dancers and musicians—Afro-Argentines, countrified Creoles, and gauchos— improvised their own steps when trying the latest dance fad from Europe. This process—which began well before independence— gained fresh impulse with the arrival of the waltz in the 1810s, the polka in the 1850s, and whatever else was all the rage later in the nineteenth century.[130]

The city's dance culture proved to be open and fluid, becoming formalized as promoters brought the crazy local mix of different cultures to dance halls, variety shows, and such semilegitimate the- aters as the Royal, the Cosmopolita, and the Roma.[131] Such inven- tions were what happened when often inebriated and lonely men sought out a raucous good time at a country dance, a slum bar, and a brothel. No formal sorting out of traditions and patterns took place; everything coexisted as the poor and dispossessed endeav- ored to ease their pain in nights of joyous delirium.[132] The tango just happened as weekend debaucheries evolved into nights at a local club and moved onstage, bringing Africanized steps and rhythms along with European dance forms.

Singing in Slang

Song accompanied dance. When dancers and musicians sang, they did so in the language that they used in everyday life. For the deni- zens of the criminal and semicriminal underworld in the poorest neighborhoods in town, this language more often than not was the Italian-based, Spanish criminal argot known as Lunfardo. As a se- cret language poorly understood by the uninitiated, Lunfardo was the jargonized vocabulary of the *compradito*—the street tough—that created an identifiable gangster style—much as so-called ghetto culture would shape the vocabulary and style of late-twentieth- century hip-hop culture. The *compadrito* uniform included a slouch hat, loosely tied neckerchief, high-heeled boots, and a knife tucked into a belt.[133]

The soldiers, immigrants, factory hands, slaughterhouse workers, herdsmen, and vagrants who joined the *compraditos* in their *arrabal* netherworld absorbed these cultural cues and learned the speech that went with their style. This was what it meant to be hip and cool in turn-of-the-twentieth-century Buenos Aires. Lunfardo—and the world of the *arrabales* that produced it—took shape more or less contemporaneously with the creation of the tango. They were part of the same cultural package, whereby criminals, criminal wannabes, and noncriminal roustabouts established their distinctive identities in a world dominated by European-oriented elites. Lunfardo offended local bourgeois sensibilities every bit as much as Afro-Argentine hip shimmies.[134]

The social historian Donald Castro observes that Lunfardo was initially a vocabulary of secret words known only to criminals. It took written form by March 1879, within the context of descriptions of *porteño* criminal life, and criminological journalistic and academic studies. Lunfardo became codified and integrated into Buenos Aires's literary canon over the next four decades. Great Lunfardo poets—such Enrique Santos Discepolo, Pascual Contursi, Celeconio Flores, and Homero Manzi, together with many others—wrote increasingly sophisticated popular verse beginning in the 1890s.[135] By the end of World War I, Lunfardo was accepted as a natural expression of *porteño* identity. This was so much the case that, in 1919, José Gobello established the Academia Porteño del Lunfardo to preserve and promote what had become a distinctive local dialect.[136] Lunfardo poems, in turn, provided the words for lyrics that were being added to tango melodies as the dance moved from bar and brothel to semirespectable dance halls and variety stages.

If the forms of verbal improvisation originated on the pampas and rhythms of the tango originated in Africa, the language of the tango came from the world of immigrants. The tango was thought by many contemporaries to be happy music when it arrived in Buenos Aires in about 1900, as one might expect, given its association with boozy carousing in déclassé neighborhoods, seedy bars, makeshift cafés, and outdoor barbeque pits.[137] Castro tells us that the first tango lyrics were about bordellos and the skills of celebrity prostitutes—they were so bawdy, in fact, that their obscenity gave more offense than the salacious gestures being made on the dance floor.[138]

Within a very short time, the tango had captured the pathos of the immigrant. Quoting Jorge Gottling, Thompson notes that classic tango themes tell of absence, presence, and departure of a woman.[139] Tango lyrics became infused with the bittersweet "mellow elation" that is the "refinement of sadness" tinged with nostalgia called *mufarse*.[140] This Argentine version of the North American "blues" is a feeling shared by country folk who come to town, immigrants who are far from home, and former slaves who have been stripped of their past and dignity.

Tango verse left the improvisation of the range to become formalized onstage, on the radio, in cinema, and in recordings into a series of stylized traditions—the *tango canción*, or the tango as written poem—built around these themes. The "industrialization" of mass culture of the early to middle twentieth century pulled the tango from the "informal" economy to find a home in the "formal." It was transformed from a sphere of "cultural production" into one more oriented toward "cultural consumption." The tango became something to be watched—and danced, to be sure—but not necessarily played by amateurs. Composers and librettists wrote tango notes and lyrics for copyright rather than inventing them in the heat of a verbal battle around a campfire or in a seedy bar.

A turning point came when Carlos Gardel recorded Pascual Contursi's "Mi Noche Trieste" in 1917. The genre continued to evolve through Contursi's subsequent explorations of unrequited love and social striving, as in his 1927 hit "La Mina del Ford" (The Girl with the Ford), about a lower-class girl who longs for the middle-class dream of an apartment with a balcony and a car.[141]

Analyses of tango themes fill many bookshelves with deep textual, class, and gender interpretations. There is little doubt that the tango is about machismo and the subjugation of woman.[142] It is, however, a more potent weave of power and impotence. The subjugated woman often gains the upper hand, which is why the songs are so laden with a sense of failure. The man doing the subjugating on the dance floor is himself the object of subjugation in life. *Mufarse* is the soul of the dispossessed, which helps to explain why so many of the city's immigrants embraced the tango as soon as they heard its plaintiff call.

As immigrants formed more and more of a following for the music and its performers, the tango and the performers became more and more influenced by the immigrants, who brought their own corners of Europe into the mix of the city and its sound. Europe similarly provided the instruments used in the tango. Originally, as the genre took shape on the Pampas and in the *arrabales*, the tango was played on guitars, violins, and flutes. Contrabasses were added—sometimes pounded like a drum—with mandolins and some drums eventually making an appearance.[143]

A breakthrough into a distinctive and unique sound that would audibly brand the tango as something all its own came about when someone brought the *bandoneón* into the mix. This accordion-like instrument became so ubiquitous in the tango that it is impossible to think of the music without at least one musician pumping away on the awkward little squeeze box perched on a lap.

Heinrich Band invented the *bandoneón* in Krefled, Germany, in the mid-1830s as a newfangled *concertina* intended to allow churches too small to have an organ to reproduce its majestic sound. Rather than attaining refined pitch by pushing compressed air through pipes, a single player could push the air through the keys of a small, lap-held box. The player uses up to eighty buttons on contemporary instruments—rather than keys, as on an accordion—to play specific notes. Within a few years, the *bandoneón* was refined into two models—the chromatic and the achromatic—and took to the road; reaching Argentina sometime in the 1860s, the *bandoneón* quickly found a new life. The chromatic version plays the same note, whether the bellows are opening or closing, while the achromatic varies in expression, depending on whether the instrument is inhaling or exhaling. It is the maddeningly difficult, achromatic version that became the "Stradivarius of the tango."[144]

The *bandoneón* is a perfect symbol of the immigrant embrace of the tango. Quickly forgotten in its homeland and surpassed by new inventions that are easier to play, the humble squeeze box traveled across the Atlantic to find new fans. Its plaintive sound accurately reflected the Buenos Aires sense of *mufarse*; its rhythmic possibilities opened up expressions of complex Afro-Argentine and Andalusian passion to small ensembles and bands of two, three, four, and five players. This humble instrument played what would become the quintessential tango sound.[145]

The tango's powerful blend of indigenous, African, and European influences produced a new synthetic whole by the first years of the twentieth century. Writing a century later, the novelist Manuel Vázquez Montalbán tried to capture the mood of the tango and the city in a passage that could just as well have been written about the Buenos Aires of the early 1900s: "The dim lights of Boca seem to have been reluctantly lit. They illuminate restaurant fronts that would be garish were it not for the eternal damp of the river. Away from the lights the rest of the neighborhood is mostly corrugated iron, with rusty patches which speak of having to survive without any sense of greatness. . . . The restaurant doors cast oblongs of yellow light on the pavements where Alma and Carvalho are walking. From inside they hear snatches of secret *bandoneón* music, smell the charcoal embers and the crucified carcasses of roasting lambs."[146] The grand kaleidoscope of Buenos Aries turned, and the tango became its most enduring legacy.

Telling the Truth About Argentina

The challenge of understanding the tango is to see it as a blend of various indigenous Argentine, African, and European elements rather than thinking of this dance as having emerged at any single moment from any single tradition. By the middle of the nineteenth century, blacks had abandoned many of their own traditions in favor of European imports such as the polka and mazurka. Meanwhile, whites often mimicked the Carnival processions and *candombe* of Afro-Argentines. Everyone improvised, drawing on whatever they saw and heard around them.[147] As much of this dancing took place in slums scattered around the city fringe, what they saw and heard came from everywhere. At some point, this blend became known as the "tango."

The tango was not Argentine; neither was it African, immigrant, or Creole. The tango was—and remains—"*porteño*," the very essence of Buenos Aires. The dance's improvisational character reflects the spontaneity of *porteño* life, the equality of encounters, and the importance of conversational exchange in local culture.

The tango scholar Brandon Olszewski explains that "in tango, a leader is not simply leading a follower around the floor, exhibiting her as an ornament. Instead, tango prescribed that both partners are active collaborators in the construction of the dance. The improvised nature of the dance makes this possible. . . . Ultimately, the process of leading and following is more of a conversation between partners, rather than a kinetic fiat issued by the leader."[148] There simply would be no tango without the urban environment that blended the traditions that eventually merged to a point of losing their distinctive identities within this dance.[149] The precise proportion of elements that went into the chemical explosion of the tango is less important than the place where this explosion took place, Buenos Aires.

The capacity to blend and create something new and distinctive has been one of the city's characteristics that have most often caught the attention of visitors. To cite but one example, upon arriving in the city after World War II, the distinguished British writer Christopher Isherwood observed that Buenos Aires is a place where "foreign elements have been blended and transformed into something indigenous, immediately recognizable, and unique."[150] The city's syncretistic essence is perhaps the greatest *porteño* gift of all—one that becomes manifest in the blending of so many otherwise alien and contradictory strains into a single conversation.

Taylor may come closest to the tango's essence when she writes that the dance

> appears to be of the genre of European, embraced dances. But danced by Argentines, it displays differences from its European counterparts. The dancers' steps are explicitly different, although danced in an embrace, but coordination is maintained principally by the male's *marca*, something that has been poorly translated as his "lead." When a male tango dancer pressures the female dancer's back, or signals her right hand with his left, more often than not the *marca* tells her to do a figure entirely different than what he himself is doing. Limbs of both male and female dancers seem to move independently of their own bodies. Torsos remain motionless while legs perform what appear to be

completely unrelated figures. Sometimes a lower leg flashes out in a counterintuitive escape. Even eye contact, when infrequently established on the dance floor as opposed to the stage, is abruptly broken. This embrace can be danced to enact and exaggerate exclusion not inclusion, objectification not intimacy, difference not sameness. In doing so, it mirrors exclusions Argentines are vulnerable to at the hands of Europeans.[151]

For all the transatlantic influences that shaped the tango as a dance form, this dance was more than a formalized ballroom romp across a polished floor, because it always inculcated an underlying New World savageness.[152]

The centennial of Argentine independence arrived with high hopes, reconfirming the modernizing ambitions of the country's European-centric elites. Gabriella Nouzeilles and Graciela Montaldo remind us that

in 1910, one hundred years after independence from Spain, Argentina offered convincing proof that modernity could take root and prosper in postcolonial Latin America. The local elites had replaced a past of poverty and violence and wastelands with a future of prosperity, cosmopolitanism, and economic opportunity. In an essay celebrating the country's remarkable achievements, the Nicaraguan poet Ruben Dario expressed his conviction that Argentina would lead the rest of the former Spanish colonies along the path of progress. To the astonishment and applause of all the nations of the world, he contended, Argentina was already flourishing and would soon become strong enough to compete even with the big brother to the North, the United States. Nobody seemed to doubt that Argentines would eventually become the "Yankees of the South." Echoing this perspective, writers at home and abroad portrayed Argentina as a homogenous and exceptional community, remarkably different from its Latin American counterparts.[153]

The country's leaders certainly agreed with Dario's assessment. The historian Juan Balestra famously proclaimed to president-elect Roque Saenz Peña on May 25, 1910, that Argentina had generated enough light to illuminate the entire world. "No one," Balestra declared, "not even in their wildest dreams had anticipated the greatness of the Argentine people. It has generated enough electricity to illuminate an entire century."[154]

The tango belied such visions of white homogeneity and European modernity. The tango, by its very existence, spoke of a very different Argentina—one, like every other place in the Americas, that had become its own blend of indigenous American, European, and African elements. The tango, rather than the centennial celebrations, revealed profound truths about the country's complex web of competing realities.

At some point, about the time when the Argentine elites were celebrating their modernity and "European-ness," the seditious tango—which represented the very essence of the "barbarians" who threatened their image of "civilization" and "modernity" — was telling a different story. The tango revealed its inconvenient truth about Argentina to the world at large. Someone took the tango to Paris.

First Tango in Paris

No one knows for sure the precise identity of that someone who took the tango to Paris. Perhaps he, she, or they were upper-class fops who had enjoyed slumming around *porteño* bars and brothels before leaving for Paris; perhaps they were returning French tourists; perhaps they were exhausted European immigrants seeking a distant home of memory, or local Argentine musicians who got a gig on a transatlantic voyage; perhaps they were a ship's crew or a touring theater group. What is known is that within months, this blend of all the factors that had turned Buenos Aires into one of the wealthiest, grandest, and most complex cities in the world—and, in the process, spurred the creation of something totally and completely new from the flash fusion of its various parts—exploded across the face of Europe in a classic moment of what is now called globalization. Within weeks of its arrival—and much to the outraged embarrassment of the Argentine elite—tango musicians and tango dancers were performing for wildly enthusiastic audiences, including political leaders, British royals, the Russian tsar and his family, the German kaiser, and the pope in Rome.

The tango came to Paris on the eve of World War I, just as fin-de-siècle decadence and lavish entertainment were reaching new heights. The city's heady mix of bourgeois and downscale nightlife had an edge not seen in the pursuit of pleasure elsewhere. Glamor and slumming mixed as every kind of social and sexual encounter found new outlets in a society that loved the shock of being shocked. The titillation of scandal was stage-managed. Ever more scandalous exotic dances swept through the Parisian scene—the waltz, polka, can-can, apache, cakewalk, *maxixe*, samba, belly dancing—simultaneously becoming tamed for social dancing.[155] Performers sought tension between virtuosity, gracefulness, and sensuality; and the bourgeoisie was ready to follow suit in more muted form at their own parties.[156]

The bohemia of Montmartre became the center of the center, the place where the French and visitors embraced any new entertainment that promised erotic pleasure.[157] The raw tango that crossed the Atlantic from *porteño* brothels was ready-made for this world of touristy, respectable unrespectability. Whoever the first tango performers and musicians were, they arrived in Paris sometime after 1905. They moved readily onto the same dance hall and music hall stages as such uninhibited Parisian performers as La Loulue, Jean Avril, and Nini Patte en l'Air.[158] Seekers of exoticized debauchery and vulgarity immediately took to the tango. In doing so, they gradually sanitized its passion, so that by 1914, even Pope Pius X could watch the dance in the Vatican.[159] To return to Marta Savigliano: "The tango was originally poor but moving upwards, urban with some traces of ruralness, white with some traces of color, colonized with some traces of a native barbarian in the process of being civilized. . . . The tango was a versatile, hybrid, new kind of exotic that could adopt the manners of the colonizer while retaining the passion of the colonized, both at heart and on the surface."[160]

The British writer Artemis Cooper records that the first genuine *tangueros* to arrive in Paris from Buenos Aires—Angel Villoldo and Alfredo Gobbi, and, a short time thereafter, Gobbi's wife, Flora

Rodriguez de Gobbi—showed up in the French capital in 1907 to cut records using the most advanced technology of the era.[161] Their presence underscores a direct link between the rise of the tango and the popularization of new entertainment media—first the Victrola, and, by 1920, the radio. Within a year, the tango was danced for the first time in a Parisian theatrical review; and by 1910, it was being performed by cabaret stars before European royalty.[162] The tango thus arrived simultaneously with Sergei Diaghilev's Ballets Russes, which similarly responded to the Parisian love of sensuality and exoticism.[163] And like Diaghilev and Igor Stravinsky with their *Firebird*, sometimes the tango sparked a violent backlash. Among fisticuffs and moralistic journalistic and academic debates, the tango represented everything that was both right and wrong about Europe.

The tango was anathema for the sorts of Argentines who hung out in Paris at the time. Shocked that their urbane, modern culture was being portrayed through the raunchy medium of a brothel dance, Argentines such as the diplomat Don Carlos Ibarguern protested loudly that the dance was becoming a symbol of their homeland.[164] Argentine nationalists who wanted to be honored for the centennial of independence were chagrined to find themselves linked to the savage dance, as when Tsar Nicholas II, on having been presented with the new Argentine ambassador in Saint Petersburg, allegedly responded, "Argentina. . . . Oh yes, the tango!"[165] Argentine ambassadors banned the tango from the country's embassies, while diplomats everywhere doggedly denied it was Argentina's own.

Argentine performers and musicians responded more quickly than their diplomatic representatives. Having gotten word that "tangomania" was sweeping Europe, they immediately made their way to Paris, London, Madrid, Marseilles, Nice, and Barcelona. Matronly, wealthy New Yorkers brought the tango to North America from Paris, and not from Buenos Aires.[166] The dance became all the rage throughout European ballrooms, slowly becoming domesticated, even as it shocked.[167] Tango manuals popped up everywhere, as did "authentic" Argentines, who discovered that they could make a good living claiming to know their supposed "national dance." Tango cocktail dresses, tango colors (a red-orange), and "tango teas" quickly followed.[168]

The Parisian understanding of the tango's origins missed many of the dance's complexities. Parisians liked their tango, an ultimate urban cultural form, to be performed by musicians and dancers in gaucho costumes. Proper Englishmen and Englishwomen returning from wicked weekends on the Continent brought the dance with them, as did Russian aristocrats and Spanish grandees.[169] Their tango had less the raw bump and grinds of the free-flowing *arrabal* brothel and more the elegance and studied steps of the European ballroom. The tango, to some degree, was losing its raw core as it passed through Europe and North America.[170] Suave, proud, moneyed Argentines had to come to terms with their new symbol. This task was made somewhat easier by the fact that *tout* Paris had made it their own.

Beyond the European heartland, Japan and Finland embraced the tango with particular verve—and both countries remain major tango centers today. In the case of Japan, the tango represented an exotic import that was both "uncivilized" and suave. The tango had the further advantage of not being from the United States, which allowed it to thrive as the increasingly nationalistic Tokyo government prepared for, and ultimately, fought the Great Pacific War. The tango became surrogate foreign popular music and won adherents who carried the performance forward.[171] The melancholy mood of the later tango touched the Finnish soul during the 1920s following Finland's hard-fought wars of independence. The Finns began writing their own tangos during the difficult years of the Great Depression and World War II, continuing a love affair with the dance into the twenty-first century.[172]

The tango exploded across Europe like a starburst, and lasted about as long. Paris and other European capitals did not seem quite so gay after the guns of August 1914 ended the party. Tango films were being made, Argentine performers still arrived—Carlos Gardel, for example, made his movie debut in 1917 in the Parisian-produced silent *Flor del Durzano*—but the age of carefree debauchery was over.[173] The tango still had its following in Europe, for sure; but postwar imports such as the Charleston and American jazz became more fitting symbols for the "roaring" decade of the 1920s that followed victory, won in large measure by American dough boys. Defeated Germans and Austrians—to say nothing of the puritanical postrevolutionary Bolsheviks in Russia—seemed less ready to dance.

Returning Home

Argentine performers slowly drifted home from war-torn Europe, bringing a more formalized tango with them. The tango had moved from the bar and brothel to the drawing room and music hall stage in Europe; it had become less spontaneous and more scripted. Its embourgeoisement and newfound respectability had softened the more ribald and raunchy corners of the dance and the music. The tango was reinvented to find a place just within middle-class respectability rather than outside it. It had won the grudging endorsement of Argentine elites, who realized that the art form of the slums—rather than the architecture of the boulevards—gave them legitimacy in Europe.[174] Having traveled to the metropolis to win approval, the tango became acceptable in Argentina.

The tango in Europe had encountered the new mass communication and entertainment technologies that would create a global popular culture in the decades ahead.[175] This was a time when, as the historian of Weimar Germany, Eric Weitz, has noted, "All across the developed world and beyond, the post–World War I era showered people with new sounds and images. Britons, too, flocked to the radio and the cinema, Argentines danced to recorded as well as to live music, and wherever there was a movie projector and something resembling a screen, audiences laughed at Charlie Chaplin."[176]

The tango—to be successful on the phonograph—had to be contained within the parameters of a wax cylinder and a vinyl disc. The tango—in order to travel to new audiences over the radio airwaves—needed words and new mores so as to capture but not insult mass audiences. The tango—to win over the emerging movie audience—needed dramatic flair that could be captured in the silent film. The tango's domestication was driven as much by technology as by its jaunt to the Continent.

The year 1917, which launched the age of world revolution in Saint Petersburg and Moscow, proved to be a momentous one for the tango as well, as the threads of the tango came together in a transformational moment. Buenos Aires boomed, because it was benefiting from being at peace and supplying the European combatants.[177] Local theatrical life flourished, not yet having been challenged by electronic media, which would bleed patrons steadily away over the next century. Carlos Gardel recorded Contursi and Castriota's classic tango anthem "Mi Noche Triste," and made his film debut in the silent *Flor del Durzano*.

Donald Castro captures the meaning of 1917 as a pivotal moment for the tango, observing that,

> in its earliest stages (1880–90), the tango can be considered folk culture; it its next stage, *tango-danza* (1890–1917), it can be characterized as a form of popular culture by virtue of its wider acceptance in the culture of the *suburios* (lower- and working-class neighborhoods) of Buenos Aires. The massification of the tango, if you will, began with its transformation into a popular form, the *tango-canción*, after 1917, when it began to be disseminated through the new electronic media of radio, film, and sound recordings. By the 1930s, the popularity of sound films and radio made the *tango-canción* a national (and international) popular culture phenomenon.[178]

The changes in the tango did not come about simply because of its European adventures. Its *porteño* breeding grounds were also changing. Buenos Aires reached an apogee of sorts in the late teens of the twentieth century, as the city became "an embodiment of advanced civilization."[179] British investment and interest in Argentina were at their height, a modernizing political elite ensured a stable form of managed democracy, business ruled the day, and agriculture boomed.[180] The city's North Side, long home to the *gente bien*, sported some of the grandest urban mansions in the Americas. The Center and the West Side were home to a booming middle class—the largest on the continent—which included successful immigrant strivers of decades past. The South Side housed a growing working class tied to factories and the ports. Immigrants moved into small-scale manufacturing and retail (there were about 40,000 shopkeepers in 1914, four-fifths of whom foreign born).[181] Their increasingly well-educated offspring climbed the ranks of the professions; how-ever, in a sign of troubles to come for the Argentine economy in the years ahead, they did so by signing onto the exploding government service rather than by pursuing careers in the private sector. The working class—some 400,000 strong—remained overwhelmingly male and immigrant. The realities of blue-collar life to the south of town ultimately shaped the tenor of the city more than the elegant mansions and facades to the north.

All was not as well as it seemed. Unions and working-class mobilization disrupted public life as the country became saturated with cheap labor. An expanding middle class challenged the rul-ing oligarchy through the new Radical Party and other political organizations.[182] The best land had been gobbled up; manufactur-ing remained overly dependent on exports in a country of only 8 million inhabitants on a land mass roughly the size of Western Eu-rope. Within a decade, the political order would unwind—with the first of numerous military coups overthrowing President Hipólito Yrigoyen in September 1930—opening the door to authoritarian populist nationalism.[183]

The Great Depression prompted democracy's fall. Nonethe-less, economic stagnation arrived in Argentina earlier. Highly de-pendent on British capital, Argentina suffered from the transfer of capital's global headquarters from London to New York following the war. The country never again quite attracted the same level of international investment that had turned it into a symbol of wealth and success. And its nationalist disdain for the United States led to increasing tensions, as when Yrigoyen slighted US president-elect and former commerce secretary Herbert Hoover during Hoover's late 1928 tour to promote trade.[184]

The tango held its own trajectory, entering a "golden age" in the years after World War I. For many *porteños*, life was unbelievably good, especially during the 1920s. Those with disposable incomes "flocked to bars, cafés, cinemas, and theaters to listen to their favor-ite groups. The tango lovers who wanted to dance," as the cultural anthropologist Maria Susana Azzi tells her readers, "went to what were called *dancings* (dance halls) as well as to somewhat more el-egant *salones de baile* and cabarets. More and more dance venues sprang up every year. One of the most famous tango centres was the El Nacional Café, next to the El Nacional Theatre in Corrientes Street [sometimes called "Latin America's Broadway"]. . . . The best tango bands performed at the cabarets, which mushroomed in the Centre in the 1920s. The influence of Paris is evident in their names, the Abbaye, Maxim, Montmartre, the Petit Parisen, Pigall, the Tabaris, and the Folies Bergere."[185] They were egged on by radio and cinema, which brought the worlds of the *arrabales* and the drawing room together. Mass media transformed the tango from the dance of a male underworld into the popular entertainment of bourgeois housewives. It cleaned it up and moved it out of the slums. The tango became a form of cultural consumption as much as it was a form of cultural production and expression.[186]

Simon Collier notes that the

> tango began as a dance (in due course it also became a color, a letter in the international radio alphabet, and even, in some countries, a soft drink and a chocolate bar) and for most of the people in the world it has always remained just that, a dance, its original sensual nature long since tamed into ballroom respectability. In Argentina, however, the tango also tended to be viewed from an early stage as a tradition of popular music. The lively tunes and irresistible rhythms of this music called out for words to be added. In due course, they were.[187]

A number of poet-lyricists were led by Pascual Contursi, a clerk in a shoe shop who devoted as much spare time as possible to mounting puppet shows.[188] Contursi proved to be a gifted poet, spicing his verse with Lunfardo slang to give it an air of authenticity. After having met Gardel and Razzano by chance in Montevideo in January 1917, Contursi convinced Gardel to sing his "Mi Noche Triste" for a recording. The song became a hit, one of Spanish America's first of the phonograph-radio era. The record promoter Max Glucksmann recorded Gardel and Razzano again and again, with the tango replacing their more countrified repertoire from earlier years.[189] Others—often quite-talented lyricists, composers, and singers in their own rights—followed suit. Their music was "the song of a city, and of that city's life."[190] The great urban mixing bowl of Buenos Aires had prompted the tango to evolve further. The tango song was born, and with it, the legend of the tango king Carlos Gardel.

International Popular Music's First King

Carlos Gardel—"Carlitos," "El Zorzal" (the Song Thrush), "the king of tango," "El Mago" (the Magician), and "El Mudo" (the Mute)—dominated the tango and Argentine popular culture as no single performer did before or has done since (figure 15). Gardel was born Charles Romuald Gardes on December 11, 1890, in Toulouse, as the illegitimate son of his mother Berthe Gardes's liaison with married businessman Paul Lasserre.[191] Intent on escaping social disgrace and stigmatization in the claustrophobic world of provincial France, Doña Berra—as she would become known to her son's fans and admirers—picked her two-year-old son up and boarded the transatlantic steamer *Dom Pedro* for a new life in one of the greatest immigrant cities of the era, Buenos Aires. Berthe Gardes and her son Charles arrived in the New World on March 9, 1893—one of those dates that would mark a profound cultural turning point for their new country—though no one was aware of it at the time, least of all the single-parent Gardes immigrant household.

Doña Berra rented a cheap room in the lively and colorful immigrant, working-class Abasto market district and started a career of precarious jobs ironing clothes, serving as a cardboard maker's assistant, working as a watchmakers' apprentice, and learning the craft of typography. Charles became Carlos, El Francesito ("Frenchie"), as he moved from school to school, picking up a posse of neighborhood childhood and teenage buddies.[192] France must have appeared shrouded in the fog of a distant past, though Doña Berra seems to have remained in some sort of contact with her European relatives, because Carlos eventually would track them down and visit whenever he was performing nearby.

Carlos led the typical hardscrabble childhood of a poor immigrant kid, not doing particularly well in school, skirting the law, and learning how to hold his own on the at-times-violent streets of his tough, working-class neighborhood. But he was different, in one respect: He discovered the theater in general, and opera in particular.[193]

Figure 15. The tango singer and actor Carlos Gardel, shown with the actress Anita Campbell, was one of Argentina's most popular cultural figures during the twentieth century.
Source: La fotografía en la Historia Argentina, Archivo General de la Nación.

Opera was omnipresent in a city dominated by Italian immigrants and a Creole elite brandishing its European pretensions by building grand theaters, such as the spectacular Teatro Colon opera house, which opened in 1908. Immediately considered among the half-dozen premier opera houses in the world, the Colon offered Carlos and his fellow *porteños* opportunities to hear the best singers of the era (he would later surprise more than a few opera stars by breaking into his own variations on their leading roles, having learned classical operatic librettos in his youth).

Carlos linked up with Luis Ghiglione, a shadowy theatrical figure who hired folks such as Gardel to applaud at performances and to work as stagehands. Gardel may have appeared in some minor roles on the Colon stage.[194]

At some point along the way, Carlos started singing in local cafés and bars in his neighborhood—eventually landing a permanent gig at the O'Roudeman Café, at the corner of the streets named simply Agüero and Humahuaca—now a pilgrimage site of sorts.[195] He discovered the indigenous *payada* tradition, meeting Ezeiza, José Bettinoti, Arthru de Nava, and other masters of the genre.[196] His repertoire of folksongs grew, as did his mastery of the guitar and his reputation.

Sometime around 1911, Carlos hooked up with another local youth who was winning fans singing in local bars—José "El Oriental" Razzano.[197] In another moment of legend, Razzano, a native of Montevideo (hence his nickname), met the wealthy Francisco Taurel on the street. Taurel was looking for someone to sing at a party that night. Razzano suggested that Gardel join him. Taurel agreed. Razzano and Gardel showed up at the ritzy Confitería Perù and continued on with the group—which included a senator, police officials, local bards, and the proprietor of city's most famous brothel, Madame Jeanne—before adjourning to the Armenonville cabaret.[198] The proprietors of the Armenonville offered the duo a well-paid, long-term engagement. Argentina's most popular singing act—the Razzano-Gardel duo—was born.

Razzano and Gardel started to tour, performing in Cordoba, Rosario, and Montevideo—where Gardel seems to have been shot in a dance hall altercation—as well as in Brazil and in any two-bit provincial theater within a day's train ride of Buenos Aires.[199] Both men understood the power of recording their songs, and by 1912 or 1913 they had begun doing so, both together and separately. They were joined much of the time by the Afro-Argentine guitarist José "El Negro" Ricardo. They were stars, singing as often as they could to any sort of audience, from the denizens of a dusty down-on-its-luck town at the edge of the Pampas to the prince of Wales and the maharaja of Kapurthala.[200] By late 1924, El Oriental's voice had given out, leaving Gardel on his own. Having already enjoyed commercial success with his rendition of Contursi's and Castriota's tango anthem "Mi Noche Triste," the now-single Gardel began to sing more and more tango songs (the preponderance of his nearly one thousand recorded songs would come from the tango repertoire).[201]

Gardel enjoyed success singing in France and Spain; and in 1929, he participated in some of the most successful and opulent shows on the Paris stage. He and Osvaldo Fresedo started spending time with Charlie Chaplin during an engagement in Nice, prompting Gardel to become interested in the new entertainment medium of sound cinema. He signed with Paramount, eventually staring in seven films made in France and the United States, including Adolph Zukor's *The Big Broadcast of 1935*, which featured such Hollywood and Broadway stars as Bing Crosby, George Burns, Gracie Allen, and Ethel Merman.[202]

In April 1935, Gardel embarked on a studio-sponsored tour of the Caribbean, after having spent several months making films in New York.[203] Poignantly, the year before, among his New York recordings for the film *Cuesta abajo* had been an homage to his adopted hometown, "Mi Buenos Aires Querido" (My Beloved Buenos Aires). Gardel had written the music for the tune, to which Alfredo Lepera added the lyrics: *Mi Buenos Aires querido / cuando you te vuelva a ver / no habrá mas penas ni olvido* (My beloved Buenos Aires / the day I see you again / there will be no more sorrow or forgetfulness).[204]

But the tango king would not see his beloved city again. On June 24, 1935, while in the Colombian city of Medellín on the Caribbean tour promoting his films for Paramount, Gardel died in a fiery crash when his plane ploughed into another one during takeoff.[205] His internment in Buenos Aires attracted tens of thousands of mourners, despite a rare snowstorm, prompting some to proclaim that a voice like that of Gardel would only be heard once more when it snowed again in the city. His cortege moved slowly past the quiet multitude from the docks through downtown and the Abasto district to La Chacarita Cemetery.[206] His grave—including a life-size bronze statue, to which pilgrims have attached a lighted cigarette nearly every day for the past seven decades—has become a sacred space honoring both Gardel the man and Gardel the myth, as well as a mythical Buenos Aires of tango lore.[207]

Gardel's life and career are intertwined with the rise of the tango as a mass phenomenon in the ever-expanding popular culture of the globalized twentieth century.[208] He dominates the tango story for many reasons, not the least being his talent and charisma. Just as important, he personified the very Buenos Aires that had created the tango—offering the quintessential immigrant success story, rising from *porteño* streets to elegant Parisian and New York theaters, star-studded restaurants, and internationally renowned soundstages.

Going Global

Although Gardel's personal odyssey looms large over the tango, there is much more to the story than Gardel himself. Gardel was but one of many talented musicians performing around the world and embracing the new technologies of the recorded voice, the silver screen, and the radio. Together, they told the world—as well as Buenos Aires, and Argentina itself—what it meant to be a *porteño*.

Recording companies and, during the 1930s, radio stations promoted any number of singers as the music industry was transformed into a world dominated by ratings and sales. Male and female singers—such as Gardel's great rival Ignacio "El Galan" Corsini, Juan Carlos Cobian, Mercedes Simone, Libertad Lamarque, Ada Falcon, the cross-dressing Azucena "La Nata Gaucha" Maizani, and Rosita Quiroga—had their devoted followers and ardent fans. They were joined by an endless pool of extraordinarily talented musicians, many Afro-Argentine—such as Horacio Salgan, Osvaldo Pugliese, Guillermo Barbieri, "El Negro" Ricardo, the bandleader Juan D'Arenzo, and the "Charlie Parker of the *bandoneón*," Anibal "El Gordo" Troilo—and dancers—such as the legendary José Ovidio "El Cachafaz" Bianquet (considered perhaps the best tango dancer ever), Carlos "Petroleo" Estevez, and Mingo Pugliese—elevating the tango to ever-higher levels.[209]

Perhaps adding more to the art form as stylists than as innovators, these great performers enriched the tango with the still-fecund cultural environment of Buenos Aires. And more important, these gifted entertainers of the 1920s and 1930s reached ever-wider audiences, not just abroad but also within Argentina itself. As the tango moved from live performance to the airwaves, it reached further and further into the Argentine hinterland. Its macho, brothel-dominated origins were softened as recordings and broadcasts found a powerful new following among middle-class housewives.[210]

The new media promoting the tango were doing far more. For the first time, the traditional gap between Creole and immigrant culture, between the culture of the *gente del pueblo* and the *gente decent*, was being bridged. As elsewhere, the mass culture produced in sound studios and on film stages around the world created an increasingly homogenized national (and eventually global) culture out of the scattered fragments of localized cultural expression. A distinctly "Argentine" culture began to emerge—one shared by all Argentines—with the tango leading the way.[211]

This new tango for the masses perhaps appeared to have been somehow denuded. Yet the great city always managed to add its own voice. Initially disappointed by the reality of the tango, a visiting Englishman, Philip Guedalla, found that he was lamenting the city's seemingly sanitized voice as presented to outsiders for mass consumption. He continued:

> Yet Buenos Aires has a voice that you may catch, if you listen hard. Somewhere in a gallery above that dismal dancing floor violins of an incomparable band beat to a slow pulse of music; a strange air creeps across the throbbing undertone of strings; and above the music a deep voice utters its complaint. It is an education in the tango to have heard Porque at Ta-ba-ris. Or a wilderness of dreary vaudeville is brightened by the sudden interruption of a marching air sung in a hoarse Spanish voice, a woman's voice that rises to a wailing minor or falls to a reproachful bass, as the air marches to its close. That is the voice of Buenos Aires; and it is the world's misfortune that outside Buenos Aires it is rarely heard.[212]

If the tango could still move people, it was because it remained profoundly connected with those in the city who made it work. The Polish novelist Witold Gombrowicz was taken with this aspect of the city as he found refuge in Buenos Aires at the outbreak of World War II. Setting a scene of his 1953 novel *Trans-Atlantyk* in a vast dance hall at the time of his arrival on the eve of war, he writes, "So vast the hall, so great its space that from one end to the other— as in the Mountains when from a height, the highland, the eye in a Valley there strays, drowns—people like unto ants, . . . and from the distance comes a Hum, and the voice of music strays. Workers, maids, vendors, apprentices, and Sailors aplenty, and Soldiers, also clerks, seamstresses, or *Vendeuses*, and by the tables they sit on in the midst turn themselves to the time of the music; when the Music breaks off, they stop."[213]

The quarter century following the Armistice in Europe had become the tango's "Epoca de oro" — its "Golden Age." The tango had become Argentina; and it did so just as Argentina began to change politically and economically — no longer looking to Europe for validation and investment but seeking a brighter future through myths of national glory and state-dominated economic investment. The conservatives who overthrew President Hipólito Yrigoyen initially proved themselves to be adept at managing Argentina's economy through the traumatic first years of the Great Depression. Real gross domestic product collapsed by 14 percent between 1929 and 1932, but recovered quickly, being 15 percent higher than in 1929 and 33 percent higher than in 1932 at the close of the decade.[214] The country's urban unemployment rate — never much over 5 percent — remained far lower than that in Europe and the United States.

This rebirth was predicated on an industrial strategy that looked to reorient the national economy around state-controlled manufacturing. Factories began to draw thousands of rural migrants to the capital and other cities, submerging *porteño* culture yet again under tens of thousands of newcomers who brought social and cultural traditions with them. Giant industrial housing complexes replaced the *arrabales* as industry-led expansion led the city's population to explode. The city's population had grown by just 5 percent between 1914 — when it stood at 1,973,000 — and 1935. But it soared by 37 percent before 1947, by which time it had reached 4,643,000.[215] The increasingly powerful state created a Central Bank in 1934 to gain a hold over the money supply and concluded a number of bilateral agreements to promote meats and cereals. Tellingly, the United States refused to enter into such negotiations, so the country found itself yet again dependent on European markets damaged by the Depression and eventually destroyed by World War II.

Economic nationalism accompanied chauvinistic rhetoric. Argentines began to believe that their country was predestined by nature and by God for power and greatness. The rise of mass labor, industry, and xenophobic nationalism represented a new Argen-

tine reality—one far less congenial to the tango than the local, political, and social realities of the *porteño* fin-de-siècle.

Don't Cry for Me

Argentina did its best to sit out World War II; the country only
joined the hostilities in March 1945, when it was more than evident
that the Allied victory had been assured. Much taken with Italian
corporatist fascism—and later, sympathetic to Hitler's more viral
fascist incarnation—Argentine elites did all that they could to support the Axis Powers, just short of taking on the United States.[216]
The internal political situation—already destabilized by the massive social and economic dislocations unleashed by rapid industrialization—became ever more precarious as the world at large set
about to destroy itself.

On June 4, 1943, the military intervened in national politics, as a
coup led by General Arturo Rawson overthrew the government of
President Ramón Castillo. Three days later, the ruling junta under
the United Officers' Group (Grupo de Oficiales Unidos) overthrew
Rawson, turning the presidency over to Pedro P. Ramírez.

Initially, the new regime seemed to be just one more in an increasing succession of military-led governments. This time, however, events would take a more ominous course as a young colonel, Juan Domingo Perón, settled into a leadership position at the
Department of Labor. He discovered that his department—with its
ties to both trade unions and the national treasury—was an advantageous base of operations for a charismatic, ambitious, nationalist
populist.[217]

Perón, in the words of Castro, "saved the revolution of 1943
from becoming a traditional lackluster repressive military regime.
He gave the revolution its social reason and orientation. The power
base for Perón's power was founded in the previously ignored laboring class and in the emerging industrial-oriented middle class.
. . . In addition, the revolution initiated in 1943 seemed to be tied
to a value system that was based on Catholic ethics and Creole virtue."[218] The cosmopolitan, sexually tinged tango—with its roots
deep in the slums and brothels frequented by Africans, indigenous
peoples, and *compadritos*; and which was sung in the criminal slag—
hardly conformed to their image of Argentina.

Having left the *arrabal* for the film studio and radio station—having moved in twenty-first-century lingo from the "informal" economy to the "formal"—the tango depended on official endorsement as never before. Censors controlled public virtue on the airwaves, at the recording studios, and on movie soundstages. Popular soap operas and music disappeared from view; and with it, so too did the tango. In their place, classical music and songs with lyrics conforming to good Spanish and the morals endorsed by Monsignor Gustavo Franceschi—the most zealous of the regime's thought police—gained a monopolist position in an increasingly state-controlled culture.[219] University linguists favored by the regime—such as the Spaniards Amado Alonso and Americo Castro—toiled vigorously for the "purification" of Argentine Spanish. The tango seemed doomed.[220]

Musicians fought back. The Argentine Association of Musicians and Writers of Music (Sociedad Argentina de Autores y Composttores de Musica)—which included Homero Manzi and Enrique Santos Discepolo from the tango, along with representatives of other popular music forms—worked their way up the new regime's hierarchy, meeting with bureaucrat after bureaucrat until eventually sitting down with Colonel Perón himself.[221] Not much happened, despite Perón's promises to the contrary (though Manzi and Discepolo were won over by the force of Perón's personality). The tango remained banned from broadcasts until after 1946, when it was permitted back, in a muted form. Meanwhile, the airways filled up with folk music and heroic tales from the interior, because gauchos made a better symbol than *compraditos* for the "New Argentina" being created by the Catholic, populist nationalists in power.

A native of the Province of Buenos Aires, and grandson of Sardinian immigrants, Perón was forty-eight years of age when Rawson seized power. His family had moved to Patagonia, where they tried unsuccessfully to run a sheep ranch, before returning to Buenos Aires Province. He entered military school and went directly into the military service. His first wife died in 1929. Perón began traveling as an observer of various authoritarian governments around Europe, becoming especially familiar with Benito Mussolini's regime in Rome.[222]

Perón took advantage of his position as head of the Department of Labor to build an alliance with left-leaning labor unions, and he actively promoted labor reform. He rallied celebrities to support the victims of a January 1944 earthquake in San Juan, meeting the radio actress Eva Duarte in the process. When General Edelmiro Farrell unseated Ramírez as president, Farrell promoted Perón to the vice presidency. In October 1945, rivals in the junta moved against the rising star, having him arrested for four days. Trade unionists organized massive demonstrations on October 17, securing his release.[223] The next day, Perón announced that he would run for president; and five days later, he married "Evita" Duarte.[224]

Evita was an illegitimate daughter of poor parents in rural Los Toldos. She moved to Buenos Aires in the mid-1930s to pursue a career on the stage and screen. She built a powerful political base by appealing to low-income workers—the *descamisados*, or "shirtless ones"—and became an outspoken advocate for the poor and for women. She operated an extensive network of charitable activities through the Charitable Society (Sociedad de Beneficencia), which had predated her arrival in power and operated with public and private funds under the auspices of a succession of the country's first ladies.[225] She converted the society into her own Eva Perón Foundation, which she used for both good works and to reward her supporters.[226]

The visiting Christopher Isherwood described the atmosphere in an account of meeting her shortly after she became first lady. "She may have been a bad actress once," he wrote, "but today she is a highly efficient demagogue. She may have been vulgar and noisy and temperamental; now she is coldly vindictive, ruthless, and ambitious. . . . Señora Perón is extremely shrewd. She has built up her personality like a great star, and she advertises it daily through the Press and the radio, and by frequent personal appearances. Her pictures are plastered all over the city."[227]

Perón won the election and became president on June 4, 1946.[228] He consolidated power around his "Third Way" agenda of social justice and economic independence, while avoiding alliances with either the United States or the Soviet Union. Exports fell as the combination of Argentine government policies and the growing success of the Marshall Plan cut off the county's access to European markets, eventually undermining economic growth, with the gross domestic product falling by a fifth between 1948 and 1952. Strikes became commonplace as the Peróns sought to mobilize the poor, the dispossessed, and workers on their behalf.

An increasingly divided Argentine nation became ever more at odds with itself. Perón, often using union thugs, moved against intellectuals, wealthy rural interests, and other opponents with increasing vigor and brutality. His opponents, in turn, withheld investment.[229] For many in the country, Evita and her legacy were of greater concern than Juan. "Evita," as Miranda France puts it, "did more than anyone to muddy the waters."[230]

Perón swept on to a second term buoyed by the votes of women who were voting for the first time, in part because of Evita's campaign for women's rights. The opposition to Perón solidified within the corridors of power, using Evita's death on July 26, 1952, to push for advantage.[231] Two bombs exploded at a massive Perónist rally on the Plaza de Mayo on April 15, 1953, killing seven and wounding close to one hundred, unleashing a rampage throughout the city. Such opposition landmarks as Socialist Party headquarters and the ritzy Jockey Club burned to the ground.[232]

With the economy beginning to recover, Perón stage-managed the election of a new vice president and launched many industrial developments with renewed foreign investment, including an expansion of the automobile and oil industries. Proposals to legalize divorce and prostitution led to his excommunication from the Roman Catholic Church on June 15, 1955. The next day, navy jets bombed a massive Perónist rally in the Plaza de Mayo, killing 354. The crowd, in return, took its vengeance on Catholic churches, destroying many in the process. On September 16, 1955, nationalist Catholics joined with army and navy officers in a revolt that began in the country's second-largest city, Cordoba.[233] Perón managed to escape via gunboat to Paraguay, leaving a permanently divided and scarred nation behind.[234]

The military government outlawed Perónism, preventing either Juan or Evita's name from appearing in public and banning Perónist parties from public life. Perón made his way to Venezuela and, eventually, to Spain. Evita's body embarked on an even more convoluted journey around Argentina and Europe.[235] Ever more authoritarian military dictatorships replaced ever more inept democratically elected governments, as the country fell into a grinding, slow-motion the civil war.[236] Finally, after a violent outbreak of leftist violence in the late 1960s and early 1970s, the military negotiated to allow Perón and his new wife Isabel (whom he married in 1961) to return to the country.[237]

For every Discepolo and Manzi who had supported the regime, there was a Libertad Lamarque who had gone into exile (reputedly after a contretemps with Evita).[238] Discepolo and Manzi died just before Perón fell from power; but others were not so lucky. Although Perón and his minions did their best to destroy the careers of those *tangueros* who did not join their side, his successors sought retribution against those—such as Catulo Castilo—who did.[239] More than just another passing junta of military officers, Perón's government introduced a powerful ideology that sparked internal Argentine culture wars that would last for a half century. As Borges eloquently warned in 1946 as Perón was gathering power, "Dictatorships breed oppression, dictatorships breed servility, dictatorships breed cruelty; more loathsome still is the fact that they breed idiocy."[240]

The tango was no different from other aspects of Argentine life during this era; it suffered from the ongoing political strife that often left decisionmaking and the setting of taste in the hands of the servile, the cruel, and the idiots on both sides of the growing political divide. But the tango faced three main serious challenges well beyond who was sitting in the presidential chair in the Pink House.[241]

First, the economic transformation taking place, as giant state-run factories came to dominate the economy, brought waves of migrants into the towns—poor, rural workers who brought their own music and culture with them. Because nearly two-thirds of these migrants ended up in Buenos Aires, they ruralized the city rather than the city urbanizing them, as had been the case before. The tango had not been part of their world and, with few cues indicating that it should be, it remained outside their interest.

Second, many of the great musicians, dancers, and songwriters from the tango's Golden Era were aging and dying off, and there were fewer and fewer younger performers coming along to take their place. Officially favored folklore, rather than the disreputable tango, became the genre of choice for many aspiring musicians and dangers.

Third, as everywhere in the world, the well-financed American entertainment machine—emboldened by the United States' new position at the pinnacle of the international order—flooded local theaters, radio stations, and record shops with the popular music of the Yankee North. Frank Sinatra, Elvis Presley, and, later, the Beatles dominated Argentine teenage life, as everywhere else in the world.

Azzi captures the slow evisceration of the tango's Golden Age during these multiple upheavals in Argentine politics, society, and cultural life:

> The Golden Age of the tango now drew to a close. Tango cafés closed, as did cabarets, *confiteras, salones de baile,* and *dancings;* soccer and other sports clubs could no longer afford to stage the huge gatherings of the previous decade. Although in 1950 Perón decreed that 50 percent of all music played on the radio was henceforth to be Argentine in origin, and though this act of cultural protectionism might, in principle, have boosted tango music in the 1950s, in fact, its real beneficiaries were the new generation of folk musicians now putting together the magnificent tradition of neofolklore—so soon to challenge the tango in public affections. Folk music was given more air time than the tango; tango bands recorded less and less and the market for the records that were made was greatly diminished. . . . A further and vital factor in the tango's decline was the virtual assimilation of the immigrant community into Argentine society, a process that greatly reduced the function of the tango as a means of bringing many disparate nationalities together.[242]

Society and politics changed. Dynamic art forms proclaimed dead many times over rarely die. Indeed, the tango did not disappear so much as it transformed itself. Talented and versatile musicians—such as the Afro-Argentines Horacio Salgan and Osvaldo Pugliese—moved the music forward, exploring its boundary with North American jazz through joint performances with such stars as

Ella Fitzgerald while encouraging younger musicians to continue the tradition.[243] The music lived, often on career-honoring television broadcasts and at retrospective concerts. The tango suffered to the extent that it no longer held pride of place in the musical life of the members of younger generations who were disaffected from the Argentine past and their dictatorial present.

The science fiction writer and poet Thomas Disch's observation in relation to the so-called demise of the Broadway musical is similarly appropriate for the fate of the tango in Buenos Aires. "A city is a machine that works by inertia," Disch writes. "By virtue of their solidity and expense, large buildings act as a brake on social change." And yet, he concludes, "finally, however, no single building, no street, no neighborhood, can hold its own against the glacial advance of larger social forces."[244]

If, as Azzi puts it, "in earlier decades the people themselves had been active participants in the tango, they now simply paid the admission price and sat and listened," yet the tango nonetheless lived.[245] The debauched party music of the brothel and its more inhibited cousin of the soundstage and screen has been converted into a form of Argentine concert music.

A Society in Exile

Like much of Argentine society, the troubled postwar decades forced the tango into exile—internal exile, in small concert halls and on basement stages; and external exile, in countries as diverse as Japan and Finland, where the tango found new energy and life. Marta Savigliano explores the phenomenon of tango and exile in her study of the "political economy of passion": "Tango and exile (in the sense of 'being away from home' for whatever reason) are intimately associated. On a personal level, it is more than common for any *argentino* living abroad to connect the experience of longing and nostalgia to the tango. It is a recurrent pattern, even for those of us who do not consider ourselves connoisseurs or fans of the tango, to be affected by the tango syndrome after being deprived for a while of our *argentino* 'environment.'"[246]

This syndrome has been more than personal. Savigliano explicitly links the dance's fate to the political upheavals at home.

"In the 1970s and 1980s," she writes, "a battered generation took hold of tango as an expression of experiences of political terror and exile lived during the most recent military government. As a result, tango went through a revival in Europe and some sensitive *argentino* artists and astute impresarios launched successful shows in the United States, Japan, and Buenos Aires. In addition, successful shows produced by both *argentino* and foreign directors situated tango at the core of their symbolism. These events brought the tango back."[247]

Events tied the dance to the spirit of the new democratization that would sweep through Argentina in the 1990s. This ambiguous relationship between local authenticity and world notoriety made the tango the perfect expression of an emerging *porteño* global consciousness that accompanied the end of the brutal military regimes that had formed with vicious rapidity following Perón's fall.[248]

Argentina entered a new era when the military decided it had no choice but to let Perón return. After extensive negotiations, Perón's stand-in candidate, Héctor Cámpora, handily won the general elections on March 11, 1973, taking office on May 25. Cámpora invited Perón to return from exile in Spain. About 3.5 million Argentines showed up at Ezeiza Airport to welcome him back on June 20, 1973.[249] The Perónists, now divided among leftists and rightists, broke into open fighting while they waited for the leader's plane to land. More than 12 people were killed, and another 365 were injured in this massacre. Cámpora and his vice president resigned, opening the way for a new election, which Perón won handily. He took over as the country's president on October 12, 1973, with his wife Isabel serving as vice president.

Perón's health was already failing when he returned. The bitter divisions in the country were too deep for the old magic to return. He died after a series of heart attacks on July 1, 1974, with his wife succeeding him.[250] Juan Perón had revealed his right-wing inclinations upon his return, a direction that continued to be pursued under his ineffectual wife. The military took over once again in March 1976, launching the so-called Dirty War that brutalized the country. Between 9,000 and 30,000 Argentines—predominantly young and intellectual—"disappeared" during a bloody reign of terror that lasted until civilian rule was restored in 1983. The military leadership was completely discredited following a catastrophically disastrous seventy-four-day war with the British over the Malvinas/Falkland Islands, which resulted in 257 British and 649 Argentine deaths.[251]

Not surprisingly, the four decades of political strife associated with the rise and fall of the Peróns devastated the Argentine economy, which was ravaged by inflation and eroded by declining access to export markets. Buenos Aires lost its luster, as it more and more appeared to be a city of the past.[252] The first democratically elected president, Raúl Alfonsín, succeeded in rebuilding the mainstays of a democratic regime, including launching inquiries into the horrors of the Dirty War. Democracy seems to have been assured by Alfonsín's defeat of an attack on La Tablada barracks, in an event that secured the legitimacy of civilian government for the foreseeable future.[253]

Alfonsín was less successful in taming the economy, as inflation skyrocketed to more than 700 percent, the highest rate in the world at the time.[254] A drought and a decline in exports deepened economic disorder, as Argentina fell from the ranks of developed to middle-income countries.[255] These difficult economic realities led to a peaceful democratic transition to Perónist rule under Carlos Menem. The collapse of the country's economy touched off another period of political instability. The Perónists regained power following the election of Néstor Kirchner as president in 2003 and, more recently, that of his widow, Cristina Fernández de Kirchner.[256] Argentina once again opened itself up to the world in the process of democratic consolidation. A new Argentina and a new Buenos Aires slowly took shape—as did a new tango.

The Neo-Tango Revolution

The tango continued to evolve, absorbing, as the *milonga* had done before it, fresh influences until they renewed and enriched the whole dance. Ástor Piazzolla became the best known among many masters of this "neo-tango." He even may prove to be as important for the long-term vitality of the music and dance as Gardel had been a half century before.

Piazzolla was born to Italian immigrant parents in the Atlantic coast city of Mar del Plata on March 11, 1921.[257] The family moved to New York, where he fell in love with jazz. His father gave him a *bandoneón* after a run-in with the police for trying to steal a harmonica. Living in the tough world of Depression-era Hispanic New York, the young Ástor held a number of odd jobs as he drifted in and out of school. His adventures brought him into contact with the Mexican artist Diego Rivera, who was painting controversial murals in the lobby of the new RCA Building in Radio City. He tracked down every major musician of the day, including Carlos Gardel. Piazzolla landed a bit part as a newsboy in Gardel's 1935 film *El dia que me quieras* (*The Day You Loved Me*). But the *bandoneón* remained his first love, so he happily returned to Argentina with his family in 1937.

Once back in Buenos Aires, Piazzolla started playing with tango orchestras and, in the process, discovered the music of the *bandoneón* master Anibal "El Gordo" Troilo. After having seen Piazzolla at his nightly gigs at Café Germinal, in 1939 El Gordo invited Ástor to audition after one of his sidemen had walked out. Piazzolla played Gershwin's *Rhapsody in Blue* on the *bandoneón* and immediately signed onto the band. He would stay with Troilo until 1944, and he started his own group in 1946.[258]

Piazzolla befriended the classical pianist Arthur Rubinstein, who was living in Buenos Aires at the time, and, on Rubinstein's advice, Piazzolla convinced the Argentine composer Alberto Ginastera to accept him as a student. Building on his study of composition with Ginastera, Piazzolla was accepted by the master Parisian composition teacher Nadia Boulanger in 1954.[259] Piazzolla's career lasted until his death in 1992, bringing his new synthesis of the tango, jazz, and classical music to a world of admirers.[260]

Other musicians working on the edge of the tango and other genres—such as the former Piazzolla protégé Pablo Ziegler and the younger Pablo Aslan—performed from such diverse bases as Buenos Aires, Berlin, and New York.[261] The tango no longer can be contained within itself. After Piazzolla, *porteño* musicians played with major jazz and classical artists. Tapes from late night jam sessions during the 1940s, 1950s, and 1960s with such greats as Gerry Mulligan and Dizzy Gillespie have earned a cultlike following among jazz aficionados. Classical masters such as Placido Domingo, Yo Yo Ma, and Daniel Barenboim have cut tango records of their own.

Simultaneously, *porteño* dancers followed the global interest in the tango to move from the dance halls of Buenos Aires to stages in Paris, London, New York, and Tokyo. Perhaps the most successful included Juan Carlos Copes and María Nieves, whose worldwide hit show *Tango Argentino* took Paris by storm in November 1983. Their show continued to win new audiences around the world as it moved on to Broadway, Tokyo, and elsewhere.[262]

Copes and Nieves took the world of the tango by storm when they unexpectedly won a tango contest at Buenos Aires's legendary Luna Park arena at the beginning of the 1950s. Located at the beginning of Corrientes, and just as well known for boxing and celebrity concerts, Luna Park gave the couple instant notoriety, and they became widely recognized as the king and queen of the tango. Along the way, they joined forces with Piazzolla, Troilo, Pugliese, and other great Argentine artists, catching the attention of prominent dancers and entertainers such as Gene Kelly, Liza Minnelli, and Mikhail Barishnikov. Performing abroad both together and separately, Copes and Nieves took the tango back to the world. Successful appearances on the Ed Sullivan and Arthur Murray television shows in the United States helped Copes and Nieves land performance contracts with several Broadway shows in the 1960s.

Wanting to reinvigorate the tango, facing growing economic and political uncertainty at home, and having myriad international contracts on which they could build, the duo assembled some of the greatest *tangueros* of the 1980s—including Salgan, Sexteto Mayor, Virulazo y Elvira, Roberto Goyeneche, Miguel Zotto, Milena Plebs, and Jovita Luna—and headed off to Paris, where their show exploded across the city's cultural scene. Similarly successful in New York, the troupe continued on despite some internal bickering, spawning any number of imitators.

Celebrities—such as the Hollywood actor Robert Duvall—embraced the tango around this time, putting it in their films and hosting tango parties around the world.[263] Duvall in particular enjoyed inviting tango aficionados (ranging from fellow actors to university professors, such as the historian Joseph Tulchin) to his farm outside Middleburg, Virginia, for extended dance weekends.[264]

The tango, in other words, was no longer a *porteño* phenomenon. Nor was Buenos Aires the cultural mixing bowl it had been a century ago. The tango nonetheless continues to convert the ambiguity of its components into a generous blend.

The tango is back. Buenos Aires is now the metropolis of a democracy—and, depending on the economic crisis of the day, is affordable for tourists from North America, Europe, and Japan—and attracts ever more tourists. Foreign visitors want to do the tango. They have discovered the old tango neighborhoods La Boca and San Telmo. The San Telmo of our imaginary immigrant Alberto holds particular appeal, with its giant Sunday flea market. Old tango hands—such as Barnabel "Gardelito" Ferreya, who began singing in 1972 around San Telmo's Plaza Dorrego—are joined by younger tango bands—such as the Orquesta Tipica Fernández Fierro—and scores of street dancers to entertain the tourists and, as just important, reinvigorate their own art. Dozens of tango shows are staged at the old tango bars, such as the Almacén, Bar Sur, and the nearby Café Tortoni, as well as the Confitería Ideal and other old tango haunts along Suipacha downtown.

The Genius of Detached Tolerance

Buenos Aires always has had a complex, layered tradition of the *milongas*, not as a dance form but as dance places. These often-run-down, semipermanent dance halls pop up around town—sometimes on a schedule (as in, after 11 pm on every fourth Thursday of the month) and sometimes by happenstance. They appear all over the city, sometimes lasting for years and other times for only one night. This was where serious *porteños* went to dance. The tradition of moving around in a semiclandestine manner proved to be a successful survival strategy during the difficult years of dictatorship. International *tangueros* have brought new life and revenue to the *milongas*.

Outside observers often are confused by what they see upon entering such a club. Tomás Eloy Martinez captured the scene perhaps as well as anyone in his novel *The Tango Singer*:

On the top floor of El Rufian there was a dance practice going on. The women had slim waists and understanding eyes, and the guys, though they wore their sleepless nights on their worn-out sleeves, moved with a marvelous delicacy and corrected partners' errors by whispering in their ears. Downstairs, the bookstore was full of people, like almost every bookstore we'd seen. . . . Once dance finished and the couples separated as if they had nothing to do with each other. I'd found that ritual disconcerting when I saw it in films, but in reality it was stranger still. Between one tango and the next, a man would invite a woman to dance with a nod that seemed indifferent. It wasn't. The disdain was feigned to protect their pride from any slight. If the woman accepted, she would do so with a distant smile and stand up, so the man would come over to her. When the music began the couple would stand waiting for some seconds, one in front of the other, making small talk without looking at each other. Then the dance began and a somewhat brutal embrace. The man's arm encircled the woman's waist and from that moment she began to back away. She was always on the retreat; sometimes, he arched his chest forward or turned sideways, cheek to cheek, while his legs sketched tangled figures that the woman would have to repeat in reverse. The dance demanded great precision and, most of all, a certain talent for divination, because the steps didn't follow a predictable order, but were either up to the one who was leading to improvise or choreographed from infinite combinations. With couples who understood each other best, some of the dance's movements mimicked copulation. It looked like athletic sex, tending towards perfection but with no interest in love.[265]

Many outsiders have found the tango's combination of disinterest and intimacy to be disconcerting. For the dyspeptic Miranda France, the dance as performed in *porteño milongas* is as loveless as a one-night stand.[266] Nonetheless, detachment and familiarity stand at the core of its forced intercultural mixing. Feigned disdain ensures survival in a world where slights—intended and not—lurk around every corner and people from different worlds try to survive alongside one another.

Now well into the twenty-first century, the Buenos Aires tango scene remains dynamic. A century ago, the tango was an expression of sadness shared not in public performances but in private moments of drunken release. It was a way to let off steam—both economic and emotional—for the poor and the marginal. Under dictatorships, the tango remained something that one did in older South Side neighborhoods such as San Telmo. It was something students did; something that intellectuals and bohemians did. Respectable people did not do the tango in public. But in the globalizing, democratic present, the tango has been taken into the broader society and into the neighborhoods where the rich and the middle class live. Now, the tango is everywhere in the city, with the old tango haunts of San Telmo and La Boca being relegated to tourists.

Having survived economic collapse and dictatorship several times over, the tango, like Buenos Aires itself, still captivates. As in the past, Buenos Aires is, in the words of the late-twentieth-century writer Juan José Saer, a city where

> incongruity is the norm. On each block, heterogeneous structures, raised, or maintained, by the economic means, the manual dexterity, the aesthetics and even the whimsy of their proprietors, coexist. A twenty-story building rises up, improbably stable, next to a modest house with a small front garden, which has been needing a paint job since the forties, and this house in turn shares a dividing wall with a two- or three-story house built at the turn of the century, judging from the niches, angels, and moldings that crowd its façade. Even in the middle of downtown, though to a lesser degree, architectural anarchy is the norm. The straightness of the streets is the only rigor that contains this vertiginous variety, as a square mold holds in an amorphous substance. And if, to be generous, the whole lacks interest, its details surprise, delight, and even dazzle at each step.[267]

Like its hometown, instead of passing away quietly, the tango lives anew. As at its birth more than a century ago, the tango now allows the disjointed differences of an immigrant metropolis awash in modernity to be fashioned into a congenial unity. The tango, like Buenos Aires itself, keeps finding new ways to convert diversity from a problem into an asset. The tango—and its birthplace, Buenos Aires, to which it is so invariably linked—reveal how the delirium caused by the collision of hostility and difference becomes neutered, sanitized, detoxified, and, eventually, converted into an advantage for everyone.

The tango today is no more Andalusian, African, Mediterranean, or even Argentine than it was when it emerged on the edge of a growing metropolis at the edge of the world. The tango is what happens when an urban culture and a metropolitan place force people who can barely stand one another to embrace. They might look ahead rather than into each other's eyes; but they blend together nonetheless. Complex and, at times, brutal, the tango is more than anything else beautiful. Its beauty is caused by the constant precariousness and delirium of life in a city where the kaleidoscope of cultural differences spins too quickly.

There's a Boat That's Leaving Soon for New York

Oh Lord
I'm on my way
I'm on my way
To a Heav'nly Land.

—Porgy, *Porgy and Bess*, 1935

New York's Alvin Theatre was only a few weeks shy of its eighth anniversary on October 10, 1935, when it hosted one of the most important performances in the history of American musical theater: the Broadway premiere of George and Ira Gershwin and DuBose Heyward's "American folk opera" *Porgy and Bess*, based on Charleston literary notable Heyward's 1925 best-selling novel *Porgy*.[1] The Alvin (now the Neil Simon Theatre), which opened at the height of Broadway's most prolific season in 1927, sits on the south side of West 52nd Street between Broadway and Eighth Avenue in the heart of New York's raucous Theater District.[2] A survivor, this landmark playhouse has, over the years, witnessed many a memorable evening since Alex Aarons and Vinton Freedley (ALex + VINton = Alvin) launched their new stage, with Fred and Adele Astaire hoofing their way through George and Ira Gershwin's *Funny Face*. Ethel Merman, Lucille Ball, and Liza Minnelli all made their Broadway debuts on its famous stage, while Cole Porter and Neil Simon opened some of their most successful productions there. But no evening has had as lasting an impact on American—and indeed world—musical theater as *Porgy and Bess's* gala premiere.

Those present knew they were witnessing history. Gershwin's

reputation and ambition suggested that his opera was possibly a work for the ages. An earlier play, *Porgy*, which Heyward and his wife Dorothy had based on the novel, had been a hit in 1927. And the opera's tryout had opened to rave reviews in Boston just days before.

Everyone who was anyone on the New York cultural and social scene wanted to be at the premiere; and many were. Major news-papers dispatched their most important drama and music critics, such as Alexander Woolcott, Brooks Atkinson, Virgil Thomson, and Olin Downes.[3] The Hollywood film actors Leslie Howard, Joan Crawford, and Katherine Hepburn joined the opera singer Lil Pons and the playwrights Elmer Rice and Ben Hecht, and the novelists Edna Ferber and J. B. Priestly, as well as the musicians Fritz Kreisler, Jascha Heifetz, Paul Whiteman, and Fred Waring. Boisterous cur-tain calls seemingly lasted for ever. And the all-night cast party, at Condé Nast's Madison Avenue penthouse, attracted the likes of William Paley, Marshall Field III, and Averell Harriman.[4]

For the past three quarters of a century, many questions have hung over everything that transpired onstage that evening: What, precisely, is *Porgy and Bess*? A musical? An opera? High-brow— or middle-brow—culture? A sympathetic and path-breaking treatment of African American life, or a racist regurgitation of demeaning stereotypes? Enthusiastic audiences aside, critics were divided about *Porgy and Bess* from the beginning, often disparaging George Gershwin as little more than an overly ambitious pop music parvenu.[5] If he had written an "opera," then why was it being staged in a music hall? Given its large scale and decidedly mixed reviews, *Porgy and Bess* unsurprisingly lost money during its 124-performance New York run. Its investors only earned back their money from the successful national tour that followed.[6]

Careers have been made as scholars, critics, musicians, poli-ticians, and social commentators have struggled to define this "American classic."[7] But questions about one undeniable dimen-sion of the *Porgy and Bess* tale were answered definitively as soon as Abby Mitchell launched into the opening notes of the show's first melody, "Summertime." No matter how one responds to the ques-tions swirling around *Porgy and Bess*, no one can deny the transcen-dental beauty of George Gershwin's score.

The opera's creators sat nervously toward the back of the or-chestra seats—that is, the ground floor seats—that first night try-ing to discern how others were reacting to their creation. George Gershwin was next to Kay Swift, the leading woman in his life, who was herself an author of musical dramas. The events and paths that brought Gershwin together with his cocreators—including his brother Ira, the Heywards, a number of Russian-trained musicians and directors, and dozens of exceptionally talented and highly skilled African American performers—constitute a prototypical tale of how twentieth-century America transformed world culture by mixing and matching previously unblended traditions into a vibrant, innovative, cohesive whole.[8] And it is a story of how one city—New York—enabled immigrants and their children to trans-form Americans' views of themselves and the world around them.

Theater is a product of collaboration among many artistic as-sociates, and this was especially true of *Porgy and Bess*.[9] The sto-ry's first creator—the sickly DuBose Heyward—inherited con-siderable social prominence and little wealth from his distin-guished Charleston family (his great-great-grandfather signed the Declaration of Independence).[10] Having decided to become a writer, Heyward tossed aside his job selling insurance so he could devote time to his new craft. And looking for a tale to tell, he picked up the *Charleston News and Courier* on his way to have breakfast one morning at his sister's place down the street from an eighteenth-century building with a courtyard, known as Cabbage Row, that was inhabited by African American workers and servants. He read a story about how a memorable crippled beggar named Samuel Smalls—who was well known for getting around town in a goat-drawn cart—had been arrested for aggravated assault after having attempted to shoot a woman named Maggie Barnes. DuBose and his wife Dorothy—an Ohio-born playwright whom he had met at New Hampshire's MacDowell Colony, a retreat for all kinds of art-ists—collaborated on writing what became one of 1925's top liter-ary hits, the novel *Porgy*. Dorothy saw *Porgy*'s theatrical potential and adapted the tale for the stage. The play *Porgy*—which was then produced by New York's prominent Theatre Guild and directed by a gifted young Armenian, Rouben Mamoulian—proved to be one of the great successes of one of Broadway's most successful seasons, in 1927–28.[11] That remarkable year witnessed an all-time high of 264 plays and musicals, including what was arguably the best traditional musical of all times, *Show Boat*.[12]

Porgy's success rested on more than a compelling, if melodramatic, story. DuBose had been fascinated since childhood by the African Americans on whom every white person in Charleston depended in any number of ways.[13] His mother, Jane, had become something of an amateur specialist on the region's distinctive Gullah language and culture, which had been handed down from generation to generation among the descendants of the slaves who were brought from West Africa to South Carolina to farm rice. The word "Gullah," which was probably derived from "Angola," refers to a form of English infused with vocabulary and grammatical structures preserved from several West African languages. African inheritances also marked the communal arrangements and religious practices of the people who spoke—and speak—Gullah. Like all Charleston children of his social station, DuBose grew up surrounded by Gullah-speaking nannies, servants, and workers.

DuBose's stories—he also wrote other African American–oriented works, such as *Jasbo Brown and Other Poems* (1924), *Mamba's Daughters* (1929), and the screenplay for Eugene O'Neill's *The Emperor Jones* (1933)—appeared at a time when most white Americans knew little or nothing about African American life and culture.[14] Although DuBose's works are dated and have long been open to charges of promoting derogatory racial and social stereotypes, they nonetheless stand out from the white writing of their era as the works of an author who was unusually knowledgeable about and sympathetic to African American culture.

The animosity of most native-born whites toward African Americans' cultural achievements during that period is difficult to grasp today, from the distance of decades, when American culture has been thoroughly infused by blends of black and white, and "high" and "low," culture. And this scorn ran deep, just as it did among Argentine elites toward their own African compatriots.

As the critic-historian Joseph Horowitz has noted, many white Americans at the time believed that African American music was "essentially white melodies appropriated by ignorant slaves."[15] The slight white interest in black music that did exist usually took the form of a white performer appropriating black music and earning money from it, rather than anything approaching true cross-racial collaboration. Significantly, prominent European observers of American music had no difficulty appreciating how any American national musical style would need to blend indigenous, European, and African traditions. As Horowitz tellingly adds, the act of immigration afforded "a clarity of understanding unencumbered by native habit and bias."[16]

The accomplished Czech composer Antonín Dvořák presciently captured this future American national musical style most succinctly when, during his time in New York in the 1890s, he declared that "Negro melodies" would create a distinctive "American school" of operas, symphonies, art songs, and chamber works.[17] Perhaps Dvořák, a butcher's son, was more open to the accomplishments of outsiders; or perhaps, as an outsider, he simply could hear what prejudiced native ears could not.[18] But in any case, what he heard and said was unwelcome, and native-born American white musicians and critics dismissed Dvořák as hopelessly naive.[19] The imposingly authoritative Boston music critic Philip Hale went so far as to call the Czech composer a "Negrophile," which is how a proper Brahmin would have mimicked the redneck "n_____ lover," and is no less repugnant even though expressed with Hale's unmatched erudition.[20]

Yet Dvořák was hardly alone in his prophetic views. Any number of the immigrant artists who transformed the twentieth century's performing arts enthusiastically collaborated with African Americans. To cite just a handful of examples, the celebrated Georgian Russian choreographer George Balanchine, who had danced with Josephine Baker in Paris, worked closely on several projects with Ethel Waters, Katherine Dunham, the Nicolas brothers, and Todd Duncan.[21] The master songwriter and son of German immigrants Jerome Kern, together with Oscar Hammerstein II, joined African American performers to tackle such taboo subjects as interracial marriage in *Show Boat*.[22] And the German-born composer Kurt Weill formed a partnership with the African American poet Langston Hughes to turn Elmer Rice's play *Street Scene* into a musical and to write the "black" musical *Lost in the Stars*.[23] And among the immigrants and children of immigrants who saw value in African American culture was a certain George, the Brooklyn-born son of poor Jewish parents from Saint Petersburg, who soaked up the sounds of his hometown as his family moved around, from Brooklyn's East New York to Manhattan's Lower East Side and Harlem.[24]

George Gershwin demonstrated his musical acumen as soon as he sat down at a newly purchased second-hand family piano for the first time at the age of twelve and immediately started playing songs. By fifteen, he was playing in bars and took jobs in Tin Pan Alley, the hub of New York's popular music industry. He connected with the legendary Irving Berlin and Jerome Kern, among many composers and lyricists, and he soon began writing tunes for Broadway shows.[25]

All the time he was engaged in these activities, George was also following the city's emerging jazz scene uptown in Harlem and scouting New York's vibrant Yiddish musical theater downtown on lower Second Avenue.[26] Early-twentieth-century Yiddish theater set standards for innovation unmatched on Broadway. And because these Yiddish works were often more accessible to highly trained Eastern European professionals than English-language theater, innovators such as the seminal stage designer Boris Aronson, the son of the grand rabbi of Kyiv, and the director Jacob Adler, an Odessa native, conducted their most protean experiments on Yiddish stages, from the upper Bronx to Lower Manhattan.[27] As a young man, Aronson—who later designed the original productions of *Fiddler on the Roof* and *Cabaret*—had been part of Kyiv's vibrant, revolutionary avant-garde theatrical scene. He studied with the legendary designer Alexandra Ekster, and he worked in Moscow in the Constructivist orbit of Vsevolod Meyerhold and Alexander Tairov, before moving to Berlin and, in 1923, to New York.[28] Gershwin thus drew on the multiple influences from these artists as he tried to define for himself what it meant to be an American musician.

Responding to a commission from Paul Whiteman for a concert piece bringing together jazz and classical forms, Gershwin wrote his now-iconic *Rhapsody in Blue* (1924), which he followed with *Concerto in F* (1925) and the concert piece *An American in Paris* (1928). These works, to cite Horowitz once more, contributed to a growing American "vibrant piano repertoire, deeply inflected by slave song, and ranging from [Louis Moreau] Gottschalk's *Banjo* and [Scott] Joplin's *Maple Leaf Rag* to the Transcendental profundities of Ives's *Concord Sonata* and the jagged urban rhythms of Aaron Copland's *Piano Variations*."[29]

Now set on writing an American opera, Gershwin began looking for a story to put to music.[30] One night, unable to fall asleep, he picked up a recent best seller, *Porgy*. The next morning, he wrote to the Heywards, initiating a creative journey that would last nearly a decade.

By the time he had completed *Porgy and Bess*, Gershwin—now the toast of Broadway and Hollywood—was a wealthy and respected man. He moved from success to success on the Broadway stage and the Hollywood screen, and he was saluted at the most famous European concert halls. Yet he was still nothing if not musically ambitious, and he cared deeply about creating a distinctive American classical tradition. It was in this context that he set out to write the "great American opera."

The term used by Gershwin in labeling his masterpiece—a "folk opera"—has deeply confused American critics. But Dvořák and other Slavic creators would have needed little explanation, as they simultaneously drew on local folk music and traditions to create distinctive national operatic traditions.

Gershwin was well aware of these connections, comparing *Porgy and Bess* to *Boris Godunov* and *Carmen* (indeed, the Gershwin opera closely tracks Bizet's *Carmen*).[31] Such comparisons made little sense to insecure Americans, who measured cultural accomplishment against what they romanticized to be Germanic and British standards. However, those who were more familiar with the national operatic traditions then emerging in Southern and Slavic Europe better appreciated the close connections between opera and folk traditions.

Unsurprisingly, *Porgy and Bess* gained recognition as a major operatic triumph throughout Europe.[32] Eventually, Americans could no longer deny the significance of this masterpiece that had been validated enthusiastically on the stages of Milan, Venice, Vienna, Berlin, Copenhagen, London, and Paris.[33] Thus, after circling the globe and being performed across the United States, George Gershwin's monumental folk opera was finally added to the repertoire of New York's exalted Metropolitan Opera in 1985, more or less simultaneously with its first performance in Charleston, and a full half century after it premiered at the Alvin Theatre.[34]

To bring their libretto and music to the stage, Gershwin; his brother, the lyricist Ira; and the Heywards enlisted dozens of tremendously talented people. George Gershwin insisted on an all–African American cast, a stipulation that has remained central to the granting of performance rights.[35] The composer's demand both made *Porgy and Bess* a launching pad over the years for prominent African American performers—ranging from William Warfield (Porgy) and Leontyne Price (Bess) to Maya Angelou (Carla) and Lorenzo Fuller Jr. (Sportin' Life)—and also kept such white performers as Al Jolson from performing the role of Porgy in blackface.[36]

Although many white critics questioned whether there were sufficient numbers of African American performers to fill out an opera cast, Gershwin had little doubt as he sought out his singers and actors. The legendary original cast featured a Howard University music professor, Todd Duncan, as Porgy; a Baltimore-born Juilliard School student, Anne Wiggins Brown, as Bess; a Mississippi-born Juilliard graduate, Ruby Elzy, as Serena; a classically trained singer, Abby Mitchell, as Clara; and a graduate of the New England Conservatory of Music, Warren Coleman, as Crown (figure 16).[37] They were joined by the veteran vaudeville star John W. Bubbles as Sportin' Life and were backed by Harlem's Eva Jessye Choir and Charleston's Jenkins Orphanage Band.[38] The presence of so many talented and highly trained African Americans came as a revelation to many critics and audience members—one that helped to transform how white Americans and Europeans viewed black American talent.

Americans born in the Russian Empire similarly played a pivotal role in bringing Gershwin's score to production.[39] Rouben Mamoulian, who had directed the Heywards' earlier play *Porgy*, grew up in a prominent Armenian theatrical family in Tiflis (today's Tbilisi). As a young man, he moved to Moscow, where he studied with the legendary Evgenii Vakhtangov at the Studio Theater of the Moscow Art Theater.[40]

Serge Sudeikin had become a prominent stage designer in Saint

Figure 16. A scene from *Porgy and Bess*, a Theater Guild production, 1935. *Source: Library of Congress.*

Petersburg before joining Serge Diaghilev and his fabled Ballets Russes in Paris. He is still remembered in Saint Petersburg for his wall paintings at the renowned futurist watering hole the Stray Dog Cabaret, where he would have spent time discussing emerging cultural fashions with such notable writers from the Silver Age of Russian/Soviet literature as Nikolai Gumilov, Mikhail Kuzmin, Vyacheslav Ivanov, Vladimir Mayakovsky, Boris Pasternak, Maria Tsvetaeva, Sergei Esenin, and Alexander Blok, as well as the dancer Tamara Karsavina.[41]

A Saint Petersburg native, Alexander Smallens, who was brought to the United States as a child, conducted the orchestra for the original 1935 production of *Porgy and Bess*, as well as those for its Broadway revivals in 1942 and 1953 and its 1952 world tour. And Gershwin studied musical composition with the Kharkov native Joseph Schlinger—and regularly sought counseling from the Kyiv-born psychiatrist Gregory Zilboorg—throughout the period when he was writing the opera.

These "Russians" who were involved in the production were connected both directly and indirectly to the artistic explosion of early-twentieth-century Moscow and Saint Petersburg, which turned so much of the creative world on its head as the century's decades passed. Their influence on Gershwin's folk opera, though often subtle, proved to be notable.

Igor Stravinsky reported that he conversed with Gershwin in Russian from time to time, adding that George had picked up the language growing up in his Yiddish-, English-, and Russian-speaking household.[42] And Gershwin regularly spent time with a number of other Russians, including the composer Sergei Rachmaninoff and the violinist Jascha Heifetz.

All were familiar with the Russian tradition of opera-*skazka* (folk tales), which had been initiated by Catherine II, who wrote four librettos herself.[43] The genre reached maturity with the great Russian operas of the nineteenth century, which were written by such composers as Mikhail Gilnka, the members of the "Balakirev Circle"—Mily Balakirev, César Cui, Modest Mussorgsky, Nikolai Rimsky-Korsakov, and Alexander Borodin—and their students, including Alexander Glazunov, Igor Stravinsky, and Sergei Prokofiev.[44] Collectively, they defined a vibrant operatic tradition that combined orchestral music and folk traditions.

For Gershwin, the notion of an "American folk opera" had precise meaning, even if his American critics couldn't grasp the concept. It represented the fusion of European and American traditions that immigrants trying to find their way in a new country would understand far better than pretentious native-born cultural gatekeepers.

Together, these artists brought American musical theater closer to the Russian concept of "total theater," which is not surprising, given how many gifted immigrants working on the New York stage during the first half of the twentieth century had worked or trained with Moscow theater giants, such as Vakhtangov (Mamoulian, the producer), Konstantin Stanislavsky (Michael Chekhov, an actor; and Joshua Logan, the director), Vladimir Nemirovich-Danchenko (Alla Nazimova, an actress), and Aleksandr Tairov (Boris Aronson, the designer).[45] Stanislavsky's influence solidified when the master himself visited Gotham with a troupe of Moscow Art Theater actors in 1923 and again in 1924.[46]

For all their crucial importance in the development of truly inclusive American performing art, *Porgy* the play and *Porgy and Bess* the opera were hardly the only successful collaborations among African Americans and Russians on the New York stage. For instance, the seminal 1940 Broadway production *Cabin in the Sky* brought the towering Russian-born trio of the composer Vernon Duke (Vladimir Dukelsky), the designer Boris Aronson, and the choreographer George Balanchine together with the Richmond-reared lyricist John Latouche and a stellar African American cast featuring Ethel Waters, Todd Duncan, and Katherine Dunham, under Balanchine's direction. The actors were bemused and confused by the constant bickering in Russian between Duke, Aronson, and Balanchine—who, it seemed, could not make it through a rehearsal without arguing "a half dozen times." *Cabin in the Sky*, which told the story of the Lawd's and Lucifer's agents fighting over the soul of a Southern scamp, drew heavily on African American folklore. Its modest Broadway success—its run lasted 156 performances—led to its successful national tour and its even more notable film version, which was directed by Vincente Minnelli.[47]

The Russian influence on American theater is not unique. Joseph Urban, for example, achieved noteworthiness as an architect and designer in imperial Vienna before arriving in Boston in 1911 to work for the Boston Opera.[48] Then he moved to New York once his Boston commissions had run their course. His stage work, which introduced new aesthetic textures and lighting effects into New World stage productions, included sets for Ziegfeld's famous showgirls, the epic musical *Show Boat*, and fifty productions at the Metropolitan Opera—as well as sleekly erudite art deco architectural designs infused with Viennese elegance and sophistication.

The Gershwins, the Heywards, and the other creators of *Porgy and Bess*—together with the Aronsons, the Urbans, the Nazimovas, and their creative partners—worked in New York during the Golden Age of the Broadway musical theater, a period that arguably began with the settlement of the 1919 Actors' Equity strike formalizing labor relations on the Great White Way.[49] This era continued until the curtain came down in 1963 on Oscar Hammerstein II and Richard Rodgers' final production, *The Sound of Music*.

Yet this "age" was in no way seamless. Broadway defined American entertainment during the Roaring Twenties, but following the 1929 stock market crash, the key Broadway contributors headed west to Hollywood, where they shaped the launching of "talking" movies.[50] New York stages never again mounted as many productions as they did during the 1927–28 season. For some time, actors, producers, directors, writers, and designers shuttled back and forth between the two American coasts, but eventually the new sound film industry produced its own artistic leaders.

Another outburst of creativity elevated Broadway to new artistic heights throughout the decade and a half following World War II, aided by the newborn television industry, which provided New York–based entertainers with much-appreciated supplemental income.[51] However, by the time Oscar Hammerstein II died in 1960, New York was on its way to becoming a poster child for urban decline. Although New York's flagship cultural invention—the Broadway musical—would be transformed and rejuvenated by new economic, social, and technological realities, the city's stages never again achieved quite the same pride of place in American culture.

For nearly a half century, the New York stage defined American culture. Significantly, many of the New Yorkers creating this culture were born abroad, or were the children of immigrant parents. The fact that so many among those who created *Porgy and Bess* could trace their roots back to the Russian Empire is unexceptional. Some 1,500 musicians emigrated from war-and-revolution-torn Europe between 1933 and 1944, and many settled in New York.[52] Broadway was full of ambitious immigrants.[53]

Why? Perhaps these immigrants were more observant of the American reality that they sought to enter, and perhaps they drew on their previous connections and traditions in their homelands to provide the cultural and social capital they needed to make their way in the New World. Perhaps, as in Argentina, these outsiders were less shaped by the myths of local elites. Or perhaps an entertainment business dominated by immigrants was more open to outsiders than other realms of American life, such as finance, business, and the law. Most critically, perhaps these immigrants' new hometown—arguably, the most successful immigrant city the world has ever known—created plentiful opportunities for them to shine.

New Amsterdam

The city that became New York was born as an afterthought embedded in an obsessive drive to colonize the world. European sailors dispatched by various monarchs to beat other rulers to Asia had found themselves bumping up against various corners of the Americas ever since Columbus sailed in 1492 (earlier arrivals—such as probable Viking incursions in North America—predate the Age of Discovery). In the 1520s, Giovanni da Verrazzano, an Italian explorer in the service of the French crown, and Esteban Gomez, a Portuguese captain commissioned by Charles I of Spain, both visited the estuary that would become New York Harbor. But it wasn't until September 3, 1609, that the Europeans came to stay, when Henry Hudson, a British sea captain looking for a western route to Asia for the Dutch East India Company, sailed into the estuary and, eventually, up what is now the Hudson River almost as far as today's state capital of Albany.

Early Dutch visitors recorded a fecund landscape overflowing with bounty, including whales, seals, porpoises, gigantic oysters, a variety of lobsters, woods and marshlands full of bears, wolves, foxes, raccoons, otters, beavers, quail, partridge, turkeys, swans, and geese.[54] Not surprisingly, humans had found the area a congenial place to live for several millennia, with a number of Native American nations—primarily the Lenape—thriving when Hudson first cast his anchor off what seems to have been known as Mannahata, for "hilly island."[55]

Most of the peoples who greeted Hudson spoke Munsee, a dialect of the Delaware language, and called themselves simply "men" or "people." They identified themselves as members of autonomous groups of between a dozen and several hundred people, based largely on kinship. They moved seasonally along trails running throughout the region, from campsite to campsite, in impermanent settlements that conformed to no European notion of village or town.[56] Living on the move in a world of supernatural abundance, the Lenape had not seen a need to develop notions of private "ownership" of land and hierarchies of domination and exploitation. They did, however, order gender roles in ways that were familiar to the newly arriving Europeans, with the women taking care of cooking, childrearing, and agricultural work while the men hunted and fished. They lived in a world of networks dominated by custom yet subject to constant negotiation. Given this idyllic context, it didn't take long for Hudson's clumsy and acquisitive crew to encounter hostility, ranging from rampant theft to fusillades of arrows.[57]

Yet a more immediate menace for the Lenape was closer at hand. Slightly more than a quarter century before Hudson would arrive, the grasping and considerably less pastoral Native American nations living to the north of the Lenape had formed a new alliance under the leadership of an Iroquois-speaking Huron tribe prophet, Denganawidah. They had done so partly in response to pushy French colonists, who were claiming the Saint Lawrence River Valley as their own. The consequent Iroquois League—uniting the Mohawk, Oneida, Onondaga, Cayuga, and Seneca nations—encompassed well-defended, semipermanent, stockade-like villages stretching from the Hudson River to Niagara Falls.[58]

Though they were fecund, the Lenape lands held little exploratory promise for Hudson and his employers back in Amsterdam. The river did not lead to Asia, the harbor was far removed from larger territorial prizes in the Caribbean and Brazil, and there was no gold. There was, however, the promise of great wealth from the fur pelts to be claimed from the area's robust animal life. As the French had discerned in earlier decades, European demand for fur was limitless. By trading modest supplies—such as blankets, knives, combs, and eventually guns and alcohol—for beaver and other pelts, French traders had been able to undermine the lucrative monopoly of Baltic merchants peddling Siberian skins.[59]

Beyond whatever lurked on the American shores, the Dutch were engaged in a fierce global battle for independence from Spain, which coincided with a merciless war between Protestants and Catholics across Europe.[60] By 1614, Amsterdam's merchants had created the precursor of the Dutch West India Company (Geotroyeerde Westindische Compagnie) to control trade with West Africa and the Americas—in parallel with the Dutch monopoly for trade east of the Cape of Good Hope, the United East India Company (Vereenigde Oost-Indische Compagnie), which had been established in 1602. Together, in what are today Indonesia and Brazil, these early multinational corporations protected Dutch commerce with fortified outposts that supported lucrative business operations. Both companies were charged with making money and making war by harassing Spanish outposts around the world.[61]

Two essential elements in this foundational tale of New York have continued to be central throughout the city's existence: This urban enterprise is predicated, first and foremost, on commerce; and to succeed, it must draw participants of unknowable diversity from wherever they can be lured. From the beginning, the settlement on Manhattan incorporated an ease with diversity, a way for people to tolerate one another based on necessity as much as on any idealized notion of equality and justice.[62] This city has always been a place of pragmatic pluralism rooted in its capacity to derive benefit from contacts among individuals or groups that otherwise consider each other personally loathsome—a product of a diverse urban environment that tosses those in competition with one another into relationships dependent on cooperation as much as rivalry.[63]

As the New York historians Edwin Burrows and Mike Wallace explain, "New York would not become a warrior city, living by raids on its hinterland. Even when, centuries later, it emerged as an imperial center, it was never a military stronghold. . . . Nor would New York become an urban theocracy, a citadel of priests. . . . Nor would New York become a great government hub. . . . New York would become a city of deal makers, a city of commerce, a City of Capital."[64] Thus, it became a city whose founding myth rests on the Dutch buying Manhattan from the Native Americans for beads worth $24—that is, the supposed purchase with seemingly useless trinkets of an indeterminate amount of real estate from residents with no notion that land could be bought or sold (Burrows and Wallace calculate the value in late-twentieth-century dollars as $669.42, rather than the more famous nineteenth-century calculation of $24).[65] And the city's history of dubious commercial practices extends from this opening moment straight through to the trickeries leading to the financial crises of 2008.

Coming from a tiny country with limited resources, New Amsterdam's merchants became adept at using whatever was at hand to turn a profit, including labor recruited without regard for religion, nation, race, or language. Their tolerance was one of pragmatism rather than conviction; and, to turn a profit, they were as willing as other Europeans to trade in human lives—witness the essential role of slavery in New Amsterdam's economy from the very beginning (figure 17).

Figure 17. Slaves appearing in court in New York, defending themselves against charges of committing arson in a 1741 slave uprising. Although there was no hard evidence, eleven slaves were burned and eighteen were hanged.
Source: Library of Congress.

Amsterdam was Europe's most tolerant and diverse city at the time the Dutch laid claim to Manhattan. Again, quoting Burrows and Wallace, "religious outcasts of every denomination--Walloons (French-speaking Protestants from what is now Belgium), Huguenots (French Protestants, many of whom joined Walloon churches), Baptists, Quakers, Sephardic Jews, and a party of English Calvinists (known to their day as Separatists and to ours as Pilgrims)—all were drawn by the city's tolerance for diversity and dissent."[66]

The West India Company's new settlement took shape as Corneliis May and Willliem Verhulst steered several company ships across the North Atlantic between 1623 and 1625. Their arrival quickly precipitated the naming in 1626 of a forceful new director, in the person of Peter Minuit, for the company's North American operations, following several bookkeeping irregularities (another persistent theme in New York history).[67]

The city they established "had a good claim to being the motliest assortment of souls in Christendom. Probably only a narrow majority of the heavily male European population was Dutch.... The rest were Walloons, English, French, Irish, Swedish, Danish, and German, among others," plus at least one Muslim mulatto of mixed Dutch and Moroccan ancestry, a Catholic or two, and, soon, Jewish residents. The West India Company imported African slaves starting in the settlement's earliest days.[68]

The same global forces that determined the fates of Naples and Buenos Aires—and, as will become apparent in chapters to come, Cape Town—were at work in New York. Consequently, the Dutch commitment to their North American colony was never strong, and weakened considerably as the Netherlands began to lose advantage in the era's wars. Eventually, the Dutch would be driven from Brazil and would see their access to the Atlantic circumscribed by expanding British naval power. Their interests, attentions, and investments began shifting to more lucrative imperial adventures in what is today Indonesia. And their sporadic, bloody engagements with Native Americans—who were facing unfamiliar diseases and rapacious colonists—made continued investment in New Amsterdam increasingly uncertain.[69]

Two decades after the uneasy start of the West India Company's colony, the company's directors dispatched a tough-minded, grizzled veteran of previous imperial adventures, Peter Stuyvesant, to replace the colony's director-general, Willem Kieft, and to bring order from growing unruliness and obstreperousness.[70] The peg-legged Stuyvesant—who had lost part of his right leg during a failed invasion of the Spanish-held Caribbean island of Saint Martin launched from Curaçao—would serve as the colony's severe director-general until British warships sailed into the Upper Bay in September 1664.

After the fall, Stuyvesant returned to Amsterdam briefly to report to the West India Company's officers about his tenure overseeing their lost colony before removing to his Manhattan farm, the Great Bouwerie, north of which then constituted the city on the island's lower tip. He remained in New York until his death in 1672. The last known descendent living on Manhattan to share his surname died nearly three hundred years later, in 1953.

When Stuyvesant hobbled down the gangplank onto Manhattan's shore for the first time in August 1647, he found a settlement in disarray. Makeshift huts huddled around muddy paths, along which an unsavory combination of inebriated humans and unkempt farm animals competed for the right of way. What appeared on paper as a fort had fallen in disrepair. The town was overrun with several hundred refugees from nearby rural areas, who had fled their farmsteads following continuous attacks by angry Native Americans. The willful governor set out to convert this "New" Amsterdam into "the kind of community that would appeal to the Dutch taste for well-regulated urban life."[71] He would largely succeed through authoritarian means, which, from time to time, provoked partially successful demands for greater autonomy and citizenship (though the settlement always remained a "company town").[72]

Burrows and Wallace captured Stuyvesant's achievement in an attempt to describe what the seventeenth-century imperial outpost must have been like. They write:

By the mid-1650s, New Netherland's population had claimed to perhaps thirty-five hundred men, women and children; a decade later, to nine thousand. Of that number some fifteen hundred lived in New Amsterdam alone, roughly three times as many as Stuyvesant found fifteen years earlier. Only one-fourth of the town's three hundred adult white males could claim to have lived there longer than he had. The newcomers were as diverse as ever, too: half of them hailed from Germany, England, France, and the Scandinavian countries. By the mid-1660s, indeed, only 40 percent of New Netherland's population was actually Dutch, while 19 percent was German and 15 percent was English. But these weren't the same kind of people who had been drawn to the colony during its first twenty or thirty years. Seventy percent came over in family groups, many of them couples in their early twenties with small children. Only one in four was a single male, and for the first time a small but significant proportion, about 6 percent, were single women. Better than half were farmers or skilled craftsmen (a few fishermen showed up as well). Only one in eight was a laborer or servant. The rest were soldiers. Travelers disembarking at the new East River pier in these years would have found themselves near the heart of a bustling, cosmopolitan little seaport.[73]

Stuyvesant's lively and colorful port nurtured an embryonic social structure dominated by a mercantile elite that was "unmistakably Dutch in taste, manner and outlook," followed in order of status by white working people—including craftsmen, innkeepers, surgeons, and the like—a shifting white laboring class, farmhands, indentured servants, and African slaves.[74] This robust community looked outward to the sea rather than inward to the prosperous countryside.

The colony's ribald social life and entertainment preferences centered on the tavern and the home hearth. The Dutch penchant for public kissing, gambling and gaming, lewd talk, and a hearty embrace of drunkenness and inebriation frequently scandalized other Europeans.[75] And in New Amsterdam, the Dutch colonists exhibited even fewer inhibitions than at home in the Netherlands. New Amsterdam's residents—to the condemnation of governor-generals Kieft and Stuyvesant and various pastors of the official Dutch

Reformed Church—enjoyed all number of public amusements and festivals (including the Feast of Saint Nicholas, Saint Valentine's Day, and Pinkster, or Shrove, Tuesday).[76] Such Rabelaisian folk celebrations remained fundamentally domestic, celebrated at home or at the tavern.

Righteous defenders of virtue—whether from the Church or the West India Company—exerted little control over how the people in the crowd chose to enjoy their private moments. They could, however, prevent more organized manifestations of the Devil's work—such as theater. From beginning to end, "popular culture in New Amsterdam centered on the town's always numerous taverns, grogshops and pothouses, where noisy, pipe-smoking crowds of men and women drank, gambled, and played games like backgammon, hardball, and bowling."[77] Music and performances of all kinds were ubiquitous, only not on the stage.[78]

Almost from the beginning, the Dutch claim to their corner of North America was challenged by energetic and industrious British colonists in New England who were on the prowl for new lands to cultivate.[79] The inevitable transpired when, in the late 1660s, Charles II restored the British monarchy following the death of Oliver Cromwell and set out on a campaign of ambitious acquisition both at home and abroad. Capturing the tenor of the new times, Connecticut governor John Winthrop Jr. launched an effort to grab previously Dutch-held lands on Long Island and in Westchester County.

In March 1664, James, the duke of York—the king's younger brother—was awarded proprietorship of all territory between the Delaware River and Connecticut River. By September, British ships and soldiers under the command of Colonel Richard Nicolls arrived to take possession of these Dutch lands for the British. Recognizing that he had few resources with which to fight, the pugnacious Stuyvesant reluctantly accepted reality, and New Amsterdam became New York.[80]

The orderly transfer of power left much in place. New York would be a fundamentally commercial city and thriving seaport, supported by the labors of a hugely diverse population drawn from the four corners of Europe and Africa. Unlike on the Continent, however, religious and ethnic tolerance was the accepted norm for daily intercourse. The island village had become, in the words of the historian Russell Shorto, "the first multiethnic, upwardly mobile society on America's shores, a prototype of the kind of society that would be duplicated throughout the country and around the world."[81]

Dutch cultural tastes, social etiquette, and familial ties continued to thrive in New York for decades, contributing to expanding demands for citizenship rights for all white colonists. Simultaneously, a lively slave trade and expanding commercial connections with an increasingly British-controlled Caribbean brought wealth to New York's shippers and merchants while these activities were entrenching the economic and social subordination of Africans and their descendants.

British New York

The British ruled New York as a colony from 1664 to 1783 (except for a few months in the 1670s, when the Dutch briefly returned).[82] New York's period as a British colony gets short shrift in history books. A period of 119 years nonetheless represents sufficient time for a city to develop a distinctive identity.

Multiple explanations justify these lacunae in the recording of the city's history. The transition from Dutch to British rule was largely seamless, as well-off Dutch New Yorkers pragmatically leveraged opportunities to demonstrate their acceptance of British rule into new business opportunities. Furthermore, Americans generally think of their history as beginning with the Declaration of Independence. In the case of New York, such common tendencies become amplified by the fact that British troops occupied the city throughout the Revolution and an embarrassing number of pro-British Tory Loyalists called the city home. Moreover, aside from the British governor, Edward Hyde, the third earl of Clarendon—who dressed in women's clothing and took munificent bribes—British New York had few of the Dutch city's colorful characters (e.g., a peg-legged misanthropic governor, grog-house-fueled debauchery, and Saint Nicholas, who visited the frontier village every December as per Dutch custom). British control nonetheless proved to be a foundational era for the city that New York would become.

By 1776, New York had grown from a large village with a handful of a hundred residents into a considerable town of 25,000, making the city second in population only to Philadelphia—which had a population of 40,000—among the cities of the thirteen British colonies to declare themselves independent. Inhabitants became increasingly segmented by ethnicity, race, confession, and social class. A wealthy merchant class gathered ever larger shares of the colony's wealth under the king's rule, entrenching market-generated economic inequality as another among New York's signature characteristics.[83]

Greater wealth was a product of the city's insertion into the rapid, trade-driven growth that was enriching all the British domains at that time. By the early years of the eighteenth century, the city's merchants had insinuated themselves into the center of the British Empire's lucrative sugar and slave trade between the Caribbean and the home British Isles across the Atlantic.[84] The British consumption of sugar doubled at this time, and the satisfying of voracious sweet teeth had become implanted into the daily rituals of British life by the 1730s. Consequently, earnings rose and production increased.[85]

By midcentury, sugar had become the single most valuable product in British overseas trade, making West Indian planters far wealthier as a group than their counterparts cultivating tobacco and rice on the mainland. New York's port was perfectly situated to facilitate trade across the North Atlantic and down to the Caribbean, sending necessary products (including flour, pork, beef, turpentine, and lumber) south in exchange for sugar, molasses, and related products to be transshipped back to the Mother Country. Most important, New Yorkers developed and controlled the financial tools (e.g., bills of exchange, bills of credit, and warehouse certificates) that were necessary for trade to thrive. New York's merchants, bankers, wholesalers, shippers, and warehouse proprietors established their town as an indispensable financial center for the British Empire's most lucrative trading commodity.

Sugar—and the deepening relationships with Caribbean plantation owners—naturally extended to another highly lucrative commodity: human chattel.[86] Sugar production depended on African slave labor, with the same trade routes taking sugar eastward that were bringing African slaves westward. Africans—both free and enslaved—had been living in the city from the earliest Dutch times. Nonetheless, slavery remained of limited economic significance for the city before the burgeoning sugar trade of the early eighteenth century.

As the slave trade grew, the gluttonous demand of West Indies plantation owners for labor tied New York merchants ever more tightly to the Caribbean slave economy; and as it did, it enticed more and more New Yorkers to also rely on slaves at home.[87] In 1712, approximately 15 percent of the city's inhabitants were black, and 40 percent of all households owned a slave. By 1746, 21 percent of all New Yorkers were of African heritage; and New York had the highest concentration of slaves north of Virginia.[88]

New York's slaves worked as domestics, dock crew members, coopers, butchers, carpenters, and blacksmiths, as well as field hands on agricultural Long Island and in the Hudson River Valley. The slave trade and business relations with the slaveholding Caribbean and mainland Southern colonies embedded questions of race into the city's psyche. New York would become one of the last Northern states to abolish slavery, to embrace combat against the South in the Civil War, and to accept racial propinquity.

As was the case in Buenos Aires, deep racist attitudes persisted among old New York families well into the nineteenth century. These attitudes often caused the standard bearers of high culture to denigrate the achievements of African American artists, musicians, and performers. Such attitudes in the cultural realm would prove to be more pernicious than the more visible economic animosities prompted by labor market competition between African Americans and immigrants. At the dawn of the twentieth century, as New York claimed cultural preeminence throughout the Western Hemisphere, immigrants entering the arts would prove far more receptive to African American cultural achievements than well-born white Anglo-Saxon Protestant wardens of taste.

British New York became a trading center and port rather than a producer of goods of its own. Commerce experienced a growth spurt as the British wars with France spread to North America—and as British colonial armies engaged in battles with Native Americans and colonial armies in French Quebec. These struggles were central to Britain's domestic economy, because North American markets had come to account for half of all British commercial shipping at the time, including half of all British manufactures other than woolens.[89]

Reinforced by the Navigation Acts prohibiting direct imports from other European colonies, British-controlled ports such as New York thrived. With easy credit increasingly available—offered first and foremost by New York's financial managers and bankers—ships returning to British ports carried American agricultural products across the Atlantic. And New York was better situated than its rivals Boston and Philadelphia, because it linked its upstate hinterland with Caribbean plantations and British towns. The colonial city thrived as a commercial and trading center while producing little of value on its own.

Trade and finance required an advanced education; and the arrival of potential disease with each ship pulling into port demanded a growing health establishment. Thus British New York moved well along the path toward rivaling Boston and Philadelphia as a major educational and medical center. King's College (chartered by King George II, and now Columbia University) and New York Hospital (chartered by King George III) found their way to the top of the emerging North American education system, with footprints that reached deep into the Caribbean colonies. To cite but one example, young Alexander Hamilton—a native of the British-controlled island Nevis—first came to New York to attend King's College.[90]

With money to burn and the latest in British high fashion arriving at the water's edge, Colonial New York began to test Philadelphia as the continent's leading center for high fashion, high design, and high culture.[91] Although its Pennsylvania rival retained preeminence until the early days of the Republic, prerevolutionary New York was fast becoming the nascent metropolis it would grow to be in the nineteenth century.

If the Dutch had entertained themselves around the hearth at home and at the tavern, the British had wider cultural ambitions. Elizabethan London had arguably become the world's most important theater center a decade or two before Henry Hudson had sailed into the river that would one day bear his name. By the time the British arrived in New York, their capital was integrated into a pan-European music circuit, once dominated by Naples, that was producing what we now know as European "Classical" music.

Genteel Englishmen and Englishwomen came to their new colonies, bringing their cultural tastes with them. As early as 1716, the merchant William Levingston built perhaps the earliest theaters in the original thirteen British colonies in Williamsburg, Virginia.[92] Professional troupes had an easier time making a living in the South because they did not face the opposition of Puritan preachers, who condemned performances as the Devil's work.

The 1752 arrival of the Covent Garden impresario Lewis Hallam and his company on American shores proved to have lasting significance. He had formerly been the head of London's Company of Comedians, and now he, his wife, and their children—who were also in the company—landed with a troupe of ten adult performers to seek success in the New World. Their appearance in Williamsburg, Virginia, marks the beginning of professional theater in what would become the United States.[93]

Hallam brought to the Colonies the British system of theatrical companies created by actor-managers who assembled performers familiar with a repertory combining current and classic productions. They traveled together, jointly held shares in the company, and were remunerated according to their ownership. Hallam's company established several customary aspects of American theatrical life that would last into the nineteenth century: Companies were controlled by managers/producers/directors; theatrical performances featured stock companies that offered well-known repertoires of dramatic and comedic works; and financial success depended as much or more on touring as on remaining in one town or at a single stage.[94]

By the 1750s and 1760s—with the New York Harmonic Society sponsoring recitals, concerts, and fancy dress balls to celebrate the king's birthday—theater found an enthusiastic audience in Manhattan.[95] Nassau Street's New Theater, which opened in the 1730s, offered a stage for a number of itinerant companies. Touring British actors brought the latest hits—such as *The Recruiting Officer, The Beggar's Opera, Beau in the Suds,* and *The Intriguing Chambermaid*— direct from the London stage to New York audiences.

In 1753, Hallam conveyed his London Company of Comedians to a refurbished and expanded New Theater. Others followed. David Douglas, manager of the London Company, built a playhouse on the corner of Nassau and Chapel (now Beekman) streets in 1758.[96] Denizens of the cheaper upper galleries talked, sang, fought, and hurled eggs at well-dressed patrons below—prompting Douglas to add partitions to protect his wealthier audience members.[97]

Douglas continued to Philadelphia—then the continent's preeminent cultural center—where he opened the Southwark Theatre, widely regarded as the first permanent theater in the United States. Meanwhile, Hallam had died on tour in Jamaica in 1754.[98] His widow married Douglas, with Hallam's son, Lewis Jr., joining his stepfather's company as an actor. In December 1767, the younger Hallam returned to New York and opened the city's first permanent stage—the John Street Theatre. The only purpose-built theater in New York at the time, John Street hosted the first American and New York performances of numerous Shakespeare plays as well as contemporary American drama. In 1769, Lewis Jr. became the first white actor to perform an African American–styled song in "blackface" when he sang "Dear Heart! What a Terrible Life I Am Led" at the John Street Theatre."[99]

Douglas emerged over these years as the Colonies' leading producer—opening theaters in Philadelphia, Charleston, and Providence, as well as in New York—and continued to enjoy success until the Continental Congress closed his theaters in 1774. Mourning the death of his wife in Philadelphia the year before, Douglas decamped for Jamaica, where he continued to stockpile sufficient wealth to be described as a "gentleman" at the time of his death in 1789.[100]

New York remained a hotbed of Loyalism as revolt became increasingly likely.[101] Some prominent New Yorkers—such as the scions of the Livingston family, Gouverneur Morris, John Jay, Aaron Burr, and Alexander Hamilton—became Patriots from the earliest days of the American movement for independence. They nonetheless faced fierce opposition as they tried to rally the state behind the rebellion.

The revolutionary movement gained momentum in the city—as elsewhere across the thirteen British colonies—following the first and second Continental Congresses, with the New York delegation to the Second Congress supporting and signing the Declaration of Independence. The mood on the street turned toward the Patriots.

A New York mob tore down the statue of George III on Bowling Green as word of the declaration reached the banks of the Hudson.[102]

A British fleet under the command of General William Howe arrived in New York during the summer of 1776 to take command of the city and the harbor. Fierce fighting broke out between armies under the command of Howe and George Washington, with the American forces losing major battles in Brooklyn, Harlem, and White Plains.[103] Washington miraculously saved his army by stealthily abandoning his positions, first in Brooklyn and then in Manhattan, so they could fight another day. With the Patriot armies on the run, Howe established military rule that would continue throughout the war.

The city—"the Gibraltar of North America"—filled up with Loyalists fleeing the fighting elsewhere. The Tory flood tripled the city's population in just a few months. With the conflict largely confined to no-man's zones in Westchester and New Jersey, British-occupied New York became ever wealthier. The city's African American population grew as runaway slaves and freedmen fled Patriot-held territory in response to British promises of protection.[104] New York became a major staging ground for the British war effort, a refuge for Tory Loyalists, and the site of harsh British prisons (including infamous prison ships docked along the Brooklyn shore, on which 11,500 American prisoners of war perished).

Following Washington's final victory at Yorktown, British occupation forces and their Loyalist camp followers departed on what became known as Evacuation Day, November 25, 1783. New Yorkers returned to find a city that, following "seven years of enemy occupation and two calamitous fires, had been reduced to a shambles."[105] Major landmarks, including Trinity Church, had been destroyed; and private residences were all too often unfit for habitation. Hospitals and barracks and stables were in desperate need of repair, trees had been stripped bare and used for redoubts and fortifications, garbage was strewn everywhere, wharves were crumbling, and lucrative Caribbean markets had been lost.[106] Radical state legislators set about dismantling powerful British institutions—such as King's College, which was renamed Columbia; and the official Anglican Church, beginning by taking over wealthy Trinity Church on Broadway in Lower Manhattan.[107]

Some saw opportunity where many saw despair. The city filled with thousands of refugees (both those returning to pick up their lives and newcomers driven from a devastated countryside). Many new New Yorkers became economic and intellectual leaders.[108] The first New York packet ship—searching for markets to replace those lost in the British Caribbean—left for China in February 1784, returning fifteen months later with a 30 percent profit on the original investment.[109] The city's financial acumen and commercial genius quickly found fresh outlets for profit seeking.

New York's cultural revival had to wait, as a Common Council fearful of moral laxity refused a license for Lewis Hallam Jr.'s long-exiled Old American Company.[110] Moral approbation for public entertainment would not last long. New York became the last capital of the new United States under the Articles of Confederation in 1785, and the first capital under the Constitution four years later. George Washington was inaugurated as first president of the United States in Wall Street's Federal Hall on April 30, 1789, launching the new American republic (figure 18).[111]

A renewed demand for entertainment arrived with these capital functions. With only 150 actors and actresses throughout the country—all trained in British performance styles and speaking with English accents—up-and-coming New York became a city of opportunity for performers.[112] Hallam Jr. returned to the city at this time to relaunch the John Street Theater with a performance of Royall Tyler's *The Contrast*, a sentimental comedy set in the postwar city.[113]

By the time Congress and the executive branch had relocated to another temporary home in Philadelphia in 1790—and later to their permanent capital, in the new city of Washington, ten years later—New York had recovered from the ravages of war. The 1790 census revealed that New York had surpassed Philadelphia as the country's largest city. Two years later, local auctioneers, dealers, and brokers gathered under a favorite Buttonwood tree on Wall Street to establish the New York Stock Exchange; and the wars following the French Revolution unleashed yet another wave of political refugees from the Continent. [114] As the eighteenth century turned into the nineteenth, New York stood as the primary contender for Philadelphia's claim to be the American capital of capital and culture.

Figure 18. George Washington taking the oath of office as first president of the United States in Wall Street's Federal Hall on April 30, 1789.
Source: Library of Congress.

"The London of the New World"

During the seven decades between George Washington's inauguration and the start of the American Civil War, New York became, in the words of *The Times* of London, the "London of the New World" — the "empire city" of the Americas.[115] When the capital left New York for Philadelphia and, eventually, Washington, New York arguably was still second fiddle to William Penn's City of Brotherly Love. But by 1800, New York had emerged as the dominant city in the United States and, during the next half century, it perhaps became the most important city in the Western Hemisphere.

The city succeeded as a consequence of the strategic vision of local elites and an effective public–private partnership enabling leaders to respond to myriad threats to their entrepreneurial daring. New York's firms failed more often than their counterparts in Boston; its financial institutions had yet to gain hegemony over their rivals in Philadelphia; and its political power was nothing more than local in comparison with the national struggles in Washington. But New York's collective ambition and curiosity remained unmatched — and it was the city's ability to mobilize a vast array of resources around gigantic infrastructural projects that lifted the city above potential competitors.[116] The success of the Erie Canal, which opened in 1825, offers but one especially prominent example of the New York Way.

In the decades following independence, thousands of Americans rushed over the Appalachians to claim patches of some of the most fertile agricultural land on the planet, in what is now known as the American Midwest. With the opening of the Mississippi Valley to secure American settlement following the War of 1812, New Orleans seemed poised to emerge as the continent's singularly important port. Boston was further from the action than other major East Coast cities; Philadelphia assertively sought pathways west over the mountains. Baltimore, the closest of the East Coast ports to the action in the Midwest, started building the first railroad on the continent, the Baltimore & Ohio. New York's shippers and merchants already had cornered the sugar and cotton trade between the American South and Britain; but they could only combine the wheat trade with the Midwest by finding an inexpensive way of shipping goods from the Great Lakes to the Atlantic.[117]

New Yorkers were preoccupied with seeking a solution, especially as increasing Abolitionist sentiment threatened the once-lucrative slave trade (there were as many as 2,500 slaves in New York in 1800).[118] New markets needed to be found—or created. Geography and geology offered a partial solution. Up the Hudson River at Albany, where the Mohawk River feeds in from the west, lies a more-or-less level pathway west to the Great Lakes. All that the city needed to do was to build a 363-mile-long canal that would be 4 feet deep and 40 feet wide from Albany to Lake Erie. In addition to digging the ditch, engineers and workers eventually would add sixty-three stone locks and eighteen aqueducts.[119] With President Madison refusing to invest federal funding in the project, a consortium of promoters led by Gouverneur Morris convinced the New York State authorities to invest and build the canal on their own.

On November 4, 1825, New York governor DeWitt Clinton poured two casks of Lake Erie water into New York Harbor from the first flat barge to make the trip from Buffalo east through the canal and south on the Hudson, touching off a wild celebration. Within a year, shipping costs plummeted from $100 a ton to under $9. Forty-two barges were moving through Utica each day, carrying 221,000 barrels of flour, 435,000 gallons of whiskey, 562,000 bushels of wheat, and thousands of passengers.[120] No other city could compete, not even New Orleans, where the entire Midwestern river system emptied into the sea.

The Erie Canal secured New York's position as the continent's leading harbor for at least half a century, until the railroads came to dominate continental shipping.[121] When the railroads arrived, New York merchants, led by the tug boat tsar Commodore Vanderbilt, ensured that they would control the action yet again. Peter Cooper built his first steam engine for the road starting from Baltimore using New York's iron foundries; the finance that secured the necessary investment, and the insurance that guaranteed the railroad could run, were both Manhattan based.[122] Chicago became the nation's rail hub following the American Civil War, on the shoulders of New York's finance and control.[123]

New York–based capital investment—which created the foundation for hemispheric financial dominance—did not stop with any singular achievement. In 1811, a group of commissioners appointed by the city authorities laid out a grid plan covering all of as-yet-undeveloped Manhattan in a pattern that commodified real estate as no one had ever done before.[124] America's first suburb took shape on the heights of Brooklyn, tied to the offices in Manhattan by the first steam ferries in the country launched by Robert Fulton. Industrial suburbs grew up across the Hudson in New Jersey.[125] City and state authorities brought clean water into town via the Croton Aqueduct and related systems. Local shippers began the first regularly scheduled sailings to Liverpool with the Black Ball Line in 1818; and they simultaneously expanded the China trade.[126]

New York entrepreneurs looked to South America once the British had closed off their Caribbean colonies to American trade.[127] New York managed to secure a 60 percent increase in ship tonnage following the 1849 Gold Rush in faraway California.[128] Grasping New York cupidity knew no bounds as the city claimed a continent as its backyard.

The insatiable New York business elite—bringing together two distinctly different cultural groups, the more liberal-minded, Dutch-descended "Knickerbockers"; and the offspring of puritanical, New England Protestant "Yankees"—unified to ensure that business got whatever business needed.[129] More of the wealthiest Americans lived in New York by the 1820s than anywhere else.[130] If private funds were insufficient for some task, business leaders turned to the public till. If markets proved too unregulated to limit shenanigans, investors enhanced enforcement through stronger trading institutions, including the ever-expanding New York Stock Exchange. When national financial institutions—such as the collapsed first and second Banks of the United States—failed, New York's financiers swooped in to pick up the pieces. If the workforce was too unskilled to do what was needed, they expanded public education. If there simply were not enough workers, they opened the city to migrants from the interior—the so-called buckwheats— as well as opening it to immigrants from abroad.

By midcentury, commerce was pouring into the city from around the world; and with it, people from around the globe. Three-quarters of the 667,000 immigrants arriving in the United States between 1820 and 1838 came through New York. But that was just the beginning, for between 1840 and 1859, 4,242,000 immigrants—40 percent Irish, 32 percent German, and 16 percent British—came to American shores; many stayed in the city. Some 157,000 immigrants were making New York their home in any average year leading up to the American Civil War.[131]

The so-called Five Points neighborhood on the Lower East Side of Manhattan symbolized the immigrant city as much as San Telmo and La Boca did in Buenos Aires. An explosion of poor Catholic immigrants from Ireland following the Potato Famines between 1845 and 1852 disrupted social and economic arrangements throughout New York. The slow emancipation of New York's African American slaves reached fruition on July 4, 1827 (though black New Yorkers chose to celebrate Emancipation Day each year on July 5 so as not to call undue attention to themselves).[132] Increasingly organized around churches and self-help groups, the black community remained subject to harsh discrimination (e.g., they could not ride the new omnibuses) and faced a constant threat of kidnapping by bounty hunters scouring the city for anyone who looked like a fugitive slave. Settling around Five Points and other isolated corners of the metropolis, African Americans found themselves living in close proximity to—and competing for the lowest-paying jobs in the city with—impoverished Irish arrivals.

A major German community—Kleindeutschland, or Little Germany—took shape elsewhere on the Lower East Side, replenished by refugees fleeing the political upheavals of 1848.[133] The German-speaking community included a large number of respectable Jews, who climbed in social status to a point from which they could cast disdain on their later-arriving coreligionists from Eastern Europe.[134] Newly arriving New Yorkers demanded that educational, health, and social services be at the ready to contribute to the city's dynamic economy; and the city did its best to respond through a plethora of public, private, and civic institutions.[135]

Confronting hard-hitting competition from other cities—such as Boston, Philadelphia, Baltimore, and New Orleans—New Yorkers rallied to defend their city's position at the top of the American urban hierarchy with a mix of tough-mindedness, inventiveness, ruthlessness, and cunning. On the eve of the American Civil War, New York was home to the most successful and diversified urban economy in the Western Hemisphere.[136] Those who made it happen wanted to be entertained—whether they were among the Knickerbockers and Yankee wealthy; were members of the rising, native "buckwheat"; were British, Jewish, and German bourgeois (fully one-quarter of the top 10,000 New York taxpayers were foreign born by 1855[137]); or were hard-pressed blacks and Irish immigrants at the bottom of the economic pecking order.

The city's reliance on trade necessitated the continuing expansion of information and communications networks. Promoting the growth of the nation's largest and most timely newspapers and news agencies, these networks expanded into an ever-growing publishing industry, which in turn lured may of the country's best and most prolific writers to live in the city for the sake of their livelihoods.[138]

The great Exhibition of the Industry of All Nations—modeled after London's Crystal Palace—opened on the site of what is today Bryant Park, on Sixth Avenue between 40th and 42nd streets. On July 14, 1853, President Franklin Pierce cut the ribbon to open the New York Crystal Palace, which was larger than the London original. The pavilion had been developed by a consortium of prominent New Yorkers, including Theodore Sedgwick, August Belmont, Edward Collins, William Cullen Bryant, and various Schuylers, Livingstons, and Hamiltons. The palace became New York's first major tourist attraction until it was destroyed by fire in 1858.[139]

Tourists and visitors stayed in some of the nation's most elegant hotels, shopped at its most stylish shops, and ate at its most accomplished restaurants. When they sought entertainment, they turned to taverns as well as to theaters and music halls. With so many wealthy and educated residents and visitors—the very sorts who consumed local newspapers and the latest local, national, and British literary achievements, fed by the New York printing houses—the city fostered a congenial environment for a vibrant performing arts community.

New York had few cultural competitors on the continent. Boston's Protestant leaders discouraged—or even outlawed—musical and stage performances. New Orleans—with its Creole tradition of supporting Italian Opera—was too far away and too distinctive in its origins to count.[140] Only Philadelphia—with the country's oldest professional musical organizations and legitimate theaters, including Benjamin Latrobe's elegant Chestnut Street Theatre—could challenge New York's preeminence in the arts.[141] Antebellum New York was well on its way to continental cultural domination.

As noted above, the city's oldest theaters—such as John Street—dated back to British times, while British touring companies made New York a must stop from the earliest days of the republic. John Street was joined by a growing number of newer theaters, including Stephen Price's Park Theater. Price had taken over that troubled stage following the bankruptcy of one of its managers, William Dunlap, in 1808.[142] Price outmaneuvered the British actor Thomas Apthorpe Cooper, who had taken over as the Park's manager in 1815, and set out to make his playhouse the most important in the country.[143]

These machinations would prove to be a turning point in the development of the American stage. The autocratic Price—whom the writer Washington Irving called "King Stephen"—expanded the Park's performance schedule, from three to six days a week (Sunday remained a day of rest, so as not to bring on the ire of Protestant preachers). He imported George Frederick Cooke, an alcoholic British matinee idol, from London and followed with a continuing parade of other British stars, including the luminescent Edmund Kean in 1820 and 1825. By doing so, he created what became the American "star system," in which leading stage names were more important in attracting audiences than the stock companies with whom they were making guest appearances. By the time of his death in 1840, Price had all but guaranteed the ascendancy of the star system over the more traditional stock companies.[144]

Other frontrunner stage managers and promoters competed with Price—such as William Mitchell, who launched the Olympic Theatre in 1839, despite the lingering effects of the financial Panic of 1837; William E. Burton, who promoted "low" Irish and ethnic comedy; and John Lester, who took over John Brougham's Lyceum in 1852. Together, these men converted the orchestra seating areas on the first floor into a "pit" for cheaper ticket holders, created a rowdy new variety theater—which became known as "burlesque"—parodying everyday life, and sponsored all-star benefit performances to raise money for imperiled actors. They moved their theaters further uptown, initially establishing an entertainment district around

Union Square by midcentury (from whence the Theater District move further uptown along Broadway to Times Square a half century later).[145]

Opera simultaneously came to New York, arriving in the 1830s, when numerous leading New York musical institutions took shape. Lorenzo Da Ponte—the Venetian-born librettist for Mozart's three great operas, *Don Giovanni*, *The Marriage of Figaro*, and *Così fan tutte*—settled in the city before the War of 1812, after having unsuccessfully tried his hand at running a grocery store in Sunbury, Pennsylvania.[146] Da Ponte, though Jewish by birth, had been ordained a Catholic priest while teaching in Venice. Banished from his hometown, Da Ponte enjoyed considerable success in Vienna, as he had also done in Naples and Venice. After the deaths of his collaborator, Mozart, and his patron, the Austrian emperor Joseph II, Da Ponte attempted to make a living in London with varied theatrical and publishing ventures. Now the father of four children with his companion, Nancy Grahl, Da Ponte was forced to flee his debts in Britain in 1805. He, Grahl, and their children ventured to America, like many immigrants, to start a new life.

Opening a bookshop in New York, Da Ponte befriended well-placed locals, who helped him secure appointment as the first professor of Italian literature at Columbia University (he was also the first Roman Catholic priest and the first Jewish-born scholar to be appointed to the university's faculty). In 1833, Da Ponte arranged the New York premiere of *Don Giovanni* at a new Italian Opera House.[147] The first theater built exclusively for opera in the United States, Da Ponte's auditorium sported a Greek-style, white-columned exterior and an opulent, gas-lit interior. The company disbanded after only two seasons, leaving Da Ponte bankrupt yet again. He would die in 1838, being laid to rest after a large funeral service in Old Saint Patrick's Cathedral on Mulberry Street.

Da Ponte's unsuccessful attempt to establish grand opera on American shores paved the way for the New York Academy of Music and the New York Metropolitan Opera to follow. His dramatic story represents the first among many journeys whereby highly accomplished immigrants in the performing arts would enrich the New York stage.

Popular Performances

If New York wasn't quite ready for opera, the city was already home to a vibrant performance culture. Five theatrical genres enjoyed success on New York stages during the first half of the nineteenth century: (1) British imports, beginning with Shakespeare's plays; (2) American minstrelsy; (3) melodrama; (4) the misadventures of country hicks who had come to the big city; and (5) Irish and other ethnic performances.

British companies started touring American shores during the colonial period, and they continued to do so following the American Revolution. At times, setting up semipermanent homes in cities such as Philadelphia, Charleston, and New York, British performers brought the latest plays from London as well as classics by Shakespeare and others. For example, John Gay and Johann Christoph Pepusch's 1728 satirical super hit *The Beggar's Opera* toured continuously around the American colonies within months of its opening at Lincoln's Fields Theatre. For much of the early nineteenth century, John and Mary Ann Duff—successes on the London and Dublin stages—dominated the American stage. The *Mayflower* descendent Charlotte Cushman—who won fame performing Lady Macbeth—was an important native-born exception.[148] Cushman and other American performers assimilated British plays, often reshaping them for a local audience. To mention only a single example, the major hit of 1843—*Macbeth Travestie*, at the city's most popular theater, William Mitchell's Olympic Theater—used stereotypical New Yorkers, such as market women as the witches, to transform Shakespeare's tragedy into a lampoon on contemporary American life.[149]

New Yorkers of various social classes embraced different styles and rallied around favored actors, who frequently became surrogates for deeper conflicts. In May 1849, one of the worst riots in the city's history exploded, as Irish and American working-class supporters of the native-born actor Edwin Forrest surrounded and attacked the Astor Opera House, where the British actor William Charles Macready was performing *Macbeth* before an audience of upper-class Anglophiles.[150] The three-sided melee—pitting immigrant, nativist, and upper-class New Yorkers against one another—

left 25 dead and 120 injured before the city police and state militia restored order. The immediate cause was the serendipitous appearance of the era's two leading Shakespearean actors performing the same role in theaters just a few blocks from one another on the same night. New York had become a city increasingly divided by class, race, and national origin, divisions that would continue to disturb public order in the decades ahead.[151]

Minstrelsy represented a second popular type of theater, of purely American invention. Minstrel bards had wandered across Europe from the time of the Middle Ages, singing of love, longing, and historical triumphs and tragedies. Similar forms of musical storytelling crossed the Atlantic with French, British, and Dutch colonizers, blending, by the beginning of the nineteenth century, into what would become American folk music. This art moved to the music halls and theatrical stages of the newly formed United States, as an increasingly commercial venture. However, minstrelsy—which remained the country's most popular theatrical form throughout the nineteenth century—assumed an extraordinarily pernicious meaning as it became inexorably entwined with American racism.

By the 1840s, a Cincinnati bookkeeper named Stephen Foster began writing songs for monetary profit. Foster's songs—such as "Oh! Susanna," "Camptown Races," "Old Folks at Home," "My Old Kentucky Home," and "Old Black Joe"—became part of the American musical canon and continue to be sung and enjoyed more than a century and a half later.[152] They proved to be well suited for the "blackface minstrel" variety shows that dominated American popular culture, both in its original and in its evolved form as so-called vaudeville variety theater. Minstrelsy and vaudeville dominated American entertainment until the emergence of film early in the twentieth century.[153] Foster found an easy alliance with the circus promoter and celebrity clown Dan Rice, who gained fame and fortune in part by singing "Negro songs" in blackface as the character Jim Crow.[154] Other popular blackface characters sported a host of offensively named figures.

At the outset of the 1850s, Foster entered into a contract to write songs for the Christy Minstrels, perhaps the most influential "blackface" performers in the English-speaking world at the time.[155] In

1825, Edwin Pearce Christy had moved at the age of ten from his native Pennsylvania to New Orleans, arriving in that Caribbean-tinged city reflecting its French, Spanish, and African origins.[156] The young Northern boy was drawn to the famous African drumming circles that gathered every Sunday afternoon on Congo Square. After joining the touring Purdy, Welch & Delavan Menagerie and Circus in 1832, Christy returned to New Orleans and found a job supervising slaves at a local rope works. In 1846, he set out for Buffalo, where he formed Christy's Minstrels, who quickly moved to New York to start a ten-year run as one of the most popular shows in town.

In a pattern that would be repeated far too often, white Christy refashioned the songs that he had heard enslaved Africans singing, reharmonized them, and scored them before selling them without attribution. He performed those songs in "blackface," together with works written by Foster and others, in syncopated choreographed dances with stereotyped movements that had been stolen, yet again, from the African slaves he watched in New Orleans.

Christy established a formula that subsequent minstrel shows would follow for decades to come. Each show was divided into three distinct acts that were followed by a concluding "walkaround," in which company members organized themselves into a semicircle onstage and stepped into the center for a final competitive dance, as Louisiana's African slaves had been doing for more than a century at Congo Square. The "Cake Walk," which eventually became a popular dance, originated from this format (figure 19).[157] Christy's success found immediate imitators across North America and Britain, creating a standard for minstrel shows that would last in its pure form—and be translated into such spin-off genres as vaude-ville and variety shows—for decades.

Melodrama rivaled minstrel shows as a third dominant genre on the American stage, and continued to do so well into the twentieth century as popular entertainment moved from the playhouse to the movie palace, and later, to the living room.[158] What became known as "melodrama" existed before the French created a word for it—*mélodrame*—two centuries ago.[159] By often featuring ordinary people confronting extraordinary situations, melodrama uses a surface realism to tell simply drawn morality stories bathed in

Figure 19. Contestants for the Cake Walk crown in the 1890s.
Source: New York Public Library (unknown photographer).

emotion, in which starkly drawn plots dominate character development.[160] These melodramatic plays were widespread in France during the eighteenth century, and they became popular even earlier in England during the Restoration of Charles II in 1660, who permitted serious plays to be staged only at a handful of theaters.[161]

Although the genre populated the repertoire of British companies and their imitators from the beginning of theater in America, melodrama became codified within American theatrical culture following the arrival of Dion Boucicault in New York, first in the 1853, and later in 1872.[162] Boucicault, a native of Dublin, managed his own company, both writing and directing his own plays. Augustin Daly, a native of North Carolina, arrived in New York following the Civil War and similarly managed, directed, and wrote what many consider to have been the first recognizably "American" plays.[163]

Throughout the last third of the nineteenth century until his untimely death in 1899, Daly's works joined with those of Boucicault to provide popular vehicles for the leading actors of the day—including, most notably, Maurice Barrymore, Maude Adams, Tyrone Power Sr., Isadora Duncan, and the indomitable Mrs. (Minnie Madden) Fiske.[164] Boucicault, Daly, and their contemporaries codified melodrama as an American art form during the second half of the nineteenth century by building on the already well-established expectations created by *Uncle Tom's Cabin*, perhaps the most famous American play of the century.[165]

The impact of Harriet Beecher Stowe's antislavery novel *Uncle Tom's Cabin* is difficult to appreciate more than a century and a half after it appeared in 1852. By some estimates, Stowe's tale about the sale of a beloved slave family headed by "Uncle Tom" to a trader to pay for their owner's debts—and the family's determination to escape and reunite—was the largest-selling American novel of the nineteenth century, and the second-largest-selling book in America throughout the century, behind only the Bible.[166] Given the absence of international copyrights, the book quickly appeared in several languages and hopped around the world to become the century's most-read American novel abroad as well as at home.

The story and its lead characters—Uncle Tom, Simon Legree, and Little Eva—were absorbed into the American lexicon as symbols of obsequiousness, brutality, and innocence. The novel was quickly transferred to the stage, and its theatrical version toured the country in well-polished professional productions as well as in simple community theaters; as musicals, as stage plays, and eventually in film. A favorite for blackface minstrel companies, the play dominated the American cultural scene into the twentieth century. More Americans—perhaps as many as 3 million—saw a production of *Uncle Tom's Cabin* than read the book or saw any other play.[167] These highly emotional productions secured a permanent taste among American theatergoers for the sort of morality tales produced by Boucicault, Daly, and others.

The genre of country-hick-come-to-town stories constitutes a fourth major type of popular entertainment. New Yorkers enjoyed watching country rubes try to negotiate the perils of Manhattan. The actor Big Mose's portrayal of *Davy Crockett* ("half-horse, half-alligator, a little touched with snapping turtle") defined the American frontier spirit.[168] Alternatively, Benjamin Baker's 1848 smash *A*

Glance at New York ran for several seasons, tracing the missteps of a country greenhorn coming to town from Connecticut only to fall prey to all sorts of locals. Recast as *New York As It Is*, Baker's play—one of the most successful in the history of the Manhattan stage—featured elaborate sets and props in which good eventually triumphed over evil. The genre continued into the twentieth century, becoming a precursor to dozens of plays and films in a direct line leading to such tales as Neil Simon's 1970 comedy film *The Out-of-Towners*, which featured the misadventures of an Ohioan suburban couple played by Jack Lemmon and Sandy Dennis.[169]

The immigrant tale, in which performers mimicked the travails of being a newcomer in a new land before audiences of their compatriots, became a fifth mainstay genre of the New York stage. Irish and German immigrants filling the Lower East Side viewed the music hall and theater stage as a place of release, and a venue for recalling who they were. Stages presented evenings of Irish hijinks and song; and German drama and music. They fashioned New York as a central venue for immigrant theater, and they started to bring the immigrant stage front and center in New York's theatrical life.[170]

The creation of New York theater across the early decades of the nineteenth century parallels the establishment of New York as the all-encompassing urban metropolis linking the wealth of the Old and New worlds. New York was indeed becoming the London of the New World. Like London, New York was home to urban pathology as well as urban glory—embedded in a society full of its own contradictions and overwhelmed at times by political strife. The city's role in America's next war—a war with itself, known as the Civil War—would further consolidate New York's position as America's "Empire City."

"A House Divided Against Itself Cannot Stand"

Quoting words attributed to Jesus in the Gospels, a rising Illinois politician, Abraham Lincoln, secured his party's candidacy for the US Senate in June 1858 by declaring that "this government cannot endure, permanently half slave and half free."[171] As the nation's leading city, New York reflected the divisions that so worried Lincoln. Too many among New York's merchants, financiers, and bankers were too closely connected to the Southern economy to welcome the severing of ties among the regions; and too many among New York's immigrant working classes—and elites, for that matter—were too deeply racist to welcome African American equality. Although Lincoln eventually would attract passionate backers within the city, he failed to win a majority of the local electorate in both the 1860 and 1864 elections. Only upstate voters enabled him to squeak by in statewide vote counts to carry New York's votes in the Electoral College.[172]

New York was never a wartime front-line city, such as Washington; and it was never caught directly in the shifting lines of open warfare, such as any number of Southern cities. The city nonetheless did not escape open conflict, stark divisions, and economic booms and bust throughout the war and its immediate aftermath.

The city's Republican leaders—led by Horace Greeley and William Cullen Bryant—embraced Lincoln's candidacy following the Illinoisan's conciliatory speech at Cooper Union in Lower Manhattan in February 1860.[173] Although his attractive appearance during his New York stopover won numerous supporters around the city, many among New York's richest businessmen worked vigorously for his defeat, often drawing on racial hatred to mobilize voters against the Republican ticket.[174] The president-elect's second visit to the city on his way to his inauguration in early 1861 touched off a flurry of efforts by prominent New Yorkers to head off the inevitable war. New York financial interests turned their backs on their Southern business partners only after the possibility emerged for the South to join the British Empire (which would have disrupted existing financial networks). A final blow came when the newly formed Confederate government announced punitive tariff policies soon after its declaration of secession.[175] For many of the city's most important economic leaders, money was more important than principle.

The beginning of hostilities changed the calculation of New York's moneyed classes. Financiers in New York, Boston, and Philadelphia enriched themselves by loaning the US Treasury funds and by playing money markets around the government's new "greenbacks," currency that was not backed by precious metals. New York's dominance of the nation's communications industry grew more secure; and bankers and manufacturers reoriented themselves around war-related profiteering.

With the exception of the merchant marine—which had depended on Southern trade—New York's economic leaders found ways to leverage the war to become even wealthier.[176] In 1863, the top 1 percent of income earners (some 1,600 families) had accumulated nearly two-thirds of all the city's wealth. If, in 1860, there had been a few dozen New York millionaires, there were several hundred by the time the war ended, including some worth more than $20 million.[177]

The city's immigrants and workers were less invested in the conflict. Initially, German, Hungarian, Swiss, and Irish immigrants enthusiastically rallied to the war effort as a way to demonstrate loyalty to their new land. Many benefited directly from jobs produced by the boom in war-related production.[178] But New York's foreign born became increasingly hostile as the fighting ground on, human losses mounted, and the slavery question moved center stage in the conflict.[179] Race and class tensions exploded in mid-July 1863 over the issue of the draft, within days of the Union's all-important victory at Gettysburg, fueled in part by resentment over Lincoln's Emancipation Proclamation at the beginning of the year.[180]

The National Conscription Act authorized draft lotteries in which the wealthy could pay a recruitment bounty to escape military service, being replaced on the battlefield by draftees who could not afford to do the same. The lottery began amid high tensions on Saturday, July 11, with protests growing after 1,236 of the nearly 3,500 spots allotted to the city had been filled.[181] Following a break for the Sabbath, the lottery recommenced on Monday. Thousands of immigrants left behind their harsh homes in the city's tenements and attacked symbols of the rich (e.g., Brooks Brothers), tore up rail lines, and besieged the city's limited police force.

Before long, crowds turned their anger on the city's African Americans, in what would become one of the worst race riots in a national history punctuated by racial warfare.[182] It would not be until three days of chaos had passed that troops could be pulled from the battlefield at Gettysburg to restore peace in New York. In the interim, untold atrocities were committed against the city's African

Americans, who were beaten, killed, mutilated, hanged, and had their schools, churches, and homes burned to the ground.[183] Officially, 119 people were verified as having died during the riots, although observers at the time believed the death toll to be several hundred.[184]

Lincoln was concerned about further alienating the New York electorate in the face of an uphill battle in the impending 1864 presidential election, so he eschewed establishing military rule in the city. Democratic leaders in City Hall and the State House in Albany were left to manage an uneasy peace. The Republicans, meanwhile, successfully lobbied for the open enlistment of African American soldiers, who disembarked for the fronts to the south following a huge rally in Union Square in March 1864.[185]

Many in New York and Washington worried that the Confederates would disrupt the 1864 presidential elections. Fresh off victories on the battlefield, Lincoln was able to eke out an electoral victory, carrying New York State despite losing the city. Southern agents dispatched to the city withheld their attack until late November, when conspirators set fire to more than a dozen hotels, several theaters—including the popular Niblo's and the Winter Garden—and scores of industrial facilities. The city withstood this assault, and the conspirators were tracked down in Canada and elsewhere, and were arrested or killed.[186] Together with much of the Union, New Yorkers joined in celebrating Lincoln's second inauguration on March 6, 1865.[187]

Jubilation would not last, as Lincoln would be assassinated just a few days following the North's triumph in April 1865. The famous actor Edwin Booth's brother, a fellow actor named John Wilkes Booth, shot the president during a performance of Tom Taylor's *Our American Cousin* at John Ford's theater in downtown Washington (this theater was a former Baptist meeting house that had been built in 1833 and converted into a playhouse just a few months before the tragedy).

Laura Keene originally produced the play. Keene counted herself as one of a small yet influential number of women among New York's theatrical impresarios. *Our American Cousin* ran for 150 performances in New York and 496 more in London, and then traveled to Washington as a stop on its national tour. The evening's playbill featured Joseph Jefferson in the lead role of the "rustic American," Asa Trenchard, with the promoter Keene playing his daughter, and a British actor, E. A. Sothern, playing "an idiotic English nobleman," Lord Dundreary. Sothern's success in the role made "Dundreary" synonymous in British and American popular culture with malapropisms, which became known as "dundrearies."

Jefferson, for his part, began his stage career acting in blackface as a child opposite Thomas Rice in some of Rice's original "Jim Crow" performances. He would become famous for his portrayal of Washington Irving's *Rip Van Winkle* on stages around the English-speaking world. The ill-starred performance that evening thus brought together the various ways in which American theater had matured. The production took what was happening in New York to the rest of the country, thereby shaping broad popular culture in the process. Keene, Jefferson, and Sothern were products of the growing entertainment industry based in New York, which welcomed men and women, Americans and foreigners, and reached out to Britain and the world beyond.[188]

On April 25, Lincoln's funeral train reached New York on its way back to Illinois. A procession up Broadway from City Hall to 14th Street carrying the martyred president's body proved to be one of the largest in the city's history. Initially, the City Council shamefully prohibited African Americans from joining the massive parade. But in the end, a small representation of Freedmen was allowed to bring up the rear of the official procession. Frederick Douglass and other African Americans held their own ceremony at Cooper Union.[189] After having tried to play both sides of the war, as they had done during the American Revolution and the War of 1812, New York's elite collectively positioned themselves as staunch defenders of the victors.

New York emerged from the Civil War more dominant economically than before. Its wealthy were wealthier, its manufacturers had more orders, its newspapers enjoyed larger readerships, and its financial institutions were more in control. Yet the metropolis was more divided by race and class than ever before, leaving scars that would haunt the city—and its popular culture—for decades to come.

American Metropolis

The years following the American Civil War pushed the United States to the brink of becoming a global power, and carried New York to the top of the global urban hierarchy. But this path was hardly linear, as the city lurched from the financial booms to the crushing busts of the country's largely unregulated market economy. The trend line, however, carried the nation forward as it consolidated its control over the West with the help of the US Calvary and myriad railroad companies (often controlled by New York financiers), and extended America's power for the first time far beyond its national borders.

New York, for its part, emerged as the unquestioned leader of every aspect of American life—except the political.[190] Corporations and industries founded elsewhere—ranging from Ohio's oil companies and Pittsburgh's steelmakers to the South's tobacco growers and Boston's bankers—found it necessary to relocate to Manhattan in order to gain access to the city's remarkable talents, ranging from typists and stenographers to financial wizards and communication gurus.[191]

Louis Keller launched *The Social Register* in 1887 to differentiate the city's top two thousand socialite families that really mattered from the merely wealthy.[192] Housed in newfangled skyscrapers and neo-Renaissance faux palaces—and serviced by expanding networks of underground steam pipes, transit systems, bridges longer than elsewhere, and water pipes—these elites inhabited a city that felt more secure than any other in the world.[193] By the 1890s, more than 1 million people were pouring into Manhattan's office districts every day, returning to homes flung further and further across a vast metropolitan region.[194]

Driven by an accumulation of wealth that was almost unprecedented in world history, New York competed with Buenos Aires and other cities to attract all varieties of newcomers, both foreign and domestic. Traditional immigrant groups, such as the Germans, poured into the city (about 1.4 million during the 1880s).[195] The Irish continued to arrive as well (about a quarter of a million a year into the 1880s).[196]

They were followed by new groups—such as Jews from the Russian Empire's Pale of Settlement—who increased from tens of thousands in the 1870s to more than 200,000 each year in the 1890s. Their arrival set off a round of cultural and social conflicts between German and Eastern European Jews that defined much of the city's immigrant culture.[197]

Italian immigrants fleeing the miseries of the Southern Italian Mezzogiorno started to arrive in the 1880s and 1890s—again by the tens of thousands.[198] European immigrants were joined by thousands of Chinese—often by way of California—and large numbers of African Americans fleeing the harsh realities of a racist and defeated Jim Crow American South.[199]

The flow would not abate until the 1920s, when US laws restricted immigration. Even with that, an estimated 12 million immigrants passed through New York between 1892 and 1956, many remaining in the metropolitan region.[200] Foreign immigrants were joined by talented and ambitious white Americans looking to make it to the top. Each group competed among themselves and with one another to find a physical, social, cultural, and economic place in the big city. The world had never seen anything like it. New York, the "Empire City," had become by the turn of the twentieth century the preeminent immigrant city in the world.

Before the century had time to turn, in 1898, Manhattan joined the Bronx (which was carved out from Westchester County), Queens, Brooklyn (by then the fourth-largest city in the country), and Staten Island to form a consolidated city.[201] And New York's growth did not stop. As Europe bankrupted itself fighting World War I, governments and industrialists seeking capital had no choice but to turn to New York for money. By the end of that conflict, New York had emerged as the wealthiest city the world had ever seen. If the city had once been the London of the New World, London was now the New York of the Old World.[202] With so much talent and wealth, the city simultaneously became the undisputed center of American culture—most especially theater.

Show Business Is Business

Post–Civil War America was becoming an increasingly integrated system, tied together by railroads and telegraphs and financial institutions, which extended their reach beyond any particular region. Over time, large organizations came to dominate daily life. Corporations were driven by powerful logic to push competitors from the playing field and establish themselves as uncontrolled monopolists. The world of theater could hardly escape these deeper and powerful socioeconomic forces reshaping American society.

Producers extended their reach beyond their own backyards as they established their theaters in major towns and cities across the nation. Tom Maguire, for example, opened the Jenny Lind Theatre (which the Swedish nightingale never visited) in San Francisco in 1848. His Lind Theater and other regional playhouses were important for giving new talent—such as playwrights David Belasco and James A Herbe—their starts.[203] Over time, local theaters became affiliated with—and often were owned by—booking syndicates. Maguire successfully ran such a circuit, bringing star power ranging from minstrel shows to grand opera to stages around the country until forced into bankruptcy in 1882.[204]

William Chapman found another way of taking the show on the road. Moving with his family from London to the United States in 1827, the former Covent Garden actor ended up in Pittsburgh, where he purchased a flat-bottomed boat to serve as a home and theater for his clan. In 1831, he launched his "floating theater." Combining the Shakespeare plays he had once performed in Britain with new melodramas, he relied on his extended family to fill in the roles. *Chapman's Floating Palace* sprang from success to success for five years, becoming a prototype for the showboats that dominated the nation's waterways before and after the Civil War.[205]

Shows that began in New York were going on the road, often for long runs. Producers, musicians, actors, and investors converted loss into profit by extending a show's natural life, running from town to town. This expanding American entertainment machine required constant attention. Within a few years, a group of theater managers—including John Duff, A. M. Palmer, and Charles Frohman—had transformed how the business would be run. Such entrepreneurs proved to be the Goulds, Carnegies, Morgans, and Rockefellers of the new show business that was being run for profit. They collected talent from around the country to stock their productions in New York, and dispatched them across the country. Their hub was Manhattan's Union Square, and their reach extended to the Pacific Coast.[206]

Entertainment empires sucked up the oxygen required to sustain a once-vibrant colonial and antebellum stock company scene as theater moved from preindustrial to industrial modes of production. Those with ownership wanted greater control and fewer surprises. Their solution—as was happening over and over again throughout the American economy—was to establish trusts to exert monopoly control over their industry.[207]

For theater, the formational moment came over lunch at the Holland House Hotel on August 31, 1896, when six leading promoters formed what would become known as the Theatrical Syndicate. Jointly, the luncheon guests Abraham Lincoln Erlanger, Charles Frohman, Al Hayman, Marc Klaw, Samuel (Nirdlinger) Nixon, and Fred Zimmerman controlled thirty-three theaters, plus fractions of hundreds of productions that went on the road. Frohman alone owned eight theaters in New York, three in Boston, two in Chicago, three in London, and one in Paris.[208]

All six producers were Jewish, had been born on the eve of the Civil War, and had entered through management doors in theaters far from Manhattan.[209] As Jews and Midwesterners, they had arrived in New York and shared the experience of being outsiders. They had produced some of the best-known works of the American stage (including *Dracula*, *Ben-Hur*, *The Jazz Singer*, *Peter Pan*, and *Erminie*), and had made theater into a national business headquartered in a small section of New York City, along Broadway.

Frohman perished on the *Lusitania* in 1915, followed by Hayman in 1917, Zimmerman in 1925, Erlanger in 1930, Nixon in 1931, and Klaw in 1936. Competitors, the emergence of the film industry and radio, and also the Great Depression following the stock market crash of 1929, weakened the Theatrical Syndicate's hold over the industry by the time Erlanger, Nixon, and Klaw passed on. Their legacies proved to be enormously important in shaping how Americans experienced live entertainment for decades to come.[210]

The difficulty in operating a monopoly lies in the inability to choke off competition. New trendsetters, fresh sources of finance, technological innovation, and labor unrest eventually eroded the syndicate's control. Initially, the ability of the Theatrical Syndicate to dominate its industry was challenged by newcomers who also were claimants to monopoly, the Shubert Brothers.

In 1882, Duvvid Schubart, his wife Katrina Helwitz, and six of their eventual seven children arrived in New York from Vladislavov, Russia (now Kudirkos Naumiestis, Lithuania), to set up a household in Syracuse.[211] Three of Duvvid and Katrina's sons—Lee, Sam, and Jacob—were drawn to the theater. Taking a lease on the Herald Square Theater on Broadway in 1900, the brothers—now known as the Shuberts—set out to break the Theatrical Syndicate's monopoly position in entertainment. Despite Sam's untimely death in a 1905 train accident, Lee and Jacob unrelentingly pursued their goal. By 1914, they controlled 350 theaters—including the marquee Winter Garden—and sponsored 150 productions from coast to coast. Within a decade, they would be running more than 1,000 theaters nationwide, overtaking the syndicate's survivors, Klaw and Erlanger, as masters of the American theater.[212] The consolidation of theatrical ownership and management proved attractive to newly robust capital markets, making theater an attractive investment throughout the years leading up to the Depression.[213]

Although the economic tumult of the 1930s would take its toll on their organization, the Shuberts nonetheless controlled half of New York's forty legitimate theaters when World War II broke out (in addition to such prominent out-of-town showcases as the Forrest in Philadelphia and the National in Washington). Only federal enforcement of antitrust laws could limit the Shuberts' ambition. Following a 1956 consent decree, the corporation divested many of its theaters in New York, Boston, Philadelphia, Chicago, Cincinnati, and Detroit, and disposed of its booking agency.[214] Yet the Shubert Organization still thrives, more than a century after its founding.

Established businesses resist innovation. Broadway and touring companies concentrated on popular romantic and musical comedies, melodramas and spectacles, revues and star vehicles. Interest in more "serious" plays was pushed to the "little theater" movement, which had been launched in Europe in the 1880s and had reached American shores on the eve of World War I.[215]

Gathering in and around the incipient "bohemian colony" of Greenwich Village, several theater mavens—including wanna-be actors, writers, and directors—met; produced small plays in rented community centers, church halls, and school basements; and generally challenged the uptown commercial theater scene. In 1919, a small group coalesced around the creation of the Theatre Guild, an independent enterprise that had been formed to promote productions that would never make it to Broadway's commercial stages. With Lawrence Langner, Rollo Peters, Philip Moeller, Helen Freeman, Helen Westley, Justus Sheffield, and Lew Simonson on the guild's board—undergirded by financial support from Maurice Wertheim and Therese Helburg—the guild secured the Garrick Theatre on West 35th Street and set out to transform American theater.[216]

The Theatre Guild succeeded in its mission, retaining the loyalties of a small group of dedicated actors, directors, and designers. As the theater historian Mary Henderson tells the story, the guild gave

> the American theater *Porgy and Bess* and *Oklahoma!* It had premiered many of Shaw's plays and introduced other European plays no commercial producer would touch, had presented works by the mature O'Neill and the nascent Saroyan, had made stars of many actors and the careers of many more, and had reached out to millions throughout the country through its Theatre Guild on the Air in the 1940s and its television productions in the 1950s. . . . Its everlasting and monumental achievement was in elevating the taste of American audiences and in creating a climate that stimulated the professional producer into taking changes on new American voices struggling to be heard.[217]

Others followed, and not just in New York.[218] In 1915, George Cram Cook founded the Provincetown Players, a group that introduced many of Eugene O'Neill's most important works, and brought together the journalist John Reed, the writers Louise Bryant and Max Eastman, and the painter Marsden Hartley.[219] Following runs on Cape Cod, the group took their plays to New York, building up a stable subscription audience appreciative of their dedication to serious drama.[220] Their contemporary, the Washington Square Players, similarly expanded the reach of the "little theaters" in Broadway's shadow during its operation between 1914 and 1919.[221]

Regional companies followed, often associated with an expanding list of university-based drama schools that came into beginning during the early years of the twentieth century.[222] George Pierce Baker taught the first playwriting course in the country at Harvard in 1905. Yale's Dramatic Association, founded in 1900, evolved into the school's Department of Drama in 1924 once Baker had moved to that university.[223] Farther afield, the University of North Carolina began teaching playwriting in 1918, founding the Carolina Playmakers, which began touring the South in the 1920s.[224] Maurice Browne and Ellen Van Volkengburg established the seminal Chicago Little Theatre in 1912.[225] Collectively, these noncommercial, educational, and regional institutions expanded the reach of the American theater and provided an important alternative to the commercial stages dominated by a few organizations on and around Broadway.

Organized management prompted labor unions to organize in the theater, as in so many other American industries. Actors created the Actors' Equity Association in 1913; composers and musicians joined together as the American Society of Composers, Authors, and Publishers (known as ASCAP) a year later; and the Dramatists Guild of America split off from the Authors' League of America in 1921. In 1926, a militant group of playwrights negotiated a Minimum Basic Agreement (known as MBA), which would govern their financial relationship with producers, with minor adjustments, until the 1980s.[226] These—and numerous more specialized unions to follow—made labor in the field of entertainment among the most highly organized sectors in the United States.

In 1919, Actors' Equity joined the American Federation of Labor and called for a strike against the Producing Managers' Association, led by Erlanger and Claw.[227] The resulting conflict proved to be a transformative moment for determining how theater in New York would function.[228]

Actors had enough to complain about. They were not paid for rehearsals; nor were they compensated for extra performances added during holidays. Once a tour was over, they frequently had to make their way home on their own. The profession was divided between well-paid stars and struggling performers trying to make ends meet. And conditions worsened after Edward F. Albee—the "tyrant of vaudeville"—busted a strike of his performers and blacklisted its leaders.[229]

With livelihoods ever less secure, Frank Bacon and other workaday actors concluded that they needed to force an improvement in work compensation and conditions in order to survive. On August 6, 1919, Actors' Equity went out on strike. Chaos issued. The Theatre Guild, having already reached a separate agreement with Equity, continued its run of St. John Ervine's *John Ferguson* at the Garrick. Within a few days, the owners of the Hippodrome cut their own deal with their nearly four hundred musicians and stagehands and turned their lights back on.[230] Other theaters stayed dark for a month, deeply dividing the community. George M. Cohan took the strike as a personal affront, and sailed to London. Stars such as Zelda Sears, Laura Hopes Crews, and Janet Beecher deserted Equity to join with the Shuberts and Flo Ziegfeld in trying to bring injunctions against the recalcitrant actors.

But Actors' Equity held together. The union earned funds for its striking members with benefit shows at the Lexington Avenue Opera House featuring some of theater's brightest stars. Eddie Cantor, Lillian Russell, Eddie Foy, Ed Wynn, Lionel and Ethel Barrymore, W. C. Fields, and Marie Dressler stood by the union. Modern economic relationships imposed by the resulting labor agreements defeated the feudalism of the nineteenth-century stage.[231] The strike, the arrival of the little theater movement from Europe, the appearance of fresh American writers such as Eugene O'Neill, and new competition from the nascent film industry combined to transform American theater into a far different endeavor than it had been before.[232]

American theater entered the 1920s as a well-organized entertainment business with set rules for the game that gave structure and coherence to this traditionally disorganized, inchoate cultural enterprise. Owners, investors, actors, writers, directors, and audiences now knew what to expect from one another. Real estate developers constructed a record number of theaters following the lead of the irrepressible opera and musical promoter, the German immigrant Oscar Hammerstein I, who had built his grandest theater—the Olympia—on an undeveloped patch of dusty land east of Seventh Avenue between 44th Street and 45th Street.[233] By the time Hammerstein was done and the *New York Times* had opened a headquarters nearby, the subway had opened its first stations. The area—once known as Longacre Square—was rechristened Times Square. The young century had a new, indisputable center for the city's never-ending nightlife.[234]

New York began an era when everyone who had survived World War I wanted to celebrate having done so. The floodgates opened onto the Roaring Twenties, Broadway's Golden Age. Two thousand plays reached Broadway during that decade, a peak achievement not likely to be matched again.[235]

Blending the Stages and Sounds of the World

The period between the Civil War and World War I added fresh creative life to American theater, bringing new musical forms that would blend into a distinctive brand of American musical comedy. Long-standing popular genres—such as imported British hits, minstrelsy, melodrama, comedies focusing on honest-yet-simple country folk moving to confusing cities, and ethnic theater tied to specific immigrant communities—played off one another and incorporated unexpected influences to produce types of theater unknown before. By 1920, Tom Taylor's *Our American Cousin* would have struck audiences as hopelessly out of date, given that American theater generally—and New York theater in particular—were becoming supercharged by the ever-changing surrounding society. New organizational forms created unprecedented opportunities for theater to address society's contemporary sensitivities.

For example, at the end of his career, the master American lyricist Alan Jay Lerner—whose achievements included collaborations on *My Fair Lady, Gigi, Camelot,* and *On a Clear Day You Can See Forever*—wrote an engaging history of American musical theater in which he identified three essential European influences on his art form: the works of Jacques Offenbach, Johann Strauss (the younger), and the British collaborative team of William Gilbert and Arthur Sullivan.[236] Their impact was direct—works by these four composers and librettists were performed on New York stages—and indirect—their works represented models that reshaped how Americans approached their craft.

Offenbach's immigrant story is similar to that of many of the creators of American musical theater a century later. Born in 1819 into the family of a cantor at a synagogue in Cologne, Jacob changed his name to Jacques upon entering the Paris Conservatoire as a child protégé cellist at the age of thirteen.[237] He dropped out of school after a year of study to pursue a successful recital career.

His performances took him to London, where he appeared before Queen Victoria and fell in love with the French stepdaughter of the British concert manager John Mitchell, Hérminie d'Alcain. In 1844, he converted to Catholicism and married Hérminie, whose birth father had been the Spanish ambassador to France and a Carlist general. Hérminie inspired Offenbach's first successful tune, "À Toi" (To You), leading Lerner to quip that "marital love, as an inspiration, seems to be more rare than one would imagine. To my knowledge, only two popular composers actually wrote love songs to their wives, Irving Berlin and Harold Rome." The couple, Lerner continues, "had five children and lived happily ever after, despite an occasional wander by Jacques from the straight and narrow."[238]

Offenbach enjoyed success as a performer and composer before and after returning to Cologne for two years following the July Revolution of 1848 in France. In 1855, as Paris prepared for an international exhibition that was sure to attract tourists, Offenbach found backers to lease and remodel the diminutive wooded Théâtre Lacaze off the Champs-Élysées. According to city regulations, the theater's limited seating capacity required that there be no more than three actors with speaking parts appearing onstage at one time (this restriction was later modified to permit four speaking characters at a time). Converting the venue to the Théâtre des Bouffes-Parisiens, Offenbach created miniature one act comedies bringing together music, speaking, and pantomime. His first play, *Les deux aveugles* (*The Two Beggars*), was an instant hit.

Offenbach produced more than forty works satirizing his

times over the next six years. Emperor Louis-Napoléon Bonaparte (Napoléon III) and Empress Eugénie revealed that they had joined the ranks of his admirers by constantly praising his shows to their American dentist, Dr. Tom Evans.[239] Offenbach's fame and creative influence spread across Europe, influencing Lerner's other seminal figures, Richard Strauss (the younger) in Vienna and William Schwenk Gilbert and Arthur Seymour Sullivan in London. At the time of his death in 1880, the composer was at work on one of his most influential works—*The Tales of Hoffman*—which was among more than a hundred operettas, countless songs, and orchestral works that he left behind.[240]

Johann Strauss (the younger) was among those inspired by Offenbach's innovations. Strauss's father was a popular composer who, together with Joseph Lanner, became a Viennese idol by converting an awkward, traditional Austrian Tyrolean dance in three-quarter time, the Lander, into the gracefully erotic Viennese waltz. Strauss the Elder was orphaned by the age of twelve and taken in as an apprentice to a bookbinder. He started to study the violin and viola in his teenage years. Johann the Elder eventually became a deputy conductor to Lanner's string orchestra, which was known for playing rustic dances, and, increasingly, recently stylish waltzes. He struck out on his own during the 1826 Carnival, moving from success to success before forming his own orchestra, which toured widely throughout Europe.[241] His *Radetzky March* remains a mainstay of Viennese New Year's celebrations.

The strong-willed senior Strauss wanted his son to be a banker rather than a musician. The younger Strauss, however, had exceptional talent and began to study surreptitiously with Franz Amon, a member of his father's orchestra. His mother encouraged her son's musical studies once the elder Johann had left home with a mistress.

The younger Johann began studying with some of the most rigorous music teachers in Vienna and, once he began to perform his own music, never looked back. During the Revolution of 1848, Johann the Elder remained loyal to the royalists, while Johann the Younger was briefly jailed for his support of the revolutionaries. Hindered by having backed history's losers, Junior accepted commissions at Pavlovsk outside Saint Petersburg (returning every year between 1856 and 1865). He constantly toured Europe and, in the 1870s, extended his performances to the United States. He was by then known as "the Waltz King," a monikter that had been secured by such famous waltzes as "The Blue Danube" (1866) and "Tales from the Vienna Woods" (1868). He would in all compose five hundred waltzes, polkas, and other dance music.[242]

Viennese operetta is said to have come into being on the evening of November 24, 1860, with the premiere of Franz von Suppé's *Das Pensionat* (*The Boarding School*). Popular at the time, this and other von Suppé operettas were regularly performed in London, Paris, and New York. Von Suppé established a joyous musical and stage style that became a signature for Viennese light opera. His works were generally weak on storyline and noteworthy for their inferior librettos.[243] Strauss the younger, who was well versed in von Suppé's and Offenbach's works, began writing operettas in 1870 with *Indigo und die vierzig Räuber* (*Indigo and the Forty Thieves*), based on the Ali Baba tales. He would write eleven operettas, which collectively defined the Viennese version of the genre.[244]

Strauss the younger's most enduring stage work, *Die Fledermaus* (1874), ran for a scant sixty-eight performances in the Austrian capital before attaining thunderous success in Berlin, where it ran more than two hundred performances. The operetta moved to London before two years had passed, and, within a decade, it was being performed regularly in New York, becoming part of the repertoires of the world's leading grand opera companies.[245] In 1899, Strauss caught double pneumonia conducting this opera at an outdoor anniversary performance, and died. More than a hundred thousand attended his funeral cortege as it wound through the streets of Vienna.[246]

Lerner's third major European influence, leading to the development of a uniquely American musical theater, needed no translation. The British operetta—which had begun with John Gay's long-running musical *The Beggar's Opera* (1728)—attained its pinnacle accomplishment when the promoter Richard D'Oyly Carte of London's Royalty Theatre invited the collaboration of William Schwenk Gilbert and Arthur Seymour Sullivan in 1875.[247] The duo—who had at best a distant personal relationship—set about writing some of the wittiest musical plays in the English language in a business-like fashion, often exchanging draft scores and lyrics by Royal Post. They would create fourteen exceptional comic operas between 1871 and 1896—including the towering *HMS Pinafore* (1878), *The Pirates of Penzance* (which opened on December 31, 1879, in New York, and in London in 1880), and *The Mikado* (1885).[248] In 1881, D'Oyly Carte opened the Savoy Theatre, which was dedicated to their works. The composer Sullivan died in 1900, and the librettist Gilbert lived until 1911. Neither individually would approach their joint achievements.[249]

Gilbert and Sullivan enjoyed immediate success in New York, as evidenced by the opening of *The Pirates of Penzance* in Manhattan before its London debut. In an era without recognition of copyright restrictions, their plays frequently appeared in makeshift productions around the English-speaking world. American producers were especially prone to promoting bootlegged and pirated productions.[250]

As influential as Offenbach's, Strauss's, and Gilbert and Sullivan's works were in the United States—together with other European works, such as the Viennese master Franz Lehár's popular and frequently performed hit *Die lustige Witwe* (*The Merry Widow*)—their works remained firmly within the European tradition.[251] Even sketchy productions of Gilbert and Sullivan's comic operas were American presentations of European art forms. Their works became incorporated into American musical theater in myriad ways, of course; and were Americanized in the process.

The first genuinely American "book musical" generally is thought to be *The Black Crook*. Produced at Niblo's Garden in 1866, the spectacle ran for an unprecedented 474 performances, and was reprised often in New York and around the country. Thought of as the prototypical American musical, this show by Thomas Baker, Giuseppe Operti, George Bickwell, and Theodore Kennick took shape when a Parisian ballet troupe became stranded in New York after a fire destroyed the New York Academy of Music and left them without a performance venue.[252] Combining forces with the New York producers Henry C. Jarrett and Harry Palmer, the play's creators tossed everything they could into a single mix. For some in the record-setting audience, the draw may have been solos by two ballerinas from La Scala in Milan; for others, a weakened tale drawn from Goethe's *Faust* and Weber's *Der Frieschütz* may have been sufficient. For many more, scantily clad chorus girls undoubtedly served as a sufficient reward for enduring the five-and-a-half-hour marathon.[253]

Other pastiche musicals followed. Two plays produced at Chicago's Grand Opera House in 1902 and 1903—*The Wizard of Oz*, based on L. Frank Baum's fantasy about Chicago politics; and *Babes in Toyland*, featuring Victor Herbert's famous "March of the Wooden Soldiers"—moved to Broadway and, over subsequent decades, to Hollywood and into the core of American popular culture.[254] But something else still had to happen before a uniquely American musical theater could take shape: Outsiders had to become insiders on Broadway.

Lerner got to the heart of the matter in his history of the American musical:

> I cannot believe that almost three centuries of man's inhumanity to man, which reached a peak of organized violence with the Civil War, is worth a single bar of music. But without the presence of the black race in America, there never would have been the popular music or the popular musical that we know today. Nor did the American eagle flap its wings in joyous welcome to the other major contributors to the popular musical theater, the Jews. Barred from all major industry well into the twentieth century, they turned their energies to unrestricted professions such as medicine and the law, shopkeeping and entertainment, both creative and interpretive. That social suppression was the father of artistic expression would be a hard case to prove, but, nevertheless, the overwhelming number of great composers and lyricists of the popular musical theater of the twentieth century were Jewish. So were the theater owners, so were the producers, and so were the visionaries who founded the motion picture industry.[255]

Surpassing Minstrelsy and Escaping Shtetls

Africans and their descendants had been present in New York since the earliest days of Dutch settlement. Africans and their descendants had contributed to a distinctive American musical sound since their arrival on slave ships accompanying the earliest British colonies. Their talents were at best denigrated and at worst appropriated for the benefit of white pretenders. From the time of Stephen Foster and Edwin Pearce Christy, white performers had enriched themselves by presenting African American musical genius as their own. Having been institutionalized in popular blackface minstrelsy, African American cultural achievements almost never appeared before whites without being mocked and degraded.

The decades following the Civil War saw the emergence of autonomous African American institutions devoted to educating and promoting newly freed slaves. An increasingly powerful network of African American church, educational, civic, and cultural establishments—which sometimes were associated with the post–Civil War Freedmen's Bureau, at other times were associated with religious groups, and frequently were embraced by philanthropists—enabled talented African Americans to connect to the larger world. These organizations sustained vibrant communities at the height of the Jim Crow era of legal segregation, which stretched from the collapse of Reconstruction in 1877 until the successful judicial campaigns for equal rights beginning in the late 1940s. They represent important points of light in the dark era labeled by the Howard University historian Rayford Logan as the "nadir of American race relations."[256]

Initially considered as little more than niche "race" music, African American melodic creativity remained largely unknown to the larger white society. But this imposed isolation did little to inhibit the artists' creative desire. Harnessed by African American institutions—especially schools, colleges, universities, and churches—black music attained ever higher levels of achievement. In his history of African American music, *Black Song*, John Lovell Jr. notes that

> in the ten years following the Civil War, a number of church organizations decided to dedicate themselves to the education of the new freedmen. One of these was the American Missionary Association, established by the then–Congregational Church. One of its first acts was the founding of Fisk University. Voted into being in 1865, Fisk opened

its doors to students irrespective of race in January 1866. Like most such colleges and universities, it became immediately engaged in a death struggle for funds. Although many of its teachers worked for little or nothing, Fisk University was on the verge of bankruptcy and closing by 1870. George L. White, a music teacher, suggested a student concert tour to raise funds and publicize the school.[257]

White and nine ex-slaves left Fisk's Nashville campus and traveled to Cincinnati to start their concert tour on October 6, 1871. Their concerts featured a mix of spirituals, sacred anthems, sentimental songs, temperance songs, and patriotic tunes. They reached New York in December, and were on their way to international fame.[258]

The group would become known worldwide as the Fisk Jubilee Singers, with "Jubilee" referencing the word's association in Leviticus 25:10 with the year when slaves were to be freed. The Fisk Singers would perform for American presidents, Queen Victoria, British prime ministers, and European royalty. They steamed their way as far afield as Cape Town—where, as is discussed in the chapters titled "Humanity Is Coloured" and "Windsongs" below, they transformed South African music.[259] No-less-talented imitators followed, most notably Orpheus Myron McAdoo and the Hampton Jubilee Singers. McAdoo's repeated tours throughout South Africa prompted well-placed community and religious leaders there to embrace music as a form of social uplift.[260]

Shunned by white critics and audiences, African American musicians slowly gained recognition from white institutions, bringing them closer to the cultural mainstream. Will Marion Cook, the son of Howard University Law School dean John Harwell Cook, left segregated Washington to study musical composition at Oberlin College. Fellow Washingtonian Frederick Douglass and members of the First Congregational Church raised funds to send Cook to study at Berlin's Hochschule für Musik between 1887 and 1889. Returning to New York, Cook studied with Antonín Dvořák at the short-lived National Conservatory.[261]

Cook's career included numerous significant contributions to the American stage. In 1898, he joined with fellow-Washington denizen Paul Laurence Dunbar to compose *Clorindy; or The Origin of the Cakewalk,* a one act musical with the first all-black cast to appear on Broadway.[262] Cook and Dunbar collaborated on the bustout hit *In Dahomey* in 1903, which featured one of the era's most popular entertainers, the Bahamian-born Bert Williams.[263]

Washingtonian James Reese Europe—who coincidentally grew up a few doors down the street from John Philip Sousa near the US Marine Corps Barracks on Capitol Hill in Washington—became part of New York's black theater scene. Reese Europe eventually gained international fame with the Harlem 369th Regiment in France, where, during World War I, he and other musical soldiers transformed European musical tastes as they played during interludes from the fighting.[264]

Other noteworthy African American productions followed. These included Noble Sissle and Eubie Blake's 1921 hit *Shuffle Along*; Lew Leslie's *Blackbirds Revues* (in 1926, 1928, 1930, 1933, and 1939), featuring such performers as Florence Mills, Bill "Bojangles" Robinson, and Littie Gee; and impressive African American casts in works by whites.[265]

Black accomplishments transcended musical comedy.[266] Paul Robeson's towering performance in Eugene O'Neill's *The Emperor Jones* (1920) and Charles Sidney Gilpin's exceptional turn as a North Carolina farmer in Paul Green's Pulitzer Prize–winning *In Abraham's Bosom* (1927) caught the attention of critics and audiences alike.[267] None of these achievements protected their soaring creators from abuse and degradation at the hands of a racist society and city. Cook and Dunbar's hit plays were performed to segregated audiences; Williams—upon reaching the top of the entertainment work in 1910 by joining Flo Ziegfeld's previously all-white *Follies*—was forced to perform in blackface.[268] Robeson left the country at several pivotal moments in his tumultuous career.[269]

A different musical explosion occurred in New Orleans, where African, American, Caribbean, and European musical traditions and instrumentation came smashing together to create an entirely new musical form, eventually known as "jazz." New Orleans musicians sought their fortune by riding the descendants of William Chapman's original "floating palaces"—now popularly known as "showboats"—up and down the Mississippi River. The music spread to other river towns and cities, including Memphis and Saint Louis.

In 1897, the City of New Orleans concentrated its brothels in a central district known as ""Storyville," named for a city councillor, Sidney Story, who imposed zoning ordinances designed to contain the city's vice district within strict boundaries. Local proprietors sought out the lively music being played by so-called spasm bands. Opportunities to play music for a living evaporated in October 1917, when Storyville was shut down at the insistence of Secretary of the Navy Josephus Daniels, who railed against the district's "bad influence."[270] Consequently, New Orleans' musicians left town, traveling by train farther afield and taking their music to Chicago, New York, and the world.

This mix of influences on the ever-innovative African American musical culture came together in the works of the Saint Louis–based Scott Joplin, whose ragtime piano tunes combined African and European notions of musical composition in a distinctive American sound (figure 20). His 1899 tune "Maple Leaf Rag" was the first American-composed sheet music to sell more than 1 million copies. In 1907, he set his sights on Broadway and moved to New York. By 1910, he had completed the score of an ambitious opera, *Treemonisha*.

But New York audiences were not ready for a black opera. *Treemonisha* would not be performed in its entirety until 1972, following a chance rediscovery of the score; and it would not enter the operatic repertoire until a lush Houston Grand Opera production in 1982.[271] Joplin would need to be celebrated posthumously; he died in New York in obscurity at the age of forty-nine in 1917.

Jews, like Africans, had been among the first residents of Dutch New Amsterdam. For many years, Jewish immigrants were largely German in origin, and the Jewish community assimilated into New York life. But this situation changed when tens of thousands of Central and Eastern European Ashkenazi Jews arrived in the late nineteenth century. To escape intolerance and violence in the Russian and other European empires—and to seek economic opportunity in America—Jews from these regions came to New York in unprecedented numbers during the decades leading up to World War I. As they did, they brought with them the bountiful stage traditions of the Yiddish theater.[272]

The thespian craft underlying Yiddish theater has numerous

Figure 20. The composer Scott Joplin in 1903.
Source: Library of Congress.

roots, beginning with Purim plays performed for centuries in synagogue courtyards during the holiday commemorating the Jews' salvation from a Persian plot to destroy them. Yiddish-speaking theatrical troupes emerged in and around Warsaw, Vienna, Odessa, and
other urban centers of Eastern European Jewish life, drawing on
the vitality of the Yiddish literary language. Abraham Goldfaden
founded the first professional Yiddish troupe in Bucharest in 1876.
Goldfaden's actors performed in L'viv, Vilna, and New York, and
many cities in between. Yiddish theater companies were established
in Odessa, London, Manchester, Glasgow, and Warsaw. Immigrants
arriving in New York—including the same playwrights, directors,
and actors who had been performing across Europe—brought their
energetic performance art with them.[273] By the first decade of the
new century, three Yiddish theaters were thriving on the Bowery,
producing a wide variety of plays, ranging from variety shows, co-

medic reviews, and satirical looks at the immigrants' new home to light opera and historical and melodramatic plays.[274]

Writing in 1905, a radical social critic, Hutchins Hapgood, noted that Yiddish-speaking audiences

> vary in character from night to night rather more than in an uptown theater. On evenings of the first four days the theater is let to a guild or club, many hundreds of which exist among the working people of the East Side. Many are labor organizations representing the different trades, many are purely social, and others are in the nature of secret societies. Some of these clubs are formed on the basis of a common home in Russia. . . . Then, too, the anarchists have a society, there are many socialistic orders. . . . Two or three hundred dollars is paid to the theater by the guild which then sells the tickets among the faithful for a good price. . . . These performances are called "benefits." On Saturday and Sunday nights, the theater is not let, for these are the Jewish holidays and the house is always completely sold out. . . . On those nights the theater presents a peculiarly picturesque spirit.[275]

Yiddish theater maintained its own star system—with Jacob Adler and Boris and Bessie Thomashefsky among the most prominent actors—and provided a comfortable halfway house for theater professionals making their way in New York from abroad (e.g., the master stage designer Boris Aronson worked both on the Bowery and on Broadway).[276] To those who could compare, the Thomashefskys' performances in a wide repertoire—including *Uncle Tom's Cabin, Faust, Parsifal*, an adaptation of *Hamlet* called *Der Yeshiva Bokher* (*The Yeshiva Student*), and Adler's *Lear* and *Othello*—were considered as memorable as those on any stage in the city.

Such figures as the Gershwin brothers, the Marx brothers, Zero Mostel, and Irving Berlin regularly followed New York's Yiddish theaters. Luminaries of Yiddish literature, such as Sholem Aleichem and the Nobel laureate Isaac Bashevis Singer, were incorporated into the swirl around the New York Yiddish stage. Yiddish influences on the American performing arts were wide, at times direct, and often deeply personal. For instance, the Tomashefskys' first son, Henry, moved to California to work in the film industry, while their third son, Ted, became a stage manager and the father of the conductor Michael Tilson Thomas.[277] More generally, Yiddish performers and traditions transformed stage—and eventually screen—humor from the homespun to the wisecrack, as performers from within the Yiddish tradition—such as the Marx Brothers and Jimmy Durante—took their wisenheimer antics into the world.[278]

Without African American musical sensibilities and Yiddish theatrical culture, the New York musical would have remained a somewhat cheap imitation of European operetta and comic opera. But the sounds and sights of black and Jewish America transformed how music and storytelling came together onstage. Looking back from the twenty-first century, their consequence is clear: Without the inventive talents of African Americans and Jews, there would not have been distinctive Broadway and Hollywood musical traditions.

On the Eve of a Golden Age

By the dawn of the twentieth century, a number of trend lines converged around Manhattan's primary Theater District surrounding the Times Square crossroads of Broadway and 42d Street. The city's leading socialite gathering point—the Metropolitan Opera—sat at 39th Street and Broadway; and its primary concert venue, Carnegie Hall, was a short walk north, at 57th Street and Seventh Avenue. New theaters were putting on dozens of plays every night; and clubs and stages further afield featured the transformative art of the Jewish stage, Irish musicians, and African American culture.

Producers—such as the legendary David Belasco—knew what audiences wanted: spectacles, musicals, circuses, and good times.[279] Vaudeville thrived, featuring such famous comics as Edward "Ned" Harrigan and Tony Hart, as well as Joe Weber and Lew Fields.[280] Revues followed current events, with George Lederer's *The Passing Show* and *The Belle of New York* leading the way.[281] New York promoters and producers determined what popular music would get published and which plays would be seen around the country. The business of culture had been codified, with producers, actors, writers, and composers all becoming well organized. Tin Pan Alley and Times Square shaped the theatrical culture of a nation. The results of these developments included the coming of age of American playwrights such as Eugene O'Neill; the elevation of the minstrel and variety spectacle to new artistic levels, as evidenced in productions by impresarios like Florenz Ziegfeld; and the appearance of new forms of musical comedy, as found in the works of composers such as Irving Berlin.

Eugene O'Neill established a distinctive American voice in dramatic theater.[282] O'Neill combined realism with in-depth knowledge of the fringes of American society to create forceful portrayals of the disillusionment and despair that accompany failure in a culture that celebrates success. His stories and characters are profoundly American, as is evident in his use of vernacular American speech. He was the forerunner of such twentieth-century giants as Arthur Miller, Tennessee Williams, and others who made American theater "American."[283]

O'Neill was a product of the forces that were converging on Manhattan to generate a distinctive theatrical tradition. He was born in October 1888 at the Barrett Hotel at 1500 Broadway, in the heart of Longacre—later Times—Square. His Irish immigrant father was an actor married to a woman of Irish descent. O'Neill grew up in New York, attending Catholic boarding school. He went off to Princeton for a year, before his personal demons surrounding alcohol and chronic illness began to interfere with his life. He shipped off to sea, became a union organizer, and started writing plays while recovering at a sanatorium in 1912. Drawn to the art of stagecraft, he entered George Baker's playwriting course at Harvard in 1914. Then he returned to Greenwich Village, where he became involved in radical politics and the little theater movement that was flourishing there.

The Provincetown Players produced his early works, which then moved to Broadway. He would win the Pulitzer Prize for Drama for *Beyond the Horizon* (1920) and *Anna Christie* (1922). His first major hit, *The Emperor Jones* (1920), featured Charles Sidney Gilpin in the lead role of Brutus Jones. Later, Paul Robeson turned Brutus Jones into a signature role in London and on film.

O'Neill created a distinctive American dramatic voice. He

would win the Nobel Prize in Literature (1936) and a total of four Pulitzer Prizes for Drama (1920, 1922, 1928, and 1957). He actively engaged African American themes (as with his 1924 hit, *All God's Chillun Got Wings*), and he built on his own immigrant family's experience to add depth and substance to American playwriting. His mature works—*Mourning Becomes Electra* (1931), *The Iceman Cometh* (1939, first performed in 1946), *Long Day's Journey into Night* (1941, first performed in 1956), and *A Moon for the Misbegotten* (1943, first performed in 1947)—elevated the New York stage to high art.

Flo Ziegfeld Jr. raised the variety show to previously unknown heights.[284] Born in Chicago to a German immigrant father and a Belgian immigrant mother, Ziegfeld grew up in a musical family. His father was the director of the Chicago Musical College, and he also moonlit by running nightclubs—including the Trocadero, where he intended to capitalize on tourist traffic from the World's Columbian Exposition in 1893. Florenz the younger helped out at his father's nightclub business, hiring the famed strongman Eugen Sandow and the Polish-French actress Anna Held.[285]

Taking the Parisian Folies Bergère as a model, Flo Junior moved to New York in 1907 and began producing stage spectaculars known as the Ziegfeld Follies (figure 21). These annual extravaganzas—which continued until 1931—combined comedy, musical performances, and innumerable exquisitely costumed dancing women, who came to be seen as exemplifying American female beauty.[286] Ziegfeld relied on the era's top talent. Joseph Urban, the Viennese architect and stage designer we met early in this chapter, oversaw the production. Urban, together with Thomas Lamb, would build Ziegfled an extravagant theater on Sixth Avenue between 54th and 55th streets, which opened in 1927.

Ziegfeld employed the most famous comedians of the day—including Bert Williams, W. C. Fields, Will Rodgers, Eddie Cantor, Fanny Brice, and Eddie Cantor—and hired the most highly regarded composers—such as George Gershwin, Jerome Kern, and Irving Berlin. He set a high standard for spectacle that would be followed in Hollywood and Las Vegas long after his death in 1932 at the age of sixty-five years.

Irving Berlin, even more than O'Neill and Ziegfeld, was crucial in creating American popular culture. The son of Jewish immigrants

Figure 21. Mademoiselle Dazie, a Ziegfeld Follies dancer, at the turn of the twentieth century.
Source: Photograph by Otto Sarony of the New York Star, October 1908 (Wikipedia,https://en.wikipedia.org/wiki/Mademoiselle_Dazie#/media/File:Mlle_ Dazie_001.jpg).

from Russia (his father, like Offenbach's, was a cantor), Berlin defined American popular music. It was with wisdom that George
Gershwin called him "America's Franz Schubert."[287] The author of
such classics as "Easter Parade," "White Christmas," "There's No
Business Like Show Business," and "God Bless America," Berlin
had no formal musical training and scant formal education of any
kind. Jerome Kern summarized Berlin's achievements with an awe
that equaled Gershwin's: "Irving Berlin has no *place* in American
music—he *is* American music."[288]

Berlin's career began in a local saloon near Union Square in
1908. The Tin Pan Alley crowd passed in and out of the tavern as
Berlin began to write lyrics and music. His first songs appeared
in 1907, beginning with "Marie from Sunny Italy" (which earned
him royalties totaling 37 cents).[289] His rise was nothing short of
meteoric, and one top seller catapulted him beyond any competition. Writing for the *Friars' Frolic of 1911*, he penned "Alexander's
Ragtime Band." From that moment on, American popular music
left Europe behind.

Lerner captures the song's importance in his celebration of the
American musical theater:

> "Alexander's Ragtime Band" caught the scattered winds of
> ragtime and created a storm that swept the world. It pro-
> foundly influenced popular music and the popular musical
> theatre. It also changed the social life of the country, mak-
> ing people want to dance. They pulled up their carpets and
> danced at home, hotels added ballrooms, and nightclubs
> began to flourish. The world of entertainment was never the
> same again, and all because of one song. Thirty-two bars of
> music and lyrics written by a twenty-three-year-old Russian
> immigrant, who could neither write music nor read it, and
> whose formal education ceased before he was ten years old.
> If one wonders how it was possible, for once there is a sim-
> ple answer. Irving Berlin is a genius. Genius is a word that
> suffers from metal fatigue. Some people have it but few are
> it. Irving Berlin is.[290]

The more-or-less simultaneous appearance in Manhattan of O'Neill, Ziegfeld, and Berlin was no accident. All were created by — and were creators of — an American theatrical culture struggling to be born. New York's ability to mix and match previously unblended and unrelated traditions into a vibrant, innovative, cohesive whole produced a new economy, a new society, and a new urban civilization. New York's musical theater was no longer transplanted European musical comedy. Like the city itself, it had become something distinct and all its own. With unprecedented wealth and a desire for good times arriving following World War I, the stage was set for Broadway's Golden Age.

We'll Have Manhattan

We'll turn Manhattan into an isle of Joy.

—Rodgers and Hart, 1925

For Broadway, the 1920s were a glorious Golden Age—with new theaters, new plays, celebrated productions, and an ever-expanding audience.[1] Although the movies began to cut into theater audiences elsewhere, the frisson of live performances and sound kept the stage on top in New York, and would do so throughout the decade. Eventually, however, the "talkies" and the Great Depression would bring the curtain down on this unique era of the Broadway theater's cultural preeminence.

The 1920s witnessed the arrival of new talents, of men and women who would define American popular stage culture for much of the remainder of the twentieth century. Two of the newcomers—Oscar Hammerstein II and Richard Rodgers—followed remarkably similar paths to Broadway success (figure 22).

Oscar Hammerstein II was born into a theatrical family.[2] His grandfather, Oscar Hammerstein I, was a German-born impresario who famously converted the profits from a cigar-making business—as well as the successful trade publication *US Tobacco Journal*, which he founded—into the capital needed to build, open, and manage theaters.

Oscar I arrived in New York at the end of the Civil War, full of dreams of grandeur. He was initially unable to compete with theaters downtown, but he opened the Harlem Opera House in 1889 and the Columbus Theater a year later uptown on 125th Street, in a

Figure 22. Richard Rodgers, Irving Berlin, Oscar Hammerstein II (from left to right), and Helen Tamiris (in the rear), watching hopefuls being auditioned on the stage of the Saint James Theatre in 1948.
Source: Photograph by Al Aumuller of the New York World-Telegram; Library of Congress.

quickly developing middle-class neighborhood. But he was better at starting than sustaining his business enterprises, so his mercurial career ebbed and flowed between glory and failure.

Oscar I's true love was opera. So in 1893, he decided to challenge the monopoly of the Metropolitan Opera by opening his own Manhattan Opera House on 34th Street. But despite the new opera house's artistic success, the immigrant cigar maker could not withstand the counterattacks of the prestigious socialites who claimed the Met as their own. Undeterred by colossal failures, Oscar I turned his attention to the recently renamed Times (née Longacre) Square, at the intersection of Broadway and 42nd Street. In addition to the Victoria—a major vaudeville venue managed by his son, William (Willie)—Oscar I leased the Republic to David Belasco, and built the Lew Fields Theatre, named for the celebrated Weber and Fields comedy team. His Paradise Roof Garden above the Victoria and Republic theaters became a popular date spot.

Oscar I did not limit his theatrical reach to New York. He also opened opera houses in Philadelphia and London. Still dissatisfied with his treatment by the Metropolitan Opera—and in a moment of typically uninhibited braggadocio—he opened a second Manhattan Opera House in 1906. Although this house was another artistic success, he was yet again forced out of business by the baronial socialites at the Met, this time being compelled to leave grand opera for ten years. He died in 1919, having transformed New York theater by promoting Times Square as the new central focus of live entertainment.

Oscar I's two sons, Arthur and Willie, entered the business as producers, directors, and theater owners. Their father's volatile personality—as well as their own professional travails—convinced them that the Hammerstein family should move into new realms. Willie, therefore, encouraged his son, Oscar II, to become a lawyer.

The dutiful Oscar II entered Columbia University in 1912, and, upon graduation, he began studies at Columbia Law School. Then his father Willie died unexpectedly in 1914, declaring on his deathbed that Oscar II should continue his legal studies. Shortly after his father's death, Oscar II joined the company of Columbia's annual *Varsity Show*, an important training ground for aspiring thespians; and, by 1917, he had dropped out of law school to write lyrics on Broadway. His first professional collaboration—involving Herbert Stothart, Otto Harbach, and Frank Mandel—opened on Broadway in 1920 as *Always You*. Oscar II's career was launched.

Richard "Dick" Rodgers was seven years younger that Oscar II, and their paths would not cross for some time, despite having grown up near one another and moved in the same prosperous German Jewish circles in Queens.[3] The son of a successful physician, Rodgers discovered his musical talent early, heading off to Columbia University in large measure for the opportunity to participate in the famous annual *Varsity Show*. Rodgers's older brother briefly introduced Dick to his fraternity brother, "Oscie" Hammerstein, and, of greater immediate importance, to a friend of another friend, Lorenz "Larry" Hart. By 1921, Rodgers had decided that music was his destiny and was seeking to follow in the footsteps of his composer idols, Victor Herbert and Jerome Kern.

Dick Rodgers began studies at the Institute of Musical Art (now the Juilliard School) after having joined forces with Hart on their first song—"Any Old Place with You," for the 1919 musical *A Lonely Romeo*—and their first complete musical, *Poor Little Ritz Girl*, which opened on Broadway in 1920. Rodgers and Hart would continue collaborating—writing some of Broadway's and Hollywood's most memorable scores and standards—until Hart's death in 1943. Their continuous stream of his shows—including *Dearest Enemy* (1925), *The Girl Friend* (1926), *A Connecticut Yankee* (1927), *Love Me Tonight* (1932), *On Your Toes* (1936), *Babes in Arms* (1937), *I Married an Angel* (1938), *The Boys from Syracuse* (1938), the iconic *Pal Joey* (140), and their final collaboration, *By Jupiter* (1942), to name just a few of their twenty-eight stage musicals—included some of the era's most memorable songs, which are still performed regularly—including "There's A Small Hotel," "My Funny Valentine," "The Lady Is a Tramp," and "Bewitched, Bothered, and Bewildered.⁴ Their achievement is all the more remarkable given the erratic Hart's losing struggle with alcoholism, which frequently rendered him unreliable.

The Broadway world young Oscar II and Dick entered was dominated by revues modeled after Ziegfeld's famous productions as well as earlier minstrel and variety shows.⁵ Composers and lyricists would be hired to write a song or two for this production or that, with the works of various songwriters being mixed and matched for effect. Audiences were showing up for a good laugh or to catch a glimpse of a pretty girl. Storytelling resided far more frequently in dramatic productions without music. With notable exceptions, most musicals—other than stagings of European operettas—represented a mix-and-match approach by extended collaborative teams.

Oscar II, however, was drawn to an emerging genre of "book show," which was based on librettos telling a more-or-less coherent story, with music, language, and characters drawn from contemporary life. The leading masters of this musical craft—Jerome Kern, in particular—were developing a style in which works moved seamlessly "from song to play to song," as the theater historian Stephen

Citron put it, in a completely believable manner.[6] Characters were given some depth, and they spoke "in language that was authentic to themselves, the plot, and its timeframe."[7] Not surprisingly, these shows became identified with the composer, and the score, rather than with the lyricist and the libretto.

As Citron notes,

Although [Oscar Hammerstein II] had contributed lyrics and librettos to many successes and was long and highly esteemed by the critical faculty, the public at large applauded *Rose-Marie* as being an operetta by Rudolph Friml. Hammerstein conceived the books, adapted the stories and wrote the lyrics for every one of the following, yet it was Kern's *Sunny*, *Show Boat*, and *Music in the Air*, Gershwin's *Song of the Flame*, and Romberg's *Desert Song* and *New Moon*. Such was the power of music that unless the names of both composer and lyricist are teamed on the program, the public only remembers the one who wrote the tune.[8]

With an unprecedented number of shows filling Broadway stages, producers were open to experiments. Both Oscar Hammerstein II, in his collaborations with the era's most esteemed composers—including Jerome Kern, George Gershwin, Rudolf Friml, Sigmund Romberg, Vincent Youmans, and Emmerich Kálmán—and Rodgers, in his long partnership with Hart, equalized the credit being given to lyricist and composer alike. In the case of Hammerstein—who collaborated with Central Europeans such as Kern, Friml, Romberg, and Kálmán—a focus on storytelling drawn from the operetta evolved effortlessly.[9] The growing theatrical trade between Broadway and London's West End—where the operetta tradition had deeper roots—reinforced this development, which transpired slowly over time.

Hammerstein's breakthrough moment arrived with *Rose-Marie*, an operetta-style musical that, at the time, became the longest-running Broadway musical of the decade (with 557 performances in New York, beginning in 1924, and with another 581 in London, followed by successful films in 1928, 1936, and 1954).[10] Hammerstein's Uncle Arthur had long sought to promote Broadway shows in an operetta tradition (e.g., he produced the wildly successful *Merry Widow* in 1907).[11] Taken with the story of a young French Canadienne who falls in love with a Rocky Mountain miner, Arthur assembled a creative team including Friml, Herbert Stothart, and the lyricist Otto Harbach, together with his nephew Oscar II. The production's signature song, "Indian Love Call," became a classic, especially after its memorable performance by Jeanette MacDonald and Nelson Eddy on the stage and in the Hollywood film version.

Rose-Marie made its backers very wealthy.[12] Pleased with this success, Uncle Arthur paired his nephew with Jerome Kern, George Gershwin, and others to produce such hit shows (and eventually films) as *Sunny*, *Flame*, and *The Wild Rose*.[13] Hoping to cash in on the craze surrounding the silent film star Rudolf Valentino, Arthur promoted a tale from "Old Araby." Sensing that a guerrilla uprising against French rule in Morocco would recall the recently popular stories of Lawrence of Arabia, he invited the lyricist Otto Harbach, Frank Mandel, and his nephew Oscar to develop the storyline for an operetta with music by Sigmund Romberg.

Romberg, who had emigrated from Hungary, had become a fixture on Broadway, bringing a Viennese sensibility with him across the Atlantic.[14] The show's music—including the waltz-tinged title melody, "Desert Song"—won immediate popularity. Though it is perhaps difficult to imagine from the vantage point of the twenty-first century, English-speaking audiences were enchanted by the story of Islamic insurgents fighting nasty European colonists for their freedom—replete with a love interest or two and a dashing hero. *Desert Song* ran for 465 performances on Broadway, before moving to film and television multiple times in 1929, 1943, 1953, and 1955 and being revived in London and New York numerous times on both music hall and operatic stages.[15]

Lerner tellingly recounts how, despite the popular success of these early operettas, the music invariably overwhelmed the lyrics.[16] But this would soon change when Hammerstein became paired with Jerome Kern, a partnership that resulted in a production featuring some of the most accomplished music and words in the Broadway canon—*Show Boat*.

Jerry Kern

Kern's maternal grandparents, Seligman and Bertha Kakeles, emigrated from Bohemia in the 1840s, setting up their household on Delancey Street. The family was so poor that their daughters could not attend school because of their lack of winter clothing. Seligman quickly grasped much about his new country and city. By 1850, he was corresponding with Gerrit Smith, an abolitionist and philanthropist, and was beginning to make his way up the immigrant hierarchy. He eventually secured employment as a conductor on public transit, and he moved his household all over Manhattan.

Seligman's daughter Fannie—who would become Jerome's mother—was born in 1852. Seligman, by 1864, had become the sexton of the well-heeled Temple Emanu-El on 12th Street and grew in stature throughout the rest of his life. The elite of New York's German Jewish community attended his funeral in 1903; and his children included a successful surgeon and a pediatrician turned businesswoman. Kern's Aunt Sarah left more than $1 million to Mount Sinai Hospital at the height of the Depression.[17]

Kern's father Henry was born in Germany in 1842, and he made his way to New York, where he worked at stables near the present-day site of the United Nations. The family grew quickly following his marriage to Fannie. Their sixth son, Jerome—or, as he was known, Jerry—was born in 1885 in Manhattan, about a dozen years before the family moved to Newark.[18] Like so many of the innovators in New York's musical life, the Kern clan's life stories were similar to those of tens of thousands of other immigrant tales taking shape in and around Manhattan throughout the decades following the Civil War. The city was full of challenge, drama, tragedy, and untold opportunity. For talented children of recently successful immigrant families—such as Kern, Hammerstein, and Rodgers—the future was boundless.

Jerry Kern discovered a love of and gift for composing in school, writing songs for school minstrel shows and an adaptation of *Uncle Tom's Cabin* at the Newark Yacht Club. His mother ignited his musical imagination, taking him to his first Broadway musical as a gift on his tenth birthday (the Kern biographer Gerald Boardman speculates that this life-transforming visit may have been to see the popular *Little Christopher Columbus,* which had moved to New York from London).[19] Kern left high school early and set off for Heidelberg, where he began to study music formally.

After a failed attempt to work in his father's business, Jerry entered the New York College of Music (which is now part of New York University), where he studied with Alexander Lambert, Paolo Galico, and Austin Pierce. His first published song—"At the Casino"—received a copyright on September 5, 1902.[20] Like so many Broadway composers in that era—including Irving Berlin and George Gershwin—Jerry Kern's first job was as a "song-plugger" for the leading Tin Pan Alley publisher T. B. Harms; in Kern's case, his assignment was to play Harms's sheet music in Wanamaker's Department Store. His boss at Harms—Max Dreyfus—signed him on to write music for the company.[21] Kern would work with Harms for a decade, often serving as a rehearsal pianist for shows featuring the company's music.[22]

Kern spent seven months in London during 1903 and 1904, supported by Dreyfus and Harms. Will Marion Cook and Paul Laurence Dunbar's ragtime masterpiece *In Dahomey,* starring Bert Williams and George Walker, was the triumph of the season. Notably, this hit would figure prominently in Kern and Hammerstein's *Show Boat.*[23] While in London, Kern encountered the Broadway producer Charles Frohman. Kern began regular visits to London, where he met and married the daughter of the proprietor of the Swan Inn in Walton-on-Thames in 1910.[24]

Kern wrote incidental music to be played during the showings of silent films, and he fulfilled his odd song-writing duties for Harms, at times working with African American songsters.[25] His first complete score for the Shubert Brothers—*The Red Petticoat*—appeared, to limited success, in 1912.[26] In 1915, he was scheduled to sail with Charles Frohman on the ill-fated RMS *Lusitania;* but according to family legend, he missed the ship's sailing after staying up too late the night before playing poker with friends.[27] The New York music business was beginning to change. With war raging in Europe, the back-and-forth between Broadway and the West End that had been so characteristic of earlier years faded from possibility. Audience tastes were evolving, more theaters were chasing one another for consumer dollars, and labor was becoming bad-tempered. Producers began to look for new business models. As with Offenbach's Paris, it would be a small theater that would lead the way.

In 1912, the Shubert brothers contracted with the architect William Swasey to build a small theater near the Metropolitan Opera on West 39th Street that was initially intended for dramatic plays. The diminutive site constricted the possibilities, and Swasey designed a petite auditorium in an ornate style, with fourteen rows at orchestra level, a half-dozen boxes, and a small balcony with two rows. The result was a jewel—known as the Princess Theatre—in which there could be no inexpensive seats.[28]

The Shuberts were unclear what to do with the Princess, so they turned to the director Holbrook Blinn, the manager F. Ray Comstock, and the indubitable theatrical agent Elisabeth "Bessie" Marbury to come up with a plan. Marbury approached Kern to help out; and Kern, in turn, suggested that he work with the British-born lyricist Guy Bolton. The British humorist P. G. Wodehouse joined the team in 1917. Between 1915 and 1920, Kern, Bolton, and Wodehouse composed sixteen scores that were noteworthy for their intimate scale, modest productions, ingenious wordplay, light music, and clever plots—as well as for attracting knowledgeable, affluent audiences.

Kern drew on jazz harmonies to transform musical scores; Bolton connected the lyrics to storytelling; and Wodehouse added a dollop of sophisticated humor and charm. "The Princess Theatre" musicals—which included *Very Good Eddie* (1915), *Nobody Home* (1915), *Oh, Boy!* (1917), and *Oh, Lady! Lady!* (1918)—transformed American musical theater.[29] More and more, successful shows relished erudition and complexity.[30] In what was still an unusual practice at the time, Kern collaborated with the African American songwriter Ford Dabney and the composer James Reese Europe when writing *Nobody Home*. But the Princess business model could not be sustained following the settlement with Actors' Equity (see the previous chapter), and, by 1920, the theater had turned to less expensive dramatic plays.[31]

Boardman assesses the importance of the Princess musicals by noting that the "shows were not radical departures for the American musical theater. Yet at the same time, they were clearly seminal in the genre's development. They assured that reasonably believable stories about reasonably believable people would provide the sturdy frame on which everything else would be hung. Royalty, supernatural beings, and grotesque clowns were shunted aside."[32]

By decade's end, the Princess had closed.[33] After it was dark for several years, the International Ladies' Garment Workers Union purchased it and converted it into a recreation center. After several different incarnations—including a period as a cinema—the building was demolished in 1955.

Kern thrived.[34] He and his wife moved to a comfortable house in the tony Westchester suburb of Bronxville, and, following the war, they made frequent trips to visit her family in London. An avid book collector, Kern became a familiar figure to antiquarian booksellers throughout New York and London.

In 1924, Kern became embroiled in a messy copyright infringement case, in which Fred Fisher—who owned the rights to his 1919 breakaway hit song "Dardanella," written with Felix Bernard and Johnny S. Black—claimed that Kern had stolen the bass line for his song "Ka-lu-a." Following a press-frenzied trial in which Victor Herbert, among others, was put on the witness stand, the eminent jurist Judge Learned Hand ruled that bass lines retain the same copyright protection as melodies, though he limited the judgment against Kern to the absolute minimum, in the absence of mal intent by Kern and material damage to Fisher.[35]

Kern collaborated with Flo Ziegfeld, and worked on several blockbuster hits, including *The Girl from Utah* (London, 1913; New York, 1914), for which he hired nineteen-year-old George Gershwin as the rehearsal pianist.[36] The successes continued to flow. *Sally* (1920), which Ziegfeld produced and which brought Marilyn Miller lasting fame, included the mega-hit "Look for the Silver Lining." *Stepping Stones* (1923) and *Criss Cross* (1926) followed. Some plays— such as *Sitting Pretty* (1924) and *Dear Sir* (1924)—failed.[37]

Most significantly, in 1925 Kern collaborated with Oscar Hammerstein II for the first time on *Sunny*, a follow-on vehicle to *Sally* for its star, Marilyn Miller, which ran for 517 performances on Broadway and 363 performances in London.[38] The well-off Kern had by now earned a reputation for being a difficult partner, and, over the years, he rarely sustained collaborative relations with anyone other than Hammerstein. *Sally* lured Kern to Hollywood for the production of its 1930 film version. He would not return to Broadway again.[39]

Kern would compose scores to more than a dozen films, with numerous collaborators, including numbers for Fred Astaire and Ginger Rogers ("I Won't Dance," 1935), and the Academy Award–winning "The Way You Look Tonight" (1936). In 1940, he set Oscar Hammerstein's lyric "The Last Time I Saw Paris" to music, the only hit either would write that was not part of a larger score for a play or film.

On November 5, 1945, Kern collapsed at the corner of Park Avenue and 57th Street after having returned a few days before to help with the revival of his classic show *Show Boat*. Carrying only his union (ASCAP) card, he was taken to the indigent ward at City Hospital, before Hammerstein was able to get him moved to Doctors Hospital. Kern died of a cerebral hemorrhage on November 11, without having regained consciousness, at the age of sixty.[40] The revival that had lured him back from the West Coast to New York promised to make theatrical history.

"Ol' Man River"

The crowd that had gathered at intermission in the lobby of the Globe Theater on October 12, 1926, to see the premiere performance of *Criss Cross* (a musical comedy with lyrics by Otto Harbach and Anne Caldwell and music by Jerome Kern) may have been talking about the stars Fred and Dorothy Stone, or perhaps they were still chatting about the Saint Louis Cardinals' seven-game victory over the hometown Yankees a few days before. Those who were politically inclined undoubtedly were arguing about the latest imbroglio headed to the Supreme Court between President Calvin Coolidge and the US Senate over the president's authority to appoint and dismiss federal officials. But whatever their conversations might have been about, it is doubtful that anyone was aware of a casual introduction taking place that would change the history of American musical theater. That chance meeting did not focus on the play being performed, which would run for a respectful 210 performances before closing as the Yankees were taking the field again in April 1927.[41]

The composer, Jerome Kern, had just finished reading the new, best-selling novel *Show Boat*, by the rising author Edna Ferber.[42] Ferber—who had grown up in the Midwest, the daughter of a Hungarian-born Jewish shopkeeper and his Milwaukee-born wife—had started out working as a journalist covering the 1920 Republican and Democratic national conventions. Then she moved on to fiction, winning the 1925 Pulitzer Prize for *So Big*, a novel about a silent film star. That success was followed by *Minick*, as well as the season's smash novel, *Show Boat*, which would earn her a second Pulitzer. She subsequently enjoyed great success writing novels, plays, and screenplays, garnering an Oscar for her script for *Cimarron*. Among her numerous successes is the 1956 film classic *Giant*, featuring an all-star cast—including Elizabeth Taylor, Rock Hudson, James Dean, Carroll Baker, Mercedes McCambridge, Dennis Hopper, and Sal Mineo.

Although much of Ferber's fame and success lay ahead, she already was becoming a fixture on the New York literary scene (e.g., she would become a steadfast member of the famous Round Table lunch group that met daily at the Algonquin Hotel in Midtown Manhattan). In her stories, Ferber bestowed the strongest character traits on people who confronted discrimination of one sort or other. Her stories were also noteworthy for their strong women, who are both supported by—and are in conflict with—plentiful, colorfully portrayed supporting characters. As the *Show Boat* historian Todd Decker notes, "Ferber never created a woman who couldn't win on her own terms in a world of men. The children are disappointing but never embarrassing."[43] She was herself a formidable woman, who lived on her own until her death in 1968 overlooking Central Park.

The composer Kern was chatting amiably at the intermission of his latest premiere with the *New York Times* drama critic Alexander Woolcott, mentioning in passing that he would like to meet Ferber, whose book *Show Boat* he had just read. Woolcott and Ferber maintained a testy relationship, which developed into a deep feud at times before the vitriolic Woolcott's death in 1943. But at that time his relationship with the young novelist was as yet far from its nadir. Seeing Ferber across the crowded opening night lobby, he shouted to her, asking Kern to follow as he introduced the novelist and composer to one another.

Kern mentioned that he wanted to write a musical based on *Show Boat*. Ferber, though fearing a fluffy confection unworthy of her work, initially hid her incredulity and agreed to meet again. A creative partnership ensued and, before too long, Ferber granted Kern and his lyricists Oscar Hammerstein II and P. G. Wodehouse the rights to turn the story into what would become the hit musical of the next season—and of many seasons thereafter.[44]

With Broadway rushing headlong toward its greatest commercial success—more plays being performed than at any time before or since—New York's highbrow literati tittered among themselves about the absence of "authenticity" in commercial culture. The issue was brought to a head by the newfound popularity of Negro spirituals, which were coming into vogue in socially proper circles. Promoters increasingly asked African American performers to sing spirituals in formal concert settings—an honor and a paycheck, to be sure.[45] Yet some critics wondered whether a professionally trained singer such as Jules Bledso or Paul Robeson performing in a tuxedo on the stage of a concert hall reserved for the European greats constituted an "authentic" representation of music once sung by enslaved fieldhands.[46]

Ferber—who was intrigued by such questions swirling around the intersection of race, music, and identity—decided to set out a novel to bring together questions of authenticity in the artificial world of the theater.[47] After a misbegotten out-of-town tryout for her and George S. Kaufman's stage adaptation of her story *Old Man Minick,* the producer Winthrop Ames bitterly proposed that they could always take the performance to a "showboat." Ferber later recalled that she had never heard of such a thing.[48]

As noted above, floating theaters had been plying the nation's waters ever since William Chapman and his family launched their floating palace in pre–Civil War Pittsburgh. But the fashion for such entertainment waned as railroads enabled producers tied to the Theater Syndicate to gain monopoly control over the entertainment business. Fewer, but still a handful of, floating theaters remained in business as quaint reminders of an earlier era.

The intrigued Ferber dove into research and eventually spent several weeks on the Chesapeake Bay–based *James Adams Floating Palace Theater.*[49] Her novel's success resulted from a powerful com-

bination of strong characters, an unexpectedly complex and controversial story, and a watchful attention to getting the story's details
right.

Ferber's story is difficult to summarize, for it is rich in unexpected twists and turns that have been open to reinterpretation
with each retelling in print, on the stage, and on film.[50] The powerful themes that run throughout the story include the ambiguities
of race; the poorly defined boundary between appearance and performance on one hand, and reality and the authentic on the other
hand; and the impact of technological innovation.[51]

Essentially, the tale is about life on the showboat *Cotton Blossom*
plying the Mississippi River in 1887, just as Jim Crow segregation
is digging in after the end of the Reconstruction Era.[52] Upon pulling into a dock at Natchez, the *Blossom*'s Cap'n Andy and his wife,
Parthy Ann, intervene to stop an altercation after the ruffian Pete
makes a pass at Julie, the wife of the boat's leading man, Steve.

Meanwhile, an eighteen-year-old beauty, Magnolia, catches the
eye of the handsome riverboat gambler Gaylord Ravenal. Magnolia,
in turn, seeks advice from Joe, a black dock worker (who responds
by offering life's wisdom, with the classic ballad "Ol' Man River").
Joe—who had been dispatched by his wife Queenie, the ship's
cook, to buy flour—sends Magnolia to Queenie, where the young
girl sings a song known only to "colored folks," "Can't Help Lovin'
Dat Man." Why does Magnolia, a young white girl, sing like a black
woman? Is it even possible for a white singer to do so and "be authentic?"

By this early point, the story's essential riddle has crystallized:
When it comes to race, nothing is as it first seems—a powerful
theme at a time when the Ku Klux Klan was at its most virulent and
white crowds lynched a couple of dozen blacks each year.[53]

The spurned Pete runs off, only to return with the sheriff, claiming that Julie and Steve are living in violation of Mississippi's' anti-
miscegenation laws banning mixed-race marriages. After Steve and
Julie exchange blood through sliced finger tips, they and the crew
swear that they both share Negro blood. As Negroes, they must
now leave—though they have avoided jail. Soon enough, Magnolia
marries Ravenal, the scamp of a riverboat gambler. Together, they
eventually head off to Chicago.

Six years later, in 1893, the action moves to Chicago, at the height of the city's famous World's Columbian Exposition. Ravenal and Magnolia have lived the good life—and have started a family, with the birth of their daughter, Kim. But now Ravenal cuts out, leaving Magnolia and Kim to move to a rooming house. Two former *Cotton Blossom* performers, Frank and Ellie, discover Magnolia and Kim as they seek to rent the same room. They arrange for Magnolia to try out for a singing gig at the Trocadero (the same name as Ziegfeld's Chicago club of the same era). Julie, by now a star, accidentally overhears Magnolia auditioning and backs out so the younger woman can get the job. Magnolia becomes a star following her in-spired performance in a dance extravaganza titled "In Dahomey," which briefly features a young Bert Williams, who, together with his partner George Walker, would star in the Broadway hit of the same name.[54] Kern and Hammerstein thus reference both African American performers at the 1893 World's Fair who masqueraded as Africans; and Will Marion Cook and Paul Laurence Dunbar's 1903 musical hit play of the same name.

The action switches to 1927. Kim has become a leading lady on Broadway, and Magnolia wants to return to the *Cotton Blossom*. Cap'n Andy arranges for Ravenal to be backstage at Kim's debut performance in a Broadway play featuring the era's dance craze, the Charleston. Ravenal surreptitiously serenades Magnolia, who is in the boxes enjoying her daughter's stage success. Ravenal and Magnolia reunite and return to the *Cotton Blossom*.

By bringing the story into what was the present, audiences are moved from an era when black and white were separate to the con-temporary moment, when African American music—spirituals, jazz, and song and dance—were the rage on Broadway.[55] The epic story's intricacy permitted Ferber to explore a variety of the era's most troublesome cultural issues. Such convolution does not easily lend itself to the stage—especially the commercially driven theater of 1920s Broadway. Ferber's initial skepticism about the whole idea of this musical would seem well founded. The play succeeds, how-ever, because it presented a vehicle for Kern to engage more deeply than before with the African American contribution to American music.

Hammerstein, the lead lyricist, revealed a deep commitment to racial equality throughout his career. For him, *Show Boat* provided an early opportunity to do battle with racism and inequality. He aggressively reworked Ferber's novel to fit it onto the stage. He was able, in Citron's words, "to cut Ferber's book to its essence and add a sense of romance and lightness to the play without violating any of *Show Boat*'s considerable artistic principles. He eliminated whole segments, slicing off at least a decade of Ferber's story and telescoping lengthy scenes that brought the show up to date at the end. He combined characters, and most of all, he began to realize that the story's appeal lay largely in its early scenes and period setting."[56] He did so, as Lerner understood, but placing the river itself at the center of the story.

For Lerner, "'Ol' Man River'" was "the greatest folk lyric ever written in the music theatre. . . . Probably the profoundest lyric ever to emerge on the musical stage. . . . The entire score was studded with both brilliance and depth, almost as if each man had suddenly opened a door in his creative soul, behind which a greater artist had been waiting to see the sunlight."[57]

The libretto unfolded as it did in part because Kern and Hammerstein envisioned a star vehicle promoting Paul Robeson as a way to capitalize on the growing white fascination with black talent.[58] Robeson waffled on making a commitment because he was concerned, in part, by unflattering characterizations of blacks in the script and also by competing professional commitments. Jules Bledsoe gave a landmark performance in the original production, and Robeson would join the 1928 London production. Having sung "Ol' Man River" onstage, Robeson took ownership of this magisterial song, and he would continue to play the role through a 1940 Los Angeles production.[59]

Because Robeson's participation seemed ever less likely, Kern, Hammerstein, and Wodehouse moved the character of Julie center stage, especially after having signed a scandalous nightclub performer—and speakeasy owner—Helen Morgan as Julie. Just two days after the opening of *Show Boat*, Morgan was arrested when Prohibition enforcement officers closed down her Times Square after-hours club in a spectacular raid, thereby generating invaluable publicity for the new Broadway show.[60] Sitting on top of a piano and playing with a swirling scarf, Morgan made Julie's torch song

"Bill"—artfully crafted by Wodehouse and Kern for her limited talents—into a personal signature. She would carry the song and the role from production to production—from stage to Hollywood screen—until her death from alcohol-related illnesses in 1941.[61]

Race permeates *Show Boat*, from the threat of the arrest for miscegenation, and black characters "passing" for white, to demonstrations of profound wisdom by characters such as Joe and Queenie. The role of Queenie—which has long become synonymous with the illustrious screen portrayal by Hattie McDaniel (figure 23), who went on to win an Academy Award for best supporting actress for playing Mammy in *Gone with the Wind*—was initially performed in blackface by the Italian American vaudeville powerhouse Tess Gardella.[62] Gardella had gained fame for her vaudeville act, in which she played under the stage name "Aunt Jemima" (also the billing given her in the original *Show Boat* production).[63]

Figure 23. Hattie McDaniel (center)—the recipient of the Academy Award for best supporting actress in *Gone with the Wind*—pictured with the Hollywood Victory Committee's Negro Division, of which she was the chairwoman.
Source: US National Archives.

The show's opening chorus has proven far more controversial. As the *Cotton Blossom* docks, the black stevedores sing about their work, calling themselves the n-word: "N____s—all work on the Mississippi, N____s—all work while de white folks play." Was Hammerstein simply duplicating the language of the era? Or was he using the word with an ironic inflection? Robeson always refused to sing the word, often substituting "Negroes." Later productions substitute "people," or leave the chorus out altogether. The verse is blurred in the 1936 film. Hammerstein—an outspoken opponent of racial, religious, and ethnic discrimination all throughout his life—never commented on this chorus; and its presence confronts contemporary productions with vexing choices.[64]

Show Boat transformed the place of African American performers and music on Broadway. The show presented the first truly mixed cast in the history of the New York stage. Although blacks and whites had appeared onstage separately, either in their own shows or at different times during a single show, Hammerstein and Kern created a truly interracial musical in which blacks and whites appeared at the same time. And they interacted directly with one another when they did appear together. Both black and white music, dances, characters, and themes run together throughout the show. Moreover, even though whites dominate the storyline, blacks are given a significant presence throughout. African American characters often play the role of truth teller and repository of wisdom. There had never been a play like this.[65]

Show Boat demonstrated that the most popular of popular culture could still actively engage the country's most difficult topics. Kern and Hammerstein understood this possibility, turning to the impresario Flo Ziegfeld to stage their show. Ziegfeld expressed his admiration, and offered to have the show open the grand new theater that Joseph Urban and Thomas Lamb were building for him on the corner of 54th Street and Sixth Avenue. For this most opulent of all the Broadway stages, Ziegfeld wanted something a cut above the usual for its opening—and Kern and Hammerstein's show held out the promise of high art.

Unfortunately, Ziegfeld had begun to experience some of the financial difficulties that would lead him to ruin after the stock market crash in October 1929. Funds flowed only after Hammerstein and Kern paid a visit to the producer's Yonkers estate overlooking the Hudson River. Beyond financing, Ziegfeld permitted his top designer—Joseph Urban—to join the *Show Boat* production team. Tryouts in Pittsburgh, Cleveland, Philadelphia, and Washington led to endless tinkering, as the authors tried to trim and tuck the show into a more manageable package. Ziegfeld had to open his new theater in February 1927 with the now-forgotten musical *Rio Rita*. But *Show Boat* followed, on December 27, 1927, as a "Christmas present" to New York.[66] Critics immediately recognized the play as a classic with the power to last the ages.[67]

Show Boat has lived on for nearly a century. Even as it was closing in New York, the play headed to London, where its memorable 1928 production brought Robeson into the story (and he would remain in various revivals through the famous 1940 production in Los Angeles). The show has enjoyed at least eight major New York revivals, five London stagings, four Hollywood films, and numerous important stage productions in Houston, Los Angeles, and Washington.[68]

The show's film production brought Kern and Hammerstein to Hollywood. Kern would never return to Broadway—though (as already recounted above) he died after having headed east to stage the play's revival. Hammerstein failed to adapt to the West Coast, and he came back to New York to seek renewed success on Broadway. More important, *Show Boat*'s success on both stage and screen cemented the connection between the Broadway musical and the newly developing sound motion picture industry. It succeeded, as few American musicals ever have, as both popular entertainment and serious theater.

Show Boat ran for 572 performances on Broadway, covering a year and a half that ended just before the stock market crash of 1929 destroyed the good times. Broadway would never again be as central to American cultural life as it was when *Show Boat* had its initial success. The New York stage had to adapt to a world with fewer resources and more competitors, beginning with the rapid growth of Hollywood's massive film industry.

The urban historian Donald Miller summarizes Broadway's transformation resulting from the stock market crash, which bound the Great White Way and distant Hollywood together in new ways:

The Great Depression would deal a heavy but hardly fatal blow to the New York theater industry. In the entire United States there were two hundred theaters in the mid-1930s and forty four of them were in the Times Square district, but there were fewer of them every year. Many of the survivors were kept alive, as they had been for years, by movie money. It was Hollywood — "the archangel of Broadway" — that kept dozens of New York theaters in business in the late 1920s and into the 1930s. In these years, Hollywood money backed as many as a quarter of all shows on Broadway. West Coast producers used the New York stage as a "testing ground" for plays with film potential. Theater derived films would come back to Broadway as major motion pictures, packing the movie palaces that were the legitimate theaters' greatest competitors. As early as 1927, there really was no American Theater. There was only "a New York Theater," and Hollywood had a direct hand in it, both as principal supporter and damaging competitor.[69]

Other factors also undermined New York's central place in American life. Ironically, the New Deal of the New Yorker who had become president, Franklin Delano Roosevelt, redistributed wealth to the American South and West. Under Mayor Fiorello La Guardia, the city became more dependent on federal largess, setting it up for an eventual fall from grace later in the century, when more conservative Congresses ceased funding the numerous programs on which the city had come to depend.[70]

The Immigration Act of 1924 (otherwise known as the Johnson-Reed Act) limited the number of immigrants who would be admitted to the United States to 2 percent of the number of people living in the United States in 1890.[71] The result was to choke New York City off from one of its greatest sources of strength from the time of its founding as a Dutch colony: foreign-born, immigrant residents. The absence of new waves of immigrants was not immediately felt on Broadway, because the sons and daughters of immigrants continued to enter the world of New York theater for another generation. But over time, the impact would be profound.

"We'll Have Manhattan"

In 1925, Sterling Holloway and June Cochran stepped on the stage of that year's *Garrick Gaieties* and burst forth into a song about the delights of Manhattan as seen through the eyes of a young couple in love. This song—"We'll Have Manhattan"—by the new team of lyricist Lorenz Hart and composer Richard Rodgers, became an instant hit, and it has been recorded over and over again ever since (figure 24). Rodgers and Hart, who had been introduced at an amateur show at Columbia University a half-dozen years earlier, would eventually write 28 musicals and more than 500 songs, and pen numerous hit tunes for Hollywood films between 1919 and 1943, when Hart died.[72] Hart was thirty when the team took Manhattan by storm, and Rodgers was just a couple of years beyond twenty. In many ways, they exemplified Broadway and New York.

Figure 24. Richard Rodgers and Lorenz Hart in 1936.
Source: Photograph by a New York World-Telegram staff photographer; Library of Congress.

As noted above, Rodgers, the grandson of Jewish immigrants from Russia, grew up in a prosperous physician's family in Queens.[73] He attended Columbia University and the Institute of Musical Art (now the Juilliard School) before trying his hand in Tin Pan Alley. By 1919, he had teamed up with Hart, and they had begun finding a successful joint voice.[74]

Larry Hart was the son of successful Jewish German parents who moved to Harlem and could afford to send Larry and his brother Teddy (a future musical comedy star) to private school. Larry attended the Columbia School of Journalism before drifting toward Tin Pan Alley. His first job in music was to translate German plays into English for the Shuberts.[75] By 1919, he started working with Rodgers.[76] Individually and jointly, Dick and Larry personified the New York experience at its best. The sons of German Jewish families—and of immigrant parents, in the case of Hart—they thrived in middle-class neighborhoods made possible by the spreading city's subways, and advanced through a high-quality education, ending up at one of the country's leading universities. Looking to the future, their religious and ethnic backgrounds foreclosed some professions, yet many options remained open to them. Rodgers's father flourished as a respected physician, and Hart's was a successful businessman.

They had every opportunity to hear music and to see musical theater. Rodgers, while a child, attended the New York premiere of Diaghilev's Ballets Russes, heard Josef Hofmann play Tchaikovsky's Piano Concerto No. 1 at Carnegie Hall, saw Enrico Caruso at the Metropolitan Opera, and regularly attended the New York Philharmonic's free concerts at Lewisohn Stadium with his aunt.[77] Rodgers received first-rate musical training at one of the country's best conservatories, which was a quick subway ride away. New York was the sort of place where, in the late 1920s, when his wife Dorothy decided to become a sculptor, she would study with a then-struggling immigrant Ukrainian, Alexander Archipenko.[78]

Attracted to music, Rodgers and Hart gained immediate access to the most imaginative songwriters and promoters in the country—thus, they were nurtured as up-and-coming protégés by the Shuberts, Lew Fields, Jerome Kern, and Victor Herbert. Being in New York, they heard all kinds of music and saw all genres of theater. Their works drew on influences that never would have converged elsewhere.

Once Rodgers and Hart had been discovered, success created opportunities for greater accomplishment. Therefore, when the Depression undermined the economic viability of New York theater, they—like many of their colleagues—were able to use their connections to earn good livings in Hollywood.[79] Only Hart's bouts with depression and alcoholism limited their achievements.

Having been born in New York at the turn of the twentieth century (Hart in 1895; Rodgers in 1902), the world was completely open to them. They effortlessly personified the city of their birth and the musical theater of their choosing. They both created new forms of theater—and, in their small ways, new forms of city life—and were products of that same theatrical and urban tradition.[80] As they declared to the world at the end of their first hit song, "The city's glamor can never spoil the dreams of a boy and goil / We'll turn Manhattan into an isle of joy."[81] And they did. There were few more famous theater folks in the New York of the 1930s than Rodgers and Hart.[82]

Three landmark Rodgers and Hart collaborations—*On Your Toes* (1936), *Babes in Arms* (1937), and *Pal Joey* (1940)—are especially noteworthy for the ways in which they exemplified the emergent American musical art form—and reshaped it in the process. Rodgers and Hart explicitly sought to integrate varied art forms into their works. For example, they decided to form a partnership with George Balanchine after having seen a 1935 recital of Balanchine's ballet company.[83]

Rodgers incorporated jazz influences into the score of *On Your Toes*, a convoluted story about a touring Russian Ballet company in which a provincial university music teacher, Junior Dolan III, falls for the company's prima ballerina, Vera Baranova.[84] Junior's fixation on Vera unleashes the jealous rage of her lover, Morrisone, who orders a hit on Junior. The second act features a jazz ballet choreographed by George Balanchine—"Slaughter on Tenth Avenue"—in which Junior, tipped off about the plot, keeps dancing so that his potential killers won't have an opportunity to shoot him during the ballet's loud conclusion. The police arrive just in time, and Junior is united with his student Frankie and his parents.

Rodgers and Hart originally conceived of the piece as a cinematic vehicle for Fred Astaire. They took it to Broadway once Astaire rejected the concept, with a cast that included Ray Bolger and Tamara Geva (who had left Saint Petersburg with Balanchine and previously had been his wife). The play—which featured the hit "There's a Small Hotel"—ran for 315 performances before moving to London, with Jack Whiting and Vera Zorina in the lead roles, and it has been reprised on film and stage many times over.

The "Slaughter on Tenth Avenue" ballet proved to be a landmark moment in the history of American music and ballet. Balanchine formed a partnership with the African American choreographer Herbie Harper to blend jazz, tap, and ballet throughout the show.[85] Balanchine then continued to work with African American dancers and choreographers over the next several years, comfortably incorporating lessons learned from his collaborations with the brothers Harold and Fayard Nicholas and Katherine Dunham into his other work.[86] Once again, the immigrant outsider understood that there was much to learn from African American traditions, in the case of Balanchine both on Broadway and in Hollywood.

On Your Toes brought serious dance center stage on Broadway—including a memorable number of battling American stage tap and chorus dancers and Russian ballet dancers as well as the longer ballet piece—and melded jazz with ballet. Dance drove the story forward, and it was integral to the play's narrative and not merely a stand-alone confection.[87] Rodgers and Hart—as well as George Abbott, who worked on the book, and the director, C. Worthington Miner—reconfigured the boundaries between high-brow and middle-brow culture by integrating previously disparate performing arts into a cohesive whole that was innovative and original.

Rodgers, Hart, and Balanchine went even further a year later with *Babes in Arms*. The play was built around teenagers on rural Long Island who stage a show to circumvent the local sheriff's efforts to send them to a work farm. Though it was defanged in later film and stage productions, the original version of the play included explicit political dialogues, communists, and African American victims of racism. The opening production, which ran for 289 performances, featuring a racially integrated cast including Nicholas Brothers, Alfred Drake, Ray Heatherton, and Mitzi Green, among others. For Lerner, *Babes in Arms* "may well have been their [Rodgers and Hart's] greatest score."[88] Many of the musical's songs—such as "My Funny Valentine," "The Lady Is a Tramp," "Where or When," and "I Wish I Were in Love Again"—moved easily into the *Great American Songbook*.

The apogee of Rodgers and Hart's remarkable legacy came with the original Broadway production of *Pal Joey*, which starred Vivienne Segal and a newcomer, Gene Kelly.[89] Based on the work of the novelist John O'Hara, the story revolves around Joey Evans, an amoral, disreputable antihero—hardly usual fare for the Broadway stage.[90] The darkly cynical, womanizing Joey runs through a number of caddish relationships throughout the show. Simultaneously, however, Joey is charming to a fault, as is the score—including the renowned "Bewitched, Bothered, and Bewildered"—which stands in stark contrast to the shadowy tale. In *Pal Joey*, Rodgers and Hart presage the shadier heroes who came to dominate Broadway in the second half of the twentieth century.

Larry Hart fought personal demons and ill health throughout much of his adult life. Rodgers adjusted to Hart's innate unreliability, finding new ways to continue working. But by the early 1940s, his patience had run out, and Dick began looking for new ideas and new partners. In 1943, Dick was collaborating with Oscar Hammerstein II on what would become *Oklahoma!*[91] Hart, who had been close to his mother throughout his life, descended more deeply into depression following her death (so much so that he was unaware of attending his mother's funeral).[92] On November 22, 1943, Larry died from pneumonia from exposure after heavy drinking.[93] His glorious lyrics—in such hits as "Bewitched, Bothered, and Bewildered," "Isn't It Romantic?" "My Romance," and "With a Song in My Heart"—embody a search for love and acceptance that Hart never found within himself.

"Oh What a Beautiful Mornin'"

The 1930s were not as kind to Oscar Hammerstein II as the 1920s had been. After a stint in Hollywood that began with work on the screenplay for *Show Boat* turned sour, Hammerstein and his wife Dorothy discovered that they were East Coast theater people rather than Californian movie people.[94] Returning to New York, they began to split their time between Manhattan and a 72-acre working farm in Bucks County, Pennsylvania, outside Philadelphia.

Whatever peace Hammerstein found in his quiet domestic life was not being replicated in his professional life, for he wrote a series of undistinguished flops.[95] His translation of *Carmen* into an African American setting as *Carmen Jones* reflected his continuing interest in black culture. However, the project achieved more attention as a film during the 1950s than it did at its 1943 New York stage premiere.[96] Hammerstein's singular success was a poem he wrote in response to the Nazi occupation of Paris. Jerry Kern, reading the poem, added the music to what became the sorrowful hit tune "The Last Time I Saw Paris."[97] Hammerstein was looking to try something new.

The 1930s were not as kind to the Theatre Guild as the 1920s had been. The Depression, the shift of entertainment dollars to Hollywood, the movement of audiences to cinemas, and a series of less-than-successful productions left the organization with more prestige than financial resources. By the decade's end, the guild was almost bankrupt.[98] Like Hammerstein, the guild was looking to try something new.

Looking back through the files, the Theatre Guild's codirector, Theresa Helburn, rediscovered an unsuccessful play by Lynn Riggs named after a folk song: *Green Grow the Lilacs*. Though nominated at the time for a Pulitzer Prize, Riggs's play opened and closed in early 1931 after only sixty-four performances. The story of failed cowboy love in Indian Territory (later Oklahoma) at the turn of the century had never connected with Depression-era audiences. But Helburn believed in the work, thinking that it could be successful if set to music. Even more, its very American themes would play well to the wartime audiences of the early 1940s. Helburn hoped that the play could capitalize on the popularity of John Steinbeck's 1939 novel *The Grapes of Wrath* about the flight of Depression era Okies.[99]

Helburn approached Dick Rodgers to write music for the play. When Rodgers approached Larry Hart, the writer dismissed the offer to collaborate. Hart was not attracted to the play's rustic setting, was beset by personal difficulties, and left for a vacation in Mexico. "If you walk out on me now, I'm going to do it with someone else," Rodgers is reported to have responded to Hart's rejection. "Anyone in mind?" Hart asked. "Yes," Rodgers replied, "Oscar Hammerstein." "Well," answered Hart, "you couldn't pick a better man."[100] The legendary twenty-four-year collaboration between Rodgers and Hart came to an abrupt end.[101]

Hammerstein already had considered setting the Riggs play to music, only to set the idea aside when Jerry Kern turned the idea down.[102] So when Rodgers called Hammerstein, both men—who had first met years before at Columbia University but had never been more than professional acquaintances—were predisposed to take on Helburn's project. Hammerstein invited Rodgers to lunch at his farm on September 1941. Almost immediately, they reconvened at Rodgers's Fairfield, Connecticut, residence and began to work. Over the next several months, Hammerstein would write lyrics and send them to Rodgers, who would write the musical score—the opposite pattern from what either one had used with their previous collaborators, Kern and Hart.

The new musical—titled *Away We Go!*—came together quickly; but its financing did not.[103] So Rodgers and Hammerstein worked assiduously to raise the money, realizing, in the process, that they needed to become their own producers. As a result, they transformed the business side of show business. In addition to creating New York stage productions, road trips, films, sheet music, and, in significant innovations, original cast recordings and television broadcasts of their own works, Rodgers and Hammerstein produced the works of others as well.[104] Most notably, they were the business force behind Irving Berlin's classic musical *Annie Get Your Gun* (1946) and Cole Porter's *Kiss Me Kate* (1948).[105]

The artistic impact of Rodgers and Hammerstein proved to be inestimable. As the theater historian Ethan Mordden notes, of the nine stage shows they created, "one was an outright failure, another was a succès d'estime, and two were hits but did not enter the abiding repertory The remaining five form the most phenomenal success story in the musical's saga, making up a unique short list of eternally revivable classics and governing Broadway for a generation."[106] Together, they received thirty-four Tony Awards, fifteen Academy Awards, two Grammy Awards, and the Pulitzer Prize. Artistically, their collaboration elevated Rodgers to the level of recognition of his idol, Jerome Kern (while Kern was gracious in public about Rodgers and his erstwhile, longtime partner Hammerstein's success, he privately viewed *Oklahoma!* as a challenge to his own supremacy in the world of American musical theater).[107]

Helburn pulled together a creative team during the waiting period, while Rodgers, Hammerstein, and the Theatre Guild tried to secure the resources to stage the new work. Lerner tells the story well:

> Searching for a choreographer, [Theresa Helburn] had seen a ballet in the repertoire of the Ballets Russes de Monte Carlo called *Rodeo*. The choreographer was that often-replaced lady Agnes de Mille. Theresa Helburn recommended that Dick and Oscar see the ballet, which they did. They loved it. They thought Agnes was ideal. They approached her. She accepted. The guild, remembering Rouben Mamoulian's contribution to *Porgy and Bess*, suggested him as director, and there was no hesitancy. Alfred Drake, the young leading man who had sung so beautifully in *Babes in Arms*, was selected to play Curly, and Joan Roberts, who had sung the lead in Oscar's 1941 ill-fated operetta *Sunny River*, was chosen for Laurey.[108]

De Mille was the daughter of the playwright William C. de Mille and the niece of the film director Cecil B. de Mille. She grew up in California and had choreographed films before moving to theater. After she had returned from European studies, the American Ballet Theater invited her to choreograph Aaron Copland's score *Rodeo*, integrating popular dances with classical ballet.[109] *Rodeo* was an instant hit, and this success at composing a cowboy-and-cowgirl ballet made her a perfect candidate for Rodgers and Hammerstein's Western-inspired work.[110]

Although *Oklahoma!* was well received in its New Haven and Boston tryouts, Rodgers and Hammerstein continued to tinker with their work. In Boston, they added the song "Oklahoma!" and made that song the title of the show. The New York run could not have been more successful. Opening on March 31, 1943, *Oklahoma!* would run for 2,212 performances over five years, together with a successful film, extended tours, London productions, and endless reprises.[111] The play rescued the Theatre Guild and made Rodgers and Hammerstein very well off, earning a profit of $4,245,500.[112]

Oklahoma! immediately became recognized as an artistic as well as commercial breakthrough (winning a special Pulitzer Prize in 1944). It opened the floodgates on stories glorifying life in an earlier America.[113] The play set the standard for the American "book musical," building on a base set by Kern and Hammerstein in *Show Boat* a decade and a half before. Like *Show Boat, Oklahoma!* drew on American folk culture and music to enliven the traditions brought to American shores with European operetta. Indeed, as is often the case with achievements that consolidate previous innovations and launch the arts off in new directions, most of the play's constituent parts had already existed in some form or other.

In this, as in all their best work, Rodgers and Hammerstein presented coherent characters and stories in depth, partly because their works began with Hammerstein's lyrics rather than with Rodgers's music.[114] They became literary as well as musical works. Later on, the team would deal with serious issues of race, class, and cultural conflict.[115]

The success was a consequence of a true collaboration that made both Rodgers and Hammerstein better as a pair than they would have been individually. Hammerstein's approach to writing lyrics perfectly supported Rodgers's approach to writing scores. As the biographer Meryle Secrest noted about Rodgers's composition, he displayed "a gift more to be valued than speed, versatility, dramatic appropriateness, or even a subliminal understanding of the needs of his times: that of the inevitable melody. This sequence of notes so imprints itself on the ear that one cannot ever forget it, or ever wants to."[116]

Lerner goes to the heart of Rodgers and Hammerstein's achievement in his homage to the American musical theater:

> *Oklahoma!* was the most totally realized amalgamation of all the theatrical arts. The book was legitimate play writing, every song flowed from the dramatic action, and Agnes de Mille's ballet at the end of Act One, in which Curly and Laurey were skillfully replaced by two dancers as the plot

continued, was one of the most imaginative uses of choreography yet set in a theater. Whereas Hammerstein was never the wit that Larry Hart was, he was far superior as a dramatic lyricist, and lyricist, and certainly no one ever wrote a lyric that sang better. Lyrically *Oklahoma!* was a masterful work, lighter than Hammerstein had been before and with none of the "poetic" excesses that to me frequently marred some of his future writing. Dick's music adjusted itself to the new collaboration, and together they produced a new voice and a style that was distinctly their own.[117]

Oklahoma! made another, perhaps more unusual, contribution to the American stage—though one that would not be revealed for some time. A child chum of Hammerstein's son Jamie—who had been coming to visit the Hammersteins' Bucks County farm—was looking to show off before a family babysitter and called his friend to get some standing room tickets to see the hit of the season. The Hammersteins obliged, and young Stephen Sondheim took the sitter to see the musical. He was hooked and, as he frequented the Hammersteins' farm more and more often in the months and years ahead, he began turning to Hammerstein for advice about how to write musicals.[118]

Oklahoma! helped to define New York's transition from wartime to postwar prosperity. With most of its major rivals having been destroyed by the fighting, New York was securely at the top of the world's urban hierarchy, entering a run of unprecedented wealth and prestige and cultural self-confidence. "Few cities in the history of the world," the British author Jan Morris observes, "can have stood so consciously at a moment of fulfillment, looking into a future that seemed so full of reward."[119] As if to prove this point, New York became in some sense the "capital of the world" with the construction of United Nations Headquarters on the former site of the East Side's slaughterhouses.

At the Top of the World

New York was at a point of transition. In many ways, it was the same city it had been for much of the twentieth century. Fully half of Manhattan's residents were either foreign born or were children of foreign-born parents; a quarter of New Yorkers were Jewish; and about a fifth were black.[120] New York remained a town that produced goods as well as traded them. In 1940, 60 percent of New York workers held manufacturing jobs.[121] The city's population was continuing to grow—from 7,454,995 according to the 1940 census to 7,891,957 at the time of the 1950 census.[122]

Several trends, however, were beginning to make themselves felt, which, within a decade or two, would define rapid urban decline. Automobiles and suburban dreams carried more and more residents to homes outside the city; immigrants, restricted by law in the mid-1920s, began to disappear; and manufacturing fled first out of town, then to the rising American Sun Belt, and eventually abroad.

The city's population declined to just over 7 million by the 1980s, before beginning a new path of growth, driven by the financial and service sectors. The city's population would not surpass its previous 1950 high until the late 1990s, and has continued to grow, to nearly 8.5 million in the mid-2000s.[123]

A sharp decline in the percentage of New Yorkers who were foreign born represents another significant change. By 1970, less than 20 percent of the city's population had been born abroad, an all-time low. Once again, this trend reversed itself in the 1970s and 1980s, so that, by the first decade of the 2000s, more than a third of all New Yorkers had been born abroad.[124] This increase took place once President Lyndon Johnson signed the Immigration and Nationality Act (or Hart-Celler Act) of 1965, removing previous restrictions on immigration by nationality. Over time, New York benefited from the new policies as much as any place in the country, growing with the new arrivals from a wider array of countries of origin than ever before.[125] By the early twenty-first century, Asians represented the fastest-growing population group, while the white and African American populations stabilized.[126] The city never has been as diverse racially, ethnically, and religiously as it would become in recent years.[127]

When, after World War II, demand for labor continued to grow and earlier immigration patterns had been disrupted by legislative restrictions, the still-expanding demand for workers was met by rural African American and Puerto Rican migration to the city. The newly arriving African American population expanded the black community well beyond traditional patterns. Blacks moved to Brooklyn, Queens, the Bronx, and surrounding suburbs, making metropolitan New York the largest—and one of the most diverse— African American communities in the United States (encompassing more than 3.5 million people at the outset of the twenty-first century).[128]

The inauguration of inexpensive direct airline routes between San Juan and New York City prompted Puerto Ricans—who had been granted US citizenship at the beginning of American involvement in World War I in 1917—to move north. A total of 40,000 Puerto Ricans arrived in New York in 1946, 58,600 in 1952, and 75,000 in 1953. And as they brought their culture, their music, and their language to the city, New York became a major and energetic epicenter for Spanish-language culture by the end of the 1950s (e.g., the first New York Puerto Rican Day Parade was held on April 12, 1958). New York began to become something it had never been before: Latin.[129]

These trends tracked the decline of an urban economic regime dependent on federal and other public expenditures, which had ended with the city barely escaping bankruptcy during the mid-1970s. Industrial employment collapsed, so that by the 1990s just 16 percent of all private-sector jobs were in manufacturing.[130] The city that once made the things it traded had returned to what it had been during British rule: a city that added value through trade rather than production. As New York became less important to the country's economic fortunes, it also lost political clout. Only the explosion of high-technology and financial services employment beginning in the 1980s turned around the city's fortunes.[131]

These tumultuous changes—first, the end of decades of near-continuous growth; then, calamitous decline; and finally, a remarkable revival—shaped what would appear on New York stages as well as who would be in the audience. New Yorkers who were recent immigrants brought fresh energy, music, and tastes to Broadway, as they had always done before. The search for new identities transformed what people wanted to hear and see, as did new technologies—ranging from long-playing recordings to television to computer screens, the Internet, and the Cloud. New York's future never quite played out as people thought it would. Even if "you cannot be a Wonder City forever," as Jan Morris observes, New York remained one of the dynamic cultural centers on the planet, and Broadway was center stage.[132]

Yet all this was unknown as Rodgers and Hammerstein's singing cowboys danced innocently to de Mille's choreography under Mamoulian's direction. Audiences understood at the time that the war was ending; and they were at the top of the world.

Teaching Carefully

The Theatre Guild's Helburn and Lawrence Langner invited Dick and Oscar to lunch in 1944 and suggested that they bring the same creative team together for a musical based on Ferenc Molnar's hit play from earlier in the century, *Liliom*.[133] Set in a bleak fin de siècle Hungary, *Liliom* had managed to charm audiences everywhere (including in a 1921 New York production starring Eva Le Gallienne as a simple servant girl, and Joseph Schildkraut as an itinerant cad of a circus barker).[134] Rodgers and Hammerstein moved the story to a small New England coastal town in the 1870s, thereby "Americanizing" the tale at a time when American national spirits ran high.[135] They brought back de Mille—who choreographed another dream ballet—and Mamoulian, to put the pieces together.[136] Newcomers John Riatt and Jan Clayton played the lead roles of Billie Bigelow, the carnival barker, and Julie Jordan, the young and naive townie.[137] Bigelow fathers Julie's daughter Louise and is killed in a gambling fight. The "Starkeeper" in Heaven allows him to make one visit to set his now-fifteen-year-old daughter's life straight.

Carousel, as the play was renamed, opened across the street from *Oklahoma!* just days before the end of the war in Europe on April 19, 1945.[138] The first night's production was improved from meticulous and extensive revisions made during preview runs in Boston and New Haven.[139] *Carousel* would run for 890 performances, move to London, go on tour, and play on the Hollywood screen.[140]

Many close to the world of Broadway considered this to be the best among Rodgers's collaborations with Hammerstein. The play was Rodgers's favorite, though Hammerstein preferred their fourth collaboration, *Allegro* (in 1945, the pair squeezed in the successful musical movie *State Fair* for Hollywood).[141] Irving Berlin considered Hammerstein's lyrics for "You Will Never Walk Alone" (which Bigelow sings at the end of his Starkeeper-approved intervention), to be Oscar's best.[142] The extraordinarily high quality of the writing—Billy's extended "soliloquy" about becoming a father—is unmatched in the annals of American musical theater. Rodgers composed continuous music to run throughout the first act, which combined with de Mille's choreography to set a new standard for the Broadway stage.[143]

Rodgers and Hammerstein continued. *Allegro*—their third stage musical, and last for the Theatre Guild—offered another piece of Americana. Following the son of a small town doctor who goes to the big city, the play is said to be based on Hammerstein's own physician's life story. The innovative use of a Greek chorus and ingenious set design permitted a quick succession of scenes onstage. But the cast, directed and choreographed by de Mille, rebelled against her tyrannical leadership.

Allegro did not come together, even though, as noted above, Hammerstein liked it best of all among his works with Rodgers. The play has never been successfully staged, despite numerous efforts over subsequent decades. A recent 2014 staging, presented by the Classic Stage Company, fell as flat as previous attempts.[144] The play's place in Broadway history is tied more to Hammerstein permitting his protégé, Stephen Sondheim, to work backstage for the first time.[145] However, Rodgers and Hammerstein's next joint effort—*South Pacific*—would become another classic—one that explored the noisome question of race.

The Broadway stage promoted creative cooperation across some of America's deepest divisions, embracing immigrants, African Americans, and working-class and aristocratic whites alike. Consequently, from time to time, Broadway productions confronted some of the country's most deceitful demons. Flo Ziegfeld could bring Bert Williams to his stage at the very nadir of American race relations; the immigrant Irving Berlin could write Ragtime tunes; and the immigrant son George Gershwin could do it all.

As the United States came out of World War II an undisputed

global power, the American elite could ill afford withdrawing into a moated white world. African American World War II veterans would not permit it; their return in part promoted an explosion of domestic civil rights movements.[146] New non-European allies overseas would not permit it either. But how could ordinary Americans think about the complexity of a nonwhite world that they could no longer ignore?[147] Rodgers and Hammerstein's portrayal of a story from James Michener's 1947 Pulitzer Prize–winning short story collection *Tales of the Pacific* defined the challenge of what it meant to be all-American in a non-American world.[148]

Set in a United States–occupied Polynesian island at the height of fighting in the Pacific, *South Pacific* is at once very "American" — most of the characters are in the US Navy — and strikingly exotic.[149] Many audience members would have readily identified with the military setting, given their own wartime experiences. They were reminded of the imagined location's profound foreignness every time they saw and heard the single civilian woman onstage: a Tongan barkeeper, Bloody Mary (skillfully played in the original by the Juilliard-trained African American Juanita Hall), who sings about the mystical paradise always found on the next island just a little further away, "Bali Ha'i."[150]

Rodgers and Hammerstein drew most directly among Michener's stories about the love story between the Arkansas nurse Nellie Forbush — played by their spunky favorite female lead, the Texan Mary Martin — and an older, local French planter, Emile de Becque — played by the Metropolitan Opera basso Enzio Pinza. In the first of what would become a series of May/November love affairs running throughout Rodgers and Hammerstein's later works — the younger, naive Nellie falls for the older, sophisticated Emile.[151] She is shocked to discover that he has several interracial children. In the end, love triumphs over prejudice.

Nellie's ultimate rejection of racial prejudice aligns closely with Hammerstein's liberal humanitarianism and staunch opposition to discrimination and prejudice.[152] His views are spelled out in the song "You Have to Be Carefully Taught" — to become a bigot.[153] For Oscar, prejudice is learned behavior. As he wrote in a song for the Navy officer Cable to sing to Nellie after she had discovered Emile's multiracial children:

You've got to be taught
To hate and fear,
You've got to be taught
From year to year;
It' got to be drummed
In your dear little ear
You've got to be carefully taught.[154]

Of particular importance for Hammerstein, because prejudice had to be learned, it could also be unlearned—as is demonstrated by Nellie in *South Pacific*; and by the king in *The King and I*, who slowly overcomes his prejudices against the modern world. Such an equation of Nellie's rejection of Emile's children and the king's rejection of Western ways rankles many today, lending support to commentaries that Hammerstein promoted paternalistic approaches between whites and others at home and abroad. Recent staging of these works emphasize the contradictions in Hammerstein's position. At the time, his deep opposition to prejudice and discrimination identified him as at best an ultraliberal and at worst a communist sympathizer.

Ironically, in this context, Rodgers—whose next personal project was music for the 1952 World War II epic documentary film *Victory at Sea*—came under scrutiny by the US House of Representatives' Un-American Activities Committee and the Federal Bureau of Investigation.[155] Rodgers was viewed as an obvious threat to the United States after he had joined a committee of those prominent in the arts endorsing the reelection of President Franklin D. Roosevelt in 1944.[156]

Hammerstein's discomfort with *South Pacific*'s military theme led the team to invite Joshua Logan into their collaborative circle.[157] Logan had served in World War II as a public relations and intelligence officer, rising to the rank of captain. He had built on these experiences in directing the successful Broadway production of *Mister Roberts* in 1948; and had worked with Rodgers and Hammerstein Productions while directing *Annie Get Your Gun*. Earlier, Logan had directed Rodgers and Hart's *By Jupiter*.[158]

A graduate of Princeton—where he worked in student theater with James Stewart and Henry Fonda—Logan acted on the

Broadway and London stages before winning a scholarship to study with Konstantin Stanislavsky in Moscow.[159] Logan collaborated with Hammerstein, worked on the libretto, contributed to the songs, and directed the production (although he did not initially receive full creative credit at the time of *South Pacific*'s premiere).

By the time *South Pacific* reached Broadway, on April 7, 1949, the play had already set records for advanced sales. Its run of 1,925 performances in just under five years (only surpassed at the time by *Oklahoma!*) brought a record-breaking take of more than $7 million.[160] The touring company, London productions, and the successful film confirmed the play's legendary status. There hardly has been a night since when *South Pacific* hasn't been performed somewhere, including a highly successful 2008 revival at Lincoln Center.[161]

Rodgers and Hammerstein continued to explore intercultural respect and comity. Their next musical was based on Margaret Landon's *Anna and the King of Siam*, about a British governess arriving in Siam to teach the royal children during the 1860s. Unlike previous Rodgers and Hammerstein collaborations, which highlighted tightly integrated company productions, the team intended *The King and I* to serve as a star vehicle for their friend Gertrude Lawrence.[162] Lawrence fell ill with the cancer that would bring an end to her life shortly after the play began its run in 1951.[163]

The King and I, in fact, would become a star vehicle, but instead for the Russian-born Yul Brynner.[164] Brynner would play the role of King Mongkut 4,625 times over his lifetime, performing his final tour just months before his death in December 1985. Few actors would define a role as comprehensively as Brynner did that of the king, establishing the standard against which everyone else would be measured. The Japanese movie star Ken Watanabe's 2015 Lincoln Center performance ranks among the very few thought by critics to measure up.[165]

Much beloved as a play, *The King and I* nonetheless appears with the passage of time to have been condescending toward Asian culture. Another Rodgers and Hammerstein exploration of intercultural relations, this time set in San Francisco's Chinatown— *Flower Drum Song* (1959)—similarly becomes embarrassingly stereotypical in hindsight. That play nonetheless offered a number of

Asian American actors—including Miyoshi Umeki, Jack Soo, and Pat Suzuki—an unusual opportunity to star on the Broadway stage and in Hollywood films.[166]

Rodgers and Hammerstein continued to write classic musicals throughout the 1950s—works noteworthy for their craft, gravity, and pure entertainment value on the stage, on film, and via the new medium of television. Their partnership elevated the American "book musical" to a serious art form. But they were hardly the only creative partners working on Broadway.

Runyonland

By the 1950s, Broadway—like New York City—was riding high, having recovered its audiences, its profits, and its creative inventiveness after the difficult Depression years of the 1930s. Theater's place in American popular culture had been diminished by Hollywood film and, in short order, by television. Yet, even having relinquished national pride of place, Broadway still defined American theater. As the playwright Arthur Miller wrote in 1955, "The American theater occupies five side streets, Forty-Fourth to Forty-Ninth, between Eighth Avenue and Broadway, with a few additional theaters to the north and south and across Broadway. In these thirty-two buildings, every new play in the United States starts its life and ends it."[167]

Even if it might have been objectionable to some at the time, the claim that Broadway was the totality of American theater was a plausible point of argumentation in the 1950s. In just a few more years, however, no one would be able to imagine making such a claim. Broadway's mid-twentieth-century successes may have been led by—but were never limited to—the Rodgers and Hammerstein juggernaut. The street was as full of talent as it ever had been. The advent of television, which initially cut into Hollywood's stature and profits, represented a fresh challenge to Broadway producers. Television, however, generally played a positive role in supporting the New York cultural scene.

As television developed the national networks patterned on those that dominated radio broadcasting, its programming reached across multiple time zones. As those living on the East Coast could not catch up with prime time on the West Coast, national television programming originated on the Atlantic seaboard. New York's earlier media successes—from the creation of national print media in the early nineteenth century to radio networks in the middle twentieth century—supported the city's place at the center of the new communications media.

Television proved to be synergistic with Broadway in ways that Hollywood no longer could be. In the early days, the new medium's variety and talk formats—including such programs as *The Ed Sullivan Show*, which was broadcast from the heart of Broadway, and Steve Allen's *The Tonight Show*—drew heavily on Broadway talent to fill their programs. In some instances—such as *Peter Pan*, starring Mary Martin and Cyril Ritchard (musical, 1954; television, 1955–60)—musicals and plays were performed for television audiences (in fact, NBC bought, and still owns, the Broadway rights for this version of *Peter Pan*, and NBC actually produced it as a successful, limited-run live show at the Winter Garden Theater before broadcasting it on TV).[168] Television expanded employment opportunities for actors, writers, composers, directors, and producers, bringing important income to the same professionals who kept Broadway going.

There was no lack of shows coming to Broadway during these years.[169] To cite just one example, Frank Loesser composed and wrote the lyrics for *Guys and Dolls* (1950), a work that successfully promoted the Broadway scene as a unique cultural experience.[170] Based on short stories about the New York underworld of the 1920s and 1930s, with a book by Jo Swerling and Abe Burrows, *Guys and Dolls* poked gentle fun at the amiable two-bit crooks and unsuccessful gamblers who hung out around Times Square.[171] The musical made light of the criminal class drawn to the neighborhood around the theaters—lawbreakers who soon would become seen as threatening, violent, and dangerous rather than lovable.

The original Broadway production of *Guys and Dolls* featured Robert Alda, Sam Levine, Isabel Bigley, and Vivian Blaine and ran for 1,200 performances, followed by successful West End London and touring companies and a best-selling recording. A winning film version released in 1955 featured Marlon Brando and Frank Sinatra, among others. The play opened to rave reviews and enthusiastic audiences, sweeping that year's Tony Awards. However, because Abe Burrows had come under negative scrutiny from the US House of Representatives' Un-American Activities Committee for his supposedly left-leaning political views, the Pulitzer Prize Committee voted no award for drama that year rather that face the accusation that they had validated a politically suspect author.

Guys and Dolls has been revived numerous times over the years—including a 1992 staging featuring Nathan Lane—always featuring endearing two-bit lowlifes. The play's naive presentation of so-called victimless criminality speaks of an era when a confident New York sat atop the world. But within just a few years, the "criminal element" present in Times Square appeared to be decidedly threatening to a city that had entered a spiral of urban decay. The city's decline began to become visible during the late 1950s, accelerated during the 1960s, and cascaded throughout the 1970s and 1980s, calling into question the viability of the city and its theatrical life. The Broadway stage reflected these urban realities, which affected every member of the professional theatrical community and also every potential member of a Broadway audience.

Broadway during the 1950s was about drama as well as musicals. If American theater found its unique voice in the 1920s through the works of such luminaries as Eugene O'Neill, Robert E. Sherwood, and Maxwell Anderson, it achieved lasting universality during the 1950s through the works of Arthur Miller, Tennessee Williams, and Lorraine Hansberry.[172] Legendary directors—including Elia Kazan, Lee Strasberg, and José Benjamin Quintero—were at work, as were earlier innovators such as O'Neill—including his plays *The Iceman Cometh*, which was written in 1939 and first performed in 1946; and *Long Day's Journey into Night*, which was first performed posthumously in 1956.[173]

However, American theater was becoming larger than Broadway. Noncommercial theaters with seating capacities of between 100 and 499—known as Off-Broadway theaters—came into being, as regional professional theaters exploded in number. Nonetheless, the few blocks mentioned by Miller remained center stage for drama as well as musicals throughout the decade.

Miller perhaps best personifies the era's achievements in drama for the New York stage. He was born in Harlem in 1915, and his father was an Austrian Jewish immigrant who worked in the cloth trade. He traveled to the University of Michigan for college and was drawn to the playwriting seminars there. Upon graduation, he joined the Federal Theater Project, which would soon be shut down by a Congress concerned with communist infiltration. Miller gained notoriety when he married Marilyn Monroe in 1956 (a union that ended in divorce in 1961), and when his passport was revoked and he was subpoenaed to appear before the US House of Representatives' Un-American Activities Committee to testify about communist influence in the arts.

Miller's play *The Crucible* (which opened on Broadway in January 1953), about the 1692 Salem witch hunts, proved too much of a direct provocation to the Un-American Activities Committee. Thinking he had a deal not to name individuals if he spoke about general trends, Miller was held in contempt of Congress, fined, and imprisoned for thirty days after he refused under questioning to identify individuals. He was blacklisted and denied a passport. Although these sanctions proved short-lived, they inspired his later writing. He would continue to write and work in the theater throughout his life. He died in 2005 at the age of eighty-nine.[174]

Miller's postwar plays—including *Death of a Salesman* (1949), *An Enemy of the People* (1950), *The Crucible* (1953), and *A View from the Bridge* (1955)—are among the best-known and most admired works presented on the American stage. They confronted the quiet desperation of those who lost in their pursuits of the American Dream, the dysfunctionality of the American family, and the era's most profound political issues. Miller demonstrated that the Broadway stage offered a uniquely significant platform for exploring some of society's most disturbing issues.[175]

Miller's contemporary, the Mississippi-born Tennessee Williams, wrote some of the most admired plays in the American theatrical canon during this era as well—*The Glass Menagerie* (1944), *A Streetcar Named Desire* (1947), *The Rose Tattoo* (1951), *Camino Real* (1953), *Cat on a Hot Tin Roof* (1955), and *Sweet Bird of Youth* (1959).[176] Williams graduated in journalism from the University of Missouri at the height of the Depression and made his way to Saint Louis, where he enrolled at Washington University and found himself drawn to the theater. In 1939, he received a grant from the

Works Progress Administration, which had been established by the Roosevelt administration to support artists, musicians, and writers. This program brought him to New Orleans, the city that became his muse.[177]

Between 1948 and 1959, Williams brought seven plays to Broadway, two of which—*A Streetcar Named Desire* and *Cat on a Hot Tin Roof*—won the Pulitzer Prize. These initial plays were followed by additional successes in the 1960s and 1970s. Like Miller's work, Williams's plays explored the degradation of the American dream—in the case of Williams, through close examination of the toxic mix within families of too much history, too much alcohol, and too much insanity. Many of Williams's plays moved to film and have entered into the repertoire of top theater companies around the world.[178]

Lorraine Hansberry's *Raisin in the Sun* was the first play written by an African American woman to be produced on Broadway. Within two years, the play would be translated into thirty-five languages and performed worldwide.[179]

Hansberry grew up in a politically active family in the Chicago that she was later to write about, and attended the University of Wisconsin–Madison. She moved to New York to attend the New School and quickly established herself as a powerful civil rights, feminist, and gay rights activist at a time when society scorned all three. Joining the staff of the newspaper *Freedom*, she worked with several prominent African American intellectuals, including W. E. B. Du Bois, Mary Church Terrell, and Paul Robeson. After Nina Simone encountered Hansberry, a young woman of such strength and talent, Simone wrote a song about her, "To Be Young, Gifted, and Black."[180]

Raisin in the Sun—titled after a line in Langston Hughes's poem "Harlem" (sometimes known as "A Dream Deferred")—was Hansberry's searing examination of a middle-class black family in Chicago's Woodlawn neighborhood. This play recast the American conversation about race by forcing Americans to confront the reality that racial equality rested on full integration into society's mainstream. *Raisin*'s Broadway production—which was directed by Lloyd Richards and starred Sidney Poitier and Ruby Dee—launched several legendary stage and film careers.[181] Unfortunately,

Figure 25. Lorraine Hansberry.
Source: BlackPast.org (public domain; http://www.blackpast.
org/aah/hansberry-lorraine-1930-1965).

Hansberry herself died of cancer in 1965 at the age of thirty-four, leaving behind a matchless legacy in just a few years (figure 25).

The success of drama on the Broadway stage of the 1950s depended on several towering directors, who recreated American stage and film craft with their plays, films, and teaching studios. Elia Kazan made his way to New York as a child from war-torn Istanbul; Lee Strasberg made a similar pilgrimage from Galicia in today's Ukraine. Stella Adler was a local girl, the daughter of famous figures in New York's Yiddish theater. Together, they taught some of America's finest twentieth-century actors at the Actors

Studio, which was founded by Kazan, Robert Lewis, and Cheryl Crawford and was continued by Lee Strasberg in the 1950s. Adler established her own studio, which continues in Los Angeles.[182]

Having become embroiled in the politics surrounding the US House of Representatives' Un-American Activities Committee, Kazan testified, thereby severing his ties with many former colleagues, including Arthur Miller.[183] Strasburg had his own tangle of personal feuds with his colleagues.[184] Adler dealt more comfortably with her colleagues, and she often succeeded in larger institutions, as when she taught at the New School, the Yale School of Drama, and New York University.[185]

Strasberg and Adler are credited with introducing the psychological interpretations of the Russian director Konstantin Stanislavsky into the American theater—which became known, in the American context, as "method acting." Russian specialists familiar with Stanislavsky's original approach question how much of "the Method" was Strasberg and Adler and how much was Stanislavsky. At a minimum, they argue, what emerged from their schools was a uniquely American variant on the original Russian technique.[186]

Kazan, Strasberg, and Adler worked in Hollywood as well as on Broadway; and between them, they trained and directed nearly every late-twentieth-century American actor of note. They brought varied influences around the world to a city and a theatrical community that had been born and were predicated on absorbing new influences. Of particular importance for this story, the Broadway stage was still a place where they could work throughout the 1950s.

Of course, there was much more to Broadway dramatic theater during the 1950s than Miller, Williams, Hansberry, Kazan, Strasburg, and Adler—just as there was much more to Broadway musical theater than Rodgers and Hammerstein.[187] There were great actors (e.g., Marlon Brando, Bert Lahr, Lee J. Cobb, and Julie Harris), and there were other great plays that have stood the test of time on Broadway (e.g., Samuel Beckett's *Waiting for Godot*, and Jerome Lawrence and Robert Edwin Lee's *Inherit the Wind*).[188] The work mentioned here achieved international recognition and revealed the extent to which noncommercially oriented theater could still "make it" and survive on Broadway. But this possibility was beginning to change, as the economics of theater evolved and as the city itself began to become less hospitable to the sort of middle-class audience that had sustained theater for decades.

Diverse responses to the increasing economic constraints on Broadway undermined Miller's observation that American theater was contained within a few blocks of Midtown Manhattan. Not only would Broadway evolve; those writers, producers, directors, composers, and actors who were interested in pursuing less commercial ventures returned to the "little theater" and "regional theater" movements that had sprung up earlier in the century.

In 1951, the Panamanian-born and California-trained director and teacher José Benjamin Quintero, together with Theodore Mann, established the Circle in the Square Theatre in Greenwich Village.[189] Quintero's productions of O'Neill's classics, in particular, were considered among the best ever staged. Other smaller theaters also followed, so that, by the 1960s, a vibrant network of smaller, Off-Broadway professional theaters (which are defined by Actors' Equity as having a seating capacity of between 100 and 499, with different wage rates than larger theaters) had sprung up across Manhattan.[190] Many more professional theaters that were even smaller — "Off-Off Broadway," seating fewer than 99 audience members — soon followed. [191] As Broadway became more commercial and more expensive, Off-Broadway evolved into a major innovative center for American theater.

Creativity also emerged outside New York, as an expansive regional theater movement made cities such as San Diego, Minneapolis, Washington, Boston, and Chicago increasingly distinguished theater centers that were no longer dependent on New York for talent and ideas.[192] The founding of the San Diego's La Jolla Playhouse in 1947, Washington's Arena Stage in 1950, and Minneapolis's Guthrie Theater in 1963 established major creative nodes, which joined together with long-established regional powerhouses, such as Chicago's Goodman Theatre and the Cleveland Play House, to support an increasingly national theater scene. Over time, these professional stages outside New York — many producing as high a quality night at the theater as anything in the city — have exploded, from about 24 in 1960 to nearly 2,000 today.[193]

These developments would combine with changes in New York

itself to fundamentally alter the world of the New York stage in the late 1950s, the 1960s, and beyond. Yet there still remained much to come in the 1950s for the city and for the world of Broadway before anyone would notice the scent of urban decay for the first time.

On the Street Where You Live

The party was not yet over, and the 1950s were not yet done. In March 15, 1956, *My Fair Lady*, one of the grandest American "book musicals," opened at the Mark Hellinger Theatre. In remaking George Bernard Shaw's *Pygmalion* for American audiences, the lyricist Alan Jay Lerner and the composer Frederick Loewe were successful beyond any hopes. The original production ran for 2,717 performances, breaking all existing records on Broadway. And these New York triumphs were followed by a popular London run and film. In the eyes of many critics, this play set the standard for "the perfect musical."[194]

Lerner, who was born in 1918, grew up during the 1920s and 1930s in the protected world of a wealthy, if dysfunctional, family living on Park Avenue.[195] His father Joe was a partner in the Lerner Company, a large women's specialty clothing chain offering moderately priced fashions at stores throughout metropolitan New York and the nation. The Lerners manufactured much of their clothing, and they succeeded during the economic downturn of the Great Depression by remaining a midmarket line. Lerner's grandfather set up a small shop when he emigrated from Ukraine to South Philadelphia in the 1880s. His three sons continued in business as the eldest Sam moved west and established a successful carpet business, and Joe started manufacturing shirts. By 1914, the Lerners had forty shops in New York City alone.[196]

The Lerner family's wealth meant that young Alan would attend the best private schools in New York, England, and New England (he was a classmate of future American president John F. Kennedy, first at Choate, an elite boarding school in Connecticut, and later at Harvard). The Lerners' money was too "new" and too associated with the déclassé "rag trade" to grant them access to New York's highest social circles. But it was more than enough to ensure that Alan would never need to earn money to support himself, and this wealth allowed him to pursue his interest in show business, beginning with trips to Broadway plays with his dad throughout his childhood. He also carried forward a family tradition of living a tempestuous domestic life, marrying eight times and becoming a regular feature in any number of newspaper society columns, thanks to several tumultuously contested divorce settlements.[197]

As a student at Harvard, Lerner joined the school's famous Hasty Pudding Club, which produced annual farcical musicals, and he spent his summers studying musical composition at Juilliard. Drawn to the musicals he had seen with his father—especially the shows of Cole Porter, Kern and Hammerstein, and Rodgers and Hart—Lerner returned to Manhattan following graduation and found a job as a radio scriptwriter, preparing advertisements and scripts for both national and local shows. And after failing the physical examination for military service in World War II, Lerner set out to make his own way in New York.[198]

His script job allowed Lerner to move into the Lambs Club, New York's oldest theatrical club, founded in 1874 (and modeled after the older Lambs established by London actors in 1868). He remained at the Lambs for just six months, and then he moved into the Royalton Hotel across the street after marrying for the first time. While living at the Lambs, Lerner would spend time at the club's bar, where he befriended Larry Hart. Hart immediately took the ambitious young man under his wing.[199] Lerner also met the Lambs member Frederick "Fritz" Loewe, a German-born composer seventeen years his senior.[200]

Loewe had been born into a Viennese acting family in Berlin in 1901. His father was a tenor renowned for playing Prince Danilo in *The Merry Widow*. His mother wanted her son to enjoy a more stable life that that of a musician. She dispatched him to a Prussian military school, where he was ostracized for being too small and for being Jewish.[201] His talents lay with music. After having left the military cadets behind to study at the conservatory in Berlin, he became, at the age of thirteen, the youngest piano soloist to appear with the Berlin Philharmonic.[202]

Loewe worked and traveled with his opera singer father, and thus he accompanied his father, who was under a contract with David Belasco, to the United States. When his father died during rehearsals, Loewe set out on his own American adventure. He survived doing odd jobs from coast to coast (including teaching horseback riding and playing the piano for a silent movie theater in Montana).

Loewe offered invaluable connections to the young Lerner. For example, he introduced him to the circle of German theater professionals—including Kurt Weill—who had been forced into exile by the Nazis and World War II.[203] However, when Loewe met Lerner at the Lambs, the elder composer had yet to make it big in the world of New York music.[204] So the two men were good candidates for a partnership.

Lerner and Loewe were ready to collaborate to move ahead on Broadway and, though they would never become particularly close friends, they were well-suited partners. In 1947, their first collaboration to reach Broadway—*Brigadoon*—was a hit, running 581 performances. This play, which told the story of a pair of American tourists discovering a mythical Scottish village that comes alive for one day each century, combined the fresh lyrics of the New World with the polished music of the Old. Agnes de Mille added her sophisticated choreography, and the leading lady, Marion Bell, became Lerner's second wife.[205]

De Mille also choreographed their second collaboration—*Paint Your Wagon*—which was set in the American West. This play perhaps became better known as a 1969 film featuring a singing Lee Marvin and a young Clint Eastwood.[206]

Lerner and Loewe now set their sights on a bigger challenge, setting George Bernard Shaw's play *Pygmalion* to music. The problem, in the words of the theater historian Stephen Citron, was that *Pygmalion* "is a comedy of manners that concerns several heartless men—Higgins, Pickering, Doolittle—who preyed on an ambitious but vulnerable woman and is totally antiromantic."[207]

When Lerner ran into Oscar Hammerstein II at a 1952 Madison Square Garden rally for the Democratic Party's nominee for president, Adlai Stevenson, Hammerstein admitted that he and Rodgers had turned down an offer the previous month to set *Pygmalion* to music because they had concluded that it could not be done.[208] But Lerner and Loewe succeeded by turning the story, renamed *My Fair Lady*, into "a cynical Cinderella story of a cockney flower girl Eliza

Doolittle and her transformation from a squashed cabbage head to a blossomed cabbage rose who becomes a lady under the tutelage of Henry Higgins, a misogynistic phonetics professor."[209]

They succeeded in this challenging work by writing with specific performers in mind. Rex Harrison, who would define the role of Professor Higgins, was an accomplished British actor who had never sung onstage before. His fear of doing so added a certain tremor to each performance. When Mary Martin declined the role of Eliza due to conflicting commitments, Lerner and Loewe found a twenty-year-old English soprano, Julie Andrews, who eventually became better known than Martin, in large measure because of her performance in *My Fair Lady*.

The play set every record at the time on Broadway, running from 1956 to 1962. And it also enjoyed a successful run in London, in film, and on records—with a strong assist from appearances by Lerner, Loewe, Harrison, Andrews, and others on television.[210]

Lerner and Loewe followed this triumph with the successful movie *Gigi* (1958), and one more Broadway smash hit, *Camelot* (1960), a play about the knights at King Arthur's Court. Opening as it did just as Lerner's Choate and Harvard classmate John Kennedy entered the White House, *Camelot* became associated with the new American administration.[211] *Camelot* remains a popular revival into the twenty-first century.

Loewe then retired to Palms Springs, California, and Lerner looked for new partners. He supported Dick Rodgers's solo effort following Oscar Hammerstein's death, a musical about the incendiary topic of an interracial love affair—*No Strings*—which opened in 1962.[212] And Lerner formed partnerships with Burton Lane, for the successful *On a Clear Day You Can See Forever* (1965), and with André Previn, for *Coco* (1969). He later worked with Leonard Bernstein on a disastrously horrid musical about American presidents, *1600 Pennsylvania Avenue*, which was commissioned by the John F. Kennedy Center for the Performing Arts in Washington for the American bicentennial year of 1976. [213]

Lerner had not lost his touch by the 1970s; nor did he require the genius of Loewe to succeed. Rather, Broadway, American culture, and New York City were changing around him—becoming harsher and more cynical in reaction to the Kennedy assassination, the Vietnam War, and the collapse of New York's manufacturing sector and accompanying rise in criminality. Romantic myths of fanciful Scottish villages, dancing Mexicans and Americans in Gold Rush–era California, and a cockney Cinderella no longer held center stage.

Jets and Sharks

A younger generation of composers, lyricists, choreographers, directors, producers, and performers bridled against what they saw to be limitations of the masterful "book musicals" being written by Rodgers and Hammerstein, Lerner and Loewe, and Irving Berlin. Yet, for the most part, their desire to create something new and different never was directed against their mentors and their seniors. Their impatience with existing forms had more to do with the different realities they experienced having come of age more or less around the time of World War II and during the postwar era. They appreciated different kinds of music—including the sounds expressed by African Americans—and they were drawn to modern dance—as opposed to classical ballet and traditional musical dance forms such as tap. And they had been well educated, having benefited from the new theater and music programs that were being offered at the nation's top universities and conservatories—and thus they had completed courses in now-well-established drama programs and had received more inclusive music educations that moved beyond European classical training.

Most significantly, they lived in a different world—one that saw New York and the United States at the pinnacle of their global political and economic power but simultaneously moving toward the precipice of industrial decline and rapid technological change. Conventional histories of the 1960s see the decade as one of growing unrest and tumultuous political and social change, and all these trends also began to sweep across the world of Broadway.

One play among the many on Broadway captured the paradigm shift that was about to take place: *West Side Story* (1957). It represented the different, kaleidoscopic sensibilities of the members of its young creative team, bristling with as-yet-unrecognized talent, who would come to dominate the world of Broadway for decades ahead: the composer Leonard Bernstein, the librettist Stephen Sondheim, the choreographer Jerome Robbins, the writer Arthur Laurents, and the producer Hal Prince. Their ever-changing concept for the play reflected the evolution of an entertainment business and a city that were about to set off in new directions.[214]

Robbins came up with the idea of adapting *Romeo and Juliet* to the contemporary world. He approached Bernstein and Laurents in 1947, proposing that the action revolve around the conflict between Irish Catholics and Jewish families living on Manhattan's Lower East Side during the Easter/Passover season.[215] Robbins, Bernstein, and Laurents kept returning to their *East Side Story* over the next several years, talking about the project whenever competing commitments and travel schedules permitted. Eventually, they brought in the novice Sondheim to help with the lyrics.

Robbins (originally Jerome Rabinowitz) was born to Jewish immigrant parents from Russia on Manhattan's Lower East Side in 1918. The family lived briefly in a less-desirable section of the Upper East Side before his parents moved right across the Hudson to Weehawken, New Jersey, where his father and uncle Americanized the family name to Robbins and opened a corset factory. The family had a number of connections with show business, so Robbins, after having to drop out of New York University for financial reasons, turned his attention to dance. He performed in the choruses of several Broadway shows, including works choreographed by George Balanchine, and he was eventually drawn to efforts—such as *Oklahoma!*—that sought to integrate dance into musical storytelling. In 1944, he joined forces with Bernstein to choreograph the hit *On the Town* about Navy sailors enjoying shore leave for a day in New York.[216] This collaboration launched Robbins on his illustrious career as a one of the great American choreographers working in theater, film, and ballet.[217]

Bernstein, one of the preeminent American composers and conductors of his generation, was born in Lawrence, Massachusetts, in 1918 to Ukrainian Jewish immigrants. He was originally named Louis to satisfy his grandmother, but he and the family changed his name to their preferred Leonard after her death. His father owned a bookstore and took him to concerts during his youth. Bernstein attended the Boston Latin School and Harvard University, where he studied music. His final-year thesis, in 1939, which was titled "The Absorption of Race Elements in American Music," reflected the same interest in the African origins of American music that was evident among other immigrants and children of immigrants during the early years of the twentieth century. During these years, Bernstein met the American composer Aaron Copland, and he came under the influence of the conductor Dimitri Mitropoulous.

After Harvard, Bernstein went on to the Curtis Institute of Music in Philadelphia, where he studied with, among others, the conductor Fritz Reiner. Following graduation, he came to New York and, as early as 1940, began to study conducting with Serge Koussevitzky at the Boston Symphony Orchestra's Massachusetts summer retreat, Tanglewood (figure 26). In November 1943, when the New York Philharmonic's conductor, Bruno Walter, became sick, Bernstein was called on at the last moment to conduct the Philharmonic in a nationally broadcast concert. Bernstein became an instant sensation throughout the world of classical music and never looked back.

Bernstein's continuing fascination with popular music brought him close to Betty Comden and Adolph Green and, eventually, Robbins. Together, they collaborated on the hit *On the Town*.[218]

The writer Arthur Laurents was born in 1917 to middle-class Jewish parents and grew up in Brooklyn's Flatbush neighborhood. After graduating from the prestigious public Erasmus Hall High School, he went off to Cornell University. Returning to New York on the eve of World War II, he took radio scriptwriting evening courses at New York University and landed his first job at CBS Radio. But then he was drafted into the war effort, and he ended up at the US Army's Pictorial Service in Astoria, Queens, turning out training films. After leaving the Army, he turned his writing and directing efforts to Broadway, and was launched on a fruitful career both on Broadway and Hollywood. His career would have been even more successful if his name had not been mentioned to investigators for the US House of Representatives' Un-American Activities Committee, for this led to his being blacklisted and denied a US passport. Although this issue was quickly resolved, his experience demonstrates yet again the pernicious effects of the committee's investigations on the Broadway community.[219]

Figure 26. Leonard Bernstein, when he was a young conductor and the music director of the New York City Symphony.
Source: Library of Congress.

A dozen year's younger, Stephen Sondheim was the latecomer to the group. His parents had gone into the dress business, with his mother designing the apparel that his father manufactured. He lived in the upscale San Remo apartment building on Central Park West until his parents divorced. Then his mother moved to a farm near Doylestown, Pennsylvania, where he met and befriended Jamie Hammerstein, eventually becoming the informal student of Jamie's father Oscar.[220] Stephen graduated from the Quaker-run George School after having attended New York Military Academy. During summers, he shipped off to Camp Androscoggin, where he enthusiastically joined the theatrical productions. He completed the theater program at Williams College, and then headed to New York. All the while, he continued working closely with Hammerstein, who was teaching him the ropes of writing and producing lyrics and plays.[221]

Shortly after arriving in New York, Sondheim found himself at a party chatting with Laurents, who told him about the plans that he, Bernstein, and Robbins had to write a contemporary *Romeo and Juliet*. Betty Comden and Adolph Green had just declined to write the lyrics for the project because they had taken on work in Hollywood. Laurents arranged for Sondheim to meet Bernstein the next day, and he was brought onto the team. Initially, Bernstein had intended to write many of the show's lyrics, but he was distracted completing his own musical, *Candide* (1956).[222]

Sondheim, of course, would become Broadway's most successful composer and lyricist in the late twentieth century. He would write and compose such hits as *Gypsy* (1959), *A Funny Thing Happened on the Way to the Forum* (1962), *Do I Hear a Waltz?* (1965), *Company* (1970), *Follies* (1971), *A Little Night Music* (1973), *Sweeney Todd* (1979), *Sunday in the Park with George* (1984), and *Into the Woods* (1987), among many productions.[223]

By the time *West Side Story* opened for previews in Washington, Bernstein had assigned the credits (and royalties) for its lyrics to the inexperienced Sondheim. During the dinner celebrating the opening night in the nation's capital, Bernstein met Sondheim's friend, Mary Rodgers, the daughter of Richard Rodgers. He invited her to help write and produce his planned—and, ultimately, hugely successful—New York Philharmonic Young People's Concert Series for television.[224]

Hal Prince, the final member of the creative team for *West Side Story*, was closer in age to Sondheim than to Robbins, Laurents, and Bernstein, having been born in 1928. The adopted son of a successful stockbroker, Prince thrived as a young student and graduated from the University of Pennsylvania on the eve World War II at the age of nineteen. He returned to New York to enter the world of theater following military service, and began a legendary career as a producer and director on Broadway and in opera, with such hits as *The Pajama Game* (1955), *Cabaret* (1966), and Andrew Lloyd Webber's *Evita* (1980) and *The Phantom of the Opera* (1988). By the 1970s, he was teaming up with Sondheim on many of the lyricist and composer's most successful efforts. He joined the *West Side Story* team after the collaborators had difficulty finding financial backers for their increasingly path-breaking play.[225]

Robbins, Bernstein, Sondheim, Laurents, and Prince would become legendary figures in late-twentieth-century American culture. At the time they were working through their concept for a contemporary, New York–based *Romeo and Juliet*, they were merely a bunch of hotshot young New Yorkers (mostly by birth and, in the case of Bernstein, by choice). Their notions of what a musical should be were strikingly different from those of their elders and mentors. They wanted plays to connect with their generation's understanding of culture by using music that would appeal to those who were coming of age following World War II, and by combining dance, music, and speech in different ways than had ever been done before. Thus, their *West Side Story* is told as much through dance as through music and words.[226]

What had originally been conceived as *East Side Story* became *West Side Story* over time. The original story of conflict between the Irish and Jewish communities paralleled the earlier successful musical *Abbie's Irish Rose*. Robbins, Laurents, and Bernstein kept putting the project aside, though they would bring up the subject whenever their paths crossed. One such meeting between Laurents and Bernstein transpired over breakfast at the Beverly Hills Hotel. Scanning the local Los Angeles press, Bernstein had noticed growing gang violence involving Chicano gangs.

Living through the rapid growth of the Hispanic presence in New York, with the arrival in the city of large numbers of Puerto

Ricans, the pair felt more comfortable writing about Puerto Ricans rather than Mexican Americans. They decided to remake their concept around conflicting turf battles between long-established Irish gangs and the newly arriving Puerto Rican gangs, which were increasingly evident on the Upper West Side. So they set the action in the run-down neighborhood, on what would become the site of Lincoln Center a few years later.[227]

The show opened on September 26, 1957, at the Winter Garden Theater, with a stellar cast that included Larry Kert, Carol Lawrence, and Chita Rivera. It would run 732 performances and be followed by long-running London and touring productions, as well as the very successful film starring Natalie Wood in 1961. The critics were divided, recognizing with praise or condemnation the play's innovative structure, contemporary music, and focus on what, to many socially proper observers, was little more than a frightening urban underclass.[228]

Bernstein, Sondheim, Robbins, Laurents, and Prince secured their enormous success by producing a play that was innovative yet readily accessible to middle-brow audiences. *West Side Story* revealed that Broadway could succeed both artistically and financially by striking out in new directions. The era of the classic "book musical," exemplified by the works of Rodgers and Hammerstein, was coming to an end—and also, tragically, was their collaboration, for Hammerstein fell mortally ill with cancer.

The Hills Are Alive

Mary Martin had been a favorite of Oscar Hammerstein's ever since she had first auditioned at a tea party hosted by Oscar's wife Dorothy in Hollywood in 1937.[229] He had promoted her career at every opportunity ever since, often encouraging her to be cast in a leading role in his own plays with Rodgers as well as in their productions of work by others. With *Flower Drum Song* launched, Oscar and Dick were looking for an opportunity to showcase Martin again.

Maria von Trapp's German autobiography about her family singers and their escape from Nazi-controlled Europe eventually to New England enjoyed considerable success in Germany. As

Stephen Citron notes, "as the teacher of a large group of children in a household run by an imperious, tyrannical man whom the heroine eventually democratizes and falls in love with, Baroness von Trapp's story parallels the hugely successful *The King and I*. Mary could not have been immune to the idea that this plum role had brought Gertrude Lawrence much acclaim and certainly must have hoped that the premise would work as well for her."[230]

Martin discussed various options for bringing the von Trapp family saga to stage and screen. Hearing about the project, Rodgers and Hammerstein offered to take over the project, provided they could write the entire score. In other words, the production would not borrow traditional Austrian folksongs but would be completely original. What became *The Sound of Music* took shape as Rodgers and Hammerstein's next project, as a vehicle for showcasing Martin. It would be their last collaboration.[231]

Citron continues: "The simplicity and accessibility of the score of *The Sound of Music* is typical of Hammerstein's best work. Although this writer does not agree with him, Oscar often said that he had not a large vocabulary. What he meant was that he did not use a fancy word when an ordinary one would do. He most admired Winston Churchill's writing style, clarity, and lack of obfuscation. In his own work, he would spend days searching out exact words to convey the precise meaning of even his smallest thought."[232]

In August 1959, the production went into rehearsals; and in September, Oscar visited his family physician for a routine annual checkup. The examination revealed that he was suffering from grade four stomach cancer. Oscar died a year later, in August 1960. His last song would be the delicate *Edelweiss*, written with such sweet simplicity that many still believe that the tune must be an original Austrian folk song.[233]

The Sound of Music made history, running for 1,442 performances on Broadway (the longest run at the time), and it enjoyed a successful three-year national tour and a run in London of more than five years. The movie version—released in 1965, starring Julie Andrews (instead of Mary Martin) and Christopher Plummer—converted the play into a global mega-hit that is broadcast annually on television and still enchants many a young viewer.[234]

By the time *The Sound of Music* closed on Broadway, on June 16, 1963, the theatrical world that had created Rodgers and Hammerstein was fast disappearing. Rodgers and his peers continued to write with some success, and traditional book musicals of the genre that came into being in the 1920s continued to appear.[235] But the art form seemed increasingly dated.

Broadway was moving in new directions, in response to the profound changes in the larger society. As Amy Henderson and Dwight Blocker Bowers write,

In the early 1960s, American entered a period of social disquiet and dissonance. This uncertainty — in the society, political, and artistic climates — forced a jarring transition in the American musical: The time-tested formulas that had once vitalized the genre revealed themselves to be time-worn. This brought about the virtual demise of the splashy, spectacular Hollywood musical at least in the original dimensions that it had once achieved. Meanwhile, the stage musical was forced to enter a new phase of redefinition and revival, combining the familiar with the experimental in an effort to seek various new patrons to replace the rapidly disappearing broadly based middle-class audience.[236]

A curmudgeonly Lerner is more explicit in telling the tale:

In the sixties, the musical theater was regarded as the establishment and musical expression became the exclusive property of rock and deafening amplification, which made unintelligible lyrics beneficially more unintelligible. Genuine talents, such as Paul Simon, who in another age might have glorified the theater, eschewed it. When I [Lerner] was growing up in the thirties, my heroes were Larry Hart, Cole Porter, Ira Gershwin, and Howard Dietz. In the sixties, neither Oscar Hammerstein nor I, for example, was a hero of the generation behind us. Stephen Sondheim, who became the cheer leader of alienation in the seventies and who had been a pupil of Oscar Hammerstein, regarded him, as you may remember, as a man "of limited talent," and wrote of

Larry Hart: "[His] work has always struck me as being occasionally graceful, touching, but mostly technically sloppy, unfelt and silly."[237]

Both Lerner's own snarkiness—and that which he attributes to Sondheim—accurately reflect the tenor of the times. Yet they miss a larger point. Oscar Hammerstein lived in a world peopled by creative talents born as outsiders because they were the children of immigrants or were themselves immigrants, were open to the influence of African American culture, were Jewish at a time when Jews remained outsiders in American society, and mainly grew up and matured in New York, a city unlike any other in the country. Even Lerner—who grew up on Park Avenue and went to Harvard—remained an outsider to mainstream America.

The generation represented by Sondheim was more integrated into the larger society from the beginning. They took their cultural cues from the all-American Hollywood screen (and, later, from the smaller television screen) as much as they did from Broadway. They attended the best colleges and universities, where they swam easily within a larger student environment. And they were Americans at a time when the nation's major institutions were beginning to teeter, and when there no longer was a hierarchy of taste. As Lerner begrudgingly observes, they no longer looked to Broadway to find validation.

Within a few years, many who cared about the Broadway theater had discerned its impending doom. The science fiction master Thomas Disch, for example, declared Broadway dead on more than one occasion in his reviews appearing in *The Nation* and other periodicals. In one such essay, appearing in *The Atlantic Monthly* in 1991, he began,

In the 1967–68 season, fifty-eight shows opened on Broadway: forty-four nonmusical plays (twenty-five dramas, nineteen comedies) and fourteen musicals. The 1989–90 season yielded thirty-five shows; twenty-one nonmusicals (six of them revivals) and twelve musicals (four of them revivals), plus two "special attractions." Musicals seem to be holding their own but clearly "legit" drama (to use *Variety's* parlance) is an endangered species. In 1967–68, there were new plays by Harold Pinter, Tennessee Williams, Arthur Miller, Tom Stoppard, Gore Vidal, Eugene O'Neill, Joe Orton, Edward Albee, Neil Simon, Peter Nichols, Lillian Hellman, Ira Levin, Peter Ustinov (two plays), and some twenty-seven other playwrights, not counting those who wrote book for musicals. Last season, the "name" playwrights presenting new works were Larry Gelbart and Peter Shaffer. As of January 1, a time when the season is usually at its peak, only five legit dramas were playing on Broadway—three held over from last season and two survivors from among the scant four that opened last fall, one of them at Lincoln Center, which is a "Broadway" theater only by a legal fiction. The steep decline since 1967–68 represents bit a portion of a longer term downward trend. . . . There were 264 new productions in the 1927–28 season; and 187 three years later, after the double whammy of the Depression and talkies, there were sixty in 1940–41. The sixties brought a mild upsurge. . . . In the seventies there was a surplus of theaters.[238]

After reviewing various factors contributing to the decline of the Broadway stage, Disch arrives at New York—indeed, Times Square—as a major villain: "The problem of Times Square's squalor is of another magnitude, one that requires solutions on the scale in which Robert Moses worked. Indeed, bulldozers are poised to begin a Moses-style effort that will entail leveling Forty-Second Street and several blocks around, and replacing all the local low life with high-rise office towers and a convention center."[239]

No one any longer attributed Runyonesque charm and lovability to the small-time hustlers who hung out around Times Square. Broadway's decline, as Disch makes clear, was but a reflection of New York City's larger fall from grace, which became ever more visible in the years following the end of the street's Golden Era.

Epilogue

In 1987, two very different reviews of the state of the city appeared almost simultaneously. The first was a report issued by an ad hoc commission on New York in 2000 chaired by Robert F. Wagner Jr., who was the son of a beloved three-term mayor, was the grandson of a popular former US senator from New York, and was himself deeply involved in city affairs and a chair of the City Planning Commission.[240] The second review was a special issue of the distinguished Leftist journal *Dissent* edited by the author and journalist Jim Sleeper.[241] Although both reviews presented a portrait of what was recognizably the same city, their differences in orientation and interest pointed them in opposite directions. Their titles reflect their diverse sensibilities. Wagner's report was titled *New York Ascendant*, but Sleeper's journal issue bore the title *In Search of New York*.

Both reports appeared at what, in retrospect, was a turning point in the city's destiny. The economic disinvestment that was beginning to become noticeable by the end of the 1950s cascaded throughout the 1960s and 1970s; the manufacturing sector collapsed; port facilities and hundreds of critical jobs moved to New Jersey following the containerization revolution in shipping; corporate headquarters fled to the suburbs and beyond; and even the New York Stock Exchange and NBC gave serious consideration to leaving Manhattan for New Jersey. A nadir was reached with a disastrous brush with municipal bankruptcy in 1975, widespread civil breakdown during a 1977 blackout, and excessively publicized violence on the subway and in parks. A tsunami of violence accompanying a crack cocaine epidemic swept over the city, reaching its peak just as both publications appeared.

In this dire context, *Dissent*'s contributors told a tale of slow and inexorable urban decline, decay, and death. New York was no longer able to create wealth for the thousands of poor citizens struggling to make their way in the city. As the city became more starkly divided by class, it became less attractive to those who had great wealth. New York was a tough, nasty place full of paranoia, racial hatred, and economic conflict in which its residents felt under constant threat.

However, all was not lost, according to the ad hoc commission's report. The commission's members viewed the restructuring of the city's finances in response to near bankruptcy as having improved New York's ability to respond to economic change. They found the boosterism of three-term mayor Ed Koch, who held the office between 1978 and 1989, to have lifted civic identity. A New York

State tourism campaign, begun in 1977 based on the song "I Love New York"—and in which Broadway actors played a prominent role—similarly started to transform how New Yorkers and others thought about both the city and its state.

More significantly, according to the commission's report, the profound changes in international financial markets, reflecting the beginnings of what we now know as globalization—including a newly assertive capitalism unleashed by the Reagan administration, and deregulation of the financial markets—also have enabled New York to firmly secure its position as the world's financial capital against all competitors, except London. Technological changes—the beginning of the Internet age—reaffirmed New York's position at the center of global communications; and the maturation of the smart economy expanded its reach beyond Silicon Valley and Boston's Route 128 corridor, favoring the establishment of high-technology industries in New York. The opening of immigration pathways to the United States during the 1960s similarly began to reshape the city as it once more became a magnet for new Americans.

This dynamism, the commission's report argued, was gaining momentum so that, by 2000, New York would be ascendant once more. The report predicted that the city would regain 300,000 jobs (matching its peak employment in 1969 of 3.8 million) and 400,000 people, growing to 7.5 million by the turn of the millennium.[242] In fact, the city's population would reach a then-all-time high of just over 8 million.[243] This growth was largely driven by immigrants. According to some estimates, more than 3 million immigrants made their way to New York over the past half century, many remaining in the city.[244]

Despite privileging different factors, both *Dissent*'s and the commission's reviews identified many similar positive and negative trends. Both accounts lamented the absence of civility in New York life, an edginess that both saw as counterproductive for the city and its residents. These hard edges would continue to mar civic life throughout the twentieth century, softening only in the wake of the September 11, 2001, terrorist attack on the World Trade Center. Thereafter, many New Yorkers subsumed whatever differences they had under the shared experience of living in a city under assault.

For the authors of the commission's *New York Ascendant*, positive developments were offset by growing income disparities, continued high rates of crime and violence, and a floundering educational system that poorly served both the city's youth and employers. For the contributors to *Dissent*, New York was experiencing a remarkable mixing of different traditions—especially of Hispanic and African cultures—which produced unprecedented creativity on city streets. Both reviews emphasized the importance of the arts, with *Dissent* highlighting the creativity bubbling up from below and *New York Ascendant* identifying culture as a draw making the city attractive to what we now call the "creative class."

In retrospect, the commission was closer to the mark, in that New York once more emerged as the world's preeminent city. Longtime New Yorkers are not quite confident of this success, seeing what has been described as the "homogenization"—and even the "Disneyfication" or hypergentrification—of their city, as those without abundant means are forced to leave town. Whether this perception is accurate for the city as a whole, there is no doubt that Times Square has been Disneyfied—by Disney itself.

In his premature death notice for the Broadway theater, Disch sardonically noted that the bulldozers were gathering to attack the squalor of Times Square by leveling many of the blocks around 42nd Street to replace low life with high-rise towers. This is, in fact, what transpired as mayors Rudy Giuliani (1994–2001) and Michael Bloomberg (2002–13) promoted the conversion of Times Square into a tourist and corporate wonderland embodying broader transformations throughout the city. The Times Square Alliance, established in 1992, lured major corporations to the area and promoted attractions—such as giant LED screens and live television broadcasts—that would create a nonthreatening urban vibe. Bloomberg closed the square to most automobile traffic in 2009, securing the area's place as a major tourist destination.

Nonetheless, the theater has remained essential to what Times Square is and what it will become. Broadway has flourished as a tourist attraction, with the number of productions and audiences growing once again. But as Ditsch feared, spectacles for middlebrow suburban and tourist-centric audiences have pushed aside more serious fare. By the 2014–15 season, Broadway was setting new records for the number and value of tickets sold, drawing more than 13 million people paying $1.3 billion. Broadway has become so successful that there is now a shortage of theaters rather that a shortage of productions. Shows are queuing up to find a Broadway venue.[245]

Ditsch and many others, however, are more concerned about artistic success than financial profits. From this perspective, shows that are dependent on high-tech wizardry and lushly mounted re-vivals—often, of the works discussed above—do not deserve ac-colades.

If Broadway has been transformed into a tourist attraction, is it still Broadway? In many ways, the Broadway of today is a re-turn to form for Broadway and its equivalents before the Golden Age. Rather than die, Broadway has evolved. More important, New York and American theater have changed.

Serious theater has not died, either in New York (although the current financial boom may still undermine the viability of perfor-mances other than pure spectacles) or in the United States. But it has moved—it has shifted to Off and Off-Off Broadway in New York, and to regional theaters around the country. Broadway ben-efits from these networks. Shows from Washington, Chicago, and Seattle make their way to Broadway and enrich the New York scene, even as Broadway shows go on tour. There has been a maturation of American theater, in which Broadway is just a part of a larger live entertainment industry, with outposts in Austin, Las Vegas, and Nashville. American theater no longer is found only nestled among a few blocks around 42nd Street and Broadway, as Arthur Miller could say a half century ago; today, Broadway is part of a larger American theater in ways it hasn't been before.[246] Theater lives.

Enduring art forms continually prompt cries of despair over their impending death. Many times, critics have declared the im-minent death of opera, ballet, jazz, bluegrass, Kabuki, theater, and Broadway. Yet new generations come along and discover what came before them in new ways. When once asked about the de-mise of jazz, Ravi Coltrane chuckled and observed that people will be playing his and his father's music decades if not centuries from now because there will still be new discoveries, which will inspire new listeners.[247] For instance, just as some began to write off Broadway as nothing more than light diversion for tourists, Lin-Manuel Miranda came along.[248]

Miranda is a product of the exciting blend of Hispanic and black cultures celebrated by the authors who contributed to the *Dissent* report discussed just above. Miranda was born in Manhattan of Puerto Rican heritage, and he grew up in Inwood, a blue-collar neighborhood near the island's northern tip cut off by subway switching yards from downtown. The area evolved from being the home of Jewish and Irish immigrants to the home of Hispanic— often Dominican—newcomers. The basketball legend Kareem Abdul-Jabar grew up a generation ago in the same neighborhood; and a generation before Abdul-Jabar, a boyish Henry Kissinger scampered around the streets of nearby Washington Heights. This end of Manhattan has long been reserved for the latest arrivals to find their way in a new homeland, often tossing off new cultural permutations in the process.

Miranda graduated from Hunter College High School and went off to idyllic Wesleyan University—a small Connecticut school best known for educating the gentry's offspring—where he combined the hip-hop of his home turf with a solid grounding in Wesleyan's more traditional student theater company. While a sophomore at Wesleyan, he began working on a musical based on a book by Quiara Alegría Hudes that told the story of the lives of his generation in the now largely Dominican American neighborhood of Washington Heights. The show—*In the Heights*—moved from Connecticut to Off-Broadway, and then to a Broadway production in 2008, winning four Tony Awards and a Pulitzer Prize nomination. Miranda—like the Berlins, Kerns, Hammersteins, Rodgers, Harts, and Sondheims before—was setting Broadway on fire by bringing new energy from the ever-evolving life of the city around them.

The *New York Times* drama critic—Charles Isherwood—could not contain his enthusiasm at the opening performance of *In the Heights*:

> It has been lamented in certain circles that they don't make Broadway musical stars the way they used to. We'll not see

the likes of Ethel Merman again. Or Mary Martin or John Riatt. Or, for that matter, Patti LuPone or Mandy Patinkin. C'mon everybody, let's give a big, sad sigh. Oh, let's not. While the manufacture of matinee idols and worship-ready divas, not to mention the sturdy vehicles they rode to fame, may be in decline, the theater has not gone out of the star-making business entirely. If you stroll down to the Richard Rodgers Theater, where the spirited musical *In the Heights* opened on Sunday night, you'll discover a singular new sensation, Lin-Manuel Miranda, commanding the spotlight as if he were born in the wings.[249]

But *In the Heights* was just the beginning. In 2015, Miranda's hip-hop interpretation of Ron Chernow's authoritative biography of Alexander Hamilton broke every mold on Broadway, starting out with its two-month run at the Public Theater. *Hamilton* tells the story of one of the country's most overlooked founding parents through the lens of the generations infused with the sounds of DJ Kool Herc. As the play's opening verse asks:

How does a bastard
Orphan
Son of a whore and
A Scotsman
Dropped in
The middle of a forgotten
Spot in
The Caribbean by Providence
Impoverished
In squalor
Grow up to be a hero and a scholar?[250]

How Hamilton did this was by coming to New York. As Miranda understood, Hamilton's story is the same tale that has been playing out on the streets of Manhattan since the eighteenth century. It took four decades from DJ Herc's 1973 back-to-school celebration in the Bronx (see the overture above) to a rapping Hamilton, Washington, and Jefferson on Broadway in 2015, by which time the new blend of cultures that came together on New York's streets had stormed the castle.

Broadway—like all human creations and the people who make them—dies a bit every day. Simultaneously, it is reborn. For all its twenty-first-century vibe, the Miranda legend *Hamilton* follows similar storylines to those that have driven New York stage shows from the very beginning. It is the story of the newcomer who soaks up all that is happening around and creates something no one has ever seen before. Of course, it is not totally new; and yet it is. No one had made one of the most New York musical genres of all—hip-hop—work before on a Broadway stage; and no one had ever cast a black man as George Washington.

Stephen Sondheim—who has encouraged and mentored Miranda ever since meeting him as a high school student—revealed profound truths about artistic innovation when speaking about Miranda's *Hamilton*. The play "is a breakthrough," Sondheim noted, "but it doesn't exactly introduce a new era. Nothing introduces an era. What it does is empower people to think differently. There's always got to be an innovator, somebody who experiments first with new forms. The minute something is a success, everybody imitates it. It's what happened with *Oklahoma!*—everybody immediately started to write bad Western musicals. *Hair* also had that effect. But eventually people stop imitation, and the form matures."[251] This moment of empowerment of new communities and social groups leads to startling new artistic achievements—on Broadway, in Naples and Buenos Aires, and in Osaka.

Tensions between popular and serious art—between high-brow and middle-brow—have marked the New York theater scene since its beginning more than three centuries ago. Esteemed critics and mere mortals have argued over the meaning of the various changes taking place both on and off stage. A much-anticipated 2012 revival of *Porgy and Bess* by the director Diane Paulus, originating at the American Repertory Theater in Cambridge, prompted intense and learned discussions about whether Gershwin's masterpiece was a "musical" or an "opera"—an overly stylized rendering of an essentially racist story to pander to middle-brow audiences, or a transcendent moment in American musical theater.

The *New York Times* reviewer Ben Brantley captured this ambiguity in his opening night review. "Mostly," Brantley noted, the production's "modernization" of the original "has meant scrapping much of the score, using dialogue instead of recitative and reducing sets and cast to an affordable minimum. . . . The resulting two-and-a-half hour *Porgy and Bess*—originally a fat, four-hour opera teeming with layers of life and music—sometimes feels skeletal."[252] This observation about a musical theatrical production echoes much criticism about a contemporary New York that somehow feels more skeletal than teeming with layers of life.

Then "suddenly an elemental force takes possession of the stage, and its tremors course through the audience," Brantley wrote. Audra McDonald's "extraordinary Bess" is reunited with her former lover, Crown, played by Phillip Boykin (figure 27). "And no matter what they're calling it these days—a musical, I believe," Brantley continues, "*Porgy and Bess* has suddenly risen to its natural heights as towering, emotion-saturated opera."

Figure 27. Audra McDonald (center foreground) as Bess and NaTasha Yvette Williams (right foreground) as Mariah, in the 2012 revival of Porgy and Bess.
Source: Photograph by Michael J. Lutch; used by permission, courtesy of the American Repertory Theater.

No matter how much *Porgy and Bess* has been reshaped to conform to modern sensibilities, Gershwin's folk opera still bristles with transcendent moments that consume the audience's emotions. Similarly, no matter how much New York is tamed, the city still bursts forth with elemental human energy. And Broadway theater—like the city that gave it life—continues to confront and define the American experience by enabling newcomers to engage with traditions that have long been in place.

Stage Notes for Act Two

Buenos Aires and New York are quintessential New World cities drawing residents from around the world. Significantly, however, this was not always the case. Both began as distant outposts of empires. And even after they had become independent, their elites still looked to the European metropolises for validation. In Buenos Aires, the social, political, and economic elite did everything it could to define Argentina and its capital as the "whitest" on the South American continent. In New York, elites defined cultural achievement through European frames. For these elites, the social supremacy of, respectively, the Teatro Colon and the Metropolitan Opera demonstrated their city's continued commitment to remaining European, even though it was sitting on the edges of the wild and uninhibited North and South American continents.

These same elites drew their wealth from increasingly modern economies that were converting natural wealth into personal wealth through new technologies. The era's ocean-faring steamship, underwater telegraph cables, and innovative financial practices demanded openness to the world and a fluidity in social and economic practices that did not exist in Europe. Moreover, the self-satisfaction of the old European social and cultural identities rooted in postcolonial hierarchies were at odds with how the *porteños* of Buenos Aires and the Knickerbockers and Yankees of New York actually made their money.

The postcolonial migrants from Europe and elsewhere entered the New World with different expectations. As they made their way in their new lives, they oriented themselves on the basis of cultural, social, and economic cues that were quite different from the ones being proclaimed by those who stood above them in the supposed pecking orders that governed their new homes. Thus, Spaniards and white Anglo-Saxon Protestants were washed away by tidal waves of innovation that were completely detached from their older values—as Buenos Aires and New York constantly changed.

As these immigrants tried to find their own anchors in these dynamic societies, they redefined what it meant to be a *porteño* or a New Yorker. And they did so by expressing themselves through the performing arts, in which they mixed and matched traditions that they had brought with them as well as those brought by earlier arrivals, including the homegrown traditions of the dispossessed in both Argentina and the United States, as well as the pseudo-European pretensions of their betters.

Argentine music and dance only became distinctively Argentine once these sounds of the brothels on the urban periphery had been blended together with the country's other various traditions into something new: the tango. Likewise, the New York theater only found its distinctive voice once foreigners, Jewish immigrants, and African Americans had come together to create an identifiable American musical theater, which eventually became global through Broadway and its connections with the new film industry based in Hollywood.

In both cities, the seeming chaos of daily life, as defined by constant urban change and economic transformation, inspired creative souls to find new outlets for their artistic expressions. Whether, respectively, the tango or the book musical, the stages in and around Buenos Aires and New York began to show audiences something they had never seen before. And the simultaneous emergence of the first electronic communications revolution spread these innovations around the globe. For instance, Carlos Gardel and George Gershwin became household names in France via the radio airwaves full of electronic signals that, for the first time in human history, were carrying the sounds of the music these artists created.

In both Buenos Aires and New York, the curative voice of the outsider transcended that of the insider, because both cities exemplified the syncretistic melding of a multitude of traditions and art forms into a new, distinctive entirety. Both burgeoning metropolises set standards for multicultural dynamism and comity that have seldom been matched. The arts led the way toward creating fresh understandings of how to be Argentine or American. How fitting that the tango has enjoyed a renaissance in Buenos Aires of late, and that Lin-Manuel Miranda has taken Broadway by storm, just as the historians and critics were busy writing obituaries for both the tango and the Broadway musical.

The subjects of Act Three, Cape Town and Yekaterinburg, share many of the characteristics attributed in the previous chapters to Buenos Aires and New York. Both cities were founded as colonial outposts on the edge of empires. And as gateways to new continents—landlocked Yekaterinburg sits but a couple dozen kilometers inside Asia, as a portal from European Russia; and Cape Town is a principal port at the southern end of Africa—they were constantly changing as newcomers came and went. These outsiders built economic empires, and failed miserably while trying. Moreover, Cape Town and New York are perhaps not-so-distant cousins, given that they share similar Dutch and British colonial experiences. Yet they are very different.

Both Cape Town and Yekaterinburg are the products of repressive political regimes in which the powerful elites did all that they could to sustain their existing hierarchies of power through the use of unassailable force. Throughout the most authoritarian of centuries, which began with the horrors of

the Boer War and the Russian Civil War, those in power suppressed anyone other than themselves (and sometimes suppressed even their own family members) in varieties of un-
imaginably barbaric ways. In these totalitarian contexts, music and theater became subversive, giving voice to thoughts
and emotions that were deemed illegal.

In South Africa, new forms of music emerging from the
country's diverse communities encouraged the blending of
various traditions into creations that reflected a distinctive
South African sensibility. On one hand, such experimentation was forced into the exile of apartheid-imposed monoracial settlements after having sustained cross-racial contact for
decades. On the other hand, official South African broadcasters encouraged new musical forms to emerge even as they
imposed high barriers separating all music into distinct categories. Most important, the authorities destroyed the very
physical environments that promoted cross-racial contact,
thus inhibiting the sort of blending of forms that so mark the
Buenos Aires and New York experiences. Music thus became
an affront to power.

In Yekaterinburg, the theater community seized opportunities presented by the collapse of the Soviet Union to create new forms of theater that were as rough and jagged as
the society around them. Drawing on while simultaneously
transforming British in-your-face theater and other non-Rus-
sian theatrical movements, playwrights and directors created a new form of theater that was uniquely Russian, leading
many observers to write about a new golden age of Russian
drama. Though always challenging authority, these renewed
approaches to drama unsurprisingly came under attack as
Russia became more authoritarian after the return of Vladimir
Putin to the Russian presidency in 2012.

The stories of music in Cape Town and theater in
Yekaterinburg that follow provide cautionary notes for any
thoughts that the creativity spawned by urban transformation

Act Three: Putting Demons to Rest

Humanity Is Coloured:

Musical Cape Town

Cape Town's subconscious has long guessed
what contemporary social science is now confirming:
we are all the bearers of the same mixed-up genetic bredie [stew].
Humanity is Coloured.

—Jeremy Cronin, "Creole Cape Town," 2005

The end was unremarkable.[1] One early October day in 1963, an un-gainly truck rumbled up to 22 Cross Street in Cape Town's District Six, in the heart of one of the most diverse neighborhoods on the African continent. A team of brutish movers descended upon a modest but much-loved abode, climbed thirteen narrow steps to a second-floor flat, gathered up the Ngcelwane family's earthly belongings, and quickly dispatched them miles away to the distant "black" township of Nyanga West (figure 28). Mr. Ngcelwane was off at his job with the United Tobacco Company in Observatory at the time, so his wife and children took their new keys and went off to start an unwanted alien life.[2]

The Ngcelwanes were members of a community that was being written out of history. They were Africans living in a historic part of Cape Town known as District Six. Because it was more often thought of as a "coloured" area, District Six stood as an affront to the racial dogmatists who had designed South Africa's apartheid policies. The guardians of racial purity—empowered by the passage of the Group Areas Act in 1950, together with accompanying pass laws and other assorted apartheid laws—had systematically set out to obliterate everything associated with the area so that its

Figure 28. People's belongings being packed onto a truck in preparation for their being moved out of District Six in Cape Town.
Source: Photograph by E. Walker; courtesy of the District Six Museum in Cape Town (www.districtsix.co.za).

centrally located real estate could become part of a freshly cleansed, "white" central city.[3]

More than a few twenty-first-century bookworms probably feel uncomfortable reading such terms as "black," "coloured," and "white," even when they are enclosed in quotation marks to underscore their official usage by South Africa's racist apartheid regime. Such terminology offends—and it should. These racialized terms overlap with other everyday categories, which similarly give offense to many both within and outside South Africa. The very act of telling the horrific tale of forced evictions from a single Cape Town neighborhood thus itself becomes a linguistic and moral ordeal.

Although such language is offensive, it captures a fundamental moral failing: The apartheid regime endorsed an aggressively negative vocabulary, which constructed definitions of race and ethnicity that privileged those who wielded the power to define, and that dehumanized those who did not. A preoccupation with establishing immutable group boundaries destroyed any notion of social cohesion, provoking an angry backlash that wounds the country to this day.

The text that follows relies on the approach toward these linguistic and moral conundrums taken earlier in this book by the anthropologist David Coplan. At the beginning of his classic study of twentieth-century South African urban music *In Township Tonight*, Coplan offers a "Note on Terminology":

> Vernacular, colloquial, official, and analytical terms play a major role in this study, and must be carefully defined. The first group of terms includes labels for socio-cultural categories and "population groups," as they are known in South Africa. Such terms have no necessary objective value. They are used here as they are still used, with some variation, by South Africans of all categories themselves. "African," for example, refers only to native speakers of Bantu or Khoisan languages who are of reputedly complete African Negro or Khoisan ancestry. There is then, in popular parlance, no such thing as an African or European, Asian or Eurafrican ancestry. Racially based, negative terms such as "Native," "Bantu," and "*Kaffir*" are never used to refer to Africans descriptively, but appear only in quotations and historical context. "Khoisan" refers to indigenes of Khoikhoi and San origins. The pejorative terms "Hottentot" (for Khoikhoi) and "Bushman" (for San) are used only in historical quotations in context. The term "coloured" (so-called) refers to persons of mixed ancestry. The South African "Malays," descendants of East Indian and Malabari slaves imported during the seventeenth and eighteenth centuries by the Dutch East India Company, constitute a separate Islamic East Indian segment within the coloured community. The term "Malay" refers only to them, while "coloured" may refer to any person of mixed racial heritage. "Black" indicates a person either African or coloured viewed as a single category. In official usage, South Africans of Indian descent are also categorized as "black" — in the sense that they are "other than white." "Other than European" (colloquially, "non-European") refers to South Africans who are not of

complete European ancestry. "White" indicates persons of exclusive European ancestry. The term "European," a synonym for white in South African usage, appears only rarely, to avoid confusion between South African whites and present or past natives of Europe.[4]

Though Coplan is about as straightforward a guide to the complexities of South Africa's linguistic somersaults about race and identity as the uninitiated might hope to find—setting down rules of linguistic engagement to be followed here—readers should understand that virtually every word cited above can be—and has been—contested.[5] Moreover, Coplan's excursion through the dark considerations of race and ethnicity in South Africa leaves out any number of other terms used within various communities about both themselves and outsiders.

Some of those unmentionable words are derived from the dozens of languages spoken in South Africa, including but not limited to the eleven official languages inscribed in the country's 1997 Constitution.[6] Others are borrowed from abroad, including one profoundly offensive legacy word left behind by visiting nineteenth-century American minstrel groups. This word—"coon"—refers to minstrel, performance, choral, and Carnival associations and groups that have played a profound role in Cape Town's musical and cultural history for well over a century.[7] Although today's performers and their associates who continue the city's lively and distinctive New Year's celebratory traditions vociferously defend the term within the context of Cape Town, it appears again in this chapter only within quotations by others, or within the titles of cited references.[8]

Returning to the forced expulsion of the Ngcelwane family from District Six with these linguistic cues in mind, the story takes on expanded meaning. The Ngcelwanes—a working-class family of Xhosan cultural heritage from the amaBhele clan and adhering to the Protestant Christian Methodist faith that had come to town decades before—was forced to move from a neighborhood that had been home to a community of perhaps as many as 60,000 souls that included Afrikaner-speaking descendants of East African slaves, Afrikaner- and English-speaking former Dutch and British working-class colonists, Muslim merchants, and shopkeepers whose ancestors had arrived in Cape Town as Dutch chattel, Jewish immigrants fleeing Russian pogroms at the beginning of the twentieth century, Christian missionaries and their flocks, and residents of every conceivable complexion. Individual and group identities formed around jobs, clan, ethnicity, language, religious belief, gender, and birth generation. The last pre-apartheid census in 1946 officially identified 28,377 District Six residents, including 20,184 "coloureds," 1,096 "Asians," 5,957 "Europeans," and 840 "natives."[9] Holiday traditions were shared, distinct cuisines enriched one another, and a pulsating blend of musical cultures took shape.

Such a mélange of humanity could only offend those who preoccupied themselves with defining and enforcing concise racial, ethnic, religious, gender, and linguistic boundaries. When they had the power to do so, the proprietors of racial "purity" dispatched the Ngcelwanes and their neighbors to "scientifically" organized "monoracial" settlements remote from the city itself. Such official deportations—as opposed to less formalized, market- and custom-based segregation—first occurred in Cape Town with the removal of Africans from District Six in 1901 after a bubonic plague epidemic.[10] Resettlement gained ferocious regularity once Afrikaner nationalists, led by Daniel François Malan's National Party, gained control of the country's Parliament in 1948.[11]

District Six was hardly the only "mixed" South African urban neighborhood to disappear under the separation policies of the Nationalists' apartheid regime. The newly empowered authorities likewise eradicated Johannesburg's Sophiatown and Fordsburg, Port Elizabeth's South End, East London's North End, and other, smaller integrated areas.[12] In fact, District Six managed to hold on a bit longer than some similar neighborhoods, thanks in part to the stubborn resistance of Cape Town's City Council and other local leaders.[13] Overall, between 1913 and 1983, at least 3.9 million people were forcibly removed from their homes in South Africa to enforce what the ideologues of state policy defined for themselves as "racial purity."[14]

District Six was swept away every bit as thoroughly as the other areas, as those in power dispatched the Ngcelwanes and their neighbors to ethnically cleansed settlements far from the country's bleached-out downtowns. They did so as residents found their lives being ripped apart through the painstakingly methodical implementation of racial laws, bureaucratic rules, and administrative protocols.

In the case of the Ngcelwane family, a letter arrived in August 1963 requesting the patriarch to come to a nearby drill hall that had once served as a vital community center. The local authorities informed him that they would relocate his family to NY75, No. 7, Section 2, Nyanga West. Eventually, the area's "coloured" residents similarly would be dispatched to other segregated townships.[15] Mr. Ngcelwane was once able to walk to work before the family's October relocation, but he now had to pay nearly 10 percent of his wages to traverse a dozen miles on various dysfunctional and inefficient forms of public transportation in order to earn even a semblance of a living.[16]

District Six had been among the most diverse and vibrant of Cape Town's in-town neighborhoods for decades, a creation of the days when the former Dutch provisioning station had become, in the eyes of the city's Victorian and mid-twentieth-century boosters, a "tavern of the seas."[17] District residents arrived from all seven seas and beyond, providing basic services to their neighbors, laboring on the docks, and working in the warehouses and workshops that were a quick walk downhill in town.[18]

This neighborhood was precisely the sort of place that outsiders look upon with scorn.[19] The area appeared to be in a constant state of decrepitude, because its poor residents and landlords lacked the capital needed to completely upgrade their residences. The district seemed to overflow with the sort of hucksters who feed off the poor, offering up an endless variety of entertainments to be enjoyed by sailors (and by those socially proper sorts who wanted to pursue their sporting life beyond the scrutiny of family, friends, colleagues, and coreligionists). Criminals were thought to lurk in various shadows, looking for easy prey.[20]

District Six, in short, was a dynamic and culturally rich neighborhood that constantly tossed off an innovative ethos, despite offending those who claimed authority over public virtue. The neighborhood's vigor lay not in what could be seen by outsiders. Rather, it was to be found in the mutual support that its residents gave to one another. District Six was a place where family and connections mattered more than money. Though none of the administrators at the drill hall probably would have understood, each time they summoned another resident, they destroyed the very strengths that, over the centuries, had made Cape Town a creative meeting ground.

Whatever the outsiders may have thought, those being displaced knew what they were losing. The wound still stung thirty-five years later for Nomvuyo Ngcelwane when she wrote:

> The removal was going to bring a lot of change to people's lives: for immediate neighbours, there was no guarantee that they would be living together as neighbours in Nyanga West. The fear was that we would be scattered all over. To those who walked to their place of work, it meant budgeting for bus or train fares in the future.
>
> To the children, it meant making new friends and attending new schools. And what was going to happen to the Chapel Street School that held such indelible memories for the Black children of District Six?
>
> To housewives, it meant cutting down on grocery lists because the increase in rent and fares to work—with no increase in people's wages—left less money for food.
>
> To the worshippers, it meant travelling long distances to get to church. To everybody, it meant paying higher rent, adjusting to the conditions of Nyanga West, and changing their social life style.[21]

These sentiments have been repeated by Mrs. Ngcelwane's neighbors and their descendants over and over again, whenever and wherever they have been given an opportunity to speak.[22] They perhaps have found the most vivid and touching expression at the District Six Museum, which opened in December 1994 in the former Central Methodist Mission on Buttenkanrt Street.[23] Returning residents arriving at the museum lovingly mark their former homes on a giant street map of the old neighborhood that was painted on the museum's floor.[24]

A District of Multiple Personalities and Possibilities

District Six had a long history of having a substantial presence within a burgeoning British colonial city. The Municipal Act of 1867 dividing Cape Town into six districts officially designated the area at the foot of Devil's Peak, known as Kanaladorp—either from the Malay word "kanala," meaning to help one another, or in reference to the Capel Sloot ditch that ran between the Dutch East India Company's Gardens and the Castle at the waterfront—as "District Six."[25] The neighborhood was growing rapidly at the time. Kanaladorp had been largely devoid of buildings in 1840, when Cape Town had a small population of about 20,000. Just a few decades before, the area designated as an urban district in 1867 had been the site of vineyards and small farms.[26] Both the district and the city quickly filled up over the course of the nineteenth century, so that, at the end of the Second Anglo-Boer War in 1902, Cape Town and its suburbs had become home to more than 140,000 and continued to grow quickly.[27]

The neighborhood's rapid development reflected a distinctive combination of centrality and marginality within a colonial boom-town. With easy access to the harried docks yet sufficient distance to be out of the view of those who did not want to see, District Six became home to a hard-working laboring class and petit bourgeoisie. It proved to be an efficient staging ground and residence for those engaged in South Africa's flourishing trade in wool and ostrich feathers with the colonial metropolis in Britain. District residents worked in the country's exploding trade, which steadily accelerated after the discovery of diamonds and gold inland.[28] These workers and their families, in turn, depended on the services provided by the small merchants and landlords who lived in their midst.

Many residents of District Six were the descendants of slaves known locally as "Malays," who had been brought by the Dutch in the seventeenth and eighteenth centuries from their South Asian colonies. Their Afrikaans speech; Arabic education; shared occupations; distinctive sartorial, culinary, and medical practices; music and festivals; and one- and two-story flat-roofed whitewashed houses bespoke a cosmopolitanism that seemingly distinguished their area from anyplace else in the Cape Colony.[29] An identifiable and varied neighborhood of some 30,000 residents had taken shape as the twentieth century dawned.[30]

Since its founding in the second quarter of the nineteenth century, District Six had remained a densely packed mixture of all the social groups—from the wealthy through domestic servants and laborers—that characterized premodern towns. Residential segregation by class, income, ethnicity, language, and conviction necessarily remained piecemeal until the railways and tramways arrived after midcentury. By the 1870s, those who could afford to move—either because of their wealth or because of their reliance on more reliable employment—began to follow the rails to the gardens, as well as to Green Point and Sea Point to the south. Those competing for casual employment remained concentrated within walking distance of the docks and downtown. By 1900, District Six had become a densely developed community of small shopkeepers, artisans, and laborers, with doctors, clergymen, and lawyers intermittently tossed in.[31]

District Six and adjacent quarters, such as the Observatory and the Castle neighborhoods, became home to a population arriving from every corner of the globe. "By 1900," the historian Vivian Bickford-Smith records, "the largest component [of the District's population] was formed by people whom the Cape government referred to variously as 'Malay,' 'Mixed and Other,' or 'Coloured'—that is, those Capetonians of darkish pigmentation who were descendants of slaves and/or 'mixed' marriages with or between Khoi, Africans who spoke Bantu languages, and Colonists from Europe or their descendants. . . . A vast range of nationalities were represented in the District, including considerable numbers of Indians, Chinese, and Australians."[32]

The transformation to modernity initiated by commuter railroads and trams hardly improved living conditions for those left behind. Class and racial conflicts were carried back from attempts to unionize workplaces in town and also in the mines further afield. The area was overcrowded, blemished by poor public health, and impaired by municipal inattention, and its difficulties were seen as validating the era's popular social Darwinism.

Two trends that would shape District Six until its demise were pronounced by the time the Second Anglo-Boer War ground to an end. The first of many successful civil society organizations began to form around this time, as an assortment of increasingly effective local leaders—such as Morris Alexander and Abdullah Abdurahman—stepped forward to challenge authority. In return, local officials facing seemingly intractable social challenges responded by attacking the defenseless.[33] In 1901, to mention just one already-cited example, city officials dispatched "African" residents from District Six in the wake of an outbreak of the bubonic plague.[34]

Where hardly a building stood at the beginning of the nineteenth century, a full-blown community of distinct and multiple personalities had taken shape by the beginning of the twentieth century. The historian Deborah Hart notes that, on one hand, the District Six of a century ago was "impoverished, crime-ridden, dilapidated, and overcrowded." Yet simultaneously, on the other hand, the neighborhood

> hummed with the enterprise of its residents, boasting a bewildering assortment of stores that served the population far beyond its immediate boundaries. Mingled with the more commonplace small general stories, tailors, butchers, fruitiers, and fishmongers were the spice and curry shops and dimply lit herbalists' stores, reflecting the diverse cultures of their owners and patrons. Informal trading flourished as hawkers set up their barrows at nearly every street corner, bartering animatedly with great exhibitionism; and adding to the chaos of what was said to be a "river of people, cars, barrows, buses, horse-drawn cars; a bustling, laughing, shouting, chatting river of people."[35]

If Cape Town had become a bustling entrepôt on the central trade routes of the world's largest, wealthiest, and most powerful empire—a proverbial "tavern of the seas"—District Six was its déclassé roadhouse, close enough to the main road to be visited and far enough away from prying eyes to offer any good or service that the imagination of an entrepreneur and a customer might conjure. It was the space where the human diversity of the larger city intermingled, creating more than the "exotic" "local color" that so pleased colonial voyeurs.[36] It was, in fact, a vibrant and rich community that nurtured bountiful cultural expression and a potent social intelligence. It would remain (until the rambling lorries arrived to cart the inhabitants away) the very sort of productive urban jagged edge that enriches its residents and society at large, even as it forces them to struggle to thrive as well as survive.[37] In other words, it was a "zone of contact," in the sense that it was an area "commonly regarded as chaotic, barbarous, lacking in structure" that was nonetheless marked by a "co-presence" arising from a coming into contact of peoples who were "geographically and historically separated."[38]

District Six is an important introduction to a city where, more often than generally acknowledged, residents transgressed social and racial boundaries. The district—as Sandra Prosalendis, Hennifer Marot, Crain Soudien, and Anwah Nagia note—was a place where local history is "about impoverished and marginalized people managing to build a sense of community and retain their own humanity in the face of considerable state neglect and oppression, . . . a place where they were able to share their everyday experiences and to live not as 'coloured,' 'whites,' 'Africans,' or 'Indians' but as South Africans."[39] Thus, it was just the sort of place, in just the sort of city, where new ideas burst forth—even if no one in authority cared to take note.

A Feast for the Eye

Laying claim to an exclusive domain over tens of thousands of neighbors of difference is a complex task. Having constructed a "national" history around such travails as the "Great Trek" to escape British control during the 1830s and 1840s, Afrikaner ideologists argued that they were the sole couriers of a genuine South African nationhood.[40] Asserting this entitlement proved to be a knotty task. On one hand, they needed to deny the existence of those who had inhabited the region before their own arrival. On the other hand, they needed to distinguish their own privileged claim while denying the historical reality of British colonial status following the Napoleonic Wars.

Malan's ideologists were a resourceful lot. They managed to

Figure 29. A portrait of Jan van Riebeeck.
Source: A woodcut done in 1830 by A. Reid; Library of Congress.

invent just the right moment to redefine the meaning of the South African state as their own. In 1952, they seized upon a founding date for their people: the 1652 arrival of a small band dispatched by the Dutch East India Company (Vereenigde Oost-Indische Compagnie), under the command of Captain Jan van Riebeeck, to secure a provisioning station for ships shuttling between their Asian colonies and the European Dutch home ports (figure 29).

Van Riebeeck was a well-known figure to anyone who had studied in a South African school. Before 1952, as Leslie Witz explains, "Van Riebeeck had been depicted as the *volksvader* (father of the Afrikaner nation), the initiator of farming in South Africa, the bearer of Christianity to the subcontinent, and the (British) colonial founder."[41] But the Nationalists wanted him to be more.

The celebration of the tercentenary of van Riebeeck's landing was a not-unusual twentieth-century ruse used to establish "a moment of colonial discovery or founding as the font of a nation."[42] The United States embraced Christopher Columbus's 1492 crossing of the Atlantic Ocean as a foundational moment, despite the fact he did not land in what would become the United States. Australians claimed the arrival of the "First Fleet" at Botany Bay in January 1788 as their moment of creation. Afrikaans organizers faced an additional task. They simultaneously needed to use the fact of van Riebeeck's arrival to reinforce their own anti-imperialist narrative delegitimizing the British as colonizing "outsiders."[43]

The organizers of the van Riebeeck Tercentenary Festival Fair planned an extravaganza focusing on a stadium that had been hastily built adjacent to the Victoria & Albert Waterfront on Granger Bay. This festival venue would become the nerve center for street processions, exhibitions, academic conferences, and plays—a splendid "feast for the eye" (*n Fees vir die Ooog*).[44] The pageant culminated in a nationwide procession of mail coaches converging on the festival stadium that retraced, in reverse, the historic dispersion of the Afrikaner nation across the face of South Africa, thereby reconfirming how the tentacles extending from van Riebeeck's Mother City bound the "nation" together.

The accomplished, thirty-three-year-old van Riebeeck had commanded three Dutch East India Company ships when he landed at Table Bay on April 6, 1652. He arrived under instructions to establish a fortified way station for the provisioning of ships making their way between Dutch Batavia and Holland. This assignment was a nontrivial one. Treacherous waters around what is now called the Cape of Good Hope and hostile indigenous peoples on land had long discouraged Europeans from trying to colonize the area. The company had little interest in undertaking the expensive and time-consuming chore of establishing a colony. The quarter-century experiment of the parallel Dutch West Indies Company at New Amsterdam in North America similarly had proven to be too expensive to maintain, and would pass to British hands shortly after van Riebeeck had been reassigned as governor of Malacca in May 1662.[45]

Van Riebeeck fulfilled his initial assignment despite its very real challenges. He built the first fort, developed the Dutch East India Company's Gardens to grow fruits and vegetables for the visiting company ships, and established continuing—though troubled—relations and trade with the indigenous Khoikhoi and San people for livestock and other necessary goods.[46]

The provisioning of basic foods and labor remained a vexing challenge for the tiny outpost as it sought to feed both passing convoys and itself. Natural and human predators devoured flocks of sheep and other animals, so van Riebeeck and his minions turned to nearby Robben Island as a more secure "pantry" for the post. Spices and other staples had to be imported from various Dutch colonies. As a result, in October 1657, the Dutch East India Company's directors approved the grant of freehold lands along the Liesbeek Valley for agricultural purposes, creating a free Burgher society no longer in the company's employ. Little time passed before these newly independent farmers began to protest restrictions on their livelihoods put in place by the company, thus marking the beginnings of a distinct settler society.[47]

The granting of freeholds had five additional effects that would shape the outpost's future long after van Riebeeck had departed. First, the new orderly freehold farms disrupted the migration patterns of the peripatetic Khoikhoi herding communities. Second, recognizing that the Khoikhoi and San people in the region were not likely to be easily impounded into service, the Dutch East India Company's directors approved the importation of slaves from other company-controlled lands in the East Indies.[48] Third, Islam accompanied the arrival of slaves from the Malay Archipelago, Indonesia, Ceylon (Sri Lanka), and India, so Cape Town has been home to a significant Islamic community almost since the day of its founding.[49] Fourth, a handful of women joined van Riebeeck's wife, Maria de la Quellerie, in entering domestic life as the wives and daughters of senior company officers and independent Burghers.[50] And fifth, the official recognition of the Dutch Reformed Church marked the entire venture as "Christian," despite the presence of multiple confessions.[51]

Within a few years after van Riebeeck's reassignment in 1662, his early earthen, star-shaped fort had been rebuilt in stone; a small permanent settlement had taken shape; and the core elements of Cape Town's future diversity had been secured. His official gardener, Hendrick Boom, had established the fine Dutch East India Company Gardens growing fruits and vegetables to replenish passing ships, and exotic trees and shrubs have been imported continuously ever since.[52] Imperial and commercial maneuvering was transforming what initially had been intended as little more than a seventeenth-century wayfaring service station into an urban community.

This moment of settlement never represented the national founding summoned by the fervent imaginations of nationalist ideologists. Large segments of Cape Town society rejected the premises underlying the tercentenary festival. Intellectuals at the University of Cape Town joined in boycotting the event, together with civic and religious leaders of several Cape Town non-Afrikaans communities (including many from District Six).[53] Their critiques of van Riebeeck's legacy were hardly novel. A century before, in 1852, the famous Scottish missionary David Livingstone had decried van Riebeeck as worthy of excommunication rather than veneration for having condoned "robbery and murder, provided the victims had black skins."[54]

Statues of Jan van Riebeeck and Maria de la Quellerie remain standing on Cape Town's Adderley Street, and they are venerated each April 6 by ever-smaller numbers of Afrikaner nationalists. The year 1652 appears listed as the founding date for South Africa's "Mother City" in numerous popular accounts of Cape

Town's history. The seventeenth-century stone replacement for van Riebeeck's fort signifies the city's center, drawing curious tourists from around the globe to this day.[55] Perhaps their presence constitutes a fitting dénouement for the celebration that never could have been anything but a single strand in the riotously complex urban tapestry that is Cape Town.

A Maritime Caravanserai

The van Riebeeck founding myth for Cape Town and the Afrikaner nation comes up short on several fronts. Human beings had inhabited the shores of Table Bay and the slopes of Table Mountain for millennia before the Dutch even existed in Europe, let alone in Africa. In addition, the Dutch were hardly the first Europeans to land in or even to lay claim to the area. Moreover, the Dutch East India Company was a corporate enterprise that drew on a multinational labor force, so Cape Town became home to people of diverse backgrounds from the very beginning.

The lands around Table Bay and across the Cape Peninsula and Cape Flats had been inhabited by hunters and gatherers since at least the Middle Ages and Late Stone Age. Human skeletons dating from 33,000 years ago have been found throughout the greater Cape Town area, as have the remains of sheep from 1,600 years ago. Cattle appear to have arrived on what is now called the Cape of Good Hope in about AD 700, if not before.[56] The precise contour of community evolution from hunter-gatherer to pastoralist is subject to debate. In some academic accounts, hunter-gatherers adopted domestic livestock and evolved into pastoralists; in other narratives, different groups moved into the area at different times.[57]

What is indisputable is that what is now called the Cape of Good Hope was not vacant when the Dutch arrived. The Khoikhoi had developed a robust, pastoral, cattle-based economy, moving their livestock with the seasons because the local vegetation proved to be insufficiently nutritious to permit them to remain in one place all year round. The Khoikhoi drew on the accumulated wealth of their cattle and sheep to trade for other staples with peoples living further inland.[58] They developed a reputation among European visitors for being fierce defenders of their livestock—which represented wealth—and of their migration routes.[59]

The Khoikhoi shared the region with the San people (some-times called Bushmen by European settlers), hunters and gatherers who migrated throughout the southern regions of the African con-tinent. The Dutch dismissively called both groups Hottentots—or stutterers—because of the clicks used in their language.[60] Linguists include both groups in the Khoisan linguistic category for their use of click language. The Khoikhoi and the San maintained distinct cultures, religious beliefs, and livelihood strategies, despite their long contact and not-infrequent intermarriages with one another.[61] Neither the Khoikhoi nor the San were brought easily into Euro-pean service, and both faced considerable discrimination once they were.[62]

The Dutch under van Riebeeck's command had not arrived in lands that represented a "clean slate" on which they could form a new nation. Moreover, they weren't even the first Europeans to stake a claim to the area. Barolomeu Dias was the first European during the Age of Discovery to reach what later became the Cape of Good Hope in 1488, suitably giving the Cape Peninsula the name Cape of Storms. King John II of Portugal later renamed it the Cape of Good Hope, in anticipation of the riches being opened by the new route to India. Drawn to the Zambezi by gold and the slave trade, the cape remained an afterthought, a stop along the way to take on fresh water and trade for cattle and sheep with the locals. The Portuguese tended to steer clear, especially following numer-ous shipwrecks and a murderous 1510 run-in between a viceroy returning home from the East and the indigenous people that left the viceroy dead.[63]

A century or so later, in July 1620—a dozen weeks before the Pilgrims landed in Plymouth, Massachusetts—Andrew Schillinge and Humphrey Fitzherbert of the British East India Company claimed Table Bay and "the whole continent near adjoining" for the British Crown when they stopped to refresh their ships on the way to Bantam.[64] As with earlier visiting Portuguese and Dutch crews, their purpose was to gather water and food, and barter with the Khoikhoi for meat. The British left little to secure their grandiose claims—other than, tellingly, a penal colony established on Robben Island in 1615.

By the 1630s, the Dutch were throwing mutineers and other

miscreants overboard in Table Bay.[65] As competition grew among the European powers to achieve global reach, the Cape of Good Hope began to loom larger in their imaginations. The Dutch East India Company's dispatch of van Riebeeck was a preemptive strike protecting an increasingly strategic coastline from being grabbed by its competitors. There was, in other words, never one particular moment of Dutch discovery touching off the creation of a new ethnos on unknown and unpopulated land, as suggested by Afrikaner ideologists.

The Dutch East India Company's employees who arrived and stayed were not even particularly Dutch. Instead, as in New York, they were mercenaries hired from across Northern Europe.[66] The crews of the visiting ships they serviced were a motley, cosmopolitan lot. Few Europeans wanted to come to the Cape of Good Hope—there was no gold—and even fewer wanted to stay.[67]

Realizing that the Dutch were not going to leave, the Khoikhoi contested Burgher claims to their grazing land. With scant local workers and less-than-enthusiastic Dutch settlers (there were only 120 employees on the company's books in 1662), the directors made the fateful decision to import slave labor from their colonies in Dutch Batavia and the Dutch East Indies.[68] Many of the arriving slaves were political exiles, including the leaders of revolts against the Dutch in Java, Batavia, and Goa.[69] Before century's end, Sheik Joseph (Syech Yussuf), a remarkable Bantamese insurgency leader and brother of the king of Goa, was dispatched to the Cape of Good Hope, accompanied by his two wives, friends, and servants (figure 30). Yussuf is venerated as the founder of the Muslim faith in South Africa, and his tomb overlooking the Eerste River has become a pilgrimage destination.

Others seeking refuge joined together with company men, Burghers, and slaves. Persecuted French Huguenots arrived in search of a safe haven in 1688.[70] Van Riebeeck had begun viniculture in 1659, with vineyards quickly becoming a prominent feature of the new Burgher farms.[71] The displaced French families brought a taste for gracious living, an appreciation of high-quality wine and food, and a knack for growing grapes that gave them quick entrée into local society from their farms in the nearby Franschloek Valley.

Figure 30. A painting of the arrival of Sheik Joseph (Syech Yussuf) in Cape Town.
Source: Painting by G. S. Smithard and J. S. Skelton, 1909 (https://en.wikipedia.org/ wiki/Sheikh_Yusuf#/media/File:G.S._Smithard;_J.S._Skelton_%281909%29_-_ The_Coming_of_Sheik_Joseph.jpg).

Rather than serve as the homeland for a new nation, the small Dutch East India Company encampment and the scattered homesteads in the surrounding valleys established Cape Town as a lively international settlement more diverse and cosmopolitan than its diminutive size might suggest. Add to this scene the crews of visiting ships—who often stayed for several weeks—and the town was a virtual babel of nations, as was the case with New Amsterdam in North America. If Cape Town is a "mother city," its offspring is diversity. The town always has been, in the words of the historian Leonard Thompson, "a miniature Batavia—'a seaward-looking community, a caravanserai on the periphery of the global spice trade,' where diverse religions, languages, and peoples jostled, and life focused on the world outside."[72]

Drunkards, Gamblers, Burghers, and Imams

By the last quarter of the seventeenth century, the Dutch East India Company sought to offset declining returns from the spice trade with income from expanding cotton and silk commerce with India and China. The provisioning station's significance grew as the company expanded direct shipping routes passing the Cape of Good Hope, between Bengal, Ceylon, and the Netherlands. Because they were embroiled in wars with Britain and France, the Dutch expanded their commitments to defending the Table Bay colonies. They rebuilt van Riebeeck's wooden fort in stone between 1666 and 1674, expanded infrastructure investments, and set down a diminutive grid street plan to secure a permanent settlement.[73] Newly minted Burghers staked their claims to farmlands further in the interior. Cape Town became a trading and market center, with livestock and produce being brought to town in return for manufactured goods arriving by ship. A cape creole society was brought forth as the seventeenth century passed into the eighteenth.[74]

The town remained unimpressive in comparison with the Dutch East India Company's settlements in Batavia, let alone in contrast to the provincial European market towns. Cape Town nonetheless developed its own distinctive character, drawing on a mixture of styles imported from Europe and Asia that would become a precursor to later Cape Dutch vernacular design.[75] The built environment reflected a social hierarchy in which the Dutch East India Company's officers stood at the top, followed by skilled and unskilled company employees, as well as unskilled soldiers recruited from the Netherlands, various German principalities, Denmark, Sweden, Norway, Scotland, Britain, France, Switzerland, and Russia.[76]

Evidence of the colony's dependence on imported slaves from the East was ubiquitous in a town where 42 percent of the recorded urban population in 1731 were slaves.[77] A substantial Dutch East India Company slave lodge glowered across from the Castle.[78] Diminutive outbuildings were scattered about to shelter those held in domestic servitude (most urban households owned fewer than five slaves, compared with perhaps twice that number in establishments providing lodging, and vastly larger numbers on farms inland).[79]

In contrast to the larger colony, Cape Town was home as well to a significant population of *vrijwarten* ("free blacks"), including those released from bondage together with the offspring of slave and nonslave parents.[80] Some slaves simply wandered off into the vast African hinterland, often becoming integrated with indigenous peoples.[81] An unrecorded number of Khoikhoi construction crews were joined in Cape Town by a small Chinese community, as well as convicts and exiles from Batavia.[82] Among all the possible social distinctions existing in the colony, those distinguishing between "Christian" and "heathen" carried the most meaning.[83]

Various sorts of people came together in Dutch Cape Town for a single purpose: the replenishment of the trading vessels that berthed in Table Bay for some twenty to thirty days at a time.[84] There was nothing genteel about Cape life, even if a somewhat refined Burgher society took shape in the countryside.[85] Cape rural life wasn't completely elegant in any case, as growing colonies of white agricultural settlers extended their reach deeper into the northeastern and southwestern environs. Inhabiting land unable to sustain long-term agriculture, these semi-migrant pastoralists—who became known as *trekboers*—gradually replaced the native Khoikhoi over the course of the eighteenth century. Living largely independent of the Dutch East India Company, their homesteads formed subsistence communities on the edge of the colonial authority and the market-based economy in town.[86]

Cape Town itself was dominated by the trades and crafts necessary to sustain ships—including a highly profitable commerce
in slaves—and the lodgings and groggeries necessary to contain
their crews on land while vessels were being outfitted for further
voyages.[87] The town remained a raucous, at times violent, libertine
place full of drunkards, philanderers, baboon-baiters, cockfight impresarios, gamblers, and cheats. Alcohol in various forms was consumed in such large quantities that, according to legend, the first
sailor on a Dutch East India Company ship to sight Table Mountain from the sea was given 10 guilders and six bottles of wine. The
company provided all hands with a glass of brandy before they
alighted on shore.[88] Social boundaries proved more porous in actuality than various legal codes, administrative decrees, and sermons
by Reformed Church preachers might suggest.[89] In other words, the
town was just the sort of place that blends together various high
and low cultures into its own distinctive volatile mix.

Language became one measure of the town. Like its North
American colonial cousin New Amsterdam, Cape Town became
a city of competing tongues. If eighteen languages were spoken
in the 1640s under Dutch rule in the area that is now New York
City, the Cape Town of a century later was its match.[90] As Leonard
Thompson records in his seminar volume *A History of South Africa,*

> Some colonists were holding to the Dutch of the Nether-
> lands, the official language of the colony. Some indigenous
> people were still speaking their native languages. A few
> slaves were able to use their languages of origin, whereas
> Portuguese Creole had become a common means of com-
> munication among the Asian slaves. A simplified form of
> Dutch, which dropped certain inflections and vocabulary
> items, modified the vowel sounds, and incorporated loan
> words from the other languages, however, was becoming
> the dominant lingua franca. This dialect, which originated
> as a medium of oral communication between Burghers and
> slaves, would become a distinct language—Afrikaans.[91]

Significantly for the story of Cape Town's hybrid culture, the
first book to published in Afrikaans during the 1850s probably was
printed in Arabic script.[92]

Religion is another measure of a consolidating Cape culture. As in New York, the Dutch authorities were tolerant, for that age, of a variety of beliefs, despite the official authority of the Reformed Church. One result was the establishment of an energetic Islamic community embracing slaves imported from the Dutch colonies in Asia.

As noted above, the Dutch dispatched the Bantamese nobleman Syech Yussuf to the Cape Colony during the late seventeenth century. A hundred years later, they banished Abdullah Ibn Qadhu Abdus Salaam—known as *tuan guru* (master teacher)—from the Teinate Islands to Robben Island for having conspired with the British against them. A descendant of the sultan of Morocco, Salaam was incarcerated between 1780 and 1792. He subsequently established one of South Africa's first religious schools (madrassas) in his Dorp Street house, where he taught the Qur'an, Arabic philosophy, Islamic law, and the guiding principles of the Ash'ari creed of Sunnism well into the nineteenth century. The Cape Town Muslim community grew from 1,000 in 1800 to 6,000 by 1840, during which time the number of Islamic religious schools increased to more than twelve.[93]

The Bo-Kaap neighborhood surrounding Dorp Street developed into the historic center of Cape Town's Malay community, remaining the site of several significant religious institutions; Sufi burial shrines, known as *kramats*; and a broad-based Islamic cultural community. With its colorful diminutive houses sporting front stairs (*stoeps*) that were perfectly suited for neighborly conversation, the area became a tourist attraction after the end of apartheid, and today it confronts the multifaceted challenges of gentrification.[94]

Each group brought its own musical sensibilities and traditions with it, while the city's expansive tavern economy created numerous opportunities for informal and formal performances. The Portuguese explorer Vasco de Gama made note of the Khoikhoi's astonishing polyphonic flute music in 1497, long before the Dutch arrived.[95] The Khoikhoi similarly mastered the *ramkie*, a three- or four- (now six-) stringed guitar brought by Malabar slaves in the eighteenth century, as well as their own single-stringed instruments using a distinctive chin technique (figure 31).[96] Other indigenous instruments based on European examples included a bugle

Figure 31. Shepherds being entertained by the player of a *ramkie*, a three-or four- (now six-) stringed guitar.
Source: Photograph by Carol Muller; used by permission.

made of kelp, and the *t'guthe,* an adaptation of the violin. Much later, Afrikaans-speaking folk musicians would create the *velviool* by placing steenbok hide over a wooden frame. Non-European instruments—including various early forms of the *ghoema,* a distinctive, barrel-shaped drum that defines Cape minstrel music—quickly passed into the local musical repertoire.

The Dutch, for their part, generally viewed the Khoikhoi and Asian slaves as musically gifted, establishing "slave orchestras" for their own entertainment as early as 1676. Tavern owners were known to buy slaves primarily for their musical talents. The Dutch celebrated Christmas and the New Year with serenades and gift giving, often moving from house to house. They and Europeans generally brought their dance music—including quadrilles and later polkas—as well as military bands from both the Dutch East India Company's barracks and visiting ships.

One easily sees the origins of later Cape Town traditions in the blend of components dating from the time of Dutch rule.[97] As

Denis-Constant Martin notes in her history of the city's extravagant New Year's celebrations,

> The cradle of a Creole society was probably the canteens, taverns, and "smuggling houses" (unlicensed bars) in which slaves from the city and from rural areas, free blacks, sailors, and white Capetonians rubbed shoulders, gambled and got drunk together. This meant that input into the developing Creole culture came not only from the people living at the Cape but also from various outsiders. The result of this multiethnic, nonracial integration—as in New Amsterdam—was the development of an urban subculture, marginal if contrasted to the norms of the dominant classes and cosmopolitan when the variety of people who participated in its assemblage is considered. . . . It also, however, infiltrated the culture of the dominant classes, especially where language, music and cooking were concerned.[98]

The Dutch East India Company never turned a profit on its Cape venture (although its strategic position for reprovisioning ships was more valuable than monetary gain).[99] The company failed to invest adequate capital for the colony to develop self-sustainability, and few people came to settle.[100] The British arrived in June 1795 to reestablish their 1620 claim to Table Bay. Never having had to defend their town from direct attack, panic set in, rural Burgher recruits never materialized, while local militia and a Khoikhoi regiment were hardly a match for British arms. The local elite quietly swore allegiance to King George in return for a waiver of reparations.[101]

The British—like van Riebeeck before them—thought their occupation was only a transitory skirmish in larger European wars. In exchange for Ceylon, they returned the colony to the Dutch (though to Batavian colonial authorities rather than to the Dutch East India Company) under the Treaty of Amiens in 1802. The British returned to stay, as it turned out, a few years later, as part of their maneuverings against Napoleon. The Cape of Good Hope officially became a crown colony in 1814, under the terms of the grand European post-Bonaparte settlement. And Cape Town began its transformation into a respectable British provincial colonial town.[102]

From Dutch Tavern to Imperial Hub

Once the British settled in, they largely centralized power in subordination to London.[103] The British recognized the property rights and privileges of local inhabitants. As late as 1820, 90 percent of the free white population remained of Dutch and German heritage.[104]

As in New York, the Dutch and Burgher presence throughout the town and colony continued to be pronounced, even as the British undertook a number of measures intended to Anglicize the city and colony—such as the imposition of British law and language; the appointment of British officials; the replacement of Dutch garrisons with British soldiers; the increased presence of the Royal Navy; and the abolition of slavery following the enactment of the Slavery Abolition Act of 1833.[105] Enhanced maritime technologies, including the replacement of sailing ships with those powered by steam, and communication links, such as submarine telegraph cables between Britain and the Cape of Good Hope, effectively brought Cape Town closer to Britain during the third quarter of the nineteenth century.[106]

Royal dominion opened the town and colony to new immigrants from elsewhere in the empire, most especially from South Asia and the British Isles.[107] One particular group of migrants from Britain—the so-called 1820 Settlers—arrived in response to a program transporting potential tillers from the home islands and providing them upon arrival with farm plots of approximately 100 acres per household. Their presence immediately placed an emerging British agricultural class in competition with its Dutch predecessors.[108] Thus, in the words of the historian Leonard Thompson, white South Africa "acquired an ethnic problem analogous to the Anglo-French problem of Canada. But the demographic proportions were—and remained—decisively different. In the colonies that became Canada, British settlers soon outnumbered the French Canadians.[109]

It was particularly important, Thompson notes, that the British colonial enterprise in South Africa before the discovery of diamonds and gold remained miniscule in comparison with North America. As he notes, the United States had a population of more than 32 million, with nearly 53,000 miles of railroad by 1870, in comparison with 250,000 Europeans plus their descendants and fewer than 70 miles of railroads in all of Southern Africa at the same time.[110]

The British began to reshape the town physically.[111] Economic adaptation proved to be as significant as the legal, administrative, and demographic changes taking place throughout the colony. Cape Town became a hub in the diverse global economy of the British Empire, which was moving its primary trade routes from the Atlantic Ocean to the Indian Ocean.[112]

The abolition of slavery expanded the local urban economy.[113] Slaves in the town—as opposed to rural areas—primarily worked as domestic traders, artisans, and craftspeople. Their shift to wage labor increased the money earned by the Dutch and others employed in the local service and construction trades. That growth in income attracted growing numbers of poor Irish immigrants, who began to compete with local wage earners. Worden, van Heyningen, and Bickford-Smith observe that "Sydney Street in 'Irish town,' for example, was described in 1838 as a place 'where many low Irish and coloured people reside.' But there was a growing tendency for some streets and parts of town to be associated with primarily white or primarily 'coloured' residents, and it was comparatively rare for households to include both white and coloured residents (apart from live-in coloured servants in white households), even where the street itself was mixed."[114]

The compensation paid to slave owners under abolition policies pumped new capital into the local economy, creating something of a boom economy for Capetonians.[115] Although those with British and Dutch backgrounds dominated the professional and administrative commanding heights of the local economy, ethnic and racial propinquity marked the artisans and laborers who would form the core of the future Cape Town working class. These changes, in turn, transformed Cape Town from a settlement with a singular purpose—the provisioning of ships—into an increasingly varied merchant and commercial center. With these changes came social division and growing inequality, reflecting the town's varied economic ventures and social groupings.

Cape Town's burgeoning commercial economy produced more than rich and poor. As in Britain, a local middle class based in retail and trade gained a modicum of financial independence throughout the mid–nineteenth century. Joined by midranking colonial administrators and military personnel, this expanding group bought homes, employed servants, and indulged in the growing middling culture of their peers in Europe that was marked by the possession of carriages, pianos, and respectable wardrobes. The men worked and followed the horse races that had been introduced by British officers.[116] The women enjoyed a leisure-time autonomy that was unthinkable during Dutch times.[117] Education and religion became prime markers of social advance.

Both the Dutch and the British bourgeoisies spawned intellectuals who encouraged the arts and sciences as well as education.[118] Private schools catered to both groups, though middle-class British Capetonians sent their sons to Britain for a proper education whenever possible. Collectively, these institutions stimulated a sense of citizenship among proper British Capetonians while defining a distinctive identity among their Dutch neighbors that would lead to the codification of Afrikaans and the development of a distinctive national identity.

Educational opportunities for working-class children were markedly more constrained, being limited for the most part to the basic skills required to find employment.[119] The behavior of laborers of all ethnicities increasingly offended middle-class sensibilities, as in other developing bourgeois societies. As a result, the need to establish firm social boundaries to protect and preserve respectability led to the expansion of laws defining unacceptable behavior and the strengthening of constabularies to enforce these new laws. A new prison was built on Robben Island as early as 1808, with other facilities to follow.[120]

The explosion of social and economic identities was accompanied by an upsurge in religious activity that reinforced group boundaries as various denominations became associated with particular ethnic groups (e.g., Dutch Reformers, German Lutherans, British Anglicans, Irish Catholics, and Scottish Presbyterians).[121] Two early-nineteenth-century religious movements would prove of special note for the evolution of Cape Town's musical traditions. The first was Protestant evangelicalism following the arrival of preachers dispatched by the London Missionary Society as early as 1811. The second was the rapid growth of Islam. As already noted, the charismatic Master Teacher Imam Abdullah ibn Qadi Abd al-Salam took advantage of greater religious freedom under the British to promote and nurture the Muslim community.

Protestant missionaries similarly became increasingly active throughout the colony, often through the promotion of choral music, which resonated with indigenous singing traditions. Protestant and Sunni religious leaders reached out to those—such as people of color, former slaves, immigrants, and Africans from elsewhere on the continent—who were scorned by their official and properly bourgeois counterparts representing the Church of England, Dutch Reformed, and Lutheran establishments.

Victorian Cape Town

The city symbolically entered a new era—that of a provincial British imperial city similar in some ways to such colonial outposts as Toronto and Sydney—with the May 1863 celebration of the wedding of Prince Albert, then heir to the British throne and the future King Edward VII. A parade carefully reflected the colony's new social order.[122] Feasting followed, with the local government providing meals to schoolchildren, fire brigade members, and others at different spots around town, where games, countless entertainments, and, for the adults, plentiful wine held sway. Fireworks displays and celebratory bonfires brought the festivities to a close later that evening. The 1863 revelries were repeated for Queen Victoria's golden and diamond jubilees in 1887 and 1897, signifying just how much of a British colonial city the Dutch provisioning station had become.[123]

The Dutch legacy remained in the form of an increasingly self-conscious Afrikaner community that fiercely set itself off from the arriviste British through language, religion, and numerous forms of both large and small cultural expressions.[124] Capetonians of Dutch heritage worked assiduously to nurture and preserve their space within the larger city, which eventually led to the Cape Colony's 1882 adoption of Dutch as a second official language in addition to English.

Many of their rural brethren were more single-minded in their quest to escape British control. The abolition of slavery and other liberalizing reforms imposed by the British tried the patience of many among the seminomadic pastoralist Trekboers.[125] In the mid-1830s, they set out to escape British rule. Some 12,000 Voortrekkers headed to the north and east, on what would become known as the Great Trek (Die Groot Trek), to establish their own colonies free from the British. A pivotal moment came in early 1838, when the Voortrekkers defeated Zulu armies in a number of harsh battles and guerrilla raids. Other engagements among the Dutch, British, and Africans erupted throughout the period, driving the Xhosa, the Khoikhoi, and the Zulu from lands that were of interest to European settlers.[126]

The Great Trek eventuated in the establishment of the Natalia Republic, the Orange Free State Republic, and the Transvaal beyond British control. After the British annexed the Natalia Republic in 1843, the Boers, as they were becoming known, concentrated their settlements on the Highveld of the Transvaal and Orange Free State.[127]

As the Trekboer response to British rule suggests, since the British had arrived, much more had transpired than a simple transfer of colonial power. The British brought modernity with them—in every form, ranging from management strategies and modernized dock facilities to omnibuses and railroads—and expanded opportunities for overseas investors to underwrite the local economy.[128] They consolidated their administrative and economic control over the colony and the city as local wealth expanded with integration into the British Empire. Speculative, British-styled terrace housing sprung up around the town's outskirts, creating idyllic suburban wonderlands to protect the growing imperial middle class from urban "horrors" in town.

Local wealth exploded following the discovery of diamonds in Kimberly in 1868 and, even more so, after the discovery of gold in Witwatersrand in 1886.[129] These events, which repositioned Southern Africa within the global economy, had several profound effects on local life. Of foremost importance, the discovery of some of the largest diamond and gold deposits on the planet drove the British to seek control of greater swaths of the Southern African hinterland, bringing them inexorably into conflict with the newly established Trekboer states.

The rush to control mineral wealth unleashed the appetites of ever-more-ferociously ambitious imperialists such as Cecil Rhodes, the sickly son of an English provincial vicar who immigrated to South Africa in 1870.[130] Rhodes made his way quickly to the Kimberley diamond fields to launch a career that would make him one of the wealthiest men in the world. The promise of quick wealth made Southern Africa attractive to immigrants of all economic classes. In response, Afrikaners briefly rebelled against British rule in the Transvaal during the First Anglo-Boer War from December 1880 to March 1881.[131]

Locally, Cape Town emerged as the staging ground for moving supplies inland, retrieving mineral wealth, and sending it back to London. Population growth is but one important measure of Cape Town's metamorphosis from town into city.[132] The city grew physically, spinning off working- and middle-class suburbs in Salt River (home to the largest railyards in the country), Woodstock, Mowbray, and elsewhere.[133] Plebeian neighborhoods in town—such as District Six and Bo-Kaap—similarly took on large numbers of new residents.

Expanding economic opportunities attracted Africans, South Asians, and Eastern European Jews fleeing the Pale of Settlements.[134] Social, ethnic, racial, and religious divisions took greater meaning behind the city's cast iron commercial facades, which were so typical of the Victorian era.[135] Unprecedented violence broke out between the city's Muslim community and the local authorities in 1886, following a resolution issued by sanitation officials prohibiting burials in cemeteries located in the city, such as the historic Tana Baru Muslim Cemetery at the foot of Signal Hill.[136] Dutch resistance to British domination deepened, leading to further changes in local government.

The British reorganized the Colonial Office on the Cape of Good Hope as the colony evolved and grew in importance. Although nonwhites retained the right to vote, the power of their suffrage was reduced through the 1893 introduction of multiple votes for property owners based on the value of their real estate. This reform favored British businessmen over Dutch and so-called coloured residents in town.[137]

Most important for what would follow, Cape Town became an

increasingly "colonial" city in terms of residential segregation. Unlike typical colonial patterns elsewhere, Cape Town previously had not developed distinctly European and "native" quarters.[138] But Cape Town's world was about to change again, as the nineteenth century came to an end.

In 1895, a band of 600 loosely organized raiders, headed by Leander Starr Jameson, set out from Bechuanaland to take Johannesburg—then the capital of the Trekboer Orange Free State—for the British.[139] The disastrous Jameson raid turned Cape Afrikaners against the British and strengthened the resolve of the Transvaal and the Orange Free State to resist British claims. In 1897, the Transvaal and the Orange Free State formed a military alliance and began to arm themselves for what they saw as an inevitable war with the British.

On October 11, 1899, their armies marched into the Colony of Natal and the Cape Colony, engaging directly with British troops. The Boer armies enjoyed initial success, until the British deployed fresh troops into the war theater in early 1900 and moved to take the Transvaal capital at Pretoria. A brutal guerrilla war followed, in which the British systematically destroyed Boer farms and settlements and established the first concentration camps of the twentieth century. The Transvaal and the Orange Free State accepted British-imposed peace terms in May 1902, submitting to the British Empire in exchange for self-government, under what emerged in 1910 as the Union of South Africa.[140]

The Second Anglo-Boer War represented a turning of the page in global military history, denoting the first of a multitude of twentieth-century wars targeting both civilians and military combatants. The war changed Cape Town forever. In the short run, the city enjoyed the wealth that flowed from being the major port of entry into Southern Africa for the largest global empire's military machine. In the longer run, Cape Town and the Cape Colony entered into the larger South African Union, in which economic and political power inevitably would shift to the mineral-rich Witwatersrand region.[141]

"Daar Kom Die Alabama"

The first century of British rule integrated Cape Town into an expanding global economy in ways in which its earlier function as a stopping-off point for ships of the Dutch East India Company never could. Most significantly, Cape Town grew into a lively provincial city within a powerful imperial economy. It developed political institutions and social classes that mimicked those in the most modern metropole of the time, London. Parallel shifts took place in local cultural life, leading to the introduction of two new musical forms, which would cast an influence over the Cape of Good Hope for another century: minstrelsy, and Gospel choral music.

The British brought their own military traditions, beginning with military bands, military tattoos, and military parades featuring musicians playing brass instruments and drums marching in a kaleidoscope of complex formations.[142] They carried their own traditions of social dancing—including formal balls, as well as folk and "square" dancing—and religious choral music. These forms blended with the diverse musical traditions already in place (including—but not limited to—Afrikaner and "coloured" popular music as well as a Dutch form of "square" dancing derived from Scotch-Irish dancing in North America). The Southern Hemisphere summer Christmas and New Year's season emerged as an obvious time of year to enjoy such entertainments out-of-doors.

British musical forms were not the only influences to arrive on visiting ships. American—and eventually, African American—music and musicians followed. As the influence of Scotch-Irish North American square dancing on Afrikaner social dance indicates, American culture followed Atlantic trade routes to the Cape Colony from before the time the British had arrived. Various dance forms mutated as they initially crossed the Atlantic from the British Isles to North America and then crossed the ocean again to Southern Africa. American minstrelsy found fertile shores along the Cape, blending some of those same Scotch-Irish elements with African American slave culture. Minstrel music was carried by touring white American and African American groups, as well as by touring British music hall performers. South African Town music has remained in an anxious relationship with American music ever since.

Cape Town quickly proved to be a receptive overseas market for race-mocking minstrelsy (figure 32). Thomas Rice's song "Jim Crow" appeared in the popular Cape Town weekly *Die Verzamelaar* shortly after its publication in the United States at the end of the 1820s. British variety shows—often explicitly shaped by the emerging American minstrel tradition—frequently visited the Cape Colony, and, in 1848, the first African American ensemble Joe Brown's Band of Brothers arrived.[143] Groups such the American Ethiopian Serenaders and the British Harvey–Leslie Christy Minstrels followed, with Stephen Foster's songbook—both in its English original and in Afrikaans translation—passing into the local repertoire.[144] Collectively, these songs and the groups that performed them became known by the derogatory moniker attached to African Americans that was mentioned at the beginning of this chapter.

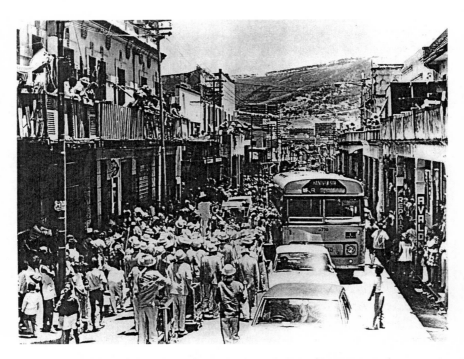

Figure 32. Minstrels walking down Wale Street in Cape Town.
Source: Photograph by I. Omar; courtesy of the District Six Museum in Cape Town (www.districtsix.co.za).

In July 1863, the Confederate privateer CSS *Alabama* appeared at the Cape, putting in for coal at the Simonstown Navy Base and landing for a second time on a return visit at Table Bay.[145] The ship was an eye-catcher, carrying state-of-the art ordnance and sailing technologies. British Capetonians, Dutch farmers, and "coloured" workers stood on the shore scanning the horizon for a glimpse of the legendary ship. Once in port, its commander, Captain Raphael Semmes, lavishly entertained sympathetic British colonial officers and Cape Town notables. The *Alabama* became a local favorite and subject of romantic legend. Pursued by the Union's USS *Kearsarge*, the *Alabama* eventually met its demise off the post of Cherbourg, France, in June 1864, after having burned sixty-five Union vessels from the South Atlantic to the Caribbean.[146] Before she disappeared, local Cape Town writers had composed one of the most enduring Afrikaner songs "*Daar Kom die Alabama*." Written in the form of a *ghoema*, or drum-based dance song, "Here Comes the *Alabama*" remains part of the repertoire of local choral and festival groups.[147]

Homegrown Cape Town "coloured" New Year's minstrel celebrations assimilated musical and dance traditions from a variety of sources. The ancestors of today's New Year's festival paraders probably drew direct inspiration from the African American Dante brothers' minstrel troupe that marched in Queen Victoria's Golden Jubilee celebrations in 1887.[148] The new minstrel groups, based in the city's working-class neighborhoods dominated by the descendants of slaves brought by the Dutch from the Indies, did more than mimic visiting American and British performers. They melded their own cultural roots to create a distinctive form of Carnival.

Cape "Coloured" communities sustained their distinct identities through shared religion, shared dress, shared cuisine, and a shared embrace of communal song.[149] Musicians in mixed neighborhoods, such as District Six and Bo-Kaap, fused Dutch wedding and folk songs, melodic revels sung at picnics (the *ghommaliedjie*), and lively comedic songs (the Afrikaans *moppie*) with American minstrel music as well as American and British brass band traditions.

New Year's Carnival groups (often taking names replete with racist innuendo from American minstrel—and later film—performers) became increasingly well organized during the 1890s.[150] Their primary festival—the Kaapse Klopse, held on Tweede Nuwe Jaar (January 2)—consistently attracted thousands of minstrels in bright garb, often carrying colorful umbrellas as they march in blackface.[151] Organized today by more than 150 competing associations, bands rehearse and plan their routines the year around.[152]

Political and financial vicissitudes forced the annual festival to move to various venues around the city. Typically, Carnival associations marched at some point during the celebration through such Malay neighborhoods as District Six and Bo-Kaap.[153] Robyn Wilkinson and Astrid Kragolsen-Kille capture the contemporary spectacle in their 2006 homage to Bo-Kaap: "The musicians, plying tambourines, saxophones, banjos, trumpets and big drums, lead the jovial marchers and dancers around the town, often throughout the night, until everyone is utterly exhausted. Batons twirl, while songs, ditties, and *moppies* (comical songs) unload current issues— triumphs and failures, the cost of living, laments and joys aired with equal fervor. A *moffie* (homosexual—but in this case a token transvestite) usually follows at the end of each procession, presenting the diversity of society."[154]

Although the precise nature of the festival parades has varied over time, Wilkinson and Kragolsen-Kille nicely capture their significance for the community, their colorful and energetic atmosphere, their wealth of musical styles and instruments drawn from a variety of cultures, their ironic portrayal of life, and their embrace of diversity. Not surprisingly, the Kaapse Klopse greatly offended arbiters of respectability and racial purity.[155]

The superficial trappings of American minstrelsy disguise a deeper, more profound foundation: the rhythms of the *ghoema* drum. John Edwin Mason emphasizes the role of the *ghoema* as the beating heart of Carnival. "*Ghoema*," he writes, "is a drum, a pulse, and some would say, a way of life. Its roots lie deep in the history of Cape Town and in the history of the people who created Carnival and keep it alive. Ancestors of the coloured people, the community from which the minstrel troupes draw virtually all of their members, invented the drum and its rhythms. For Cape Town's servants and slaves in the eighteenth and nineteenth centuries, *ghoema* was a symbol of life in the face of exile and oppression. After slavery, it came to symbolize cultural independence and continuity in the midst of segregation and apartheid."[156]

Ghoema music, in turn, is a product of Cape Town itself. "A more complete account of its origins," Mason continues, "would show how slowly it evolved over time—its rhythms, melodies and vocal inflections mirror Cape Town's polyglot culture, drawing on a variety of sources, especially Indonesia, Malaysia, Sri Lanka, India, and East Africa; areas that supplied slaves to the Cape Colony in the seventeenth and eighteenth centuries. The costumes, face-painting, and music of American blackface minstrelsy—which was a popular form of entertainment in late-nineteenth-century Cape Town—also shaped Carnival. The troupes' marching parodies the military precision of nineteenth-century British garrisons and a substantial portion of Carnival's songs originated in the Netherlands."[157] These same components were shaping a distinctive Cape Town choral tradition.

Cape Town's identity—especially "coloured" identity in Cape Town—has always been problematic because it represents a cultural fusion of various factors often delineated by others and only embraced in a piecemeal manner over decades.[158] Cape Town's New Year Carnival and its mix of sources reflect the very "constructedness" of a so-called Cape Coloured identity. Over time, as is demonstrated by its evolution throughout the twentieth century, the Carnival served as a source of pride and distinctiveness. Whatever labels might be attached to its various quintessential components, the Carnival represents the collective corporeality of Cape Town itself.[159]

Jubilee Singers Singing Songs of Faith

African American performers came to the Cape with greater regularity as steamships eased the challenges of travel and as the American Civil War came to an end with African American slaves having been emancipated. Coplan writes:

> From the mid-1870s, black American minstrelsy had taken a different direction from that of white blackface performers. With the international success of the Fisk Jubilee Singers, who performed spirituals in a Western classical style, black minstrel shows increasingly featured black religious music

of the Southern United States. As already noted, the word "jubilee" significant in the Bible (Leviticus 25:10) as the year when slaves were to be freed, began to appear in the names of black troupes, both minstrel and nonminstrel. Those companies performing sacred concerts rather than minstrel shows, such as the Louisiana Jubilee Singers, played minstrel favourites, such as "Carve Dat Possum" and Stephen Foster songs. James Bland, the greatest of all black minstrel songwriters, also composed many spirituals.[160] (figure 33)

Figure 33. An image of James Bland, on the cover of his *Three Great Songs.* Source: James Bland's *Three Great Songs (Boston: White, Smith & Co., 1879); Library of Congress.*

Orpheus Myron McAdoo and his Hampton Jubilee Singers were perhaps the most influential African American singing group to visit Southern Africa at this time.

Born in North Carolina on the eve of the Civil War, McAdoo graduated from the Hampton Institute in Virginia in 1876.[161] He turned to music after spending a decade teaching school, joining original members of the Fisk University Jubilee Singers on a three-year tour of Europe, Australia, New Zealand, and the Far East. The troupe had been formed by faculty and students to raise money for the newly founded Fisk University.[162] The American Missionary Associations established Fisk shortly after the end of the Civil War to educate freed slaves, and Fisk's choirs quickly gained national and international recognition, performing for President Grant, Queen Victoria, and a long list of other notables during the early 1870s.[163] Returning to Virginia, McAdoo gathered a new group primarily drawn from Hampton students and graduates and set out on tour once more. He and his company arrived in Cape Colony in June 1889, traveling for the next nineteen months and spreading Gospel singing in their wake.[164]

McAdoo appreciated the rush of acclaim that greeted the Hampton Jubilee Singers upon their entry into the Cape Colony. In a letter home to General Armstrong, McAdoo recorded that "the first hour of my arrival I began to work hard. I soon had friends to become interested in me. Got the support of the press by inviting them to my rehearsals. Visited Governor Locke and secured his and Lady Locke's patronage and opened in Cape Town on June 30th, to the most fashionable audience."[165] Simultaneously, McAdoo was forthright about local racism. "There is no country in the world," he continued, "where prejudice is so strong as here in Africa. The native to-day is treated as badly as ever the slave was treated in Georgia. Here in Africa the native laws are most unjust; such as any Christian people would be ashamed of."[166]

McAdoo's impact extended beyond the Cape Colony's elite. On October 16, 1890, the *Imvo Zabantsundu* of Kingswilliamston published a review of McAdoo's local concert, noting that his singers

have sung before the millions on the habitable globe the honeyed music which served to dissipate the miseries of their African forefathers in the plantations of the New World, whither they had been taken by shipload as slaves; and melodious strains they sing, diffusing sweetness wherever they are heard. It would strongly savour of presumption for a Native African of this part to venture a critique of his brethren from America, who are now visiting the quarter of their fatherland, and whose position, socially, is being deservedly pointed at on all hands as one that Natives here should strive to attain. But we may be allowed to join in the huzzas that have greeted their musical entertainments in the towns and cities they have visited. All the [people] ungrudgingly conceded that the Africans possessed musical talents of an exceptional order, which need cultivation to turn them into good account. It would appear, however, that it was reserved for our countrymen in America to give an object lesson as to the development these dormant gifts are capable of.[167]

McAdoo and the Hampton Jubilee Singers—and later, spin-off groups of his own creation—returned to the Cape of Good Hope frequently during the years leading up to the Second Anglo-Boer War.[168] They joined an ever-growing number of white and black American Protestant missionaries who preached self-improvement, race pride, and the Gospel.[169] Their impact on local music was immediate.[170] As Coplan explains, "In Cape Town, thousands of working-class coloured men joined performance clubs in the wake of McAdoo's visits. Beginning around that time, these clubs organized parades through the streets of the city every new year in the famous Cape Coon Carnival, dressed as blackface minstrels and singing American Negro songs and Afrikaans *moppies* (comic songs) to the accompaniment of Khoi-style *ghomma* drums, whistles, guitars, tambourines, and banjos."[171]

Songs of Good News

Christian missionaries had prepared the ground for McAdoo and other African American Jubilee choruses as they used choral music to reach potential converts from the days when the Cape passed from Dutch to British control. The nationalist Xhosa prince Ntsika-na, who converted to Christianity in 1816, composed one of the first hymns to combine African and Western musical attributes, "Ulko Thixo Mkulu" (Thou Great God), thereby establishing a convention for African-composed Gospel music blending both musical traditions.[172]

Choral music in Cape Town extended beyond Christian conventions. The summer holiday season in diverse working-class communities such as District Six and Bo-Kaap began with Christian processions of Christmas Carolers, followed after December 25 by Muslim Malay choirs singing in the lead-up to New Year's Eve. Their songs frequently included time-honored Malay serenades as well as the vocal accompaniments to the Khalifa, a game involving swords and skewers, at times drawing blood, that had been performed during slavery to inspire conversion to Islam.[173] Next, the Carnival Kaapse Klopse marked Twedde Nuwe Jaar (January 2).

The summer season was one of a renewal celebrated through music, dancing, and feasting that both reinforced group boundaries and shared collective goodwill with neighbors who were different.[174] As important for communal life in neighborhoods such as District Six and Bo-Kaap as the celebrations themselves, Christmas Choirs, Malay Choirs, and Carnival groups rehearsed their performances throughout the year, often parading around local streets.[175] In doing so, they created a sense of community in places marked by poverty and diversity.

Choral music appealed to the native peoples of Southern Africa in ways that transcended Western presence and endorsement. Their shared musical traditions were vocal rather than percussive. "Communal vocal music," Coplan tells us, "always involved dancing or gestures or work movements by the singers themselves. There were at least two voice parts in antiphonal, leader-and-chorus relationship to each other, and the parts frequently overlapped, producing polyphony."[176] Choral music simultaneously appealed to Cape Town's "coloured" population, which, by this time, had nurtured a strong legacy of supporting the Malay choirs that sustained traditions brought by their slave ancestors from the Dutch East Indies.[177] The musical association of groups singing with Christian missionaries additionally connected musical expressions to a growing African middle class that was being brought into existence by the educational institutions, clubs, and churches—prompted by churches and related institutions such as the South African Improvement Society.[178]

This social function was hardly limited to Cape Town and the Cape Colony. Significant choral communities also emerged in Durban, Kimberly, and the Witwatersrand region.[179] Perhaps the most celebrated hymn of the period—Enoch M. Sontonga's "Nkosi Sikel' iAfrika'" (God Bless Africa)—was composed as part of the repertoire for the composer's students at a mission school in the Nancefield district of Johannesburg. This hymn was sung following Sontonga's death at the first meeting of the South African Native National Congress (later to become the African National Congress, ANC) by the Ohlange Institute Choir under Reuben Caluza and Sol Plaayje, and was subsequently recorded in London in 1926.[180] The original version drew on African and Methodist patterns to become a signature for the ANC and the broader anti-apartheid movement around the world, eventually becoming incorporated into the post-apartheid South African national anthem.[181]

The years leading up to the Second Anglo-Boer War were a time of great social upheaval in Southern Africa, as thousands of Africans began migrating to the mines and other industrial centers for work.[182] Migrant trains carrying workers from the hinterland to the mines—convoys on rails, which Hugh Masekela still memorably calls a "motherf@#%er" in South Africa—workers' barracks, and, a little later, settlement camps, became major symbols of a deeply exploitative economic system.[183]

Young Xhosa, Sotho, and Zulu men—among many—formed support groups far away from home. Often based on kinship and hometown ties, such informal assemblies became integral to their sense of self-identity. Informal choral groups brought together a number of traditions (including indigenous Southern African vocal practices, plus, at times, vocal forms imported by missionaries). Over time, proletarian singers created a distinctive South African urban music.[184] Capetonians—though not always central to this process—participated in this invention of urban cultural forms and eagerly brought them back to their neighborhoods surrounding Table Mountain.[185]

Union and Disunion

The elaborate negotiations following the close of the Second Anglo-Boer War in May 1902 that created the Union of South Africa eight years later have proven worthy of much analytical inspection.[186] The resulting self-governing British dominion unified Cape Colony, Natal Colony, Transvaal Colony, and Orange River Colony (and, for some time after World War I, the German South-West Africa colony through a League of Nations mandate) into a constitutional parliamentary monarchy under the British throne and its representative, the governor-general.[187] The 1931 Statute of Westminster elevated the Union under a bicameral Parliament consisting of a House of Assembly and Senate to parallel status of dominion with Australia and Canada. This law prohibited the United Kingdom from enacting legislation affecting South Africa, and designated the prime minster as the Union's chief executive, thereby relegating the governor-general to little more than symbolic status.

Unlike Australia and Canada, the South African Union was a unitary state rather than a federation. Subordinate provincial councils replaced earlier semiautonomous colonial parliaments. In an arrangement that still remains in place today, the function of capital was divided among the Union's constituent members, with Cape Town serving as home to Parliament, Pretoria becoming administrative capital, Pietermaritzburg being designated as home to archival administration, and Bloemfontein hosting senior judicial functions. The dominion was reconstituted as a republic in May 1961, thus severing the historic connection to the British Crown.

The first important effect of dominion status for Cape Town was the extension of the former Cape Colony's qualified franchise system, which theoretically allowed citizens to vote without racial restriction (although property provisions effectively limited the franchise to whites). Cape prime minister John X. Merriman had sought the enlargement of multiracial voting rights to encompass the rest of the new union. Although failing in that effort, he nonetheless protected that prerogative within the former Cape Colony.[188] A second important provision transferred jurisdiction for so-called native affairs to the national government.

The South Africa Party, led by the former guerrilla fighters Louis Botha (who died in 1919) and Jan Smuts, would govern the Union of South Africa until the 1924 electoral victory of J. B. M. Hertzog's National Party.[189] Both being patronizing advocates of racial segregation, Botha, a wealthy farmer with progressive views, and Smuts, a Cambridge-trained internationalist who participated in the founding of the League of Nations, moved to restrict the ability of nonwhites to own land and implemented a number of additional "anti-native" measures. They were followed in power between 1924 and 1933 by a Hertzog administration intent on extending Afrikaners' cultural, economic, and political rights at the expense of the British and the "natives." Among many changes under National Party rule, Afrikaans joined Dutch as an official language in 1925.[190]

This period proved to be one when South Africans outside the political mainstream began to assert their rights. Activists established the future ANC in January 1912 as the South African Native National Congress. They worked with black and labor organizations before reorganizing as the ANC in 1923.[191] In Cape Town, an increasingly radicalized trade union movement emerged, as did a number of powerful civic associations (e.g., Cape Town city councillor Abdullah Abdurahman's African Political Organization).[192]

As important as any political change, the early twentieth century proved itself to be a period of insatiable demand for labor at the gold and diamond mines, and in growing industrial cities (including textile-dominated Cape Town). This demand could be satisfied only by attracting African migrants to the mines, towns, and cities.[193] White city dwellers became ever more fearful of being "overwhelmed" in their own communities. Drawing on the latest progressive theories of British city planners (i.e., zoning and garden towns), South African governments began to set aside isolated "locations," where the growing wave of African migrants could be dispatched out of view. These processes accelerated following the 1918–19 influenza epidemic, which led, in the 1920s, to the enactment of the Native (Urban Areas) Act giving local governments the right to limit nonwhite habitation in town. One result proved to be a burgeoning, male-dominated African urban culture, in which young men found themselves cut off from families or any broader life in town.[194]

Cape Town, though thoroughly involved in these developments, remained distinct from much of the Union of South Africa around it. The city's "coloured" population retained a complex identity dating back to the earliest days of slavery under the Dutch. The preponderance of African rural laborers streaming from the countryside in search of employment tended to head first to the mines, and second to large industrial concerns elsewhere. Cape Town segregated itself, though at its own pace.[195]

The Cape Town suburb of Langa (which means "sun" in Xhosa) exemplifies many of these developments. Ostensibly named after a Xhosan chief, Langalibalele, who had been imprisoned on Robben Island in 1873 for leading a rebellion against the Natal government, Langa is one of the first "townships" in South Africa. Located a 20-minute, 8-mile ride from Cape Town's main train station, Langa has served for nearly a century as a prototype of segregated settlements that are largely (if not entirely) devoted to a single ethnic community tied to the central city by a rail connection, while nonetheless remaining purposefully cut off from others by human-made and natural barriers.

Africans, having lived in and around Cape Town since long before Europeans arrived, came and went, filling menial and domestic jobs as opportunities drew them to town. Close to 9,000 Africans lived in Cape Town at the end of World War I, when the city's metropolitan population hovered at just over 220,000.[196] Various epidemics at the outset of the twentieth century frightened white Capetonians. By the early 1920s, the City Council assumed control of a "government reserve" established on the city's outskirts at Ndabeni, and it moved to construct a new "model township" to be named Langa.[197] This process accelerated following the 1923 Urban Areas Act, which enabled local authorities to clear so-called slum areas in town.

Langa, which opened in 1927, was intended to become a "respectable" township for Africans.[198] Carefully planned streets included a variety of housing types, from single-family homes to "barracks" and dormitories for single men, together with thoughtfully placed schools, churches, medical facilities, and other urban amenities. The inhabitants most often worked at unskilled jobs in town.

Though segregated by race and ethnicity, Langa has been a

predominantly Xhosa settlement since its founding. Townships became places where "'decent people' and town toughs—*tsotsis*—live all mixed up; a clergyman may have a beer brewer as his next door neighbor. Many middle-class African families find themselves compelled to bring up children in a street in which their neighbors have totally different standards of hygiene, manners, and morals."[199] Various apartheid-era laws eventually destroyed this modicum of community by limiting access to metropolitan areas and restricting movement once in town. A vicious riot in March 1960 effectively left control of Langa in the hands of those who could organize themselves, whether they were *tsotsis* criminal gangs or radicalized political organizations.[200]

Langa is hardly unique in Cape Town or in South Africa. The sprawling townships southwest of Johannesburg—in what officially would be designated in the 1960s as the SOuth WEstern TOwnships—Soweto—similarly date back to the early years of the twentieth century.[201] Closer by, townships in the Cape Flats (e.g., Nyanga, Ndabeni, Windermere, and Kensington) joined Langa in becoming home to large numbers of recent arrivals from the countryside, as well as those being displaced in town by apartheid-era policies. Many settlements were reserved for the members of a particular racially designated group. This arrangement should not disguise the complexity of local social and economic life, because residents were embedded in networks of kinship relationships that extended well beyond the Cape.

Marabi Homeboys

Writing in the early 1960s, the anthropologists Monica Wilson and Archie Mafeje note that, in Langa, "kinsmen are bound by personal ties, but they do not now form defined corporate groups other than the elementary family, and more than three-quarters of the people do not even live in families, for they are men who have left their wives and children behind in the country, or are young bachelors."[202] The result was a "homeboy" (*abakhaya*) culture, in which men from one neighborhood—often from the same village—came together under a headman to join forces for survival. Their homeboy loyalties often proved more important than tribal divisions.[203]

Men—young and old, fresh from the country as well as long-term residents of the city—sought out associations and communal bonds providing the sort of support provided by family in more traditional communities. Distinctive clubs formed in many townships, organizing job exchanges, food services, sports, music, dance, and every other aspect of local life. Frequently, such groups gathered to drink alcohol at small bars run by female bootleggers—*shebeens* (from an Irish expression for illicit whisky)—who served as surrogate wives, mothers, and daughters as they offered up a jagged domesticity for men far from home.[204] Homeboy groups organized choruses and bands, bringing new forms of music from the countryside to town.[205] The result was a rough-edged, alcohol-fueled "slumyard" culture known as *marabi* that eventually became celebrated by writers and musicians alike.[206]

The "bard of township culture," Modikwe Dikobw, begins his 1973 debut novel *The Marabi Dance*, which is set in the townships of Johannesburg in the 1940s, with a detailed description of slumyard life. "The Molefe yard, where Martha lives," he writes, "was also home to more than twenty other people. It served a row of five rooms, each about 14 by 12 feet in size. When it rained, the yard was as muddy as a cattle *kraal*, and the smell of beer, thrown out by the police on their raids, combining with the stench of the lavatories, was nauseating."

Sundays were special, for, on that day of rest, visitors "swarmed like bees in the yards and streets of Doornfontein. They stood in groups, talking loudly, greeting each other, shaking hands, kissing on the pretext that they were sisters and brothers. The drinking parties sat in the houses, the men singing as loudly as their throats would allow, swaying like tree branches in the fumes of liquor and tobacco."[207]

This scene could have been duplicated in the townships surrounding any South African city at any time following World War I, including the Cape Flats townships during the 1920s. The soundtrack to this effervescent life came from a musical style unique to the South African slumyards of the second quarter of the twentieth century: *marabi*.

Marabi is not simply a form of homegrown South African jazz based on an American model. It also contains, for example, no "blue note" (a note pitched slightly below the musical scale being played that is fundamental to black American music).[208] Many people debate its origins, contesting the meaning of the name "*marabi*" itself.[209] Rarely—if ever—caught on electronic recordings, its original sound has been lost forever.

Those who grew up with *marabi* and played *marabi* still know it when they hear it. As the trombonist Jonas Gwangwa told the visiting American musicologist Gewn Ansell, *marabi* is "an African music translated to Western instruments at the *stokvels* and the parties. There were polyrhythmic and interlocked elements, drawn from tradition, and these were fitted around the three-chord structure of modern songs and played with whatever instruments were at hand. The modern songs could be anything: the melodic line of a composed hymn or the chorus of an American pop tune; any tune that crosses my mind."[210]

Ansell continues that *marabi* "was an intimate music suited to small domestic spaces, converted kitchens, and sack-roofed backyards where the sound of piano or organ needed no amplification. However, *marabi* was not simply music but a whole lifestyle, created during the 1920s—and extinct by the end of the 1940s."[211] It is the music and culture of rural folk come to town to create a new life for themselves. It is the music to which the homeboys listened as they gathered here and there to drink, to reminisce about home, and to teach the ropes of urban life to arriving newcomers. *Marabi*, in other words, is to South African music what blues is to American music: a unique, elemental sound born of the inimitable amalgam of bewilderment and intelligence that comes from having been torn from one's societal moorings.

If a lively mix of musical genres offered a soundtrack to *marabi* culture, beer provided an animating life force. Initially, trade in homebrews offered African women with few other employment opportunities a chance to carve out a life for themselves. By the late 1930s, what had been a largely informal market had become commercialized. The authorities started to crack down on fringe settlements, beginning with an effort to clear away racially mixed areas.[212] "By then," Ansell notes, "the dynamic female entrepreneurs of the liquor trade—'*shebeen* queens' or 'aunties'—and the informal economy and autonomous culture they helped build, had established survival mechanisms that would twist but not break under new enforced living patterns."[213]

Sheeben culture, from the very beginning, depended on the camaraderie of shared roots, the fuel of cheap alcohol, and the beat of *marabi* music—just the right setting to give musicians a chance to perfect their trade (figure 34). Not surprisingly, new musical forms took shape, and hundreds of musicians found a livelihood. These musicians learned their music on the fly, often from other musicians who brought their instruments and skills with them when they moved to the city. An edgy air of protest that still marks South African music naturally took shape.

Figure 34. People at a *shebeen* in Joe Slovo Park in Cape Town. *Shebeens* are more than drinking establishments; they are central to the cultural life of black South Africans.
Source: Photograph by Discott (https://en.wikipedia.org/wiki/Shebeen#/media/File:Shebeen_in_Joe_Slovo_Park.jpg).

The *shebeens*, then, are where musicians accelerated a local tradition of "jazzing" that had begun to mark South African music from the dawn of the twentieth century.[214] The *shebeens* of the 1920s and 1930s provided an inventive opening, in which a distinctive Cape Town sound eventually would emerge.[215] Local musicians would take this sound to Johannesburg, where it would pass into an emerging South African mainstream, in part through an emerging recording industry based in the country's largest city.[216] The South African jazz culture to follow cannot be understood outside this experience.

Christopher Ballantine gets to the heart of the matter at the outset of his pioneering book *Marabi Nights: Early South African Jazz and Vaudeville*: "While no-one today [1993] listens any longer to the extraordinary music of a 1950s 'superstar' group such as the Manhattan Brothers, for some the name will still at least kindle a distant memory; but in the case of (say) the 1930s or early 1940s the names of great and seminal composers and performers such as William Mseleku, Snowy Radebe, Solomon Cele, or Griffiths Motsieloa typically cannot raise even a flicker."[217]

Perhaps this inattention is less the case now than two decades ago. If a greater appreciation of the *marabi* tradition has emerged, it is in no small measure the result of the scholarship of Ballantine himself. *Marabi*, he revealed, evolved around 1920 from the even-more-distant *marabou* music of such players as Ntebejana, Boet Gashe, Toto, Highbricks, and Nine Fingers. They developed their own sound by blending indigenous African music with the new sounds arriving from the United States, such as minstrel songs, ragtime, and early jazz.[218]

Ballantine compellingly sets out the link between early vaudeville groups of the 1910s and 1920s—such as the Palladiums, the Darktown Negroes, the African Darkies, and the Versatile Seven—with subsequent South African urban music.[219] The explosive development of a jazz band tradition in South African cities dating from the 1920s was closely allied with an equally rapid maturation of an indigenous vaudeville tradition. This melding, he records, is "one of the most astonishing features of urban black culture in the first half of the century. Surrounded by myriad other musics—styles forged by migrant workers; traditional styles transplanted from the countryside to the mines; petit bourgeois choral song; music of the church and of Western classical provenance—jazz and vaudeville quickly established themselves as the music which represented and articulated the hopes and aspirations of the most deeply urbanized sectors of the African working class."[220]

Songs of Migration

Ballantine's scholarship gives considerable weight to evolving vocal traditions as well as to embryonic instrumental practices. Far from home, migrants—whether they were Africans heading to the mines of the Rand or Eastern European Jews escaping tsarist pogroms—took their music with them.[221] James Ngcpbo, director of the internationally successful twenty-first-century musical *Songs of Migration*, found nobility in such music. In preparing his production, he discerned a common thread running through all migrant journeys as "people always carry with them the songs of their people and whilst on the trot they learn and compose new songs that form a tapestry for generations to come."[222] In early-twentieth-century South Africa, such musical forms reflected the diversity of an African population brought together by migration, shared insecurity nurtured by racial oppression, and an absence of strong social institutions in their new worlds.[223] As Coplan tells the tale,

> In Durban, workers developed new dances in traditional idiom like *isikhuze, isicathulo, isibhaca, umzani,* and *ingome* and performed country dances such as *ndhlamu* in industrial yards. Commercial employers co-opted workers' dance competitions, providing uniforms, colours, banners, transport and time off for rehearsals—all to heighten the loyalty and morale of the workforce. This system of company teams and white judges and performance standards continued into the 1980s and powerfully influenced the aesthetic of Zulu men's dancing for more than half a century. . . . Interestingly, the majority of creative innovators in competitive dance and song were not the more traditional Zulu migrants, but *amagsagza* (vagrants), marginal people who, like the Xhosa *abaphakathi* (middle ones) were neither traditional nor Christian but somewhere in between.[224]

Zulu musical influence came to Cape Town indirectly through migrants who made their way to the Cape in the mid–twentieth century, and later. When this influence arrived, it already had developed a rich and distinctive sound that, later on, would add its own flavor to the opulent musical stew of influences that would become the Cape Town sound. Reuben Caluza—among those who created modern urban Zulu music—has emerged as a quintessential and legendary figure in this story.[225]

By the 1890s, a new Zulu nationalism began to take shape—inspired, in part, by African American educational, political, and religious movements. Caluza was born in 1895 in a small village near Pietermaritzburg to a family converted by American Christian missionaries three generations before.[226] The young Rueben received his education at John Langalibalele Dube's Ohlange Institute, which had been modeled after Booker T. Washington's Tuskegee Institute. Dube, the founding president of the South African Native National Congress (precursor to the ANC), had studied at Oberlin College in Ohio and conceived of the Ohlange Institute as a hotbed for intellectuals drawn to a New African movement modeled in part on the US New Negro Movement of the era. Following in Dube's footsteps, Caluza established a boys' choir known as the Royal Singers in 1910 and, for the rest of his life until his death in 1969, excelled as a composer and as a leading contributor to a number of intellectual movements intended to give modern meaning to what it meant to be African and Zulu.[227]

Caluza's distinguished career took him all over the world, recording for HMV in London as early as 1930. He studied at the Hampton Institute and Columbia University in the United States, where he had important encounters with such African American luminaries as Paul Robeson, Roland Hayes, and W. E. B. DuBois, and performed with other Hampton students for President Franklin D. Roosevelt. His Columbia sojourn brought him into contact with the influential anthropologist Franz Boas. Through Boas, Caluza developed a long-lasting and fruitful relationship with London's School of Oriental African Studies. By 1936 he was back in South Africa at Adams College, and began working with Witswatersrand University and Gallo Record Company to record indigenous African music.

Caluza's efforts elevated African music in the eyes of intellectuals as well as African and non-African colonial elites. His achievements helped to shape the distinctive Zulu modern choral tradition.[228] Much of the vibrancy drawn to this tradition came from the broad, indigenous African working class, whose members drew sustenance on music traditions of their own.

Sleeping Lions and Gumboots

Isicathamiya—from *"catham"* or "to walk like a cat"—had become world renowned by the 1950s. "Like *marabi*, jazz, and *mbaqanga*," the musicologist Veit Erlmann argues, "this rich body of competitive song and dance is an expression of the creativity of black South Africans. Performed by male a cappella choirs, *isicathamiya* performance is also located at the core of black isiZulu-speaking migrants' social performance. Although, over the years, *isicathamiya* attracted a great deal of international attention, the culture and consciousness of South Africa's migrant labor army—the performances, leisure activities of miners, domestic servants, and so on—remain largely unknown."[229] Drawing on deep Zulu musical patterns—including call-and-response, group singing integrated with dance, and competitive singing—*isicathamiya* is what happens when traditional music, minstrel songs, Gospel music, ragtime tunes, wedding refrains, and protest songs, written by innovative composers such as Caluza, catch the ears of young men tossed together in the pressure cooker of grinding poverty and migration.[230]

Durban became the source of this new music, spawning early a cappella groups. In 1914, Lutheran minister Isaac Mzobe founded one such ensemble, the Crocodiles, at Botha's Hill outside Durban, to provide music for rural wedding ceremonies.[231] Little time passed before Mzobe had imitators, such as the Johannesburg-centered Amanzimtoti, and the Vryheid-based Bulking Waters.[232] As South Africa's manufacturing base consolidated—spinning off an ever-more-strident trade union movement, together with dance clubs and sports groups—so too did *isicathamiya*.

A seminal moment came in 1939, when thirty-year-old, Natal-born Solomon Popoli Linda accepted a job at the newly opened Gallo Recording plant in Roodepoort. Linda's singing group caught the attention of a talent scout, Griffith Motsieloa, who convinced him to record his wedding song "Mbube," commemorating "the killing of a lion cub by the young Solomon and his herd-boy friends" decades before.[233] Known as the "Wimoweh" song, and as "The Lion Sleeps Tonight," Linda had penned South Africa's most renowned song.[234] By 2000, according to some estimates, the song had been recorded at least 160 times; had been performed in thirteen movies and a half dozen television commercials; had been played on the radio hundreds of millions of times, if not more; and had been ranked among the most-beloved "golden oldies" in listener surveys by radio stations on every continent.[235]

Unfortunately, Linda rarely if ever received the royalties he deserved, because the song was stolen by non-African performers worldwide. Some—such as the American folksinger Pete Seeger—would try to pay back at least some portion of the royalties they had earned at Linda's expense. But such instances proved to be rare. The Disney Corporation, for example, only agreed to pay Linda's descendants royalties for their use of his music in *The Lion King* after a 2006 out-of-court settlement.[236] According to one calculation, Linda should have received between $10 million and $15 million in unpaid royalties.[237] As with Christy's appropriation of the Congo Square performances of his New Orleans youth, indigenous African music was viewed as much for the taking as African gold, African diamonds, and African human beings.

Linda and his group, the Evening Birds, were innovators in the small world of Durban migrant workers' music. His and other *isi-cathamiya* groups came together to create good times. They sang competitively on Saturday nights at small clubs for hard-working laborers trying to forget the realities of their jobs. Ralph Bunche—a Howard University political science professor, and future United Nations undersecretary-general and Nobel Peace Prize winner—captured one such night in his field notes about a visit to the Witwatersrand Native Labor Association in 1937 or 1938. Bunche recalls that he watched two choirs singing

Zulu songs, weird and with shuffling steps [for money that] was being paid to "buy" dances and to "buy" singers not to sing. In the hall there was a chairman (sitting before a table laden with oranges and large bottles of "Society Pop"—not Kaffir beer) to announce items and to receive cash for the request of a choir to sing or stop singing. That is, if one wishes, a choir to sing one should go up to the chairman and "buy" that choir to sing. Small sums of even a penny are accepted. If, however, one is tired or not interested in the singing of a group, one can go up and "buy" the choir "off" with a slightly higher sum than the person has bought them. There are cases where bidding in this fashion has been very keen and, of course, the highest bidder wins.[238]

The world of migrant worker clubs around Durban simultaneously produced a distinctive style of communal dancing known as "Gumboot Dance." Named after the rubber boots worn by miners, Gumboot Dance drew, according to the historian Carol Muller, "on a variety of sources: Bhaca tradition, the various missionary heritages such as that of German missionaries; dances of sailors who visited the port city of Durban such as Russian folk dance; the popular social dances that accompanied jazz music in the 1930s and 1940s such as the jitterbug; and most clearly, tap dance as performed by visiting minstrel groups of the nineteenth century and popularized through the films of Fred Astaire and Gene Kelly in the mid–twentieth century."[239]

Like *isicathamiya*, Gumboot groups were highly competitive and judged performance by their precision (in this instance, through movement rather than voice).[240] They meshed together a variety of styles, including the stamping of the feet in traditional Zulu dance, the enthusiasm of minstrel show performers, and the intricacies of Busby Berkeley's Hollywood routines.[241] The groups mimicked their workplace relationship to an authoritarian "boss boy," who determined what each dancer would do.

Decades would pass before the indigenous, Zulu-based performance styles emerging in and around Durban would gain respectability. And as African migrants increasingly moved around South Africa looking for work, some would make their way to the Cape of Good Hope's townships—and when they did, they would bring their music with them.

Windsongs

That's why my voice is so unusual—you know because it comes from far, far, far away.

> —Sathima Bea Benjamin, in *Sathima's Windsong*,
> a film by Dan Yon, 2010

With its roots in *marabi*, South Asian, and African vocal styles, *ghoema* drumming, and local Carnival music, the Cape Town sound did more than mimic what was arriving from the United States.[1] Jazz in the Cape Town of the era was about more than just music. As the oral historian Colin Miller concludes after interviewing nearly two dozen local musicians, "until this time most local traditions in Cape Town had been associated with specific ethnic or racial groups. One of the distinguishing aspects of jazz in Cape Town was that it cut across these separations. It brought together for the first time musicians of different colour who otherwise would probably have continued playing music within their own communities."[2] In this way, Cape Town jazz in the 1940s and 1950s both reflected the diverse and complex traditions of its hometown, and held out the promise of a more integrated future.

Most Capetonians throughout the first half of the twentieth century—whether they were white or "coloured"—would have been hard-pressed to explain what *marabi*, *isicathamiya*, gumboots, or even Zulu and Xhosa choral groups were about. They lived lives that seldom, if ever, came into contact with the tens of thousands of migrants arriving in townships surrounding every South African city of any size. Their musical lives were filled, instead, with the sounds of official ceremonies and religious services. Like their urban counterparts around the world, they sought out the international popular sounds offered by increasingly commercial recordings, radio, and film. Faraway Hollywood defined the jazzy life of midcentury proper Cape Town more than next-door Langa.

The era began in war, even though the main theaters of conflict during World War I were far from Cape Town. For a city and society recovering from the brutal Second Anglo-Boer War, fighting among European combatants initially seemed distant.[3] As the "War to End All Wars" dragged on, a limitless British appetite for soldiers brought home the bloodshed of the battlefields. Initially, the new South African government confronted the need to protect its borders with German South West Africa. The local Cape Town authorities faced the additional task of managing a large German community that was simultaneously viewed as consisting of enemy aliens (especially those who had not adopted South African citizenship) and as a community asset. In November 1915, the level of commitment to the war effort changed substantially when the South African Overseas Expeditionary Force set sail for the slaughter of a Europe at war.

Capetonians mobilized around homefront activities as the casualties mounted. As in Canada—where French Canadian resentment for becoming embroiled in what was seen as a British imperial adventure in Europe churned just beneath the surface—World War I exacerbated tensions between Afrikaner and Dutch Capetonians and their British neighbors. The local mood darkened following additional loss of life resulting from the postwar global influenza epidemic.[4]

The end of the war marked a moment for collective jubilation to a Cape Town participating in the euphoria that would become known as the Roaring Twenties. American popular song—especially the new genre known as jazz—exerted a profound influence over the city's musical life. Local performers sought to demonstrate their "chops"—their ability to play—by drawing on sheet music and new recordings from the United States.[5] As the anthropologist David Coplan argues,

> the artistic biographies of black instrumentalists, then as now, are filled with stories of how music-loving and -playing

parents, uncles, neighbours, community show promoters or performers recognized budding talent and fervent desire in some young future star, and gave their time and talents without payment. While white teachers were general too expensive, it is remarkable how many players managed to receive at least some formal lessons from them. . . . Among the elite, it was fondly hoped that performing arts, in the absence of other fields of self-expression, might play an important social and even political role by proving that blacks could indeed master the cultural repertoire of whites at a professional level.[6]

Cape Town's black and "coloured" musicians didn't simply mimic their white teachers; they also appropriated musical trends coming from abroad and made them their own by adding distinctive South African and Capetonian components.[7] Important players, such as the pianist Sullivan Mphahlele, built on American styles—in his case, the stride style of Fats Waller—through freeform improvisation, which took the music to a different level. Tellingly, Mphahlele enjoyed passing himself off in Cape Town as an African American musician, even as he was perfecting a distinctive African style.

Jazzing Up The Town

By the mid-1930s, a small number of black music teachers had begun to challenge the dominance of white music education. In particular, Wilfred Sentso, leader of the Synco Fans, gained considerable stature as a composer, performer, and teacher. His Bantu Sports Club—which opened branches in a number of settlements around Johannesburg in and near what became known as Soweto—promoted new styles of musicianship that were closely connected to African traditions, nurturing important future performers who eventually led the way to greater militancy within the African musical profession.[8]

Solomon "Zuluboy" Cele—another seminal figure to emerge from the Johannesburg scene, which increasingly focused on the legendary Sophiatown neighborhood—pulled together some of the most legendary township players to form the Jazz Maniacs big band.[9] The Maniacs combined South African *marabi* and American swing to heat up township municipal halls and movie theater stages. Their recording *Izikhalo Zika Z-Boy*, backed by Tsaba Tsaba No. 1, was perhaps the first South African jazz recording when it was released in 1939.[10] The Maniacs continued on in various forms long after Cele's murder on February 13, 1944.[11] Their legacy was vast and unpredictable. A Maniacs performance at the wedding reception of Lily and Nico Sikwane, for example, inspired four-year-old Hugh Masekela to decide that he wanted to play the trumpet.[12] The Maniacs and other groups of the period—including the Harmony Kings, Harlem Swing Aces, Harlem Swingsters, Merry Blackbirds, Merrymakers, and Rhythm Hot Shots—created a distinctive brand of South African musicianship.[13]

Collectively, these performers provided the backdrop for many a good time. The trumpeter Hugh Masakela recalled these early days of South African jazz by noting that "there were very different types of audiences for the Harlem Swingsters and the Jazz Maniacs and those people (figure 35). The elite didn't go to the same dances as the others. But every township had a municipal hall. The old townships maybe had five to ten thousand people. Some were too smack to have halls. But Springs, Brakpan, Benoni, Germiston, Roodeport, Randfontein, Krugersdorp, Boksburg: All those places had municipal halls. And that was the circuit of these groups. In every township on every weekend there was a concert and dance Friday, Saturday through Sunday."[14] Singing groups fronting for the Maniacs—such as the Manhattan Brothers, the Quad Sisters, the Woody Wood Peckers, and the Skylarks (which included Miriam Makeba, Abigail Khubeka, Letta Mbulu, and Mary Rabotaba)—similarly transformed South African popular music, as did other ensembles, such as the Merry Blackbirds.[15]

Cape Town was producing its own legends. The African Mills Brothers—based on the model of the American quartet the Mills Brothers—emerged a generation later than the Maniacs. The Brothers' relationship with the District Sixers was similar to that between the Maniacs and their spin-off groups with the Sophiatowners. Nomvuyo Ngcelwane devotes an entire chapter of her District Six memoirs to the group. She records:

Figure 35. The famed jazz trumpeter Hugh Masekela performing in 2009.
Source: Photograph by Tom Beetz
(http://www.flickr.com/photos/9967007@N07/6580953101/in/photostream/;
Creative Commons, https://creativecommons.org/licenses/by/2.0/).

The African Mills Brothers loved their music and because of
their generosity were loved in turn by all District Six residents. They never charged a fee when they were requested
to perform in a show organized by Black people, so they
regularly appeared free of charge at the Black Miss Cape
Town beauty pageant. They also sang at Sunday afternoon
spends at the Clyde and the Ayre Street halls, and at fund-
raising concerts organized by the Chapel Street school and
the Methodist church. But since they were known throughout Cape Town, they were sometimes invited to sing at the
Drill Hall and the City Hall. For these occasions of course
they charged a fee. Andy Masiba and his boys were real
professionals. They performed in black trousers, off white
jackets, white shirts and black bow ties. Sometimes they
preferred white trousers and floral shirts, or if the occasion
called for it, traditional wear. These outfits they purchased

out of their own pockets, because there were no sponsors
for Black performing artists those days.[16]

Ngcelwane's reminiscences highlight two important dimensions of the South African dance band scene. First, bands and singing groups were inextricably tied to their communities. Oral histories collected by Bill Nasson on behalf of the Hands-Off District
Six Committee in the late 1980s amplify this observation. Hasson's
interlocutors described a local scene that brought the commercial
culture of local cinemas together with a cacophony of street performance styles into an integrated blend. Nostalgic District Six
exiles spoke to Hasson about street entertainers of "extraordinary
variety" lining up to entertain the crowds waiting to get into local
movie theaters such as the Star, the Avalon, the British Bioscope,
and the National.[17]

Second, popular music was becoming national in scope. Beyond the passage cited here, Ngcelwane writes about Johannesburg musicians performing in Cape Town.[18] The African Mills
Brothers traveled to performances in other cities. This movement
of performers subtly produced a growing sense of shared destiny
among township audiences. Such networks produced by an increasingly common performance culture that effortlessly took on
political meaning as South African music became radicalized in the
decades ahead.

During the second quarter of the twentieth century, the increasingly unified South African entertainment space expanded beyond
earlier vaudeville and theater circuits that had been focused on a
few cities and towns. An indigenous recording industry grew up
around the Gallo Africa record company (which began operations
in 1926), and its local competitor, GRC (which was established in
1939). The South African Broadcasting Company inaugurated service in 1936, replacing the earlier African Broadcasting Corporation, which had started broadcasting in 1927.[19] Local film companies promoted South African talent throughout the Union. A growing commercialization of popular culture reached into every sphere
of artistic life. This trend was tellingly evident in the evolution of
Cape Town's New Year's Carnival during the years between the
Second Anglo-Boer War and World War II.

"Bits and Pieces," "Odds and Ends"

As noted above, the New Year's Carnival took place on the streets of District Six and Bo-Kaap at the turn of the century. Popular displays became increasingly competitive, with singers and bands forming clubs to compete with one another. As happened in New Orleans during Mardi Gras, spontaneous contests would explode whenever different choirs and bands—such as the Rosslyn Rugby Club from District Six and Arabian College from Bo-Kaap—chanced upon one another during their processions on the local streets.[20] These impulsive displays of braggadocio increasingly disturbed those who felt empowered to control the city in the name of decorum.

Beginning in 1906, the city authorities invited musicians and singers to compete at the Green Point Race Track for a trophy offered by the *Cape Argus* newspaper.[21] The following year, local officials restricted the Carnival to a single parade route from downtown to Green Point, where competitions were held under the watchful gaze of white judges.[22] The raceground competition proved to be an immediate success, with some 7,000 spectators (including some 2,000 Europeans) piling into the track in 1907, and a Festival of Lanterns being added the following year.[23] Yet, by 1909, interest waned, and the Green Point competitions were suspended until 1920, when civic leaders such as Abdullah Abdurahman seized on the event to raise money for political and community causes.[24]

Rival competitions continued throughout the 1930s, organized by various groups and featuring different types of troupes—such as "Privates," "Americans," "Bits and Pieces," and "Odds and Ends"—as well as brass bands, Christmas Carolers, and Malay Choirs.[25] Officially sanctioned spectacles became, in the words of the Carnival historian Martin, "commercial endeavours. The competitive spirit was preserved most of the time, but was channeled into a show which allowed for innovations. . . . From the end of the 1920s, a new medium was to play a decisive role in the evolution and aesthetics of the musical repertoires: the talking moving."[26] Al Jolson's performance in the debut talking movie *The Jazz Singer*, as Martin demonstrates, further validated the prominence of characters in blackface.[27]

Midcentury Carnival became another demonstration of the facility with which Capetonians assimilated fresh cultural impulses and made their own (*osvoit'* as the Russians — themselves masters at transformational assimilation — would put it). The same neighborhoods producing Carnival simultaneously were home to Muslim Malay choirs celebrating the New Year as well as Christian carolers marking Christmas. Carnival troupes, Muslim and Christian choirs, and choruses sprang up, with people moving back and forth among the various holiday amusements.[28]

In so doing, they celebrated what others might scorn: diversity. The Afrikaans intellectual Izak David Du Plessis made a career of celebrating diversity as a charming picturesqueness.[29] Constructing the notion of "Malay" as a distinctive aspect of the Afrikaans-speaking community, as he did, domesticated differences while rendering them captivatingly exotic.[30] But turning "Malay" into "coloured" during apartheid proved to be far more pernicious.[31] Cape Town's New Year's celebrations substantiate a local aptitude for blending a variety of influences into an original, vigorous, and distinguishing essence not found anyplace else.[32]

The value of creative diversity by no means remained an abstraction in midcentury Cape Town. Among the prominent twentieth-century South African cultural leaders who found Cape Town's celebrations to be an invaluable training ground were Abdullah Ibrahim (Dollar Brand), Basil "Manenberg" Coetzee, Jonathan Butler, Robbie Janson, Dudu Pukwana, Winston Mankuku, Simon Goldberg, Chris McGregor, and the members of the Eoan Group Ballet, including the director, Joseph Manca, and the opera singer Joseph Gabriels. These local holiday spectacles inspired such writers as Adam Small, Peter Abrahams, Dom Matera, Achmat Dangor, Bessie Head, Alex La Guma, and Richard Rive.[33] Such a list of cultural luminaries should inspire commendation rather than condemnation.

Commendation, alas, was not in the offing. Efforts to control street parading ebbed and flowed over the years, with a general trend toward increased restrictions. Total regulation proved difficult, given the close proximity of Carnival zones — such as District Six — to downtown areas. Moreover, these in-town neighborhoods remained alive with activity even without the Carnival, so the New Year's celebrations endured as a means for the divested to assert their presence in local life.[34]

Such anarchic spectacles greatly concerned those in authority. For whites, the Carnival became a pageant staged at Green Point Track and Rosebank Showgrounds, with seats set aside for Europeans. The Cape Town middle class could safely amuse themselves by marveling at the self-mockery of "coloured people" strutting before them.[35] Carnival thus became a leisure-time cavalcade rather than a neighborhood's declaration of self-worth.[36]

Carnival remained far more, of course. Beyond formal competitions judged by whites and the procession between Green Point and home neighborhoods, Carnival was first and foremost a neighborhood activity—troupes gathered throughout the year to practice for upcoming competitions; their associations easily extended into social, economic, and political engagement; and the underlying irony of their performance validated what was happening on local streets through hyperbole.

The informants of the oral historian Nasson make clear, in his summary of their words, that "everywhere in District Six it was a short hop from home, workplace, or classroom to the street. The street was home to absorbing sights and a vibrant communal life and it drew people like a magnet. Its noises washed over pavements, alleyways and courtyards. There were unstaged entertainments which residents could stand back and enjoy, like public squabbles between neighbours over shared street washing lines, street fights, drunks, or the sight of a fruit and vegetable barrow toppling over."[37]

World War II marked a turning point for Cape Town, as it did for so much of the world. The presence of soldiers and sailors from around the world—including African American warriors—only heightened the possibility for cross-cultural pollination. More forms of American popular culture arrived with the troops; more money flowed through town.[38] Cape Town and Capetonians of all hues gained in innumerable ways from being on the side of the victors.[39]

Afrikaner nationalism was also on the rise, fueled in part by the growing presence of the English language, brought along by British war efforts and American popular culture. For Carnival troupes, a growing reliance in their routines on American songs became an ever-more-visible affront to those for whom Afrikaans was the only suitable language for South Africa.

More perniciously, segregation—often practiced by custom—was becoming an ideological anchor for the South African regime under Prime Minister Jan Smuts, who held office between 1939 and 1948.[40] For all the international accolades granted to Smuts for his heroism in World War I, his leading role in the founding of the League of Nations, and his participation in the councils of empire, he presided between 1939 and 1948 over a government that expanded legal segregation through such laws as the Native Trust and Land Act (1936) and the Native Laws Amendment Act (1937).[41] The world that had produced the vibrant culture evident in Cape Town's New Year's celebrations—and that ran far deeper into the city's oldest neighborhoods and traditions—was about to come under unrelenting attack by Afrikaner nationalism, which was predicated on racial purity.

"Scientific" Racism

Racial separation, which had been omnipresent throughout South African history, became steadily more pronounced as the country entered the postwar era. Unable to survive in the countryside, larger numbers of Africans moved to town, often settling in new, self-made communities on the peripheries of major cities. And the formal African settlements—such as Langa—became home to far larger numbers of residents than anticipated.

The workplace—most especially in the all-important mining industry—became a primordial battlefield, as unions and other civic organizations followed racial lines. Unlike the American South, where returning veterans from World War II carried notions of integrated life with them from Europe, South Africa's war experience only hardened racial boundaries. Among whites, the contest between the Afrikaners and the British deepened as the Afrikaners became ever more bitter over the British domination that they saw being reinforced by the new international order. For those caught in between these numerous lines—such as Cape Town's "coloured" and the emerging African intellectual class—mounting tensions left less and less room to stake out an independent existence.[42]

The sustainability of segregation appeared to be called into question as South Africa emerged from the war. International pressure brought by the county's allies, for example, encouraged South Africans opposed to racial division to pursue political action. Afrikaners' sympathies for the defeated Germans rendered some of their political organizations suspect. Additionally, Smuts's personal participation in the drafting of the United Nations Charter transformed his support for segregation at home into an embarrassment abroad. Meanwhile, an educated and assertive generation of African leaders—including such rising personalities as Nelson Mandela, Oliver Tambo, and Walter Sisulu—was moving into the public realm while the South African economy was becoming ever more dependent on African labor.[43]

There were many reasons to assume that Smuts would lose the 1948 national elections. He was old; and his government had been in power for too long to sustain a sense of vibrancy. And yet, he fell narrowly to Malan's Nationalists, who won seventy (primarily rural) parliamentary seats to the governing United Party's sixty-five (primarily urban) seats. At the time of Malan's arrival in Pretoria, on June 1, 1948, every indication pointed to a short-lived and weak Nationalist government. But nothing could have been further from what transpired. The wily Malan moved boldly forward, as if he had a supermajority in the national Parliament, quickly overseeing a series of local and regional elections.[44]

Within a few years, every state institution had been Afrikanerized, nonwhites had been systematically disenfranchised, and the seats for white representatives of African and coloured voters had been abolished. By the mid-1960s, some British-heritage voters were joining with Afrikaners in supporting the harsh racialist regime.[45] Meanwhile, Smuts briefly served as the chancellor of the University of Cambridge before returning to South Africa, where he died in September 1950 a few weeks after his eightieth birthday.

The Nationalists' signature policy became quickly known as apartheid, a program of race-based social engineering largely developed by Hendrik Frensch Verwoerd.[46] Having been born in Holland and raised in South Africa, Verwoerd was trained at the leading Afrikaner university and also at German universities before he assumed a faculty position in applied psychology at his alma mater in Stellenbosch. He was a onetime sympathizer with the Nazi regime, and he used his growing reputation as a journalist and publicist to oppose Jewish immigration from Europe in the mid-1930s. He promoted republicanism in opposition to the British Crown, and helped engineer Malan's 1948 victory. As a reward, Malan appointed Verwoerd a senator and, in 1950, minister of native affairs. Empowered by his cabinet position, Verwoerd implemented the policies that would become known as apartheid. He became prime minister in 1958, overseeing the establishment of the Republic of South Africa in 1961. On September 6, 1966, a mentally disturbed parliamentary messenger assassinated him on the floor of the House of Assembly.[47]

Apartheid was more than a system of racial segregation. It applied firm racial categories that claimed, like many modernist classifications, to provide a "scientific" basis for identifying racial groups, which were to be separated into discrete realms. Beyond separation, whites in general—and Afrikaners in particular—sat at the pinnacle of the supposed racial hierarchy, which similarly was based on pseudo-scientific claims.

Apartheid became policy through the enactment of several laws during Malan's early years in power.[48] Apartheid legislation eventually led to the creation of black "homelands" in apartheid's mature stage.[49] Enforcement of these policies and laws necessitated the relocation of millions of South Africans into isolated residential, educational, and economic realms.

The government, known for its thuggish brutality and totalitarian ambition, imposed these laws and decrees without mercy. As in the Soviet Union, no aspect of human existence was too small to escape the attention of the all-powerful state. But also as in the Soviet Union, important spaces for opposition and for creative resistance nonetheless remained beyond the reach of the state—which could not control all, even though it sought to command everything. The history of South Africa's next four decades proved to be about this breach between the government's rigid, totalitarian intents and the creative, apartheid-resisting societal reality.

The history of apartheid is the history of resistance, primarily by Africans. White religious leaders outside the Dutch Reformed Church opposed the passage of the apartheid laws, and a number of white universities—especially the University of Cape Town and the University of the Witwatersrand—became focal points of resistance. Eventually, a number of business organizations criticized the policies as well.[50]

Cape Town was a center of liberal resistance to the policies, with an activist City Council and many religious, educational, and civic leaders taking stands on principle.[51] The local Cape Town urban culture—with its long history of racial propinquity and decades of British colonial rule—naturally stood as a slight to the new regime. Metropolitan Cape Town's population was approaching a half million by the time apartheid took hold, with the preponderance of Africans being male labor migrants.[52]

Simultaneously, however, many Capetonians supported—or at least acquiesced to—apartheid; and others benefited personally from the various dislocations that were being imposed from Pretoria. Previous prohibitions on Africans moving to urban areas without permits and restrictions on African ownership of land contributed to racial segregation in Cape Town, as they did throughout urban South Africa.[53] The limits of Cape Town's liberalism were evident at City Hall. Theoretically, jobs in the municipal government were open to all; but in practice, the highest-ranking nonwhite Capetonian on the municipal payroll at the end of World War II was a senior clerk.[54]

A long and complex relationship developed during apartheid among the authorities, the opposition, and Cape Town's "coloured" community.[55] Over time, African resentment grew in response to the preferential treatment of the city's "coloured" residents by the apartheid regime, in what became part of a divide-and-conquer strategy. Even today, many Africans complain that economic opportunity for black people in the Western Cape is greatly constrained; but others counter that such claims have more to do with the city and province being the lone holdouts opposing the dominant postapartheid African National Congress (ANC) governments. Significantly, Cape Town entered the apartheid period with a reputation for permeable racial and class boundaries and exited being known as among the most racist corners of the new South Africa.[56] These strains and contradictions constrained the city's musical as well as its political and economic lives.

Windsongs

The historian Carol Muller writes,

> Certainly in Cape Town in the 1940s and 1950s, the sound of
> music was everywhere: on the street, in one's home, as well
> as on the stage, in the movies, in the mosque or church. For
> young people like Sathima Bea Benjamin, even the natural
> world made its own kinds of musical sounds. Cape Town
> is known for its powerful southeasterly winds, winds that
> shape what it means to live in the city. If you have never
> experienced the power of gale force winds, it might be hard
> to imagine just how the wind can carry sounds that are like
> music to your ears. But Benjamin has vivid memories of
> such sounds, and she sings about their power in one of her
> compositions, "Windsong."[57]

Benjamin—who died in 2013—was born in Johannesburg in
1936 and raised in Cape Town. A child of mixed race, she flourished in the complex world of 1940s Cape Town, easily entering
the local music scene. After winning talent contests at local movie
theaters, she began singing at clubs and community events, eventually falling in with a number of young musicians who would define the Cape Town Sound in the years ahead—including Adolph
"Dollar" Brand, also known as Abdullah Ibrahim; Kippie Moeketsi;
Johnny Duani; and Chris McGregor. She took particular interest in
the contemporary American singers she would hear on the radio
and in the movies—such as Nat King Cole, Billie Holiday, and Ella
Fitzgerald. These American influences were filtered through her local partners to produce a distinct approach to music that reflected
the varied musical genre that had taken root on the Cape of Good
Hope.[58]

At one point in the mid-1950s, Benjamin found herself stranded
in Mozambique after having joined Arthur Klugman's unsuccessful "coloured" jazz and variety tour. Looking for musicians with
whom she could perform to earn her way home, she discovered the
Johannesburg saxophonist Kippie Moeketsi. Back in Cape Town,
she met her future husband, Brand (Ibrahim), himself a child of

Cape Town's port neighborhoods. In 1959 and 1960, Brand joined Moeketsi and Hugh Masekela to form the legendary Sophiatown group the Jazz Epistles.[59] Their *Verse 1* album is considered to have been South Africa's first—and perhaps most important—bebop recording.[60]

Within weeks, the Jazz Epistles were the hottest act in Cape Town as well as Johannesburg. Masekela would recall, years later, that "the tourists, the township folks (coloreds and Africans) from Athlone, District Six, Goodwood, Langa, and all over the Cape Flats, flocked to see us. The wealthy white folks who had suntanned along the sandy beaches all crowded into the Ambassadors nightclub. And the women—*lawd have mercy!*—the most beautiful women of every color and shade filled the joint."[61]

Benjamin and Brand were in the South African touring company of Matshikiza's "all-African jazz opera" musical *King Kong* (fully described below), and after the company disbanded in London, the couple (who were to be married in 1965) went on tour in Europe.[62] They soon enjoyed an extraordinary break while performing at Zurich's Club Africana in 1963, when Duke Ellington was in town. Ellington invited Benjamin to sing in a recording session that would not be released until 1997. But the legendary American musician also arranged to record Brand and his fellow South Africans, Johnny Gertz on bass and Makaya Ntshoko on drums, at the Barclay Recording Studio in Paris. The resulting disc—*Duke Ellington Presents the Dollar Brand Trio*—was released in 1963 and cemented their international reputations.[63] Several additional tracks not included on that recording were thought to have been lost, but resurfaced and were released in the mid-1990s.[64]

Brand and Benjamin were the products of a vibrant and multiracial Cape Town musical community that brought together the city's numerous traditions with modern American jazz. The Capetonians intermingled easily with the Sophiatown musicians from the effervescent Johannesburg scene, such as the future luminaries Masekela and Miriam Makeba (figure 36).[65] These talented players embraced Africans (e.g., Makeba), "coloureds" (Benjamin), and whites (McGregor). Many would influence the international development of jazz throughout the late twentieth century. To create their distinctive sound, unlike anything that had come before, they drew on South Africa's distinctive traditions in choral music; Cape Town's New Year's Carnivals; migrant workers' songs; rural "pennywhistle jazz" (*kwela*), played on inexpensive flutes and whistles that were popular in Sophiatown; *marabi*; and American jazz.[66]

As the July 1968 issue of the South African music magazine *Drum* noted, Cape Town jazz was both the "music of the people, the coloured people" and a creative process whereby musicians from diverse cultural backgrounds sought "a common musical identity."[67] In short, jazz and the musicians who played it represented everything that Malan's Nationalists and Verwoerd's apartheid policies opposed.

Figure 36. The singer Miriam Makeba in 1969.
Source: Photograph by Rob Mieremet (https://commons.wikimedia.org/wiki/ File:Miriam_Makeba_%281969%29.jpg).

Two distinct musical styles dominated postwar Cape Town jazz: the big band sound popular in dance halls, and experimental music better suited for chamber audiences. McGregor's Blue Notes perhaps best represent the former, while Brand's Jazz Epistles were masters of modern jazz and bop.[68] The musicians themselves crossed over such distinctions to perform improvisational music in a variety of settings, with multiple partners who changed from gig to gig. Some performers, such as Benjamin—who had sung in a college choir—integrated classical training with more contemporary playing. And this constant opportunity to move across a variety of musical styles raised everyone's performance standards.

This musical intimacy depended on having available places where the musicians could mix together and play together. But apartheid literally outlawed such proximity. Before apartheid took its full effect, however, Cape Town enjoyed a brief period when it became precisely the sort of urban jagged edge where new worlds come into being. Mixed neighborhoods such as District Six, with their numerous small clubs, provided just the sorts of congenial places where musical invention could flourish. As longtime District Sixer Eddie George told local oral historians years later,

> Socialising in all spheres in those days was pretty segregat-
> ed. . . . But the jazz session really brought all kinds of people
> together, all kinds of musicians and all kinds of audiences
> . . . . This all happened at the time that the apartheid laws
> were consolidating the segregation. It was a sort of contra-
> diction and of course jazz concerts started becoming fashion-
> able and then some people realized it would become profit-
> able. Then the commercial side came into it. Jazz flourished
> all over the world and of course South Africa legislatively
> was going in the opposite direction. . . . They couldn't cope
> with this integration. . . . All these activities, which of course
> included jazz and clubs, closed. . . . It was like death.[69]

There were many reasons why nonwhite musicians were per-forming around Cape Town, often for white audiences, despite various efforts by the white unions and the white-controlled music industry to prevent them from doing so.[70] In part, the city's long

history of multiethnic, multiconfessional, and multiracial performances dating back to the days of the Dutch raised everyone's comfort with seeing a "coloured" person with an instrument. In part,
the continued existence of urban zones of contact in neighborhoods
such as District Six facilitated the circulation of nonwhites musicians into upscale venues downtown and whites out for a night
on the town in nonwhite areas. The harsh colonial racial boundaries found around South Africa's gold and diamond mines had not
quite yet hardened in Cape Town. Apartheid's malignant impact
had yet to be fully experienced.

Tough-minded economics also played a role. As Muller explains, "In the mid- to late 1950s there was a moment where coloured musicans were hired in Cape Town clubs more frequently
than white bands because the coloured musicians would play for
less and apparently were more reliable. The clubs ranged from elite
dinner dance venues to seedy strip joints. The Balalaika and the
Navigators Den were two of the less respectable clubs. Jazz was
performed more often in the white clubs than in the coloured communities, where band music for dancing was the primary form of
'jazz.'"[71]

Public and religious institutions further expanded the spaces
for potential cross-racial musical exchanges, with community centers and church basements providing additional venues for the
sorts of celebrations that required the hot sounds of jazz. Vincent
Kolbe—himself a musician and longtime stalwart in efforts to preserve Cape Town's history in the face of apartheid's brutishness—
established the Jazz Appreciation Club at the Kew Town library,
which became the focal point of an effervescent bohemian community that included Benjamin.[72] In Johannesburg, the future Anglican
archbishop Trevor Huddleston, then the chaplain at Saint Peter's
Secondary School, gave instruments to students and invited local
musicians such as Uncle Sauda of the Johannesburg "Native" Municipal Brass Band to give lessons. Masekela got his start playing a
trumpet presented to him by Huddleston.[73]

All was not sweetness and light, however. "Coloured" musicians were dispatched to the kitchen during breaks, for example,
and curtains were drawn to separate musicians from strippers in
dives that hired white women to disrobe.[74] Yet however harsh such

restrictions seemed at the time, they paled before the absolute racial separation that would follow a few years later. More important,
such interracial mixing—limited as it was—created small spaces
where white, black, and "coloured" musicians who wanted to learn
from one another could play together.

"Black and White and Everything in Between"

Hardy Stockman, a German photographer who came to town in
1959 in search of Brand, described the Cape Town scene in his account of finding the pianist at the nonwhite Ambassador Ballroom
Dancing School in suburban Woodstock. As the South African jazz
scholar, journalist, and educator Gwen Ansell recounts the story in
Soweto Blues, Stockman recalls his first encounter with Brand and
the other musicians who were to form the Jazz Epistles. "The place
was over crowded," he told Ansell. "The band and audience were
composed of black and white and anything in between, mingling
freely like nowhere else in the land. This was all the more surprising as there was no dancing and neither food nor drink was available. You either played or you listened. There was nothing else. I
felt great; finally I had arrived 'home.'"[75]

Ansell continues that the Ambassador was far from the only notable venue on the Cape. "There were concerts at the Rondebosch
and Woodstock Town Halls," she continues, "as well as occasionally at the University of Cape Town and City Hall. Live jazz featured among others the Vortex coffee bar in the city's Long Street,
the Naaz nightclub in Salt River, and the Zambezi Indian restaurant in District Six. Tolerance, however, only stretched so far," she
adds. "When the Mermaid seafood restaurant in the upper market white coastal resort of Sea Point began featuring McGregor's
mixed group in sessions and workshops, the authorities took only
ten days to close the place down."[76]

Among the other well-known venues of the era were the Catacombs and the Tombs in the Cape Town City Bowl, plus the Three
Cellars, the Grove Club, the Chechita, the Waldorf, the Mount Nelson, and the Grand Hotel. Some venues—such as the Naaz, Zambezi, and Catacombs—were open to players of all colors, even if
nonwhite musicians were shunted to back rooms during the inter-

vals. Others—such as the Waldorf, Mount Nelson, and Grand Hotel—were generally off limits to nonwhite musicians. A few white musicians joined community and church hall Sunday jazz sessions in Langa and other townships.[77]

Musicians from Cape Town, Sophiatown, and elsewhere frequently toured the country together with traveling variety shows. Although very few individual players easily crossed the various racial boundaries, those who did—such as McGregor and Jimmy Adams—were of inordinate importance.[78] As a result, Cape Town's and Johannesburg's jazz players formed a single community, reinforcing the South African style that transformed American jazz into a new, distinctive sound.

The pianist Brand—who changed his name to Abdullah Ibrahim after converting to Islam in the 1970s—emerged as a pivotal leader in shaping the Cape Town sound. As noted, Brand was a child of Cape Town's port neighborhoods. He was raised on traditional Xhosa and Gospel music as well as the *bilal* (call to prayer) and the choral music of the Cape Town Muslim community.[79] Once in exile, he and Benjamin made New York's famous Hotel Chelsea their home base by the mid-1970s, after having returned to South Africa earlier in the decade.[80] He first penned his iconic Cape Town jazz masterpiece *Mannenberg* during one of these trips home in 1974–75.[81] Named after the Cape Flats township to which many District Six residents were being dispatched at the time, Brand recorded the song with the local players Basil Coetzee, Paul Micheals, Monty Weber, and Robbie Jensen. His tune paid stirring homage to the *marabi*-tinged sounds that were popular in the Cape Town of his youth.

Brand shared his ascendancy with the other members of the prodigious bop band the Jazz Epistles (which brought together Brand on piano, Moeketsi on alto, Gwangwa on trombone, Masekela on trumpet, Johnny Gertze on base, and Early Mabuza or Ntshoko on drums). Modeled on Art Blakey's Jazz Messengers in the United States, the group caught immediate international attention and promised to expand South Africa's prospects as a leading center in the world of modern jazz.

But the racist world surrounding jazz's diminutive sanctuary was hardening fast. In 1956, the South African government brought charges of treason against 156 leading political, union, and civic leaders—including Nelson Mandela, Oliver Tambo, Walter Sisulu, Chief Luthuli, Alex La Guma, Joe Slovo, and the Reverend James Calata. The trial dragged on until 1961, when the defendants were acquitted. The prosecutors were to prove far more effective in subsequent trials, sending many prominent anti-apartheid leaders—such as the ANC's Mandela and Sisulu—to long prison terms. Other defendants—such as Tambo and Slovo—escaped further prosecution only by going into exile.[82]

Sharpeville

On the morning of March 21, 1960, several thousand demonstrators converged on the local constabulary in the township of Sharpeville near Johannesburg to protest the enforcement of pass laws intended to control and limit the movement of blacks.[83] Both the police and the demonstrators became progressively agitated as the hours passed. Scuffles broke out after low-flying military jet planes and tear gas failed to disperse the crowd. Shooting broke out as the police attempted to arrest the demonstration's organizers. When the consequent melee was over, 69 demonstrators—including numerous women and children—had been killed, and 180 had been injured. Many were shot in the back as they tried to flee the advancing chaos.

   Sharpeville inexorably changed the larger political battle over apartheid, as the ANC and other groups made it a symbol of official brutality. The police used the events as a reason to launch ever-harsher crackdowns. Three weeks later, a failed assassination attempt convinced Verwoerd and his followers that he had been saved by God. "From that day on," Masekela wrote, "the apartheid guillotine came crashing down on the country with more venom than ever before. . . . Our [African] paranoia had now been upgraded to fear, loathing, suspicion, anger, and hate. The next month was even tenser. There was no music work."[84]

   As these events transpired, the trumpeter Matshikiza wrote the music for an "all-African jazz opera," with lyrics by Pat Williams and himself.[85] Based on Harry Bloom's book about the heavyweight boxer Ezekiel "King Kong" Dlamini, this extravagant musical told the tragic story of Dlamini's rapid rise to the pinnacle of pugilistic success, followed by his equally swift descent into alcoholism and criminality. Matshikiza's masterpiece, *King Kong*, proved to be a tremendous success, launching the career of Miriam Makeba and bringing together the Jazz Epistles' Brand (Ibrahim), Masekela, and Moeketsi with numerous other prominent South African jazz musicians as members of an enormous all-black, seventy-two-member cast.

King Kong opened on February 2, 1959, at Witwatersrand University, and it became an instantaneous triumph—winning, according to legend, an opening night endorsement during the first intermission from Nelson Mandela.[86] It played before wildly enthusiastic audiences all across South Africa before leaving for London. A New York production that was to have followed never materialized, so the cast disbanded before leaving Britain. This tour abroad enabled many cast members to obtain international passports for the first time.

Finding themselves beyond the reach of the South African authorities and facing increasingly harsh racial and political realities at home, several members of the cast—including the future international stars Makeba, Masekela, and Brand—remained in Europe or made their way to the United States into either temporary or long-term exile. Within a few years, Matshikiza would go to London and then to Zambia, while Cecil Bernard, Ntshoko, Gertze, Benjamin, Gwangwa, and McGregor would decamp for Europe.[87] As Benjamin noted years later, the departures "just happened very quickly and very naturally because the situation got very bad. . . . And it started to get very empty. And that is when we [i.e., Benjamin and Brand] moved. We would either have to shut up completely or we'd have to make peace. And that's when we decided to leave, in 1961, because it became impossible, not only to do jazz. To do any kind of music. It became very repressive."[88]

In a conventional world, Matshikiza would be remembered for having created a sophisticated yet approachable spectacle that justifiably earned South Africa's music scene the global recognition that it deserved. But in the twisted world of apartheid South Africa, *King Kong* marked the end of an era, as it scattered some of the country's most talented musicians around the world.

As challenging as the mounting weight of apartheid would prove to be for Cape Town's jazz community, it descended even more mercilessly on the city's Carnival community. Resettlement programs were beginning to disperse troupe members from in-town neighborhoods such as District Six to out-of-town townships in the Cape Flats. Their new homes placed troupe members at a great distance from one another and removed them beyond walking distance from communal rehearsal halls. Stadiums were segregated, and the city center was becoming a prohibited area for non-whites. The Cape Flats townships were falling under the control of gangs and criminal groups, which frowned on independent associations beyond their direct control.[89] Cape Town's most glorious era in jazz had come to an ignominious end.

Into Biblical Exile

As the National Party consolidated its control over Parliament throughout the 1950s, legislators passed ever-more-stringent laws designed to separate racial categories. The Separate Amenities Act of 1953 exerted an especially troubling influence over the shape of South Africa's cities. From now on, people using all facilities—ranging from maternity wards to cemeteries, from shop entrances to taxis and ambulances, from beaches and parks to pedestrian subways—were to be separated by race. Urban amenities as simple as a pedestrian bridge or a park bench needed to be produced in pairs to ensure this racial separation.

Further legislation imposed strict racial segregation on technical colleges, universities, and housing. The struggle between the government and its opponents grew fiercest in those communities with a strong ANC presence. In cities such as Cape Town, where the ANC had historically been weak, resistance remained more circumscribed.[90] The Prevention of Political Interference Act of 1968 outlawed multiracial political parties and other less formal gatherings. As a result, those little corners of the city where musicians of different races, ethnicities, confessions, and styles had previously been able to meet and play together simply disappeared.

In Table Bay, within sight of downtown, the authorities converted the Robben Island military post into a prison and place of banishment. After being turned over to the Prisons Department as a "maximum security institution" in 1959, the island became a hard labor camp for leading political opponents, such as Nelson Mandela and Robert Sobukwe, who were incarcerated together with notorious gang members and hardened prisoners under the harshest conditions. Throughout the 1960s, the government arrested those whom it deemed to be dangerous for longer periods and without due process. Liberal newspapers were shut, and intellectuals and union leaders were threatened as police surveillance over society became ever more intrusive. Cape Town, like the rest of South Africa, lived in the grip of this murderous police state.[91]

Heading into the 1960s, mass evictions from racially mixed neighborhoods began with a vengeance. Africans were relegated to township encampments on the periphery of the city, only being able to settle there on a temporary basis before being returned to their "homelands" in the interior. Cape Town's historic "coloured" neighborhoods came under official attack. After years of dispute, District Six was declared a "white area," in a land grab that was intended to turn the district's scenic lots close to downtown over to white developers and institutions.[92] The government sent thousands of longtime District Six residents, such as the Ngcelwanes, to the Cape Flats, to live in shantytowns designated by racial type (i.e., Nyanga for "coloured" and Langa for "blacks").[93]

Contradictions abounded. Churches and mosques were allowed to remain in the deserted cityscapes left behind by the wholesale destruction of racially mixed and poor communities. But because they were now far removed from their congregations, few were able to provide religious comfort to their congregants. The vibrant social and civil life that had grown up in places such as District Six—including groups such as the successor organizations to Abdullah Abdurahman's African Political Organization—disappeared.

More militant trade unions, communist cells, and ANC groups were better prepared to move their operations underground as they increasingly contested with criminal gangs for control of the townships.[94] The anthropologists Monica Wilson and Archie Mafeje captured this transformation in their study of Langa. "The attitude toward the police in a well-to-do-suburb is very different from what it is in the slums in any society," they observed. "The peculiarity of South Africa lies in the fact that all the 'decent people' of Langa, including the middle class, are in conflict with the police in only a slightly less degree than the *tsotsis* [gansters]. . . . Class distinctions plainly exist in Langa, but they are flattened by the cleavage between the colour groups."[95]

The very act of eviction and dislocation turned former residents of neighborhoods and communities such as District Six into sworn enemies of the state. As a certain "Mr. KT" told the oral historians Felicity Swanson and Jane Harries decades later, "Many people were angry and bitter after being forced out of District Six. They felt disconnected from their urban roots, cast out into the unfamiliar world of the townships on the windswept Cape Flats, almost in the biblical sense of being sent into exile."[96]

This process continued as the government became intent on removing Africans from the Western Cape altogether.[97] The removals continued to spread to communities throughout the Cape. In 1967, thousands of nonwhite residents were forced to leave the historic navy suburb of Simonstown on False Bay after nearly three centuries of multiracial settlement.[98] Mixed areas within the predominantly white suburb of Claremont were cleansed during the 1970s and 1980s, followed by Windemere, Tramway Road, and other neighborhoods.[99] In each case people, families, relationships, communities, and cultural traditions were smashed in the name of a bogus racial theory that destroyed the lives of many to enrich the lives of the few.[100]

Unable to challenge the destruction of their city, liberal-minded British and Afrikaner intellectuals and musicians turned to Cape Town's past for soulful nourishment.[101] Such memories, however, could be highly selective. By the 1960s, films and travelogues ignored the raucous New Year's festivals and the "coloured" people who celebrated them.[102]

The attractions of Western counterculture provided an alternative means of escape for some.[103] Jazz, as a fusion of various cultural influences, symbolized resistance to apartheid. "The spirit of Monk is everywhere in Africa," the bassist Herbie Tsoaeli has noted. "I feel it. When you talk about Monk, you talk about Coltrane, you talk about all the cats who were really into revolution—that's the spirit I'm talking about it. It can change the world."[104]

Simultaneously, 1960s America and Britain brought new musical forms to Cape Town and the rest of South Africa. Postwar jazz had morphed through rhythm & blues into rock 'n' roll and, eventually, harder-edged forms of rock. As in the past, South Africans fully participated in these international musical fashions, despite desperate attempts by those in power to isolate the country. The 1960s similarly brought a wave of protest-based songs (sometimes known as "folk music" in the United States), which carried powerful messages that reached the hearts and minds of frustrated South African white youth. Cut off from their nonwhite contemporaries at home, young white musicians looked to the Beatles, Rolling Stones, and Bob Dylan for musical inspiration in yet another episode of transatlantic cultural blending.

Early in the 1970s, a bootlegged copy of an album cut by an obscure Detroit singer, Sixto Rodriguez, reached South Africa. In a story retold by the 2012 Oscar-winning documentary film *Searching for Sugar Man*, South African liberal youth—predominantly white Afrikaners and English speakers—embraced Rodriguez's elegant, antiauthoritarian protest lyrics.[105] Drawing on Rodriguez's music for inspiration, his South African fans sang his songs at anti-apartheid protests, while young performers tried to copy his style and his words. Rodriguez, meanwhile, abandoned his music career after having made just two commercially unsuccessful albums. Unable to discover anything about their hero in the state-controlled South African media, his fans concocted all sorts of legends about the singer's heroic end (e.g., his having committed suicide onstage following a particularly disappointing performance).

Rodriguez, for his part, was living an honorable life of modest obscurity in his hometown of Detroit. Eventually, as the film reveals, his South African fans used their country's post-apartheid openness, combined with the power of the Internet, to track down the American singer, who was completely unaware of his fame. His emotional 1998 South African tour relaunched his career and brought a modicum of closure to apartheid's dark history for his local fans.

The Rodriguez story underscores how isolated apartheid South Africa had become from the world at large. More important, here, it reveals how isolated the once mutually engaged worlds of Cape

Town music had become from one another. The sounds emanating from Britain and the United States—whether the Beatles, the Rolling Stones, or Rodriguez—grew out of the powerful intermingling of European, white American, and African American musical forms (the Beatles and Rolling Stones being inspired in large measure by African American blues singers). Such fraternization had been a hallmark of Cape Town's music from the city's earliest days. But this mixing was no longer possible.

The destiny of the New Year's Carnival symbolizes the damage to Cape Town's culture inflicted by the imposition of apartheid. The Department of Community Development in Pretoria designated Green Point, the site of the racetrack housing the annual competition among Carnival troupes, to be a "white area." Consequently, beginning in 1968, the Carnival became invisible. The multidisciplinary scholar Denis-Constant Martin explains:

> The prohibition on the use of Green Point Track and on walking through the centre of town meant that some of the most important parts of the carnivals had been scrapped — the possibility of appearing in the mask; . . . the right of use of the streets to sing and dance and play music that was the heritage of the community; the chance of watching . . . without paying for tickets which were unaffordable for poor families; and the opportunity for reminding South Africa that Cape Town was also a coloured place and that it would not have developed without the contribution of the present coloureds' ancestors.[106]

Like the city itself, Cape Town's music scene lay grievously wounded. The troupes continued to perform where they could, often out of sight. Some years, the authorities prohibited the gathering altogether because of various emergency measures that had been imposed to prohibit public gatherings. Celebrations did not return to Green Point until 1979, with the traditional parade from the city center to Green Point stadium resuming only in 1989.[107] By the early 1970s, apartheid's stranglehold seemed unbreakable. Any collaboration among musicians of different racial categories had become impossible.[108]

The Woeful Fate of Cape Jazz

The music didn't stop in either South Africa or Cape Town; it transformed into the sound of survival. Survival, of course, had different meanings for different groups, each of which assumed hardened boundaries around themselves as apartheid policies built the walls separating South Africans higher and higher. The cross-fertilization of the postwar Capetonian jazz scene and of the colorful New Year's festivities may have been wounded, but other music still thrived.

If the improvisational freedom of jazz challenged the founding tenets of the authoritarian regime, this regime in turn challenged the improvisers. There were fewer and fewer venues where jazz players could perform (even within their own racial groups). Record companies and state-controlled media outlets stopped promoting the music and the musicians. To some extent, jazz was losing pride of place on the international music scene as the 1960s unfolded. Unlike Europe and North America, however, there were few opportunities in South Africa for jazz to survive, even as contemporary chamber music. Musicians could not get gigs; they were not being hired to teach; they were not being sought out by fans. Some of Cape Town's best jazz players stayed in town, playing for families, friends, and other musicians, whenever and wherever they could. Like their neighbors in the Carnival troupes, these remarkable and resilient performers kept the flame of jazz alive in Cape Town through the harshest apartheid times.

The attack on the microenvironments that had promoted South Africa's distinctive jazz came from a multiplicity of directions. These policies advanced several goals. First among many, they made it possible to deny South African citizenship to blacks. Second, they permitted South Africa to sidestep the collapse of European colonialism and the wave of newly independent countries that had washed across the continent in 1960.[109] The reality of these many self-governing African states across the continent profoundly changed South African race relations. They provided living alternative models, legitimacy, and sanctuary for black South African political, civic, and cultural leaders as the attacks by the country's regime on its own people ebbed and flowed after 1960.

Each reserve—or "homeland"—was to have its own administration legitimated by the promotion of a local culture.[110] The South African Broadcasting Company (SABC) assumed responsibility for promoting "authentic" music, for example, precisely at the moment when broadcasting was becoming an essential outlet for promoting and marketing the increasingly commercialized products of the growing local recording industry. Thus, "Bantu Music" was born.[111]

Gwen Ansell tells the story: "Between 1960 and 1962, the South African Broadcasting Corporation replaced the piecemeal broadcasting of generic or language-specific African programmes in mainstream broadcasting hours with the creation of English and Afrikaans stations with a whites-only menu and Radio Bantu. Eventually, thirteen 'commercial' stations, also controlled by the SABC (which occasionally played African American, but never black South African, music) later joined the broadcasting bouquet. Ethnomusicologist and university lecturer Dr. Yvonne Huskisson became the SABC's overseer of 'Bantu Indigenous Music.'"[112]

Huskisson—who had written a master's thesis on "Bantu" music education—deeply and profoundly opposed efforts to "detribalize" and "acculturize" African culture. Her policies turned state radio—and eventually television—into a potent advocate of "tribal" music and musicians.[113] Although generally hostile to jazz, Huskisson's policies promoted musicians who aligned with her own vision of authenticity. Thus, for example, the saxophonist Winston Mankunku's 1968 recording *Yakhal'Inkomo* (*The Bellowing Bull*) became the best-selling jazz recording in South African history.[114] Apolitical *isicathamiya* groups—and other "traditional" musicians—found favor, income, and audiences.[115] But the musicians associated with the urban and cosmopolitan sounds of modern jazz found themselves with fewer and fewer outlets for their music.

Some important modern players stayed in Cape Town, Johannesburg, and elsewhere, finding gigs where they could, taking on students, and keeping the local scenes alive. Ansell begins her book *Soweto Blues* with the account of the unveiling of the tombstone of one such musical legend in Langa in 2003:

Baritone saxophonist and bandleader Christopher Ngcukana, known respectfully as "Mra" and colloquially as "Chris

Columbus," lived from 1927 to 1993. He had been as great an explorer of modern music as his namesake had been of oceans. He started his career with a close-harmony group of vaudeville singers, the Bantu Young Ideas, in 1943 and by the end of the decade he was leading the first of many innovative ensembles. According to his son, Duke, a trumpeter: "When Third Stream music came along through Ornette Coleman and such people, my father knew that. He was only playing that sort of music. . . . And now few people could play with him, because he was interpreting all that old music differently."[116]

Musicians such as Ngcukana, Winston Mankunku Ngozi on reeds, Tony Schilder on the piano, and Johnny Mekoa on the trumpet are rightfully as revered as those jazz pioneers such as Masekela and Brand (Ibrahim) who found international celebrity in exile.[117] They played in segregated halls, blew their horns backstage while white musicians mimed onstage, and had their stage names Anglicized so as not to give offense to white broadcast audiences. Resilient and creative performance spaces popped up, most especially Lucky Michael's Pelican in Orlando near Johannesburg and Club Galaxy in Rylands on the Cape Flats.[118] Musicians jammed in smaller places such as coffee houses. The local players became beloved figures in their own communities, as they struggled to pass on their musical legacies to new generations. They are the central protagonists in any account of Cape Town's music because they once again incorporated the city's rich and vast traditions in their music, along with the sounds that came from abroad.

Others—such as Masekela, Brand (Ibrahim), Clegg, Makeba, Matshikiza, Bernard, Ntshoko, Gertze, Benjamin, McGregor, Gwangwa, and Sibongile Khumalo—were forced into, or chose, exile in Britain, the United States, Europe, and the newly independent African countries.[119] There, they continued Cape Town's tuneful traditions in their own ways, adding important and distinctive sounds to music around the world in what today would be considered a "virtual" Mother City, extending from the Hudson River to the River Thames to the Limpopo River.

Life in exile can be soul crushing. A number of South African jazz musicians could not compete in the rarified American jazz scene. Those in Britain, such as Clegg and McGregor, may have had a bit easier time. The Afro jazz funk "London Township" scene of the 1970s, for example, proved especially important for both South African and British music, as did various incarnations of McGregor's big bands.[120] Masekela and Makeba became international luminaries, carrying a political as well as cultural message. Masekela's 1968 hit "Grazin' in the Grass" (composed together with the fellow exiled South African Philemon Hou) rose to the top of the charts and brought him into the new funk mainstream that was developing in the United States.[121] Those musicians—such as Masekela, Gwanga, and Caiphus Semenya—who added American training to their credentials had better luck in making their transitions to life in exile.[122] Others did not.

Brand (Ibrahim) became a seminal figure in the exiled Cape Town music community.[123] Though based in New York, he combined his US appearances with travels to and from his hometown. By the 1970s, he had cut his landmark *Mannenberg* tune with Basil Coetzee, Robbie Jensen, Paul Michaels, Monty Weber, and Morris Goldberg for the new label As-Shams (the Sun) back home in South Africa. Later, he worked with bands from South Africa in Mozambique and Angola after these countries gained their independence in, respectively, 1975 and 1976. He thus provided invaluable leadership by bringing together international and South African players both at home and abroad, as well as South African jazz performers from around the country. And he was also joined from time to time by the hard-bop Sithole brothers, Cyril Magubane, and other jazz musicians who persisted in their various confrontations with authority.

Creatively, despite apartheid, South African jazz thrived in the 1960s, 1970s, and 1980s. Its performers drew on the sounds of rural Africa to reimagine *marabi* with international trends in mind, ranging from post-bop and free jazz to funk.[124] Their sounds were less distinctively Capetonian. Abroad, musicians from Cape Town became identified as more generically "South African"; at home, the integration of the various local jazz scenes that accompanied the ongoing commercialization of musical production was accentuated by the impact of the destruction of communities such as District Six and Sophiatown that had long nurtured distinctive local sensibilities.[125]

New sounds flooded into Cape Town, even as the old sounds faded. Cape Town's economy created a demand for labor that could only be met by African migrants from the countryside. Unable by law to live just anywhere, these migrants piled into increasingly self-built townships on the Cape Flats on the other side of Table Mountain from downtown. They brought their musical lives with them, sensibilities that the apartheid authorities found to be somehow "authentic." Yet, as Coplan argues, musicians subverted such official embraces to produce music that would become ever more urban as the performers themselves adopted new identities in the city.

Harmony in Disharmony

The sounds of migration embraced the choral musical traditions of the Zulu and Xhosa, who themselves absorbed the Gospel choral traditions of Protestant Christianity. *Isicathamiya* and other popular urban African choral music had arrived in Cape Town early in the twentieth century. Musicians and community groups in the townships of the Cape Flats performed and found solace in these familiar sounds. Yet the most creative energy in these musical forms was found elsewhere, in and around Johannesburg, Durban, and Natal. Rural and urban music blended in neighboring Botswana, Swaziland, and Lesotho before Capetonians would make as meaningful a contribution to these sounds. The music's leading innovators—such as Sipho Mchunu, who joined Johnny Clegg's Anglo-Zulu group, Juluka; Joseph Shabalala, who founded Ladysmith Black Mambazo; and Simon "Mahlathini" Nkabinde, an innovator in working-class Mbaqanga music—made their mark elsewhere.[126]

The startling sounds of South African singers were promoted nationally by the SABC, which found within them what their patronizing managers, programmers, and overseers thought of as an "authenticity" that could lend legitimacy to apartheid's "homelands" policies. As Coplan persuasively argues, official perceptions diverged from reality on the ground. These groups were as opposed to apartheid as other nonwhites in South Africa, and at times they effectively used their music to support the broader struggle for nonracial democracy.[127] Moreover, their music was as much a music of the city as it was of a customary culture.

Terminological differences over "authenticity," "traditional," "neotraditional," urban," and "rural" still drive much of the discussion about South African music. Whatever its strengths and insights, these and similar distinctions lie beyond the scope of a discussion of music in Cape Town. By the time the sounds of *isicathamiya* and related genres came to Capetonian musical life, they already had moved to town; they already were "urban," whether they arrived in the hearts of their performers or over the airwaves of state-sponsored radio stations. The act of seeking out this music in small venues, *shebeens*, and township halls became an act of defiance against the regime. Similarly, efforts to protect the musicians' intellectual property—such as the founding of the South African Musicians' Association in 1982—invariably opposed the stranglehold of apartheid law.[128]

Over time, the role of music in opposition to apartheid would grow and, with it, the transgression of musical boundaries would gain in significance. In Cape Town, a collective of local musicians of all genres—the Musical Action of People's Power—organized in the 1980s to perform at rallies, protests, and other events that brought together music from jazz to Zulu dance. Such efforts created new forms of "Afro-pop fusion," which blended music from many styles. Musical Action eventually became "a combined township booking agency, ensemble stable, music school, and student big band"—Musical Action for People's Progress—thereby creating new opportunities for the sort of syncretistic cross-fertilization that has marked Cape Town's music from the very beginning.[129]

Cape Town's musicians emerged among the many innovators within the African performing arts. Rinigo Madlingoze, a native of Gugulethyu Township, transformed Xhosa vocal traditions during the 1980s by integrating the sounds of Reggae and other international styles. Capitalizing on his distinctive vocal range and sound, Rinigo rejuvenated Xhosa song and, in the post-apartheid period, would become a major popular cultural figure throughout the country. Such attempts often expressed both a longing for idealized "homelands" in the past and unease over the harsh realities of "townships" in the present. "Although the environment of Johannesburg, Pretoria, or Durban was inimical to the pursuit of what they considered a properly African social life," Coplan writes, "the need to achieve permanency there was a consuming strategic motivation."[130] This determination was just as strong in Cape Town as in other major South African cities.

The groundwork for the musical breakthroughs that became so visible in the late 1980s and early 1990s was put down a decade or two earlier during the implementation of apartheid cultural policies and the backlash that such efforts generated. The SABC steadily increased the airtime for its isiZulu, Xhosa, and Sesotho broadcasting throughout the 1950s, with nationwide FM service beginning in several major African languages once Radio Bantu started broadcasting on January 1, 1962.[131] Playlists and broadcast policies set by executives such as Huskisson had their own particular ideological approaches to what constituted appropriate music—as did leading SABC broadcasters, such as the Zulu Service announcer Alexius Buthelezi.[132] Their dogmas carried over to other media once the SABC introduced television broadcasting in 1976, and the "black" station TTV 2/3 six years later.[133]

The tales of the patronizing, senseless, and generally idiotic restrictions imposed upon musicians by the SABC's executives and their government overseers duplicate similar tales from other authoritarian states bent on censorship. Among the myriad contradictions that such ideological controls produce is a need to balance philosophical purity with economic necessity. Broadcasters are compelled to have someone listen to what is being aired. In the case of Radio Bantu—as with commercial recording companies, such as the homegrown Gallo, and the multinational giants HMV and Columbia—*isicathamiya* and similar genres were undeniably popular.[134]

By the 1960s and 1970s, the most popular music groups tended to be multiethnic. They brought together varied musical traditions that had been evident in urban centers such as Cape Town for some time. The popular Mbaqanga—which contrasted melodic lines and rhythms with drive dancing—represented just such an amalgam.[135] So too did the legendary Zulu Swazi choir Ladysmith Black Mambazo, from Durban, which brought together a dozen members of the Shabalala and Mazibuko families in their Natal hometown of Ladysmith. The head of this choir, Joseph Shabalala, provided charismatic and inventive leadership that set a new standard by blending tonal and rhythmic variability with "cut-and-run" phrasing. So the choir rightfully caught the ears of Africans and Europeans alike.[136] Shabalala initially benefited from the energetic backing of the SABC's Radio Zulu and this choir's early recording contracts with Gallo. Such support reveals some of the ways in which even groups being promoted as tied to one particular culture—in this case, Zulu—drew on urban experiences blended with various Eoan group influences, such as Gospel traditions.[137]

The incandescent sounds of Johnny "la Zoulou Blanc" (the White Zulu) Clegg's collaborations with Sipho Mchunu in the group Juluka similarly brought together Zulu, British, and African traditions in a vibrant mix that reflected the emerging urban life styles of South Africa. In the case of Clegg—who was the son of a British father and a Rhodesian mother of Jewish heritage—his sound would need to receive recognition in Europe, given that interracial collaboration with Mchunu and other Zulu musicians was illegal in apartheid South Africa.[138]

Shabalala's Ladysmith Black Mambazo and Clegg-Mchunu's Juluka illustrate the irony of the status of African musical traditions under apartheid. Even as those institutions that could promote the music—such as the SABC—intended to promote the sounds of ethnic communities tied to rural places, they in fact had the unintended consequence of advancing something altogether new: "black city music."[139] These developments played out in all South Africa's cities, including but hardly limited to Cape Town, as an ever more violent and spiteful political atmosphere drove the creation of this new music.

Uprising!

The history of apartheid South Africa took a violent, tragic, and destructive turn on June 16, 1976, when the police shot and killed thirteen-year-old Hector Pieterson, an African student, during a demonstration in Soweto (figure 37). Ten thousand black Soweto school children had been peacefully demonstrating against a new policy that required half their subjects to be taught in Afrikaans. They had planned to listen to speeches, sing Sontonga's "Nkosi Sikel' iAfrika" (Lord Bless Africa, in Xhosa), and go home. Instead, the police set dogs on them and fired teargas into the crowd when they refused to disband. In the chaos that followed, the police turned to live ammunition to disperse the crowd.[140]

This protest was the consequence of years of heightening tensions between the regime and its own society. Now, however, the backlash against Pieterson's murder escalated into almost constant demonstrations nationwide—which, by February 1977, had resulted in 575 people being killed, including 134 victims under the age of eighteen. Later that year, the police arrested and killed Steve Biko, founder of the Black Consciousness Movement. He died of injuries to his skull, inflicted while he was being transported naked in police a van for 750 miles the night before.[141] As a result of these events, a growing stream of young blacks fled South Africa for military training camps in Tanzania and newly independent Angola. A long, sustained guerrilla civil war began, which eventually eviscerated the South African regime.

Attacks on the government and its apartheid policies quickly spread abroad. By 1977, the United Nations had endorsed an embargo on the sale of arms to South Africa, activists in the United States and Europe had begun to lobby successfully for disinvestment from corporations based in the country, and a series of boycotts had effectively removed South Africa from participating in most international forums. The apartheid regime was becoming an international pariah state.[142]

At home, embargoes severely damaged the local economy, while continued civil unrest and armed conflict eroded any sense of well-being among nearly all South Africans. In 1978, Prime Minister John Vorster, who had come to power after Verwoerd's assassination in 1966, resigned in a cloud of scandal, to be replaced by the mercurial Pieter Willem Botha. The country's periodic emergency measures, skyrocketing crime, clandestine wars with neighboring states, unending internal battles, censure by the international community, and cavalcade of ultimately ineffectual reforms systematically called every aspect of its apartheid policies into question.[143]

In Cape Town, tensions similarly had been rising over black and "coloured" educational policies. Large, at times violent, dem-

Figure 37. A photograph of the dying Hector Pieterson, at the Hector Pieterson Memorial in Soweto. The photo shows twelve-year-old Pieterson being carried by Mbuyisa Makhubo moments after he was shot by the South African police during a student demonstration in Soweto on June 16, 1976. Pieterson's sister, Antoinette Sithole, runs beside them.
Source: Photograph by Ina96 (https://commons.wikimedia.org/wiki/ File:HectorPieterson1030626.jpg).

onstrations immediately followed the events in Soweto, causing national and local grievances to coalesce.[144] By the mid-1970s, the disparities in the quality of education offered to Cape Town's students could no longer be disguised.[145]

The arrival of tens of thousands of labor migrants into unregulated, self-built township settlements ceded effective control to opposition groups and criminal gangs, which often fought with one another for control. The Black Consciousness and anticolonial movements offered powerful ideological lenses through which to view daily life. Clandestine connections with those battling the South African Army in Angola offered those who wanted to fight the chance to do so.[146]

By the 1980s, a new generation had formed in Cape Town that was committed to overthrowing the apartheid regime. Botha reduced "petty apartheid," adjusting several national policies: Private schools could now admit students of all racial groups; the racially discriminatory clauses of the Immorality Act were rescinded, as was the Mixed Marriages Act; and multiracial political parties became legal.[147] In Cape Town, the government unveiled a series of development plans, none of which came to fruition.

More significant, the regime's efforts to assuage the "coloured" electorate collapsed during the so-called Western Cape Rebellion in 1984, when fewer than a third of all registered "coloured" voters in the Western Cape (and even fewer in Cape Town itself) came out to vote in the August elections.[148] By 1989, a majority of Capetonians outside a limited number of regime strongholds opposed apartheid, though they did not always agree with one another about how to fight it. White voters elected anti-apartheid candidates in local elections that year, helping to set the stage for the regime's eventual collapse.[149]

As this impasse between state and society grew, so too did social and racial tensions. Labor unrest spread. The regime renewed the 1986 State of Emergency, which brought about thousands of detentions each year until 1991. A culture of resistance developed in response.[150]

During this same period, the world of music was changing dramatically, as American and British rock music spread, multinational corporations purchased local and long-independent record labels, amplified instrumentation replaced acoustic instruments as the norm in popular music, and the beginnings of the digital revolution that would transform the music industry (and so much else) appeared. As so many times in the past, Capetonian music makers absorbed and processed musical trends from across the Atlantic.

The combination of apartheid restrictions, the strengthening culture of resistance to these restrictions, the integration of the South African media space, and the transformations within music itself recharged the local Cape Town music scene. Pop music in South Africa, as everyplace else, was becoming an international hybrid of multiple styles. The 1977 Pan-African arts festival, the Second World Black and African Festival of Arts and Culture (known as FESTAC) in Nigeria had brought many exiled South African musicians into contact with the prime movers of what, in a few years, would become known as "world music." And word of these developments spread back to Cape Town, even though local musicians could not travel to the festival itself.[151]

Cape Town's groups—such as Amampondo in Langa—brought a variety of international styles—such as *marimba*—into their repertoire. Other groups followed, including the Genuines in Cape Town and Sakhile (We Have Built) in Johannesburg. "What these groups—and many others smaller and less well known across the country—had in common," Ansell suggests, "was their combination of social themes and a musical language drawing on both urban pop and rural tradition and often jazz too."[152]

In Cape Town and elsewhere, these dynamic developments spilled over into religious as well as secular music. The era's political struggles reinvigorated South African music, whether connected with the Black Consciousness Movement or to others. For example, a vibrant protest music scene emerged by the late 1970s among Afrikaans-speaking youth, with performers assuming ironically sardonic stage names such as Johannes Kerkorrel (Church Organ), Loos Kombius (Bake Oven), and Bernoldus Niemand (Nobody). These Afrikaner entertainers combined traditional folk melodies with angry lyrics, and the loud discord of heavy metal rock and punk.[153]

The regime's ever-increasing violence and brutality isolated officially promoted music from the sounds of the streets. Easily exchanged tape cassettes enabled both performers and fans to circumvent official broadcast and recording outlets. As part of the "Bantustan" policies promoting culturally distinct "homelands," officially endorsed entrepreneurs and promoters established new entertainment venues to circumvent the tight restrictions of apartheid. Such lucrative Bantu "Las Vegases" as Sun City, though widely viewed as morally compromised, initially enjoyed success. Over time, fewer and fewer musicians were willing to go along with such schemes, so even Bophuthatswana's flashy Sun City began to fray around the edges.[154]

By the 1980s, the ANC had launched an energetic cultural counteroffensive as part of a broader diplomatic initiative to rally international support for the anti-apartheid cause. The ANC's Department of Arts and Culture produced a high-visibility cultural ensemble—the Amandla! Company—which developed increasingly sophisticated music and drama programs to go on tour around the world. Under the direction of the former Jazz Epistle member Gwangwa, the ANC recruited highly skilled professionals to train aspiring musicians and actors to create an international-quality stage show. Gwangwa—who had circulated within Masekela and Makeba's community of United States–based South African exiles—eventually would be nominated for two Academy Awards for his scoring of the 1987 film *Cry Freedom*. He successfully created important struggle-inspired stage productions in London, New York, and elsewhere.[155]

To Boycott or Not

The ANC's increasing reliance on culture as a weapon against apartheid consisted of several components. As just mentioned, the ANC developed an anti-apartheid road show to captivate audiences abroad. Another approach was to isolate South Africa from the rest of the world. Following the United Nations–supported boycott of South Africa, the ANC vigorously encouraged the outside world (including South Africans living in exile) to have nothing to do with any South African performer, sports person, or institution. This stance placed the ANC on a collision course with those abroad who believed that they were assisting the cause by supporting and engaging with individual South Africans, regardless of their race.

By the 1980s, the American pop singer Paul Simon found his career floundering after his breakup with his longtime singing partner, Art Garfunkel. Looking for a new project to follow the commercial failure of his *Hearts and Bones* album, Simon found his creativity reinspired after encountering the music of the Boyoyo Boys' "Gumboots," as well as Johnny Clegg, Sipho Mchunu, and their integrated pop band Juluka. Simon, ignoring or not fully cognizant of the boycott, flew to South Africa in search of musicians for his new recording. Eventually, he gathered an eclectic group of performers around him and began recording what would become the album *Graceland*. This venture would transform Simon's career, as well as those of many of the South African musicians who worked with him.

The project did not come together easily, however, and the resulting songs combined Western pop and a capella with South African *isicathamiya* and Mbaqanga. The content of the lyrics often had very little to do with South Africa itself. The reference in the album's title is to the Memphis home of the deceased US rock icon Elvis Presley, and many of the lyrics contain more allusions to Manhattan's Upper West Side than to the West Cape. The immediate response on the part of those associated with the anti-apartheid fight was intense anger over Simon's disregard of the boycott.[156]

Joseph Shabalala's Ladysmith Black Mambazo had also caught Simon's ears. Shabalala was reinventing Zulu vocal traditions and *isicathamiya* by expanding upon the textual experimentation of other groups and bending them in new directions. He was also able to utilize technological advances in recordings to capture fresh qualities of live performances.[157] The amalgamation of Simon, Shabalala, and the other South African musicians on the album was immediate and explosive.

The impact of *Graceland* on music around the world cannot be overestimated. Few outside South Africa had ever heard anything quite like Ladysmith Black Mambazo before Simon's November 22, 1986, performance on the popular US late night television show *Saturday Night Live*. The audience was the first of many to be stunned by their grace and beauty. The recording eventually won the 1987 Grammy Award for Album of the Year, and its title track won the 1988 Grammy for Record of the Year (figure 38).

Simon then brought together the original South African *Graceland* musicians with Masekela, Makeba, and other exiles for a highly successful world tour that began with a raucous outdoor concert in Harare.[158] Simon shared credit with his African colleagues, paid them well, and opened up the possibility of international stardom not only for Ladysmith Black Mambazo but also for other South African groups. Their success brought new attention to bear on the harshly repressive South African apartheid regime and the bitter struggle against it. Nonetheless, many in the anti-apartheid movement—beginning with the ANC and the United Nations Special Committee Against Apartheid—stridently condemned Simon for having broken the cultural boycott.[159]

Figure 38. Artifacts from Paul Simon's *Graceland* album at the Rock and Roll Hall of Fame in Cleveland.
Source: Photograph by Sam Howzit (https://commons.wikimedia.org/wiki/
*File:Graceland_-_Rock_and_Roll_Hall_of_Fame_%282014-12-30_12.52.16_*
by_Sam_Howzit%29.jpg).

The participation of Masekela and Makeba in the world tour greatly enhanced Simon's legitimacy and added considerably to the tour's success. Two decades later, Masekela recalled the agonizing controversies that swirled around every stop. "The English anti-apartheid movement," he recalled in his memoirs, "had even gone to the extent of banning South African artists from performing in the United Kingdom with the hope of extending it to the rest of the world. This I found absolutely absurd. The international media jumped into the fray and began to editorialize vehemently against *Graceland*. Many press conferences took place and interviews, where we had very unpleasant exchanges with journalists. I had no doubt that our shows helped to raise the awareness of millions of people who had never heard of apartheid."[160]

Masekela goes on to observe laconically that Simon would again perform in South Africa within a few years, after the end of apartheid, and would appear at receptions hosted by President Nelson Mandela. *Graceland*'s success catapulted Ladysmith Black Mambazo to international stardom and cleared the way for the long New York run of the township-based musical *Sarafina*, which had previously enjoyed success at Johannesburg's Market Theater.[161] Yet the bitter controversy over Simon's album and the tour still stings for many, despite all that has transpired since. Its acrid legacy is but one small reminder of the powerful emotions surrounding South African music as the struggle against apartheid was reaching its zenith.

City Prophets

The *Graceland* story highlights the extent to which South African and American music continued to be in an inventively tempestuous relationship with one another even as the country became ever more isolated from the rest of the world. The significance of *Graceland* within South Africa would be quickly eclipsed by an even more compelling musical force emanating from New York City: hip-hop. While on its way to becoming the most commercially successful popular music genre in history, hip-hop made its way to Cape Town with extraordinary speed. The first sounds of American rap and the first moves of American break dancing were being heard and seen on the Cape Flats within a handful of months following the genre's foundational moment at DJ Kool Herc's legendary August 11, 1973, back-to-school party at 1520 Sedgwick Avenue in the working-class, immigrant Morris Heights section of New York City's borough of the Bronx (for more on this event, see the "Overture" above).[162]

Hip-hop found fertile ground in an apartheid Cape Town where the sounds of electrified working-class music making already gave expression to the anger and frustrations of young people marginalized by race, poverty, and predatory police. Mbaqanga—a potent blend of Zulu "traditional" music, Afropop, and wired instrumentation—gained fans throughout South Africa's most disaffected townships beginning in the late 1960s. A typical Mbaqanga group presented a choreographed female front line singing in close harmony opposite a bass solo voice, backed up by a garage band of guitar, bass, drums, and keyboards.[163] Although not overly political lyrically, Mbaqanga challenged the regime through a modern, ur-ban, and "black" aesthetic. Its practitioners faced repression, were banned from studios, and suffered from censorship before emerg-ing as one of South Africa's signature sounds following apart-heid.[164] Hip-hop and rap shared the same ethos while giving voice in the form of poetry to anger directed against the political system.

Like jazz and *marabi*, hip-hop is more than music. The genre encompasses an entire way of being in the world. More generally, hip-hop is thought to embrace four components: emceeing/rap-ping, disc-jockeying, graffiti artistry, and break dancing. Many so-cially concerned observers add "knowledge of self" as a fifth com-ponent, by which they mean "a critical consciousness about black history and the roots of racial oppression and exclusion."[165] This last element of engagement with black history, racial oppression, and exclusion can elevate hip-hop at its most socially penetrating beyond expressions of rage, lust, and power.[166] As Ncedisa Nkony-eni suggests in her oral history of Cape Town hip-hop, though "dif-ficult to pin down, 'knowledge of self' is an ideology that advocates the pursuit of spiritual and intellectual upliftment" that provides the conceptual canvas for the other elements.[167]

Hip-hop culture immediately appealed to youth in neighbor-hoods such as its birthplace in the Bronx that were plagued by pov-erty, crime, discrimination, addiction, and violence. Young men liv-ing in the Cape Flats connected with the new music and the urban culture emanating from the streets of what many considered to be the most degraded neighborhood in the United States. For Capeto-nians—both "black" and "coloured"—the new music represented nation-consciousness and self-empowerment under a regime that wanted to deny both.[168] Ready D, one of the founders of the seminal Cape Town crew Prophets of da City (POC), has repeatedly told the story of first hearing N@!*ers With Attitudes' "F#%K tha Police" in the late 1980s and immediately identifying "with that because we were going through the same things these guys were talking about."[169]

Hip-hop and, earlier, rap performers drew their power by fash-ioning an art, as the critic Adam Bradley writes, that "draws on idioms of the Africa diaspora, the musical legacy of jazz, blues and

funk, and the creative capacities conditioned by the often harsh realities of people's everyday surroundings. . . . Rap gave voice to a
group hardly heard before by Americans at large, certainly never
heard in their own often profane, always assertive words."[170] In doing so, he argues, rap returned poetry to the public space. It did so
by linking poetry to rhythm, rather than melody.[171] This connection came naturally to Southern African cultures, in which so much
music of accomplishment relied on the blending of verbal dexterity
with rhythmic complexity and group vocalization to seek a competitive edge.

Hip-hop, for course, has become a universal cultural language
and means of expression tied to defiance of authority and social
norms. Far from Morris Heights and Langa, Ukrainian hip-hop
provided the soundtrack for Kyiv's 2004 Orange Revolution.[172]
As the Ukrainian experience—among many possible examples—
demonstrates, part of hip-hop's power is its ability to simultaneously remain universal in form and local in content. As the South
African urban observer Edgar Pieterse underscores, "Throughout
the various subgenres of hip-hop music, the explication of locality
and especially community (i.e., "homeboys") is a constant reference, along with identification of who is the emcee and the 'crew'
adjoining him or her on a particular track and where they came
from."[173] This adaptive quality means that Cape Town's hip-hop is
distinct and homegrown, despite the constantly expanding commercialized, global hip-hop scene. Moreover, Cape Town's hip-hop
remains distinct from other South African scenes in Johannesburg,
Durban, and other cities.[174]

The most influential Cape Flats hip-hop crew, Prophets of Da
City, came together in 1988 when its founders, Shaheen Ariefdien
and DJ Ready D, began experimenting with cutting eight-track
tapes in a small, out-of-the-way studio. POC—whose primary
members have included Ishmael Morabe, Mark Heuvel, Shaheen
Ariefdien, Ramone, and DJ Ready D—captured the realities of a
world at war with authority in which disenfranchised young men
of different backgrounds were finding themselves. Their first re-
leases, including "Dala Flat" (Do It Thoroughly), were recorded
in Cape Afrikaans dialect and drew heavily on Mbaqanga, paying
particular homage to the Cape Town sound of Abdullah Ibrahim.[175]

From the very outset, POC, like so many Capetonian musicians in so many different genres, was about defining place and presence within a general framework coming from the United States.

Ready D's family had moved to Mitchell's Plain in 1980 as part of the apartheid-forced relocations. Like a number of local hip-hop performers, he had been largely apolitical until the music coming from the United States raised his consciousness about the oppression of dark-skinned peoples. Like so many nonwhite youths of his era, he joined boycotts, took part in increasingly violent confrontations with the police, and became committed to overthrowing the white regime. Poetry and hip-hop gave him the tools he needed to move beyond anarchic rebellion.[176]

Ready D and POC would branch out over time. They gained fame and commercial success as apartheid fell, eventually performing at the presidential inauguration ceremonies for Nelson Mandela. As hip-hop continued to develop, they spun off Brasse Vannie Kaap (BVK) ("Dudes from the Cape"), a group formed in the 1990s that rapped in Gamtaal, a Cape Flats Afrikaans dialect.[177] Dozens, if not more, of other crews emerged, often recording on POC's label, Ghetto Ruff. The bands use Afrikaans-based Gamtaal as well as nonstandard English, Xhosa, and Zulu dialects.[178] Some—such as Black Noise and Jitsvinger—are oriented toward general social commentary, while others are more overtly militant, such as POX.[179]

Hip-hop continued to evolve after the end of apartheid. Johannesburg groups such as Boom Shaka, which featured *kawaito*-style vocalists in which lyrics are rapped against a more melodic backdrop—drew hip-hop back toward its earlier, indigenous musical roots.[180] Other performers oriented themselves more squarely within global hip-hop as post-apartheid South Africa became more integrated into larger international fashions.[181]

Post-apartheid trends encouraged a second wave of Cape Town hip-hop, which incorporated female emcees. The new music sought to educate youth about social issues and to address painful concerns of the day, such as the voracious AIDS/HIV epidemic that was attacking South Africa. These young Cape Town performers employed their music to engage their audiences in deliberations about gangsterism, violence against women, globalization, social injustice, and political oppression.[182] Cape rappers generally eschewed commercialization to retain a core focus on resisting state oppression in all its apartheid and post-apartheid forms. More than many places around the world, Cape Town hip-hop has remained distinctive because of its commitment to sedition.

Tumultuous Transitions

Sedition had far more serious consequences in the post-Soweto South Africa of the 1970s than it has today; it could cost one's life. As the 1970s became the 1980s, with no end in sight to civil unrest, the underpinnings of the apartheid regime shook ever more noticeably. The international boycott increasingly isolated the country, turning South Africa into a pariah state. Inescapable demographic, political, and geostrategic realities revealed the unsustainability of a white state on an African continent of independent black states; the economy was stagnating, and, by the mid-1980s, increasing opportunities for superpower rapprochement had all but eliminated the strategic value of the South African regime to the United States. Most plainly, the regime's policies of complete segregation and the development of separate "homelands" was proving completely unworkable in a South Africa where "blacks," "whites," and "coloureds" depended on one another for their livelihoods. Malan's and Verwoerd's experiment had been tried and undeniably had failed. All but the most recalcitrant Afrikaner nationalist understood the most pressing challenge for the regime was finding a way out.[183]

Those whites looking for a negotiating partner were drawn to the ANC, as the largest and most effectively organized among all the banned African political organizations. By the mid-1980s, leading white business executives, intellectuals, clergy, and sports administrators were meeting with senior ANC officials such as Oliver Tambo and Thabo Mbeki in places like Zambia, Dakar, and New York. Radical right-wing Afrikanner groups, such as the Afrikaner Weerstand Beweging (Afrikaner Resistance Movement), sensed the impending collapse and demanded their own white state separate from the rest of the republic.[184]

P. W. Botha, who had been either prime minister or president for nearly two decades, began to lose his trademark drive and, after suffering a stroke in January 1989, stepped down from power and was replaced by longtime National Party operative Frederik Willem de Klerk. Upon reviewing the state of South African affairs, de Klerk soon concluded that the survival of the country and of Afrikaans culture and society depended on successful negotiations leading to majority rule. Within a year of taking power, on February 2, 1990, he lifted the ban on the ANC, the Pan-Africanist Congress, and the South African Communist Party. Nine days later, he unconditionally released Nelson Mandela, who had been in prison for twenty-seven years. The post-apartheid transition had begun.[185]

The regime had been negotiating with Mandela for some time. Those talks only became more complex once Mandela had been freed. Other players on the South African political scene, including the Zulu nationalist Buthelezi, had entered into the fray, trying to expand their own power and authority. A period of brutal, often violent political struggle erupted across the country—eventuating in the convening of the Convention for a Democratic South Africa, which was charged with writing a new Constitution. The country was descending into open civil war. No particular outcome appeared clear when Mandela and de Klerk signed the Record of Understanding, which led to legislative elections in April 1994 under the terms of the Interim Constitution.[186] The new South African Constitution—222 pages long, with an elaborate Bill of Rights—eventually gained ratification in 1996.

No one knew what to expect of the first post-apartheid elections, which were to be held in April 1994. Various disturbing rumors flew until the very last preelection days that one group or another would refuse to participate, thereby touching off the total collapse of civil authority. In the end, the elections were a model of open democracy, with long lines of new voters patiently waiting to cast their votes. The ANC captured just under two-thirds of the votes and 252 seats in the National Assembly, with the National Party coming in second with a fifth of the votes and 82 seats. Nelson Mandela was elected president.[187] A new South Africa was born.

Post-apartheid South Africa has remained under the ANC's control. The society has been plagued by extreme levels of violence, crime, and corruption, an HIV/AIDS epidemic that has ravaged families and communities, extremely high unemployment rates, an at-times-sluggish economy, and some of the highest levels of income inequality in the world. Nonetheless, there has been much to inspire, such as the magisterial performance of Mandela as president and moral authority. One of the most successful—though extraordinarily painful—postauthoritarian lustration processes was carried out under the auspices of the country's Truth and Reconciliation Commission. Perhaps most tellingly, the Constitution has held, even through the multiple transitions of presidential power, from Mandela to Thabo Mbeli in 1999, to Kgalema Motlanthe in 2008, and to Jacob Zuma in 2009.[188]

Post-apartheid times have proven to be as traumatic and uncertain for Capetonians of all races as they have been for all South Africans. Explosions of violence throughout the city became more pronounced as the old regime began to waiver. In the case of Cape Town, trade union activists played an especially pronounced role in events, demanding worker rights. Both white and African extremist groups—such as the Azanian People's Liberation Army—attacked multiracial congregations and other groups within the city.[189] Capetonians seldom felt sufficiently secure to gather publicly to listen to music, though music continued to be produced in new forms, including the fast-growing hip-hop scene.[190]

At the most local level, opposition parties—including the New Nationalist Party and the Democratic Alliance—have defeated the ANC within Cape Town and the Western Cape more generally, much to the consternation of South African political elites elsewhere in the country. The local electorate's rejection of the national political mainstream has led many South Africans to see a dormant—and not always passive—racism lying just underneath the surface of everyday life in this predominantly "coloured," mestizo city.[191]

Capetonians were looking elsewhere—often much closer to home—as they set out to try to reclaim their pre-apartheid history and identity. Many intuitively understood that they could only do so by appreciating their city's historically mixed culture and identity.[192] Activists—including the intrepid community activist and former jazz musician Vincent Kolbe and others—launched the Western Cape Oral History Project as early as 1984. Now renamed the Centre for Popular Memory, based at the University of Cape Town, this initiative has been instrumental in continuing the city's historic embrace of diversity by consistently empowering those who otherwise would not have able to speak.[193]

Beginning as early as the 1970s, former District Sixers opposed grand visions to redevelop the abandoned area, which included shopping centers, luxury housing, and educational institutions to be built by such international interlopers as Shell Oil. Their various organizations consistently kept alive a vision of a multicultural Cape Town that stood as an affront to those in power.[194] By recording what had been before, seeking out those who had been aggrieved by the resettlements, and opposing new projects that would have obliterated the previous landscape, these activists preserved the memory of a Cape Town where diversity was possible. By doing so, they created space for repossession of the past by the dispossessed. The 1989 establishment of the District Six Museum Foundation, leading to the 1994 opening of the museum itself in the former Central Methodist Mission on Buttenkant Street, marked moments when anguished remembering was transformed into fragile healing.[195]

The traumas, deaths, violence, folly, and wounds to the human psyche unleashed in apartheid's wake only intensified the need to find meaning through cultural expression. As the London-based Shakespearian director Antony Sher explained when bringing a production of Shakespeare's *Titus Andronicus* back to his native South Africa in 1994, "Whereas the scene can be absurd and revolting elsewhere, doing the play here in South Africa, a society which has suffered decades of atrocious violence, a strange reversal occurs. The acts of brutality, instead of being gratuitous or extreme, seem only too familiar, and the focus turns instead on to how the characters deal with that violence and the impact of grief."[196] The Roman General Titus, as channeled through the Elizabethan playwright, had much in common, it would seem, with Capetonian DJ Ready D.

A "World City's" Musical Rebirth

When, on the evening of February 11, 1990, the newly liberated Nelson Mandela stepped onto the balcony of Cape Town's City

Hall to address a throng of fifty-thousand jubilant supporters, South Africa and Cape Town changed forever.[197] Beyond the political transformations that lay ahead, Cape Town was about to enter a world where cities were being tossed into a global competition for investments, resources, and advantage. It became a "world city" dominated by a burgeoning service sector.[198] A neoliberal economic paradigm known as the "Washington Consensus" dictated that cities would sink or swim on their own, unprotected by national social and economic policies, in a worldwide competition with one another.[199] Little during the apartheid period had prepared Capetonians for this rapacious world of late-twentieth-century and early-twenty-first-century global urban capitalism.

Contemporary Cape Town has become a sprawling metropolitan region containing nearly 4 million people, around half of whom would have been classified as "coloured" during apartheid, with nearly one-third of the region's population being "black." Whites and a small Asian population make up the balance of metropolitan residents. About half of Capetonians speak English at home, whereas more than 40 percent speak Afrikaans. IsiXhosa occupies a distant third place. Unemployment remains stubbornly high, at 28 percent overall, though the rate climbs to more than 50 percent in some poor black neighborhoods.[200] Somewhere around a third of the population lives below the poverty line. With HIV/AIDS ravaging its "townships," Cape Town had one of the world's highest rates of tuberculosis at the turn of the twenty-first century. The threat of TB is amplified by poor housing and the city's chronic cold and damp winters. Tens of thousands lack access to water, electricity, and reliable public transportation, even though public service provision might be better than elsewhere in the country.[201]

Today's Cape Town is a much larger, more complex and diverse, and perhaps more socially unjust city than some of its previous iterations. Administratively, it is larger, because the post-apartheid settlement merged two dozen racially segregated municipalities and nearly seventy decisionmaking authorities into a single unit. Further negotiations followed this 1996 arrangement, as some white suburban jurisdictions had preserved their way out of the new city. Eventually, in December 2000, a stronger "Unicity" came into being, unifying the metropolitan region for the first time.[202] Simultaneously, as elsewhere around the world, municipal services have been increasingly privatized, leading to marked inequality in their distribution.[203]

Some observers of contemporary Cape Town, such as the Canadian political economist David McDonald, find the local claim to a progressive post-apartheid reputation misplaced: "Underlying this inequity is a smug white liberalism that permeates all manner of activity in Cape Town—from the pedantic treatment of black store clerks, to a suburban sense of entitlement, to policies that keep the poor 'in their place.' Cape Town smacks of a privileged elite that feels it has little to apologize for, while at the same time suggesting it has all the answers for future development."[204]

Simultaneously, others see the possibility of a future that is more progressive than the city's past. As the actor Nkululeko Mabandla has put it, "Today Cape Town has blossomed into a much more welcoming city, becoming a melting pot of multicultural diversity. It is home to an ever-increasing number of languages and dialects. Immigration, as in Australia and the United States, also had a positive impact. Multiculturalism is everywhere."[205] From this perspective, the seeds of a more hopeful future can be found in Cape Town's embrace of diversity—albeit an uneasy one. Such trends are evident in various efforts to reinvigorate the local jazz scene.

Many prominent South African musicians in exile required time to overcome skepticism about the changes taking place at home. A number of prominent jazz musicians began returning to South Africa in the months immediately surrounding Mandela's release. Such decisions about whether and when to return were personal. Masekela took some time before he was willing to commit to the new South Africa. Others, including the drummer Louis Moholo, who had established careers abroad, chose to remain in exile. Members of the Manhattan Brothers, for example, decided to remain in Britain. Significantly, several prominent musicians—such as Ibrahim, Makeba, Gwangwa, and Semenya—enthusiastically returned to nurture a renewed music enterprise.[206]

Once back in South Africa, they found a growing number of venues, including prominent clubs, that had desegregated voluntarily (e.g., Kippie's in Johannesburg, Bassline in Melville, and

Rosie's and Mannenberg in Cape Town).[207] As everywhere, jazz often proved to be a difficult product to market to mainstream audiences. The pervasive atmosphere of violence that affected urban South Africa often shrank audiences. Yet, by the late 1990s, a national and even local Cape Town circuit of venues sympathetic to jazz had come into existence.

Jazz is an apprenticeship genre that requires a multiplicity of places where a knowledgeable audience can listen to and encourage a mix of younger and older musicians moving the music along.[208] In other words, it requires players and places for them to play. The microenvironment that had made the first explosion of Cape Town jazz recreated itself as the twentieth century turned into the twenty-first. Old masters, such as the returning Ibrahim and Ngozi, held forth, along with exciting new musicians, such as the pianist Moses Taiwa Molelekwa (who died in 2001), and the saxophoniost Zim Ngqawana (who died in 2011).[209] Very quickly, a growing roster of players—such as Khaya Mahlangu, Sidney Mnisi, Zim Ngqawana, Andile Yenana, Marcus Wyatt, Feya Faku, Herb Tsoedi, Fana Zulu, Lulu Gontsana, Louis Moholo, and many others—formed a vibrant community.

As with everywhere jazz is played these days, the community often divided between those who want to guard the boundaries around jazz—such as Ibrahim—and those who are open to more promiscuous borrowings from other kinds of popular music.[210] Coplan gets to the heart of the matter when he remarks that "what post-colonial South African performers are doing is what they have done since colonial times: searching out varying combinations of elements from indigenous, Euro–North American, other African, and New World African forms as a way of inserting local currents into global stylistic streams, multiplying the estuaries of contemporary cultural identity. Performances or works are African not because they display a preponderance of 'indigenous' elements, but because Africans have chosen to perform them."[211]

This creativity takes place within a city that is inserting itself into the global economy as a major tourist center. Consequently, the large number of venues where local musicians can play has been further enlarged by the presence of tourists. The local jazz scene thus is fundamentally different from that of the pre-apartheid era.

It exists in no small measure because of the presence of both South African and international tourists who are willing to spend their money to listen. This is also true for other musical genres in Cape Town, which are supported by the city's brisk tourist trade.

This blend of local, national, and international artistic and capitalist stimuli is captured by the highly successful Cape Town International Jazz Festival, which has flourished with the large-scale sponsorship of banks and, for a while, the prominent and highly commercial North Sea Festival in the Netherlands.[212] This festival has been held each April since 2000, and it has become widely regarded as one of the top half dozen international jazz festivals, with more than 30,000 spectators attending dozens of performances by both international stars and local up-and-coming artists. This combination of the global and local under the auspices of private sponsorship personifies precisely the sort of broad, neoliberal urban development explored by McDonald.

The success of the Cape Town jazz scene—and the local music community, more generally—has depended on its ability to leverage engagement with the global to create the space for the local. Globalization in Cape Town has often seemed hollow and dispiriting, in this city of stark economic and social inequity tied to race. In music, however, the city's deep local traditions have sustained a performance culture that remains significantly local even as it has become global.

A Cultural *Bredie*

For all their complexities, some changes have brought unquestionable joy and celebration to Capetonians. By 1990, the New Year's Carnival troupes had begun to reclaim pride of place in the city's annual calendar. The Malay choirs, Christmas carolers, and minstrel strutters, like so much of South African society, were reknitting their communities together by rebuilding their pasts. Early on, some in the new regime were as questioning of the Carnival's legitimacy as their predecessors in the old regime. What could one make of an event featuring blackfaced minstrels marching under an old racist label mimicking some of the most strident racial stereotypes? For the marchers, of course, the festival had a different meaning.

Nothing was more healing for communities that had been dispatched to distant townships than to once again march through the streets of Bo-Kaap and downtown Cape Town in a colorful display of pride and celebration of life.[213]

Any lingering controversy over the minstrelsy revelries was put to rest when, in 1996, President Nelson Mandela inaugurated the annual competitions among various groups. Today, the Kaapse Klopse (Minstrel Festival) on Tweede Nuwe Jaar (January 2) is widely embraced as a major civic festival and tourist attraction. For all the commercialization and official promotion, however, Kaapse Klopse remains principally about community. Some one hundred and fifty troupes of various sizes prepare about 10,000 individual outfits. They prepare their new routines and raise their own resources in a year-round quest that enriches their own lives and the lives of their neighbors both spiritually and materially.

The Carnival has reemerged as a moment of a communal embrace so often absent in the city's history. Most important, it raises spirits. "Despite the heat, spirits are high," the historian John Edwin Mason notes about his own participation in 2007. "Laughter abounds and silliness runs rampant."[214] As Mason, Mandela, and thousands of others have appreciated, this ridiculousness is the supreme silliness of a culture being reborn—a culture that could exist in no other time or place than in contemporary Cape Town.

The city's history, from the moment Jan van Riebeeck led his motley band of Dutch East India Company employees to shore, has been marked by all the crimes, injustices, and indignities that the human mind can conjure to commit against those who are somehow different. The human mind seems capable of offering up endless criteria for asserting differences, so the city's past and present have contained far more stories of villainy than decency. Even the tiniest of tears in the stunningly beautiful surface visions of Table Mountain and Table Bay tossed up by tourism promoters exposes human cruelty in all its multitudinous forms. This is a city where many—if not most—residents have always wanted to be living someplace other than where they actually reside.

Yet the incredibly rich history of Capetonian music reveals a different story, one of improbable beauty and inventiveness. From the moment when Jan van Riebeeck arrived on the shores of

Table Bay, the town has been home to an opulent multiplicity of humankind, each seeking solace and meaning in the creation and performance of song and dance (figure 39). The intermingling of indigenous African and imported European and Asian instruments; the two-century-long absorption, adaptation, and reinvention of American musical forms that continues until today; and the stunning integration of Islamic, Christian, and African vocal forms—all speak to an uncommon Capetonian capacity to create aural beauty.

These two storylines of the Beast and Beauty initially seem contradictory. As the playwright and novelist Damon Galgut explains in a loving essay about the contemporary city, "If there is an essential quality to Cape Town, it doesn't lie in either its beauty or its tackiness, but in the tension between the two. There is always a promise, and then a denial of that promise."[215] In other words, the distressing and promising are not at all contradictory.

Cape Town has become one of the most musically inventive places on the planet precisely because it has been one of the most dastardly innovators for thinking about how to divide humankind into rigid, allegedly immutable categories. Both inclinations emerge from the realities of having thousands and thousands of people who are different in every conceivable way live on top of one another in the intimate relationships of shared destinies. Music in Cape Town became a most human response to how individuals can assert their humanity and claim the dignity that is their due in a world of constant brutish assault.

Capetonians did not just create music. They fashioned a very special kind of music. Their sound defies easy categorization by merging different traditions together in fresh and new ways. The city's New Year's Carnival troupes visually remind spectators of Carnival revelers elsewhere, in such distant jubilees as the Philadelphia Mummers' Parade and New Orleans Mardi Gras. Yet they march to a different *ghoema* beat. Capetonian jazz legends engage the music emanating from faraway New York, only without the "blue note" that makes so much of American music distinctive. African labor migrants shunted off to the dispiriting, sprawling settlements of the Cape Flats adjust Xhosian and Zulu vocal traditions in a despairing search for solace. And Afrikaans-

Figure 39. Xhosa women musicians in traditional costumes performing on the Cape Town waterfront in 2008.
Source: Photograph by Chell Hill; used by permission (https://commons.wikime-dia.org/wiki/File:2008-02-09_Xhosa_women.jpg).

speaking hip-hop artists embrace the sounds of the Bronx by changing languages and expressing local outrage.

There is more at work than rage. Speaking about the South African jazz scene today, the vocalist Melanie Scholtz notes something of perhaps even greater power: "There is something happening here—it's a very special feeling and sense of camaraderie. We young musicians see each other as like brothers and sisters getting together, sometimes uncles and aunts or fathers, even. It's really a blessing."

The musicians of Cape Town—whether fathers or mothers, brothers or sisters, uncles or aunts, or even foreign cousins—have created a distinctive Cape Town sound, one that is a celebration of syncretistic, sweeping diversity. They have done so and still do so today, despite the fact that Cape Town has always been overflowing with mean-spirited bigots who villainously deny the humanity of people they do not like. To paraphrase Jeremy Cronin, Cape Town's musical subconscious has always understood that we are all the bearers of the same mixed-up cultural *bredie* (stew).[216]

Urals Pathfinder:
Theater in Post-Soviet Yekaterinburg

If you don't close your eyes from time to time, you can see these miracles.

> — Agata Kristi Rock Band, from "Oni Letaiat,"
> on the album *Chudesa Miracles*, 1998

The mood in London the third week of March 2002 was sour.[1] Tony Blair was plowing ahead to join his friend George W. Bush in a seemingly unstoppable drive to invade Iraq. The Middle East was already in flames, as the Israelis besieged Palestinian leader Yasser Arafat's Ramallah compound. The World Meteorological Organization had released yet another, more strident, report warning against the dire consequences of global warming. The newspapers and television news shows had little to offer that could bring joy into anyone's life. But at least the first signs of spring were taking hold, as rains early in the week gave away to clear skies and temperatures climbed into the upper 50s (when measured by the scale conceived by the good physicist Daniel Gabriel Fahrenheit).

As the city gradually felt the warmth of spring, at the edgy Royal Court Theatre on its tony Sloane Square, Vasili Sigarev, a twenty-five-year-old Russian playwright from beyond the Urals, was offering the premiere of his play with a strange-sounding title — *Plasticine* — which was said to hold the promise of a new era in Russian dramaturgy. And Sigarev, despite the hubbub surrounding his arrival in London, was but one among many young provincial playwrights who were shaking up Russian theater.[2] Together with dozens more authors who had come of age as the Soviet Union collapsed, Sigarev was seeking a voice for his country's post-Soviet confusion, violence, frustration, anger, and carnivalesque debasement. Simultaneously, he and his colleagues had embraced more eternal Russian beliefs in the salvation to be found in the impact of theater as a sacral rite, in the potency of redemption, and in the transcendental power of the human soul.[3] Thus, the play *Plasticine* by Sigarev premiering that night at the Royal Court tried to square the circle between spiritual degradation and salvation.

Plasticine was not totally untried by the time it opened at the Royal Court. It had debuted in 2000, had won Sigarev the ironically revered Russian "Anti-Booker" Prize, and had already been performed at Moscow's prestigious Playwright and Director Center under the inspired direction of Kirill Serebrennikov.[4] The Royal Court, in turn, had committed itself to stage a full-fledged production of the play after hosting a successful reading of its English translation a year earlier.[5]

In writing his play, Sigarev drew on his own life to set forth a shocking tale of violence, drunkenness, hypocrisy, humiliation, rape, sadistic sexual relations, aggression, and vengeance. The play's title is derived from the material with which the hero "first molds his double, then a phallus of shocking size, and then the cast for a kuckleduster which he uses to avenge his aggressors."[6] The plot of the play is basically a coming-of-age tale in which its adolescent central characters, Maksim and Luopkha, are continually formed, un-formed, and re-formed through their muddled efforts to come to terms with violent sexual abuse and confused sexual identity.

Sigarev was a native of Verkhnaia Salda, a small city of about 50,000 souls 120 miles or so north of the Urals city of Yekaterinburg. He had left home to study at the Nizhny Tagil Pedagogical Institute, before seeking out the master dramatist Nikolai Kolyada at the innovative Yekaterinburg Theatre Institute (figure 40).[7] The city's cutting-edge cultural scene enveloped the small-town youth, who arrived just as the restrictions of Soviet life were crumbling before an onslaught led, in part, by Yekaterinburg's mercurial illustrious native son, Boris Yeltsin. Yeltsin, Kolyada, and their local protégés enthusiastically embraced the advice of the American poet Walt Whitman, to "unscrew the locks from the doors; unscrew the doors themselves from their jams!"[8] Kolyada—together with other talented local playwrights, such as Sigarev, Oleg Bogayev, and the Presnyakov brothers—was busy preparing the ground for a revolution on the Russian stage. This playwrights' revolt, which would become known as the New Russian Drama Movement, would prove to be as profound in theater as that unleashed in politics by their Urals brethren led by Yeltsin.

Figure 40. The playwright Nikolai Kolyada.
Source: Photograph by Philip Arnoult; used by permission.

London's Royal Court Theatre was an appropriate setting for bringing the New Russian Drama Movement to this arguably most important theatrical city in the world.[9] The building itself dates from 1888, having been constructed on the site of the earlier New Chelsea Theater, which itself had opened in the converted Ranelagh Chapel eighteen years before. The sort of brick-and-stone confection typical of the era, the Royal Court Theatre attained a lagniappe of elegance thanks to its Italianate style and hierarchical arrangements of stalls, dress circle, amphitheater, and gallery seating an audience of 841. The theater became known for staging some of the most innovative plays of the late nineteenth and early twentieth centuries, including several by George Bernard Shaw as well as a number of frolicking Gilbert and Sullivan musicals. But the Great Depression of the 1930s undercut its audience, so the owners switched to showing films until the roof collapsed under German bombs during World War II.

The theater architect Robert Cromie renovated the Royal Court in 1952 for a smaller audience of 500, which, after 1956, proved to be the perfect size for George Devine's English Stage Company. Devine and his actors made the Royal Court London's premier "writer's theater." Beginning in the late 1950s—and continuing until today—the very best of contemporary writers and works have found their way to British audiences at the Royal Court, with premieres of influential plays by the likes of Christopher Hampton, Athol Fugard, Howard Brenton, Caryl Churchill, Hanif Kureishi, Sarah Daniels, Timberlake Wettenbaker, Martin Crimp, Sarah Kane, Mark Ravenhill, Martin McDonagh, Simon Stephens, Leo Butler, and Edward Bond. They were joined by works from such established writers as Isaac Babel, Bertolt Brecht, Eugène Ionesco, Samuel Beckett, Jean-Paul Sarte, and Marguerite Duras, thereby cementing the Royal Court's reputation as perhaps the single most important English-language theater in the world. In addition, the legendary *Rocky Horror Show* opened in the Royal Court's small sixty-three-seat studio Theatre Upstairs in 1973. As a result, Sigarev and his play were sure to be noticed simply by virtue of the fact that they were debuting on the boards of the Royal Court.

The initial critical reaction to *Plasticine* was confused. Michael Billington of *The Guardian* was not impressed. "But the real problem," Billington wrote, "is that [the] play never analyses the source of [the main character] Maksim's alienation and at only two moments rises above a generalized portrait of urban squalor. One is when Luopkha's mother bribes a teacher with a swimming-pool pass; the other is when Maksim's gran urges the boy to buy some cheap beef reduced in price for Election Day. Suddenly you get a glimpse of the endemic corruption that has survived the collapse of the Soviet system."[10]

The Independent's Paul Taylor was more taken with what he saw as Sigarev's "bracingly clear-eyed tragicomic vision of a world where a woman would think of the local elections principally as the opportunity to grab some of the cut-prime meat the politicians offer as bribes." "Sigarev," he continues, "sees the chaos of contemporary Russia steadily, and he sees it whole. He's an exciting talent, and I look forward keenly to encountering more of his work."[11] Other critics agreed. The Evening Standard named Sigarev the "Most Promising Playwright of 2002."[12] In presenting the award to Sigarev, Tom Stoppard voiced his opinion that "if Dostoevsky were writing in the 21st century, no doubt he would have written Plasticine."[13] Billington, Taylor, and dozens of other critics would have plenty of opportunities to write about Plasticine in the years ahead, because the play—together with other Sigarev works—would be performed regularly on stages around the world.

Plasticine and other plays emerging from the New Russian Drama Movement grew out of many roots from across the enormous length of the newly formed Russian Federation. Sigarev's Yekaterinburg proved to be one particularly powerful environment for nurturing and disseminating new cultural forms that reflected the disorientation of a society in crisis. But the city's status as a hub of creativity looks much more plausible in retrospect than it did at the time. In the early post-Soviet years, for all too many observers, Yekaterinburg seemed destined for the postindustrial historical dustbin, along with the likes of Manchester and Detroit.

The Gateway to Russian Asia

Yekaterinburg, which would become Russia's fourth-largest city at the beginning of the twenty-first century, was established in 1723, late in the reign of Peter I ("the Great"), just on the Asian side of the Ural Mountains, somewhat more than 900 miles east of Moscow. The city was named after Saint Catherine, to honor Tsar Peter's wife, Ekaterina. It drew settlers from across the Russian Empire, growing slowly and achieving the status of a town only in 1796.[14] It eventually emerged as a major mining and manufacturing center, prospering from the exploitation of the rich mineral deposits throughout the Urals region, and enriching great industrial dynasties in the process.[15] The arrival of the Trans-Siberian Railroad in the late nineteenth century further secured Yekaterinburg's status as one of Russia's most important industrial centers.[16]

The city, in fact, was unusual for Imperial Russia in that it was an industrial headquarters city rather than an administrative center (Perm, where Serge Diaghilev grew up, served as the area's provincial capital for much of the period).[17] As Urals Federal University professors Sergei Kropotov and Maria Litovskaya have argued, the city's "uniqueness" lies in the fact that "it was one of the first specifically created industrial cities in the world."[18] Yekaterinburg quickly attracted a diverse population of workers and specialists—including a significant Jewish population at a time when the empire's Jews were largely prohibited from moving beyond the Pale of Settlement in the lands annexed following the final partition of Poland in the late eighteenth century.[19]

Local mine and factory owners were less concerned with the details of such imperial policies than they were with using engineering knowledge to make their businesses profitable. As the political analyst Leon Aron has noted, Yekaterinburg's "industrialists and merchants became well known for their wealth, curiosity, and civic-mindedness. They were indefatigable travelers, collectors of nature's curiosities, and connoisseurs of the arts. They founded museums, theaters, and libraries."[20] Consequently, they employed people who could do the job, no matter how much they were discriminated against elsewhere. Jews, following the extension of the military draft to men who were not Orthodox Christians in 1827, and others came to the region to serve their twenty-five-year compulsory military service and frequently never returned home.[21] Many political exiles and released prisoners similarly sought out the region's cities after having served their Siberian sentences. The city was a place where smart outsiders could thrive. Even today, local residents often claim that they judge someone only by how hard he or she works.

Yekaterinburg became the sort of melting pot of empire that promotes unrefined interethnic, interconfessional, interprofessional, and interclass propinquity. The city long has been a place where diversity has been converted into an asset. On one hand, numerous arrivals to the Urals region maintained their religious institutions and schools. According to the 1897 census, for example, between 85 and 97 percent of Jews in the four Urals provinces (*guberniia*) spoke Yiddish at home. On the other hand, residents from various backgrounds wore Russian clothes and worked alongside people different from themselves in jobs ranging from the most menial to the professions.[22]

This pattern was true for many religious and national groups, promoting a sort of rough-and-ready tolerance and mixing of cultures. As a result, some of the worst pathologies of Imperial Russian ethnic relations largely bypassed the city and region. For example, the only pogroms to take place in the city before 1917 were those provoked by police agents of the Ministry of Internal Affairs on orders from their Saint Petersburg superiors in October 1905. Attacks throughout the entire Urals region remained remarkably tame by Russian standards; only four Jews were killed in Ufa, and one Jew and one Russian perished in Yekaterinburg at the time. Only slightly higher death tolls occurred in Vyatka and Chelyabinsk.[23] Without question, local Black Hundreds, Bundist socialists, revolutionary socialists, Zionists, and Islamic Revivalists were all active in the years leading up to the outbreak of World War I; yet they never gained the traction of their brethren in other regions around the empire.[24]

Many factors promoted a frontier-like sensibility of live and let live, among them being the fact that Yekaterinburg was not as large as it was economically important. People, no matter how different, were never complete strangers to one another. Moreover, the city's intellectual achievements—though often considerable—were of a practical rather than ideological bent. Saint Petersburg, by contrast, has arguably spawned or imported every major Russian ideological movement for the past three hundred years, from Peter the Great's imperial, absolutist modernization idea to today's postmodernist hypernationalism. In Yekaterinburg, the best and brightest throughout the Urals region focused their attention on how to get things done.[25] Intellectual, ideological, political, artistic, and even architectural fashions arrived somewhat later there than in the cosmopolitan artistic centers of European Russia; and when they arrived, they often became more grounded in the realities of everyday life.[26]

Yekaterinburg nonetheless was constantly at the center of many events that shaped Russia's destiny. The city was the focal point of intense fighting during the Russian Civil War, and after the Bolshevik Revolution, the basement of one of the city's merchant houses—Ipatiev House—became the scene of the bloody execution of Russia's royal family—Tsar Nicholas, his wife Alexandra, his four daughters, and his son and trusted aides—on July 17, 1918.[27] A half dozen years later, in 1924, the city was renamed for Yakov Sverdlov, the Bolshevik who gave the final order for their execution.[28] This moniker would remain until the collapse of the Soviet Union in 1991 (though the surrounding province, or oblast, has retained the Sverdlovsk name).

During the Soviet period, Stalin's Great Leap Forward, beginning with the inauguration of the First Five-Year Plan in 1928, stimulated further growth.[29] The city became home to numerous heavy industrial plants, including the largest machinery plant in a "European economy," the giant Uralmash works.[30] The city exploded, with tens of thousands of new residents streaming in to fill the factories that were springing up all around.[31] Moreover, Uralmash, which opened on July 15, 1933, was not just a factory.[32] The project also included a gigantic new "socialist city" (*sotsgorod*) for more than 100,000 workers and their families that had been built according to the principles of "disurbanization," which called for massive decentralized housing—with commercial blocks covering between 6 and 10 hectares, on which housing surrounded by tree-lined allées opened onto green areas, with sports, education, and cultural facilities carefully spaced and mixed together with stores and worker kitchens (*fabrika-kukhnia*).[33]

In many ways, the new industrial city became Sverdlovsk, while the city's historic center evolved into an appendage (one that would eventually be connected to the industrial city by a single subway line that opened in the 1990s). This distinction between the older and newer cities underscored a central cleavage within Soviet society—between the industrial proletariat and the urban intelligentsia. For the intelligentsia, the Uralmash neighborhood and its residents were only "semicivilized."

The new socialist city that grew up around Uralmash is but part of the story of the city's Stalinist reinvention.[34] The entire town was being rebuilt, as German, Polish, and Moscow architects, representing the latest avant-garde styles, designed one of the most impressive concentrations of modernist Constructivist and Bauhausian buildings—about 140 structures—to be found anywhere.[35] Major cultural institutions sprang up, and were housed, at times, in buildings of the latest Constructivist style.[36] Although the local opera house had opened in 1912 and featured opera and ballet companies dating back many decades, the city's musical comedy theater was only founded years later, in 1932—as were its puppet theater, also founded in 1932; the local conservatory, in 1934; various literary museums, throughout the 1920s and 1930s; and its renowned folk chorus, in 1943.[37] Consequently, the city's growth as a vibrant cultural center paralleled its rise as an industrial giant. Beyond the performing arts, these institutions encouraged local youth to embrace cultural pursuits through their connections to the city's and region's vast factories and industrial enterprises that had grown up at the same time.[38]

Sverdlovsk escaped German occupation during World War II, becoming a major evacuation destination for important factories and educational and cultural institutions from cities further west, including Moscow and Leningrad. Today's modern and efficient international airport at Kol'tsovo initially served as a landing strip for Lend-Lease flights from the United States, beginning in December 1943.[39] All sorts of other facilities—together with their operating specialists—remained after the war, creating a powerful urban center dominating a vast region astride the Soviet Union's geographic center.[40] They were joined by exiled notables—including the World War II hero Marshal Konstantin Zhukov—together with engineers and mathematicians, artists and lawyers, and writers and musicians who had fallen prey to Stalin's last purges against Jewish "cosmopolitans" and other undesirables.[41] Several of contem-

Figure 41. A view of modern Yekaterinburg, with the Rastoguyev–Kharitonov Palace in the foreground.
Source: Photograph by Mntpoxnha Mapnha; used by permission.

porary Yekaterinburg's cultural luminaries—such as the popular poet-playwright-actor Vladimir Balashov—trace their familial connections to the city during this era.[42] Others—such as the local literary lion Valentin Lukyanin—arrived somewhat later to study and work in local industry.[43]

The postwar city had grown to become home to slightly more than 1 million people (figure 41). Cold War Sverdlovsk was a focal point for Soviet military industrial production, which drew on both the city's many factories and its numerous research facilities. Uralmash alone produced the famous T-34 tank and its Cold War successors, together with critical aviation and rocketry components, as well as the giant heavy machinery that propelled the Soviet industrial machine for decades.

Dynamism and Stagnation

The consequences of such a concentration of military-industrial-research capacity in the city proved to be both positive and negative. In 1979, a local research site specializing in biological warfare accidentally released anthrax into the atmosphere, leading to one of the worst biological contaminations of a civilian population in history.[44] Moreover, Soviet-era Sverdlovsk's important role in defense research and development as well as industrial production prompted the authorities to limit access to the city, which meant that foreigners and unapproved Soviet citizens were banned from crossing its boundaries.

On a more positive note, the city's overall significance for the Soviet defense effort amplified the region's political status and power.[45] Local political leaders developed their own distinctive style with roots in the region's past. As Yeltsin's biographer, Leon Aron, writes, "Yekaterinburg's unique history, demography, and industry contributed to the emergence of what might be called the Ural school of Communist Party leadership. As a rule, the Ural Party bosses were competent, tough, independent, strong, seemingly incorruptible, even austere, and direct."[46]

By the mid-1980s, the incoming Communist Party general secretary, Mikhail Gorbachev, was raiding the local elites for effective administrators. He brought Sverdlovsk's Communist Party regional first secretary, Yeltsin, to Moscow to tear apart the capital's entrenched local party elite. Gorbachev similarly summoned Uralmash's director, Nikolai Ryzhkov, to the Kremlin, where he became the general secretary's longest-serving prime minister (holding the office from 1985 until 1991).[47]

As home to the sorts of pragmatic intellectuals needed to produce giant machinery and weapons of mass destruction, the city likewise generated a vibrant theatrical and musical life. Sverdlovsk remained innovative, even during the years that became known as the "Brezhnev Era of Stagnation [zastoi]." Because it was closed to the outside world, and therefore out of the Soviet mainstream, the local scene enjoyed many more degrees of freedom of expression than larger, more open cities that were closer to the Soviet heartland.[48] This vitality was especially visible in popular music.

Brezhnev-era Sverdlovsk emerged as one of the Soviet Union's most creative centers for rock 'n' roll music, rivaled only by Leningrad (now Saint Petersburg). Its distinctive "Urals Rock" movement—led by such bands as Urfin Dzhyus, Chaif, Nautilus Pompilius, Nastya, Trek, Agata Kristi, and Smyslovye Galliustinatsii—transformed late Soviet and postindependence Russian popular music.

Beyond rock, nonconformist artists such as Evgeny Malakhin, known as "Bukashkin" (a small insect), sustained a vibrant underground art scene that was known as far away as Moscow, Saint Petersburg, and Odessa. The city's homegrown literary journal, *Ural'skii sledopyt* (*Urals Pathfinder*), established itself as the Soviet Union's leading outlet without peer for science fiction. And the region's more traditional, "thick" literary journal, *Ural*, remained one of the leading outlets for creative writing outside the political and cultural capitals of Moscow and Leningrad.

Given the Soviet policy of establishing a full range of cultural and educational institutions in cities with more than 1 million residents, Yekaterinburg simultaneously offered a complete range of official theaters, covering all major genres of dance; opera; philharmonic, choral, and chamber music; drama; musical comedy and operettas; children's theater; and the circus arts. And all these institutions were supported by the local Communist Party's leadership, though not without interference and controversy.[49] These state-supported cultural institutions steadfastly sustained high-quality companies for ballet, opera, musical comedy, modern dance, puppet, and dramatic theater. Later on, more independent ventures, such as Natalia Baganova's internationally recognized Provincial Dance Company, would also readily find audiences that had been nurtured by the larger local companies.[50]

The city's dynamism could, however, take other, less savory forms. Multigenerational criminal gangs, which would win the city the dubious title of post-Soviet Russia's "crime capital" during the 1990s, in fact were created and thrived during the Brezhnev era. The same advantages of geography that allowed the city to link east and west also attracted criminal groups, which easily penetrated its tough local working-class culture while attracting into their bands former convicts released from camps to the east.[51]

The "Second Front"

During the late 1950s, as the harshest elements of the Stalinist police state began to recede following the Great Leader's death in

1953, a distinctive Soviet youth culture at odds with official ideology began to emerge.[52] Hip *"stilyagi"* began to appear in Moscow and Leningrad, as well as in cities in western Ukraine and the Baltic Sea republics that had not been incorporated into the Soviet Union until the 1939 Stalin–Ribbentrop Pact just before World War II.[53] The term *"stilyagi,"* for funky, Soviet-style hipster fashionistas, derived from the fact that these "beatniks" wore "stylish" clothes beyond generally accepted attire.[54] Jazz dominated, though the early sounds of rock 'n' roll had reached the USSR by the time a massive youth festival brought nearly 35,000 international youth to Moscow during the summer of 1957.[55]

The first Soviet rock 'n' roll bands began to appear in Estonia and Latvia—and eventually in Moscow and Leningrad—during the early 1960s. The new music took off by mid-decade with the arrival of the Beatles over shortwave radios and, eventually, contraband cassette tape recordings.[56] As the Soviet rock critic and historian Artemy Troitsky later observed, "The Beatles' happy, harmonious vocal choir proved to be just the voice for which our confused generation was waiting, but was unable to create for itself."[57] By the 1970s, Soviet rock bands had found their own worldview. The genre swept the country, with homegrown groups such as Mashina Vremini (Time Machine), Akvarium (Aquarium), and Zvuki Mu (the Sounds of Mu) grabbing large followings. Their popularity forced the Communist Party and state bureaucrats lording over official culture to sponsor their own, tamer equivalents and to elevate politically neutral disco music and dancing to the level of a cultural icon.[58]

A quasi-underground Soviet rock scene thrived in the dark shadows of official institutions, such as those attached to Sverdlovsk's massive factories—in restaurants and workers' clubs, in palaces of culture, and on festival stages often controlled by Young Communist League (Komsomol), trade union, and factory officials. Rock music and video salons became a meaningful source of income for official institutions as well as for their officers.[59] Some speculate that these revenues became the basis for the primitive accumulation of capital during the Gorbachev years, eventually enabling officials to move into the privatization of metals, coal, natural gas, and oil as the Soviet Union collapsed.[60]

Ever more portable recording technologies allowed musicians to spread their sound across the entire Soviet Union so that, by the 1980s, a robust, complex, and varied rock music culture had taken root, ranging from ubiquitous disco groups to punk and everything in between.[61] Soviet rock survived a round of repression unleashed in 1984 by disgruntled cultural overlords who had taken advantage of the rapid turnover of Communist Party general secretaries following Brezhnev's death in late 1982.[62]

In some ways, the Soviet rock scene reached its apotheosis with the internationally televised charity concert staged to assist the victims of the 1986 Chernobyl' nuclear accident.[63] This landmark event highlighted some of the limits of rock's reach in Soviet society because its top headliner—Alla Pugacheva—represented a much more popular style. Pugacheva became the Soviet Union's and the Russian-speaking world's most enduring and popular performer. Her music blends elements of rock with strains of the era's most beloved musical genre, a bouncy yet nostalgic and sentimental blend known in Russian as *estrada*, or "variety show" songs.[64] Underground poet bards—such as Alexander Galich, Bulat Okudzhava, and Vladimir Vysotksy—gave more fulsome voice to the era's discontent through their gravelly storytelling ballads about workers, prisoners, soldiers, drivers, alcoholics, and the intelligentsia generally and the artistic intelligentsia in particular, as well as others among the Soviet alienated and dispossessed. Their songs were quickly passed from hand to hand on low-quality cassettes and tape recordings.[65]

It was rock, as the American historian of Russia Richard Stites argues, that became "the driving force behind youth culture in large Soviet cities."[66] And this was especially true in closed cities such as Yekaterinburg. Writing about the similarly closed industrial city Dnepropetrovsk in Ukraine, the Russian historian Sergei Zhuk notes that rock became a way of creating a new youth identity through a "process of selective borrowing and appropriation, translation, and incorporation into the indigenous cultural context."[67] According to Zhuk, music and other Western cultural products tore through closed societies such as the Soviet Union in general, and large defense industry cities such as Dnepropetrovsk and Yekaterinburg in particular. The music "contributed to the spread of cynicism among young people. The oppressive ideological atmosphere of Dnepropetrovsk as a closed city contributed not only to ideological and cultural confusion but also to the moral issue of ideological cynicism."[68]

Yekaterinburg's rock scene remained distinctive in important ways. By the early 1980s, a number of talented and creative bands had emerged in the city, which combined a pop sound with sharp critiques of social problems. Vyacheslav Butusov's *Nautilus Pampilius* in the 1980s and the Samoilov brothers' *Agata Kristi* in the 1990s brought together the gloomy longings of a "lost generation" with songs of love and social protest. The group Chaif (from the local slang word for "pleasure," derived from the Russian word for tea)—perhaps the longest-running group, dating back to the 1980s and still continuing on the stage for a third of a century and more—proudly declared its connection to its native city, both in song and in charitable activities.

These bands—and others like them—were the creations of the "technical intelligentsia" that so dominated the city. Some band members were trained architects; others were conservatory graduates. For instance, Yulia Chicherina—a descendant of Lenin's and Stalin's commissar of foreign affairs, Georgii Chicherin—spent her childhood years as a serious music student and later formed the popular band named Chicherina that continues to perform around Russia today. Bands like hers combined philosophical thought, social criticism, musical sophistication, and a drive for a rollicking good time to create songs that distinguished the "Urals Rock" sound from other Russian rock styles. Collectively, their music reflected the preoccupation of youth with an urban culture and intellectual sensibility who seek to integrate a sharp critical perspective while not shying away from the ugly realities of life. They have helped to define their city's special sense of self, which the local writer Valentin Lukyanov has identified as its distinctive "soul."[69]

The "Provincial" Written Word

Struggling to gain control over an entrenched Communist Party elite, the rising leader Nikita Khrushchev undertook the first of what would become an unending, three-and-a-half-decade stream of failed reforms that sought to make the Soviet economy more efficient while breaking the stranglehold of the party's elite (*nomenklatura*) over the country. In January 1957, Khrushchev announced that he would reorganize the country's economic system by separating agricultural and industrial bureaucracies into parallel sets of regional economic councils (*sovnarkhozy*), which simultaneously would merge several political regions into larger transregional units. Despite subsequent refinements, the new system created more chaos than efficiency, helping to lead to the October 1964 internal Communist Party coup that removed Khrushchev from office.[70] As one of the designated *sovnarkhoz* seats, Yekaterinburg was poised to receive recognition normally reserved for the capitals of the various union republics (e.g., to use their post–Soviet Union names, Kyiv in Ukraine, Almaty in Kazakhstan, Tbilisi in Georgia, and Bishkek in Kyrgyzstan). Literary journals were among the accoutrements of status.

During the days of the USSR, the preponderance of literary publications in the Russian Federation had been based in Moscow and Leningrad, with new regional journals being launched in Vladivostok at the end of World War II, and in Arkhangelsk to the far north in 1965.[71] As a result, "provincial" writers had little opportunity to publish their works independently from the official overlords in Moscow. Some regional journals from the early Soviet era—such as Sverdlovsk's *Shturn* and *Ural'skii sledopyt*—held on until Stalin centralized cultural institutions during the mid-1930s. And a number of annual literary almanacs—such as Sverdlovsk's *Ural'skii sovremennik*, which would continue to be published for thirty-seven years—sprang up around the country to fill this gap. But none of these publications attained the reverence preserved in Russian literary circles for the sacred "thick" journal—the name evoking its serious literary intent as well as its physical heft—which, since the late nineteenth century, has been the preferred outlet for Russian creative writing.[72]

Moscow's and Leningrad's prestigious thick journals—such as *Novyi Mir*, *Znayia*, and *Druzhba narodov*—led the literary explosion of publishing once-banned works that would become known as "the Thaw." Seeing an opportune moment, Sverdlovsk's and its region's writers moved quickly to replicate the success of the central journals at a regional level, using the city's new status as a *sovnark-hoz* center to leverage support from regional party and state authorities. Thus, in 1977 Vadim Ocheretin and other writers relaunched *Ural'skii sledopyt*, a journal that had managed to run for nine issues in 1935 before succumbing to Communist Party censorship.[73] Ocheretin and his successor Soviet-era editors—Vladimir Shustov, Ivan Akulov, and the two-decade-serving Stanislav Meshavkin— firmly established the reborn journal as the premier outlet for science fiction writing in the Soviet Union, gaining international recognition for their efforts. By publishing homegrown Soviet authors as well as translations of international writers, *Ural'skii sledopyt* developed a cult following that reached far beyond the Urals region. The journal's Aelita Festival became the Soviet Union's premier event showcasing science fiction, bringing the genre's most talented writers to Yekaterinburg each year.[74] They simultaneously used the journal as a platform to promote a discussion of environmental concerns, both within the region and nationally throughout the Soviet Union, while focusing on regional literary history from time to time.[75]

In addition, the Regional Communist Party Committee (Obkom) designated Ocheretin as the editor of a second, broad-based thick literary journal, *Ural*, which was intended to showcase regional writers and themes. Given that it was managed by the local division of the official Writers' Union and was overseen by party officials, *Ural* focused on promoting a regional identity among local writers.[76] After a number of political interventions by the party, including reprimands and dismissals of early editors, the journal firmly secured its stature as a leading regional literary journal once Valentin Lukyanin assumed its editorship in 1980. Lukyanin set out to promote the works of young authors; expand *Ural*'s focus to include plays as well as short stories, novels, and poems; and reach out to a wider community through discussion clubs and other events.[77] He, too, would prompt political controversy.

In 1982, Lukyanin serially published Konstantin Lagunov's novel *Bronzovyi dog* (*The Bronze Mastiff*) in *Ural*'s August, September, and October issues.[78] The journal included almost documentary reportage tied together by fictionalized narratives, offering a "portrayal of the true face of the oil barons" of the West Siberian petroleum belt in the neighboring Tyumen' Region. In his chronicle of shocking transgressions against "communist morality," many of Lagunov's characterizations presaged the behavior of post-Soviet Russian oil oligarchs. Tyumen' party and state officials immediately expressed their outrage with the regional party first secretary, Georgii Bogomyakov, probably telephoning his Sverdlovsk counterpart Yeltsin about the matter. Meanwhile, the journal's readership skyrocketed, and letters of support started pouring in from around the country.

The Lagunov Affair had hardly simmered down when Lukyanin proposed publishing Nikokai Nikonov's story (*povest'*) "Starikova gora" (The Old Man's Mountain) in the journal's January 1983 issue. Set in the fictional village of Makarovka, Nikonov's tale exposed the social pathologies and degradations of Soviet rural life a half century after collectivization, ending with the line "The land was waiting for its owner."[79] Given the brutality of collectivization in the region—the infamously legendary *pioner* (scout) Pavlik Morozov, who condemned his father by denouncing him to the authorities, lived in the region's Gerasimovka village—Nikonov was poking at an even rawer nerve than Lagunov had.

Uncertain censors turned the galley proofs of the January 1983 *Ural* issue over to the Regional Party Committee, which deleted approximately one-sixth of the text. Once published, *Ural* became the object of an array of attacks by the Communist Party and KGB. Eventually, in May 1983, Lukyanin was summoned to a meeting of the committee's Executive Bureau, where he was excoriated by First Secretary Yeltsin and other members of his team for four and a half hours. After a public admission of serious shortcomings, Lukyanin held onto his editorial position, while Lagunov and Nikonov avoided official sanctions. And copies of the January 1983 issue of *Ural* remained hidden away in most regional libraries, despite a Communist Party order that they be destroyed.

Despite—or, perhaps, because of—these political interventions, *Ural* exerted a primal force of gravity, around which the region's literary life could grow and flourish. It published articles focusing on local and regional history as well as traditions, cultural life, and peculiarities, thus giving definition to a distinctive regional identity. Its offices and events came to play the role of the legendary renegade hangouts Gavan and Café Saigon in Leningrad, while never turning its back on more traditional writers and cultural figures.[80] Its very existence provided an outlet for the range of the region's various authors of competing styles and temperaments from across Siberia, both young and old.[81]

Lukyanin's catholic embrace of a regional literary vision proved to be especially important for promoting local writers during the height of the Brezhnev era, when Moscow-based journals and publishing houses were held captive by the capital's increasingly ossified cliques.[82] Consequently, as with rock music, nonconformist artists, local novelists, short story writers, poets, literary and theatrical critics, and playwrights maintained their distinctive voices. These efforts gained additional outside support from many prominent writers from throughout the Urals and beyond, such as Lev Davydychev in Perm, Evgenii Ananyev in Tyumen', and Viktor Astafyev in Krasnoyarsk.[83]

Ural became such a beloved institution that, in the late 1990s, when its existence was in question due to the various economic and other uncertainties of post-Soviet life, prominent local authors stepped in to breathe new life into the journal. The internationally renowned Yekaterinburg playwright and dramatist Nikolai Kolyada took over the journal's editorial offices in July 1999, at a time when its official subscription numbers had dropped to a mere three hundred, and when there were no more manuscripts in the queue to be published. He parlayed his connections to attract new writers, linking the journal to theater festivals and generally making *Ural* essential reading for anyone interested in the New Russian Writing movement. A decade later, he passed the journal along to the worthy hands of his protégé, the internationally renowned local playwright Oleg Bogaev, who is expanding the journal's readership on the Internet.[84]

Uncontrolled Cartels

Both *Ural'skii sledopyt* and *Ural* served as important resources for the local theater community as Yekaterinburg moved into the post-Soviet world. Like the various theater companies and venues that took shape during the middle years of the twentieth century, these journals and the networks nurtured by them provided a powerful base on which new forms of drama could take shape.

Brezhenev-era Sverdlovsk was home to more than posses of writers. As mentioned above, the city had a reputation as one of the most criminally violent in the entire Soviet Union.[85] The same factors that enriched its economic and cultural life also made it a natural center for vice.[86] The city was sufficiently far from Moscow to be beyond its direct control, yet close enough to remain within reach and close enough to the Siberian prisons to become a magnet for newly released prisoners. It stood astride major transportation routes connecting narcotics-growing fields to the south and east and drug markets to the west, with a vast population of factory workers and their families who were beginning to feel the first indications of a national economic collapse that would shut down their factories. Everything about the city promoted the emergence of vast, disciplined, aggressive, and malevolent bands of armed criminals, hangers-on, and wannabes.[87]

As the Soviet industrial economy collapsed in the late 1980s and early 1990s, criminal cartels—known in Russia as *"mafiyas"* — quickly moved in to lay claim to the region's vast mineral wealth; to seize and dismantle the vast factories that could only be used as scrap; to sell off light and heavy weaponry from military bases that were no longer under any form of discernible control; to traffic in desperate human beings trying to find some way to survive; to push drugs, and to launder their profits; and to extort more.[88] The larger *"mafiyas"* —such as Tsentral'nye (which grew up around the Central Market), the Afgantsy (made up of Afghan war veterans), the Siniye (a gang of former prisoners), and the Azerbaizhantsy (consisting of criminals from the former Soviet republic)—branched out into many areas.[89] Other gangs, which were often rooted in specific enterprises—such as the powerful and massive Uralmash gang, and the less potent Miko-Invest and Sakirtan cartels—tended to specialize in their operations.[90]

The transition taking place in the criminal world paralleled the larger transformations in the Soviet and post-Soviet economy. The Centrals (Tsentral'nye) dominated the city during the late Soviet period as they exerted control over an energetic black market trade in goods and services that initially was based at the central market and spread out from there. With the decline of the Uralmash plant, a group of former professional sportsmen, their friends, and relatives from the neighborhoods surrounding the factory began to seize the assets of the once-gigantic plant. Their gang, which coalesced by 1991, entered into turf battles with the older Centrals, unleashing a brutal and massive gang war between the two groups following the June 16, 1991, assassination of the Uralmash boss Grigorii Tsyganov. Explosions, shootings, and murders became a daily occurrence from 1992 until 1994, with Yekaterinburg becoming known as the most criminal-plagued city in Russia.[91]

The Uralmash gang emerged victorious by late 1994, forcing the Centrals out of much of their original territory. Uralmash operatives allegedly expanded their horizons, reputedly laying claim to various local, regional, and national political positions. Having become increasingly secure, Uralmash began to go "legit," reportedly taking over legal real estate; hotels and industrial, financial, and construction businesses in Russia and abroad in Europe and the United States.[92]

Gang control of the native city hardly disappeared, even as tactics evolved from less-licit to more-licit activities. By the late 1990s, an estimated 60 percent of all enterprises in Yekaterinburg were controlled by criminal organizations, while between 70 and 80 percent of private and privatized firms and commercial banks were said to pay protection money to criminal groups, corrupt officials, and racketeers.[93]

More generally, numerous successful gangs expanded their drugs and arms trading worldwide through outposts in Cyprus, India, the United States, Poland, Germany, and China.[94] Many still busied themselves by victimizing local residents. In November 1997, a quarter of all city residents claimed to have themselves been victims of crime.[95] This mayhem would came under official control slowly during the late 1990s and early 2000s, as local, regional, and national political leaders began to persistently impose coherence on the Russian state.

By the time Vladimir Putin became Russian president, the Uralmash gang in particular had become well situated to avoid a direct confrontation with the more centralized Russian state—in large measure because it had already left its more overtly criminal activities behind. But its underlying network of criminal power undoubtedly remained in place.[96]

Foot soldiers were easily recruited in a city where tens of thousands of young factory workers could not find a job. *Mafiya* bands—some associated with the Centrals, others associated with Uralmash, and others not associated at all, including at least seventy-six organized and countless more unorganized groups—fought over turf, leading to an especially pernicious outburst of widespread urban violence, death, and havoc that surpassed that found even in out-of-control Moscow and Saint Petersburg.[97] As younger and younger gang members fell in this onslaught, a local culture grew up promoting opulent funeral services, in which the deceased gangsters were laid to rest under ever more ornate tombstones.[98] Two competing cemeteries on the opposite sides of Yekaterinburg filled up with the extravagant graves of criminals who had been rubbed out by other criminals. The 1994 tombstone of Central boss Mikhail Kuchin, for example, is a 10-foot-high malachite monument encrusted with precious stones, with Kuchin's carved visage holding the keys to his beloved Mercedes-Benz and wearing a designer suit over an unbuttoned shirt displaying an Orthodox Christian cross.[99]

At least one local gangster, Evgenii Monakh, turned his attention to writing detective stories. The son of a well-placed family that included a teacher of philosophy in a Communist Party school, he turned to a life of crime, and in 1994 he began to write about his experiences with vibrant, colorful style. Two years later, he was dead, the victim of the sort of story he himself celebrated as an author.[100] His last story, "Smiling before Death," appeared in a special double issue of *Ural*, bringing local literary and criminal life full circle.[101]

A world in spectacular meltdown places all sorts of human vice on prominent display and forces survivors to find meaning wherever they can. Where is human dignity to be found in a world so full of violence and degradation? Does it matter? Are there limits to unbridled cynicism? What does it mean to be human? How can one show the human being at his or her absolute most perverse and still find honor? Such themes, not surprisingly, came to dominate local literature and dramaturgy in Yekaterinburg. They provided the fodder for the creative impulses that could be supported by the institutional foundations provided by journals and theaters, enriched by a distinctive urban "soul" fervently being expressed in pop music and culture.

As was the case everywhere across Russia, after the demise of the Soviet Union, local leaders in Yekaterinburg were left on their own to confront the terrible dislocations of post-Soviet deindustrialization. They tried with varying degrees of success to parlay connections with their former colleagues in Moscow to open the city and its economy to the world at large, in order to sustain a population hovering above 1 million souls.[102] Two decades later, the city's continued vitality demonstrates these local leaders' general success. At a time when many Russian cities were losing population, Yekaterinburg slowly grew, in no small measure due to the arrival of migrants from neighboring Central Asian countries.[103] In 2009, census takers counted 1,332,264 residents in the city (just below third-ranked Novosibirsk, which had 1,397,191 residents; and just ahead of fifth-place Nizhny Novgorod, which was home to 1,272,527).[104] The American political scientist Thomas Remington, in an analysis of those regional components of the Russian Federation that are more democratic than would be predicted based on levels of economic modernization, identified Yekaterinburg's Sverdlovsk Region as the top "democratic achiever" during the two decades beginning in 1991.[105]

Soviet-era cultural institutions, struggling to find their way in the new post-Soviet environment, spun off a number of semilegitimate theater companies and music clubs that gave voice to some of the most creative Russian playwrights and rock musicians of their generation. Yekaterinburg nurtured many of the voices who would define post-Soviet Russia. The leading local playwrights Vasily Sigarev (whom we met at the start of this chapter), Oleg Bogayev, and the Presnyakov brothers wrote for the Volkhonka Chamber Theatre. Nikolai Kolyada created his own highly celebrated theater, which performs his own works together with those of other contemporary and classical Russian and international authors. They enjoyed critical success and global acclaim, in part because of their accomplishments at home, and in part because they helped to create something new that spanned Russia as a whole. Their success was only partially homegrown. It also was promoted by the national New Russian Drama Movement, which would catapult local playwrights onto the stages of such global theater centers as Moscow, London, and New York.

The New Russian Drama Movement

Plasticine's London premiere, described above at the start of this chapter, was more than happenstance. Its author, Sigarev, was but one of a score of young Russian playwrights identified with a drama movement that had been formed in response to funding opportunities provided by the British Council in cooperation with the Royal Court Theatre in London.

As the drama-film and Russian studies scholars Birgit Beumers and Mark Lipovetsky observe in *Performing Violence*, a study of the New Russian Drama Movement, innovation in theater lags behind economic, social, and political upheavals by a decade or so.[106] This lag represents the amount of time required for new voices to be heard; for established and fresh writers to assimilate society's profound transformations, so that they can form and express a new point of view; and for more-established cultural figures to hear and come to terms with what is being said.

As Beumers and Lipovetsky argue,

> Looking back at the history of the twentieth century, the best plays were written not at the beginning of the 1920s but at the end of that decade and the early 1930s. . . . The best plays were written not at the peak of the [Khrushchev-era] thaw or the early 1960s . . . but at the end of the 1960s and early 1970s. . . . In Europe, the heyday of intellectual theater occurs not during the vibrant 1920s, but in the depressive atmosphere of the 1930s. . . . And the emergence of the Theatre of the Absurd—probably the most important event in dramatic writing of the postwar—coincides not with the revolutionary 1960s, but the stagnant 1950s.
>
> Perhaps drama becomes the main field for literary experiments precisely when—after rough times, revolution, upheavals, and shifts—there comes a period of stabilization (stagnation, depression). This writing reacts to the hardening of a new sociality, previously nonformalized and open

to change. When drama is on the rise, it almost always focuses on unfulfilled hopes and aspirations. It is interested in those people who pay for the social shift, who receive slaps in the face, who have been pushed somewhere into the gutter or abandoned there as history toppled: In the beginning they beckoned, when they were cast aside.[107]

By the late 1990s, Russia had no shortage of those who had been slapped in the face, pushed into the gutter, and abandoned during the post-Soviet collapse—and no shortage of writers and artists trying to give form and meaning to their travails.

Theater requires more than setting down ideas from a single mind with pen and paper (or keyboard and screen). Plays are social acts, requiring playwrights and actors and directors and sponsors, and stages, and audiences, and money. Early in the 1990s, many observers argued that Russian theater was just one more victim of the post-Soviet transition. Because it seemed commercially unviable and bereft of fresh ideas, Russian theater entered a period that to many was marked by death throes of excruciating pain.

But just as some were sounding the death knell for the Russian stage, the New Russian Drama Movement was coalescing around the nexus of several momentous events—the booming late-1990s economy, which spun off dozens of new cultural venues in Moscow and beyond; talented writers and directors liberated by the end of censorship that accompanied the collapse of communism; actors increasingly exposed to the rich tapestry of competing styles, unencumbered by the legacy of the Soviet stage's ossified psychological realism; and audience members trying to find their own lives amid the wreckage of post-Soviet culture being overrun by the most degraded and least creative artifacts of increasingly globalized pop culture.[108] The movement's dominant feature has been "its neo-naturalistic aesthetic, with unprecedented prominence given to representations of violence," whereas its "main thematic preoccupation is the deep crisis of identity that has characterized post-Soviet society."[109]

Each of these developments needed to come together at just the right moment to produce a genuinely innovative dramatic form. After all, the extraordinary theater of the Gorbachev years in the late 1980s was followed in the early 1990s by the collapse of the theater scene, particularly in Moscow, as increasingly impoverished audiences had little patience to sit through an evening of "filth" (*chernykha*). Psychological realism, which had become the only permissible Soviet theatrical style during the 1940s and 1950s, had been both preceded and succeeded by periods rich with the grotesque, the symbolic, and the political.

The late 1990s, then, were years when a number of theatrical tendencies that fed into the New Russian Drama Movement aligned in unprecedented patterns. These events occurred simultaneously, with the establishment in 1998 of the Playwright and Director Center by the veteran Moscow playwrights Mikhail Roshchin and Alexei Kazantsev. Roshchin and Kazantsev's success prompted the creation of other new venues, such as Teatr.doc, the Praktika Theatre, and influential performance spaces.

The British Are Coming! The British Are Coming!

The New Russian Drama Movement nonetheless required a defining event, when the various elements flowing into it could coalesce into an identifiable phenomenon. This moment came in July 1997, over the course of a six-day seminar, supported by the British Council and led by a delegation from the Royal Court Theatre, which met in the ramshackle remains of Konstantin Stanislavsky's country estate in Liubimovka, near Moscow.[110]

Within months, the first Russian Festival of Documentary Theatre would open, with support from the George Soros–supported Open Society Institute; theater festivals and workshops would convene; and, in February 2002, Elena Gremina and Mikhail Ugarov would open the basement Teatr.doc on central Moscow's Trekhprudnyi Pereulok. Their success was followed in October 2005 by the opening of Eduard Boyakov's Praktika Theatre nearby, as well as the creation of countless similar companies around the country, such as Saint Petersburg's Chelovek.doc Theatre and ON.TEATR, Kemerovo's Lozhe Theatr, Chelyabink's Baby Theatre, and the subsequent Kinoteatr.doc cinema movement.[111]

As Sasha Dugdale—who was then a British Council Moscow program officer—tells the story,

In 1998, when I was working at the British Council in Russia, I was introduced to Elena Gremina and Alexei Kazantsev, two playwrights who devoted themselves to supporting a culture of playwriting in Russia. Kazantsev and Gremina together with other playwrights and critics had set up Liubimovka in 1992—a retreat for playwrights and directors, where young writers, chosen from the quality of their work, rehearsed readings of their plays with actors and directors. Liubimovka was named after Stanislavskii's estate, just outside Moscow, where the retreat took place. At the times when I attended a wild and shambolic event, a storm of creativity studded readings of the plays, which would become legendary in Russia's New Writing tradition, and after the reading a protracted and heartfelt discussion of the play would ensue.[112]

The British Council brought the Royal Court Theatre to Russia. Already having won the "Europe Theatre Prize," the Royal Court had been running workshops around the world, taking such leading British writers as Sarah Kane, Mark Ravenhill, and Jez Butterworth along with them. They tried to encourage others to adapt the documentary theater style known as "verbatim," whereby a text taken directly from the street would be spoken onstage.[113] The resulting theater became associated with an aggressively shocking style of drama that had emerged in Britain during the 1960s, known as "In-Yer-Face" theater. Moving to the mainstream of British theater by the 1990s, "In-Yer-Face theater shocks audiences by the extremism of its language and images, unsettles them by its emotional frankness and disturbs them by its acute questioning of moral norms."[114]

Although the Royal Court had experienced only sporadic success in proselytizing verbatim documentary theater—primarily in the Balkans and Poland—Russia immediately proved to be exceptionally fertile soil for such theatrical aggression.[115] Both nineteenth-century revolutionaries and later Soviet cultural bureaucrats promoted sending writers out to the countryside, to factories, and to provincial cities as a way of connecting the arts with "the Narod" (the People). The notion that writers and theater troupes should interact with everyday life and not just amuse comfortable patrons has a distinguished history in Russia, one very consistent with the style of verbatim documentary theater being promoted by the Royal Court.[116]

Newcomers to the stage from fringe areas—such as Sigarev, and Vladimir and Oleg Presnyakov, from Yekaterinburg; Maxim Kurochkin and Natalia Vorozhbit from Kyiv; Yury Klavdiev, and Vyacheslav and Mikhail Durnenkov, from Togliatti; Evgenii Grishkovets from Kemerovo; Yaroslava Pulinovich from Omsk; and Ivan Vyrypaev from Irkutsk; together with the already-established, incomparable Olga Mukhina, who had grown up in the Far North—found a coherent new voice to express the traumas and pathologies of their daily lives during the post-Soviet collapse (figure 42).[117] Though it had never been characterized by overtly political documentary theater, the New Russian Drama Movement nonetheless provided a means for discussing the country's cascading traumas, such as the war in Chechnya and the innumerable injustices of the corrupt judicial system.[118]

Within a matter of months, documentary theater swept across Russian stages. The British Council's support led directly to the translation of plays into English, and their production at the Royal Court. The Royal Shakespeare Company similarly commissioned and performed a number of new works by young Russian playwrights.[119] Just as important, the Liubimovka workshops connected the new writers to Moscow's mainstream theaters, leading to the production of New Russian Drama Movement scripts in such venues as Svetlana Vragova's Theatre on Spartakovskaya Square, Oleg Tabakov's Studio Theatre, Anatolii Vasiliev's School of Dramatic Art, Sergei Artsybashev's Theatre on Pokrovka, Mikhail Shepenko's Chamber Theatre, Petr Fomenko's Workshop Theatre, Mark Rozovskii's Theatre at Nikitskii Gates, and Sergei Zhenovach's Theatre Art Studio in converted factories near Taganka Square that had once been owned by the Stanislavskii and Alekseev families.[120] Plays by authors associated with the New Russian Drama Movement soon were being performed on stages around the world.

How "Russian" Can a Play at the Royal Court Be?

Unsurprisingly, the New Russian Drama Movement was not to everyone's taste. Russian nationalists complained about its asso-

Figure 42. The playwright Olga Mukhina.
Source: Photograph by Philip Arnoult; used by permission.

ciation with Britain, especially at a time when NATO planes were bombing fellow Slavs in Serbia; others simply deplored the playwrights' fascination with sex, violence, depravity, and general *chernykha* (filth).[121] In June 2013, perhaps reflecting a general hardening of cultural and political policies following Vladimir Putin's return as president the year before, the Saint Petersburg authorities closed ON.TEATR, a particularly significant showcase for documentary theater, for alleged safety violations.[122] Yet the New Russian Drama Movement was never merely derivative of British verbatim documentary and In-Yer-Face theater—in four main ways, it was uniquely and distinctively Russian.

First, audiences in search of Russian-language cultural expressions had begun to flock to theaters at the initial signs of the post-Soviet economic recovery the decade before. This new theater emerged from an increasingly vibrant Russian scene, which had spawned dozens of studio theaters, scores of theater festivals, and hundreds of innovative works by more established companies. Talented playwrights—such as Liudmila Petrushevskaia, Alexei Kazantsev, Eduard Radzinsky, and Vladimir Sorokin—had begun to transform Russian theater before the Soviet Union had come to an end; and Olga Mukhina's landmark plays *Tanya Tanya* and *You* had appeared well before visitors from the Royal Court arrived in Liubimovka.[123]

Second, Russian verbatim documentary theater is never quite verbatim. Russian authors simulate verisimilitude, characters, and circumstances rather than merely lifting them straight from life and placing them on the stage. In contrast to their British counterparts, Russian writers are much more likely to juxtapose languages, events, and texts from a number of different sources and to meld them into something new and distinctly their own.[124]

Third, and perhaps most important, many of the authors and plays categorized as constituting the New Russian Drama Movement seek to reveal more than the pathologies of their own society. Their characters retain a core human dignity in the face of the most degrading circumstances. Plays are infused with a larger spirituality, in mocking contrast to the events taking place onstage. This fascination in discovering the meaningful within the mundane often takes writers and actors far from moments of high drama. For example, in her 2012 play *Take Me In*, Ekaterina Vasileva effectively captures the humdrum daily dramas of domestic life by recounting family squabbles that occur against the backdrop of preparations for New Year's celebrations.[125]

Commonplace arguments over money and studying abroad reveal one level of post-Soviet Russian family life; plays dramatizing the traumas of violence, disease, and other horrors require grander appeals to the humanity of all human beings. At the close of the Togliatti playwright Yury Klavdiev's powerful 2006 play *The Polar Truth* about the ugly underside of Russian life, the HIV-positive character "Kid" proclaims in the closing monologue: "The truth? That's what we are. Those of us who live. Who work. Who earn wages. It's people who don't beg for anything from anyone—gimme money, gimme trust, gimmie an office, gimme taxes, gimme soldiers, gimme, gimme, gimme, and I'll just go and do as I please. People like that don't know anything about life—look at all the sciences they went out and invented. Organizations. Administrations. Welfare offices. All that to explain to us why we still keep living so stupidly. But we don't live stupidly. We just live."[126]

This underlying attitude of profound humanity beneath the surface horror of post-Soviet life attracted audiences back to theaters—just the opposite from how, a decade before, the era of aggressive and frank theater had simply driven people away. The new works proved to be about more than portraying society's "filth." *Chernykha* was coming to serve a larger end rather than just to shock; it was coming to create moments for redemption.

In Klavdiev's *Martial Arts*, to cite another example, a ten-year-old boy and girl are saved from the vengeance of elders, drugs dealers, addicts, thieves, thugs, and corrupt policemen by the magical Queen of Spades, who intervenes just as they are about to be killed by their tormentors.[127] Although the appearance of this traditional Russian folk heroine could have made a mockery of the entire tale (can only a miracle save us?), Klavdiev instead drew on the imagery to humanize and domesticate a situation of unbelievable horror.

Fourth and finally, Russian directors—traditionally the dominant force in the national theater tradition—have, over time, creatively interpreted the texts of the plays they direct. As a result, performances have moved further and further away over the course of the past decade from the documentary stance encouraged by the Royal Court's missionaries.[128]

The New Russian Drama Movement was, without question, "new." Many of the playwrights that belonged to it consciously sought to abandon long-standing cultural references from past Russian and Soviet traditions as a means for embracing a contemporary Russian reality that is distinct from what preceded it.[129] Yet they could not escape the powerful force of a great theatrical tradition. References to Chekhov, for example, abound in the work of many movement playwrights. In Nikolai Kolyada's 2011 play *Baba Shanel'* (*The Old Gal Chanel*), one of the members of the Ordzhonikidze District Invalid Folk Ensemble, "Naitie," joins in the celebration of the group's tenth anniversary following a wildly successful performance at the Omsk Institute for the Deaf by speaking conversationally only in the verse of the iconic twentieth-century Russian bards Anna Akhmatova and Marina Tsvetaeva.[130] Such devices melded the new with the old in Russian life.

Equally important, the movement's playwrights were not content to limit their creative horizons to Russia. International connections and the integration of several movement playwrights into the global theatrical community amplified the movement's impact. Performances at London's Royal Court and commissions from the Royal Shakespeare Company ensured a lasting impact that would have been impossible in the isolation of any one country. Moreover, continuing support from the Goethe Institute, the German counterpart to the British Council, brought Russian contemporary theater and its creators onto Berlin stages when British support waned in the wake of the British Council's forced departure from Russia in 2008, which resulted from allegations by Russia's Federal Security Service that the council was a cover for British intelligence.[131] Similarly, the New York–based Trust for Mutual Understanding—frequently working with the legendary Philip Arnoult's Center for International Theater Development in Baltimore—promoted new Russian playwrights and their works in the United States.[132]

At the same time, the New Russian Drama Movement remains profoundly "Russian" in innumerable ways. Beyond its portrayal of Russian circumstances and characters, its practitioners retain a deeply Russian fascination with spirituality in the face of degradation. This "Russian-ness" rests, as well, on the provincial backgrounds of so many of its leading lights. Several of its playwrights were born and raised in a provincial Russia far removed from Moscow, and their preoccupations are those of Russian life outside the capital.[133] They are first and foremost products of alternative cultural centers in places that generally are not thought of as having a culture at all. This pattern is nowhere more evident than in Yekaterinburg, a city that, it turns out, somewhat surprisingly has produced a post-Soviet culture that now circles the globe.[134]

The Power of Personality

The master dramatist Nikolai Kolyada, whom we have encountered several times earlier in this chapter, became a center of gravity around which much of the new drama world of Yekaterinburg revolved. He was born in 1957 in the bleak and remote provincial settlement of Presnogor'kovka in the Kustanay Region, just across the Russian/Kazakh border south of the Siberian city of Chelyabinsk.[135] He trundled off to the Sverdlovsk Theatre School at a young age, graduating at twenty to begin a career on the stage with the Sverdlovsk Academic Theatre of Drama. As an aspiring actor, he played the sorts of wide-ranging, ever-more-prominent roles that are typical of the Russian repertoire, including increasingly important parts in plays by Nikolai Gogol, Alexander Ostrovsky, and Mikhail Bulgakov. But Kolyada was also drawn to writing, so he enrolled in the prestigious Gorky Literary Institute in Moscow to study with the prominent writer Vyacheslav Shugaev. This move brought him to Moscow at the height of the excitement and ferment prompted by Mikhail Gorbachev's *glasnost'* (openness) and *perestroika* (restructuring) policies.

Kolyada immediately became a cause célèbre. An early play, *Slingshot* (1986), which was sympathetic to a gay relationship, shocked Moscow readers and was prohibited from being staged.[136] Then Roman Viktyuk, a controversial Moscow director born in the Western city of L'viv when it was still part of interwar Poland, arranged for this work to be performed at the San Diego Repertory Theater. Kolyada found an enthusiastic reception, and he became an international sensation for the first time.[137] After graduating from the Gorky Institute in 1989, he returned to Sverdlovsk and, since 1994, has taught at the Yekaterinburg Theatrical Institute, offering one of the few playwriting and dramaturge curricula in Russia.

Once back in the Urals, Kolyada began to write plays (more than one hundred, of which more than half have been performed in Russia and abroad), to teach others to write and act (his students include some of Russia's most exciting young playwrights, e.g., Anna Baturina, Anna Bogcheva, Oleg Bogyaev, Nadezhda Koltysheva, Yaroslava Pulinovich, and Vasilii Sigarev), to direct and produce plays, to organize theater festivals (e.g., the Eurasian Drama Competition Festival, which began in 2003, as well as the Kolyada-Plays Festival, which began in 2006, together with the earlier Real Theater Festival, which has been an annual event since the beginning of the decade), and to serve as an intellectual leader in the Urals region (as confirmed by his decade-long editorship of the journal *Ural*).[138] These theatrical events have often been joined by other festivals for any number of additional artistic forms, such as the First Ural Industrial Biennial of Contemporary Art, which was convened during the fall of 2010. [139]

In December 2001, Kolyada founded his own company, the Kolyada Theatre, which initially performed at Pushkin House in a historic Yekaterinburg neighborhood. In 2004, the company moved to its own small stage in a nineteenth-century mansion, where it performed a contemporary repertoire for adults and children's plays for younger audiences. But trouble loomed, with the company being displaced after a fire, only regaining cramped temporary quarters after raucous protests, hunger strikes by Kolyada himself, and the eventual intervention of Sverdlovsk governor Alexander Misharin in November 2010. Though operating with almost no state funding, Kolyada kept his company together, at times by asking its members to bring in any items that they no longer needed at home, and by drawing on the considerable international interest in his work to secure support for his actors and protégés. Following the announcement of a new 2012 tour in France, one of his lead actors evidently exclaimed, "What, Paris again?"[140] Plans for a newly constructed permanent home for the company were announced in March 2011.[141]

Kolyada soon attracted controversy yet again. Unlike many

among the Russian intelligentsia, he publicly and enthusiastically embraced the 2012 candidacy of Prime Minister Vladimir Putin for a return term as Russian president. Appearing on the popular local TV talk show *Enin,* Kolyada explained that he believed "we cannot find a better leader. I will vote for him that is my opinion and my right. All others on offer seem absolutely unworthy to assume such a position."[142] The move brought Kolyada a wave of outrage and approbation from many former supporters, combined with charges that he had sold out to those in power in order to secure his new theater. This anger threatened to undermine many of Kolyada's other projects, such as local festivals.

Leaving aside the politics of a new venue, Kolyada will face a severe challenge in sustaining his company's quirky energy in a more formal setting. *San Francisco Bay Guardian* theater critic Robert Avila captured the personality of Kolyada's theater after witnessing a 2013 production of *Hamlet.* "I wait sometimes a long time for a moment in a theater that's as satisfying as this," Avila told *Moscow Times* theater critic John Freedman. "I heard before going that some people like [Kolyada's] style and other people maybe not. But I don't think you can deny that it is a very rich and serious aesthetic." He continued on to note that the theater itself is part of the show: "There is also the astonishing foyer and entrance that is packed ceiling-high with artifacts, photos, paintings, sculptures, toys, videos, trinkets, utensils, and who knows what else." Avila then compared the "quirky, individual, playful and rich space full of a lot of care and excessive energy" to "a children's playroom or a basement."[143] Such an eccentric personality may prove impossible to re-create in a more official setting.

Kolyada's plays have demonstrated a strength and vigor quite distinct from the actions of their author, focusing, as they do, on the inner disorientation of post-Soviet life. As Birgit Beumers and Mark Lipovetsky suggest, "Kolyada's characters fail to communicate with each other and with the world because of . . . problems of transfer and reception. They resort often to performative ways of expressing their inner world, exploring the borderline between reality and the imagination."[144]

In Kolyada's play *The Old Hare,* for example, the audience sees two newly arriving guests at a less-than-deluxe provincial hotel bump into each other while they're wandering the halls trying to figure out how to get service from the hotel staff. They strike up a conversation that begins with complaints about telephones and quickly becomes a discourse about the meaning of post-Soviet life. At one point late in the play, the woman—an actress from Moscow—becomes unwound, declaring one of the central realities of the last Soviet generation: Everyone lived and lives in fear. "Cursed life!" she explodes," Cursed life! Hellish life! For what, for what, for what is all this—this, this torment, for what? Sir, I have lived my entire life in fear. This isn't just because I am an artist. Even if I were not an artist, I would have lived my entire life in fear just the same, in fear, in fright just to survive."[145]

As important as Kolyada has been for the theatrical and cultural scene in Yekaterinburg, his ambitions extend far beyond its boundaries. He is seeking to free Russian theater from its traditional fixation on director-producers (*rezhissery*) so that it can find a new focus on writers. Although many abroad think of great Russian playwrights such as Anton Chekhov, the national theatrical tradition—in a pattern reinforced during the Soviet period—has tended to elevate director-producers to a higher status than actors and writers. The New Russian Drama Movement is revolutionary in part because of its fascination with the underside of life, but even more because of its attention to the act of writing—as revealed in Kolyada's activities in Yekaterinburg.[146]

This commitment to writing becomes especially evident in the city's Eurasian Drama Competition, which has become a showcase for Russian-language playwrights living in Russia as well as abroad and attracts as many as five hundred submissions from aspiring authors each year. Winning plays are published in *Ural*, thereby promoting their performance far beyond local stages.[147] The Kolyda-Plays Festival concentrates more directly on the work of Kolyada himself and his students. For example, the 2011 festival presented twenty-three productions and readings of works by his top students—Vasily Sigarev, Yaroslava Pulinovich, Oleg Bogayev, Vladimir Zuyev, and the twenty-six-year-old Anna Baturina.[148]

These efforts have built on the success of the Real Theater Festival, which was spurred by the Liubimovka workshops at the start of the previous decade to showcase works by authors participating in the then-emerging New Russian Drama Movement.[149] This festival, which is organized by the city's Young Spectator Theater for children, has become a leading international showcase for new works by the teens of the twenty-first century, being featured in the highly successful US–Russian "Beyond the Capitals" arts program featuring companies outside traditional cultural capitals such as Moscow and New York.[150]

One powerful example of these festivals' collective power can be seen in Konstantin Kostenko's 2011 play *Jazz*, which explores the complicity of society in the long-lasting horror of dictatorships. In once scene, the "Man with a Tie" tells "Homeless Woman" that

> you know, it seems to me that such people as Hitler . . . or the other vampires, . . . such as some sort of Pol Pot, Stalin. . . . They do not exist by themselves. Their dictatorial bloodthirsty systems are propped up every minute by thousands of devoted calves. Leucocytes with red corpuscles. Entire armies of lackeys: security, advisors, secretaries, personal photographers. . . . Here, by the way, it is possible to include those who in moments of patriotism sit on their sofas watching *Swan Lake*. Who is this Hitler? I mean the concrete person Adolph Aloizovich. Who is he? The typical nonentity with a small mustache and swollen eyes. Typical mediocrity. Hitler at the same time wasn't a person, but a mass trend. Those who save their dreams and worship Hitler, all of these security guys, and thugs—they are also part of his essence, Hitler, and his immediate continuation. Those who smile and bump by him in the corridors of his personal bunker—they too are Hitler. The women who wrote to him love letters full of sighs are also Hitler. And so on and so forth. What happened at Nuremburg, but an idea that must encompass everyone? Among those who went to the gallows, how many were sufficiently contemptuous to spit in Hitler's face in order to redeem themselves? Hitler, Hitler is an illness. An illness of the spirit, of the mind, . . . a chessman with a moustache and, all the same, a pimple on a sick body. One that, step by step, grows, swells, . . . seems overfilled. At the same time it is antihuman pus. No, at the end it is

unavoidable but to raise the hand of the surgeon and with a quick, short movement scalp it, cauterizing it with iodine. . . . And the wound will remain deep and the wound will scar. The body of humanity is completely covered with such pock-marks. It looks at itself in the mirror, is ashamed, and covered with disgust.[151]

A number of leading playwrights as well as lesser authors have emerged from Kolyada's "incubator," as Yana Ross has called it.[152] Their works include plays about troops returning from Chechnya, haunting encounters by soldiers with their past, living spirits and dying souls, the tragedy of terrorism (e.g., plays about the 2004 attack on a school in the Caucasus town of Beslan), and harsh depictions of corruption, infidelity, alcoholism, drug abuse, the indignities of age, and social inequality.[153]

In the end, these plays are about how society relates to events more than about the events themselves. Sonya, in Pavel Kazantsev's *Hero*, speaks of a fundamental conundrum of life in contemporary Russia as being a strange detachment from reality. Speaking with her new lover, a returning war hero, Egor, Sonya declares, "When I watch stories about the war on the news, it seems to me that nothing is real. Well, in the sense that there are tanks, and soldiers, and destruction everywhere, and shooting every day, and it is dangerous to be out on the streets. But you hear this on television, eating a large sausage and cheese sandwich. It's simple. It's all the same for you."[154]

More than just telling a story, however, the writers seek humanity among even their most questionable characters. In Kazantsev's and Yaroslava Pylinovich's *The Cleaners*, a young man and woman meet in a supermarket, where the woman apparently is trying to buy a new dress. As the play unfolds, the audience learns that both are shoplifters. The man, who is driven less by material vanity than by a need to survive, finally confronts the young lady. "What do you want?" he asks. "A magical wand? A sling with arrows? That's all I know, all I learned from you. The rest is improvisation. . . . The world exists even without money, but money does not exist without the world. Your money can open a theater, a cinema studio, a kindergarten; but you, except for your money, are nothing of interest."[155]

At the same time, there is often a humane sympathy for an older generation that survived the travails of life in the Soviet Union. In Nina Sadur's *Pilot*, which was published in early 2011, eighty-year-old Paolo berates thirteen-year-old Lena for criticizing her father for his life during the Soviet period. "He knew how to dream," Paolo tells Lena, as if the youngster does not. Paolo continues:

> He believed in Stalin. I excuse you—what do you know about him? You didn't live then! He would say: It is so cold and lonely driving trucks along the roads of our motherland. It happens, he told me, when he was a young long-range driver that he would drive for days without meeting anyone. He told me about all he had on those long routes was a portrait of Comrade Stalin flapping on the rearview mirror, watching over him as he flew along—as he was flying somewhere through the endless deserts of this land. And Comrade Stalin had such a harsh gaze. You looked at him and you could not fall asleep. This is the country you were born in.[156]

Sadur—who was born in 1950, well before many practitioners of the New Russian Drama Movement, and has no direct connection to Yekaterinburg—is well respected by many who identify with the New Russia Drama Movement, despite being considerably older. She chose to publish her work in *Ural* in recognition of the journal's national scope and reputation.

Students and Disciples

The local theater scene remains far more vibrant than the political controversies swirling around Kolyada might imply. Beyond Kolyada himself, several Yekaterinburg playwrights have contributed to the transformation of writing for the Russian stage. At least four among them—Vassily Sigarev, Oleg Bogayev, and the Presnyakov brothers, Vladimir and Oleg—have become international sensations on their own terms.

As noted at the start of this chapter, Sigarev set the London stage world abuzz with the premiere performance of *Plasticine* at the Royal Court Theatre. Born in 1977, the native of the small Sverd-lovsk Region settlement of Verkhnaia Salda made his way to study with Kolyada via a two-year stint at the Nizhny Tagil Pedagogical Institute.[157] Segarev had grown up in the home of an electrician fa-ther, a collective-farm worker mother, and a drug-dealing brother. Taken by Stephen King's horror novels, he had begun to write be-fore he had started studying in Nizhny Tagil. He moved to Yekat-erinburg after seeing a poster for Kolyada's playwriting courses at his school.[158]

Sigarev was a fully formed writer by the time he came to work with Kolyada. In 2000, he completed *Plasticine*, which immediately began to attract attention in Russia. The play was produced in Mos-cow's Playwright and Director Center after it received the Russian "Anti-Booker" Prize, and from there was translated into English and brought to the Royal Court.[159] Simultaneously, Sigarev wrote two other successful plays, *Black Milk* and *Ladybird*, both of which similarly won considerable praise in London. More recently, he has expanded his writing to include screenplays. He won international praise and attention for both his writing and his film direction with his 2009 film *Wolfy*, a tale about a young girl left to her own devices by an alcoholic and abusive mother.[160]

Of all these works, *Black Milk* perhaps has had the most suc-cess internationally, being staged across Europe and North Amer-ica (figure 43).[161] One of its first US productions, at Washington's Studio Theater in early 2005, brought particular acclaim, helping to promote the play to other theaters around the country.[162] The story transpires in a provincial train station, from which two small-time con artists—a young couple representing the urban "sophis-tication" of the "new" Russia—travel to small towns around Rus-sia, selling outrageously priced and ultimately useless toasters in order to bamboozle the unsophisticated locals. The play paints an especially bleak picture of post-Soviet Russia, where everyone, it seems, is a ruthless, sleazy, violent, and/or alcoholic predatory con artist, and where even the wise old peasant lady selling train tick-ets turns out to have been selling poisoned moonshine from under the counter. A moment of possible redemption—after the toaster saleswoman gives birth, claims to have seen God, and proclaims her desire to remain in the virtuous countryside—collapses, so that

Figure 43. John Brambery and Anna Wilson in *Black Milk* in 2014.
Source: Photograph by Carol Rosegg; used by permission (http://www.stageand-cinema.com/2012/07/26/black-milk/).

at the end, the message is clear: One new child — or many — will not alleviate Russia's physical and spiritual suffering.

Oleg Bogayev, whose play *Russian National Postal Service* also was staged by the Studio Theater during its 2004–5 season, presents a no-less-chilling account of human relationships in Boris Yeltsin's Russia.[163] Bogayev takes us to the cluttered, tiny apartment of a lone retiree, Ivan Zhukov, who, like many of his generation, worked all his life only to end up with nothing following the collapse of the Soviet economy. Living on an inadequate pension that barely covers the cost of his food, he holes up at home, slowly entering into a fantasyland in which the queen of England, Lenin, a cosmonaut, Martians, and others visit for tea. He continues his friendship with these imaginary characters once they depart his abode through correspondence sent via the Russian National Postal Service. And he quietly slips from life as his upstairs neighbors are busy loudly celebrating New Year's Eve (and the dawn of a "new" Russia). Bogayev's dark and offbeat humor humanizes an otherwise tragic character who has been degraded, like many of his compatriots, by age, insanity, and economic collapse.[164]

Bogayev simultaneously is playing his own game with classical Russian literature. Zhukov shares his name with the protagonist of Anton Chekhov's short story "Van'ka Zhukov." As the dramatist Andrei Maleev-Babel has observed, the character in Chekhov's story, an abused boy, writes a letter to his grandfather, who lives in the village, asking the grandfather to come to town to rescue him. The boy addresses the letter "To my grandfather, at the village," and takes it off to the post office to mail it, absolutely convinced that the letter will reach his grandfather. This hopeless situation is repeated in the *Russian National Postal Service*, which makes the play in part a holistic reference to Chekhov and his work.[165]

These works earned Bogayev several awards, including the Russian "Anti-Booker" Prize and Russia's highest theatrical award, Moscow's Golden Mask, as well as leading to his being celebrated at the Royal Court Theatre. The success of his works at Washington's Studio Theater has led to numerous other performances around the United States. Several of his three-dozen plays have had wide success around Russia, Europe, and North America, including an especially well-received production of *Maria's Field* at Chicago's highly regarded Tuta Theater.[166]

Bogayev, who was born in 1970, retains a strong commitment to his native Yekaterinburg despite this wider success. He was one of the first graduates of Kolyada's program at the Yekaterinburg State Theatre Institute, and he has continued to work with the local drama scene, mentoring younger writers, producers, and directors. He began serving as editor of *Ural* after Kolyada stepped down from that position in August 2010.[167] The journal has continued to promote young writers and playwrights under his stewardship.

The Presnyakov brothers—Oleg, born in 1969, and Vladimir, born in 1974—represent yet another face of the Yekaterinburg theatrical scene. The Presnyakovs are not students of Kolyada, and in fact have even had a tumultuous relationship with their elder. Following the New York run of their play *Terrorism*, Murph Henderson wrote in *American Theatre* magazine that the Presnyakovs once had visited the editorial offices of *Ural* to ask Kolyada if they could call themselves his students, even though they had never studied with him. "Three years later," Henderson reports, they "publicly disavowed the connection, declaring Kolyada's theater a *kolkhoz* — that is, a [Soviet-era collective] farm worked by peasants — and calling themselves 'intellectuals.' Kolyada has posted a sign above his office door at the theater that reads 'head of the *kolkhoz.*'"[168] The Presnyakovs subsequently moved to Vienna.

The Presnyakov brothers were sons of an Iranian mother and a Russian father, and they graduated from the Philological Faculty at Urals State University, where they have both taught. Oleg completed graduate school in literature, while Vladimir studied pedagogy in graduate school.[169] Their most successful plays — *Playing the Victim, Killing the Judge*, and *Terrorism* — make direct references to the Russian classics. By drawing on one of the grand themes of Russian literature — conflict among the generations — the Presnyakovs bring a bittersweet sensibility to conflicts that often prove fatal.[170] Their version of the fairy tale *The Humpbacked Little Horse* revealed a similar compelling sympathy for the more magical dimensions of Russian cultural and literary traditions. Several of their plays have moved successfully from the stage to film, with Kirill Serebrennikov's retelling of *Playing the Victim* earning major awards at film festivals in Sochi and Rome.[171]

The success of several of the Presnyakovs' plays abroad speaks to their ability to address fears shared by many far beyond the boundaries of today's Russian Federation. In *Terrorism*, a group of disgruntled passengers and policemen bicker, commit adultery, make fun of one another, and even commit suicide — all while delayed by an airport bomb scare. Deeper connections among the passengers slowly emerge once the plane finally takes off. In *Playing the Victim*, a university dropout finds work with the police playing the victim in the reconstruction of murders. The young Silver Age poets Andrei Bely and Alexander Blok, and his mother, Alexandra Kublitskaia-Piottukh, roam through a cheerful farce in *Captive Spirits*, and the carnival of contemporary Russian life is portrayed in *Europe-Asia*. On one level, these works are about a "global f*#k-up" that is shared by all twenty-first-century humans; on another, they offer a penetrating critique of violence and an emerging Russian fascism.[172]

As the Presnyakovs' evolving relationship with Yekaterinburg suggests, the local theater scene is far wider than any single writer or group of writers and performers. The Kolyada group thrives within a wide theatrical scene, in which all varieties of performing arts engage the city around them. Beyond classical drama, the city is home to a highly innovative and artistically successful puppet theater that has won various national and international prices, including the Golden Mask.[173]

The Yekaterinburg Theatre of Musical Comedy similarly collected many honors under the talented directorship of Vladimir Kurochkin during the late Soviet period. Kurochkin was the first Soviet director to bring *Hello, Dolly* to the city, in 1974, and he tried but failed to follow with *Cabaret* and *Fiddler on the Roof*.[174] The theater has continued to garner awards such as the Golden Mask in more recent times, while pushing the boundaries of the Russian musical.[175] For example, the production by the composer Sergei Dreznin and the lyricists Mikhail Roshchin and Alexander Anno of the sprawling epic *Catherine the Great* proved as controversial for its slyly satirical stance toward Russian history as told by contemporary "patriots" as for its widespread use of the latest staging techniques from London's West End and New York's Broadway.

Catherine the Great was considered by some critics to be Russia's first homegrown musical, as the genre is understood in the Anglo-American world, and the Yekaterinburg production raised standards for musicals to the level of the "Hollywood blockbuster or a West End hit."[176] Yet even after being nominated for seven Golden Masks in 2009, the production ultimately challenged too many Russian assumptions about history and musical drama to find acceptance in Moscow.

A Wondrous Mirror

Yekaterinburg theater seasons during the 2000s have included new directors, new plays, new writers, and new stars, as the local opera company, ballet company, academic dramatic theater, children's theater, and smaller chamber theaters (e.g., those organized by Kolyada and the Presnyakovs) and have generated, in the words of the critic Kasia Popova, "a living and disturbing organism which has its own laws that are no less wondrous than those of the laws of nature."[177]

As Popova concludes in a review of the 2006–7 drama season, Yekaterinburg theater, in all its rich diversity, has become a mirror for the city itself. Local productions—whether they are tragedies or dark comedies, multi-act or single-act productions, allegories or high realism—share a concern with the joys and pains of everyday life as seen in a turbulent society. They emerge from the individual keyboards of writers who are embedded in the wider community of writers and theatrical institutions—writers who are engaged in a common search for meaning in a city, society, and country where every marker of stability and identity has vanished.[178]

One young man in Oleg Bogayev's *Thirty Three Happinesses* captures the ethos of the twenty-first-century Yekaterinburg stage when he declares, "You know, . . . there is nothing. There is nothing in our flags, in our laughs, in our songs, . . . around any home, any person, any song, are the slogans of an important language. All around us in any city there is nothing of ours. We have awoken in a different country. They tell me that we live in a new world. We now live in a capitalist country."[179] The New Russian Drama Movement—as it has blossomed in Yekaterinburg and elsewhere—is a search for how to make this new country one's own.

The message of these works parallels Valentin Lukyanin's city "soul," about which he wrote in an ode to Yekaterinburg. "In fact," the city's literary master penned, "we need to recognize that nothing real has changed for the past twenty years in the urban environment. Maybe there is graffiti, but in fact everything is what it was. We have our socialist capital, or our 'almost Chicago,' and all of what we see is a result of not just policy, but of human activity, how we live in our city and how we use it." Yekaterinburg's message to post-Soviet Russia seems to be to move beyond policies and politics and to focus on how to live, how to make use of life. Only then does humanity glimmer in even the bleakest landscape.

Yekaterinburg's playwrights, directors, producers, and actors are hardly unique on the Russian stage, in that the travails of post-Soviet Russian life have inspired one of this new century's most vibrant national theater scenes. The Togliatti writers—Iurii Klavdiev, Mikhail and Vyacheslav Durnenkov, Rostov-na-Donu's Sergei Medvedev, Khanty-Mansiysk's Bulat Shiribazarov, and Nizhny Tagil's Ekaterina Vasilyeva, to name just a few—have written works that have electrified, shocked, disturbed, and inspired audiences on stage, screen, and television.[180] Yekaterinburg's longtime Urals competitor city, Perm, made an ambitious commitment for a time to the visual arts by allocating 3 percent of the regional budget to promote cultural development.[181] These policies are producing a vibrant and noteworthy theatrical world all its own.

There is now fear that the period of the New Russian Drama Movement, in which Yekaterinburg has played such a central role, came to an end following the return of Vladimir Putin to the Russian presidency. The tensions around Putin's revived presidency exploded in Ekaterinburg when Kolyada supported Putin's candidacy. As that episode revealed, the Russian theatrical community is part of larger Russian society and reflects some of the same divisions as its society. More tellingly, a number of Russian cultural policies—including bans on obscenity in artistic works, limits on nonstate funding for cultural institutions, and the growth of a xenophobic nationalism consolidated by conflict with Ukraine in 2014—marked the end of an era in Russian theater.

The critic John Freedman marked the end of an era in July 2014, when he wrote:

> The number of major playwrights that Russia put up over the last 15 to 18 years may make all other eras in the history of Russian drama pale by comparison. If this hasn't been a golden age, then quickly sell off your hoard because gold is no longer a standard. . . . The avant-garde led by the new playwrights of the 2000s was dubbed "new drama." It's an amorphous phrase that causes as much confusion as clarity. But there is no denying that the bold, iconoclastic writers who tilled new ground by stretching the limits of language, by introducing controversial new themes, and by expanding the genre of drama to include many methods heretofore unknown in Russia, and, indeed, done something new, and their business was drama. . . . The community of theater writers is under attack; key values and aspirations no longer unite it. . . . A break has occurred, and now we wait to see what comes next.[182]

Tellingly, Russia's and Yekaterinburg's new theatrical life existed largely beyond the reach and control of Moscow's artistic Mandarins. Kolyada, Sigaryev, Bogayev, the Presnyakovs, and their counterparts elsewhere around Russia created their own direct paths to the outside world. Collectively, Russian playwrights gave meaning to life in an era of Russian history when nothing other than material wealth seemed of value. Through their frank, bleak, and brutal portrayals of everyday life outside Russia's "two capitals" (Moscow and Saint Petersburg), they infused magic, spirituality, truth seeking, a sense of awareness, and humanity into the Russian sense of self. That legacy remains as a primary building block for whatever Russian theater becomes in the years ahead.

Yet as important as these individual writers and the cities that inspire them may have been, Yekaterinburg remains the leading center of a new approach to theater and to writing that holds the promise of a new golden age for the Russian stage.[183] Because it is a city full of the most troubling and vexing contradictions of Russia itself, Yekaterinburg's turning of the urban kaleidoscope has been just fast enough to produce the urban delirium that has prompted human creativity for centuries. A foundation in gritty daily reality simultaneously prevents even the most soaring flight of urban fancy from leaving the orbit of human existence. Time is required to know whether or not this tradition will survive President Putin, as it outlived Communist Party satraps before.

Encore

Outsiders Creating for Insiders

Having an outsider on the inside can never be bad for the arts.

—Shermin Langhoff, artistic director of
Berlin's Maxim Gorki Theater, 2015

More than two decades ago, in 1993, the Harvard government professor Robert Putnam published his now-classic study *Making Democracy Work: Civic Traditions in Modern Italy.*[1] Trying to answer the question of why Northern Italian cities developed vibrant civic traditions, which came to support the growth of democratic institutions, but Southern Italian cities did not, Putnam was surprised to find a strong correlation between civic health and choral societies. Putnam masterfully argued that choral societies emerged from the same broad reservoir of social capital that is required to support civic vitality.

Appearing just as countries throughout the former communist world were struggling to create new democracies, Putnam's work became something of a Holy Grail for promoters of a new political order. The problem, however, was that Putnam's work failed to sufficiently explain how such civic virtue and social capital could be created in the first place.

Perhaps hard-nosed democracy advocates pursuing measurable advances toward institutionally bounded representative institutions considered music little more than white noise. If so, they may have missed part of a solution to Putnam's seemingly unanswered challenge. Song, after all, has bound humans together for millennia, and the social interaction required to create vocal beauty can be transferred to other activities. Choral societies are not just a reflection of civic health, but may in reality be central to its origins.

The significance of social capital for civic well-being is more than theoretical conjecture. A growing body of evidence drawn from the responses to such recent disasters as Hurricane Katrina and Superstorm Sandy suggests that those communities that have the highest stores of social capital before suffering a communal trauma recover most quickly following both human-made and natural disasters. This capital, in turn, does not require deep knowledge of one another so much as a casual sociability that allows neighbors and colleagues to turn to one another in times of crisis. The performing arts encourage just such a geniality by bringing together audiences and performers to share a moment of conviviality. They open pathways for outsiders to become insiders, adding new creative energy to cities. They convert urban delirium into an asset, as can been seen for each of the cities and performing arts explored in this volume.

The dynamism of eighteenth-century Naples and Osaka reflected the energy of new political regimes and the broadening of commerce. Their wealth drew tens of thousands of migrants from the surrounding countryside into town and created new social classes. Opera and Kabuki responded to the desires of ambitious, rising nouveaux bourgeoisie as they dreamed of ascending ever higher in the social hierarchy. The broad comedies of opera buffa were sung in the language of the street by characters lifted out of everyday life. Kabuki was still closer to the ground, having originated in the Tokugawa sex trade. Both opera and Kabuki were intensely urban in their character from the very beginning. Opera, of course, initially began at court, often in small towns. It secured its place in European culture in the grand cities of the era—first in Venice and Naples; and later in London, Paris, and Vienna. Kabuki, from its earliest performances in Kyoto, always was about pleasing audiences of townspeople.

New York and Buenos Aires a century ago were the very definitions of urban intensity, as tens of thousands of immigrants arrived from across Europe. These outsiders challenged assumptions about every aspect of daily life. In coming to the New World, they joined societies predicated on integration. Culture throughout the

Americas for a couple of centuries before had formed around locally distinctive blends of native, African, and European elements—a
process heightened in the urban pressure cookers of Buenos Aires
and New York.

Twentieth-century Cape Town and Yekaterinburg were products of colonial projects united by some of the harshest social and
political experimentation of the twentieth century. Because these
cities' performing arts were set in regimes in which insiders sought
to keep outsiders permanently under heel, performing gave voice
to those who otherwise could not speak. In both cities, jazz and
rock performers, and theater directors and playwrights, uttered the
unutterable. They created public spaces where those who were to
be kept apart nonetheless came together. They literally created the
social capital necessary to motivate political and economic transformation.

As noted at the outset to this book, Rem Koolhaas has argued
in his path-breaking evocation of New York during the 1970s, *Delirious New York*, that "the Metropolis strives to reach a mythical
point where the world is completely fabricated by man, so that it
absolutely coincides with his desires."[2] So, too, do the arts, which
are kinetic expressions of unconscious desires and fears. As collective expressions, the performing arts enable community members to impose their own inner world on a cityscape of immense
complexity. The contradictions of urban life are a wellspring of
invention, converting the sudden and disconcerting juxtaposition
of opposites—of high and low culture, good and evil, foreign and
domestic—into an asset that enriches the cityscape.

The chapters presented here have drawn on histories of the
performing arts—opera, dance, theater, and music—to provide insight into the creativity of urban life. They tell the story of moments
when the urban kaleidoscope has turned with such delirious speed
that the city has become the muse for many among its most creative
inhabitants.

This volume opened on the corner of 7th and T streets, NW, in
Washington, as the freshly renovated Howard Theatre reopened.
The stories that have been told in the subsequent chapters have
contemporary meaning, even if they have been rooted in different
continents and centuries. Back in Washington, looking around at

the happy crowd that made David Akers smile, it was easy to lose sight of the heated tensions surrounding the city's vibrant popular culture. Music in Washington has long had an insurrectional accent, giving voice to disenfranchised outsiders to be used against those who hold power. And this was especially true during the century when the city was run by a troika of unelected commissioners appointed by the federal government.

During the late 1960s, with revolt in the air, the local musician Chuck Brown created an infectious musical style combining a distinctive Latin-tinged beat with a call-and-response vocal track that came to be known as "go-go." A subgenre of funk and a distant cousin of hip-hop, go-go emerged on Washington's streets and in its rough-and-tumble nightclubs as the city was reeling from crushing economic decline, massive civil unrest, and the arrival of crack cocaine. Go-go quickly became the anthem of Washington's African American working class.

For many, the go-go scene was alarming, with disorder and crime often seen as associated with go-go venues. The Washington police carefully tracked performances, working with various licensing authorities to shut down clubs following violent incidents. Then, several popular go-go haunts along the Anacostia River waterfront were demolished to make way for a new baseball stadium for the Washington Nationals, which opened in 2010. There even have been reports that an Advisory Neighborhood Commission in Northwest Washington's rapidly gentrifying Petworth area voted to recommend that the Liquor Control Board grant a liquor license, provided that the club in question not allow go-go to be performed. Such a provision would be particularly ironic, given that Petworth had been home to an especially vibrant go-go scene just a few years before.

At the same time, Washingtonians of all classes, races, genders, and generations now take pride in the city's distinctive soundtrack. The outsiders have become insiders, defining what it means to be from and live in the city—all because of music.

New art forms, emerging during periods of profound economic change, fill the vacuum left by conflicts over power. They express the frustrations and struggles of social groups that are at the losing end of such skirmishes; and they do so in ways that are unvarnished and potent. Their practitioners mean to offend—and they do. In response, the authorities present themselves as preserving public safety and virtue by ensuring that some in-your-face forms of cultural expression are removed from view.

Go-go is far too new and local to know how secure a future the genre will have. Like many American musical forms—such as jazz, bluegrass, opera, and chamber music—critics are certain to write its obituary long before its actual death. Go-go will live on and find fertile ground for renewal, as it has already done, pushing out of Washington into its nearby suburbs, and beyond.

Struggles over new urban cultural forms are often more about the underappreciated using the arts as a way of forcing themselves to respectability. David Akers smiled when he saw the statue of Duke Ellington in front of the newly honored Howard Theatre. Yet Ellington and his music were underappreciated when he was starting out. His name is now attached to a significant bridge and a high school in Washington, and is found on various historical plaques and memorials scattered around his hometown. Chuck Brown—the "godfather of go-go"—similarly has become a treasure. In August 2014, the DC government dedicated a monument, amphitheater, and memorial park honoring Brown in Northeast DC's Langdon Park. A go-go beat, like all the art forms explored in this book, outlasts politicians. It is art that endures.

Notes

Preface: The Devil Is a Local Call Away

1 The epigraphs for the book and for this preface are from, respectively, these sources: Edgar Pieterse, "Youth Cultures and the Mediation of Racial Exclusion or Inclusion in Rio de Janeiro and Cape Town," in *Urban Diversity: Space, Culture, and Inclusive Pluralism in Cities Worldwide*, ed. Caroline Wanjiku Kihato, Mejgan Massoumi, Blair A. Ruble, Pep Subirós, and Allison M. Garland (Washington and Baltimore: Woodrow Wilson Center Press and Johns Hopkins University Press, 2010), 187–211, at 209; and Cess Nooteboom, "Amsterdam," in *De Filossof Zonder Ogen*, 1997, trans. Manfred Wolf and Virginie Kortekaas, in *Amsterdam: A Traveler's Literary Companion*, ed. Manfred Wolf (San Francisco: Whereabouts Press, 2001), 3–4.

2 Blair A. Ruble, *Soviet Trade Unions: Their Development in the 1970s* (New York: Cambridge University Press, 1981).

3 Blair A. Ruble, *Leningrad: Shaping a Soviet City* (Berkeley: University of California Press, 1990).

4 Blair A. Ruble, *Money Sings: The Changing Politics of Urban Space in Post-Soviet Yaroslavl* (Washington and New York: Woodrow Wilson Center Press and Cambridge University Press, 1995).

5 Blair A. Ruble, *Second Metropolis: Pragmatic Pluralism in Gilded Age Chicago, Silver Age Moscow, and Meiji Osaka* (Washington and New York: Woodrow Wilson Center Press and Cambridge University Press, 2001).

6 Blair A. Ruble, *Creating Diversity Capital: Transnational Migrants in Montreal, Washington, and Kyiv* (Washington and Baltimore: Woodrow Wilson Center Press and Johns Hopkins University Press, 2005).

7 Blair A. Ruble, *Washington's U Street: A Biography* (Washington and Baltimore: Woodrow Wilson Center Press and Johns Hopkins University Press, 2010).

8 Olga Grushin, *The Dream Life of Sukhanov* (New York: G. P. Putnam's Sons, 2005), 345.

9 Benjamin R. Barber, *If Mayors Ruled the World: Dysfunctional Nations, Rising Cities* (New Haven, Conn.: Yale University Press, 2013), 294.

David Akers's Smile: Urban Delirium and Cultural Innovation

1   Blair A. Ruble, *Washington's U Street: A Biography* (Washington and Baltimore: Woodrow Wilson Center Press and Johns Hopkins University Press, 2010). The epigraph for this chapter is from Manuel Vázques Montalbán, *The Buenos Aires Quintet*, trans. Nick Caistor (London: Serpent's Tail, 2003), 3.

2   These Odessa Web sites include the World-Wide Club of Oddessites, http://www.odessitclub.org/archive/static_welcome.php; Odessa on the Horizon (Odessa na gudzone), http://www.odessitka.net/; and Odessites, http://odessit.in.ua/.

3   *The Odessa Tales* and Babel's other works may be found in *The Complete Works of Isaac Babel*, ed. Isaac Babel, Nathalie Babel, and Peter Constantine (New York: W. W. Norton, 2002). Andrei Maleev-Babel's philosophy of theatrical production may be seen in his study *Yevgeny Vakhtangov: A Critical Portrait* (London: Routledge, 2012).

4   Tanya Richardson, *Kaleidoscopic Odessa: History and Place in Contemporary Ukraine* (Toronto: University of Toronto Press, 2008).

5   Rebecca Stanton, "Identity Crisis: The Literary Cult and Culture of Odessa in the Early 20th Century," *Symposium*, Fall 2003, 117–26; Rebecca Stanton, "Odessan Selves: Identity and Mythopoesis in Works of the Odessa School" (PhD diss., Columbia University, New York, 2004). Stanton subsequently published her study as *Isaac Babel and the Self-Invention of Odessan Modernism* (Evanston, Ill.: Northwestern University Press, 2012). Richardson's and Staunton's concept of the kaleidoscopic is closer to Henri Lefebvre's conceptualization of heterotropy than that of Michel Foucault; For a comparison, see Henri Lefebvre, *Révolution urbaine / The Urban Revolution* (Minneapolis: University of Minnesota Press, 2003); and Michel Foucault, *Les Mots et les choses: Une archéologie des sciences humaines* (Paris: Gallimard, 1966).

6   Anselm Gerhard, *The Urbanization of Opera: Music Theater in Paris in the Nineteenth Century* (Chicago: University of Chicago Press, 1998), trans. Mary Whittall, 14–15.

7   Tanya Richardson, *Kaleidoscopic Odessa: History and Place in Contemporary Ukraine*, p. 6.

8   The story of Odessa's first century and a quarter are well told by Patricia Herlihy, *Odessa: A History, 1794–1914* (Cambridge, Mass.: Harvard Series in Ukrainian Studies, 1991).

9   Charles King, *Odessa: Genius and Death in a City of Dreams* (New York: W. W. Norton, 2011), 18.

10 Ibid., 19.

11 This is a process known in religious discourse as "syncretism." For

an introduction to syncretism, see Eric Maroney, *Religious Syncretism* (London: SCM–Canterbury Press, 2006).

12 Samuel C. Ramer, "Meditations on Urban Identity: Odessa/Odesa and New Orleans," in *Occasional Paper 301: Place, Identity, and Urban Culture—Odesa and New Orleans*, ed. Samuel C. Ramer and Blair A. Ruble (Washington: Kennan Institute at Woodrow Wilson International Center for Scholars, 2008), 1–7, at 5.

13 Lawrence Powell, *The Accidental City: Improvising New Orleans* (Cambridge, Mass.: Harvard University Press, 2012), 120.

14 Louis Eric Elie, "Here They Come, There They Go," in *Unfathomable City: A New Orleans Atlas* ed. Rebecca Solnit and Rebecca Snedeker (Berkeley: University of California Press, 2013), 25–33, at 25.

15 Scott Cowen, *The Inevitable City: The Resurgence of New Orleans and the Future of Urban America* (New York: Palgrave MacMillan, 2014), 187.

16 Powell, *Accidental City*, 97–98.

17 Ned Sublette, *The World That Made New Orleans: From Spanish Silver to Congo Square* (Chicago: Lawrence Hill Books, 2008).

18 Freddi Williams Evans, *Congo Square: African Roots in New Orleans* (Lafayette: University of Louisiana at Lafayette Press, 2011).

19 Susan C. Pearce, "Saxophones, Trumpets, and Hurricanes: The Cultural Restructuring of New Orleans," in *Racing the Storm: Racial Implications and Lessons Learned from Hurricane Katrina*, ed. Hillary Porter (New York: Lexington Books, 2007), 115–33, at 119.

20 Evans, *Congo Square*, 107.

21 Charles B. Hersch, "Jazz and the Boundaries of Race," *Perspectives on Politics* 10, no. 3 (September 2012): 701–8, at 703.

22 Johari Jabir, "On Conjuring Mahalia: Mahalia Jackson, New Orleans, and the Sanctified Swing," *American Quarterly* 61, no. 3 (2009): 649–70.

23 Jason Berry, Jonathan Foose, and Tad Jones, *Up from the Cradle of Jazz: New Orleans Music since World War II* (Lafayette: University of Louisiana at Lafayette Press, 2009, 1–142; Ned Sublette, *The Year Before the Flood: A Story of New Orleans* (Chicago: Lawrence Hill Books, 2009), 144–57.

24 This point is powerfully made by George Porter Jr., "The Floating Cushion," in *Unfathomable City*, ed. Solnit and Snedeker, 116–20.

25 Ibid.

26 Garnette Cadogan, "Where Dey At," in *Unfathomable City*, ed. Solnit and Snedeker, 121–26.

27 Ibid., 121.

28 Sublette, *Year Before the Flood*, 193–200; Kelefa Sanneh, "New Orleans Hip-Hop Is the Home of Gansta Gumbo," *New York Times*, April 26, 2006.

29 Sublette, *Year Before the Flood*, 198.

30 Ibid., 198–216.

31 Ibid., 227.

32 Ibid., 195.

33 Caroline Wanjinku Kihato, *Migrant Women of Johannesburg: Life in an In-Between City* (Johannesburg: Wits University Press, 2013), 115.

34 This point is underscored by Jim Flynn, *Sidewalk Saints: Life Portraits of the New Orleans Street Performer Family* (New Orleans: Curbside Press, 2011).

35 John Swenson, *New Atlantis: Musicians Battle for the Survival of New Orleans* (New York: Oxford University Press, 2011), 12–15.

36 The ongoing battle over "vice" a century ago between respectable New Orleaneans and the city's African American and Italian immigrant communities is compellingly retold by Gary Krist, *Empire of Sin: A Story of Sex, Jazz, Murder, and the Battle for Modern New Orleans* (New York: Crown, 2014).

37 Thomas Brothers, *Louis Armstrong's New Orleans* (New York: W. W. Norton, 2006), 220–21.

38 Pierre Manent, *Metamorphoses of the City: On the Western Dynamic*, trans. Marc Lepain (Cambridge, Mass.: Harvard University Press, 2013), 18.

39 Kristof Van Assche and Petruţa Teampău, *Local Cosmopolitanism: Imagining and (Re-)Making Privileged Places* (New York: Springer, 2015), 95.

40 Philip Sheldrake, *The Spiritual City: Theology, Spirituality, and the Urban* (Chichester: Wiley/Blackwell, 2014), 13.

41 Ibid., 153.

42 Jeff Chang, *Can't Stop, Won't Stop: A History of the Hip-Hop Generation* (New York: St. Martin's Press, 2005), 68-72; Sublette, *Year Before the Flood*, 186–89.

43 Juan Flores, "Rappin', Writin', & Breakin'," in *Dissent Special Issue: In Search of New York*, Fall 1987, ed. Jim Sleeper, 580–84.

44 Eric D. Weitz, *Weimar Germany: Promise and Tragedy* (Princeton, N.J.: Princeton University Press, 2007), 50.

45 Adam Bradley, *Books of Rhymes: The Poetics of Hip Hop* (New York: Basic Civitas, 2009), 13–14.

46 The links between West African *griot*, Jamaican dub, New York street culture, and technology are explored in articles collected by Raquel Cepeda and Nelson George, eds., *And I Don't Stop: The Best American Hip-Hop Journalism of the Last Years* (New York: Faber & Faber, 2004).

47 Jacques Attali, *Bruits: Essai sur l'économie politique de la musique* (Paris: Presses Universitaires de France, 1977), translated as Jacques

Attali, *Noise: The Political Economy of Music*, trans. Brian Massumi (Minneapolis: University of Minnesota Press, 2011).

48 Marshal Berman, *All That Is Solid Melts into Air: The Experience of Modernity* (New York: Simon & Schuster, 1982), 175.

49 Ibid., 194–95.

50 See, e.g., Catriona Kelly, *St. Petersburg: Shadows of the Past* (New Haven, Conn.: Yale University Press, 2014), 257–62; Anatoli Yurchak, *Everything Was Forever, Until It Was No More: The Last Soviet Generation* (Princeton, N.J.: Princeton University Press, 2005), 82–148); and Elena Zdravomyslova, "The Café Saigon *Tusovka*: One Segment of the Informal-Public Sphere of Late-Soviet Society," in *Biographical Research in Eastern Europe: Altered Lives and Broken Biographies*, ed. Robin Humphrey, Robert Miller, and Elena Zdravomyslova (Burlington, Vt.: Ashgate, 2003), 141–78.

51 Kama Ginkas and John Freedman, *Provoking Theater: Kama Ginkas Directs* (Hanover, N.H.: Smith and Kraus, 2003), 213–14.

52 Robert Alter, *Imagined Cities: Urban Experience and the Language of the Novel* (New Haven, Conn.: Yale University Press, 2005), 17.

53 Nikolai Gogol's 1842 recollections of Rome can be considered Russia's first major example of "urbanological" thought. Andrei Ivanov explores Gogol's contributions to Russian thinking about cities in his masterful comparison of street life in Odessa and Baku: Andrei Ivanov, *Dve Gogolia: Sredinnye ulitsy posdbeimperskogo gorod (Odessa/Baku)* (Moscow: Vash Poligraficheskii Partner, 2010).

54 As first used by Mary Louise Pratt in the early 1990s, the notion of a "contact zone" refers to those spaces where "cultures meet, clash, and grapple with each other, often in contexts of highly asymmetrical relations of power, such as colonialism, slavery, or their aftermaths"; Mary Louise Pratt, "Arts in the Contact Zone," *Profession 91*, 33–40, as republished by David Bartholomae and Anthony Petrosky, ed., *Reading the Lives of Others* (Boston: Bedford Books of St. Martin's Press, 1995), 180–95, at 182–83. Pratt observes that such zones, which are "commonly regarded as chaotic, barbarous, lacking in structure," are often full of improvised relationships and "co-presence" that mark the coming into contact of peoples "geographically and historically separated, . . . usually involving conditions of coercion, radical inequality, and intractable conflict"; Mary Louise Pratt, *Travel Writing and Transculturation* (New York: Routledge, 1992), 6–7.

55 Donna Leon, "Music," in *My Venice and Other Essays*, by Donna Leon (New York: Atlantic Monthly Press, 2013), 61–63, at 63.

56 Rem Koolhaas, *Delirious New York* (New York: Monacelli Press, 1994; orig. pub. 1978), 293.

57 Peter Schneider, *Berlin Now: The City After the Wall*, trans. Sophie Schlondorff (New York: Farrar, Straus & Giroux, 2014), 272.

58 Daniel Snowman, *The Gilded Stage: A Social History of Opera* (London: Atlantic Books, 2009), 2–7.

59 Lewis Mumford, *The City in History* (New York: Harcourt, Brace & World, 1961).

60 Peter Hall, *Cities in Civilization* (New York: Pantheon Books, 1998).

61 Ibid., 285.

62 Ibid.

63 Ibid.

64 P. D. Smith, *City: A Guidebook for the Urban Age* (New York: Bloomsbury Press, 2012), 253.

65 This is a turn of phrase that was used by Yasunari Kawabata in describing the Asakusa district of his Tokyo youth during the late 1920s and early 1930s. See Yasunari Kawabata, *The Scarlet Gang of Asakusa*, trans. Alisa Freedman (Berkeley: University of California Press, 2005), 30.

A Paradise Inhabited by Devils: Opera in Viceregal and Bourbon Naples

1 I would like to take this opportunity to thank research interns Raughley D. Nuzzi and Elizabeth Hipple for their support and assistance in the preparation of this chapter. I also would like to acknowledge the thoughtful comments and enthusiastic support of readers Daniel Spikes and Janet Spikes. The epigraph for this chapter is from Barringer Fifield, *Seeing Naples* (Napoli: Electra, 1996), 13.

2 Michael F. Robinson, *Naples and Neapolitan Opera* (New York: Oxford University Press, 1972), 1.

3 Fifield, *Seeing Naples*, 11; Peter Robb, *Street Fight in Naples: A City's Unseen History* (London: Bloomsbury Press, 2011), 80–92.

4 Benjamin Taylor, *Naples Declared: A Walk Around the Bay* (New York: G. P. Putnam's Sons, 2012), 5.

5 Fifield, *Seeing Naples*, 11–13.

6 Taylor, *Naples Declared*, 13.

7 Fifield, *Seeing Naples*, 14.

8 Robb, *Street Fight*, 205.

9 Jordan Lancaster, *In the Shadow of Vesuvius: A Cultural History of Naples* (New York: I. B. Tauris, 2005), 1–6. The significance of Vesuvius for the city and its psychology are also discussed by Shirley Hazzard, *The Ancient Shore: Dispatches from Naples* (Chicago: University of Chicago Press, 2008), 35–40.

10 This is a phrase from Shelly's 1820 "Ode to Naples," as quoted by Lancaster, *In the Shadow of Vesuvius*, 191.

11 Hazzard, *Ancient Shore*, 51.

12 Ibid., 55.

13 Taylor, *Naples Declared*, 13.

14 Robb, *Street Fight*, 218–22.

15 Moses Gates, *Hidden Cities: Travels to the Secret Corners of the World's Great Metropolises — A Memoir of Urban Exploration* (New York: Penguin, 2013), 123.

16 Robb, *Street Fight*, 214–18.

17 Fifield, *Seeing Naples*, 14–15.

18 For an overview of these regimes, see Benedetto Croce, *History of the Kingdom of Naples*, trans. F. Frenaye (Chicago: University of Chicago Press, 1972).

19 John Julius Norwich, *The Middle Sea: A History of the Mediterranean* (New York: Doubleday, 2006), 97.

20 Fifield, *Seeing Naples*, 21–24.

21 See, e.g., the contrasting of Northern and Southern Italy in the seminal work by Robert Putnam, *Making Democracy Work: Civic Traditions in Modern Italy* (Princeton, N.J.: Princeton University Press, 1994). Such criticism may not be always well placed. As Jordan Lancaster reports, Neapolitan public finances were the best in Italy at the time of the Risorgimento; Lancaster, *In the Shadow of Vesuvius*, 198.

22 The Medieval origins of this long-standing cliché about the city and region are discussed in detail by Jennifer D. Selwyn, *A Paradise Inhabited by Devils: The Jesuits' Civilizing Mission in Early Modern Naples* (Aldershot, UK: Ashgate, 2004), 21–53. Although the underlying myth of a Neapolitan heaven inhabited by uncivilized and immoral residents dates to at least the fourteenth century, the actual turn of phrase "a paradise inhabited by devils" is attributed by the esteemed Neapolitan historian Benedetto Croce to the Florentine Bernardino Daniello in a letter sent in 1539. Selwyn discusses Daniello's reaction to Naples — as well as Croce's exposition of that notion — nearly four centuries later, in ibid., 22–26. Also see Tommaso Astarita, *Between Salt Water and Holy Water: A History of Southern Italy* (New York: W. W. Norton, 2005), 159–87.

23 Enrico Bacco, Cesare D'Engenio Caracciolo, and Others, *Naples: An Early Guide*, trans. Eileen Garniner (New York: Italica Press, 1991), 9; Helen Hills, *Invisible City: The Architecture of Devotion in Seventeenth-Century Neapolitan Convents* (New York: Oxford University Press, 2004), 3–9, 13–23, 120–60.

24 Rosario Villari, *The Revolt of Naples* (Cambridge: Polity Press, 1993); Robb, *Street Fight*, 30–32; Croce, *History*, 37.

25 Lancaster discusses the relationship of all of these accomplished Neapolitan citizens and visitors—and many more—in her cultural history of the city; Lancaster, *In the Shadow of Vesuvius*. Many also dominate Robb's exploration of sixteenth-century Naples; Robb, *Street Fight*.

26 Peter Robb, *Midnight in Sicily*, 2nd ed. (New York: Farrar, Straus & Giroux / Picador, 2007), 205. The claim that Naples invented ice cream is spurious, as it probably was invented around 200 BC in China. However, the Neapolitans quite likely did invent chocolate ice cream in the 1690s.

27 Robb, *Street Fight in Naples*, 7.

28 Ibid., 3–12.

29 Ibid., 6–7.

30 Lancaster, *In the Shadow of Vesuvius*, 121–23.

31 Ibid., 125–71.

32 Cordelia Warr and Janice Elliott, "Reassessing Naples 1266–1713," in *Art and Architecture in Naples, 1266–1713: New Approaches*, ed. Cordelia Warr and Janis Elliott (Chichester: John Wiley & Sons, 2010), 1–15, at 10–11. For a more detailed discussion of how the search for "magnificence" shaped specific artistic works, see John Nicholas Napoli, "From Social Virtue to Revetted Interior: Giovanni Antonio Dosio and Marble Inlay in Rome, Florence, and Naples," ibid., 101–24.

33 John A. Marino, *Becoming Neapolitan: Citizen Culture in Baroque Naples* (Baltimore: Johns Hopkins University Press, 2011), 1–27, 234–44.

34 Ibid., 9.

35 Lancaster, *In the Shadow of Vesuvius*, 87–93; Astarita, *Between Salt Water and Holy Water*, 159–60; Hills, *Invisible City*, 120–60; Warr and Elliott, "Reassessing Naples," 9.

36 Nicholas Bock, "Patronage, Standards and *Transfert Culturel*: Naples between Art History and Social Science Theory," in *Art and Architecture*, ed. Warr and Elliott, 152–75, at 169–70.

37 Marino, *Becoming Neapolitan*, 9–10.

38 Robb, *Street Fight*, 15.

39 Ibid., 27–30.

40 Ibid., 39.

41 Astarita, *Between Salt Water and Holy Water*, 166–67.

42 Kate Williams, *England's Mistress: The Infamous Life of Emma Hamilton* (New York: Ballantine Books, 2006), 121–22.

43 For an overview of the evolution of the Spanish Empire at this time, particularly in the Americas, see Hugh Thomas, *Golden Empire: Spain,*

Charles V, and the Creation of America (New York: Random House, 2010).

44   Astarita, *Between Salt Water and Holy Water*, 161–62.

45   This is a point argued by all the contributors to *Art and Architecture*, ed. Warr and Elliott. For a summation of the argument, see the volume's introduction, by Warr and Elliot, "Reassessing Naples." For a discussion of the especially important role of Vasari in denigrating Neapolitan cultural achievement, see the volume's essay by Aislinn Loconte, "The North Looks South: Giorgio Vasari and Early Modern Visual Culture in the Kingdom of Naples," 16–38.

46   Marino, *Becoming Neapolitan*, 234–35.

47   Robb, *Street Fight*, xiv.

48   Bock, "Patronage," 152.

49   Cathleen A. Fleck, "The Rise of the Court Artist: Cavallini and Giotto in Fourteenth-Century Naples," in *Art and Architecture*, ed. Warr and Elliott, 38–61.

50   Tanja Michalsky, "The Local Eye: Formal and Social Distinctions in Late Quattrocento Neapolitan Tombs," in *Art and Architecture*, ed. Warr and Elliott, 62–82; Bianca de Divitiis, "Building in Local *All'Antica* Style: The Palace of Diomede Carafa in Naples," ibid., 83–100.

51   Mary Beard, *Pompei: The Life of a Roman Town* (London: Profile Books, 2008), 33.

52   Fifield, *Seeing Naples*, 14.

53   Warr and Elliot, "Reassessing Naples," 3–4.

54   Robb, *Midnight in Sicily*, 311–12.

55   Marino, *Becoming Neapolitan*, 119–68.

56   Astarita, *Between Salt Water and Holy Water*, 167–68; Lancaster, *In the Shadow of Vesuvius*, 115–18; Hills, *Invisible City*, 90–19; Otis H. Green, "The Literary Court of the Conde de Lemos at Naples, 1610–616," *Hispanic Review* 1, no. 4 (1933): 290–308.

57   Lancaster, *In the Shadow of Vesuvius*, 97–99.

58   Ibid., 96; Astarita, *Between Salt Water and Holy Water*, 164.

59   Lancaster, *In the Shadow of Vesuvius*, 96–98, 119–21; Robb, *Street Fight*, 249–54, 297–304, 313–23; Marino, *Becoming Neapolitan*, 230–32.

60   Helen Hills, "'The Face Is a Mirror of the Soul': Frontispieces and the Production of Sanctity in Post-Tridentine Naples," in *Art and Architecture*, ed. Warr and Elliott, 125–51.

61   Marino, *Becoming Neapolitan*, 64–157.

62   Robb, *Street Fight*, 218–22.

63   Lancaster, *In the Shadow of Vesuvius*, 101. Mary Beard similarly emphasizes the important role of theater in nearby Pompeii; Beard, *Pompei*, 253.

64　Fifield, *Seeing Naples*, 129.

65　Marino, *Becoming Neapolitan*, 22.

66　Ibid., 192–95; Lancaster, *In the Shadow of Vesuvius*, 26–27.

67　Ibid., 117.

68　Ibid., 45, 109–10.

69　Ibid., 109–17.

70　Anna Maria Rao, "The Feudal Question, Judicial Systems and the Enlightenment," in *Naples in the Eighteenth Century: The Birth and Death of a Nation-State*, ed. Girolamo Imbruglia (New York: Cambridge University Press, 2000), 95–117, at 97–98.

71　Fifield, *Seeing Naples*, 49–50; Lancaster, *In the Shadow of Vesuvius*, 125–26; Harold Acton, *The Bourbons of Naples (1734–1825)* (London: Methuen, 1957), 23–28; Dino Carpanetto, "Reform in the First Half of the Eighteenth Century," in *Italy in the Age of Reason, 1685–1789*, ed. Dino Carpanetto and Giuseppe Ricuperati and tr. Caroline Higgitt (London: Longman, 1987), 140–209, at 179–82.

72　Lancaster, *In the Shadow of Vesuvius*, 126.

73　Dino Carpanetto, "Demography, Economy, Classes, and Institutions in Eighteenth Century Italy," in *Italy*, ed. Carpanetto and Ricuperati, 1–76, at 17–18.

74　Astarita, *Between Salt Water and Holy Water*, 159–79.

75　Fifield, *Seeing Naples*, 99–100.

76　Robb, *Street Fight*, 24–25.

77　The place of Neapolitan social thinkers within the context of Enlightenment Europe is explored by John Robertson, *The Case for The Enlightenment: Scotland and Naples 1680–1760* (New York: Cambridge University Press, 2005).

78　Koen Stapelbroek, *Love, Self-Deceit, and Money: Commerce and Morality in the Early Neapolitan Enlightenment* (Toronto: University of Toronto Press, 2008); Lancaster, *In the Shadow of Vesuvius*, 115–17; Girolamo Imbruglia, "Enlightenment in Eighteenth-Century Naples," in *Naples*, ed. Imbruglia, 70–94; Elvira Chiosi, "Intellectuals and Academies," in ibid., 118–34; and Giuseppe Ricuperati, "Political Ideas and Pressure from Reform in the First Half of the Eighteenth Century," in *Italy*, ed. Carpanetto and Ricuperati, 77–139.

79　David Gilmour, *The Pursuit of Italy: A History of a Land, Its Regions, and Their Peoples* (New York: Farrar, Straus & Giroux, 2011), 122.

80　Taylor, *Naples Declared*, 114–22.

81　The importance of Vico's work for broader European intellectual trends is explored by David L. Marshall, *Vico and the Transformation of Rhetoric in Early Modern Europe* (New York: Cambridge University Press, 2010).

82 The role of the urban conditions found in Naples in provoking innovative social philosophy is examined by Barbara Ann Naddeo, *Vico and Naples: The Urban Origins of Social Theory* (Ithaca, N.Y.: Cornell University Press, 2011).

83 Annabel S. Brett, *Changes of State: Nature and the Limits of the City in Early Modern Natural Law* (Princeton, N.J.: Princeton University Press, 2011).

84 Helen Langdon, *Caravaggio: A Life* (New York: Random House, 1998), 319–20.

85 Carpanetto, "Demography," 18.

86 Lancaster, *In the Shadow of Vesuvius*, 131–35.

87 Carpanetto, "Demography," 126–28; Acton, *Bourbons*, 31–34; Hazzard, *Ancient Shore*, 40–47.

88 Acton, *Bourbons*, 35–43.

89 Fifield, *Seeing Naples*, 24.

90 Robinson, *Naples and Neapolitan Opera*, 1.

91 Dinko Fabris, *Music in Seventeenth-Century Naples: Francesco Provenzale* (Aldershot, UK: Ashgate, 2007), 1.

92 This is as quoted by Jeanne Chenault Porter, ed., *Baroque Naples: A Documentary History, 1600–1800* (New York: Italica Press, 2000), 108.

93 Lancaster, *In the Shadow of Vesuvius*, 131–35.

94 This left many subsequent observers, such as Benjamin Taylor, to conclude that Naples under Charles was at its most brilliant, perhaps even becoming the most exciting city in Europe, during his reign from 1734 to 1759. Taylor, *Naples Declared*, 124.

95 Gilmour, *Pursuit of Italy*, 122.

96 Norwich, *Middle Sea*, 431.

97 Lancaster, *In the Shadow of Vesuvius*, 142.

98 Kate Williams, a twenty-first-century biographer of Lady Emma Hamilton, presents a powerful and accessible portrait of Queen Maria Carolina; see Williams, *England's Mistress*, 170–229.

99 This is as reported by Acton, *Bourbons*, 148.

100 Current scholarly reflection on this period may be found in the informative essays compiled in *Naples*, ed. Imbruglia.

101 Lancaster, *In the Shadow of Vesuvius*, 144.

102 Martha Feldman, *Opera and Sovereignty: Transforming Myths in Eighteenth-Century Italy* (Chicago: University of Chicago Press, 2007), 5–6.

103 Ibid., 6.

104 Ibid., 7.

105 Ibid., 190–92.

106 Acton, *Bourbons*, 36–37. Pietro Colletta's account of the same story

dating from 1825 may be found in translation; see Desmond Seward, *Naples: A Travelers' Companion* (New York: Atheneum, 1986), 165.

107 This is an argument made by Susan McClary, "Afterword: The Politics of Silence and Sound," in *Noise: The Political Economy of Music*, by Jacques Attali and trans. by Brian Massumi (Minneapolis: University of Minnesota Press, 2011), 149–58, at 154–56.

108 Carolyn Abbate and Roger Parker, *A History of Opera* (New York: W. W. Norton, 2012), 35–42.

109 Paul Strathern, *The Venetians: A New History, From Marco Polo to Casanova* (New York: Pegasus Books, 2013), 277–78.

110 Donal Hay Grout and Hermine Weigel Williams, *A Short History of Opera*, 4th ed. (New York: Columbia University Press, 2003), 33–38.

111 Irina Naroditskaya, *Bewitching Russian Opera: The Tsarina from State to Stage* (New York: Oxford University Press, 2012), 7–14.

112 Ibid., 16–17.

113 Ibid., 85.

114 Ibid., 85.

115 Abbate and Parker, *History of Opera*, 39–40.

116 Daniel Snowman, *The Gilded Stage: A Social History of Opera* (London: Atlantic Books, 2009), 11–12.

117 Strathern, *Venetians*, 278–79.

118 Snowman, *Gilded Stage*, 12–19; Abbate and Parker, *History of Opera*, 41–43; Grout and Williams, *Short History of Opera*, 41–47.

119 Grout and Williams, *Short History of Opera*, 44, 62–81; Snowman, *Gilded Stage*, 24–31.

120 Abbate and Parker, *History of Opera*, 43–45.

121 For more information about Monteverdi's music and career, see John Whenham and Richard Wistreich, eds., *The Cambridge Companion to Monteverdi* (Cambridge: Cambridge University Press, 2007).

122 Snowman, *Gilded Stage*, 13–25.

123 Strathern, *Venetians*, 279–81.

124 Venice's first public opera house opened in 1637. Venetian composers and theaters produced more than 350 operas during the remainder of the seventeenth century, with at least six opera troupes in continuous operation for one dozen to three dozen weeks a year. During this period, opera once again became a favorite Carnival-time activity for Venetians and foreign visitors alike; Grout and Williams, *Short History of Opera*, 83–84.

125 Ibid., 47–48.

126 Abbate and Parker, *History of Opera*, 48–59.

127 Margaret Doody, *Tropic of Venice* (Philadelphia: University of Pennsylvania Press, 2007), 68–69.

128 Snowman, *Gilded Stage*, 24–26.

129 Ibid., 34.

130 Abbate and Parker, *History of Opera*, 63.

131 Grout and Williams, *Short History of Opera*, 102; Robinson, *Naples and Neapolitan Opera*, 2–5.

132 Lancaster, *In the Shadow of Vesuvius*, 109–10.

133 John Troughton, *The Mandolin Manual: The Art, Craft, and Science of the Mandolin and Mandola* (Ramsbury, UK: Crowood Press, 2002), 145.

134 This is as quoted by Lancaster, *In the Shadow of Vesuvius*, 118.

135 Robinson, *Naples and Neapolitan Opera*, 38.

136 Ibid., 14–15.

137 Marino, *Becoming Neapolitan*, 228.

138 Williams, *England's Mistress*, 122–23.

139 Astarita, *Between Salt Water and Holy Water*, 178–80.

140 Fabris, *Music in Seventeenth-Century Naples*, 10–13.

141 Feldman, *Opera and Sovereignty*, 146–47.

142 Ibid., 152–53.

143 Roberto Paganno, *Alessandro and Domenico Scarlatti: Two Lives in One*, trans. Frederick Hammond (Hillsdale, N.Y.: Pendragon Press, 2006), 90.

144 Fifield, *Seeing Naples*, 31.

145 Ibid., 135; Warr and Elliott, "Reassessing Naples," 10–12.

146 Robinson, *Naples and Neapolitan Opera*, 15–17.

147 Fabris, *Music in Seventeenth-Century Naples*, 15–16.

148 Ibid., 15.

149 Snowman, *Gilded Stage*, 33–34.

150 William Joseph Dent, *Alessandro Scarlatti: His Life and Works* (London: Edward Arnold, 1960); Lancaster, *In the Shadow of Vesuvius*, 132–33.

151 Fabris, *Music in Seventeenth-Century Naples*, 79; Fifield, *Seeing Naples*, 102–4.

152 Doody, *Tropic of Venice*, 69–70.

153 Robinson, *Naples and Neapolitan Opera*, 28–29.

154 Doody, *Tropic of Venice*, 69–70.

155 Ibid., 13–17.

156 Fabris, *Music in Seventeenth-Century Naples*, 80; Snowman, *Gilded Stage*, 3, 6–41.

157 Lancaster, *In the Shadow of Vesuvius*, 134–35.

158 Fabris, *Music in Seventeenth-Century Naples*, 81; Hanns-Berrtold Deitz, "Review: *Naples and Neapolitan Opera* by Michael F. Robinson," *Journal of the American Musicological Society* 28, no. 3 (1975): 552–57.

159 Gordana Lazarevich, "The Neapolitan Intermezzo and Its Influence on the Symphonic Idiom," *Musical Quarterly* 57, no. 2 (1971): 294–313.

160   Robinson, *Naples and Neapolitan Opera*, 47–48.
161   Ibid., 299.
162   Gaia Servadio, *Rossini* (New York: Carol & Graf, 2003), 47.
163   Anselm Gerhard, *The Urbanization of Opera: Music Theater in Paris in the Nineteenth Century* (Chicago: University of Chicago Press, 1998), trans. Mary Whittall, 69.
164   Philip Eisenbeiss, *Bel Canto Bully: The Life and Times of the Legendary Opera Impresario Domenico Barbaja* (London: Haus, 2013), 50–65.
165   Ibid., 8–19.
166   Ibid., 32–45.
167   Servadio, *Rossini*, 47–50.
168   Eisenbeiss, *Bel Canto Bully*, 45–50.
169   Servadio, *Rossini*, 47–50; Abbate and Parker, *History of Opera*, 188–214.
170   Eisenbeiss, *Bel Canto Bully*, 149–70.
171   Ibid., 50–65.
172   Servadio, *Rossini*, 72.
173   Eisenbeiss, *Bel Canto Bully*, 73–87.
174   Ibid., 101–41.
175   Ibid., 173–211.
176   Ibid., 71.
177   Gerhard, *Urbanization of Opera*, 2–21.
178   Ibid., 6.
179   Arnold Jacobshagen, "The Origins of the 'Recitativi i Prose' in Neapolitan Opera," *Acta Musicologica* 74, no. 2 (2002): 107–28, at 107–11.
180   Gerhard, *Urbanization of Opera*, 39.
181   For a concise overview of the Bonaparte engagement with the Italian Peninsula, see Gilmour, *Pursuit of Italy*, 126–37.
182   Ibid., 171.
183   Robinson, *Naples and Neapolitan Opera*, v–vi; William Dean, "A View of Naples: Review of *Naples and Neapolitan Opera* by Michael F. Robinson," *Musical Times* 114, no. 1561 (1973): 261–63.
184   Selwyn, *Paradise Inhabited by Devils*, 211–42.
185   Feldman, *Opera and Sovereignty*, 35.
186   Naples's operatic rival, Venice, similarly was known for its extravagant theatricality throughout the seventeenth and eighteenth centuries. See, e.g., the discussion of this Venetian trait by Doody, *Tropic of Venice*, 74–81.
187   Snowman, *Gilded Stage*, 40–45.
188   Fabris, *Music in Seventeenth-Century Naples*, 1-12.
189   Ibid.

190 Ibid.; Paganno, *Alessandro and Domenico Scarlatti*; Ralph Kirkpatrick, *Domenico Scarlatti* (Princeton, N.J.: Princeton University Press, 1953).

191 Paganno, *Alessandro and Domenico Scarlatti*, 93.

192 Kirkpatrick, *Domenico Scarlatti*, 3.

193 Lancaster, *In the Shadow of Vesuvius*, 133–34.

194 Snowman, *Gilded Stage*, 42–43.

195 Robinson, *Naples and Neapolitan Opera*, 36–71.

196 Grout and Williams, *Short History of Opera*, 207–9; Abbate and Parker, *History of Opera*, 96–102.

197 Grout and Williams, *Short History of Opera*, 207.

198 Abbate and Parker, *History of Opera*, 63–64.

199 Eisenbeiss, *Bel Canto Bully*, 32–49.

200 Ruggero Vene, "The Origin of 'Opera Buffa,'" *Musical Quarterly* 21, no. 1 (1935): 33–38.

201 Abbate and Parker, *History of Opera*, 121–24.

202 Carpanetto, "Demography," 64.

203 Vene, "Origin of 'Opera Buffa,'" 36; Abbate and Parker, *History of Opera*, 121–22.

204 Vene, "Origin of 'Opera Buffa,'" 37; Abbate and Parker, *History of Opera*, 121–22.

205 Abbate and Parker, *History of Opera*, 136–44; Sebastian Weer, "Neapolitan Elements and Comedy in Nineteenth-Century Opera Buffe," *Cambridge Opera Journal* 14, no. 3 (2002): 297–311.

206 Lazarevich, "Neapolitan Intermezzo."

207 Robinson, *Naples and Neapolitan Opera*, 178–204.

208 Acton, *Bourbons*, 35–36.

209 This is as reported in ibid., 38.

210 Robinson, *Naples and Neapolitan Opera*, 108–26.

211 Ibid., 6.

212 Ibid.

213 Ibid., 10.

214 Acton, *Bourbons*, 166–67. In this regard, Charles was following the Parisian fashion of the moment. Ballet, which emerged in grand European courts more or less contemporaneously with opera, was identified primarily as a French art form. Beloved by the French Bourbon monarchs—King Louis XIII was himself an accomplished dancer and performer—the ballet world revolved around Paris and Versailles, while opera quickly became identified with Venice, Naples, Milan, and other Italian cities. For a history of the emergence of ballet, see Jennifer Homans, *Apollo's Angels: A History of Ballet* (New York: Random House, 2010), 3–48.

215 Robinson, *Naples and Neapolitan Opera*, 127.

216 Snowman, *Gilded Stage*, 18; Grout and Williams, *Short History of Opera*, 253–73; Acton, *Bourbons*, 166–69; Renato di Benedetto, "Music and Enlightenment," in *Naples*, ed. Imbruglia, 135–53.

217 Owen Connelly, *The Gentle Bonaparte: A Biography of Joseph, Napoleon's Elder Brother* (New York: Macmillan, 1968), 80; Jacobshagen, "Origins of the 'Recitativi i Prose.'"

218 Acton, *Bourbons*, 676–78.

219 Snowman, *Gilded Stage*, 122–23.

220 Victor Records, *The Victor Book of The Opera* (Camden, N.J.: Victor Talking Machine Company, 1915), 361–62.

221 Feldman, *Opera and Sovereignty*, 206–7.

222 These issues are discussed in the collections of essays found in *Italy*, ed. Carpanetto and Ricuperati, as well as in *Naples*, ed. Imbruglia.

223 Feldman, *Opera and Sovereignty*, 206–7.

224 Ibid., 194.

225 As reported in ibid., 210.

226 Ibid., 211–12.

227 Connelly, *Gentle Bonaparte*; Taylor, *Naples Declared*, 130–31.

228 Ibid., 131–32.

229 Ibid., 132–36; Gilmour, *Pursuit of Italy*, 140–42.

230 Taylor, *Naples Declared*, 141–47.

231 Ibid., 191–99.

232 Ibid.

233 Gilmour, *Pursuit of Italy*, 191–99.

234 Ibid., 238–39.

235 Fifield, *Seeing Naples*, 115.

236 Elena Ferrante, *The Story of a New Name*, trans. Ann Goldstein (New York: Europa Editions, 2013), 456.

237 Fascist inattention—followed by Nazi brutality, urban warfare, American occupation, rampant organized criminality, and inattention by the postwar republic in Rome—amplified Neapolitan suffering throughout much of the unfortunate twentieth century. A hint of the challenges faced by the city during the last hundred years or so are given by Taylor, *Naples Declared*, 166–71—among many commentaries on the city.

238 Tanya Richardson, *Kaleidoscopic Odessa: History and Place in Contemporary Ukraine* (Toronto: University of Toronto Press, 2008), 6.

239 Rem Koolhaas, *Delirious New York* (New York: Monacelli Press, 1994; orig. pub. 1978), 293.

240 Giuseppe "Pino" Daniele, "*Napule é*," 1977, as translated by Jeannette Corell-Giuliano, in the version found on the "Napoli Unplugged" Web site, http://napoliunplugged.com/Napule-E.html.

A Passionate and Slippery City: Puppetry and Kabuki Theater in Tokugawa Osaka and Beyond

1 I would like to take this opportunity to acknowledge the enthusiastic response of University of Pittsburgh professor emeritus J. Thomas Rimer, University of Hawaii Kabuki specialist Julie Iezzi, and Kyoto University professor Kengo Akizuki, and to thank them for their good-spirited reaction to this project, and to acknowledge their thoughtful comments and suggestions. Portions of this text appeared previously in *Second Metropolis: Pragmatic Pluralism in Gilded Age Chicago, Silver Age Moscow, and Meiji Osaka*, by Blair A. Ruble (Washington and New York: Woodrow Wilson Center Press and Cambridge University Press, 2001). The epigraph for this chapter is from Alex Kerr, *Lost Japan* (Oakland: Lonely Planet, 1996), 217.

2 John Simon, "Theater," *New York Magazine*, November 7, 1988.

3 John Rockwell, "Music: 'The Warrior Ant,' by Breuer and Telson," *New York Times*, June 18, 1986.

4 Eileen Blumenthal, "Theater: Ants Invade BAM, Puppets in Cahoots," *New York Times*, October 16, 1988.

5 Ibid.

6 Ibid.

7 Ibid.

8 Ibid.

9 Ibid.

10 Reiko Hayashi, "Provisioning Edo in the Early Eighteenth Century: The Pricing Policies of the Shogunate and the Crisis of 1733," in *Edo and Paris: Urban Life and the State in the Early Modern Era*, ed. James L. McClain, John M. Merriman, and Kaoru Ugawa (Ithaca, N.Y.: Cornell University Press, 1994), 211–33; Takeo Yazaki, *Social Change and the City in Japan: From Earliest Times Through the Industrial Revolution* (New York: Japan Publications, 1968), 233–40; Takeo Yazaki, *The Japanese City: A Sociological Analysis* (Rutland, Vt., and Tokyo: Japan Publications, 1963); Jeffrey E. Hanes, "From Megalopolis to *Megaroporisu*," *Journal of Urban History* 19, no. 2 (February 1993): 56–94, at 59–65.

11 Kenneth B. Pyle, *The Making of Modern Japan* (Lexington, Mass.: D. C. Heath, 1978), 30–31.

12 The notion that Chicago's Board of Trade is the world's oldest futures market is often repeated in Chicago economic histories. See, e.g., Bob Tamarkin, *The New Gatsbys: Fortunes and Misfortunes of Commodity Traders* (New York: William Morrow, 1985); and Jonathan Lurie, *The Chicago Board of Trade, 1859–1905: The Dynamics of Self-Regulation* (Urbana: University of Illinois Press, 1979), 24. The eighty-two

businessmen who convened on the first Monday of April 1848 to form the Chicago Board of Trade (Tumarkin, *New Gatsbys*, 19) undoubtedly had no knowledge of the Osaka experience.

13 Al Alletzhauser, *The House of Nomura: The Inside Story of the World's Most Powerful Company* (London: Bloomsbury Press, 1990), 27.

14 A fundamental observation concerning Osaka's urban morphology is explored by David Rands, *Function-Based Spatiality and the Development of Korean Communities in Japan: A Complex Adaptive Systems Theory Approach* (New York: Lexington Books, 2014).

15 James L. McClain and Wakita Osamu, "Osaka across the Ages," in *Osaka: The Merchants' Capital of Early Modern Japan*, ed. James L McClain and Wakita Osamu (Ithaca, N.Y.: Cornell University Press, 1999), 1–21, at 1–3.

16 Ibid., 3–4.

17 McClain and Osamu, "Osaka," 6–8.

18 Wakita Haruko, "Ports, Markets, and Medieval Urbanism in the Osaka Region," in *Osaka*, ed. McClain and Osamu, 22–43, at 23.

19 Ibid., 34–39; McClain and Osamu, "Osaka," 8.

20 McClain and Osamu, "Osaka," 9–16; Stephen Turnbull, *Japanese Warrior Monks AD 949–1603* (Oxford: Osprey, 2003).

21 Stephen Turnbull, *Samurai Invasion: Japan's Korean War 1592–1598* (Oxford: Osprey Publishers, 2008).

22 Earle Ernst, *The Kabuki Theatre* (Honolulu: University of Hawai'i Press, 1974), 3–4; Anthony J. Bryant, *Sekigahara 1600: The Final Struggle for Power* (Oxford: Osprey, 1995).

23 Stephen Turnbull, *Osaka 1615: The Last Samurai Battle* (Oxford: Osprey, 2006).

24 Marius Jansen, *The Making of Modern Japan* (Cambridge, Mass.: Belknap Press of Harvard University Press, 2002), 32–33.

25 James L. McClain, "Space, Power, Wealth, and Status in Seventeenth-Century Osaka," in *Osaka*, ed. McClain and Osamu, 44–79, at 44–46.

26 Matthew Stavros, *Kyoto: An Urban History of Japan's Premodern Capital* (Honolulu: University of Hawai'i Press, 2014), 173–84.

27 McClain and Osamu, "Osaka," 17–20.

28 Rands, *Function-Based Spatiality*, 23.

29 Jansen, *Making of Modern Japan*, 96–126.

30 Wakita Osamu, "The Distinguished Characteristics of Osaka's Early Modern Urbanism," in *Osaka*, ed. McClain and Osamu, 261–71, at 263–64.

31 McClain, "Space," 56–58, 65–67.

32 Ibid., 73; Takeo Yazaki, *Social Change and the City in Japan* (Tokyo: Japan Publications, 1968), 233–40; William B. Hauser, "Osaka Castle

and Tokugawa Authority in Western Japan," in *The Bakufu in Japanese History*, ed. Jeffrey P. Mass and William B. Hauser (Stanford, Calif.: Stanford University Press, 1985), 153–72, 242–45.

33 Alletzhauser, *House of Nomura*, 26.

34 Ibid., 27.

35 Yazaki, *Social Change*, 233–40.

36 McClain, "Space," 59–61.

37 William B. Hauser, "Osaka: A Commercial City in Tokugawa Japan," *Urbanism Past and Present* 5 (Winter 1977–78): 23–36.

38 Ibid., 24.

39 Tanizaki Junichiro, *Quicksand*, trans. Howard Hibbett (New York: Vintage Books, 1993), 38.

40 Shiraishi Bon, "Merchants of Osaka," *Japan Quarterly* 5, no. 2 (April–June 1958): 169–77, at 170–71.

41 Inoue Hiroshi, "Osaka's Culture of Laughter," in *Understanding Humor in Japan*, ed. Jessica Milner Davis (Detroit: Wayne State University Press, 2006), 27–36.

42 For an informative history and examination of the contemporary status of Rakugo, see Lorie Brau, *Rakugo: Performing Comedy and Cultural Heritage in Contemporary Tokyo* (New York: Lexington Books, 2008).

43 McClain, "Space," 79.

44 Ronald Cavaye and Paul Griffith, "Nō," in *Guide to the Japanese Stage: From Traditional to Cutting Edge*, ed. Ronald Cavaye, Paul Griffith, and Akihiko Senda (New York: Kodansha International, 2004), 162–80, at 162–64; Yoshinobo Inoura and Toshio Kawatake, *Traditional Theater of Japan*, 3rd ed. (Warren, Conn.: Floating World Editions, 2006), 5–13, 46–80.

45 Cavaye and Griffith, "Nō," 163.

46 Ibid., 164–65.

47 Ibid.; Inoura and Kawatake, *Traditional Theater of Japan*, 104–5; Yoshio Yoshikawa, *Tourist Library 6: Japanese Drama*, trans. E. T. Iglehart and I. Matsuhara (Tokyo: Board of Tourist Industry of Japanese Government Railways, 1935), 16–17.

48 Cavaye and Griffith, "Nō," 164–65; Inoura and Kawatake, *Traditional Theater*, 13–14, 89–95.

49 Andrew T. Tsubaki, "The Performing Arts of Sixteenth-Century Japan: A Prelude to Kabuki," in *A Kabuki Reader: History and Performance*, ed. Samuel L. Leiter (Armonk, N.Y.: M. E. Sharpe, 2002), 3–15, at 4–6.

50 Ibid., 168–71.

51 Ibid., 172–81.

52 Ronald Cavaye and Paul Griffith, "Kyōgen," in *Guide to the Japanese*

Stage, ed. Cavaye, Griffith, and Senda, 181–206; Inoura and Kawatake, *Traditional Theater*, 81–88.

53 Cavaye and Griffith, "Nō," 171–72.

54 Ibid.

55 Ernst, *Kabuki Theatre*, 3–7.

56 Yoshikawa, *Tourist Library 6*, 21–24; Inoura and Kawatake, *Traditional Theater*, 141.

57 Samuel L. Leiter, "Introduction," in *Kabuki Reader*, ed. Leiter, xxi; Tsubaki, "Performing Arts."

58 Tsubaki, "Performing Arts," 3. Tsubaki continues on in his article to explore in some detail the earlier art forms that may have contributed to Okuni's performance.

59 Ibid., 13–14; Leiter, "Introduction," xxii; Michael Hoffman, "Japan's First Popular Culture," *Japan Times*, February 13, 2011; Ronald Cavaye and Paul Griffith, "Kabuki," in *Guide to the Japanese Stage*, ed. Cavaye, Griffith, and Senda, 21–98, at 25–27.

60 Cavaye and Griffith, "Kabuki," 22–24.

61 Toshio Kawatake, *Kabuki: Baroque Fusion of the Arts*, trans. Jean and Frank Hoff (Tokyo: International House of Japan Press, 2006), 87–88.

62 Ibid.

63 Barbara E. Thornbury, "Actor, Role, and Character: Their Multiple Interrelationships in *Kabuki*," in *Kabuki Reader*, ed. Leiter, 230–37, at 232.

64 Donald H. Shively, "*Bakufu* versus *Kabuki*," in *Kabuki Reader*, ed. Leiter, 33–59, at 36–37.

65 Ernst, *Kabuki Theatre*, 164–66; Leiter, "Introduction," xxi; Samuel L. Leiter, "Female-Role Specialization in Kabuki: How Real Is Read?" in *Frozen Moments: Writings on Kabuki, 1966–2001*, ed. Samuel L. Leiter (Ithaca, N.Y.: East Asia Program of Cornell University, 2002), 146–56; Cavaye and Griffith, "Kabuki," 26–28.

66 Samuel L. Leiter, "From Gay to *Gei*: The *Onnagata* and the Creation of Kabuki's Female Characters," in *Kabuki Reader*, ed. Leiter, 211–29, at 211–12; Yoshio Yoshikawa, *Tourist Library 6*, 24–27.

67 Tsubaki, "Performing Arts," 13.

68 Leiter, "From Gay to *Gei*."

69 Leiter, "From Gay to *Gei*," 212–13.

70 Ernst, *Kabuki Theatre*, 11; Cavaye and Griffith, "Kabuki," 27–28.

71 Leiter, "From Gay to *Gei*," 212–13.

72 Ernst, *Kabuki Theatre*, 4–7.

73 The history of such regulation is explored by Shively, "*Bakufu* versus *Kabuki*."

74 Cavaye and Griffith, "Kabuki," 28–30.

75 Ernst, *Kabuki Theatre*, 127–63.
76 Yoshikawa, *Tourist Library 6*, 46–47.
77 Kawatake, *Kabuki*, 49.
78 Cavaye and Griffith, "Kabuki," 95–98; Inoura and Kawatake, *Traditional Theater*, 184–86.
79 Cavaye and Griffith, "Kabuki," 95.
80 Samuel L. Leiter, "Suwa Haru's 'The Birth of the Hanamichi,'" in *Frozen Moments*, ed. Leiter, 205–29.
81 Kawatake, *Kabuki*, 49.
82 Ernst, *Kabuki Theatre*, 92.
83 Kawatake, *Kabuki*, 36–38.
84 Ernst, *Kabuki Theatre*, 92–93.
85 Cavaye and Griffith, "Kabuki," 98–99; Inoura and Kawatake, *Traditional Theater*, 186–88.
86 Leiter, "Introduction," in *Frozen Moments*, ed. Leiter, 2; Samuel L. Leiter, "*Keren*: Spectacle and Trickery in Kabuki Acting," in *Frozen Moments*, ed. Leiter, 74–91.
87 The spirit of the older stages can still be found outside Japan's major cities in carefully preserved village theaters around the country. For more information about the older stages, see Samuel L. Leiter, "The Kanamaru-za: Japan's Oldest Kabuki Theatre," in *Frozen Moments*, ed. Leiter, 231–56; and Samuel L. Leiter, "Gimme That Old-Time Kabuki: Japan's Rural Theatre Landscape," in *Frozen Moments*, ed. Leiter, 257–94.
88 Kawatake, *Kabuki*, 60–73.
89 Ibid.
90 Ibid., 112–14.
91 Yoshikawa, *Tourist Library 6*, 352–55.
92 Ernst, *Kabuki Theatre*, 113.
93 Cavaye and Griffith, "Kabuki," 87–89.
94 Kawatake, *Kabuki*, 88–90.
95 Cavaye and Griffith, "Kabuki," 91–92.
96 Samuel L. Leiter, "Four Interviews with Kabuki Actors," in *Frozen Moments*, ed. Leiter, 11–31.
97 Ibid., 17–18.
98 Ibid., 19–21.
99 Kawatake, *Kabuki*, 88–90.
100 Ernst, *Kabuki Theatre*, 115–16; Inoura and Kawatake, *Traditional Theater*, 174–77.
101 Cavaye and Griffith, "Kabuki," 89–91.
102 Tsubaki, "Performing Arts," 9.
103 Kawatake, *Kabuki*, 93–99.

104 Ernst, *Kabuki Theatre*, 114.
105 Kawatake, *Kabuki*, 94–95; Inoura and Kawatake, *Traditional Theater*, 178–80.
106 Kawatake, *Kabuki*, 107.
107 Ernst, *Kabuki Theatre*, 9.
108 Ibid., 164–69.
109 Samuel L. Leiter, "The Frozen Moment: A Kabuki Technique," in *Frozen Moments*, ed. Leiter, 59–73; Leonard C. Pronko, "*Kabuki*: Signs, Symbols and the Hieroglyphic Actor," in *Kabuki Reader*, ed. Leiter, 238–52.
110 Ibid., 171.
111 Ibid., 78–80.
112 Cavaye and Griffith, "Kabuki," 53–55.
113 Ernst, *Kabuki Theatre*, 173–77.
114 Kawatake, *Kabuki*, 162–72; Leiter, "Female-Role Specialization"; Leiter, "From Gay to *Gei*."
115 Ernst, *Kabuki Theatre*, 192–93.
116 Kawatake, *Kabuki*, 107–10.
117 Ibid., 110–13; Cavaye and Griffith, "Kabuki," 69–78.
118 Ernst, *Kabuki Theatre*, 82.
119 Ibid., 200–204; Samuel L. Leiter, "Ichikawa Danjūrō XI: A Life in Kabuki," in *Frozen Moments*, ed. Leiter, 32–43; Samuel L. Leiter, "Parallel Lives: Sir Henry Irving and Ichikawa Danjūrō IX," in *Frozen Moments*, ed. Leiter, 44–55; Cavaye and Griffith, "Kabuki," 64–69.
120 Leiter, "Introduction," in *Kabuki Reader*, ed. Leiter, xxii–xxiii.
121 Brian Powell, "Communist *Kabuki*: A Contradiction in Terms," in *Kabuki Reader*, ed. Leiter, 160–69.
122 Ernst, *Kabuki Theatre*, 219–22.
123 Ibid., 17–23.
124 C. Andrew Gerstle, "Takemoto Gidayu and the Individualistic Spirit of Osaka Theater," in *Osaka*, ed. McClain and Osamu, 104–24.
125 Yoshikawa, *Tourist Library 6*, 37–41.
126 Tsubaki, "Performing Arts," 3–15, at 13–14.
127 Ronald Cavaye and Paul Griffith, "Bunraku," in *Guide to the Japanese Stage*, ed. Cavaye, Griffith, and Senda, 99–120, at 104.
128 Ibid.
129 Donald Keene, *Nō and Bunraku: Two Forms of Japanese Theatre* (New York: Columbia University Press, 1990), 120.
130 Cavaye and Griffith, "Bunraku," 101.
131 Tsubaki, "Performing Arts," 8–10.
132 Cavaye and Griffith, "Bunraku," 102–3.
133 Ibid.

134 Ibid., 103.
135 Ibid., 104–5.
136 Leiter, "Four Interviews," 25.
137 Ibid., 114–16; Inoura and Kawatake, *Traditional Theater*, 150–51.
138 Leiter, "Four Interviews," 110–12.
139 Ibid.
140 Ibid., 108–9; Inoura and Kawatake, *Traditional Theater*, 147–48.
141 Gerstle, "Takemoto Gidayu," 104–13.
142 Cavaye and Griffith, "Bunraku," 103–4; Inoura and Kawatake, *Traditional Theater*, 135–39.
143 Tsubaki, "Performing Arts," 8–10; Yoshikawa, *Tourist Library 6*, 342–43. For two insightful discussions about the process of transferring plays from the puppet to the Kabuki stage, see Janet E. Goff, "Conjuring Kuzunoha from the World of Abe no Seimei," in *Kabuki Reader*, ed. Leiter, 269–83; and Stanleigh H. Jones Jr., "*Miracle at Yaguchi Ferry*: A Japanese Puppet Play and Its Metamorphosis to Kabuki," in *Kabuki Reader*, ed. Leiter, 284–327.
144 Ibid., 105–6; Kawatake, *Kabuki*, 215–16.
145 Gerstle, "Takemoto Gidayu."
146 Cavaye and Griffith, "Kabuki," 30; Zoë Kincaid, *Kabuki: The Popular Stage of Japan* (London: Macmillan, 1925), 243–49.
147 Paul B. Kennelly, "*Ehon Gappō ga Tsuji*: A Kabuki Drama of Unfettered Evil," *Asian Theatre Journal* 17, no. 2 (2000): 149–89.
148 Timothy T. Clark and Osamu Ueda with Donald Jenkins, Naomi Noble Richard, ed., *The Actor's Image: Print-Makers of the Katsukawa School* (Chicago: Art Institute of Chicago, 1994), 14.
149 Cavaye and Griffith, "Kabuki," 56–64; Ernst, *Kabuki Theatre*, 205–16; Samuel L. Leiter, "Kumagai Jinya: Form and Tradition in Kabuki Acting," in *Frozen Moments*, ed. Leiter, 157–82.
150 Kawatake, *Kabuki*, 149–51; Yoshikawa, *Tourist Library 6*, 34–36.
151 Kawatake, *Kabuki*, 178–81; Samuel L. Leiter, "What Really Happens Backstage: A Nineteenth-Century Kabuki Document," in *Frozen Moments*, ed. Leiter, 92–109.
152 Cavaye and Griffith, "Kabuki," 49–52.
153 Ibid.; Leiter, "Introduction," in *Kabuki Reader*, ed. Leiter, xx; Laurence R. Kominz, "Origins of Kabuki Acting in Medieval Japanese Drama," in *Kabuki Reader*, ed. Leiter, 16–32; Holly A. Blumner, "Nakamura Shichisaburō I and the Creation of Edo-Style *Wagoto*," in *Kabuki Reader*, ed. Leiter, 60–75; Nakamura Genjirō III, "Preface," in *Kabuki Heroes on the Osaka Stage, 1780–1830*, ed. C. Andrew Gerstle (Honolulu: University of Hawai'i Press, 2005), 7; Inoura and Kawatake, *Traditional Theater*, 189–93.

154 Kominz, "Origins," 16–32.
155 Cavaye and Griffith, "Kabuki," 49–52.
156 Ibid.
157 Gary P. Leupp, "The Five Men of Naniwa: Gang Violence and Popular Culture in Genroku Osaka," in *Osaka*, ed. McClain and Osamu, 125–55.
158 Ibid., 154–55.
159 Samuel L. Leiter, "Beautiful Cruelty: Suicide, Murder, Torture, and Combat on the Kabuki Stage," in *Frozen Moments*, ed. Leiter, 110–45; Samuel L. Leiter, "From the London Patents to the Edo Sanza: A Partial Comparison of the British Stage and Kabuki, ca 1650–1800," in *Frozen Moments*, ed. Leiter, 297–319; Leonard C. Pronko, "Kabuki and the Elizabethan Theatre," in *Kabuki Reader*, ed. Leiter, 329–39.
160 For a more extensive examination of the story of the forty-seven *rōnin* and the various ways in which it has become a central theme in Japanese popular culture, see John Allyn, *The Forty-Seven Rōnin Story* (Boston: Charles E. Tuttle, 1989).
161 Masakatsu Gunji and Chiaki Yoshina, *Kabuki* (Tokyo: Kondansha, 1985), 208.
162 "Kagamiyama kokyo no nishiki-e," performance at the National Bunraku Theatre, Osaka, April 30, 2012.
163 "Ehon Taiko Ki," Osaka Kabuki Theatre Program, May 5, 2012, 85–86.
164 Kawatake, *Kabuki*, 198–200; Ernst, *Kabuki Theatre*, 53–58; Hoffman, "Japan's First Popular Culture"; Brau, *Rakugo*, 62–65.
165 Clark et al., *Actor's Image*, 28.
166 C. Andrew Gerstle, "Foreword and Acknowledgments," in *Kabuki Heroes*, ed. Gerstle, 8–9; Leiter, "Introduction," in *Kabuki Reader*, ed. Leiter, xxiii.
167 Gerstle, "Foreword and Acknowledgments," 8–9.
168 Clark et al., *Actor's Image*, 17–23.
169 C. Andrew Gerstle, "Flowers of Edo: Eighteenth-Century Kabuki and Its Patrons," in *Kabuki Reader*, ed. Leiter, 88–111.
170 C. Andrew Gerstle, "Kabuki Culture and Collective Creativity," in *Kabuki Heroes*, ed. Gerstle, 10–29, at 10.
171 Pronko, "Kabuki and the Elizabethan Theatre"; Leiter, "From the London Patents to the Edo Sanza."
172 Katherine Saltzman-Li, "The *Tsurane* of *Shibaraku*: Communicating the Power of Identity," in *Kabuki Reader*, ed. Leiter, 253–68.
173 Gerstle, "Kabuki Culture," 28–29; Charles J. Dunn, "Episodes in the Career of the Kabuki Actor Nakamura Utaemon III, Including His Rivalry with Arashi Rikan I," in *Kabuki Reader*, ed. Leiter, 76–87.

174 Gerstle, "Kabuki Culture," 11–15.
175 Ibid., 16–17.
176 Leiter, "Introduction," in *Kabuki Reader*, ed. Leiter, xxiv; Susumu Matsudaira, *Hiiki Renchū* (Theatre Fan Clubs) in Osaka in the Early Nineteenth Century," in *Kabuki Reader*, ed. Leiter, 112–22.
177 Yōko Kaguraoka, "Osaka Kabuki Fan Clubs and Their Obsessions," in *Kabuki Heroes*, ed. Gerstle, 30–35.
178 Gerstle, "Kabuki Culture," 14–17.
179 Ibid., 22.
180 Kaguraoka, "Osaka Kabuki Fan Clubs," 33–34.
181 Timothy Clark, "Ready for a Close-Up: Actor 'Likenesses' in Edo and Osaka," in *Kabuki Heroes*, ed. Gerstle, 36–55.
182 Uchida Kusuo, "Protest and the Tactics of Direct Remonstration: Osaka's Merchants Make Their Voices Heard," in *Osaka*, ed. McClain and Osamu, 80–103, at 80.
183 Osamu, "Distinguished Characteristics," 80–103.
184 Ibid., 202.
185 Ernst, *Kabuki Theatre*, 219–22.
186 Ibid.
187 Ibid., 253–54; J. Thomas Rimer, "Chekhov and the Beginnings of Modern Japanese Theatre, 1910–1928," in *A Hidden Fire: Russian and Japanese Cultural Encounters, 1868–1926*, ed. J. Thomas Rimer (Stanford, Calif., and Washington: Stanford University Press Woodrow Wilson Center Press, 1995), 80–94.
188 Senda Akihiko, "Contemporary Theater," in *Guide to the Japanese Stage*, ed. Cavaye, Griffith, and Senda, 207–58, at 251–55.
189 Ernst, *Kabuki Theatre*, 248–52; the author's personal communication from a peer reviewer of the present volume.
190 Faith Beach, "Breaking the *Kabuki* Actors' Barriers: 1868–1900," in *Kabuki Reader*, ed. Leiter, 152–66.
191 Yoshikawa, *Tourist Library 6*, 66.
192 Powell, "Communist *Kabuki*," 170–71; the author's personal communication from a peer reviewer of the present volume.
193 Isabella L. Bird, *Unbeaten Tracks in Japan: An Account of Travels on Horseback in the Interior Including Visits to the Aborigines of Yezo and the Shrines of Nikkō and Isé with Map and Illustrations* (New York: G. P. Putnam's Sons, 1881), vol. 1, vii.
194 Ibid., 60.
195 Ibid., 62–63.
196 Ibid., 63.
197 Yuichirō Takahashi, "*Kabuki* Goes Official: The 1878 Opening of the Shintomi-za," in *Kabuki Reader*, ed. Leiter, 123–51.

198 Ibid., 143; Inoura and Kawatake, *Traditional Theater*, 221–22.
199 William Lee, "Kabuki as National Culture: A Critical Survey of Japanese Kabuki Scholarship," in *Kabuki Reader*, ed. Leiter, 359–89, at 359.
200 Takahashi, "*Kabuki* Goes Official," 145.
201 Cavaye and Griffith, "Kabuki," 31–32.
202 Powell, "Communist *Kabuki*," 168–69.
203 Ibid., 172–73; Yoshikawa, *Tourist Library 6*, 372–73.
204 Powell, "Communist *Kabuki*, 174–79.
205 James R. Brandon, *Kabuki's Forgotten War, 1931–1945* (Honolulu: University of Hawai'i Press, 2009), 17–23.
206 Ibid.
207 Ernst, *Kabuki Theatre*, 219–22; David G. Goodman, "Russian–Japanese Connections in Drama," in *Hidden Fire*, ed. Rimer, 80–94.
208 Ernst, *Kabuki Theatre*, 251–52.
209 Lady [Kate] Lawson, *Highways and Homes of Japan* (London: T. Fisher Unwin, 1910), 206.
210 Brandon, *Kabuki's Forgotten War*, 3–4.
211 Hismatsu Issei, "Takatsuki," Osaka Kabuki Theatre Program, May 5, 2012, 85–86.
212 Brandon, *Kabuki's Forgotten War*, 5–7.
213 Ibid., 262–95.
214 Ibid., 317.
215 Ibid., 345–56; Ernst, *Kabuki Theatre*, 257–69; Eiji Takemae, Robert Ricketts, and Sebastian Swann, *The Allied Occupation of Japan* (New York: Continuum, 2002), 390–91.
216 "Yamamoto Shugoro, Yurei Kashiya," Osaka Kabuki Theatre Program, May 5, 2012, 84.
217 Leiter, "Introduction," in *Frozen Moments*, ed. Leiter, 1–5, at 1.
218 Brandon, *Kabuki's Forgotten War*, 347–53; the author's personal communication from a peer reviewer of the present volume.
219 Cavaye and Griffith, "Bunraku," 105.
220 Ibid., 105–6.
221 Ibid.
222 Ibid., 106.
223 Ibid.
224 Ayako Takahashi, "Komanosuke Takemoto: A Rare Voice of Tradition," *Japan Times*, January 22, 2014.
225 Rei Sasaguchi, "Bunraku Legend Gets Set for His Grand Finale," *Japan Times*, May 7, 2014.
226 Ayako Takahashi, "Top Bunraku Artist Ensures His Master's Name Lives On," *Japan Times*, March 27, 2015.

227 Takahashi, "Komanosuke Takemoto."

228 Hauser chronicles Osaka's late Tokugawa decline in great detail; see William B. Hauser, *Economic Institutional Change in Tokugawa Japan: Osaka and the Kinai Cotton Trade* (New York: Cambridge University Press, 1974).

229 Milton W. Meyer, *Japan: A Concise History* (Lanham, Md.: Rowman & Littlefield, 1993), 151.

230 Johannes Hirschmeier, *The Origins of Entrepreneurship in Meiji Japan* (Cambridge, Mass.: Harvard University Press, 1964), 28–37; G. V. Navlitskaia, *Osaka* (Moscow: Nauka, 1983), 130–34; E. Herbert Norman, *Japan: Emergence as a Modern State — Political and Economic Problems of the Meiji Period* (New York: Institute of Pacific Relations, 1940), 54–58, 107–11.

231 Jeffrey Eldon Hanes, "Seki Hajime and the Making of Modern Osaka" (PhD diss. in history, University of California, Berkeley, 1988), 1.

232 Mortimer Menpes, *Japan: A Record in Colour* (London: Adam & Charles Black, 1905), 102.

233 Anthony Sutcliffe, "Introduction: Urbanization, Planning and the Giant City," in *Metropolis, 1890–1940*, ed. Anthony Sutcliffe (Chicago: University of Chicago Press, 1984), 1–18, at 7.

234 This is a point made by Henry Rosovsky, *Capital Formation in Japan, 1868–1940* (Glencoe, Ill.: Free Press, 1961), 21.

235 W. Mark Fruin, *Kikkoman: Company, Clan, and Community* (Cambridge, Mass.: Harvard University Press, 1983), 51–67.

236 Hugh Patrick, "An Introductory Overview," in *Japanese Industrialization and Its Social Consequences*, ed. Hugh Patrick, with the assistance of Larry Meissner (Berkeley: University of California Press, 1976), 1–17, at 14; Irwin Scheiner, *Christian Converts and Social Protest in Meiji Japan* (Berkeley: University of California Press, 1970), 2.

237 Hiroshi Hazama, "Historical Changes in the Life Style of Industrial Workers," in *Japanese Industrialization*, ed. Patrick, 21–51, at 38.

238 Dallas Finn, *Meiji Revisited: The Sites of Victorian Japan* (New York: Weatherhill, 1995), 118–21; Hauser, *Economic Institutional Change*; E. Patricia Tsurumi, *Factory Girls: Women in the Threat Mills of Meiji Japan* (Princeton, N.J.: Princeton University Press, 1990).

239 Osaka Hotel Company, *A Guide to Osaka, Japan* (Osaka: Osaka Shiyakusho, 1913), 35; Osaka Municipal Office, *Present-Day Osaka* (Osaka: Osaka Shiyakusho, 1915), 35.

240 Yuzo Mima, "Meiji Koki Osaka no Kogyo," in *Shinshu Osakashishi*, ed. Shinshu Osakashishi Hensei Iinkai (Osaka: Osaka City Government, 1994), vol. 7, chap. 2, sec.2, sub.1, 234–46, at 235.

241 Osaka Municipal Office, *Great Osaka: A Glimpse of the Industrial City* (Osaka: Osaka Shiyakusho, 1925), 45.

242 As Jeffrey E. Hanes observes, the Japanese "*Megaroporisu*" offers a distinctly Japanese accent to the familiar Megalopolis pattern of urban expansion. See Hanes, "From Megalopolis to *Megaroporisu*."

243 As Rands argues, Osaka's large Korean community remained distinctive within Japan in its size and self-organization; Rands, *Function-Based Spatiality*. Concerning the arrival of Koreans in Osaka in large numbers, see Michael Weiner, *The Origins of the Korean Community in Japan, 1910–1923* (Atlantic Highlands, N.J.: Humanities Press International, 1989).

244 The emergence of the *zaibatsu* system has been examined by numerous observers of the Japanese scene. This discussion is based on the work of Yazaki Takeo, who relates the growth of integrated financial cliques to the evolution of Japanese cities in general, and Osaka in particular. Yazaki, *Social Change*, 384–409.

245 Chubachi Masayoshi and Taira Koji, "Poverty in Modern Japan: Perceptions and Realities," in *Japanese Industrialization*, ed. Patrick, 391–437, at 403–5.

246 Osaka Hotel Company, *Guide to Osaka, Japan*, 5.

247 Ruble, *Second Metropolis*, 207–30.

248 Jeffrey Hanes, *The City as Subject: Seki Hajime and the Reinvention of Modern Osaka* (Berkeley: University of California Press, 2002), 203–4.

249 This finding, contained in a study conducted by the International Association of Traffic and Safety Sciences, is mentioned by Taras Grescoe, *Straphanger: Saving Our Cities and Ourselves from the Automobile* (New York: Henry Holt, 2012), 180.

250 Brandon, *Kabuki's Forgotten War*, 188–232. One significant exception to this characterization were visits by small Kabuki companies to Hawaii as early as the 1890s; see James R. Brandon, "Kabuki Changes and Prospects: An International Symposium," in *Kabuki Reader*, ed. Leiter, 343–58, at 344.

251 Kawatake, *Kabuki*, 253–80; Ernst, *Kabuki Theatre*, 248–77.

252 Gerstle, *Kabuki Heroes*, 8–9.

253 Brandon, *Kabuki's Forgotten War*, 17–20.

254 Michael Craig, "Meyerhold, Biomechanics, and Russian Theater," London Theater Blog, February 8, 2009, www. Londontheatreblog. co.uk/meyerhold-hiomechanics-and-russian-theatre/.

255 Gerstle, *Kabuki Heroes*, 8.

256 As quoted in ibid.

257 For further discussion of the Soviet theatrical avant-garde, see Lars Kleberg, *Theater as Action: Soviet Russian Avant-Garde Aesthetics* (New York: New York University Press, 1993); and Konstantin Rudnitsky, Lesley Milne, and Roxane Permar, *Russian and Soviet Theatre: Tradition*

and the Avant-Garde (New York: Thames & Hudson, 2000). For one introduction to the general avant-garde experiment in Russia, see Abbott Gleason, Peter Kenez, and Richard Stites, eds., *Bolshevik Culture: Experiment and Order in the Russian Revolution* (Bloomington: Indiana University Press, 1985).

258 Leiter, "Introduction," in *Kabuki Reader*, ed. Leiter, xix.

259 Samuel L. Leiter, "Authentic Kabuki: American Style," in *Frozen Moments*, ed. Leiter, 183–92; Samuel L. Leiter, "Terakoya at Brooklyn College," in *Frozen Moments*, ed. Leiter, 193–201.

260 Toshio Kawatake begins his exploration of Kabuki as a "baroque fusion of the arts" with an in-depth examination of Kabuki's international tours beginning in 1960. Kawatake, *Kabuki*, 3–21.

261 Brandon, *Kabuki's Forgotten War*, 355.

262 Powell, "Communist *Kabuki*," 179–81.

263 Tomoko Otake, "Revamped Kabukiza Theater Aims to Charm a New Audience," *Japan Times*, March 29, 2013.

264 Leiter, "Introduction," in *Kabuki Reader*, ed. Leiter, x; Natsuko Inoue, "New (Neo) *Kabuki* and the Work of Hanagumi Shibai," in *Kabuki Reader*, ed. Leiter, 186–207; Brandon, "*Kabuki:* Changes and Prospects," 343–58.

265 Natsume Date, "Super Kabuki 'Spells Fun,'" *Japan Times*, March 12, 2014.

266 Natsume Date, "Rising Stars of Kabuki Run New-Year Asakusa Gauntlet," *Japan Times*, January 14, 2015.

Stage Notes for Act One

1 Tomoko Otake, "Revamped Kabukiza Theater Aims to Charm a New Audience," *Japan Times*, March 29, 2013; the author's personal communication from a peer reviewer of the present volume.

Milonga: The Buenos Aires Conversation of Diversity

1 I would like to take this opportunity to thank research interns Yan Slavinskiy and Oleksandr Chornyy for their support and assistance in the preparation of this chapter. I also would like to acknowledge the thoughtful comments and enthusiastic support of Joseph Tulchin, Mauricio Varea, and Valeria Varea. The epigraph for this chapter is from Robert Farris Thompson, *Tango: The Art History of Love* (New York: Pantheon Books, 2005), 133–35.

2 Concerning the impact of the expulsion of the Jesuits on the region of

the Rio de la Plata, see David Rock, *Argentina, 1516–1987: From Spanish Colonization to Alfonsin* (Berkeley: University of California Press, 1987), 53–64.

3   For a discussion of the emergence of the *conventillo*, see James R. Scobie, *Buenos Aires: Plaza to Suburb, 1870–1910* (New York: Oxford University Press, 1974), 52–58, 148–57.

4   This was his schedule because it was summer; in the winter, he would have left for work at 6:30 am. Ibid., 150.

5   Robert Anthony Orsi, *The Madonna of 115th Street: Faith and Community in Italian Harlem, 1880–1950* (New Haven, Conn.: Yale University Press, 1985), 22.

6   Scobie, *Buenos Aires*, 121–25.

7   Ibid., 52, 150–207. Crowding in Buenos Aires tenements was intense, with as many as 350 persons living in dwellings built to house 25 family members and servants and later converted to a *conventillo*, as described here (ibid., 149–50). Sometimes, as many as 207 inhabitants crammed into thirty rooms in *conventillos* built specifically for immigrants in newer neighborhoods such as La Boca; ibid., 52.

8   Miranda France, *Bad Times in Buenos Aires: A Writer's Adventures in Argentina* (Hopewell, N.J.: Ecco Press, 1998), 93–94. Concerning the blue-collar essence of early-twentieth-century Buenos Aires, see Richard J. Walter, "The Socioeconomic Growth of Buenos Aires in the Twentieth Century," in *Buenos Aires: 400 Years*, ed. Stanley R. Ross and Thomas F. McGann (Austin: University of Texas Press, 1982), 67–126, at 99–103.

9   On the importance and development of Lunfardo for Tango Culture, see Donald S. Castro, *The Argentine Tango as Social History, 1880–1955: The Soul of the People* (Lewiston, Me.: Edwin Mellen Press, 1991), 15–88; and Jason Wilson, *Buenos Aires: A Cultural History* (Northampton, Mass.: Interlink Books, 2007), 36–38, 194–95.

10   Discepolo's famous verse is quoted by Thompson, *Tango*, 26.

11   The importance of the Genoa–Barcelona–Buenos Aires immigration route is discussed by José C. Moya, *Cousins and Strangers: Spanish Immigrants in Buenos Aires, 1850–1930* (Berkeley: University of California Press, 1998).

12   Walter, "Socioeconomic Growth," 70, 99.

13   Thompson, *Tango*, 185–86.

14   Thompson credits the Afro-Argentine José Santa Cruz with being the first documented *bandoneón* musician in Argentina, playing the instrument as a soldier during the War of the Triple Alliance in 1865. Ibid., 185.

15   Simon Collier, "The Tango Is Born 1880–1920s," in *Tango!* ed. Simon

Collier, Artemis Cooper, Maria Susana Azzi, and Richard Martin (London: Thames & Hudson, 1995), 19–66, at 33–35; Carlos Fuentes, *The Buried Mirror: Reflections on Spain and the New World* (New York: Houghton Mifflin, 1992), 289–90; Scobie, *Buenos Aires*, 16–20; Wilson, *Buenos Aires*, 194–96.

16 George Reid Andrews, *The Afro-Argentines of Buenos Aires, 1800–1900* (Madison: University of Wisconsin Press, 1980), 166–67.

17 For an overview of the internal and foreign wars of the period, see Rock, *Argentina*, 79–117. For a discussion of Argentina's initial racial composition, see Andrews, *Afro-Argentines*. For a discussion of the drive to redefine Argentina as a "European" society, see Nicolas Shumway, *The Invention of Argentina* (Berkeley: University of California Press, 1991); and Gabriela Nouzeilles and Graciela Montaldo, "Introduction," in *The Argentina Reader: History, Culture, and Politics,* ed. Gabriela Nouzeilles and Graciela Montaldo (Durham, N.C.: Duke University Press, 2002), 1–14. Concerning the waves of newly arriving immigrants, see Wilson, *Buenos Aires*, 18–19.

18 For a general overview of immigration to Buenos Aires, see Moya, *Cousins and Strangers.*

19 Ibid., 125.

20 Ibid., 136.

21 Ibid., 149.

22 Concerning Buenos Aires's development as the "back door" of empire, see Rock, *Argentina*, 39–188.

23 Marta E. Savigliano, *Tango and the Political Economy of Passion* (Boulder, Colo.: Westview Press, 1995), xiii.

24 Simon Collier, *The Life, Music, and Times of Carlos Gardel* (Pittsburgh: University of Pittsburgh Press, 1986), 55–57.

25 Julie Taylor, *Paper Tangos* (Durham, N.C.: Duke University Press, 1998), 67.

26 Collier, "Tango Is Born," 19.

27 This is to recall the perspective provided by Tanya Richardson, *Kaleidoscopic Odessa: History and Place in Contemporary Ukraine* (Toronto: University of Toronto Press, 2008).

28 Wilson, *Buenos Aires*, 11–13; Scobie, *Buenos Aires*, 4–8.

29 Wilson, *Buenos Aires*, 11–13.

30 Ibid., 9–10.

31 Gustavo Verdisio, *Forgotten Conquests: Rereading New World History from the Margins* (Philadelphia: Temple University Press, 2001), 117–19.

32 Rock, *Argentina*, 39–43.

33 Ibid., 43–46; Jonathan C. Brown, "Outpost to Entrepôt: Trade and

Commerce at Colonial Buenos Aires," in *Buenos Aires*, ed. Ross and McGann, 3–17.

34 Rock, *Argentina*, 67–72.
35 Susan Migden Socolow, *The Bureaucrats of Buenos Aires, 1769–1810: Amor al Real Servicio* (Durham, N.C.: Duke University Press, 1987).
36 Susan M. Socolow, "Buenos Aires at the Time of Independence," in *Buenos Aires*, ed. Ross and McGann, 18–29; Scobie, *Buenos Aires*, 6–8; Andrews, *Afro-Argentines*, 4.
37 Wilson, *Buenos Aires*, 15–16; Rock, *Argentina*, 72–76; Shumway, *Invention of Argentina*, 9–18.
38 Rock, *Argentina*, 73–77. The junta was led by Cornelio Saavedra, Mariano Moreno, Juan José Paso, Manuel Alberti, Miguel de Azcuénaga, Manuel Belgrano, Juan Josée Castelli, Domingo Matheu, and Juan Larrea.
39 John Lynch, *San Martín: Argentine Soldier, American Hero* (New Haven, Conn.: Yale University Press, 2009).
40 Rock, *Argentina*, 91–93.
41 Andrews, *Afro-Argentines*, 12–14.
42 Rock, *Argentina*, 79–131.
43 Susan Migden Socolow, *Merchants of Buenos Aires, 1778–1810: Family and Commerce* (New York: Cambridge University Press, 2009).
44 Fuentes, *Buried Mirror*, 262–64; Shumway, *Invention of Argentina*, 24–111.
45 Thomas Whigham, *The Paraguayan War* (Lincoln: University of Nebraska Press, 2002); Shumway, *Invention of Argentina*, 223–49.
46 Rock, *Argentina*, 103–17; Shumway, *Invention of Argentina*, 58–110; John Lynch, *Argentine Caudillo: Juan Manuel de Rosas* (New York: Oxford University Press, 1981).
47 Rock, *Argentina*, 104.
48 Fuentes, *Buried Mirror*, 265–66.
49 Andrews, *Afro-Argentines*, 66.
50 Ibid., 24–30.
51 Ibid., 32–37.
52 Ibid., 42–46.
53 Ibid., 52–59.
54 Ibid., 66–67.
55 Ibid., 68.
56 Ibid., 70–93, 138–55.
57 Ibid., 178–200.
58 Ibid., 113–37.
59 Ibid., 82.
60 Ibid., 156–77.

61 Patricio Downes, "Negros en el país: Censan cuántos hay y cómo viven," *Clarin*, April 2, 2005.
62 Andrews, *Afro-Argentines*, 97–102.
63 Ibid., 97.
64 Ibid., 97–98.
65 Ibid., 160.
66 Ibid., 163–64.
67 Rock, *Argentina*, 105–12.
68 Ibid., 112–14.
69 Andrews, *Afro-Argentines*, 103.
70 George Reid Andrews, *Blackness in the White Nation: A History of Afro-Uruguay* (Chapel Hill: University of North Carolina Press, 2010), 50–85, 112–40.
71 Rock, *Argentina*, 118.
72 Ibid., 162–213. Those presidents were Bartolomé Mitre, Domingo Faustino Sarmiento, Nicolás Avellaneda, Julio Argentino Roca, Miguel Juárez Celman, Carlos Pellegrini, Luis Sáenz Peña, José Figueroa Alcorts, Roque Sáenz Peña, and Victorino de la Plaza.
73 Shumway, *Invention of Argentina*, 250–96.
74 Rock, *Argentina*, 154–61.
75 Collier, "Tango Is Born," 20–21.
76 Fuentes, *Buried Mirror*, 289.
77 Shumway, *Invention of Argentina*, 250–96.
78 Edwin Williamson, *Borges: A Life* (New York: Viking, 2005).
79 Scobie, *Buenos Aires*, 13–69.
80 Ibid., 160–206; Walter, "Socioeconomic Growth."
81 For further discussion of this concept of urban modernity during the "second industrial revolution" of the late nineteenth and early twentieth centuries, see Miriam R. Levin, "Dynamic Triad: City Exposition, and Museum in Industrial Society," in *Urban Modernity: Cultural Innovation in the Second Industrial Revolution*, ed. Miriam R. Levin, Sophie Forgan, Martina Hessler, Roget H. Kargon, and Morris Low (Cambridge, Mass.: MIT Press, 2010), 1–12.
82 France, *Bad Times*.
83 Wilson, *Buenos Aires*, 19.
84 Albert Londres, *The Road to Buenos Ayres: The Story of White Slave Traffic* (New York: Blue Ribbon Books, 1928), 119.
85 Christopher Isherwood, *The Condor and the Cows* (London: Methuen & Co., 1949).
86 Petr Vail', *Genii mesta* (Moscow: Kolibri, 2007), 223. This passage was translated by Blair Ruble.
87 Moya, *Cousins and Strangers*, 181.

88   Laura Podalsky, *Spectacular City: Transforming Culture Consumption and Space in Buenos Aires, 1955–1973* (Philadelphia: Temple University Press, 2004), 33.
89   Wilson, *Buenos Aires*, 126–27.
90   Tomás Eloy Martínez, *The Tango Singer*, trans. Anne McLean (New York: Bloomsbury Press, 2004), 71.
91   Savigliano, *Tango*, 161.
92   Ibid., 160.
93   Castro, *Argentine Tango*, 95–97.
94   Collier, *Life, Music, and Times of Carlos Gardel*, 18.
95   Ibid., 55.
96   Thompson, *Tango*, 94–96.
97   Collier, *Life, Music, and Times of Carlos Gardel*, 56.
98   Thompson, *Tango*, 94–96.
99   Ibid., 122–31.
100 Collier, *Life, Music, and Times of Carlos Gardel*, 27–29.
101 Ibid., 27–30.
102 Savigliano, *Tango*, 30.
103 Ibid., 38–40.
104 Ibid., 50–56.
105 Thompson, *Tango*, 48.
106 Collier, *Life, Music, and Times of Carlos Gardel*, 161–65.
107 Taylor, *Paper Tangos*, 3.
108 Vicente Rossi, *Cosas de Negros*, new edition (London: I. B. Tarus, 2001).
109 Castro, *Argentine Tango*, 92–98.
110 Collier, "Tango Is Born," 42.
111 Thompson, *Tango*, 8–10.
112 Collier, "Tango Is Born," 41–42; Thompson, *Tango*, 82–83.
113 Thompson, *Tango*, 82–83, 231.
114 Ibid., 96–97.
115 Collier, "Tango Is Born," 41.
116 Ibid., 41–42.
117 Andrews, *Afro-Argentines*, 163–64.
118 Ibid., 156–57.
119 Thompson, *Tango*, 61–62.
120 Ibid., 69–75, 85–86.
121 Andrews, *Afro-Argentines*, 97–102, 160–64.
122 Thompson, *Tango*, 78–89.
123 Andrews, *Afro-Argentines*, 157–59.
124 Thompson, *Tango*, 111–12.
125 Ibid., 66–76.

126   Ibid., 107–9.
127   Ibid., 111–12, 160–62.
128   Collier, *Life, Music, and Times of Carlos Gardel*, 19–21.
129   Collier, "Tango Is Born," 35–36.
130   Ibid., 40; Thompson, *Tango*, 228.
131   Collier, "Tango Is Born," 37–38.
132   Thompson, *Tango*, 228.
133   Collier, "Tango Is Born," 37–38.
134   Castro, *Argentine Tango*, 9–10.
135   Ibid., 55–87; Thompson, *Tango*, 26–40.
136   Castro, *Argentine Tango*, 16–19.
137   Ibid., 27–28.
138   Castro, *Argentine Tango*, 55–57; Wilson, *Buenos Aires*, 194–95.
139   Gottling identifies nine master narratives in tango: (1) skepticism, (2) the angelic mother, (3) the breakup of a love affair, (4) the lovers' reencounter, (5) revenge, (6) the barrio knife, (7) the fleeting quality of love, (8) retreat into alcohol, and (9) gambling—as reported by Thompson, *Tango*, 26–27.
140   Ibid., 37–38.
141   Castro, *Argentine Tango*, 66–68.
142   Savigliano, *Tango*, 166–67.
143   Thompson, *Tango*, 173.
144   Ibid., 168–69.
145   Collier, *Life, Music, and Times of Carlos Gardel*, 56.
146   Manuel Vázquez Montalbán, *The Buenos Aires Quintet* (London: Serpent's Tail, 2003), 48.
147   Collier, "Tango Is Born," 43–44.
148   Brandon Olszewski, "*El Cuerpo del Baile*: The Kinetic and Social Fundaments of Tango," *Body & Society* 14, no. 2 (2008): 63–81, at 70.
149   Collier, "Tango Is Born," 42.
150   Christopher Isherwood, *The Condor and the Cows* (London: Methuen & Co., 1949), 168.
151   Taylor, *Paper Tangos*, 65–66.
152   This is a point well argued by Marta E. Savgliano, *Angora Matta: Fatal Acts of North–South Translation* (Middletown, Conn.: Wesleyan University Press, 2003), 158–59.
153   Gabriela Nouzeilles and Garciela Montaldo, "General Introduction," in *The Argentine Reader: History, Culture, and Politics*, ed. Gabriela Mouzeilles and Graciela Montaldo (Durham, N.C.: Duke University Press, 2002), 1–14, at 2.
154   This is as quoted by Joseph Tulchin, "The Origins of Misunderstanding: United States–Argentine Relations, 1900–1940," in *Argentina Be-*

tween the Great Powers, 1939–1946, ed. Guido DiTella and D. Cameron Watt (Oxford: Macmillan, 1989), 34–55.

155 Taylor, *Paper Tangos*, 65–68; Savigliano, *Tango*, xiii.

156 Savigliano, *Tango*, 119–20.

157 For recent accounts of this well-recorded story, see Stanley Meisler, *Shocking Paris: Soutine, Chagall, and the Outsiders of Montparnasse* (New York: St. Martin's Press, 2015); and Sue Roe, *In Montmartre: Picasso, Matisse, and the Birth of Modernist Art* (New York: Penguin Press, 2015).

158 Savigliano, *Tango*, 102–6.

159 Artemis Cooper, "Tangomania in Europe and North America, 1913–1914," in *Tango!* ed. Collier et al., 166–205; Thompson, *Tango*, 241–42.

160 Savigliano, *Tango*, 110–11.

161 Cooper, "Tangomania," 67–68.

162 Ibid., 81–88.

163 Ibid., 67–68.

164 Ibid., 91–98.

165 Ibid., 96.

166 Ibid., 94–95.

167 Savigliano, *Tango*, 119–20.

168 Ibid., 125; Cooper, "Tangomania," 81–87.

169 Concerning the Russian reaction to the appearance of the Tango, see Mark D. Steinberg, *Petersburg Fin de Siècle* (New Haven, Conn.: Yale University Press, 2011), 180–81.

170 Taylor, *Paper Tangos*, 10–11.

171 Savigliano, *Tango*, 169–96.

172 Stacy Teicher Khadaroo, "Finland's Tango Fever," *Christian Science Monitor*, June 26, 2009.

173 Cooper, "Tangomania," 101–2.

174 Savigliano, *Tango*, 136–68.

175 For a stimulating discussion of the impact of these technological changes on the "political economy" of music, see Jacques Attali, *Bruits: Essai sur l'économie politique de la musique* (Paris: Presses Universitaires de France, 1977), translated as Jacques Attali, *Noise: The Political Economy of Music*, trans. Brian Massumi (Minneapolis: University of Minnesota Press, 2011), 87–106.

176 Eric D. Weitz, *Weimar Germany: Promise and Tragedy* (Princeton, N.J.: Princeton University Press, 2007), 249.

177 Rock, *Argentina*, 192–97.

178 Castro, *Argentine Tango*, 6–7.

179 Rock, *Argentina*, 162.

180 Ibid., 174–75.

181 Ibid.
182 Ibid., 183–210.
183 Ibid., 210–12.
184 Ibid., 211–12.
185 Maria Susana Azzi, "The Golden Age and After, 1920s–1990s," in *Tango!* ed. Collier et al., 115–70, at 115–16.
186 Ibid., 118–20.
187 Collier, *Life, Music, and Times of Carlos Gardel*, 58.
188 Ibid.
189 Ibid., 62–65.
190 Ibid., 161.
191 Azzi, "Golden Age," 122–23.
192 Collier, *Life, Music, and Times of Carlos Gardel*, 3–26.
193 Ibid.; Azzi, "Golden Age," 122–23.
194 Collier, *Life, Music, and Times of Carlos Gardel*, 3–26; Azzi, "Golden Age," 122–23.
195 Castro, *Argentine Tango*, 129–31.
196 Azzi, "Golden Age," 123–24.
197 Collier, *Life, Music, and Times of Carlos Gardel*, 27–54.
198 Azzi, "Golden Age," 123–24.
199 Ibid., 124–25; Collier, *Life, Music, and Times of Carlos Gardel*, 27–54.
200 Azzi, "Golden Age," 123–24.
201 Ibid., 123–24; Collier, *Life, Music, and Times of Carlos Gardel*, 58–88.
202 Collier, *Life, Music, and Times of Carlos Gardel*, 89–246.
203 Ibid., 215–70.
204 "Mi Buenos Aires Queirdo / My Beloved Buenos Aires," lyrics by Carlos Gardel and Alfredo Lepera, trans. Joseph Del Genio, 1934.
205 Azzi, "Golden Age," 125–26.
206 Ibid., 123–24; Collier, *Life, Music, and Times of Carlos Gardel*, 271–99.
207 Azzi, "Golden Age," 126–27.
208 Castro, *Argentine Tango*, 129–31.
209 Thompson, *Tango*, 174–79; Azzi, "Golden Age," 140–55.
210 Castro, *Argentine Tango*, 140–42.
211 Gustavo Sosa-Pujato, "Popular Culture," trans. Mark Falkoff, in *Prologue to Perón*, ed. Mark Falcoff and Ronald H. Dolkat (Berkeley: University of California Press, 1975), 136–63.
212 Philip Guedalla, *Argentine Tango* (London: Hodder & Stoughton, 1932), 151.
213 Witold Gombrowicz, *Trans-Atlantyk*, trans. Carolyn French and Nina Karsov (New Haven, Conn.: Yale University Press, 1994), 42–43.
214 Rock, *Argentina*, 214–15.
215 Ibid., 234.

216 Ibid., 238–45.

217 Ibid., 214–61.

218 Castro, *Argentine Tango*, 208.

219 Ibid., 211–12.

220 Ibid., 214–15.

221 Ibid., 215–16.

222 Joseph Page, *Perón: A Biography* (New York: Random House, 1983).

223 Rock, *Argentina*, 252–59.

224 Ibid., 259–61.

225 France, *Bad Times*, 114–19.

226 For more on the career of Eva Perón, see Mary Main, *Evita: The Woman with the Whip* (New York: Doubleday, 1952); Julie M. Taylor, *Eva Perón: The Myths of a Woman* (Chicago: University of Chicago Press, 1979); and Nicholas Fraser and Marysa Navarro, *Evita: The Real Life of Eva Perón* (New York: W. W. Norton, 1996); as well as the work of fiction by Tomás Eloy Martinez, *Santa Evita: The Novel*, trans. Helen Lane (New York: Alfred A. Knopf, 1996).

227 Isherwood, *Condor and the Cows*, 185.

228 Rock, *Argentina*, 262–302.

229 Ibid., 303–12.

230 France, *Bad Times*, 117.

231 Rock, *Argentina*, 307–8.

232 Ibid., 312–19.

233 Ibid., 316–19; Wilson, *Buenos Aires*, 27–29.

234 Rock, *Argentina*, 320–66.

235 Martinez, *Santa Evita*.

236 Rock, *Argentina*, 320–66.

237 Ibid., 357–58. The atmosphere in the city at this time is captured in the novel by Elsa Osorio, *A veinte años, Luz*, translated by Catherine Jagoe as *My Name Is Light* (New York: Bloomsbury Press, 2003).

238 Azzi, "Golden Age," 154–55.

239 Castro, *Argentine Tango*, 241–42.

240 Jorge Luis Borges, "*Sur 142*," translated by Edwin Williamson as *Borges: A Life* (New York: Viking, 2004), 295.

241 Walter, "Socioeconomic Growth," 67–126, at 107–22; Castro, *Argentine Tango*, 225–27.

242 Azzi, "Golden Age," 155–57.

243 Thompson, *Tango*, 194–201.

244 Thomas M. Disch, "The Death of Broadway," *Atlantic Monthly*, March 1991, 92–104, as reprinted in *The American Stage: Writing on Theater from Washington Irving to Tony Kushner*, ed. Laurence Senelick (New York: Library of America, 2010), 754–70, at 754–55.

245   Azzi, "Golden Age," 157.
246   Savigliano, *Tango*, xiii–xiv.
247   Ibid., 12–13.
248   Savigliano, *Angora Matta*, xi.
249   These events are recounted in the work of historical fictional by Tomás Eloy Martinez, *The Perón Novel*, trans. Helen Lane (New York: Alfred A. Knopf, 1998).
250   Rock, *Argentina*, 357–74.
251   Ibid., 374–84; Simon Jenkins and Max Hastings, *The Battle for the Falklands* (New York: W. W. Norton, 1984).
252   For a description of the city at this time, see Joseph S. Tulchin, "How to Know the City," in *Buenos Aires*, ed. Ross and McGann, 152–59.
253   Rock, *Argentina*, 384–403.
254   Wilson, *Buenos Aires*, 29–31.
255   Daniel K. Lewis, *The History of Argentina* (London: Palgrave Macmillan, 2003), 151–86.
256   Vito Tanzi, *Argentina: An Economic Chronicle — How One of the Richest Countries in the World Lost Its Wealth* (New York: Jorge Pinto Books, 2007).
257   Thompson, *Tango*, 205–8.
258   Azzi, "Golden Age," 157–58.
259   Ástor Piazzola, *A Memoir*, trans. Natalio Gorin (Portland: Amadaeus, 2001), 70–71.
260   Azzi, "Golden Age," 158–59.
261   Thompson, *Tango*, 214–16.
262   Ibid., 262–74.
263   Ibid., 13–24.
264   Personal correspondence with Joseph Tulchin, October 19, 2010.
265   Martínez, *Tango Singer*, 13–15.
266   France, *Bad Times*, 92.
267   Juan José Saer, "The Boundless River," trans. Marina Harss, as published in *Argentina: A Traveler's Literary Companion*, ed. Jill Gibian (Berkeley, Calif.: Whereabouts Press, 2010), 74.

There's a Boat That's Leaving Soon for New York

1   This chapter title is borrowed from the song "There's a Boat That's Leaving Soon for New York," Music and Lyrics by George Gershwin, Ira Gershwin, and DuBose and Dorothy Heyward (1935). I would like to take this opportunity to thank Philip Arnoult of the Center for International Theater Development in Baltimore and Barbara Lanciers

of the Trust for Mutual Understanding in New York for their assistance and wise advice in writing this chapter. The epigraph for this chapter is from *Porgy and Bess* (1935), by George Gershwin (music), DuBose Heyward (libretto), and Heward with Ira Gershwin (lyrics). Joseph Horowitz demonstrates that the opera's final words were added by the director, Rouben Mamoulian, during rehearsals for the 1927 production of DuBose and Dorothy Heyward's play *Porgy*, which was based on DuBose Heyward's 1925 novella *Porgy*. Joseph Horowitz, "On My Way": The Untold Story of Rouben Mamoulian, George Gershwin, and Porgy and Bess (New York: W. W. Norton, 2013), 232–43. Among the numerous accounts of *Porgy and Bess*'s opening night, one of the most complete is given by Hollis Alpert, *The Life and Times of Porgy and Bess: The Story of an American Classic* (New York: Alfred A. Knopf, 1990), 3–7.

2   William Morrison, *Broadway Theatres: History and Architecture* (New York: Dover, 1999), 154–55.

3   Their reviews would prove to be decidedly mixed, with drama critics tending to write more favorably about the production than music critics, who were often confused by how to categorize this unprecedented work. Alpert, *Life and Times*, 113–22.

4   Ibid., 4–5.

5   Ibid., 123–24.

6   Ibid., 113–22.

7   Ibid., 4–5.

8   This is a point argued by Horowitz, "On My Way."

9   Alpert's account of *Porgy and Bess*'s creation and subsequent "life" provides a comprehensive overview of how the opera came into being and continued to evolve. Alpert, *Life and Times*.

10   Ibid., 11–22.

11   Ibid., 61–68.

12   Larry Stempel, *Showtime: A History of the Broadway Musical Theater* (New York: W. W. Norton, 2010), 192–201.

13   Alpert, *Life and Times*, 20–24.

14   James M. Hutchisson, *DuBose Heyward: A Charleston Gentleman and the World of Porgy and Bess* (Oxford: University of Mississippi Press, 2000).

15   Joseph Horowitz, *Artists in Exile: How Refugees from Twentieth-Century War and Revolution Transformed the American Performing Arts* (New York: HarperCollins, 2008), 3.

16   Ibid.

17   John Lovell Jr., *Black Song: The Forge and The Flame—The Story of How the Afro-American Spiritual Was Hammered Out* (New York: Macmillan, 1972), 23.

18   Horowitz, *Artists in Exile*, 20.

19 Horowitz, "On My Way," 26–28.
20 Ibid., 2.
21 Horowitz, Artists in Exile, 42; Nancy Reynolds and Malcolm McCormick, No Fixed Points: Dance in the Twentieth Century (New Haven, Conn.: Yale University Press, 2003), 692–93.
22 Stempel, Showtime, 195–291.
23 Ibid., 299; Horowitz, Artists in Exile, 138–59; Horowitz, "On My Way," 53–64.
24 Alpert, Life and Times, 25–30.
25 Gerald Boardman, Jerome Kern: His Life and Music (New York: Oxford University Press, 1980).
26 Alpert, Life and Times, 25–30.
27 Horowitz, Artists in Exile, 340–42.
28 John E. Bowlt, "Scenic Transformation and the Ukrainian Avant-Garde," in Staging the Ukrainian Avant-Garde of the 1910s and 1920s, ed. Myroslava M. Mudrak and Tetiana Rudenko (New York: Ukrainian Museum, 2015), 82–95, at 82.
29 Horowitz, Artists in Exile, 96.
30 Alpert, Life and Times, 4–5.
31 Ibid., 4; Horowitz, "On My Way," 209–13.
32 Horowitz, "On My Way," 41–44.
33 Alpert, Life and Times, 143–230.
34 Ibid., 319–29.
35 Ibid., 62–72.
36 Ibid., 179–242.
37 Ibid., 99–118.
38 Ibid., 101–3.
39 Horowitz, "On My Way," 160–65.
40 Mamoulian subsequently would direct the landmark musicals Oklakoma! (1943) and Carousel (1945), as well as several seminal films, including Applause (1929), City Stories (1931), and Love Me Tonight (1932). Ibid., 13–17. On the importance of Yevgeny Vakhtangov for the Russian and world stage, see Konstantin Rudnitsky, Russian and Soviet Theater, 1905–1932 trans. Rozane Permar (New York: Harry N. Abrams, 1988); Andrei Malaev-Babel, Yevgenyy Vakhtangov: A Critical Portrait (London: Routledge, 2012); and Andrei Malaev-Babel, The Vakhtangov Sourcebook (London: Routledge, 2011).
41 Catriona Kelly, St. Petersburg: Shadows of the Past (New Haven, Conn.: Yale University Press, 2014), 259.
42 Horowitz, "On My Way," 161.
43 Inna Naroditskaya, Bewitching Russian Opera: The Tsarina from State to Stage (New York: Oxford University Press, 2012).

44 Stephan Walsh, *Musorgsky and His Circle: A Russian Musical Adventure* (New York: Alfred A. Knopf, 2013).
45 Horowitz, *Artists in Exile*, 331–36, 342–43, 367.
46 Ibid., 337–43.
47 Ibid., 374–78.
48 John Loring, *Joseph Urban* (New York, Harry N. Abrams, 2010); Randolph Carter and Robert Reed Cole, *Joseph Urban: Architecture, Theatre, Opera, Film* (New York: Abbeville Press, 1992).
49 Ethan Mordden, *All That Glittered: The Golden Age of Drama on Broadway, 1919–1959* (New York: St. Martin's Press, 2007), 11–16.
50 Ibid., 167–96.
51 Ibid., 261–327.
52 Reinhold Brinkmann and Christoph Wolff, eds., *Driven into Paradise: The Musical Migration from Nazi Germany to the United States* (Berkeley: University of California Press, 1999), 21, as quoted by Horowitz, *Artists in Exile*, 96–97.
53 A partial list of prominent immigrants shaping Broadway theater, music, and dance, and eventually Hollywood, would include such figures as Jacob Adler, actor, Ukraine; Boris Aronson, designer, Ukraine; George Balanchine, choreographer, Russia; Ernest Belcher, choreographer, England; Irving Berlin, composer, Russia; Guy Bolton, playwright, England; Yul Brynner, actor, Russia; Vernon Castle, dancer, England; Michael Chekhov, actor, Russia; Noël Coward, playwright, England; Hugh Cronan, actor, Canada; Alfred Drake, actor, Italy; Vernon Duke, composer, Belarus; Michel Fokine, dancer and choreographer, Russia; Rudolf Friml, composer, Czech Republic; Tamara Geva, actor, choreographer, and dancer, Russia; Anna Held, actor, Poland; Oscar Hammerstein I, impresario, Germany; Victor Herbert, composer, Ireland; Arthur Hill, actor, Canada; Bob Hope, actor, England; John Housman, actor/director, Romania; Al Jolson, actor, Lithuania; Emmerich Kalman, composer, Hungary; Elia Kazan, director, Turkey; Ruby Keeler, actor, Canada; Thomas W. Lamb, architect, Scotland; Angela Lansbury, actor, England; Eva Le Gallienne, dancer, England; Gertrude Lawrence, actor, England; Vivian Leigh, actor, England; Lotte Lenya, actor, Austria; Frederick Loewe, composer, Austria; Galt MacDermot, composer, Canada; Rouben Mamoulian, director, Georgia; Raymond Massey, actor, Canada; W. Somerset Maugham, playwright, England; Gian Carlo Menotti, composer/librettist, Italy; Ferenc Molnár, playwright, Hungary; Alla Nazimova, actor, Ukraine; Mike Nichols, director, writer, and producer, Germany; José Quintero, director, Panama; Albertina Rasch, dancer and choreographer, Austria; Max Reinhard,

actor and director, Austria; Lloyd Richards, director, Canada; Sigmund Romberg, composer, Hungary; Edward G. Robinson, actor, Romania; Jacob, Sam, and Lee Shubert, producers, Lithuania; Alexander Smallens, conductor, Russia; Lee Strasberg, actor, Ukraine; Jule Styne, composer, England; Serge Sudeikin, designer, Russia; Jessica Tandy, actor, England; Bessie Thomashefsky, actor, Ukraine; Boris Thomashefsky, actor, Ukraine; Sophie Tucker, actor, Poland; Joseph Urban, designer, Austria; Kurt Weill, composer, Germany; and Bert Williams, actor, Bahamas.

They were joined by the children of immigrants, e.g., Stella Adler, actor, Ukraine; Adele and Fred Astaire, dancers, Austria; S. N. Behrman, playwright, Lithuania; David Belasco, impresario, England; Leonard Bernstein, composer, Ukraine; Fanny Brice, actor/comedienne, Hungary/Alsace; Eddie Cantor, actor, Russia; Paddy Chayefsky, playwright, Ukraine; Howard Da Silva, actor, Russia; Robert Fosse, choreographer, Norway and Ireland; Ben Gazzara, actor, Italy; George Gershwin, composer, Russia; Ira Gershwin, lyricist, Russia; Adolph Green, lyricist, Hungary; Otto Harbach, lyricist, Denmark; Lorenz Hart, lyricist, Germany; Moss Hart, playwright, England; Arthur Hopkins, director, Wales; Gene Kelly, dancer, Canada and Ireland; Jerome Kern, playwright, Germany; Anton and Johann Kliegl, stage lighting inventors, Germany; Bert Lahr, actor, Germany; Frank Loesser, songwriter, Germany; Karl Malden, actor, Serbia; Walter Matthau, actor, Lithuania and Russia; Arthur Miller, playwright, Poland; Paul Newman, actor, Slovakia; Chico, Harpo, Groucho, Gummo, and Zeppo Marx, actors, Germany and France; Zero Mostel, actor, Poland; Clifford Odets, playwright, Russia; Eugene O'Neill, playwright, Ireland; Joseph Papp, producer, Lithuania and Poland; Cyril Ritchard, actor, Australia; Jerome Robbins, choreographer, Russia; Rosalind Russell, actor, Ireland; Phil Silvers, actor, Russia; Michael "Mike" Todd, impresario, Poland; Gwen Verdon, dancer, Canada; Mae West, actor, Germany; Ed Wynn, actor, Romania; and Florenz Ziegfeld Jr., impresario, Germany.

54 Edwin G. Burrows and Mike Wallace, *Gotham: A History of New York City to 1898* (New York: Oxford University Press), 1–5.
55 Ibid., 15.
56 Ibid., 8–10.
57 Ibid.
58 Ibid., 12–13.
59 Ibid.
60 Ibid., 15.
61 Ibid., 19–120.

62 Russell Shorto, *Amsterdam: A History of the World's Most Liberal City* (New York: Doubleday, 2013), 195.
63 Blair A. Ruble, *Second Metropolis: Pragmatic Pluralism in Gilded Age Chicago, Silver Age Moscow, and Meiji Osaka* (Washington and New York: Woodrow Wilson Center Press and Cambridge University Press, 2001), 20.
64 Burrows and Wallace, *Gotham*, xvi.
65 Ibid., xv.
66 Ibid., 16.
67 Ibid., 20; Shorto, *Amsterdam*, 48–61.
68 Burrows and Wallace, *Gotham*, 31–32.
69 Ibid., 33–39.
70 Shorto, *Amsterdam*, 146–58.
71 Burrows and Wallace, *Gotham*, 43.
72 Ibid., 43–49.
73 Ibid., 50.
74 Ibid., 54.
75 Ibid., 33–35.
76 Ibid.
77 Ibid., 54.
78 Mary C. Henderson, *The City and the Theatre: The History of New York Playhouses—A 250-Year Journey from Bowling Green to Times Square* (New York: Back Stage Books, 2004), 11.
79 Burrows and Wallace, *Gotham*, 70–72.
80 Ibid., 72–74.
81 Shorto, *Amsterdam*, 3.
82 Burrows and Wallace, *Gotham*, 75–262.
83 Ibid., 87–89.
84 Ibid., 92–122. For a critical discussion of recent works examining the role of sugar in the eighteenth-century European colonial project in the Americas, see Jerry F. Hough and Robin Grier, *The Long Process of Development: Building Markets and States in Pre-Industrial England, Spain, and Their Colonies* (New York: Cambridge University Press, 2015), 164–69.
85 Burrows and Wallace, *Gotham*, 92–122.
86 Ibid., 126–67.
87 Ibid., 126.
88 Ibid., 127.
89 Ibid., 170–71.
90 Ibid., 171–72.
91 Ibid., 172–75.
92 Mary C. Henderson, *Theater in America: 200 Years of Plays, Players, and Productions* (New York: Harry N. Abrams, 1986), 236–39.

93 Ibid., 11.
94 Ibid.
95 Burrows and Wallace, *Gotham*, 174–75.
96 Henderson, *Theater in America*, 237–39.
97 Burrows and Wallace, *Gotham*, 174–76.
98 Henderson, *Theater in America*, 237–39.
99 Eileen Southern, *The Music of Black Americans: A History* (New York: W. W. Norton, 1997), 89.
100 Henderson, *Theater in America*, 12.
101 Burrows and Wallace, *Gotham*, 220–35.
102 Ibid., 232–33.
103 Ibid., 234–44.
104 Ibid., 240–49.
105 Ibid., 267.
106 Ibid.
107 Ibid., 269–70.
108 Ibid., 274–76.
109 Ibid., 275–76.
110 Ibid., 269–70.
111 Ibid., 277–97.
112 Henderson, *Theater in America*, 142.
113 Burrows and Wallace, *Gotham*, 300.
114 Ibid., 310–13.
115 Ibid., 450.
116 Ibid.
117 Ibid., 335–46.
118 Ibid., 346–47.
119 Ibid., 429–31.
120 Ibid., 431.
121 Ibid., 430–33.
122 Ibid., 563–65.
123 Ibid., 432–34, 562–69.
124 Ibid., 420–24.
125 Ibid., 449–50, 582–89, 662–68.
126 Ibid., 435–36, 650–51.
127 Ibid., 427–36.
128 Ibid., 653.
129 Ibid., 454–55, 577–80.
130 Ibid., 577–80.
131 Ibid., 542–46, 735–36.
132 Ibid., 456–63.
133 Ibid., 736–47.

134 Ibid., 748–50.
135 Ibid., 737–39.
136 Ibid., 739–44.
137 Ibid., 739.
138 Ibid., 757–58.
139 Ibid., 669–71.
140 Henderson, *Theater in America*, 251–52.
141 Many at the time considered Latrobe's Chestnut Street Theatre, completed in 1793, to be the finest theater in the country. Ibid., 238–40.
142 Laurence Senelick, ed., *The American Stage: Writing on Theater from Washington Irving to Tony Kushner* (New York: Library of America, 2010), 13.
143 Henderson, *Theater in America*, 13–14.
144 Ibid., 14–15.
145 Ibid., 13–17.
146 Anthony Holden, *The Man Who Wrote Mozart: The Extraordinary Life of Lorenzo Da Ponte* (London: Orion, 2007).
147 Burrows and Wallace, *Gotham*, 584–86.
148 Henderson, *Theater in America*, 152–53.
149 Burrows and Wallace, *Gotham*, 757.
150 Henderson, *Theater in America*, 146–52.
151 Burrows and Wallace, *Gotham*, 761–66.
152 Ken Emerson, *Doo-dah! Steven Foster and the Rise of American Popular Culture* (New York: Simon & Schuster, 1997).
153 Lovell, *Black Song*, 459–61.
154 David Carlyon, *Dan Rice: The Most Famous Man You've Never Heard Of* (New York: Perseus Book Group, 2001).
155 Emerson, *Doo-dah!*
156 Freddi Williams Evans, *Congo Square: African Roots in New Orleans* (Lafayette: University of Louisiana at Lafayette Press, 2010), 43–45.
157 Camille F. Forbes, *Introducing Bert Williams: Burnt Cork, Broadway, and the Story of America's First Black Star* (New York: Basic Books, 2008), 64–68.
158 Henderson, *Theater in America*, 44–47.
159 Peter Brooks, *The Melodramatic Imagination: Balzac, Henry James, Melodrama, and the Mode of Excess* (New Haven, Conn.: Yale University Press, 1995), xv; Rollin Lunde Hartt, "Melodrama," in *American Stage*, ed., Senelick, 186–202.
160 Ben Singer, *Melodrama and Modernity: Early Sensational Cinema and Its Contexts* (New York: Columbia University Press, 2001), 44–53.
161 Sue Owen, *A Companion to Restoration Drama* (Oxford: Blackwell, 2001).

162 Henderson, *Theater in America*, 42–43.

163 Ibid., 44–50.

164 Ibid., 44–45, 94–97.

165 Ibid., 50–52.

166 Gail K. Smith, "The Sentimental Novel: The Example of Harriet Beecher Stowe," in *The Cambridge Companion to Nineteenth-Century American Women's Writing*, ed. Dale M. Bauer and Philip Gould (New York: Cambridge University Press, 2001), 221.

167 Eric Lott, *Love and Theft: Blackface Minstrelsy and the American Working Class* (New York: Oxford University Press, 1993), 211–33.

168 Burrows and Wallace, *Gotham*, 759–60.

169 Neil Simon, writer, Arthur Hiller, director, and Paul Nathan, producer, *The Out-of-Towners*, Paramount Pictures, 1970.

170 Burrows and Wallace, *Gotham*, 758–60.

171 "House Divided Speech, Springfield, Ill., June 16, 1858," www.abrahamlincolnonline.org/lincoln/speeches/house.htm.

172 Burrows and Wallace, *Gotham*, 865, 901–4.

173 Ibid., 864–65.

174 Ibid., 865–66.

175 Ibid., 866–75.

176 Ibid., 974–79.

177 Ibid., 877.

178 Ibid., 869–75.

179 Ibid., 875–83.

180 Ibid., 883–85.

181 Ibid., 888–89.

182 Ibid., 890–92.

183 Ibid., 892–95.

184 Ibid., 895.

185 Ibid., 896–98.

186 Ibid., 902–4.

187 Ibid., 904–5.

188 Henderson, *Theater in America*, 16–19.

189 Burrows and Wallace, *Gotham*, 904–5.

190 Ibid., 1041–45.

191 Ibid., 1045–50, 1059–70.

192 Ibid., 1073.

193 bid., 1050–57, 1076–88.

194 Ibid., 1058.

195 Ibid., 1011–12.

196 Ibid.

197 Ibid., 1012–20.

198 Ibid., 1120–26.
199 Ibid., 1112, 1126–32.
200 New York City Mayor's Office on Immigrant Affairs, *A Blueprint for Immigrant Integration* (New York: Office of the Mayor of the City of New York, 2013), 4.
201 Burrows and Wallace, *Gotham*, 1118–1235.
202 Ibid., 1236.
203 Henderson, *Theater in America*, 20.
204 Ibid.
205 Ibid., 21–23.
206 Ibid., 25–27.
207 Ibid., 23–24.
208 Ibid., 25–26.
209 Erlanger was born in Buffalo in 1859; Frohman entered the world in Sandusky, Ohio, in 1856; Hayman was born in Wheeling, West Virginia, in 1847; Klaw hailed from Paducah, Kentucky, where he was born in 1858; Nixon was born in Fort Wayne, Indiana, in 1848; and Zimmerman, the eldest, was born in 1843 and raised in Philadelphia.
210 Henderson, *Theater in America*, 26–27.
211 Jerry Stagg, *The Brothers Shubert* (New York: Ballantine Books, 1968).
212 Henderson, *Theater in America*, 28–29.
213 Ibid., 30–32.
214 Ibid., 29–30.
215 Ibid., 32–33.
216 Ibid., 32–34.
217 Ibid., 33.
218 Mordden, *All That Glittered*, 80–89.
219 Henderson, *Theater in America*, 67–77.
220 Ibid., 42–44; Edna Kenton, *The Provincetown Players and the Playwrights' Theatre, 1912–1922* (New York: McFarland, 2004).
221 Senelick, *American Stage*, xxii–xxiii.
222 Henderson, *Theater in America*, 66–67.
223 Ibid., 64–65.
224 Walter Spearman, *The Carolina Playmakers: The First Fifty Years* (Chapel Hill: University of North Carolina Press, 1970).
225 Henderson, *Theater in America*, 105–6.
226 Ibid., 67–68.
227 Amy Henderson and Dwight Blocker Bowers, *Red, Hot & Blue: A Smithsonian Salute to the Musical* (Washington: Smithsonian Institution Press, 1996), 61–66.
228 Henderson, *Theater in America*, 34–35.
229 Mordden, *All That Glittered*, 10–12.

230 Ibid., 9–10.

231 Ibid., 13–14.

232 Ibid.

233 Henderson, *City and The Theatre.*

234 Oscar Andrew Hammerstein, *The Hammersteins: A Musical Theatre Family* (New York: Black Dog & Leventhal, 2010), 36–53; William R. Taylor, *Inventing Times Square Commerce and Culture at the Crossroads of the World* (Baltimore: Johns Hopkins University Press, 1991).

235 Henderson, *Theater in America*, 110.

236 Alan Jay Lerner, *The Musical Theatre: A Celebration* (New York: Da Capo Press, 1986), 12–31.

237 Ibid., 14–20; James Harding, *Jacques Offenbach: A Biography* (London: John Calder, 1980).

238 Lerner, *Musical Theatre*, 14.

239 Ibid., 16–17.

240 Ibid., 17–19.

241 "About Johann Strauss I (1804–1849)," Johann Strauss Society of Great Britain, www.johann-strauss.org.uk/strauss.php?id=121.

242 Egon Gartenberg, *Johann Strauss: The End of an Era* (University Park: Penn State University Press, 1974).

243 Lerner, *Musical Theatre*, 21.

244 Ibid.

245 Ibid., 22–23.

246 Ibid., 24.

247 Cyril R. Rollins, and John Witts, *The D'Oyly Carte Opera Company in Gilbert and Sullivan Operas* (London: Michael Joseph, 1961).

248 Michael Ainger, *Gilbert and Sullivan: A Dual Biography* (Oxford: Oxford University Press, 2002).

249 Lerner, *Musical Theatre*, 30–32.

250 Ibid., 32.

251 Mordden, *All That Glittered*, 4–9; Lerner, *Musical Theatre*, 39–44.

252 Reynolds and McCormick, *No Fixed Points*, 676–78.

253 Mordden, *All That Glittered*, 13–28.

254 Ibid., 46–47.

255 Lerner, *Musical Theatre*, 33–34.

256 Rayford W. Logan, *The Negro in American Life and Thought: The Nadir, 1877–1901* (New York: Dial Press, 1954).

257 Lovell, *Black Song*, 402.

258 Ibid., 402–8.

259 Ibid.

260 Josephine Wright, "Orpheus Myron McAdoo: Singer, Impresario," *Black Perspective in Music* 4, no. 3 (Autumn 1976): 320–27.

261 Maurice Jackson, "'Great Black Music' and the Desegregation of Washington, D.C.," *Washington History* 26 (Spring 2014): 13–35.

262 Ibid., 15.

263 Louis Chude-Shokei, *The Last "Darky": Bert Williams, Black-on-Black Minstrelsy, and the African Diaspora* (Durham, N.C.: Duke University Press, 2005).

264 Jackson, "'Great Black Music.'"

265 Henderson and Bowers, *Red, Hot & Blue*, 66–67.

266 Alain Locke, "The Negro and the American Stage [1926]," in *American Stage*, ed. Senelick, 350–56.

267 Alpert, *Life and Times*, 49–50.

268 Forbes, *Introducing Bert Williams*, 167–332.

269 Locke, "Negro and the American Stage"; Robeson Paul Jr., *The Undiscovered Paul Robeson: An Artist's Journey, 1898–1939* (New York: John Wiley & Sons, 2001); Robeson, *Undiscovered Paul Robeson*.

270 Al Rose, *Storyville, New Orleans* (Tuscaloosa: University of Alabama Press, 1978).

271 Edward A. Berlin, *King of Ragtime: Scott Joplin and His Era* (New York: Oxford University Press, 1996).

272 Joel Berkowitz, ed., *Yiddish Theatre: New Approaches* (London: Littman Library of Jewish Civilization, 2003).

273 Ibid.

274 Hutchins Hapgood, "The Spirit of the Ghetto: Theatres, Actors, and Audience [1905]," in *American Stage*, ed. Laurence Senelick, 172–83.

275 Ibid., 174.

276 Jacob Adler, *A Life on the Stage: A Memoir*, trans. Lulla Rosenfeld (New York: Alfred A. Knopf, 1999); *The Thomashefskys, Musical Portrait of Yiddish Stage*, television program, PBS, March 29, 2012.

277 *The Thomashefskys*.

278 Mordden, *All That Glittered*, 57–72.

279 Ibid., 38–44.

280 Burrows and Wallace, *Gotham*, 1141–46.

281 Henderson and Bowers, *Red, Hot & Blue*, 17–21.

282 This discussion of Eugene O'Neill is based on Virginia Floyd, ed., *Eugene O'Neill: A World View* (New York: Frederick Unger, 1979); and Stephen A. Black, *Eugene O'Neill: Beyond Mourning and Tragedy* (New Haven, Conn.: Yale University Press, 2002).

283 Mordden, *All That Glittered*, 88–100.

284 This discussion of Ziegfeld and his legacy is based on Randolph Carter, *Ziegfeld, the Time of His Life* (London: Bernard Press, 1988).

285 Cynthia Brideson and Sara Brideson, *Ziegfled and His Follies: A Biography of Broadway's Greatest Producer* (Lexington,: University of Kentucky Press, 2015).

286 Reynolds and McCormick, *No Fixed Points*, 681–85.

287 This is as requoted by Lerner, *Musical Theatre*, 45.

288 This is as requoted in "Pop View: Irving Berlin's American Landscape," *New York Times*, May 10, 1987.

289 Lerner, *Musical Theatre. A Celebration*, 45.

290 Ibid.

We'll Have Manhattan

1 The title of this chapter is borrowed from the song "We'll Have Manhattan," music and lyrics by Richard Rodgers and Lorenz Hart (1925). The song was introduced by Sterling Holloway and June Cochrane. I would like to take this opportunity to thank Philip Arnoult of the Center for International Theater Development in Baltimore and Barbara Lanciers of the Trust for Mutual Understanding in New York for their assistance and wise advice in writing this chapter. The epigraph for this chapter is also from the song "We'll Have Manhattan"; for more information about this song, see Dominic Symonds, *We'll Have Manhattan: The Early Work of Rodgers & Hart* (New York: Oxford University Press, 2015).

2 This account of the Hammerstein family story is based on the book by Andrew Hammerstein, *The Hammersteins: A Musical Theatre Family* (New York: Black Dog & Leventhal, 2010), 1–93.

3 This account of Rodgers's early life is based on the book by Meryle Secrest, *Somewhere for Me: A Biography of Richard Rodgers* (New York: Applause, Theatre & Cinema Books, 2001), 1–41.

4 Ibid., 403–6.

5 Amy Henderson and Dwight Blocker Bowers, *Red, Hot & Blue: A Smithsonian Salute to the Musical* (Washington: Smithsonian Institution Press, 1996), 40–61; Ethan Mordden, *All That Glittered: The Golden Age of Drama on Broadway, 1919–1959* (New York: St. Martin's Press, 2007), 44–52; Ethan Mordden, *Anything Goes: A History of American Musical Theatre* (New York: Oxford University Press, 2013), 98–106.

6 Stephen Citron, *The Wordsmiths: Oscar Hammerstein 2nd and Alan Jay Lerner* (New York: Oxford University Press, 1995), 7.

7 Ibid.

8 Ibid., 4.

9 Ibid., 9–10.

10 Hammerstein, *Hammersteins*, 106–11.

11 Nancy Reynolds and Malcolm McCormick, *No Fixed Points: Dance in the Twentieth Century* (New Haven, Conn.: Yale University Press, 2003), 678–80.

12 Citron, *Wordsmiths*, 45–48.
13 Ibid.; Hammerstein, *Hammersteins*, 108–10.
14 Alan Jay Lerner, *The Musical Theatre: A Celebration* (New York: Da Capo Press, 1986), 71–72.
15 Mordden, *Anything Goes*, 122–24.
16 Lerner, *Musical Theatre*, 71–72.
17 Gerald Boardman, *Jerome Kern: His Life and Music* (New York: Oxford University Press, 1980), 6–10.
18 Ibid., 11–13.
19 Ibid., 13–17.
20 Ibid., 24–26.
21 Mordden, *Anything Goes*, 83–84.
22 Boardman, *Jerome Kern*, 27–31.
23 Ibid., 30–32.
24 Ibid., 60–63.
25 Ibid., 55–60.
26 Ibid., 74–79.
27 Chuck Denison and Duncan Schiedt, *The Great American Songbook* (Bandon, Ore.: Robert D. Reed, 2004), 21–22.
28 Mordden, *Anything Goes*, 87–97.
29 Reynolds and McCormick, *No Fixed Points*, 686–88.
30 Mordden, *All That Glittered*, 109–38.
31 Boardman, *Jerome Kern*, 106–24.
32 Ibid., 170.
33 After the theater was dark for several years, the International Ladies' Garment Workers Union purchased it and converted it into a recreation center. Then, after several different incarnations—including a period as a cinema—the building was demolished in 1955.
34 Boardman, *Jerome Kern*, 125–239.
35 Ibid., 240–41.
36 Ibid., 158; Mordden, *Anything Goes*, 85–87.
37 Boardman, *Jerome Kern*, 244–63.
38 Ibid., 263–67.
39 Ibid., 350–405.
40 Ibid., 405–6.
41 Ibid., 271.
42 Julie Goldsmith Gilbert, *Edna Ferber and Her Circle: A Biography* (New York: Hal Leonard, 2000).
43 Todd Decker, *Show Boat: Performing Race in an American Musical* (New York: Oxford University Press, 2013), 16.
44 Boardman, *Jerome Kern*, 275–76.
45 Decker, *Show Boat*, 3–5, 20–22.
46 Ibid.

47 Ibid.
48 Ibid., 13–16.
49 Ibid., 13–14.
50 Ibid., 17.
51 Ibid., 13–16.
52 Miles Kreuger, *Showboat: The Story of a Classic American Musical* (New York: Oxford University Press, 1977).
53 Robert L Zangrando, *The NAACP Crusade Against Lynching, 1909–1950* (Philadelphia: Temple University Press, 1980).
54 Camille F. Forbes, *Introducing Bert Williams: Burnt Cork, Broadway, and the Story of America's First Black Star* (New York: Basic Books, 2008), 32, 99–128.
55 Decker, *Show Boat*, 2.
56 Citron, *Wordsmiths*, 64.
57 Lerner, *Musical Theatre*, 69.
58 Decker, *Show Boat*, 29–58.
59 Ibid., 125–69.
60 Ibid., 58–59.
61 Ibid., 57–70.
62 Ibid., 114–27.
63 Ibid.
64 Stephen Holden, "'Show Boat' Makes New Waves," *New York Times*, September 25, 1988.
65 Decker, *Show Boat*, 248.
66 Ibid., 72.
67 Ibid., 72–100.
68 Ibid., 4.
69 Donald L. Miller, *Supreme City: How Jazz Age Manhattan Gave Birth to Modern America* (New York: Simon & Schuster, 2014), 288.
70 Kenneth T. Jackson and David S. Dunbar, eds., *Empire City: New York Through the Centuries* (New York: Columbia University Press, 2005).
71 Aristide Zolberg, *A National by Design: Immigration Policy in the Fashioning of America* (Cambridge, Mass.: Harvard University Press, 2006).
72 Symonds, *We'll Have Manhattan*.
73 Secrest, *Somewhere for Me*, 1–41.
74 Ibid., 403–6.
75 Ibid., 33–35.
76 Frederick Nolan, *Lorenz Hart: A Poet on Broadway* (New York: Oxford University Press, 1995).
77 Secrest, *Somewhere for Me*, 21–23.
78 Ibid., 118.
79 Ibid., 140–60; Reynolds and McCormick, *No Fixed Points*, 708–43.

80 Symonds, *We'll Have Manhattan.*
81 See www.lorenzhart.org/manhattansng.htm.
82 Secrest, *Somewhere for Me*, 182–91.
83 Lerner, *Musical Theatre*, 138.
84 Mary C. Henderson, *Theater in America: 200 Years of Plays, Players, and Productions* (New York: Harry N. Abrams, 1986), 132–34.
85 Reynolds and McCormick, *No Fixed Points*, 690–91.
86 Ibid., 692.
87 Ibid., 139–40.
88 Lerner, *Musical Theatre*, 138.
89 Reynolds and McCormick, *No Fixed Points*, 692–93.
90 Henderson and Bowers, *Red, Hot & Blue*, 111–14.
91 Secrest, *Somewhere for Me*, 238–40.
92 Ibid., 227.
93 Nolan, *Lorenz Hart.*
94 Citron, *Wordsmiths*, 113–21.
95 Ibid., 122–31.
96 Ibid., 129–30.
97 Ibid., 126.
98 Henderson and Bowers, *Red, Hot & Blue*, 141.
99 Citron, *Wordsmiths*, 132–33.
100 This is as reported by Hammerstein, *Hammersteins*, 152.
101 Ibid., 136–37.
102 Henderson and Bowers, *Red, Hot & Blue*, 142.
103 Hammerstein, *Hammersteins*, 153–55.
104 Secrest, *Somewhere for Me*, 277–86.
105 Mordden, *All That Glittered*, 172–74.
106 Ibid., 157.
107 Boardman, *Jerome Kern*, 394.
108 Lerner, *Musical Theatre*, 152.
109 Henderson and Bowers, *Red, Hot & Blue*, 144–45.
110 Hammerstein, *Hammersteins*, 156–58.
111 Henderson and Bowers, *Red, Hot & Blue*, 145.
112 Secrest, *Somewhere for Me*, 256–57.
113 Boardman, *Jerome Kern*, 394–95.
114 Lerner, *Musical Theatre*, 153.
115 Mordden, *All That Glittered*, 157–77.
116 Secrest, *Somewhere for Me*, 383.
117 Lerner, *Musical Theatre*, 153.
118 Meryle Secrest, *Stephen Sondheim: A Life*, 2nd ed. (New York: Vintage Books, 2011), 32–33.
119 Jan Morris, *Manhattan '45* (New York: Oxford University Press, 1987), 11.

120 Ibid., 91, 105.
121 Richard Harris, "Industry and Residence: The Decentralization of New York City, 1900–1940," *Journal of Historical Geography* 19, no. 2 (April 1993): 169–90.
122 Campbell Gibson, *Population of the 100 Largest Cities and Other Urban Places in the United States, 1790 to 1990* (Washington: US Census Bureau, 1998).
123 Ibid.; Sam Roberts, "City Population Barely Grew in the '00s, Census Finds," *New York Times*, March 24, 2011.
124 New York City Department of City Planning, *The Newest New Yorkers, 2000* (New York: New York City Department of City Planning, 2005).
125 Kirk Semple, "City's Newest Immigrant Enclaves, From Little Guyana to Meokjagolmok," *New York Times*, June 8, 2013.
126 Roberts, "City Population Barely Grew."
127 Michael Howard Saul, "New York City Population Hits Record High," *Wall Street Journal*, March 27, 2014.
128 New York Public Library Schomburg Center for Research in Black Culture, *The Black New Yorkers: The Schomburg Illustrated Chronology* (New York: John A. Wiley & Sons, 1999).
129 Carmen Teresa Whalen and Victor Vázquez-Hernandez, *The Puerto Rican Diaspora: Historical Perspectives* (Philadelphia: Temple University Press, 2005).
130 Harris, "Industry and Residence."
131 Robert F. Wagner Jr., *The Commission on the Year 2000: New York Ascendant* (New York: Commission on the Year 2000, 1987).
132 Morris, *Manhattan '45*, 270.
133 Hammerstein, *Hammersteins*, 162–63.
134 Secrest, *Somewhere for Me*, 270–71.
135 Hammerstein, *Hammersteins*, 170–71.
136 Henderson and Bowers, *Red, Hot & Blue*, 146–48.
137 Hammerstein, *Hammersteins*, 162–78.
138 Ibid., 173.
139 Citron, *Wordsmiths*, 178.
140 Hammerstein, *Hammersteins*, 173.
141 Ibid., 175–79; Henderson and Bowers, *Red, Hot & Blue*, 147.
142 Citron, *Wordsmiths*, 175–79.
143 Secrest, *Somewhere for Me*, 275.
144 Ben Brantley, "'Allegro,' Rarely Staged Rodgers and Hammerstein Musical, Hometown Boy, Recycled," *New York Times*, November 19, 2014.
145 Secrest, *Somewhere for Me*, 270–77.
146 Richard Kluger, *Simple Justice: The History of* Brown v. Board of

Education *and Black America's Struggle for Equality* (New York: Random House, 1975).

147 Henderson and Bowers, *Red, Hot & Blue*, 148.

148 Hammerstein, *Hammersteins*, 198.

149 Henderson and Bowers, *Red, Hot & Blue*, 148–51.

150 Citron, *Wordsmiths*, 194–95.

151 Ibid., 189–94; Hammerstein, *Hammersteins*, 196–98.

152 Hammerstein, *Hammersteins*, 198.

153 Henderson and Bowers, *Red, Hot & Blue*, 148–51.

154 Amy Asch, ed., *The Complete Lyrics of Oscar Hammerstein II* (New York: Alfred A. Knopf, 2008), 341.

155 Secrest, *Somewhere for Me*, 304–7.

156 Ibid., 301–2.

157 Citron, *Wordsmiths*, 195–96; Hammerstein, *Hammersteins*, 198.

158 Henderson and Bowers, *Red, Hot & Blue*, 148–51.

159 Joshua Logan, *Josh: My Up and Down, In and Out Life* (New York: Delacorte Press, 1978).

160 Hammerstein, *Hammersteins*, 199–205.

161 Ben Brantley, "Optimist Awash in the Tropics," *New York Times*, April 4, 2008.

162 Secrest, *Somewhere for Me*, 308–13.

163 Hammerstein, *Hammersteins*, 206–10.

164 Secrest, *Somewhere for Me*, 322–35.

165 Ben Brantley, "'The King and I,' Back on Broadway," *New York Times*, April 16, 2015.

166 Hammerstein, *Hammersteins*, 214–17.

167 Arthur Miller, "The American Theater (1955)," reprinted in *The American Stage: Writing on Theater from Washington Irving to Tony Kushner*, ed. Laurence Senelick (New York: Library of America, 2010), 548.

168 Bruce K. Hanson, *The Peter Pan Chronicles: The Nearly 100 Year History of the Boy That Wouldn't Grow Up* (New York: Birch Press, 1993), 213–14. For more on the NBC version of Peter Pan, see "Peter Pan (1955 TV Movie) Trivia," see http://www.imdb.com/title/tt0287870/trivia.

169 Mordden, *Anything Goes*, 182–94.

170 Susan Loesser, *A Most Remarkable Fella: Frank Loesser and Guys and Dolls in His Life* (New York: Donald I. Fine, 1993).

171 Mordden, *Anything Goes*, 192–93.

172 This argument is developed by Mordden, *All That Glittered*.

173 Ibid., 227–35.

174 Martin Gottfried, *Arthur Miller: A Life* (New York: Da Capo Press, 2003); Christopher Bigsby, *Arthur Miller: A Critical Study* (New York: Cambridge University Press, 2005).

175 Mordden, *All That Glittered*, 276–84.

176 Ibid., 270–84.

177 John Lahr, *Tennessee Williams: Mad Pilgrimage of the Flesh* (New York: W. W. Norton, 2014).

178 Harold Bloom, *Tennessee Williams* (New York: Chelsea, 2007).

179 Michael Anderson, "Lorraine Hansberry's Freedom Family," *American Communist History* 7, no. 2 (2008): 267.

180 Lorraine Hansberry, *To Be Young, Gifted, and Black* (New York: Signet Classics, 2011).

181 Lorraine Hansberry, *A Raisin in the Sun*, Modern Classics (New York: Methuen Drama, 2001).

182 Stella Adler, *The Art of Acting* (New York: Applause Theatre & Cinema Books, 2000).

183 Richard Schickel, *Elia Kazan* (New York: HarperCollins, 2005).

184 Cindy Heller Adams, *Lee Strasberg: The Imperfect Genius of the Actors Studio* (New York: Doubleday, 1980).

185 Harold Clurman, *The Fervent Years: The Group Theatre and the Thirties* (New York Da Capo Press, 1983).

186 Andrei Malaev-Babel, *The Vakhtangov Sourcebook* (London: Routledge, 2011).

187 Mordden, *All That Glittered*, 276–328.

188 For a sense of the era, see the articles collected by Senelick, *American Stage*, 548–717.

189 Henderson, *Theater in America*, 187–91.

190 Thomas S. Hischak, *Enter the Playmakers: Directors and Choreographers on the New York Stage* (New York: Scarecrow Press, 2006); New-York Historical Society Community History Webpage, www.nyhistory. org/community/off-broadway.

191 Christopher Olsen, *Off-Off Broadway: The Second Wave, 1968–1980* (New York: CreateSpace Independent Publishing Platform, 2011); David A. Crespy, *Off-Off-Broadway Explosion: How Provocative Playwrights of the 1960s Ignited a New American Theater* (New York: Back Stage Books, 2003).

192 Henderson, *Theater in America*, 281–96.

193 Richard Zoglin, "Bigger Than Broadway!" *Time*, May 27, 2003.

194 Mark Steyn, *Broadway Babies Say Goodnight: Musicals Then and Now* (London: Routledge, 1999), 119.

195 Henderson and Bowers, *Red, Hot & Blue*, 157–58; Citron, *Wordsmiths*, 97–99.

196 Citron, *Wordsmiths*, 98–99.

197 Ibid.

198 Henderson and Bowers, *Red, Hot & Blue*, 158–59.

199 Citron, *Wordsmiths*, 146–47.

200 Ibid., 148.

201 Ibid., 148–50.

202 Benny Green, "Frederick Loewe: A Prince of Musical Comedy," *The Guardian*, February 16, 1988.

203 Lerner, *Musical Theatre*, 176–79.

204 Citron, *Wordsmiths*, 149–50.

205 Ibid., 237–38; Henderson and Bowers, *Red, Hot & Blue*, 159–63.

206 Henderson and Bowers, *Red, Hot & Blue*, 215; Citron, *Wordsmiths*, 238–40.

207 Citron, *Wordsmiths*, 242.

208 Ibid., 242–45.

209 Henderson and Bowers, *Red, Hot & Blue*, 159–60.

210 Ibid., 159–64.

211 Mordden, *Anything Goes*, 198–200; Citron, *Wordsmiths*, 324–25.

212 Citron, *Wordsmiths*, 331–33.

213 Ibid., 339–48.

214 Mordden, *Anything Goes*, 197–98.

215 Henderson and Bowers, *Red, Hot & Blue*, 184–89.

216 Reynolds and McCormick, *No Fixed Points*, 734–37.

217 Amanda Vaill, *Somewhere: The Life of Jerome Robbins* (New York: Broadway Books, 2006).

218 Schuyler Chapin, *Leonard Bernstein: Notes from a Friend* (New York: Walker, 1992); Meryle Secrest, *Leonard Bernstein: A Life* (New York: Alfred A Knopf, 1994).

219 Arthur Laurents, *Original Story by Arthur Laurents: A Memoir of Broadway and Hollywood* (New York: Alfred A. Knopf, 2000).

220 Hammerstein, *Hammersteins*, 186–94.

221 Secrest, *Stephen Sondheim*.

222 Henderson and Bowers, *Red, Hot & Blue*, 187–89.

223 Secrest, *Stephen Sondheim*; Mordden, *Anything Goes*, 223–30; Hammerstein, *Hammersteins*, 186–95.

224 Bruce Weber, "Mary Rodgers, Author and Composer in a Musical Family, Dies at 83," *New York Times*, June 27, 2014.

225 Carol Ilson, *Harold Prince: A Director's Journey* (New York: Limelight Editions, 2000).

226 Henderson and Bowers, *Red, Hot & Blue*, 187–89.

227 Arthur Laurents, *Mainly on Directing: Gypsy, West Side Story, and Other Musicals* (New York: Alfred A. Knopf, 2009).

228 Henderson and Bowers, *Red, Hot & Blue*, 188–89.

229 Citron, *Wordsmiths*, 297–99.

230 Ibid., 301.

231 Ibid., 302–4.
232 Ibid., 308.
233 Ibid., 302.
234 Hammerstein, *Hammersteins*, 224–26.
235 Secrest, *Somewhere for Me*.
236 Henderson and Bowers, *Red, Hot & Blue*, 199.
237 Lerner, *Musical Theatre*, 224.
238 Thomas M. Disch, "The Death of Broadway," in *American Stage*, ed. Senelick, 754–70, at 755–56.
239 Ibid., 769.
240 Wagner, *Commission on the Year 2000*.
241 Jim Sleeper, ed., *Dissent Special Issue: In Search of New York*, 1987, 407–639.
242 Wagner, *Commission on the Year 2000*, 9.
243 Sam Roberts, "Region Is Reshaped," *New York Times*, December 14, 2010.
244 William B. Helmreich, *The New York Nobody Knows: Waking 6,000 Miles in the City* (Princeton, N.J.: Princeton University Press, 2013), 22.
245 Michael Paulson, "Tourism Boom Gives Broadway Record Season," *New York Times*, May 27, 2015.
246 Miller, "American Theater."
247 "Ravi Coltrane, Interview," in *Oxygen for the Ears: Living Jazz*, dir. Stefan Immler (Washington: Giganova Productions, 2012).
248 Jody Rosen, "The American Revolutionary," *New York Times Style Magazine*, July 19, 2015, 54–59.
249 Charles Isherwood, "The View From Uptown: American Dreaming to a Latin Beat," *New York Times*, March 10, 2008.
250 Rosen, "American Revolutionary," 54.
251 Stephen Sondheim, "On the Musical," *New York Times Style Magazine*, July 19, 2015, 56–59.
252 Ben Brantley, "A New Storm's Brewing Down on Catfish Row," *New York Times*, January 12, 2012.

Humanity Is Coloured: Musical Cape Town

1 I would like to single out the late James Miller of George Washington University for encouraging me to undertake this chapter on music in Cape Town. I also would like take this opportunity to thank my research intern, Irina Kuzemkina, for her support and assistance in the preparation of this chapter. In addition, I would like to acknowledge the thoughtful comments and enthusiastic support of the chapter's

readers, especially Steve McDonald. The epigraph for this chapter is from Jeremy Cronin, "Creole Cape Town," in *A City Imagined*, ed. Stephen Watson (Johannesburg: Penguin Books, 2005), 45–54, at 50.

2 Nomvuyo Ngcelwane, *Sala Kahle District Six: An African Woman's Perspective* (Cape Town: Kwela Books, 1998), 130–33.

3 Sean Field, "Oral Histories of Forced Removals," in *Lost Communities, Living Memories: Remembering Forced Removals in Cape Town*, ed. Sean Field (Cape Town: David Philip, 2001), 11–14; Vivian Bickford-Smith, "Mapping Cape Town: From Slavery to Apartheid," in *Lost Communities*, ed. Field, 15–26.

4 David B. Coplan, *In Township Tonight: South Africa's Black City Music and Theatre*, 2nd ed. (Chicago: University of Chicago Press, 2007), xi.

5 As with every other aspect of life in South Africa, language is deeply contested. An edgy contemporary commentator on South African life, Rian Malan, gets to the heart of the matter in the foreword to a collection of his essays; see Rian Malan, *The Lion Sleeps Tonight and Other Stories of Africa* (New York: Grove Press, 2012), where he writes: "Every inch of our soil is contested, every word in our histories likewise; our languages are mutually incomprehensible, our philosophies irreconcilable" (p. x).

6 These languages are Afrikaans, English, Ndebele, Northern Sotho, Sotho, Swazi, Tswana, Tsonga, Venda, Xhosa, and Zulu.

7 The word "coon" has sometimes been associated with the North American mammal of the procyonid family known for its distinctive masklike facial markings, and the use of this term as a racial slur may have originated with the Portuguese word for the cages holding slaves for sale, *barracão*. A popular 1830s minstrel song, "Zip Coon," about a "free" (nonslave) black "putting on airs," cemented the word's derogatory associations with African Americans. The label arrived in Cape Town with the numerous British and American minstrel groups that began to visit the city in the mid–nineteenth century.

8 Carnival chronicler Denis-Constant Martin takes the opposite approach toward the word, adopting the position of "a famous Cape Town composer," who stated forthrightly that "the Americans come and they don't want us to use the word 'Coon' because it's derogatory for the people. Here, 'Coon' is not derogatory in our sense. For us the minute you talk Coon, he sees New Year's Day, he sees satin and the eyes and mouth with circles in white, the rest of the face in black, like the American minstrels." Denis-Constant Martin, *New Year in Cape Town: Past to Present* (Cape Town: David Philip, 1999), 4.

9 Ibid., 132. According to some estimates, as many as twice as many Capetonians lived in the district a decade and a half later.

10 Bickford-Smith, "Mapping Cape Town," 15.

11 Leonard Thompson, *A History of South Africa*, 3rd ed. (New Haven, Conn.: Yale University Press, 2000), 187–89.

12 Gwen Ansell, *Soweto Blues: Jazz, Popular Music, and Politics in South Africa* (New York: Continuum, 2005), 11; Lucien le Grange, "District Six: Urban Place and Public Memory," in *Recalling Community in Cape Town: Creating and Curating the District Six Museum*, ed. Ciraj Rassool and Sandra Prosalendis (Cape Town: District Six Museum, 2001), 106–12.

13 Deborah M. Hart, "Political Manipulation of Urban Space: The Razing of District Six, Cape Town," in *The Struggle for District Six: Past and Present*, ed. Shamil Jeppie and Crain Soudien (Cape Town: Bunchu Books, 1990), 117–42, at 124–28.

14 Sean Field, "'I Dream of Our Old House, You See There Are Things That Can Never Go Away': Memory, Restitution, and Democracy," in *Lost Communities*, ed. Field, 117–24, at 119.

15 Ngcelwane, *Sala Kahle District Six*, 132.

16 A monthly train ticket from Nyanga to central Cape Town approached 10 percent of an unskilled laborer's wages at the time. Monica Wilson and Archie Mafeje, *Langa: A Story of Social Groups in an African Township* (Cape Town: Oxford University Press, 1963), 6.

17 Lawrence G. Green, *Tavern of the Seas* (Cape Town: Howard B. Timmins, 1948). For a discussion of how Anglophone middle-class visitors found the residents of the "lower-class" neighborhoods of the early industrial era "exotic 'others'" in British, North American, and Australian cities, see Vivian Bickford-Smith, "Providing Local Color? 'Cape Coloreds,' 'Cockneys,' and Cape Town's Identity from the Late Nineteenth Century to the 1970s," *Journal of Urban History* 38, no. 1 (2012): 133–51.

18 Ngcelwane, *Sala Kahle District Six*, 67–73.

19 Amelia M. Lewis, "Reflections on Education in District Six, 1930s to 1950s," in *Struggle*, ed. Jeppie and Soudien, 185–91.

20 Ngcelwane, *Sala Kahle District Six*, 84–88.

21 Ibid., 131.

22 Many similar agonized cries of loss may be found, e.g., in the oral histories contained in *Lost Communities*, ed. Field.

23 Sofie M. M. A. Geschier, "'I There I Sit in a Catch-22 Situation': Remembering and Imagining Trauma in the District Six Museum," in *Imaging the City: Memories and Cultures in Cape Town*, ed. Sean Field, Renate Meyer, and Felicity Swanson (Cape Town: HSRC Press, 2007), 37–56.

24 Peggy Delport, "Signposts for Retrieval: A Visual Framework for Enabling Memory of Place and Time," in *Recalling Community*, ed.

Rassool and Prosalendis, 31–46; Peggy Delport, "Digging Deeper in District Six: Features and Interfaces in a Curatorial Landscape," in *Recalling Community*, ed. Rassool and Prosalendis, 154–64.

25 Vivian Bickford-Smith, "The Origins and Early History of District Six to 1910," in *Struggle*, ed. Jeppie and Soudien, 35–43, at 35–36; Crain Sondien, "District Six and Its Uses in Discussions about Non-Racialism," in *Coloured by History, Shaped by Place: New Perspectives on Coloured Identities in Cape Town*, ed. Zimitri Erasmus (Colorado Springs: International Academic Publishers, 2001), 114–30, at 117–18.

26 Coraj Rassool and Jos Thorne, "A Timeline for District Six: A Parallel Text," in *Recalling Community*, ed. Rassool and Prosalendis, 96–158, at 98–100.

27 Bickford-Smith, "Origins," 35.

28 Rassool and Thorne, "Timeline," 104–6.

29 Bickford-Smith, "Providing Local Color?" 138.

30 Bickford-Smith, "Origins," 35–36.

31 Ibid., 36–37.

32 Ibid., 37.

33 Rassool and Thorne, "Timeline," 110–11.

34 Ibid.; Bickford-Smith, "Origins," 40–43.

35 Hart, "Political Manipulation," 117–42, at 121–22.

36 Bickford-Smith, "Providing Local Color?"

37 In the conceptualization of Mary Louise Pratt, District Six is a classic "zone of contact," or a space where "cultures meet, clash, and grapple with each other, often in contexts of highly asymmetrical relations of power, such as colonialism, slavery, or their aftermaths." Mary Louise Pratt, "Arts in the Contact Zone," *Profession* 91: 33–40, republished in *Reading the Lives of Others*, ed. David Batholomae and Anthony Petrosky (Boston: Bedford Books, 1995), 180–95.

38 Mary Louise Pratt, *Travel Writing and Transculturalation* (New York: Routledge, 1992), 6–7.

39 Sandra Prosalendis, Jennifer Marot, Crain Soudien, and Anwah Nagia, "Punctuations: Periodic Impressions of a Museum," in *Recalling Community*, ed. Rassool and Prosalendis, 74–94, at 84.

40 Leslie Witz, *Apartheid's Festival: Contesting South Africa's National Pasts* (Bloomington and Cape Town: Indiana University Press and David Philip, 2003), 11–18.

41 Ibid., 15.

42 Ibid., 17–21.

43 Ciraj Rassool and Leslie Witz, "The 1952 Jan Van Riebeeck Tercentenary Festival: Constructing and Contesting Public National History in South Africa," *Journal of African History* 34, no. 3 (1993): 447–68.

44 Witz, *Apartheid's Festival*, 80–143, 180–242.

45 Ibid., 30–35.

46 Nigel Worden, Elizabeth van Heyningen, and Vivian Bickford-Smith, *Cape Town: The Making of a City* (Claremont, South Africa: David Philip, 1998), 19–20.

47 Ibid., 18–24.

48 I. D. DuPlessis, *The Cape Malays: History, Religion, Traditions, Folk Tales — The Malay Quarter* (Cape Town: A. A. Balkema, 1972).

49 Robyn Wilkinson and Astrid Kragolsen-Kille, *Bo-Kaap: Inside Cape Town's Malay Quarter* (Cape Town: Struik, 2006), 17–18.

50 Worden, van Heyningen, and Bickford-Smith, *Cape Town*, 28–30.

51 Ibid., 30.

52 David Biggs, *This Is Cape Town* (London: New Holland, 2000), 12–13.

53 Witz, *Apartheid's Festival*, 144–79.

54 As quoted in ibid., 40.

55 Lalou Meltzer, *The Castle of Good Hope, Cape Town* (Saxonwold: Art Link, 1997).

56 Worden, van Heyningen, and Bickford-Smith, *Cape Town*, 16–17.

57 Ibid.; Thompson, *History of South Africa*, 13–16.

58 Worden, van Heyningen, and Bickford-Smith, *Cape Town*, 16–17.

59 Ibid., 21.

60 John Western, *Outcast Cape Town* (Berkeley: University of California Press, 1966), 31–32.

61 Thompson, *History of South Africa*, 10–13.

62 Ibid., 37–39, 62–65; Carol A. Muller, *South African Music: A Century of Traditions in Transformation* (Santa Barbara, Calif.: ABC-CLIO, 2003), 62–63. For an overview of this history, see Richard Elphick, *Kraal and Castle: Khoikhoi and the Founding of White South Africa* (New Haven, Conn.: Yale University Press, 1977).

63 Thompson, *History of South Africa*, 31–32.

64 Worden, van Heyningen, and Bickford-Smith, *Cape Town*, 12–13.

65 Ibid.

66 Ibid., 50–51.

67 Ibid., 20.

68 Ibid., 26.

69 Du Plessis, *Cape Malays*, 3–6.

70 Biggs, *This Is Cape Town*, 23.

71 Ibid., 28.

72 Thompson, *History of South Africa*, 39.

73 Meltzer, *Castle of Good Hope*.

74 Worden, van Heyningen, and Bickford-Smith, *Cape Town*, 36–49.

75 Graham Viney, *Historic Houses of South Africa* (New York: Abbeville Press, 1997).

76 Worden, van Heyningen, and Bickford-Smith, *Cape Town*, 51–52.
77 Ibid., 60.
78 Biggs, *This Is Cape Town*, 12.
79 Worden, van Heyningen, and Bickford-Smith, *Cape Town*, 47–49, 61.
80 Ibid., 64; Martin, *New Year in Cape Town*, 53–54.
81 Thompson, *History of South Africa*, 42–43.
82 Worden, van Heyningen, and Bickford-Smith, *Cape Town*, 67–68.
83 Ibid., 69.
84 Ibid., 53–54; Thompson, *History of South Africa*, 33–34.
85 Worden, van Heyningen, and Bickford-Smith, *Cape Town*, 67–69.
86 Thompson, *History of South Africa*, 345–50.
87 Worden, van Heyningen, and Bickford-Smith, *Cape Town*, 63–65, 79–80.
88 Green, *Tavern of the Seas*, 110.
89 Worden, van Heyningen, and Bickford-Smith, *Cape Town*, 75–78.
90 The language census for New Amsterdam is cited repeatedly in a number of works, including those by Thomas Bender, *The Unfinished City: New York and the Metropolitan Idea* (New York: New Press, 2002), 192; and Russell Shorto, *The Island at the Center of the World: The Epic Story of Dutch Manhattan and the Forgotten Colony That Shaped America* (New York: Doubleday, 2004), 2.
91 Thompson, *History of South Africa*, 51.
92 Martin, *New Year in Cape Town*, 57.
93 Worden, van Heyningen, and Bickford-Smith, *Cape Town*, 124–26.
94 Wilkinson and Kragolsen-Kille, *Bo-Kapp*; Biggs, *This Is Cape Town*, 13–14.
95 Martin, *New Year in Cape Town*, 58.
96 Coplan, *In Township Tonight*, 14–16.
97 These observations are reported by Martin, *New Year in Cape Town*, 58–61.
98 Ibid., 53–54.
99 Thompson, *History of South Africa*, 33.
100 According to the Dutch East India Company's records, the entire colony was home to only 13,830 Burghers (4,032 men, 2,730 women, and 7,068 children) in 1793. Ibid., 35–36.
101 Worden, van Heyningen, and Bickford-Smith, *Cape Town*, 86.
102 Ibid.
103 Ibid., 88.
104 Ibid., 89.
105 Ibid., 90–93; Thompson, *History of South Africa*, 56–66; Tristram Hunt, *Cities of Empire: The British Colonies and the Creation of the Urban World* (New York: Henry Holt, 2014), 141–82.

106 Thompson, *History of South Africa*, 53–54.
107 Worden, van Heyningen, and Bickford-Smith, *Cape Town*, 96–97.
108 Thompson, *History of South Africa*, 56–57.
109 However, the demographic proportions were—and remained—decisively different. In the colonies that became Canada, the British settlers soon outnumbered the French Canadians. In greater South Africa, Afrikaners have always formed at least 55 percent of the white population. In Canada, the whites became overwhelmingly more numerous than the native population at an early stage, whereas in South Africa the white population never amounted to more than about 20 percent of the total. Ibid., 56.
110 Ibid., 53.
111 Green, *Tavern of the Seas*, 76–88, 99–101; Biggs, *This Is Cape Town*, 13–15; Hunt, *Cities of Empire*, 141–82.
112 Within a decade of British rule, Cape wine benefited from imperial preferential tariffs to become a major export (accounting for nearly two-thirds of Cape exports by 1820). Later, a vibrant trade in locally produced wool and ostrich feathers developed with the metropole. Worden, van Heyningen, and Bickford-Smith, *Cape Town*, 99.
113 Hunt, *Cities of Empire*, 141–82.
114 Ibid., 111.
115 Ibid., 102–12.
116 Ibid., 142–44.
117 Ibid., 128–29.
118 Ibid., 132–36.
119 Ibid., 135–36.
120 Ibid., 133–38.
121 Ibid., 123.
122 Ibid., 152–53.
123 Ibid., 152–54.
124 Ibid., 156–61.
125 Thompson, *History of South Africa*, 67–69.
126 Ibid., 70–88.
127 Ibid., 94–109.
128 Worden, van Heyningen, and Bickford-Smith, *Cape Town*, 160–74.
129 Thompson, *History of South Africa*, 110–21.
130 Biggs, *This Is Cape Town*, 25.
131 Thompson, *History of South Africa*, 132–35.
132 If, at the time of its municipal charter in 1840, the city and surrounding area were home to approximately 20,000 residents, Cape Town's population reached 45,000 in 1875; 67,000 in 1891; and 171,000 in 1904. Worden, van Heyningen, and Bickford-Smith, *Cape Town*, 212.

133 Ibid., 212; Western, *Outcast Cape Town*, 160–201.
134 Worden, van Heyningen, and Bickford-Smith, *Cape Town*, 212–13; Thompson, *History of South Africa*, 100, 114.
135 Worden, van Heyningen, and Bickford-Smith, *Cape Town*, 213–16.
136 Ibid., 210–12.
137 These observations are found in ibid., 226–27.
138 Ibid., 221–29.
139 Thompson, *History of South Africa*, 137–41; Elizabeth Longford, *Jameson's Raid: The Prelude to the Boer War* (London: Weidenfeld & Nicolson, 1982).
140 For an introduction to the Anglo-Boer Wars, see Thomas Pakenham, *The Boer War* (New York: Random House, 1979).
141 Thompson, *History of South Africa*, 141–45.
142 Coplan, *In Township Tonight*, 16–20.
143 Ibid., 49–50.
144 Ibid., 50–51.
145 Du Plessis, *Cape Malays*, 43.
146 William Marvel, *The Alabama & the Kearsarge: The Sailor's War* (Chapel Hill: University of North Carolina Press, 1996).
147 Wilkinson and Kragolsen-Kille, *Bo-Kapp*, 84.
148 Coplan, *In Township Tonight*, 50–51.
149 Du Plessis, *Cape Malays*, 41–42.
150 Green, *Tavern of the Seas*, 14–15.
151 John Edwin Mason, *One Love, Goema Beat: Inside the Cape Town Carnival* (Charlottesville: University of Virginia Press, 2010), 10–11.
152 Wilkinson and Kragolsen-Kille, *Bo-Kapp*, 79–80.
153 Martin, *New Year in Cape Town*.
154 Wilkinson and Kragolsen-Kille, *Bo-Kapp*, 80.
155 Martin, *New Year in Cape Town*, 132–36.
156 Mason, *One Love, Goema Beat*, 10.
157 Ibid., 19.
158 The complexities of "coloured" identity in Cape Town are explored in detail by the contributors to Zimitri Erasmus's collected volume, *Coloured by History*.
159 Zimitri Erasmus, "Re-Imagining Coloured Identities in Post-Apartheid South Africa," in *Coloured by History*, ed. Erasmus, 13–28, at 22–23.
160 Coplan, *In Township Tonight*, 50.
161 Josephine Wright, "Orpheus Myron McAdoo: Singer, Impresario," *Black Perspective in Music* 4, no. 3 (Autumn 1976): 320–27.
162 John Lovell Jr., *Black Song: The Forge and the Flam — The Story of How the Afro-American Spiritual Was Hammered Out* (New York: Macmillan, 1972), 402–6.

163 Andrew Ward, *Dark Midnight When I Rise: The Story of the Jubilee Singers, Who Introduced the World to the Music of Black America* (New York: Farrar, Straus & Giroux, 2000).

164 Wright, "Orpheus Myron McAdoo," 320.

165 Ibid., 322.

166 Ibid.

167 Ibid., 323.

168 Lovell, *Black Song*, 407–12.

169 Ansell, *Soweto Blues*, 15–17.

170 Coplan, *In Township Tonight*, 52.

171 Ibid.

172 Ansell, *Soweto Blues*, 8–9.

173 Martin, *New Year in Cape Town*, 72.

174 Mason, *One Love, Goema Beat*, 10–20.

175 Martin, *New Year in Cape Town*, 133–35.

176 Coplan, *In Township Tonight*, 34.

177 Ansell, *Soweto Blues*, 16–17.

178 Coplan, *In Township Tonight*, 53.

179 Ibid., 54–57.

180 Ibid., 56–63.

181 Ibid., 62–63.

182 This is as referenced in ibid., 64.

183 The image of a train as a bone crusher has been used often in South Africa. In this instance, the reference is to the statement made by Hugh Masekela during a performance of *Songs of Migration* at the John F. Kennedy Center for the Performing Arts in Washington on October 20, 2012. The play originally had been produced by the Sibojama Theatre on the basis of a production at the Marketplace Theater in Johannesburg. That production, in turn, was based on a review of a century of South African song produced by the South African State Theater. The production presents a selection of songs complied by Hugh Masekela and James Ngcobo. They are available on a 2011 compact disc released by Ear Theatre Records.

184 Coplan, *In Township Tonight*, 64–66.

185 Ibid., 66–67.

186 For an authoritative—if now dated—account, see Leonard Thompson, *The Unification of South Africa, 1901–1910* (New York: Oxford University Press, 1960).

187 Thompson, *History of South Africa*, 147–53.

188 Janet Robertson, *Liberalism in South Africa, 1948–1952* (Oxford: Clarendon Press, 1971).

189 These population data were drawn from Thompson, *History of*

South Africa, 153. For more on Botha and Smuts, see Basil Williams, *Botha, Smuts, and South Africa* (London: Hodder & Stoughton, 1946); for more on Smuts, see Antony Lentin, *General Smuts: South Africa* (London: Haus, 2010).

190   Thompson, *History of South Africa*, 158–65.
191   Heidi Holland, *The Struggle: A History of the African National Congress*, 2nd ed. (New York: George Braziller, 1990).
192   Nigel Worden, Elizabeth van Heyningen, and Vivian Brickford-Smith, *Cape Town in the Twentieth Century: An Illustrated Social History* (Claremont, South Africa: David Philip, 1999), 70–83.
193   Thompson, *History of South Africa*, 166–71.
194   Ibid., 169–70.
195   Worden, van Heyningen, and Brickford-Smith, *Cape Town in the Twentieth Century*, 62.
196   Wilson and Mafeje, *Langa*, 2.
197   Ibid., 3–4; Western, *Outcast Cape Town*, 122–24.
198   Wilson and Mafeje, *Langa*, 7–10.
199   Ibid., 7–8.
200   Ibid., 9–13.
201   Thompson, *History of South Africa*, 178.
202   Wilson and Mafeje, *Langa*, 75.
203   Ibid., 47–48.
204   Ansell, *Soweto Blues*, 20–23.
205   Wilson and Mafeje, *Langa*, 125–27.
206   Ansell, *Soweto Blues*, 29.
207   Modikwe Dikobe, *The Marabi Dance* (Ibadan: Heinemann, 1973), 1.
208   Coplan, *In Township Tonight*, 105.
209   Ansell, *Soweto Blues*, 29.
210   Ibid.
211   Ibid.
212   Ibid., 32–36.
213   Ibid., 36.
214   Christopher Ballantine, *Marabi Nights: Early South African Jazz and Vaudeville* (Johannesburg: Ravan Press, 1993), 1–2.
215   Ansell, *Soweto Blues*, 29–30.
216   Coplan, *In Township Tonight*, 116–17.
217   Ballantine, *Marabi Nights*, 2.
218   Ibid., 6–7.
219   Ibid.
220   Ibid., 11.
221   The universal character of migrants finding solace in their home music across time and space formed the basis of a popular twenty-

first-century South African—and ultimately international—musical *Songs of Migration*. Celia Wren, "'Songs of Migration' Offers a Wistful, Buoyant Journey," *Washington Post*, October 18, 2012. As noted above, the play originally had been produced by the Sibojama Theatre on the basis of a production at the Marketplace Theater in Johannesburg. That production, in turn, was based on a review of a century of South African song produced by the South African State Theater. The production presents a selection of songs complied by Hugh Masekela and James Ngcobo. They are available on a 2011 compact disc released by Ear Theatre Records.

222 James Ngcpbo, "Director's Note," Program for Songs of Migration at John F. Kennedy Center for the Performing Arts, October 20, 2012.

223 Coplan, *In Township Tonight*, 79.

224 Ibid., 83–84.

225 Ibid., 88–105.

226 Ibid., 89–90.

227 Ibid., 88–105.

228 Ballantine, *Marabi Nights*, 26–27.

229 Veit Erlmann, *Nightsong: Performance, Power, and Practice in South Africa* (Chicago: University of Chicago Press, 1966), xv.

230 Ibid., 57; Muller, *South African Music*, 122–27.

231 Erlmann, *Nightsong*, 57.

232 Ibid., 58–61.

233 Ibid., 61–62.

234 Muller, *South African Music*, 121–31.

235 Rian Malan, "Where Does the Lion Sleep Tonight?" *Rolling Stone*, May 25, 2000.

236 Malan reports on the Disney settlement in a postscript to his 2000 article appearing in a collection of his essays; see Rian Malan, "In the Jungle," in *The Lion Sleeps Tonight*, 57–86, at 84–86.

237 Malan, "Where Does the Lion Sleep Tonight?"

238 As quoted by Erlmann, *Nightsong*, 74–75.

239 Muller, *South African Music*, 157.

240 Ibid., 158.

241 Ibid., 170–71.

Windsongs

1 I would like to single out the late James Miller of George Washington University for encouraging me to undertake this chapter on music in Cape Town. I also would like take this opportunity to thank my

research intern, Irina Kuzemkina, for her support and assistance in the preparation of the chapter. In addition, I would like to acknowledge the thoughtful comments and enthusiastic support of the readers, especially Steve McDonald.

The music material discussed in this sentence is from Colin Miller, "'Julle kan ma New York toe gaan, ek bly in die Manenberg'": An Oral History of Jazz in Cape Town from the Mid-1950s to the Mid-1970s," in *Lost Communities, Living Memories: Remembering Forced Removals in Cape Town*, ed. Sean Field (Cape Town: David Philip, 2001), 143–44. And the epigraph for this chapter is as quoted in *Sathima's Windsong*, a film by Dan Yon, 2010.

2 Ibid., 146.
3 Nigel Worden, Elizabeth van Heyningen, and Vivian Bickford-Smith, *Cape Town in the Twentieth Century: An Illustrated Social History* (Claremont, South Africa: David Philip, 1999), 50–58.
4 Ibid., 58–59.
5 David B. Coplan, *In Township Tonight: South Africa's Black City Music and Theatre*, 2nd ed. (Chicago: University of Chicago Press, 2007), 146–48.
6 Ibid., 146–47.
7 Ibid., 145–58.
8 Christopher Ballantine, *Marabi Nights: Early South African Jazz and Vaudeville* (Johannesburg: Ravan Press, 1993), 34–58.
9 For an overview of the role of Sophiatown in mid-twentieth-century South African culture, see Coplan, *In Township Tonight*, 170–223.
10 Gwen Ansell, *Soweto Blues: Jazz, Popular Music, and Politics in South Africa* (New York: Continuum, 2005), 51.
11 Ballantine, *Marabi Nights*, 60–62.
12 Hugh Masekela and D. Michael Cheers, *Still Grazing: The Musical Journey of Hugh Masekela* (New York: Crown, 2004), 3–4.
13 Ibid., 70–71.
14 Ansell, *Soweto Blues*, 46.
15 Ibid., 46–56.
16 Nomvuyo Ngcelwane, *Sale Kahle District Six: An African Woman's Perspective* (Cape Town: Kwela Books, 1998), 90.
17 Bill Nasson, "Oral History and the Reconstruction of District Six," in *The Struggle for District Six: Past and Present*, ed. Shamil Jeppie and Crain Soudien (Cape Town: Bunchu Books, 1990), 44–66, at 57–58.
18 Ibid., 92–93.
19 Ballantine, *Marabi Nights*, 3–55; Coplan, *In Township Tonight*, 162–66.
20 Denis-Constant Martin, *New Year in Cape Town: Past to Present* (Cape Town: David Philip, 1999), 97.

21 Ibid.
22 Vivian Bickford-Smith, "Providing Local Color? 'Cape Coloreds,' 'Cockneys,' and Cape Town's Identity from the Late Nineteenth Century to the 1970s," *Journal of Urban History* 38, no. 1 (2012): 133–51, at 146.
23 Martin, *New Year in Cape Town*, 101–2.
24 Ibid., 103–5.
25 Ibid., 107–11.
26 Ibid., 112.
27 Ibid., 113–14.
28 Denis-Constant Martin, "What's in the Name 'Coloured'?" in *Social Identities in the New South Africa, Volume One: After Apartheid*, ed. Abebe Zegeya (Colorado Springs: International Academic Publishers, 2001), 149–268, at 255–56.
29 See, e.g., I. D. DuPlessis, *The Cape Malays: History, Religion, Traditions, Folk Tales — The Malay Quarter* (Cape Town: A. A. Balkema, 1972).
30 Shamil Jeppie, "Reclassifications: Colored, Malay, Muslin," in *Coloured by History, Shaped by Place: New Perspectives on Coloured Identities in Cape Town*, ed. Zimitri Erasmus (Colorado Springs: International Academic Publishers, 2001), 80–96.
31 This becomes apparent in the essays compiled in *Coloured by History*, ed. Erasmus.
32 Thiven Reddy, "The Politics of Naming: The Constitution of Coloured Subjects in South Africa," in ibid., 64–79.
33 This list is taken from Martin, "What's in the Name 'Coloured'?" 258.
34 Shamil Jeppie, "Popular Culture and Carnival in Cape Town: The 1940s and 1950s," in *Struggle*, ed. Jeppie and Soudien, 67–87, at 70.
35 Ibid., 74.
36 Ibid., 85.
37 Nasson, "Oral History," 56.
38 Coplan, *In Township Tonight*, 181–83.
39 Martin, *New Year in Cape Town*, 120–24.
40 Ibid., 119–22.
41 Leonard Thompson, *A History of South Africa*, 3rd ed. (New Haven, Conn.: Yale University Press, 2000), 180–81.
42 Ibid., 178–86.
43 Ibid., 181–84, 207–8.
44 Ibid., 185–87.
45 Ibid., 186–88.
46 Ibid., 189–200.
47 C. Marx, "Hendrik Verwoerd's Long March to Apartheid: Nationalism and Racism in South Africa," in *Racism in the Modern World: Historical*

Perspectives on Cultural Transfer and Adaptation, ed. Manfred Berg and Simon Wendt (New York: Berghahn Books, 2011), 285–91.

48   The Population Registration Act of 1950 introduced identity cards specifying racial groups; the Group Areas Act of 1950 required South Africans to live in settlements set aside for their own group. The Prohibition of Mixed Marriages Act of 1949 and the Immorality Act of 1950 criminalized sexual relations between groups. The Reservation of Separate Amenities Act of 1953 forced the designation of separate public facilities for only one group (as in "whites only" public amenities). In order to empower authorities to quell political opposition, the Suppression of Communism Act of 1950 prohibited groups that were thought to support communism, defined in such a manner as to mean all who opposed government policies. The 1953 Bantu Education Act established separate university systems for each group, while the Bantu Authorities Act of 1951 created distinct government structures for whites and blacks. John Western, *Outcast Cape Town* (Berkeley: University of California Press, 1966), 70–120.

49   Thompson, *History of South Africa*, 189–200.

50   Ibid., 205–9.

51   Worden, van Heyningen, and Bickford-Smith, *Cape Town*, 122–24.

52   The 1946 census reported almost 400,000 residents within the municipal boundaries, with another 60,000 in surrounding communities. The census takers undoubtedly undercounted African migrants. White women were beginning to compete successfully for teaching and nursing positions once held by "coloured" and Indian men. In general, there were proportionally fewer whites in unskilled positions and more whites in skilled jobs Worden, van Heyningen, and Bickford-Smith, *Cape Town*, 118–23.

53   Ibid., 124–25; Western, *Outcast Cape Town*, 55–56.

54   Worden, van Heyningen, and Bickford-Smith, *Cape Town*, 122.

55   Ibid., 135.

56   Lydia Polgreen, "Cape Town Journal: In A Divided City, Many Blacks See Echoes of White Superiority," *New York Times*, March 23, 2012.

57   Carol A. Muller, *South African Music: A Century of Traditions in Transformation* (Santa Barbara, Calif.: ABC-CLIO, 2003), 62.

58   Ibid., 61–68.

59   Ibid.

60   Giovanni Russonello, "South African Jazz: Our Music Has No Limit," *Jazz Times* 44, no. 10 (December 2014): 44–51, at 47–48.

61   Masekela and Cheers, *Still Grazing*, 102.

62   Muller, *South African Music*, 95–97.

Notes 603

65   For more on the Sophiatown scene of the era, see Coplan, *In Township Tonight*, 211–14.

66   Ibid., 194–99.

67   Miller, "'Julle kan ma New York toe gaan, ek bly in die Manenberg,'" 133–49, at 143–44.

68   Muller, *South African Music*, 85–88.

69   "Yesterday's District Six: A Patchwork of Visual and Oral Memory," in *Struggle*, ed. Jeppie and Soudien, 17–34, at 25.

70   Miller, "'Julle kan ma New York toe gaan, ek bly in die Manenberg,'" 133–35.

71   Muller, *South African Music*, 90.

72   Ibid., 91–92. Kolbe remained a seminal figure on the Cape Town scene until his death in 2010. His humanity and accomplishments are movingly captured in John Edwin Mason's heartfelt obituary, which Mason posted on his Web site on September 4, 2010; John Edwin Mason, "Vincent Kolbe, Musician, Librarian, Activist, & Sage: 1933–2010," http://johnedwinmason.typepad,com/john_edwin-Mason-Photogra/2010/09/Vincent-kolbe-1933-2010.html.

73   Masekela and Cheers, *Still Grazing*, 56–69; Ansell, *Soweto Blues*, 95–100.

74   Muller, *South African Music*, 91.

75   Ansell, *Soweto Blues*, 124.

76   Ibid.

77   Miller, "'Julle kan ma New York toe gaan, ek bly in die Manenberg,'" 140–42.

78   Muller, *South African Music*, 98–99.

79   Ansell, *Soweto Blues*, 124–25.

80   Carol A. Muller, *Focus: Music of South Africa*, 2nd ed. (New York: Routledge, 2008), 116.

81   Ibid., 153–55.

82   Thompson, *History of South Africa*, 209–11.

83   Ibid., 210–11.

84   Masekela and Cheers, *Still Grazing*, 108.

85   Coplan, *In Township Tonight*, 214–15.

86   Ibid., 214–18.

87   Ansell, *Soweto Blues*, 133.

88   Muller, *Focus*, 103.

89   Coplan, *In Township Tonight*, 126–31.

90   Worden, van Heyningen, and Bickford-Smith, *Cape Town*, 150–81.

91   Ibid., 180.

92   Deborah M. Hart, "Political Manipulation of Urban Space: The Razing of District Six, Cape Town," in *Struggle*, ed. Jeppie and Soudien, 117–42, at 123–30.

93   Worden, van Heyningen, and Bickford-Smith, *Cape Town*, 181–83.

94   Ibid., 156–70.

95   Monica Wilson and Archie Mafeje, *Langa: A Study of Social Groups in an African Township* (Cape Town: Oxford University Press, 1963), 150–52.

96   Felicity Swanson and Jane Harries, "'Ja! So Was District Six! But It Was a Beautiful Place': Oral Histories, Memory, and Identity," in *Imaging the City: Memories and Cultures in Cape Town*, ed. Sean Field, Renate Meyer, and Felicity Swanson (Cape Town: HSRC Press, 2007), 62–80, at 78.

97   Vivian Bickford-Smith, "Mapping Cape Town: From Slavery to Apartheid," in *Lost Communities*, ed. Field, 15–26, at 26.

98   Albert Thomas, "'It Changed Everybody's Lives': The Simon's Town Group Areas Removals," in *Lost Communities*, ed. Field, 81–99.

99   Felicity Swanson, "'Mense van die Vlak': Community and Forced Removals in Lower Claremont," in *Lost Communities*, ed. Field, 110–16.

100 Sean Field, "'I Dream of Our Old House, You See There Are Things That Can Never Go Away': Memory, Restitution, and Democracy," in *Lost Communities*, ed. Field, 117–24.

101 Richard Rive, "District Six: Fact and Fiction," in *Struggle*, ed. Jeppie and Soudien, 110–16.

102 Vivian Bickford-Smith, "Providing Local Color?" 145–46.

103 Worden, van Heyningen, and Bickford-Smith, *Cape Town*, 194–95.

104 Russonello, "South African Jazz," 45.

105 *Searching for Sugar Man*, directed by Malik Bendjelloul, Sony Film Classics, 2012.

106 Martin, *New Year in Cape Town*, 150–51.

107 Ibid., 161–62.

108 Russonello, "South African Jazz," 49.

109 Thompson, *History of South Africa*, 190–200.

110 Vervoerd's 1953 Bantu Education Act segregated "tribal" education and endorsed curricula intended to convince "natives" that "European" culture was "alien" to their own. Ibid., 196–98; Ansell, *Soweto Blues*, 110–11.

111 Ibid., 109–10.

112 Ibid., 109.

113 Coplan, *In Township Tonight*, 227–29.

114 Ansell, *Soweto Blues*, 132.

115 Ibid., 132–33.
116 Ibid., 1.
117 Ibid., 3–4.
118 Ibid., 152–53.
119 Ibid., 133–34.
120 Ibid., 243–44; Coplan, *In Township Tonight*, 225, 232.
121 Ansell, *Soweto Blues*, 230–31.
122 Coplan, *In Township Tonight*, 232–33.
123 Ibid., 232.
124 Ansell, *Soweto Blues*, 155–62.
125 Coplan, *In Township Tonight*, 225.
126 Ibid., xi–xiii.
127 Ibid., 1–2.
128 Ibid., 9–10.
129 Ibid., 299–300.
130 Ibid., 307.
131 Veit Erlmann, *Nightsong: Performance, Power, and Practice in South Africa* (Chicago: University of Chicago Press, 1966), 250–52.
132 Ibid., 253–54.
133 Ibid., 255.
134 Ibid., 244–45.
135 Coplan, *In Township Tonight*, 236–37.
136 Ibid., 241–42; Erlmann, *Nightsong*, 91–94.
137 Coplan, *In Township Tonight*, 242–43.
138 Ibid., 242–44.
139 Ibid., 260.
140 Ansell, *Soweto Blues*, 164.
141 Thompson, *History of South Africa*, 212–13.
142 Ibid., 221–40.
143 Ibid.
144 Worden, van Heyningen, and Bickford-Smith, *Cape Town*, 200.
145 Annual government expenditures on education in the Cape, e.g., were just R28.56 for every African child, and R199 for every "coloured" child, as opposed to R496 for every white child. Ibid., 199.
146 Ibid., 199–200.
147 Ibid., 204–6.
148 Ibid., 207–13.
149 Ibid., 218–19.
150 Ansell, *Soweto Blues*, 181.
151 Ibid., 172–75.
152 Ibid., 187.
153 Ibid., 205–6.

154 Ibid., 217–18.
155 Ibid., 248–49.
156 The *Graceland* story is compellingly retold by the documentary film *Under African Skies: Paul Simon's Graceland Journey*, A&E Television Networks, 2012.
157 Erlmann, *Nightsong*, 92–93.
158 Masekela and Cheers, *Still Grazing*, 343–44.
159 Coplan, *In Township Tonight*, 303–4.
160 Masekela and Cheers, *Still Grazing*, 345.
161 Ibid., 346–48.
162 Jeff Chang, *Can't Stop Won't Stop: A History of the Hip-Hop Generation* (New York: St. Martin's Press, 2005), 68–72.
163 Louise Meintjes, *Sound of Africa! Making Music Zulu in a South African Studio* (Durham, N.C.: Duke University Press, 2003), 5–19.
164 Ibid., 13.
165 Edgar Pieterse, "Youth Cultures and the Mediation of Racial Exclusion or Inclusion in Rio de Janiero and Cape Town," in *Urban Diversity: Space, Culture, and Inclusive Pluralism in Cities Worldwide*, ed. Caroline Wanjiku Kihato, Mehjan Massoumi, Blair A. Ruble, Pep Suberiós, and Allison M. Garland (Washington and Baltimore: Woodrow Wilson Center Press and Johns Hopkins University Press, 2010), 187–211, at 194.
166 Ibid., 188–89.
167 Ncedisa Nkonyeni, "Da Struggle Continues into the 21st Century: Two Decades of Nation-Conscious Rap in Cape Town," in *Imaging the City*, ed. Field, Meyer, and Swanson, 151–72, at 153.
168 Ibid., 154–55.
169 Pieterse, "Youth Cultures," 197.
170 Adam Bradley, *Books of Rhymes: The Poetics of Hip-Hop* (New York: Basic Civitas, 2009), xix.
171 Ibid., 5–9.
172 Adriana Helbig, "The Cyberpolitics of Music in Ukraine's 2004 Orange Revolution," *Current Musicology* 82 (2006): 81–101.
173 Pieterse, "Youth Cultures," 199.
174 Ibid.
175 Chippie Waterman, "Ready D on Prophets of da City: The 'Understand Where I'm Coming From' Video and Hip-Hop Culture," *Cape Argus Big Noise*, February 1, 1997.
176 Nkonyeni, "Da Struggle Continues," 155–61.
177 Pieterse, "Youth Cultures," 198.
178 Adam Haupt, "Black Thing: Hip-Hop Nationalism, 'Race,' and Gender in Prophets of da City and Brasse runnie Kaap," in *Coloured by History*, ed. Erasmus, 173–91, at 173.

179 Pieterse, "Youth Cultures," 197–98.
180 Coplan, *In Township Tonight*, 328–30.
181 Ibid., 332–34.
182 Nkonyeni, "Da Struggle Continues," 165–68.
183 Thompson, *History of South Africa*, 241–44.
184 Ibid., 244–46.
185 Ibid., 246–48.
186 Ibid., 248–58.
187 Ibid., 258–64.
188 Ibid., 288–91.
189 Worden, van Heyningen, and Bickford-Smith, *Cape Town*, 217–20.
190 Ansell, *Soweto Blues*, 261–304.
191 Polgreen, "Cape Town Journal."
192 Martin, *New Year in Cape Town*, 170.
193 Vincent Kolbe, "Foreword," in *Lost Communities*, ed. Field, 7–8; Sean Field, "Preface," in ibid., 8–10; Sean Field, "Oral Histories of Forced Removals," in ibid., 11–14.
194 These groups evolved from the District Six Defence Committee to the District Six Association, the Friends of District Six, and Hand's Off District Six Campaign. Crain Soudien, "District Six from Protest to Protest," in *Lost Communities*, ed. Field, 143–84.
195 Crain Soudien, "The First Few Years of the District Six Museum Foundation," in *Recalling Community in Cape Town: Creating and Curating the District Six Museum*, ed. Ciraj Rassool and Sandra Prosalendis (Cape Town: District Six Museum, 2001), 5–6; Lucien le Grande, "The Collective Spirit of a Museum," in ibid., 7–9; Terrence Fredericks, "Creating the District Six Museum," in ibid., 13–14; Vincent Kolb, "Museum Beginnings," in ibid., 15–16; Charmine McEachern, "Mapping the Memories: Politics, Place and Identity in the District Six Museum, Cape Town," in *Social Identities*, ed. Zegeya, 223–47.
196 Antony Sher and Gregory Doran, *Woza Shakespeare! Titus Andronicus in South Africa* (London: Methuen Drama, 1996), 130.
197 "On This Day: 11 February, 1990," BBC News, http://news.bbc.co.uk/onthisday/hi/dates/stories/February/11/newsid_2439000/2539947.stm.
198 David A. McDonald, *World City Syndrome: Neoliberalism and Inequality in Cape Town* (London: Routledge, 2008).
199 Ibid., 15–47.
200 Pieterse, "Youth Cultures," 191.
201 McDonald, *World City Syndrome*, 135–75.
202 Ibid., 99–130.
203 Ibid., 271–31.

204 Ibid., xviii.
205 Nkululeko Mabandla, "The Mist, the Wind, and the Two Oceans," in *A City Imagined*, ed. Stephen Watson (Johannesburg: Penguin Books, 2005), 184–96, at 188.
206 Coplan, *In Township Tonight*, 340–41.
207 Ibid., 341–44.
208 Ibid., 345, 353–54.
209 Ibid., 344–45; Russonello, "South African Jazz," 49–50.
210 Coplan, *In Township Tonight*, 344.
211 Ibid., 355.
212 Ibid., 365.
213 Martin, *New Year in Cape Town*, 22–28.
214 John Edwin Mason, *One Love, Goema Beat: Inside the Cape Town Carnival* (Charlottesville: University of Virginia Press, 2010), 93.
215 Damon Galgut, "My Version of Home," in *City Imagined*, ed. Watson, 12–20, at 16.
216 Jeremy Cronin, "Creole Cape Town," in *City Imagined*, ed. Watson, 50.

Urals Pathfinder: Theater in Post-Soviet Yekaterinburg

1 I would like to take this opportunity to acknowledge a continuing debt to Pilar Bonet, the longtime Moscow correspondent for *El País*, who has shared her knowledge and love of contemporary Russian theater with me, introducing me to its vibrant post-Soviet scene over the course of some two decades. She has been a genuine colleague and friend. So too has been Philip Arnoult, a force of nature and legendary Baltimore theater figure, who established the Center for International Theater Development that has played a critical role in bringing Russian theater to American audiences (and much more).

I similarly would like to thank a number of generous colleagues, readers, and interlocutors for their assistance, comments, and goodwill during the preparation of this chapter, particularly Leon Aron, the resident scholar and director of Russian studies at the American Enterprise Institute and author of *Yeltsin: A Revolutionary Life*, for his insights into Soviet-era Yekaterinburg; Leonid Bykov and Valentine Lukyanin, Yekaterinburg writers and literary leaders extraordinaire, for their colorful and thoughtful observations about the city's Soviet-era cultural scene; John Freedman, the *Moscow Times* theater critic, for his assistance in preparing my discussion of post-Soviet theatrical life; Maxim Khomiakov and Elena Trubina of the Urals Federal University, as well as Natalya Vlasova of the Urals State Economics University, for their insights concerning how culture, academic life, and political power mix in today's Yekaterinburg; Nikolai Kolyada, dramatist, teacher, and playwright, for his generous hospitality; Andrei Malaev-Babel, of Florida State University's Asolo Conservatory for Acting Training and editor of *The Vakhtangov Sourcebook*, for his help in the discussion of late Soviet and post-Soviet theater; and Sergei Zhuk, of Ball State University's History Department and author of *Rock and Roll in the Rocket City*, for his help in the preparation of the discussion of late-Soviet rock music.

I also would like to acknowledge the support and collaboration of the Kennan Institute research associate Liz Malinkin in conducting research about contemporary Yekaterinburg and her comments on various drafts of this chapter, as well as of Kennan Institute intern Irina Kuzemkina for her energetic research.

I have employed the Library of Congress Transliteration System exclusively in the notes as well as generally in the text. However, alternative transliterations for several place and personal names have become widely accepted in British and American usage (e.g., Chelyabinsk instead of Cheliabinsk; Bogayev instead of Bogaev; Kolyada instead of Koliada; Lukyanin instead of Luk'ianin; Presnyakov instead of Presniakov; and, most important, Yekaterinburg instead of Ekaterinburg). I have used more generally accepted transliterations in the text in such instances.

The epigraph for this chapter is from "Oni Letaiat,'" on the 1998 Agata Kristi Rock Group album *Chudesa* (*Miracles*).

2   Brigit Beumers and Mark Lipovetsky, *Performing Violence: Literary and Theatrical Experiments of New Russian Drama* (Chicago: Intellect, 2009), 152–59; John Freedman, "Contemporary Russian Drama: The Journey from Stagnation to a Golden Age," *Theatre Journal* 62, no. 3 (October 2010): 389–420.

3   Beumers and Lipovetsky, *Performing Violence*, 27–44.

4   Ibid., 152.

5   Ibid.

6   Ibid., 156.

7   Ibid., 152.

8   Walt Whitman, *Song of Myself*, 1855 edition.

9   For a history of the Royal Court, see Philip Roberts, *The Royal Court Theatre and the Modern Stage* (Cambridge: Cambridge University Press, 1999).

10   Michael Billington, "Plasticine," *The Guardian*, March 22, 2002.

11   Paul Taylor, "Plasticine, Royal Court Upstairs, London," *The Independent*, March 27, 2002.

12 Philip Fisher, "Plasticine by Vassily Sigarev," *Theatreworld*, April 2002.

13 Hedy Weiss, "A Voice from Mother Russia," *Chicago Sunday Sun-Times*, November 21, 2003.

14 A. A. Starikov, V. E. Zavgel'skaia, L. I. Tokmenninova, and E. V. Cherniak, *Ekaterinburg: Istoriia goroda v arkhitekture* (Yekaterinburg: Sokrat, 2008).

15 Dmitrii Bavil'skii, "Demidovskii vremennik," *Ural*, 1996, no. 2.

16 Edward Ames, "A Century of Russian Railroad Construction: 1837–1938," *American Slavic and East European Review* 6, nos. 3–4 (1947): 57–74, at 67.

17 Irina Antropova, "Iz istorii evreev Urala," *Ural*, 2004, no. 11.

18 Sergei Kropotov and Maria Litovskaya, "Urban Space and Production of a Dream," in *First Ural Industrial Biennial of Contemporary Art 9.09–10.10.2010: Special Projects*, curated by Alisa Prudnikova (Yekaterinburg: National Center for Contemporary Art, 2010), 43–57, at 43.

19 For an overview of the history of the Pale of Settlement, see Nathaniel Deutsch, *The Jewish Dark Continent: Life and Death in the Russian Pale of Settlement* (Cambridge, Mass.: Harvard University Press, 2011).

20 Leon Aron, *Yeltsin: A Revolutionary Life* (London: HarperCollins, 2000), 12.

21 Antropova, "Iz istorii evreev Urala."

22 Ibid.

23 Ibid.

24 Ibid.

25 This observation is developed further by Arkadii Bartov, "Mif Sankt-Peterburga: Etalon giperreal'nosti i kul'tura vtorichnosti," *Ural*, 2005, no. 8. The practicality of intellectual life in the Urals is reflected in the region's primary prerevolutionary scientific honor, an annual award established by Imperial chamberlain Pavel Nikolaevich Demidov in 1831. The awards promoted the work in physics, chemistry, geology, biology, astronomy, and the earth sciences before being suspended in 1866 in accordance with the original bequest a quarter century after Demidov's death. Reconstituted in 1993, the contemporary incarnation of the Demidov Prize more often recognizes work in the humanities and social sciences. For discussion of this award and its history, see Andrei Ponizovkin, "Sobitie: Laureaty demidovskoi premii," *Ural*, 1996, no. 2.

26 This point is expanded upon along various dimensions of cultural life in such articles as that by Ol'ga Bukharkina, "Vdol' po ulitse po glavnoi," *Ural*, 2000, no. 12; and Sergei Beliaev, "Vecher budetlian: Nemuzykal'nie sametko o muzykal'nom zale," *Ural*, 2005, no. 11.

27 Robert Service, *A History of Twentieth-Century Russia* (Cambridge, Mass.: Harvard University Press, 1997), 107. Boris Yeltsin, then the Sverdlovsk regional party first secretary, dispatched wrecking crews in the middle of an autumn 1977 night to tear the house down on orders from then–KGB chairman Iurii Andropov. This story is told by Aron, *Yeltsin*, 112–14.

28 James R. Harris, *The Great Urals: Regionalism and the Evolution of the Soviet Union* (Ithaca, N.Y.: Cornell University Press, 1999), 102.

29 Kropotov and Litovskaya, "Urban Space," 45–46.

30 R. W. Davies, "Industry under Central Planning, 1929–1941," in *The Economic Transformation of the Soviet Union, 1913–1945*, ed. R. W. Davies, Mark Harrison, and S. C. Wheatcroft (New York: Cambridge University Press, 1994), 135–57; Helena Krzhivitskaia, Galina Molchanova, Ksenia Fedorova, and Andrey Shcherbenok, "The Ural Heavy Engineering Plant (UZTM, Uralmashzavod)," in *First Ural Industrial Biennial of Contemporary Arts*, curated by Prudnikova, 91–100.

31 Valentin Luk'ianin, "Gorod i dusha: Chelovek stroit gorod—gorod stroit cheloveka," *Ural*, 2008, no. 8.

32 Kropotov and Litovskaya, "Urban Space," 51–54.

33 Andrei Rastorguev, Liudmilla Tokmeninova, and Astrid Fol'pert, "Nasledie eksperimenta: Iz istorii arkhitekturnogo avangarda na Uralem," *Ural*, 2011, no. 6.

34 Luk'ianin, "Gorod i dusha."

35 Ibid.; Andrei Rastorguev, "Nasledie eksperimenta: Iz istorii arkhitekturnogo avangarda na Urale," *Ural*, 2011, no. 8; John Freedman, "Yekaterinburg, the Capital of Constructivism," *Moscow Times*, June 22, 2013.

36 Helena Krzhivitskaia, Galina Molchanova, Ksenia Fedorova, and Andrey Shcherbenok, "Center of Culture 'Ordzhinikidzevskiy,'" in *First Ural Industrial Biennial of Contemporary Arts*, curated by Prudnikova, 101–3.

37 See Raisa Gilyova, "Boites' snobizma: Otbiraite istinno prekrasnoe," *Ural*, 2010, no. 12; Igor Turbanov, "Ekaterinburg: Piat' blikov," *Ural*, 2010, no. 4; Sofid Demidova, "Deistvo v Sverdlovske," *Ural*, 2011, no. 6; Valentin Luk'ianin, "Zhizn' posle zhizni (o 'donnykh ottozhenniakh' uralskoi literatury)," *Ural*, 1996, no. 4; Aron, *Yeltsin*, 106–8; and these Web sites: www.uralopera.ru, www.muzkom.net, and culture.ekburg.ru/institutions/theatre/.

38 Valentin Luk'ianin, "Smotrie chashche v nebo, gospoda," *Ural*, 2002, no. 10.

39 Inna Gladkova, "Belyi dom iz krasnogo kirpicha," *Ural*, 2000, no. 11.

40 Harris, *Great Urals*, 32–36.

41 Aron, *Yeltsin*, 13.

42 Luk'ianin, "Smotrie chashche v nebo, gospoda."

43 Luk'ianin, "Gorod i dusha."

44 Jeanne Guillemin, "The 1979 Anthrax Epidemic in the USSR: Applied Science and Political Controversy," *Proceedings of the American Philosophical Society* 146, no. 1 (2002): 18–36.

45 Aron, *Yeltsin*, 52–105.

46 Ibid., 14.

47 Ibid., 48–128.

48 Luk'ianin, "Gorod i dusha."

49 Aron, *Yeltsin*, 106–8.

50 John Freedman, "Russia's 'Third Cultural Center,' Yekaterinburg," *Moscow Times*, May 26, 2013.

51 Stephen Handelman, *Comrade Criminal: Russia's New Mafiya* (New Haven, Conn.: Yale University Press, 1995), 73–92, 234–37, 332–47.

52 The heading above, "The Second Front," is the name of the local rock band's Agata Kristi's 1988 debut album, *Vtoroi front*.

53 Artemy Troitsky, *Back in the USSR: The True Story of Rock in Russia* (Boston: Faber & Faber, 1988), 13–23.

54 Viktor Slavkin, *Pamiatnik neizvestnomu stiliage: Istoriia pokoleniia v anekdotakh, legendakh, baikakh, pesniakh* (Moscow: Artist, 1996).

55 S. Frederick Starr, *Red and Hot: The Fate of Jazz in the Soviet Union* (New York: Oxford University Press, 1983); Pia Koivunen, "The 1957 Moscow Youth Festival: Propagating a New, Peaceful Image of the Soviet Union," in *Soviet State and Society under Nikita Khrushchev*, ed. Melane Ilic and Jerremy Smith (New York: Routledge, 2009), 46–65.

56   Troitsky, *Back in the USSR*, 22–29.

57 Ibid., 23.

58 Ibid., 30–50.

59 This is a point underscored by Sabrina Ramet, *Rocking the State: Rock Music and Politics in Eastern Europe and Russia* (Boulder, Colo.: Westview Press, 1994), as well as in Ruslan Trushchev's 2006 documentary film about the Soviet rock scene for MuzTV, *Blizhe k Zvezdam: Otpetye Devyanostie*.

60 Such was the case in other Soviet industrial cities, such as Dnepropetrovsk in Ukraine. Anecdotal evidence similarly suggests that rock music revenues formed the basis of capital later used in the privatization of industries and resources in Yekaterinburg. Personal correspondence on August 10, 2011, with Sergei I. Zhuk, author of *Rock and Roll in the Rocket City: The West, Identity, and Ideology in Soviet Dnepropetrovsk, 1960–1985* (Washington and Baltimore: Woodrow Wilson Center Press and Johns Hopkins University Press, 2010).

61 Troitsky, *Back in the USSR*, 50–96.
62 Ibid., 97–100; Richard Stites, *Russian Popular Culture: Entertainment and Society since 1900* (New York: Cambridge University Press, 1992). Locally, the KGB brought trumped-up criminal charges against the Sverdlovsk bard Aleksander Novikov in a case that quietly collapsed following General Secretary Yurii Andropov's death in 1984. This incident is recounted by Aron, *Yeltsin*, 125–26.
63 Troitsky, *Back in the USSR*, 117–31.
64 Stites, *Russian Popular Culture*, 156–57.
65 Ibid., 157–60.
66 Ibid., 192.
67 Zhuk, *Rock and Roll*, 308.
68 Ibid., 317.
69 Luk'ianin, "Gorod i dusha."
70 Andrei Markevich, *Ekaterina Zhuravskaia: Career Concerns in a Political Hierarchy—A Case of Regional Leaders in Soviet Russia* (Moscow: New Economic School, 2009).
71 Valentin Luk'ianin, "*Ural*: Ural' fragment knigi," *Ural*, 2008, no. 1.
72 Ibid.
73 The chronology here is from the *Ural'skii sledopyt* Web site, www.uralstalker.ru.
74 Ibid.
75 Ibid.
76 Naum Orlov, "V teatre moei pamiaty . . . Ustnye passkazy, sapisannye Dmitriem Bavil'skim," *Ural*, 2002, no. 3.
77 Valentina Artiushina, "Dva resiatiletiia v *Ural* sovetskogo perioda," *Ural*, 2007, no. 8.
78 This account of the Lagunov controversy is based on the discussion by Aron, *Yeltsin*, 118–20.
79 This account is based on ibid., 119–23. Nikonov's full uncensored text may be found in a collection of his novellas: Nikolai Nikonov, *Povesti* (Sverdlovsk: Sredne-Ural'skoe Izdatel'stvo, 1990).
80 E. Kiseleva, "Strannyi gorod," *Ural*, 1996, no. 4.
81 Lidia Slobozhaninova, "Ural': Yavlenia obshchenatsional'noe," *Ural*, 2008, no. 1.
82 Naum Leiderman, "Blagodaria i vopreki: Provintsial'nyi zhurnal v gody zastoiia," *Ural*, 2000, no. 11.
83 Ibid.
84 Nikolai Nokyala, "Zhurnalu *Ural*: 50 let," *Ural*, 2008, no. 1.
85 James O. Finckenauer and Yuri A. Voronin, *The Threat of Russian Organized Crime* (Washington: National Institute of Justice of US Department of Justice, 2001), 3–16.

86 Blair A. Ruble, "Institutional Weakness, Organized Crime and the International Arms Trade," in *Urbanization, Population, Environment, and Security: A Report of the Comparative Urban Studies Project,* ed. Christina Rosan, Blair A. Ruble, and Joseph S. Tulchin (Washington: Woodrow Wilson International Center for Scholars, 1999), 6–7.

87 Yuriy Voronin, *Organized Crime: Its Influence on International Security and Urban Community Life in the Industrial Cities of the Urals,* Comparative Urban Studies Occasional Paper 17 (Washington: Woodrow Wilson International Center for Scholars, 1998).

88 Ibid.

89 Ibid., 7–8.

90 Ibid.

91 "Yekaterinburg: Istoriya dvukh gruppirovok," Fotografii tiuremnykh nakolok Web site (www.nakolochka.in).

92 "Organized Criminal Group or Social-Politial Party 'Uralmash,'" Afery poddelki kriminal Web site (www.aferizm.ru/criminal).

93 Voronin, *Organized Crime,* 8.

94 Ibid., 6–7.

95 Ibid., 12.

96 Adrian Bloomfield, "Russian Mafia Killings Threaten Putin Legacy," *Telegraph* (London), February 22, 2008.

97 Voronin, *Organized Crime,* 7.

98 Yekaterinburg's cemeteries became the subjects of photo essays in many of the world's leading newspapers—such as Samuel Hutchinson, "Whacked but Not Forgotten," *New York Times Magazine,* April 13, 1997; variants in the German magazine *Forum,* March 29, 1997; and the *Sunday Times Magazine* in London, April 20, 1997.

99 Olga Matich, "'Whacked but not Forgotten': Burying the Mob," paper delivered at Conference on Russia at the End of the Twentieth Century: Culture and Its Horizons in Politics and Society, Stanford University, Stanford Calif., October 1998.

100 Pilar Bonet, "Evgenii Monakh prevratil svoi kriminal'nyi opyt' v pisatel'skuiu zolotuiu zhilu," *Ural,* 1996, nos. 11–12.

101 Evgenii Monakh, "Ulibnis' pered smert'iu: Povest," *Ural,* 1996, nos. 11–12.

102 The official population figure of 1.3 million is found in the 2002 All-Russian Census: Federal'naia sluzhba gosudarstvennoi statistiki, *Vserossiiskaia perepis' naseleniia 2002 goda: Chislennost' naseleniia Rossii, sib"ektov Rossisskoi Federatsii v sostave federal'nykh okrugov, raionov, gorodskikh poselenii, sel'skikh naselennykh punktov—raionnykh tsentrov i sel'skikh naselennykh punktov s naseleniem 3 tysiachi i bole chelovek* (Moscow: Federal State Statistical Service, 2002).

103   Izol'da Drobina, "Gastarbaitery domoi ne toropiatsia," *Urali'skii raobchi,* January 23, 2009; Irina Artemova, "Patent dlia migranta," *Ural'skii rabochii,* December 21, 2010.

104   Federal'naia sluzhba gosudarstvennoi statistiki, *Vserossiiskaia perepis' naseleniia 2009 goda: Goroda s chislennost'iu postoiannogo naseleniia 1 mil. Chelovek i bolee* (Moscow: Federal State Statistical Service, 2010), tablitsa 17, 80–88, at 80.

105   Thomas F. Remington, *The Politics of Inequality in Russia* (New York: Cambridge University Press, 2011), 195–96.

106   Beumers and Lipovetsky, *Performing Violence,* 27–34.

107   Ibid., 27–28.

108   Ibid., 103–29.

109   Vitaly Chernetsky, "Review: Brigit Beumers and Mark Lipovetsky, *Performing Violence,*" *Theatre Journal* 62, no. 3 (October 2010): 478–80.

110   Beumers and Lipovetsky, *Performing Violence,* 211–12; Freedman, "Contemporary Russian Drama"; John Freednam, "Lending an Ear to Russian Tradition," *Plays International* 21, nos. 9–10 (2006): 18–19.

111   Yana Ross, "Russia's New Drama: From Togliatti to Moscow," *Theater,* no. 1 (2006): 27–43; Valerii Kichin, "Izobrazhaya klassiku: Kino," *Rossiiskaya gazeta,* June 20, 2006; Beumers and Lipovetsky, *Performing Violence,* 211–12, 231–35.

112   Sasha Dugdale, "Preface," to *Performing Violence,* by Beumers and Lipovetsky, 13–25.

113   Ibid., 15.

114   In-Yer-Face Theatre Web site, www.inyerface-theatre.com/what.html.

115   Dugdale, "Preface."

116   This observation was made by the *Moscow Times* theater critic John Freedman in personal correspondence, September 3, 2011.

117   Ross, "Russia's New Drama"; Freedman, "Contemporary Russian Drama."

118   E.g., Elena Fremina and Mikhail Ugarov, "September.doc," about the 2004 Beslan school massacre; and Elena Gremina, "One Hour Eighteen," about the 2009 death of defense attorney Sergei Magnitsky during pretrial detention.

119   Freedman, "Contemporary Russian Drama."

120   Beumers and Lipovetsky, *Performing Violence,* 28–29; Towson University Center for the Arts and Center for International Theater Development, *New Russian Drama Conference Program* (Baltimore: Center for International Theater Development, 2010).

121   Dugdale, "Preface," 16–17; Seth Graham, "*Chernukha* and Russian Film," *Studies in Slavic Cultures* 1, no. 1 (2000): 9–27.

122 John Freedman, "St. Petersburg Theater by the Numbers," *Moscow Times*, July 30, 3013.
123 Ross, "Russia's New Drama"; Freedman, "Contemporary Russian Drama."
124 Beumers and Lipovetsky, *Performing Violence*, 100–101.
125 Ekaterina Vasil'eva, "Zaberi menia k sebe," *Ural*, 2012, no. 4.
126 Yury "Strike" Klavdiev, *The Polar Truth: A Play*, trans. John Freedman, as performed at Towson University Center for the Arts and Center for International Theater Development, New Russian Drama Conference, Baltimore, 2010.
127 Towson University Center for the Arts and Center for International Theater Development, *New Russian Drama Conference Program*.
128 John Freedman, "Winners at 19th *Moscow Times* Theater Awards," *Moscow Times*, August 4, 2011.
129 Freedman, "The Search for What Might Be True: Thoughts from Inside and Era of Change," unpublished manuscript, November 2010.
130 Nikolai Kolyada, *Baba Shanel'*, as performed in its premiere at the Kolyada Theatre, Yekaterinburg, September 13, 2011.
131 Ross, "Russia's New Drama." Concerning the British Council's expulsion from Russia, see Mark Franchetti, "British Council 'Front for Spying in Russia,'" *Sunday Times*, January 20, 2008.
132 Towson University Center for the Arts and Center for International Theater Development, New Russian Drama Conference Program. In the spirit of full disclosure, the author was an adviser to the Trust for Mutual Understanding between 1999 and 2011, and has been a trustee since 2011.
133 Marina Romanova, "Okolyadovannye," *Ekspert-Ural*, 2008, no. 27.
134 Kristina Matvienko, "Novaya Drama v Rossii: Kratkii kurs v nedavnee prosloe i eskiz nastoiashego," *Piterburgskii teatralnyi zhurnal*, 2008, no. 52.
135 This biography is based on the official Web site of the Kolyada Theater, www.kolyada-theatre.ru.
136 Beumers and Lipovetsky, *Performing Violence*, 144–48.
137 Ross, "Russia's New Drama."
138 Zlata Demina, "Klubinchnyi dnevnik P'esa v odnom deistvii," *Ural*, 2011, no. 6; John Freedman, "Kolyada-Plays Festival Under Way in Yekaterinburg," *Moscow Times*, June 26, 2011; Nadezhda Koltysheva, "Kaki a prishla robotat' v zhurnal 'Ural,'" *Ural*, 2008, no. 1.
139 The catalogue for the 2010 festival was published as *First Ural Industrial Biennial of Contemporary Art 9.09–10.10.2010: Special Projects*, curated by Alisa Prudnikova (Yekaterinburg: National Center for Contemporary Art, 2010).

140   "Nikolai Koliada: Vse eto nachinalos' s nulia, s nulia, s nulia," *Novaia gazeta*, November 28, 2011.

141   "Building for Kolyada-Theater 'Will Begin in 2012,'" Russian Opinion Web site, http://mysouth.su/2011/03/building-for-kolyada-theater-quot-will-begin-in-2012/.

142   Quoted by John Freedman, "A Playwright for Putin," *Moscow Times*, January 24, 2012.

143   John Freedman, "An American Critic on Nikolai Kolyada," *Moscow Times*, June 2, 2013.

144   Beumers and Lipovetsky, *Performing Violence*, 142–44.

145   Nikolai Kolyada, "Staraia ziachikha: P'esa v odnom deistvii," *Ural*, 2006, no. 8. Act 1; this passage was translated by Blair Ruble.

146   Ross, "Russia's New Drama."

147   "Ot redaktsii," *Ural*, 2007, no. 6. For examples of winning plays, see Zlata Demina, "Bog liubit: P'esa v odnom deistii," *Ural*, 2004, no. 5; Vladimir Zuev, "Mamochi: P'esa v odnom deistvii," *Ural*, 2006, no. 5; Sergei Medvedev, "Parikmakherska. Monolog s 13 kartinkami," *Ural*, 2007, no. 7; Ol'ga Pogonia, "Glinianaia iama: P'esa," *Ural*, 2007, no. 7; Andrei Il'enkov, "Pestraia lentochka, ili Dvorets beremennykh," *Ural*, 2007, no. 7; Anna Bogacheva and Iyrii Alesin, "Shpandrik i Klim: Gorodskaia skazka," *Ural*, 2009, no. 6; Vladimir Zuev, "Chernaia dyra: Traikomediia v odnom deistvii," *Ural*, 2009, no. 6; Oleg Kaporeiko, "Seraia sovushka: P'esa-skazka v odnom deistvii, semi kartinnakh s prologom," *Ural*, 2009, no. 6; Mikhail Durenkov, "Samyi legkii sposob brosit' kurit': P'esa v odnom deistvee," *Ural*, 2011, no. 3; Nadezjda Kol'tsheva, "Tarakanishcha. Neveroiatnaia istoriia dlia detei i vzyroslykh v dvukh deistviiakh," *Ural*, 2011, no. 4; and Tat'iana Vdovina, "Motylek: Skazka v odnom deistvii," *Ural*, 2011, no. 6.

148   Freedman, "Kolyada-Plays Festival Under Way."

149   Elena Krivonogova, Mariia Milova, Alena Berliand, and Natal'ia Vasil'eva, "Ekho festivalia 'real'nyi teatr,'" *Ural*, 2001, no. 12; Lilia Menchenko, "Pis'ma real'nogo teatra," *Ural*, 2006, no. 1.

150   Freedman, "Russia's 'Third Cultural Center.'"

151   Konstantin Kostenko, "Dzhas: P'esa v odnom deistvii," *Ural*, 2012, No. 1. Kostenko was born in Khabarovsk in the Soviet Far East and presently lives and works in Moscow.

152   Ross, "Russia's New Drama."

153   Ibid. See, e.g., Aleksander Arkhipov, "The Dembel Train," about the demobilization of soldiers either for fulfillment of their service or for injuries sustained in battle. Aleksandr Arkhipov, "Dembel'skii poezd: P'esa v odnom deist'vii," *Ural*, 2004, no. 5.

154 Pavel Kazantsev, "Geroi: P'esa," *Ural*, 2006, no. 12, act 1, scene 4; this passage was translated by Blair Ruble.
155 Pavel Kazantsev and Yaroslava Pylinovich, "Moishchiki: P'esa v odnom deistvii," *Ural*, 2007, no. 2, act 1; this passage was translated by Blair Ruble.
156 Nina Sadur, "Lyotchik," *Ural*, 2011, no. 1, act 1, scene 5; this passage was translated by Blair Ruble.
157 Beumers and Lipovetsky, *Performing Violence*, 152–53.
158 Ellen Barry, "Wrenching Tales from Russia's Rust Belt," *New York Times*, July 30, 2012.
159 Ibid.
160 Ibid., 166; Peter Knegt, "Russian 'Wolfy' Conquering Karlovy Vary Pack," indieWire Web site, July 9, 2009, www.indiewire.com.
161 Barry, "Wrenching Tales."
162 Paul Harris, "Black Milk," *Variety*, January 15, 2005.
163 Peter Marks, "Russian National Postal Service," *Washington Post*, September 14, 2001; Kenneth Jones, "Epistolary Elegy: Russian National Postal Service Makes US Debut at DC's Studio Theatre," *Playbill*, September 8, 2004.
164 "The Russian National Postal Service by Oleg Bogarev," http://nitish.9g.com/rich_text_2.html.
165 Andrei Maleev-Babel offered this observation in correspondence in August 2011.
166 Albert Williams, "Maria's Field," *Chicago Reader*, January 27, 2009.
167 "Ot redaktsii," *Ural*, 2010, no. 9.
168 Murph Henderson, "Who Needs Moscow? A Guru of Russian Playwriting Holds Court in Distant Ekaterinburg," *American Theater*, March 2006, 58–61.
169 Beumers and Lipovetsky, *Performing Violence*, 273.
170 Ross, "Russia's New Drama."
171 Beumers and Lipovetsky, *Performing Violence*, 273.
172 These plays are discussed in detail by Beumers and Lipovetsky, *Performing Violence*, 273–300.
173 Ol'ga Didkovskaia, "Komichnyi i tragichgnyi Don Zhuan," *Ural*, 1997, no. 7.
174 Aron, *Yeltsin*, 106–7.
175 Natal'ia Reshetnikova, "Moi dragostennye liudi: Liriko-teatral'nye zametki," *Ural*, 2002, no. 10; Alla Lapina, "Nostal'gicheskie zametki na poliakh teatral'noi programmy," *Ural*, 2001, no. 11.
176 Shaun Walker, "Catherine the Great Sings and Dances in Russia's First Musical," *The Independent*, December 8, 2007.
177 Kasia Popova, "Teatr kak zerkalo zhizni," *Ural*, 2007, no. 8.

178 Konstantin Bogomolov, "Interv'iu s Olegom Bogaevym i Olegom Paiberdinym," *Ural*, 2000, no. 7.

179 Oleg Bogaev, "Tridsat'tri chast'ia: Tragikomediia v dvukh deistviiakh," *Ural*, 2004, no. 5, Act 1, scene 5, p. 9; this passage was translated by Blair Ruble.

180 Freedman, "Contemporary Russian Drama"; Towson University Center for the Arts and Center for International Theater Development, New Russian Drama Conference Program; Beumers and Lipovetsky, *Performing Violence*, 168–75; Sergei Medvedev, "Zhena: Komediia," *Ural*, 2009, no. 6; Bulat Shiribazarov, "A potom my poletim na Mars . . . P'esa v dvykh destviiakh," *Ural*, 2009, no. 6; Ekaterina Vasil'eva, "Ya—idiotka: P'esa v odnom deistvii," *Ural*, 2009, no. 6.

181 Finn-Olaf Jones, "A Bilbao on Siberia's Edge?" *New York Times*, July 22, 2011.

182 John Freedman, "New Era Looms After Golden Age of 'New Drama," *Moscow Times*, July 31, 2014.

183 *Moscow Times* theater critic John Freedman is among the first to refer to the contemporary period as a "Golden Age" for Russian drama; see Freedman, "Contemporary Russian Drama."

Outsiders Creating for Insiders

1 Robert D. Putnam, *Making Democracy Work: Civic Traditions in Modern Italy* (Princeton, N.J.: Princeton University Press, 1993). The epigraph for this chapter is from Shermin Langhoff, artistic director of the Maxim Gorki Theater in Berlin, as quoted in "Christopher D. Shea, 'At Home, At Last, in Berlin,'" *New York Times*, April 26, 2015.

2 Rem Koolhaas, *Delirious New York* (New York: Monacelli Press, 1994; orig. pub. 1978), 293.

Index